The Structure of Spanish History

The Structure of
Spanish History

Américo Castro

TRANSLATED BY EDMUND L. KING

PRINCETON, NEW JERSEY

PRINCETON UNIVERSITY PRESS

1954

✦

Based on ESPAÑA EN SU HISTORIA

(Cristianos, moros y judíos)

PRINTED IN THE UNITED STATES OF AMERICA

BY PRINCETON UNIVERSITY PRESS, PRINCETON, NEW JERSEY

To My Wife

Preface

ALTHOUGH this book is based upon *España en su historia* (Spain in Her History) published in 1948, many modifications and additions have been introduced into the text. An increased interest in the theoretical problem of history has made necessary a change of title. Every historian, consciously or unconsciously, is backed by some previous theory of history, original or borrowed, which in most cases remains unexpressed. Consequently, no matter what the risk, the historian should attempt to reveal whither his history is heading. The urge to narrate or to discover "what has happened" causes the historian to forget sometimes the authentic reality of facts, or deeds, a reality only graspable by history when it is located within the human structure in which it exists, and connected with the values in which it acquires meaning. Pirandello has one of his characters make the following statement: "But a fact is like a sack which won't stand up when it is empty. In order that it may stand up, one has to put into it the reason and sentiment which caused it to exist."

Human facts must be referred to the life in which they happen and exist. This life emerging from the generic universal background of the human is, in turn, something concrete and specified. This is true of a people or an individual, and is also true of a work of art or of thought. If, for example, one discovers in a writer of stature something borrowed, it would be advisable, before questioning his originality, to ascertain the function which the borrowed thing serves within the total compass of the work. It would be necessary also to see how the borrowed element fits into the whole of the significant activities of the writer. To plagiarize is rather to transplant something valuable to a humanly sterile soil.

The determination of the essence of reality is a problem for philosophers. Yet whatever conclusion they come to in this regard, it seems unquestionable that the "historical" aspect of reality is always a matter of situation, though, to be sure, it is the situation of something that necessarily *is* before it is historically situated. The *in* where the "historical" of human life is situated may be called the "dwelling-place of life," that is, the center and the agent from which the history of each people takes its continuous start (see Chapter 2). One cannot really speak of history without referring to a "dwelling-place" where one can situate the otherwise unconnected fragments of human reality—be they what archeologists discover or what is contained in the morning paper. To take a different point of view, the fossilized remains of an animal cannot

[vii]

achieve full reality until the scientist is able to reconstruct the totality of the skeleton.

For this reason it seems historically futile to regard as Spaniards the Iberians or the other inhabitants of the Iberian Peninsula before the arrival of the Romans. Linguistic fragments, the archeological remains of historically silent peoples, the scattered remains of Roman historians about such peoples—these are like furniture without a house. Without some sense of the living context from which these things have been torn, we find it impossible to grasp their historical meaning. For us, then, they have no historical reality, that is, no inwardly human location. The Roman historical "dwelling" is the oldest one in the Iberian Peninsula, and Romans were not Spaniards. To determine how and when Spaniards began to exist, and how they are situated within themselves, is what this book attempts to do.

From this approach and in this perspective I speak of historical reality, of its inward functioning and of its revealing manifestations through a certain kind of deeds and works. In each history one has to look for the "dwelling-place" in which spontaneous activities are originated, in which new and old, native and foreign ideas and feelings are either adopted or rejected. Each people, from and in the workshop of its "dwelling-place," deals with ancient or modern *civilization* in its particular way. Traditions are human creations, and, like all things human, they never appear as essences but as situated essences, adjusted to the special functioning of each human community. Roman traditions did not "realize" themselves in the same way in the several national spheres in which the former Empire had been split up. The same holds true of Greek civilization after its rediscovery during the fifteenth and sixteenth centuries.

I do not question the validity of the concept of *races*, but only as a concept it is not useful in the study of history. For example, Negroes are not situated in Brazilian life as they are in American life; they are very different, although they are equally black. And Negroes of both North and South America show no inclination to return to Africa, the former "natural" location of their race.

The same applies to the idea of *generations*, that is, to the mode of experiencing past and present time, and of being situated in each of them. To be old is felt as a blessing in China, as a curse in America. The past, the present, and the future are not realized, actualized, lived and experienced everywhere in the same way. Consequently, the vital rhythm of past-present lacks both uniformity and universality.

Climate, just as any other *natural circumstance*, hangs—historically speaking—chiefly on man, and not vice versa. German towns in Brazil do not look Brazilian but German. Inhabitants may make a land valuable more frequently than land makes prosperous a people. All natural things being equal, changes in population bring about different kinds of human values—for better or worse. "The sabbath was made for man, and not man for the sabbath."

In short, this history is viewed and organized from within and not as a result of natural or economic causes, or of the operation of abstract ideas allegedly valid above time and space. The history of Spain (through a series of interrelated references) has been chosen to exemplify this way of understanding history. But any other people—provided one knows and likes their deeds—could furnish the necessary human material for a similar historical analysis. Whatever *is*, according to logic, metaphysics, or science, becomes for the historian a "to be situated," a "to be dwelling" in a vital station.

The most important differences between this book and the first Spanish edition are these: Chapters 2, 3, and 15 are new; most of Chapters 12 and 14 have been rewritten. In Chapter 8, the section "The Difference between Hispanic Integralism and Moorish Integralism" is new. The comparison of Spanish and French literary style has been enlarged in order to show the different way in which the same theme is situated within each historical "dwelling-place." The recently discovered Mozarabic poetry is discussed in Chapter 10; Spanish-Jewish thought, in Chapter 14. Many other small changes have been introduced.

Acknowledgments

I want to express my gratitude to those who have written about *España en su historia* in journals and newspapers, or have lectured about it. Professors P. K. Hitti, G. Levi della Vida, Irfan A. Kawar, and F. J. Ziadeh have helped me to interpret certain Arabic words. Mrs. María Rosa Lida de Malkiel has contributed certain of the notes in Chapter 13. Mrs. Carmen Castro de Zubiri, the late Professor Amado Alonso, and Professors J. M. Blecua, G. Bonfante, J. Ferrater Mora, Stephen Gilman, R. Lapesa, R. Menéndez Pidal, Ira O. Wade, and X. Zubiri have made valuable suggestions regarding the matter of the book, and Professor R. S. Willis has given much-heeded advice concerning the phrasing of the English. To all of them I owe heartfelt thanks.

Special acknowledgment and thanks are due to Professor Edmund L. King for his untiring patience in translating this book and in our long work together to produce a text as accurate as possible.

I am grateful to the University Research Fund for financial assistance granted to me for the purpose of preparing the manuscript.

Contents

[xi]

CONTENTS

Illustrations

The Structure of Spanish History

Spain, or the History of
an Insecurity

THE MAJOR PEOPLES OF EUROPE have acquired historical images which display clearly defined features. There exists, for example, a "canonical" version of the history of England, or of France, based upon certain formal characteristics and upon functional contents that are accepted by everyone as perfectly valid. The Englishman, or the Frenchman, views his past with a firm belief in its validity, a belief reflected in apparently well-established formulas such as empiricism and pragmatism, or rationalism and clarity. Until about 1935 the major peoples of Europe lived, and to a great extent still live, in the belief that they possessed a normal and progressive history founded on treasured premises that only a reckless outsider would dare to question. In the prevailing view, the past is regarded as a preparation for a future of wealth, culture, and power. The past is felt as an auspicious ante-present.

But how different has been the history of the Iberian Peninsula. For three centuries mistresses of half a world, Hispania and Lusitania arrived at the present epoch with less political and economic vitality than, for example, Holland or Scandinavia, which are integral parts of highly polished Europe. The Hispano-Portuguese people have outlived the political prestige of a past that is at once glorious and, for many, not a little enigmatic. The high level of their art and literature, and the personal and exemplary merit of their individuals, past and present, are widely recognized; their scientific and technical accomplishments have less prestige; and their economic and political competence is visibly negligible. A situation such as this cannot but be felt as a problem. The past, when contemplated from what might thus be called a problematical present, turns into a pure problem itself, one which compels the observer to look more sharply, for, seemingly, even the most prodigious deeds of remote Hispanic history prophesy an inevitable ultimate decline.

The past is felt to be the augury of nothing assured—nothing assured, that is, with respect to material prosperity and to the feeling of happy placidity to which the nineteenth-century European grew more and more accustomed as the century went on. But the past augurs certainly and affirmatively with respect to the Spaniard's capacity for creating forms to express the awareness of his existence, or the conflict between the sense of the temporal and the sense of the eternal. The rigorous thought that served other Europeans to penetrate into the problem of the nature of reality and of the rational articulation of all that is, or is in, the world, had as its counterpart for the Spaniard an impulse to express the consciousness of his existence in his own world. Instead of contemplating with clear vision the timeless present of being, the Spaniard lives his life out as an anxious movement through the moral region of the ought-to-be. The characteristically European activity of doing and reasoning, in which the agent or thinker is unmindful of his empiric presence in his work, has as its counterpart in Iberia a personalized activity which is not evaluated according to its useful results, but rather according to what the person involved is or wants to be, whether *hidalgo*, mystic, artist, dreamer, or conqueror of new worlds to include within the panorama of his own life. The Spaniard has always lived either in the tension of the actual performance of deeds of valor or in the expectation of opportunities to perform them, opportunities which for most people never come. The degenerate aspect of all this is to be seen in three types: the *picaro*, the vagabond, and the idler, who had all fallen into a state of inert passivity. There is a profound meaning in the Spanish saying, "either prince or peasant," that is to say, either to be exalted to the highest degree, or to sit idly by and watch the years as they move through the orbit of an indifferent destiny.[1]

It is understandable that such a structure of life[2] should always be a

[1] In reply to Napoleon III, Eugenia de Montijo, a woman of rare beauty, said that if he judged her not worthy enough to be the Empress of France she felt herself too worthy to be the mistress of an emperor. The lovely countess from Granada did, in fact, become the Empress of France.

[2] "Life" does not mean here "biological or temporal life" but the reality of man, the human, as distinguished from the physical or animal, existence. Four main aspects are involved: (1) the inescapable acceptance or rejection of the possibilities life always faces; (2) the faculty of planning and creating even against instinctive or physical urges; (3) the incorporation of the effects of all such living activity into the very course of life's progress; (4) the appearance to our consciousness of any given life—either individual or collective—as a function whose consistency is inseparable from its structure. To illustrate, if a ship, its engine, its rudder, its captain, the shipyard, the port from which it sails, the course of the ship as determined by the ship's seaworthiness and the weather conditions—if all these things could be integrated

problem for the very people who were living it, filled, as they were, with uncertainty and passionate desire. For Spain was a part of Europe, with which she was in close contact, and with which she continually interacted. In one way or another Spain has never been apart from Europe; nevertheless her physiognomy has always been peculiar, though not with the peculiarity that characterizes England with respect to France, or France with respect to Germany or Holland. The direct consequence of such phenomena is the fact that it has not been possible to arrange the history of Spain into a structure that is valid for all peoples. A sharp relativism characterizes everything that refers to her; in her own people, arrogance, melancholy, suspicion, and ill temper towards foreigners; in foreigners, an air of disdain, a stubborn incomprehension, an inexactness of statement that has amounted to calumny, and at times an unrestrained enthusiasm.

If we take as a criterion of historical judgment the instrumental pragmatism of the last century, the Iberian past consists in a series of political and economic errors, the results of which were failure and decadence, which the other European peoples avoided because they were free from bellico-religious passion and static and seignorial personalism. The wonderful works whose creation has been made possible by the Hispanic life-stream are admired without cavil only when they attain the extreme limits of perfection (Cervantes, Velazquez, Goya), and when they do not run against the inability to understand, the vanity, or the interests of other, more powerful, countries. But it will not be freely admitted, for example, that in several Hispanic-American countries there were cities which, by reason of their extraordinary architecture, were the most beautiful in America, for this would force the admission that the Spanish domination was not merely a matter of colonial exploitation. Similarly the surprised delight that Baron von Humboldt took in the Hispanic world a century and a half ago has not found its way into our books nor into the conversations of our contemporaries. The way has been blocked by the Anglo-Americans' attitude of superiority, and by the resentment of the majority of Spanish-Americans, who find in the colonial past an easy excuse for their present political and industrial

---

into a single idea-intuition, the result would be approximately the kind of notion I am trying to convey, a notion not to be grasped solely by logical reason.

The word "vital" as I use it does not mean "important." I use it in its strictly etymological sense, "of or pertaining to life," with "life" to be understood according to my explanation above. "Live," "living," and related words should be understood within the same frame of reference.

[5]

weakness. A further obstacle was the state of unawareness in which Spain lived with respect to herself and her past during the nineteenth century, an unawareness for which the rhetorical gestures of today's self-justifying politics are no compensation. On the other hand, the missions, forts, and government buildings in Louisiana, Florida, Texas, New Mexico, and California—trifling leftovers from the banquet-table of Spain's artistic greatness—are preserved by the Americans with a care and tenderness that neither Spain nor Spanish-America shows with respect to their inestimable treasures.

Thus, matters which have been considered beyond dispute in the Spanish past are often not really so. For almost three hundred years the best paintings of El Greco have remained buried under indifference, paintings conceived in, and because of, Spain; and it was not until the twentieth century that El Greco's art entered the realm of universal values.[3] So far as literary history is concerned, my own teachers used to tell me, and used to write in their books, that the *Soledades* of Don Luis de Góngora were no more than the vagaries of a sick and capricious mind. A critical appraisal more in accord with the artistic truth, a judgment that today is beginning to be shared by Spaniards as well as foreigners, has only in recent years begun to reach the public. All this proceeds from the fact that the greatest phenomena of Spanish civilization cannot be appraised rationally, but only vitally; and thus it is that nothing makes its appearance in Spanish history that is undisputed and securely established.

The fact is that this history, with radical personalism as its foundation, and in contact with the European world based on the victory of man over natural obstacles, fell into a state of progressive despair. In the seventeenth century, and even before, the Spaniard had begun to feel the inanity of his collective achievements;[4] ever since then Spanish

---

[3] This renascence was not brought about exclusively by the so-called "Generation of 1898" (as is claimed, for instance, by Hans Jeschke, *Die Generation von 1898 in Spanien*, 1934). With respect to this matter the year 1908 is a significant date on account of the revealing book of M. B. Cossío, *El Greco*. And Cossío and his teacher Francisco Giner de los Ríos had been talking about the whole thing for more than twenty years (after the very Spanish custom of entrusting to oral expression what the rationalist, rational European puts into books). The circle of Giner de los Ríos was frequented by the famous novelist Emilia Pardo Bazán, who writes in her little read *Nuevo teatro crítico*, July, 1891, p. 55: "*The Burial of the Count of Orgaz* need envy nothing in the execution of the best works of the painter of *The Spinners* [Velázquez]. . . . All modern painters seem impotent to me when I contemplate that divine page called *The Burial of the Count of Orgaz*."

[4] Don Francisco de Quevedo writes on 21 August 1645: "Very bad news, and

[6]

national life has consisted in trying to ward off the blows of an evil destiny, which is to say that Spain has continually opposed the irresistible advance of those who have habitually projected reason into life and who, with their technology, have constructed the powerful western states of modern time. But in spite of the melancholy reflections of Quevedo and many other writers of the seventeenth century, Spanish mettle continued to extend the Empire and keep it on its feet throughout the eighteenth century. When Spain lost her dominions in America in 1824, the Spaniards in Hispanic-America were in a position to take over the inheritance of three centuries of civilizing colonization, in spite of the persistent attacks of England, France, and Holland. This means that the line of the critical and anguished reflections of Spanish thinkers did not coincide with the vital impulse of those other Spaniards who as late as the eighteenth century (in a nation that was on its home ground almost a desert and a pauper) pressed the extension of Spanish sovereignty in Louisiana and California, and brought about at home the cultural renascence of the reign of Charles III, with its books, sciences, buildings, and, to climax the whole, the extraordinary genius of a Goya. Naïve commonplaces are shattered when they are applied to the history of Spain, whose existence has always been locked within the antagonistic and enigmatic embrace of living and dying.

We find ourselves, then, facing a history that at once both affirms and destroys itself in one swan song after another. In 1499, the desperate, vanishing soul of Spanish Jewry poured itself out in the immortal *Celestina*, a work by the Jewish convert Fernando de Rojas. In 1605, in the twilight that played upon the scene where the Renaissance was struggling with forces that opposed its spirit, the *Quijote* appeared, as the eternal incarnation of the rationally impossible made possible poetically. At the end of the eighteenth century, in an Empire already a skeleton and shadow of itself, Goya rose above all the ruins with the unique art of his painting. Near the start of the twentieth century, Spain was described by Lord Salisbury as a "moribund nation," and precisely during this agony a movement was gathering the strength which would enable it, in the realm of the arts, the sciences, and philosophy, to obtain for Spain by the year 1930 an international repute not enjoyed since the sixteenth century. There is no similar case of such a patent contradiction

---

passing bad, is written in from everywhere, and the worst of it is that everyone was expecting it to be this way. There are many things which, while seeming to exist and have being, are now nothing but a name and a shape." (*Obras en prosa*, edited by Astrana Marín, p. 1616.)

between living and not living, all the more strange if one thinks of the mass of internal and external causes which from the seventeenth century on "logically" ought to have reduced Hispania to a land of peasants, of fellahs, with no possibility of interesting visitors except for her ruins and her picturesque customs.

One must not be surprised, then, if such a strange kind of history can be examined only if we somewhat forget ideas of material progress and decadence, political power, and technological efficiency. The collective will of the Spaniards, never fully integrated even before the seventeenth century, has, since then, been manifestly in a state of disintegration. Outside the Peninsula, Holland and the Franche Comté broke away from the Spanish crown; then, inside the Peninsula, the example of the Portuguese secession in 1640 was all but followed by Catalonia. The myth of a universal empire sustained by the Catholic faith—and this faith rather as it was *felt* by the Spaniards than as it was *understood* by the Church of Rome, regardless of the dogmatic agreement between one and the other—had lost its efficacy. Once the solidity of the collective will was cracked in the seventeenth century, it was never again put back together. From then on, some Spaniards would want one thing and others the opposite.[5] Many desired nothing at all, and lived in the inertia of custom and belief, without worrying about doing or learning anything new; in some parts of Spain in the twentieth century people were still plowing with the Roman plow and threshing with oxen.

Although I shall return later on to a problem that is so central, what I have said will serve, I hope, as a warning not to apply here the usual methods for understanding history. I mean such notions as this: that civilizations are born, they progress, they wither. To understand this, let us take the example of France, in one sense near by Spain and in another, remote. The goal of the French people had been from the eleventh century to constitute a nation united under royal authority, and embracing politically everything that French civilization and language had previously conquered in a conquest that found more inspiration in earthly interests than in religious beliefs. From Henry IV on, the national aspiration was rationalized, and the learned class, strongly supported by the monarchy—following the neo-stoic pattern of the Renaissance—took charge of the direction of the masses. From that time on people were to live and even to talk according to rationally established

---

[5] In the eighteenth century some tried to raze the edifice of mythic and a-rational culture by importing the rationalist Enlightenment. But most people preferred to continue within the tradition that was falling into ruin.

principles, uniform for everyone, through whose channels authority would automatically descend from the crown at the peak to the least of the subjects. The idea of the State (absolute monarchy) and so-called classicism in literature are aspects of the same impulse. In France, living consisted in knowing and applying the principles deduced by an autonomous reason according to a logical, rigorous, and clearly explainable process. Every human act with a collective dimension would have to fit into schemes previously worked out, even at the cost of the greatest sacrifices. All the words that the *savants* said should be excluded were in fact destined to be excluded from the language, and thus the French language of earlier centuries was to become unintelligible. Man was converted into a reflective being who paid scant attention to elemental, varied, and individualized living.[6] Art and public life followed rigorous norms. There came a day when rationalism decided that it was necessary to lop off heads, beginning with the king, and thus it was done. Later the geographical division of the country was made uniform, as were education, customs, and even manners. French history, in its essential aspects, has been lived by rule and compass, and thus France became a great nation. To articulate and explain a history that is so open and obvious in its structure, be it ever so complex, is a relatively easy task. The will to power was allied with the proposal to know. Hence the heights of genius attained by rational thought (Descartes); hence the impossibility of France's producing a work of art that embraces the totality of all that is human, which is rational thought plus many other things. Nothing in France is comparable to Dante, Michelangelo, Cervantes, Shakespeare, or Goya. Indeed, it is precisely to the lack of figures of this kind that France owes the harmonious continuity of her own highly perfected civilization.

With an analogous method, although we would confront greater complexities, we could schematize the history of England and of the other peoples of Western Europe. But when we come to Spain, such procedures serve only to a very limited extent, and we must take other paths. They must be taken because whatever, in the last analysis, may be the vital structure of those other peoples (it is not my purpose to treat of this), it would always be true that to their history is conjoined the optimism

[6] La Rochefoucauld's pen ran away with him once when he was writing, and his manuscript reads: "comme *les rhumes* et les maladies contagieuses." The printed text reads simply "maladies contagieuses," an abstract concept that eliminates the connotation of coughs, sneezes, and sniffling. We are in the kingdom of "bon goût," where the passions are kept under control.

and confidence of the historian, as the result of a sustained and ascending process of evaluation. The historian takes as his starting point his intuition that France (let us take her as an example) is a successful realization, and thanks to this a priori optimism it can even happen that he will overvalue things that would be underestimated if France had been a poor and powerless nation. When one is a great and powerful lord, even the nonsense that one says passes for wit and wisdom. Thinking coldly— that is, anti-vitally—one would see that the greater part of the innumerable volumes of Voltaire are full of insignificant prose and verse. But no, since Voltaire enjoyed well-deserved prestige—based on several admirable works—and also because of the intellectual rule he exercised at a time that was suited for it, it is not the custom to point out the enormous mass of commonplaces and insipidities that fill his excessive production. Yet on the other hand, any inconsequential historian will dare to attack Lope de Vega for his excessive fecundity, his haste in composing plays, his superficiality, and many other failings. Many years ago I wrote elsewhere that if Spain had possessed a powerful armed force and economic resources, the tone of the foreign historians would have been otherwise.

But it is so because life is so, and we should face life as an integrated complexity. An essential factor in the history that one writes is the vital attitude of the historian within the time in which he writes. In the sixteenth century, the Seigneur de Brantôme adjudged the meals and inns in Spain to be excellent, while Cervantes and many others thought they left much to be desired. The enthusiasm of Brantôme does not surprise us, who know the vital attitude of that strange personage. And this does not mean that we are falling into any kind of relativism; for when relativism is absolute and total, then it ceases to be relativism, and another name must be found for it, something such as integralism, or the integration of the person who lives and the life that he lives, within which latter is included what he thinks.

We have only to adopt such a way of looking at the matter to perceive immediately that the best historical writing about Spain of late years is tinged, or rather is determined, by an old tradition of melancholy which appears in a very visible form in the major contemporary historians of Spain. Into the contemplation of history is injected the wish that it might have been different from what it was, a wish that springs not out of the caprice or sentimentality of these learned men, but out of the fact that the history of Spain has for centuries consisted—among many other things—of a tendency to what we can term in Spanish, *desvivirse*: to roll back its own living process, to live in disagreement with its own self. The ideas of "greatness" and "decadence" are not good for much in these circumstances.

"Vivir desviviéndose"

Before we can consider any single historical feature of a people, we must have a view of that people as a whole and of that people's values. Even this does not guarantee that we will be able to answer all the questions we may be asked, but it is this principle that leads me now to pursue the understanding of the facts of Spain rather than the knowledge of those facts. For many long years I have written now and again about specific aspects of linguistic, literary, religious, and even pedagogical history inside the Hispanic world. Yet, when some time ago I was asked to express in an essay my ideas concerning the Renaissance in Spain, I saw clearly, as never before, that such a task was impossible if it was not articulated, illuminated, in a general view of Hispanic history. Otherwise one would fall into anecdote and arbitrariness, into denigration or overestimation. For this reason, my projected article on the Renaissance has been converted into the present book—a personal detail of no interest, which I mention only to emphasize the importance that I attach to insight and my lesser zeal for gathering snippets of information. It might be justly said that one of the characteristics of the present time is the disequilibrium between what we "know" and what we "understand."

The first thing to surprise the observer is that as early as the fifteenth century the Castilians should have felt the necessity of characterizing Spain. They had no doubt reached the conviction that they had rounded the cape of uncertainty in their struggle with Islam, and that a splendor-filled future was approaching. But precisely at that time the Castilians who spoke for Spain began to be preoccupied not only with the form of their existence but also with what they had to do in order to exist. What surprised me first of all was that in 1459 the well-known humanist Alonso de Palencia should say that Spain was a "province that is not inclined to take rational points of view," and this he said in a book significantly entitled *Perfection of Military Triumph* (Perfección del triunfo militar).[7] But much earlier, in 1434, Don Alonso de Cartagena, Bishop of Burgos, had pronounced a famous discourse before the Council of Basel justifying the precedence of Castile with respect to England.

[7] See my book *Aspectos del vivir hispánico* (Aspects of Hispanic Existence), Cruz del Sur, Santiago de Chile, 1949, p. 21.

His petition brings us the first description of the characteristic features of Spain. As is well known, Don Alonso was a new-Christian, or convert, and the son of another illustrious convert, Don Pablo de Santa María, who had occupied a very high position among the Spanish Jews, and in the Church he attained a rank of equal eminence. Without entering now into the complexity of that fact, let us note that Don Alonso, great jurist that he was, argued like a good diplomat filled with patriotic fervor: for centuries the Spanish Jews had stood out as excellent ambassadors of the Christian and Moslem kings. Let no one believe that the Bishop of Burgos recited an insincere speech to his Basel audience. His words were an overflow of Hispanic awareness, and the preferences and contempt expressed in them are the very ones that were characteristically Spanish then and for long afterwards: "Spaniards are not wont to prize great wealth, but rather, virtue; nor do they measure a man's honor by the store of his money but rather by the quality of his beautiful deeds; wherefore riches are not to be argued in this matter (as the English argued them); for if we should mete out the precedences according to riches, Cosimo de Medici, or some other very rich merchant, mayhap would come before some duke."[8]

The spirit of nobility, united with a scorn for commercial activities, already marks the abyss that will separate Spain from capitalist Europe: so far as this Jewish arch-Spaniard ecclesiastic was concerned, Cosimo de Medici was but a contemptible merchant. No visible trace of insecurity exists in this expression of awareness of what it means to be a Spaniard: "The kings of Spain—amongst which the principal and first and greatest one is the King of Castile and Leon—have never been subject to the Emperor; for this singularity do the kings of Spain have, that they have never been subject to the Holy Roman Empire, nor to any other, but rather have they won and raised up their kingdoms out of the jaws of their enemies" (p. 214), a very acute observation the meaning of which will later become apparent. "In the time of the Goths, many of the princes of Spain were called emperors" (p. 215). Actually, however, Leon and Castile—as it will be seen—were only nominally a continuation of the Visigothic kingdom; for their spiritual strength and their political titles, including the imperial ones, had their foundations in the city of Santiago, the resting place of St. James the Apostle, which was

[8] "Discurso pronunciado por don Alonso de Cartagena en el Concilio de Basilea acerca del derecho de precedencia del Rey de Castilla sobre el rey de Inglaterra" (Discourse pronounced by Don Alonso de Cartagena at the Council of Basel, Concerning the Right of Precedence of the King of Castile over the King of England), in the journal La Ciudad de Dios, 1894, xxxv, 122-542.

for those monarchs what Rome was to the Holy Roman Empire. For Don Alonso de Cartagena the strength of Castile was grounded less on material realities than on the spiritual and transcendent virtue of the monarchy; otherwise it would not have occurred to him to bring up as a great Spanish merit, and against England, that "the Castilians and Galicians and Biscayans are different nations, and they use completely different languages" (p. 350). In this statement is implicit the idea that was to be expressed a century later by Gonzalo Fernández de Oviedo, to wit, that the only thing that harmonized the discordant variety of the Hispanic peoples was the fact that they were subjects of the king of Spain. Moreover, in the words of the Bishop of Burgos can be traced already the future imperial policy of Charles V, a policy aimed at the spreading of a belief rather than at the establishment of a system of human interests: "The lord and king of England, although he makes war, yet does not make that *divine* war . . . for it is neither against the infidels nor for the glorification of the Catholic faith, nor for the *extension of the boundaries of Christianity, but rather is it made for other interests*" (p. 353).[9] Belief is thus a firm base upon which rises the collective life; its efficacy in the struggle against the infidel brought riches and power, reflected in turn in the spectacular prestige of the monarchy and its surrounding aureole of nobility: "I say nothing here concerning the beauty and grandeur of his court, for, to speak reverently and without offense of all the princes, I could say that in that part of the world known to us, except that it be for the tumult and movement of warfare, there is no prince's court so much visited and so full of so many prelates and counts and barons and other noblemen, and of such a throng of townspeople, as is the royal court of Castile" (p. 351). The court was like a temple to which one repaired in order to obtain earthly benefits just as one visited the house of God to win heavenly favors; the transcendent powers under which the Spaniard found refuge showed their visible form in the nobility and the priesthood. Reflecting such splendors, the Bishop of Burgos succeeded in persuading the Council of Basel to recognize the precedence of Castile with respect to England.

Against the Castilians, the English argued that their own land was richer and more productive, and to this the Bishop answered: "I did not wish to argue the abundance of land, because it seemed to me a *base argument*,

---

[9] See also *ibid.*, p. 526. There are other curious observations on England: "Even though it may be a noteworthy island (for it is called *Anglia* which some say means 'more vainglorious of money'), there are not in it so many provinces nor such broad ones" (p. 349). I know no basis for Don Alonso's curious semantic interpretation of Anglia, but the legend of "English gold" is, for that matter, quite ancient.

for it is not of peasants but of very noble kings that we are speaking; honor comes not from the abundance of the field but from the virtue of man" (p. 533). It is not easy for Don Alonso to descend to the plane of material things, but since the English wish it, he adduces "the vineyards and olive groves, of which there is a great abundance in the kingdom of Castile, and which have been exiled forever from the kingdom of England. . . . And all nations know the esteem which, amongst all the things that belong to the abundance of the earth, is enjoyed by wine and olive oil. If they should speak of those skilled in the making of cloths, I would perhaps grant them something, for there are in our land no weavers who can make cloth so fine as London scarlet; but even that product which we call *grana* (Kermes dye), from which the scarlet receives the sweetness of its odor and the flame of its color, has its birth in the kingdom of Castile, whence it is carried to England. . . . I might speak of metals, but in my judgment such a base and earthly argument is not proper to such an exalted subject" (pp. 533-534). In the last analysis, riches are something secondary, a possession which "abets in the exercise of virtue, but they are not to be adduced as a principal thing"; in any case, Castile is rich, perhaps in excess, since some fear lest "such an abundance of riches as there is today in Castile may do some harm to virtue." So that nothing may be lacking in this first and most faithful picture of the Hispanic soul—drawn by a Jew, it must not be forgotten—Don Alonso ends his harangue—for it is more this than an argument—with a gesture of supreme arrogance: "I shall bring no other evidence save this embassy, for from a poor kingdom such ambassadors do not usually come forth" (p. 536).

I do not believe that at the beginning of the fifteenth century any other European people had revealed such a complete and precise awareness of itself. Castile felt the ineluctable necessity to go forth into the world. With firm step and voice she faced those who tried to diminish her dignity; she recognized the primacy of the Holy Roman Empire, an ideal continuation of the Roman Empire, and of France, a direct outgrowth of the Carolingian Empire, but nothing more. Indirectly, nevertheless, the words of the Bishop of Burgos reveal, behind the arrogance of his attack, a passionate desire for justification and a defensive purpose. It is this element that appeared still more clearly in the confidential paper that Fernando de la Torre addressed to Henry IV of Castile in 1455, when the latter was getting ready to inaugurate his reign.[10]

[10] See the *Cancionero y obras en prosa de Fernando de la Torre* (Fernando de la Torre's Book of Songs and Prose Works), published by A. Paz y Melia, Dresden,

This document seems to contain the first critical analysis of Spanish life and character, the first effort toward overt justification in the face of foreign censures, examples of which its author was forced to hear when he was at the court of Charles VII of France. Castile was beginning to acquire international renown, and she attracted the curiosity of other courts on the occasion, in 1453, of the execution of the Constable Don Alvaro de Luna, the all-powerful favorite of Don Juan II. The French were unfavorably surprised by the fact that the Constable had accumulated such a mass of riches in his castle of Escalona when not even the king of France possessed so much. Fernando de la Torre warms to the argument, highly pleased to contend "against the most great and excellent kingdom of Christians, which is that of France." What he writes is not a rhetorical harangue but rather an evaluative description of Spanish peculiarities. He mentions natural wealth: iron, steel, wool, wheat, wine, olive oil, fruit, mercury, and, to cap them all, "exceptional horses and mules." It seems at first that the author is going to give us one more version of the *Laudes Hispaniae*, so frequent in the Middle Ages, although one observes very soon how patriotism is combined with an attitude that is both critical and modern, formerly unthinkable. Besides, there is talk here not only of the products of the earth but also of the condition of the people.

The fifteenth century was an epoch of great changes: in addition to the suprahuman, which had long held the interest, contemporary reality, that which exists within immediate time and space, was beginning to be interesting. The Marquis of Santillana composed a poem about a battle that was fought in his own times, the battle of Ponza; and the *Romancero* provides a poetic gloss of events that are contemporary and nearby. The chronicles were interested in the lives of contemporary personages (Don Alvaro de Luna, Pero Niño, the Constable Miguel Lucas de Iranzo),[11] and they speak thus not only of the past but also of the current events that the people of the time had seen. Such a phenomenon I call the spirit of contemporaneity. It is from this new vital point of view that Fernando de la Torre launches into telling us for a second time what Spain is and how she appears to be when she is compared with other nations. His words have the tender charm of something newly born. I know no

---

1907. The attentive rereading of the works of Fernando de la Torre confirms me in my idea that the author belonged to the class of new Christians.

[11] The preoccupation with the biography of contemporaries appears in Fernán Pérez de Guzmán's *Generaciones y semblanzas* (Generations and Portraits) and in Fernando del Pulgar's *Claros varones de Castilla* (Worthy Men of Castile).

document prior to this in which a subject permits himself to advise a king of Spain concerning what his people expect of him, and that takes as its foundation that which the country really seems to be, and not abstract ideas of virtue and good government. The thesis of Fernando de la Torre is that Castile (which to all intents and purposes was already Spain) possessed two supreme values: a provident and extremely fertile land and a magnificent courage in warfare. The fact is, nevertheless, that alongside these natural or spontaneous conditions there were rather serious limitations, for the value of Castile lay primarily in what it humanly *was*, and not nearly so much in what it produced with the labor of its people: "The vanity of the Castilians, intensified by their pride, and by the superabundance of their land, leads them to delight in luxuries and ostentation, and therefore they do not refrain from using the products manufactured in other lands out of Castilian raw materials. It is nothing to them to acknowledge that such products are finished by foreigners with much greater polish. Most of the products leave Castile in the shape of raw materials, and in the foreign lands they are turned into finished products, while in Castile people use and consume much more of such goods than in any part of the world. As, for example, from the country of Flanders, satin, tornai cloth, tapestries, and fine cloths; from Milan, harnesses; from Florence, silk; from Naples, leather trappings for horses. They could easily do without all these things, or they could make them, if they but wished to set about the task, to judge by the great means that they have. For, there would be finished goods made out of wool and dyes and juicy plants and other things as are necessary, if the Castilians knew how to transform them technically as the Flemish do; for Castile has such primary materials. There would be iron and steel goods if they knew how to forge and temper them, as the Milanese do, for Castile has such primary materials. There would be goods of silk and silver with gold if they knew how to weave and to fashion as the Florentines do, for it is certain that the Castilians have such primary materials. There would be valuable leathers from the largest and finest bulls in the world, if they knew how to tan and dress them as the Neapolitans do, for there are such bulls and they are killed in Castile; and so with other things." Castile *is* courageous, she *possesses* natural wealth, but she does not *make* things that demand ingenious effort. The weak style of Fernando de la Torre stiffens when he thinks of horses, the noble complement of the knight in warfare: "a perfect horse there is not in any other place except in Castile, for *heart*, body, and fleetness . . . ; for these qualities will not be found in the horses of

Apulia, though they be taller and broader, and are even less to be found in the German ones, which are wild and have large heads, and still less in the Sicilian ones, which are neither swift, nor adequately suitable for battle."

But the author does not limit himself to enumerating merits and defects. With an inquiring mind and in a style inconceivable a hundred years earlier, he seeks to find a reason behind the Spaniards' lack of technical skill: "From whence does this emanate and proceed save from the fertility of the Castilian land and, in other kingdoms, from want. This want, the people know how, by their labors, to convert into wealth and income; and in Castile, the fatness of the land causes them, in a certain fashion, *to be proud and slothful and not so ingenious or industrious.*" That is, from necessity is born technology; and from the excess of easily obtained goods, pride and indolence. In 1455 is said for the first time and very crudely what is to be repeated for centuries both inside and outside the boundaries of Spain. The strange thing in this case is that Fernando de la Torre, in order to compensate for the deficiencies in the deeds of his countrymen, converts the fertility of the soil into something magical and dazzling: "not once a year but three times in some places does the earth or can the earth bear wheat and the trees fruit." Castile is sufficient to herself, whereas other peoples have to import what she produces. Yet even so, and in spite of the enthusiasm that he displays, De la Torre writes from a defensive position. He subtly perceives the difference between Spain and Western Europe; he feels himself attacked, and he counterattacks. For the first time is posed the question, what is Spain and what is her worth, a question that is still open today. Into the conscious awareness[12] of his own history De la Torre incorporates his grief over feeling incapable of providing certain cultural necessities; to be much, to do little.

We ought not for this reason to say that pessimism is predominant in our critic. If greatness does not come to Spain from her industrial skill and her commercial wealth, it does come from her lofty spirit and her grandeur, "for if you read the Roman histories, you will indeed find that from Castile have gone forth, and in Castile were born, men who were emperors of Rome, and not one, but seven; and even in our own times we have seen in Italy and in France and in many other places very

---

[12] "Conscious awareness" is used here and hereinafter to translate Spanish *vivencia*, German *Erlebnis*, in the sense this word has in the works of Wilhelm Dilthey. The German word has been variously rendered into English by others as "livingness," "living experience," and "lived experience." An approximate definition of the term might be "one's awareness of one's own experience."

great and valiant captains."[13] This already sounds like imperial language, announcing the great enterprises of the next century. Before Fernando de la Torre, Fray Diego de Valencia had already said that if the Castilian people could agree among themselves,

> I know not a single corner in the world
> That they might not conquer, including all Granada.

And a little later Gómez Manrique (1468) desires Prince Alfonso to conquer Cismaritime lands and Outremer, from the barbarian nations.[14] The Spanish Empire, founded by Ferdinand and Isabella, was not a happy accident but the same form of Spanish living, enlarged at the moment when Spain was becoming aware of herself vis-à-vis the other peoples of Europe. A land of brave bulls, of horses with eyes and hearts of fire, a land filled with men who even in the fifteenth century caused wonderment with their deeds of prowess—was anything lacking? Impetuous valor, like boundless faith, is not satisfied with limits and national boundaries, for it seeks the infinite in time and space, precisely the opposite of what the reasoning mind pursues with its measurements, limitations, and conclusions. Castile, in the middle of the fifteenth century, felt sure of her valor and her will, and she aspired to nothing less than an infinite dominion—"Cismaritime lands and Outremer." The Catalonian-Aragonese imperialism in the Mediterranean, in the fourteenth and fifteenth centuries, and the Castilian and Portuguese in the fifteenth and sixteenth provided tasks that gave satisfaction to certain wills that were untamable, and incapable of rationally modifying the natural world in which they found themselves. (We shall see the reason for this later.) The Castile of the fifteenth century craved only a leader

---

[13] The author was most likely thinking of knights such as Rodrigo de Villandrando, Count of Ribadeo, who fought magnificently in France without ceasing to be a loyal vassal of John II of Castile, or Don Pero Niño, Count of Buelna. Juan de Mena mentions, in stanzas 198 and 199 of *Las Trescientas* (The Three Hundred), Juan de Merlo, a knight of the times of John II, who died fighting on the border of the Moorish kingdom of Granada, according to the commentary of Hernán Núñez, who adds that "once when there was war between the two kingdoms of France and Castile, the famous knight Juan de Merlo went out of the kingdom and, in Bala(?), a village in the County of Brabant between Germany and France, he challenged and conquered a German knight named Enrique de Remestién; and another time in Arras, he conquered an important knight named Mosior de Charni." *Las CCC del famosísimo poeta Juan de Mena, con glosa* (The Three Hundred of the Most Famous Poet Juan de Mena, with a Gloss), Granada, 1505, fol. 99r.) Literature does not register the activities of the Castilians in war in Europe before the fifteenth century.

[14] See my remarks in *Aspectos del vivir hispánico* (Aspects of Hispanic Existence), pp. 21-22.

who would bind together the dispersed wills of her people and sound the order to attack.[15] Hence, De la Torre, avid for deeds of prowess, dared to advise the unfortunate Henry IV, a poor scrap of a king in a country clamoring for clear command and direction. But with great perspicacity the diligent counselor observes that the Castilian monarchy may aspire to high enterprises because it does not share its power with the great lords, as had been the case in France, "for the king is the supreme authority in criminal and civil justice for all people; and although he may have granted a few towns and jurisdictions as favors to his dukes, counts, marquises, and other noblemen, the court of appeal and the sovereignty always remain attached or subject to his chancellory and royal crown." The king of France, on the other hand, lacked jurisdiction over the duke of Burgundy, and obtained from him 700 or 800 lances, at the most, in case of war. Thus it came about that the army of Castile was numerous and strong, for "there is not in the world another people so skillful at arms"; besides, it was the only army in which "horses and harnesses were continually maintained," even though there might be no war going on. This means that as early as the middle of the fifteenth century people noticed the Spanish peculiarity of possessing a kind of permanent army, which Ferdinand the Catholic further developed at the end of the century and thereby made Spanish expansion in Europe possible. De la Torre predicts that Castilian arms could destroy "the nearby lands and even those far removed, if they would set themselves to the task with thought and hard work and unity."[16] This does not occur "because of the sins and pride of the Spanish nobility, or because of the internal divisions between the grandees of Castile." Otherwise, the young king Henry IV would put "under royal subjection and hand that kingdom of Granada." This passionate will to have a leader who will command and guide, will give to the advent of Ferdinand and

[15] Fernán Pérez de Guzmán was already lamenting that Henry III (1379-1406) did not "have the strength of body and spirit to prosecute the war" against Portugal and conquer that kingdom.

[16] Spanish Jews yearned for the imperial expansion of Castile, and wished for peace and concord inside their country—the dream of not being persecuted. Rabbi Arragel, glossing the Bible, thus ponders the fruits of harmony and mutual accord: "The people of that tower [of Babel], although they persisted against God and in their idolatries, yet were without hatred and ill-will one for another; and lived in concord, and protected one another's goods; wherefore our Lord wished that a memorial of them should remain; but those of the flood robbed one another, and despised one another; wherefore no memorial of them was left." (*Biblia*, translated by Rabí Arragel [1422-1433?], published by the Duke of Alba, 1920, I, 119a.)

Isabella the air of a fulfilled prophecy, or of a Messiah who at last appears.

But just as De la Torre previously described in detail the natural wealth of Spain, he will now show us with some insight the structure of the monarchical regime. The court is rich, and in its shelter live "infinite numbers of people who in time of peace are permanently employed in the royal house and court . . . ; with so much of ornaments and tapestries and tableware . . . that it is known to all people everywhere; and one must marvel at how even the common people are dressed and maintained."[17]

Those who did not participate in such splendor, who were the majority, "*go about idly*; and not only in the court but in all the towns, villages, and lands, *they are countless in number*; without robbing or stealing or doing any other evil deed, they are perpetually maintained out of the fatness of the land." It is evident that in order to dazzle the French chevaliers with whom he debated at the court of Charles VII, Fernando de la Torre sketched an idyllic picture, almost a picture out of the Golden Age, as he spoke of the host of vagabonds who simply lived off the provident earth. Although here, as before, when he spoke of the lack of technology, it is not very clear where the line is to be drawn between his praise of what Spain possesses and his bitterness over her lack of things that others possess. Concerning the people miraculously maintained in a state of idleness, he adds: "this is not done, I believe, in any other part of the world, where everyone lives, especially in France, *according to orderly rule*,[18] in the houses of the lords; and outside them, according to profession and trade."

[17] It is the moment of great luxury in living, unknown before John II. There is an awareness of wealth (as we have seen in De la Torre), Morisco customs abound (as I shall later point out), and the chivalric usages of France are imitated. The embellished expression of all this is found in the *Coplas* of Jorge Manrique:

Gifts unmeasured,	Las dádivas desmedidas,
The royal buildings	los edificios reales
Full of gold,	llenos de oro,
Dishes so burnished,	las vaxillas tan febridas,
The golden coins	los enriques y reales
Of the treasury,	del tesoro,
The caparisons, the horses	los jaezes, los cavallos
Of her people, and finery	de su gente, y atavíos
In such excess,	tan sobrados,
Where shall we find them now?	¿dónde iremos a buscallos?
What were they but the dew	¿qué fueron sino rocíos
Of the meadows?	de los prados?

[18] It is worth noting that even at that time a Spaniard should observe that in

By the middle of the fifteenth century Spain presented the same aspect that was to characterize her for centuries: a superabundance of people employed in the court, in the noble houses, and in the Church. The necessity for playing a role in society, inherent in the Hispanic condition, brought the lords to surround themselves with a multitude of servitors and clients. In the epistle of Fernando de la Torre there are precise data: a French viscount with an income of 15,000 crowns had with him only ten guardsmen at the siege of Cadillac; and in time of peace he maintained no more than ten attendants, and they and he "ate by assignment in the servants' dining room or the hall of the king." "What knight is there in Castile who with a third of the French viscount's income does not take three times as many guardsmen, and does not ordinarily maintain six times as many people, and does not regard it as degrading for him and his attendants to eat in the dining hall of His Lordship?" The Spanish knight, for reasons that will continue to appear in the course of this book, must needs envelop himself in a transcendent aura, a halo of prestige, either religious, regal, or of personal honor. He had to feel himself a part of a magical remoteness, and as if in suspension over the face of the earth—wherefore his disdain for mechanical, commercial, or even intellectual activities. Anticipating what I shall have to say later, I would point out here that De la Torre is a clear example of what I shall later call "Hispanic integralism," for he is filled with joy and a sense of plenitude by the vital unity he observes among the prestige of the monarchy, the boldness of the knight, and the magical wealth of the Spanish earth. In Castile living was cheap, and with less money one would acquire more things than in France. "From whence does this proceed save from the noble and bountiful earth? And where are there greater incomes, and where is there greater splendor than there is in noble Castile?" To be sure the duke of Burgundy collects large sums in Flanders, "but these moneys come from trafficking and swindling in the trading of goods, and from the taxes levied on them; the goods are not native to the place; the Germans bring them, the Italians transport them, and the Castilians send them." Commercial traffic, evidently, uproots man from his own land, severs him from his vital context, draws him away from nature, and causes him to participate in frauds. Here we have the seeds that later were to flower in dreams

---

France people lived "according to orderly rule," that is, in conformity with reason. I attach considerable importance to these references to what I call the "functional structure" of each people, a structure which persists throughout the changes in the content of history.

of the Golden Age of Antiquity, in disdain for the court and song in praise of the rustic life, in the pastoral, and in Don Quixote's horror of firearms. Those who do not derive their whole substance from the land on which they live, in the end cease to be themselves; they disintegrate. When the day foreshadowed came, man would be felt to be the meeting point of the strong reek of the earth with the magical beam of belief,

> for there would be no captain
> if no one tilled the soil.
>> (Calderón, *The Mayor of Zalamea*)

Where an earth made divine marched with a heaven made human, the Spanish soul ran its course. We have seen how Fernando de la Torre proclaimed his pride in the bounty of the Spanish earth; but before him the Arabs had already made their own the theme of the fertility of the soil, cultivated in Al-Andalus with loving care. The land of Seville was compared to that of Syria for its productivity, and all that "is sowed therein, bursts forth, grows, and is magnified." In some places fruit trees come up without having been planted, but only with working and improving the soil.[19] In the *Description of Spain*, by the anonymous chronicler of Almeria (twelfth century), it is related that in Zaragoza, "among other extraordinary things that happen there, nothing ever spoils, neither fruits nor wheat. I have seen wheat more than a hundred years old, and grapes that have been hanging for six years. Such is the abundance of cereals, wines, and fruits, that in all the inhabited earth there is no country more fertile."[20] This element of magic and marvel is lacking in the well-known *Laus Hispaniae*, of Saint Isidore, subsequently amplified in the *Crónica general* of Alphonse the Learned: "the valleys and the plains . . . bear much fruit and are abundant . . . Spain overflows with grains, and enjoys the sweet taste of fruits" (p. 311). Here one does not yet sense the mystic trembling of the Orient. Yet according to Leon Hebreo, a Spanish Jew of the fifteenth century, the celestial virtues pass through the other elements, "but they are stopped only in the earth, because of her thickness and because she is in the center; and against her all the rays strike most surely. So that she is the true wife of the heaven, and the other elements are his concubines; for in her, Heaven engenders all, or the greater part, of his generation; and she is adorned with so many and such divers things."[21] The sexual sublimation of the earth, in

---

[19] *La Péninsule Ibérique au Moyen Âge* (according to) Al-Ḥimyarī, translation of Lévi-Provençal, Leyde, 1938, pp. 3, 5, 27, 29.

[20] See René Basset, in *Homenaje a don Francisco Codera*, 1904, p. 643.

[21] "Diálogos de amor," in the *Nueva Biblioteca de Autores Españoles*, xx, 314.

spite of neo-Platonic reminiscences, shows the stamp of Islamic-Judaic thought and feeling.

If all the references to the earth in Spanish literature were to be grouped together, the peculiarity of their approach and style would become obvious. It is even characteristic for a sixteenth-century humanist as learned as Juan Ginés de Sepúlveda to think of agriculture as an "occupation that is very virtuous and near to nature, and that usually invigorates the body and the spirit and prepares them for work and for war: to such a degree that the ancients preferred labor in the field to commerce, and the Romans drew many consuls and dictators from among the ploughmen."[22]

Lope de Vega pondered the richness of the Spanish soil, with the same exaltation as the medieval Moslems:

> It is a fertile land, which never tires
> Of producing food, silver, and gold . . .
>
> What think you, milady, of this land?
> Does its agreeable sight not give you joy,
> Its plants, fertile and fair,
> Such diversity of fruits and trees?
> Do you not marvel to see such grandeur?[23]

In other instances the earth appears as an "alma mater" worthy of being venerated. A victim of shipwreck in *El anzuelo de Fenisa* (Fenisa's Fishhook) says:

> I know that land awaits me,
> Land I want to kiss. . . .
> The land is after all a mother,
> And like a mother she gives sustenance.

Rural life was a theme of primary importance in the art of Lope de Vega, and generally in all the literature of the sixteenth and seventeenth centuries, not only because it echoed Vergil or because the Renaissance exalted nature and the Golden Age of antiquity, but also because the peasant was felt to be the cultivator of a soil magical, eternal, and provident, the giver of fine-tasting fruits and wines, just as the cultivators of the invisible divinity brought down graces from heaven as the product of their labors. As early as the Middle Ages, the Spanish

[22] *De appetenda gloria*, Madrid, 1780, IV, 206.
[23] The examples come from the plays *Roma abrasada* (Rome Burned) and *El molino* (The Mill), and are quoted by R. del Arco, *La sociedad española en las obras dramáticas de Lope de Vega*, p. 59.

Christian scorned mechanical, rational labor that was without mystery, without a background of eternity to transcend it. No; for him, earth or heaven. The importance of the farmer and of everything rustic in Spanish life and letters went hand in hand with the equally pervasive presence of the priestly. Earth and heaven resolved their opposition in a unity of faith. If a passionate longing for infinitude and transcendence had not underlain the Spaniard's notion of the earth, Mateo Alemán— Jewish by race—would not have written the following passage, as admirable as it is gloomy:

"It has always been considered a hard thing to do, to find a faithful and true friend. . . . I have found only one who is the same substance as ourselves, the best, the most generous, the truest, the most reliable of all, who never forsakes us, *who stands forever unchanged*, who never tires of giving us gifts; and that friend is the earth. . . . She accepts and suffers everything from us, good treatment and bad. She is silent to everything. . . . And all the wealth that is ours in the earth is the gift of the earth. Finally, when we lie stinking in death, when there is neither wife nor father nor son nor kinsman nor friend who will suffer us, and all reject us, fleeing from us, then she protects us, receiving us into her own womb, where we repose under her faithful watch till she may give us up again in new and eternal life." (*Guzmán de Alfarache*, II, 2, I.)

In the notion of the *patria*—fatherland—the accent fell more strongly on the land than on the ancestors. For subtle, sensitive Lope de Vega, the greatness of even a Charles V, grandson of Ferdinand and Isabella, did not make up for the defect of his being born in another country: "If it were possible for a man, he ought to seek to be born in France, to live in Italy, and to die in Spain. To be born in France because of the French nobility, who have always had a *king born in their own land* and who have never brought in foreign blood; to live in Italy for Italian liberty and fertility; and to die in Spain *because of the faith there*, which is so Catholic, so firm, and so true."[24]

Spain was a faith, a belief, fed by life and by death, by heaven and by earth; it was the land of the cult of the Eucharist and of the cereal

[24] *El peregrino en su patria* (The Pilgrim in His Native Land), 1604, p. 304. When Lope de Vega intuits the existence of Spain as a unity, he sees it as a hollowness just as Quevedo does (a national monarchy, general welfare, and liberty are lacking); but all the negations become affirmations in his art, in a paradoxical compensation possible only in that country in which censure and praise of all that pertains to the country paradoxically coexist. Disillusion or even despair never had in Spain the consequences that modern rational thought would expect.

that lent that Sacrament its material substance. Calderon wrote *El mágico prodigioso* (The Prodigious Magician), a drama of complicated and highly subtle art, to be performed in the village of Yepes (Toledo) before rustics who tenderly tilled the soil; and who found in the bosom of the land a sense of eternity, not the same as the heavenly eternity, but possessed, like the latter, of an infinite perspective. Among the innumerable beliefs which make up the vital framework of Spain, the land was a very essential one; it is for this reason that the rustic and the royal-divine are always intermingled in the seventeenth-century theater just as they are in the previously quoted folk-saying: "Prince or peasant." Unamuno, with a powerful, intuitive sense for the Hispanic reality, wrote in 1927: "On few peoples of the earth has the divine, or, if you wish—it amounts to the same thing—the demoniac earth left a deeper imprint than on the peoples forged by Hispania," because Spain is "this land under heaven, this land full of heaven, this land which, being a body, and because of being a body, is a soul." This is not whimsical and beautiful lyricism but the expression of a life, and not less real and historical than that described in the chronicles; underneath this lyricism, as I have just demonstrated, throb ten centuries of yearning existence.

In the light of this, a considerable depth of meaning is to be found in the fact that Fernando de la Torre, the first Spaniard to try to reflect in earnest, if only to a degree, about his country, should take as his point of departure the Spanish earth—its reality, the emotion it evoked in him, and its magical powers. At the same time, the dutiful counselor was aware of the price Castile had to pay for being what she was. De la Torre expected everything from the new young king. In spite of the blessed "fatness of the land," the solution for Spain's difficulties had to fall from heaven. Our fifteenth-century Spaniard is the first one to contemplate his country with trusting satisfaction and at the same time critically and with anguish.[25] That uneasiness with respect to one's own existence has continued in a trembling but unbroken line from the fifteenth century down to the present time. In view of this, it seems to me that history ought first of all to take into account the following primordial phenomenon: here is a people whose initial and constant problem is its insecurity and anguish concerning its own existence, its uncertainty, its living in a state of alarm caused by its doubt. It will be

[25] "Anguish" is used here with the connotations it has in the writings of Kierkegaard, whose English translators have sometimes preferred the term "dread." Cf. German *Angst*. The connotation of "anxiety" as the term is used in psychology is especially to be avoided here.

said that other peoples, even the most productive and flourishing ones, were not free from an occasional lash of dissatisfaction and self-criticism. But with them such reflections are marginal voices alongside the steady stream of the collective life, which follows its course, indifferent to the admonitions and insults that are hurled from the shore. The matter of Spain was and is something else: it is rather as if the river should never cease wondering whether its waters are really following the course they ought to be following.

Half a century ago, a book such as this would have been taken as an expression of pessimism, and the reader would have looked upon it with puzzlement, or with a pity verging on ridicule—a culture whose primary feature consisted in its not being sure of itself. But fifty years ago it was believed that only what was clear and what was optimistic had value, and that the system of western life bore an assurance of indefinite progress. Today, after many tragic experiences, we know that this is not true. We know moreover that there can be forms of art and life of the highest quality, whose very basis is the anguished and the radically problematical. And, besides, whatever may be the vital peculiarity of Spain, it would be senseless to approach it with any save a purely objective attitude. The person who expects to understand history must submerge himself in it, must get rid of patriotism, as well as bitterness. And especially in studying a historic life that consists in insecurity must the historian rid himself of all insecurity. He must accept the totality of the data in all their fullness, the noble with the paltry, thinking of how the two interlock. In the heyday of the Spanish Empire (1569) Gonzalo Jiménez de Quesada, conquistador of what was to become Colombia and founder of Bogota, wrote that Spain had not been given credit for her victories in Europe—from France to Poland, from Germany to Italy. "Most shocking of all is the fact that the same thing happens in our West Indies, where their barbaric people try to minimize the greatness of their conquerors." (*El Antijovio*, Bogota, 1952, pp. 21-24.)

In 1609 Quevedo commented thus on the expulsion of the Christianized Moors: "And in the end, if the Moors who came into Spain in 711 deprived Spain of people by beheading them, the Moors that Spaniards ejected deprived it of people because they themselves left. The loss was Spain's; the only difference was the knife," *Chitón de las tarabillas*[26] (The Babblers' Stopper). Quevedo, then, feels Spain as a hollowness in a nonexistent mass. The same nihilistic reduction of the

---

[26] Included in the edition of his *Obras*, Madrid, 1936, the edition referred to here.

social reality occurs in *El Criticón* (The Book of Critics) of Baltasar Gracián (1657), who has as one of his most significant themes the hatred of the common people, of what today is called the masses: "The common people are nothing but a synagogue[27] of pretentious ignoramuses who, the less they understand of things, the more they discuss them" (II, 5).

Time and again Gracián denounces the multitude, smothering it with reproaches: "credulous, barbarous, foolish, loose, sensation-mongering, insolent, garrulous, dirty, loud-mouthed, lying, despicable" (II, 5). The serious thing for Gracián is that "men of high birth, those of good blood, those of illustrious houses, who, however little assistance they may get, are bound to attain great worth, and who, since they are all lent a hand, are bound to have a hand in all"—the grave thing is, "that these yield to vices, they humble themselves, and bury themselves alive in the cavern of nothingness" (III, 8). This whole class of people, who could become a valuable elite and did not, Gracián casts into the "cavern of nothingness." For him, as for Quevedo, the world that surrounds him is a play of inane figures, of pure shadows.

Much earlier than these two was the admirable Fernán Pérez de Guzmán, in whose *Generaciones y semblanzas* (Generations and Portraits, 1460) is to be found an anticipation of the thesis (expressed by some contemporary writers) concerning the Spanish hatred for any kind of select personality: "And not only this noble knight was ruined in these uprisings in Castile, but many other houses, both great and middling, were ruined: for Castile does better at making new gains than she does at keeping what she has gotten. For often those whom she herself has built up, she herself destroys." The last statement is no more than a gloss of what Don Alonso Fernández Coronel said as he was going to be executed by order of the king of Castile, Peter the Cruel: "This is Castile, which makes men and wastes them."[28] And so, for six

---

[27] "Synagogue" is used here in the Greek, etymological, sense of "meeting, assembly." The author, aristocratic in attitude, protects himself from the object he defines, removing himself some distance from it by means of a learned Hellenism, impenetrable to the mob.

[28] "Generaciones y semblanzas" (Generations and Portraits), in *Clásicos castellanos*, LXI, pp. 90 and 110. Other correlations no less significant could be established. Fernán Pérez de Guzmán says: "In Castile there has always been little effort made to preserve antiquities, which is a great pity. . . . Without doubt, it is a noteworthy deed and praiseworthy to preserve the memory of the noble lineages or of the services rendered to the kings and to the republics—of which little care has been taken in Castile" (pp. 50-51). Gracián is no more satisfied with history written by Spaniards: "I assure you that there have not been more, nor more heroic, deeds than those done by the Spaniards, but none have been worse recorded than by the Spaniards them-

centuries Spaniards have been aware of the difficulties that hinder the prosperity of the man who stands out from the masses. It is useless, for my purpose, to start an argument about this, and to compare lists of persecuted and nonconformist citizens in different European countries: Saint John of the Cross, cruelly harassed by the Carmelite monks; Giordano Bruno, burned alive in Rome; Luis de León, a victim of the inquisitorial furor of the mob at the University of Salamanca; Galileo, tyrannized by the Roman cardinals; Miguel Servet, burned by Calvin; Descartes, a refugee in a foreign land; and so on. I must emphasize that for the purpoes of my analysis it makes no difference whether the Spaniards of the fifteenth, the seventeenth, or the twentieth century have or do not have an objective basis for writing what they write; the important thing is to take note of the sensation of an emptiness in life that those and other illustrious Spaniards experienced. The *vital* truth of their judgment is what interests us.

To enumerate all the motives that at one time or another have been alleged by way of explaining Spain's misfortunes or her peculiarity would be a lengthy task. People have spoken of the climate, of her indolence, of her resistance to accepting the lights of reason, of her fanaticism, of the absence of the Renaissance. In the sixteenth century the Moors were blamed for the ills of Spain. Hernán Pérez de Oliva— a good humanist—says that if all the cities had resisted the Saracens as did Cordova, his ancestral home, "they would not have driven our holy religion out of our temples, they would not have given us cause to weep in the blood of our own even down to our own days."[29] The use of the word *our* four times in two lines reveals the degree to which Master Pérez de Oliva felt the Moors to be foreigners. He wanted to eject them far and away from his own life. Some historians of the present day continue to believe that Arabic domination harmfully deflected the

---

selves. Most of these histories are like bacon that is all fat and no lean, and turns the stomach after two bites." (*El criticón*, III, 8.) The common feature that lends unity to these foregoing quotations is that in the fifteenth century, and in the seventeenth, written history does not satisfy three ill-humored observers of the life around them.

[29] *Razonamiento sobre la navegación del Guadalquivir* (Discourse on the Navigation of the Guadalquivir), in *Obras*, II, 2. For Fernán Pérez de Guzmán the occupation of Spain by the Moors was:

A history sad and lachrymose,
Unworthy of scribes in meter and prose.

("Loores de los claros varones de España," in *Nueva Biblioteca de Autores Españoles*, XIX, 718)

course of Spanish history. I believe that without the presence of the Arabs this history is not understandable.

Other historians have had recourse to the idea of a Spanish essence, a prior substratum or stage on which Spain has played out the game of her history. Much has been said about Iberianism, about individualism, about tendencies incompatible with the forms of good society. The ancients talked about it, and some moderns have seized that unreal human substantialism. They connect the Iberia known to Strabo with the Iberian Peninsula of today. Thus we fall into a mythic fatalism, into an invisible history prior to the given life in the long centuries within our reach today. The truth is that the Spaniard has created himself within, and in the course of, the history of his doings, and not on a foundation of "race."

My own purpose now is more modest and less dogmatic, for I aspire to describe what has happened to the Spaniard, and what the circumstances in which destiny placed him offered him as bases of life. Only thus shall we be able to contemplate history as a realization of values, and not as the ugly reverse side of a tapestry. What is important to us is what the Spaniard is and what he has done, for his achievements are indissolubly wedded to his misfortunes and failures. Rebellious to law and to any norm of the state, the Spaniard was docile to the voice of tradition and to the imperative of his absolute person. If he had not been like this, the Peninsula would have been converted into a prolongation of Africa, or into an extension of France, or perhaps of England. The Spaniard welded himself to his legendary, religious, and artistic beliefs, as did no other European people. He fortified himself in the castle of his own person, and in his own person he found the impetus and faith to build a strange and immense colonial empire that lasted from 1500 to 1824. He preserved without essential changes his thirteenth-century language, and with it he hammered out artistic creations of universal validity. The Spaniards did not let themselves be rationally unified by means of reason, knowledge, law, or a net of economic links, but rather by beliefs which enfolded and motivated them. All this fits in rather badly with the concept of "individualism," forged by nineteenth-century thought from other points of view and to resolve other problems, as we shall see, especially in the last chapter.

Before delving into the historic life of Spain, I have sought to make understandable the fact that many Spaniards, some of them very eminent, have tried to explain the existence of Spain as a chronic ailment. These Spaniards who resort to this explanation then loom up as outstanding instances of "Vivir desviviéndose," which is to say that their explanation of Hispanicity is a function of their Hispanism. It has not befallen any other great civilization to live for century after century feeling all the while that the very ground under its feet was missing, and creating at the same time such first-class values. This people, on more than one occasion, has marched to its own destruction as to a jubilant saturnalia. But for the moment let us not worry ourselves about this, nor let us say whether this manner of existing is evil or good. Let us, rather, bring in some theoretical points of view which, I hope, will support my special method of studying history.

The Historical Approach

Fundamental Assumptions

To THE UTMOST OF HIS ABILITY the historian must make evident the "reality" of the history he is trying to write; he must endow it with meaning that will light the way for the reader to proceed, without stumbling over obstacles, from the detail to the whole, from the single event to the total life of the subject-agent, of which the single event is an expression. History is, first and foremost, a mesh of interconnected values, into which the existence of a people is articulated, whilst the people manifest their reality by accomplishing valuable actions that have actual extension in time and space.

It does not matter that we cannot all agree upon the nature and form of these values and that, consequently, we cannot render them acceptable to everyone. It is enough if the historian have faith and belief in the faith that a people have objectivized in their life, a faith justified in great achievements that stand for all to see, or even in a profound fear of being unable to realize great achievements. A people, like a tragic hero, must show themselves worthy of confronting their inescapable destiny—their eventual extinction, not as people in the physical sense, but as high value, an extinction in which they will cease to be an authentic subject for history.

History is where are realized, in many ways, man's possibilities for achieving great deeds and works that endure and radiate their values afield, works that effectively quicken and make fruitful in other men the capacity for reasoning and the longing to break out of the common round of daily insignificance, in other words, that can affect the mind, the imagination, or the soul.

History can become universal; it does not, however, attain universality through the unification of the peoples who are engaged in creating history, but rather by virtue of the fact that values can be universalized, can spread, near or far, from people to people, who might be said to be like trees touching branch tip to branch tip, but whose roots are not twined together deep down in the dark. An example of universalization is the Jewish belief in the Messiah (whose advent is an accomplished fact for many people). So, too, have the exact forms of Greek thought become universal. And many other things have spread abroad, both important and insignificant, from the use of the wheel to certain kinds of dance.

It is necessary, then, to presuppose that some kind of important value exists, before one can set about describing and trying to understand the process of history in a human collectivity, which at first glance is a confused chaos of fragments of life that in themselves are *not yet history*. The undertaking is risky since one can never arrive at certainties of the kind that will be valid for everybody, as a judgment in exact science is valid.

Those who do not have in advance a kindred feeling for the historical deeds of a people will not accept as valuable what was achieved by that people, no matter how high we may heap praises thereon. Unless it finds in the reader an adequate receptivity for a certain kind of values, the history of a people may glance off his sensibility just as Shakespeare's works did off the spirit of a number of eighteenth-century rationalists. Certain great values of the Asiatic peoples of today leave the majority of cultivated Westerners cold and indifferent.

This being the situation, I aspire in the present history to do no more and no less than satisfy the requirements I have set for myself. I take it for granted that the Hispanic people have accomplished things of high value, and that this work has gone on for the most part under difficult, harassing conditions. Thus it has been necessary to devise a historical structure that will accommodate the possibility of both valuable developments and their opposites. As the center and the subject-agent of this history, I have taken the whole workshop in which the history has been fashioning itself, and not fragmentary psychological traits, always generic and meaningless in their isolation. Nor have I considered external circumstances as separable from the very course of life itself, as if the latter were a given, substantial "reality" on which causes and motives act. My idea is that a Frenchman, or a Spaniard, handles the circumstances about them according to the possibilities of their peculiar structure of life. Historical life consists in an inner trajectory or process in which the external motivations acquire form and reality; that is, they are converted into deeds and events that have a meaning.

These deeds and events trace out the peculiar physiognomy of a people and make evident the "inwardness" of their life, never identical with that of any other human community. This "inwardness" is not a static and finished reality analogous to the classic substance; it is a dynamic reality, analogous to a function or, as I later shall point out, to an "invariance." But "inwardness" is an ambiguous term. It may designate *the fact of living* within certain vital possibilities (preferences) and impossibilities (reluctances), and in this case I shall call it the "dwelling-place of life" (morada); or it may designate *the mode according to which* men live within this dwelling-place, and then I shall call it "living structure," or "living functioning" (vividura). Both the dwelling-place and the living structure of a community of people are made manifest in the way the community speaks, thinks, believes, and makes or does for itself certain things in preference to others.

The metaphors of the dwelling-place and the functional structure will clarify, I hope, the thought that has called them forth. All peoples have a vital dwelling-place. Sometimes the dwelling-places of different peoples appear to be similar, even to the point of having the same kind of human "furniture." Certainly we find today, almost all over the world, railroads, airplanes, temples, schools, libraries, doctors, orchestras, governors, diplomatic corps, armies, etc. This leads us to think that the world is one, or at least that it will become one when the benefits of civilization are even farther extended. It should be observed, however, that much of what we see among the vital "furnishing" in a given dwelling-house does not derive authentically from the possibilities of the living structure that fills it. Sometimes vehicles and technical tools are mere importations; if not these, then the conductors of symphony orchestras, or the music they perform. Examples are too obvious to require accumulation. Bringing our vision into still sharper focus, we shall see that even if one people produces certain things similar to the products of another (philosophy, sciences, machines, etc.), these productive activities do not occupy the same volume in the totality of the respective lives; and, especially, they do not stand in the same relationship to the respective hierarchies of value. In certain dwelling-places scientific or industrial activities fill almost all the vital volume; in others they figure as an uncommon luxury, or they are relegated to back rooms, the cellar, or the garret. The same is true of everything else that goes to make up the broad orbit of life: warlike spirit, political and social morality, sense of personality, literary and artistic distinction, encouragement of intellectual activity; various kinds of religiosity.

Something of all these things may be found in a people, but always in an arrangement that reflects a particular system of capabilities and preferences. This means that our primary concern here is not the *what* and the *how much* of vital activities, but the peculiar way in which these activities go on. Ideas—so-called civilization—function one way in one place and another way in another place.

In this book I shall use, as the occasion for them arises, the terms "dwelling-place," "living structure," "functional structure," and "vital disposition and way of life." I avoid the terms "character" and "psychological traits," because they point to something already fixed, given, typed; or to something that is partial and perceptible only in its results. I am interested in life as movement, course, and direction—as something variable yet combined with an "invariance" (to borrow a term from mathematics) that makes it possible to grasp an identity as it passes through one mutation after another. I am pursuing a vital constant, not a logical univocal concept, a modality and not a substance. The dwelling-places of my metaphor are not closed or cut off from those of their neighbors. The dwellers go forth and return, they bring in or allow in "furnishings" of the most varied sorts besides their own. But when such surges of activity subside and the dweller is again established in his dwelling-place, he will prefer certain rooms to others as his normal habitation, for he feels more at home in them, more comfortable performing certain tasks than others. The dweller's freedom will depend upon the possibilities and limitations of his dwelling-place, no matter what is brought into it from the outside.

For all that, how is it possible for a people's "dwelling-place"—the helm of collective life—to become a new and different one? Our experience shows, however, that some of the main Western human groups (French, Italian, Spanish) are new historical departures. Language, in this case, has been a decisive innovation and a symptom of a breach in the collective state of mind. The fact of not understanding Latin meant that people had stopped being Roman. Centuries intervened between the time when Romance languages began to be written and the time in which orators spoke literary Latin and were understood. In the meantime an impoverished Latin was written by a minority whose daily language was no longer Latin. During this long period there were no literary works which expressed the life of the people in a language at the reach of all the people. Had such works existed, the *Chanson de Roland* and the *Aeneis* would have been linked by such a series of historical continuities as exist between the works of Marcel Proust and the *Chanson de Roland*. But this has not been the case. Between the romanized Gauls and the Capetian French there has been a gap in the collective consciousness. On the other hand, between the French of the year

1000 and those of today there has been a series of gradual transitions during which each generation understood the literary expression of the previous one. The "dwelling-place" of life was not torn down; its contents were renewed but, as we shall see later on, the decisive hierarchy of values was preserved—a down-to-earth and, at the same time, well-balanced sense of values. "Dwelling-places" of life change as a result of great and protracted cataclysms. When that occurs, people lose the consciousness of what they have been and no longer behave in the old way. They, moreover, fall under the sway of invaders whose force and prestige cannot be challenged. In this way "dwelling-places" of life have been rebuilt.

Historical life being the way it is, the valuable activities and qualities of one people cannot always be incorporated into the life of another. The values of one dwelling-place can be transplanted only to new and deeply plowed soils. Our experience confirms this when we notice that within a particular country certain valuable activities are kept in isolation or enjoy but meager cultivation when, in respect to the country's dominant values, they are felt as exceptional or as unexpected: the sciences in Spain, mysticism and "Pascalian" spirit in France, philosophy in the United States, music among the Anglo-Saxon peoples, etc. Contrariwise, when a phenomenon happens to be in phase with the current of a people's life, the authentically beloved values are multiplied and diffused with an easy spontaneity and in terms of high achievements: natural and experimental science has flourished in England from the thirteenth century till today; theoretical thought filled nine centuries of Greek history; the epic tension of the Spaniard was maintained from the tenth century to the eighteenth; and so, in other well-known instances.

A people maintain their preferred modes of valuable activity as long as their vital impetus lasts, or until they are inwardly modified by other people mingling with them, or until they are destroyed by some kind of cataclysm. The final upshot of the Germanic invasions was a modification of the living structure of the Roman people; the Franco-Normans changed the structure of life on the British Isles; tribes from the north of the Iberian Peninsula, engaged in centuries of interaction with Moors and Jews, worked out the special vital disposition of the Spaniards.

Corollaries

In the preceding chapter I have tried to make the reader feel the vexatious, problematical situation of those who expressed their conscious awareness of the nature of Spanish existence. Those several Spaniards living between the fifteenth and twentieth centuries manifestly find themselves caught in unhappy straits. These persons are aware that they have a past marked with difficulties and that they are colliding with a harsh present. What is their situation? What is the correlate of their awareness? The person in question does not refer to some untoward event befalling him, but rather to the totality of his life. The recurrence of such a phenomenon through the centuries confers on these manifestations of intimate experience the value of a historic reality: the person manifests himself existing *in* his history.

In the face of the tendency to make history consist in cultures and civilizations only, one must accentuate the reality of the fact that cultures are inseparable from the peoples that create and sustain them and feed their own lives from them. Rome became extinct the moment the Romans ceased existing as Romans. What happens to a people existing as the Roman Empire, for instance, or as a Greek city, is something singular and unrepeatable. A people wins admiration; it wins contempt; it drags along inertly; it disappears. These happenings are for each people unique. Rome and Athens, besides being different from each other because of their "cultures," possessed the singularity that their peoples existed as Romans and Greeks respectively. This observation, at first simple and apparently naïve, turns into an unmanageable problem as soon as one tries to give it a justifiable meaning. Human life is not a "thing," nor a substance that can be accounted for in a definition; it is pure activity, and not a physical, psychic, or ideal object (tree, desire, triangle). Many of us believe today that the human reality is given in life: "The totality of the psychico-physically given cannot be said to *be*, but rather to *live*; and this constitutes the starting point of historicity. An autognosis, directed not towards an abstract I but to the fullness of my self, will *encounter* me historically determined; physics, on the other hand will come to *know* me cosmically determined."[1]

The life that is spoken of here is not only the correlate of conscious

[1] From the correspondence of Dilthey with Count York von Wartenburg, as quoted by F. Heinemann, *Neue Wege der Philosophie*, p. 198. Heinemann (pp. 189ff.) has a good exposition of Dilthey's historical thought, of history as autognosis —self-knowledge—*Selbstbesinnung*: "Im Erlebnis sind die seelischen Zustände unmittelbar gegeben," in which *Erlebnis* would be the awareness of our immediate and lived experience of something. For an English account of Dilthey's thought, see H. A. Hodges, *Wilhelm Dilthey: An Introduction*, New York: Oxford University Press, 1944, especially pp. 11-35. This work is particularly useful in the understanding of Dilthey's terminology. In Spanish, see W. Dilthey, *El mundo histórico*, Mexico, 1944, pp. 308-312.

awareness (Erlebnis). It is, further, that which embraces humankind and in which humankind exists. In life are found the thinking I, as well as what gives rise to thought; everything exists and is given in the basic and all-embracing totality of life, which is contained in itself and which is the ultimate limit that man can reach in living and living self-consciously. The only possible way to proceed from here is to conceive (or dream) of life as being anchored in a beyond which is prior to it and ineffable; or as moving toward a superhuman destiny—superhuman, that is, at the same time that it is perfectly human.

A brief statement of what we understand by historical life must here suffice: a functional activity whose reason for existence consists precisely in its immanent continuous tending toward a future, from a present that includes its past. When I use the term "form" in this connection, it is with reference to an inner arrangement, an arrangement in which form and content are inseparable both from activity and its ends, and from the structure of the function. The unrestrainable process of human existence (and we must conceive of this as the existence of a human group, of a unity that is always singular in its structure) can move either in the direction of progress or towards the stagnation and ruination of values.

The inadequacy of our historical ideas makes some people confuse the idea of historical structure with a naïve determinism, of a biological or essentialist type. But my thought follows other paths. The life structure that I postulate is not a biologico-natural reality, in which, as Bergson would say, "its future is contained in its present." The human life process is, insofar as values are concerned, creation, unforeseeable and incommensurable by natural laws. The latter are an object of knowledge (scientia); the human element, on the contrary, is given in the consciousness (Bergson), in the autognosis (Dilthey).

The Presence of the Functional Structure

In dealing with such a slippery matter, it is a good idea to mention a few instances in which the reality of what I call "functional structure" is shown. Some historians have occasionally felt the presence of the functional structure when they have tried to make certain "facts" intelligible, that is, when they have tried to articulate the facts with the life of a people whose history they aspire to construct. Franz Cumont is the author of a splendid book on Roman history: *Les religions orientales dans le paganisme romain* (fourth edition, 1929). As is well known, the

Romans adopted a host of religious beliefs that came from Asia Minor, Egypt, Syria, and Persia, which interfused with the traditional religion of the Romans and displaced it. Cumont does not limit himself to recording the facts, describing the worship, etc; he poses, besides, the problem of what the existence of those beliefs was like within the Roman life process—the question, I would say, of what is their historico-human reality. The worship of the Eastern divinities spread through many countries; but the way in which the gods are articulated with the existence of the people is different in each country: "The Romans, in this respect different from the Greeks *in all the epochs of their history,* judged theories and institutions above all according to their practical results. For theorists they *always* felt that contempt which men of war and men of trade feel for them. It has been frequently observed that in the Latin world philosophy departed from metaphysical speculations in order to concentrate all its attention on ethics. Later, in the same fashion, the Roman Church (that is to say, the Christianized Romans) will leave to the subtle Hellenes the interminable controversies over the essence of the divine Logos, or over the dual nature of Christ. The questions that impassion and divide the Christians of Rome are those that refer to the conduct of life, such as the doctrine of Grace" (p. 31).[2] The Roman gods were less poetic and more "honest" than the Greek ones; "by temperament and by tradition, the Roman spirit felt the necessity of using religion as a support for morality and the State" (p. 34). The "invariance" of the Roman vital attitude thus stands out against the variation in its contents, in this case, religion. If the historian were not conscious of such an "invariance," he would not be able to articulate his history as Roman. The necessity to use religion for certain ends reveals the presence of an inclination to direct life through certain channels, and to this purpose religion, or any other form of culture, is subordinated. The truth of the judgment is confirmed by reading the correspondence of Quintus Aurelius Symmachus (345-405), the heart of whose existence continues to beat with a Roman rhythm when the Empire is on the point of disappearing. Symmachus, prefect of Rome and consul (!), was building mansions for eternity (in aevum mansura), and he tried to combine Christianity with the traditional worship of the gods, a symbol of the triumph of the State: "consuetudinis amor magnus est."[3]

[2] For this question, see X. Zubiri, *Naturaleza, historia, Dios,* Madrid, 1944, pp. 472ff.

[3] Symmachus does not seem to realize that Rome is in agony. Never were there more schools or more instruction. "We truly live in a century devoted to virtue," etc. (See Gaston Boissier, *La fin du paganisme,* ii, 192.)

The reality which we are trying to grasp is in itself fleeting and hard to express, although it is not a question of any kind of "spirit" floating in the void of abstraction. The initial difficulty lies in harmonizing the idea of humankind with the circumstance that we can perceive only the "specifications" of it, temporo-spatially given, that is, in collective historical lives. These units or specifications of mankind are not assemblies of parts, nor are they determined by final causes. They are rather total activities in which all that is circumstantial to them, and the ends to which they are directed, both acquire meaning. These activities are unthinkable without the idea of certain constant habits which limit the action at the same time that they create it. It is not enough to reduce the modalities of life to types of Weltanschauungen, for the specified functional structures present themselves not only as conceptual contents but also as sheer dynamic play between possibilities and impossibilities.[4] To understand this, it would then be necessary to establish a correlation between a determined vital direction, and the unpredictability of the contents motivated by that direction or tendency.

The functional structure of a vital "dwelling-place" becomes at times very obvious in what I have called the dynamic play of possibility and impossibility.[5] The Romans, to return to the preceding example, did not resign themselves to being a people of juridically and politically organized agriculturists. I do not know how that group of Italic peoples who spoke Latin acquired their efficient, expansive, cohesive, political capacity. But not until we encounter a people who live predominantly, evidently, in this functional structure do we encounter the people we call Roman. This functional structure disappears when those who were occupying and came to occupy the land of the ex-Empire initiated modes of existence created by a new structure. Although the people who do this living are in large part biologically connected to the old Romans, we cannot call them Romans.

[4] I leave to one side the fact that there are human groups doubtless coherent and possessing some sort of physiognomy, albeit a vague and uncertain one. The insistence on conceiving of history only as universalizable "culture" leaves out these half-done portraits, as it were, of peoples whose lives are drowsily expressed, or who pretend to be what they are not.

[5] The following statement of Dilthey's does not seem accurate to me: "Since no nation reckons with its own death, the position of plans and ends in its life is quite different from what it is in the life of the individual. These have always only a temporal, relative relationship to the inner nation, which is capable of unlimited possibilities." So long as the idea goes uncorrected that everything is possible to man (a relic, perhaps, of the immoderate pretensions of that phantom, the so-called "Renaissance man"), it will not be possible for historical knowledge to adapt itself to its object.

In spite of the unvarying functional disposition, there were enormous differences between the Rome of the Punic Wars and the Rome of Constantine. Rome had begun to be peacefully invaded, even before the Empire, by peoples, religions, institutions, customs, and objects, proceeding from the vast extension of lands which the dominating Roman was continually conquering. It has been said, and with reason, that the history of the first three centuries of the Empire was a peaceful penetration of the West by the East.[6] The Romans scorned technics and pure science, but they could not get along without importing men of learning from the East—astronomers, mathematicians, physicians, philosophers, architects, even jurists, from the third century to the fifth. Included among those who during the Empire passed as representatives of the spirit of the Greeks (Porphyry, Plotinus, Iamblichus, Galen, Dioscorides, Lucian) were Egyptians, Syrians, or Asiatics. The cultivated Romans knew Greek and spent their lives fascinated by the wonders of Attica. One need only read Book V of *De Finibus*, in which Cicero describes the pilgrimage he and his friends made through the "holy places" of vanished Athenian wisdom—"tanta vis admonitionis inest in locis." Greece and the Near East were present in Rome for centuries with their wisdom and their fascination, and as was "vitally" logical, the functional structure of the Roman reached the limit of its elasticity in its effort to Hellenize itself; it sought to surpass itself, and it did not succeed.[7] What ties Symmachus dynamically, vitally, with Cicero and the other Romans of the past—who are different in quality, in content, and in value—is what I call the vital "dwelling-place," functional structure of life. Without that, all that is "Roman" in the history of Rome would evaporate.

Thus we come to the conclusion that a history adequate to its historical object cannot consist in a relation of the successive events (in themselves nothing but meaningless anecdotes), nor in merely showing the achievements of a civilization out of the context of life, nor in the search for physical or economico-social causes, nor in dissolving the particularities of the life of a people in the universality of the human. History is understood if we contemplate it creating itself from within its peculiar

[6] F. Cumont, *op.cit.*, pp. 2-7.

[7] In a passage from Cicero it can be clearly perceived how Greece was articulated in the vital structure of the Roman: "Out of them [the Greek peripatetic philosophers] came orators, generals, and rulers. *Descending to a lower plane*, mathematicians, poets, musicians, and even physicians were made in that shop, as it were, of all the arts and crafts." (*De finibus*, v, 7.) Such is the hierarchy of social values for a profoundly Hellenized Roman.

mode of behavior, and not from without. There is no such thing as a Gothic, a Renaissance, a Baroque, or a Neo-classicism that, from an unreal space, conditions the flow of history as the moon intervenes in the tides. Nor is it certain, either, that geography or economy radically determine the future of men. These and other factors will be given *in* history, but the functional activity of a collective life is what will transform or will not transform in their present and their future the possibilities that circumstances offer them.

The possibility or impossibility of behaving in a certain way is intuited by us in some degree when we come in contact with another person. We notice immediately whether the other person belongs inside or outside our historic "field." The agreements and resistances that we expect from him, the sympathy or suspicion that he elicits, will be related to that primary intuition. Two men of the same tongue, whatever the difference between them, will begin their conversation on a basis different from that which supports one who notes in his interlocutor a foreign accent. Granted that the foreign historian can be on occasion more competent than the native, does not the historian of a people not his own stumble against the same problem? The *human being* in the abstract is not an object of the intuition and of the conscious awareness of the historian; the latter must always contend with people under the form of Romans, Italians, Spaniards, or whatever may be the modality of their existence.[8]

The knowledge of history has relied excessively on abstract and generalizing logic, supported, moreover, by the laudable intention of understanding and organizing the human species as a universal brotherhood. The Stoics thought of this in early times, and the Church Fathers called the Church catholic, universal. It is possible, for all I know, that the noble aspiration to unify the human species will someday be realized. But until this problematic event does take place, the history of man will have to be concerned with man's structural groupings. Franco-German intellectualism, idealism, and materialism of the nineteenth century conceived of man as a being unified in the common denominator of psychology, of the ideal, of economics, of the State, or of a single social class. It would seem that today's philosophy seeks to reduce history

[8] As early as 1796 Joseph de Maistre reacted against the abstract way of approaching the reality of man: "La constitution de 1795, tout comme ses aînées, est faite pour l'*homme*. Or, il n'y a point d'*homme* dans le monde. J'ai vu dans ma vie des Français, des Italiens, des Russes, etc.; je sais même, grâce à Montesquieu, qu'on peut être Persan: mais quant à l'homme, je déclare ne l'avoir rencontré de ma vie." (*Considérations sur la France*, edit. 1861, p. 88.) An idea like this has existed in France, but it has not occupied a preferred room in the French "dwelling-place."

to the idea of the radical and generic historicity of man. It is thus easy to see why we have few instruments that will enable us to say with any strictness what existence consists in for a Chinese, an Aztec, a Hungarian, a Hispanian, etc. But we will not arrive at a knowledge of this by studying and evaluating the Chinese, Aztec, and other civilizations, or by seeking to characterize peoples "psychologically" as writers have been doing since antiquity. And precisely for this reason there is a great disproportion between the terrifying amount of knowledge about cultures and our knowledge of how the people have inwardly lived who have realized their lives in those cultures.[9]

A few German philologists, some twenty years ago, tried to determine the permanent features, as it were, of the physiognomy of the Romanic peoples. With a view to the historical and geographical articulation of the languages of Latin provenience, the German romantics created Romanic philology as a collection of encyclopedic culture methodically parallel to that of Germanic philology, Semitic philology, etc. The initial intention was to provide linguistic details having the most universal meaning possible: languages realize the *idea* of language, and thus they perpetuate the structure of preceding languages. French, according to Meillet, is the Latin of the twentieth century as it is spoken in France; Latin is the Indo-European spoken in Rome, etc. All that the languages had in common and all that was generically a property of languages thus left in the background the particular existences of the languages, the living and systematic relationship between the speaker and his expression.

The criticism by certain Germans of the aforementioned efforts to determine the *essence* of French and German is connected with the universalizing purpose of the traditional German philologists.[10] Let us not argue over the success of those efforts. It is of interest only that, without repercussion, so far as I know, outside of Germany, they were

[9] In a different connection Wilhelm von Humboldt writes: "There is also the danger of evaluating inexactly the different situations of human society. Civilization or culture have often had attributed to them that which cannot have come from them because it has been the work of a *force* to which they themselves owe their existence." (*Ueber die Verschiedenheit des menschlichen Sprachbaues*, edit. by A. F. Pott, Berlin, 1876, II, 33.)

[10] I think that the idea was started by E. Wechssler, in *Esprit und Geist*, 1927, an essay on the ontology (Wesenskunde) of the Frenchmen and the German. Then came the *Handbuch der Frankreichkunde*, edited by Hartig-Schellburg, 1928-30, followed by Curtius-Bergstrasser, *Frankreich*, 1930, and E.-R. Curtius, *Essai sur la France*, 1932. See also *Neue Jahrbücher für Wissenschaft u. Jugendbildung*, 1932, VIII, 51-69.

challenged by a few scholars in Germany; the problem of the peculiarity of French and German was denied, and the traditional philological historians continued to interest themselves in generic aspects and in isolated anecdote, paying less attention to the vitally ordered structure of each language, which is the uniqueness that cannot be reduced to generalities. The confusion created by the aforementioned criticism grows, I think, out of not saying more precisely what we mean when uttering the word "permanent" (dauerhaft) with reference to that which we call French, Spanish, etc. If it is applied to an essence, to contents with a fixed stability, of a biologico-racial type, substantial in some way or other, then we err, because the objectifiable content of human activities is unforeseeable—the intelligence or the stupidity, the goodness or badness, the heroism, the faintheartedness, the baseness of an action. For life does not consist solely in doing this or that (including doing *nothing*), motivated by the inescapable attraction of an immediate future, the lodestone of life which forces one to go on living. Life presupposes, in addition, a projection from the historical "dwelling" in which man finds himself placed.

Not from an essence, but from the conscious awareness of a functional structure could the Spanish saying be born, "Church or sea or royal service," expressive of the courses possible for a Spaniard in the sixteenth century, that is, of a vital panorama that, in its general lines, functioned down to the nineteenth century. Less familiar is another expression: "Six Spanish adventurers, and one goes to the Indies, another goes to Italy, another goes to Flanders, another is in prison, another is engaged in lawsuits, and another is taking religious vows. And in Spain there are no other kinds of people save these six mentioned."[11]

Such judgments, formulated out of the conscious awareness of a collective situation, possess validity as a vision of the future linked with the present. They reveal, above all, the security of perceiving the stable channels through which the lives of the people are to unroll, at first glance, lives that are thick with unforeseeable possibilities. Such possibilities are unforeseeable as long as we think of the content of each individual, unique, unrepeatable life. Imagine the difference it makes whether it is Gonzalo de Cordova, or Miguel de Cervantes, or the Duke of Osuna, or Don Francisco de Quevedo who goes to Italy. But it is no less certain that the goals of these men as well as those of thousands of

[11] Such is the title of a book said to have been written in the middle of the sixteenth century by an eccentric named Vasco Díaz Tanco de Fregenal. (See B. J. Gallardo, *Ensayo de una biblioteca española de libros raros*, ii, 784.)

others never went beyond the limits of what I call Spanish "possibilities." Heroic lives there were in abundance, blissfully running the greatest of risks for the God and the King of Spain. But in vain will one look for an Andreas Vesalius, or heroes in the realm of thought such as Campanella, Giordano Bruno, or Galileo. This, in its turn, is another aspect of the Spanish "dwelling-place" of which there has been a clear and widespread awareness: "Spain is a province that is not inclined to take rational points of view" (Alonso de Palencia, 1459). "Let us hope that Spain, a country of light and of melancholy, may decide, one day, to rise to the level of metaphysical concepts" (Xavier Zubiri, 1933). "The capacity of the men Spanish in language for the *other* human things, a capacity so superior to their capacity for the sciences, in particular the exact and experimental sciences" (José Gaos, 1941). The reader will spare me now the monotonous task of filling out with quotations the whole period extending from 1459 to 1941. It is important for us only to realize the conscious awareness of the perdurability of what I call functional structure, and its objective validity.

Every man begins his conscious life enclosed in a collective situation, and within this enclosure he will be able to be anything from a paragon of virtue to a professional murderer. But if we look a little closer at the matter, we observe that he will realize these and other activities from his "dwelling-place" as a Spaniard, an Italian, or an Anglo-Saxon. As long as the man is very young he will be able to interrupt his molding in one structure in order to enter another. By the time he comes of age, he will be situated in life as an individual stationed in the historic situation that belongs to a people, a collective tradition. Any course that he undertakes will have as its starting point the way in which he is situated within the life of a human group. If we reject, for fear of falling into naturalistic determinism, this idea of inevitable station in an existence, we shall end up with an abstract or chaotic conception of history. The ordered structure in the "dwelling-place" of which I speak is not determined by anything exterior or transcendent to it; for it consists in the very reality of the existence of peoples. Dilthey called this the "awareness of social community," "national awareness, national feeling." The assembly of individuals "act in this field as single individuals." The nation "is capable of *unlimited possibilities*. . . . Each generation *forgets the experiences of the preceding ones*" (*Gesammelte Schriften*, VII, 283-284). Here Dilthey conceives of history as coincidences, as the awareness of horizontal social communities; *from* his station in the Germanic structure of life he sees history as the dramatic "awareness of what at a given moment is for the group a supreme good. This can happen under the influence of a collective mood, or under the leadership of a great man, as in the times of Luther or of Bismarck. . . . The feeling of the social community comes in the common adoption of an end" (p. 283).

Dilthey, to whom historiology owes so much, has to be rectified at this very moment. Each generation "will forget the experiences of the preceding ones." The history of a people would then be a superposition of horizontal human layers, connected we know not how—perhaps by the continuity of "culture." But even thus, the problem would persist: what is it that causes us to call certain generations of the twelfth century German even as we do certain generations of the twentieth?

There is a latent continuity in the way in which a man is stationed in his language, in his customs, and in his estimations. Stability is to variability as the stem of a verb is to its conjugated forms. Thus, however unexpected may be the *what* in the history of a people, their *how* presents a structural meaning that serves as a functional link. With this approach to historical understanding, I should like to avoid several traps: the conversion of the history of a people into a paralytic and abstract essentialism, or into an atomization of discontinuities, or into a sea of vague humanity, or into "unlimited possibilities" which, so far, no people have shown in their history.

In Search of the Hispanic Peculiarity

An individual or a collective human personality—one person or a people—is something unique, a form of life that is never repeated. Through the power of initiative the human being—unlike the bird, the tree, the rock—may create, or destroy, his own life. Hence the problem as to whether the reality of a people or an individual can be captured in concepts, those pincers used by reason to grasp the invariable and the permanent. As soon as the units of life, be they individual or collective, are conceptualized, they turn into corpses. When we reduce cultures to types, when we synthesize *Weltanschauungen*, we are proceeding as if to form a museum of desiccated plants or animals. The history of the totality of an individual or of a people offers the same difficulty as the history of literature or the fine arts. We say that the cathedrals of the thirteenth century were gothic, but the truth is that no one of them is like another. Notre Dame, York, Toledo, or Batalha—each possesses its own reality. When we stylize them in our concepts of "gothic, medieval," we blur their peculiar charm. But since it is impossible to express anything fully without using concepts, the only solution is to use them cautiously. It is therefore desirable, when we wish to write the history of the existence of a people, to listen to the people as they feel themselves existing. As in a novel, it is the characters and not the author who have to make their presence felt. A book of history should have its foundations, in so far as possible, on the expressions of awareness of personal and collective existence. Only thus will the meaning of the "facts" become clear; "facts" by themselves are like lost creatures wandering about in search of a shelter. If the history that is written is to keep life alive, it must also try to avoid falling into the disconnected and the arbitrary. Let us not believe, for example, that everything that happens and has happened on the soil now called Spain is Spanish, nor Italian that which the past staged on the soil of old Italy. The past of a people appears to us as an uninterrupted continuity, given in a space that is geographically stable. Since the stage of history is never empty, the spectator naïvely believes that the play is always the same. Hence the paintings in the Caves of Altamira are called Spanish; hence Trajan, Saint Isidore of Seville, and Viriathus are thought of as Spaniards exactly as are Cervantes, Unamuno, and the members of the Royal Spanish Academy, who have defined the meaning of the word "Spanish" (español).

What is the meaning of the term "Spanish," or "Hispanic"? Or, more precisely, what are the content and the semantic bounds of the term "Spanish," and what is the historico-human reality to which it univocally refers? The problem is one of hermeneutics, strictly philological, although up to now the philologists have neglected it, or have thought it either already solved or nonexistent. There is no ready-made answer, consequently, to the questions of what do the adjectives "Spanish," "French," "English" mean, and exactly what do they point out.

I think that the adjective "Spanish" (español) cannot be strictly applied to those who lived in the Iberian Peninsula prior to the Moorish invasion. If we call the Visigoths, the Romans, the Iberians, etc., Spanish, then we must find another name for the people in whose lives is articulated everything that has happened and everything that has been created (or destroyed) in that Peninsula from the tenth century till today. When we state that the bust of the Lady of Elche (la Dama de Elche) or the *Etymologies* of Saint Isidore are Spanish works, what is meant is that both were the work of people who inhabited what is today called Spain, and that to us they appear as links in the continuous chain called the History of Spain. Very well. Let us imagine in an excess of fantasy that it were made possible for one of the more learned Spaniards of today to witness the life of the Iberian Peninsula between the Roman and the modern periods, sojourning in Numantia during the period of the Celtiberic domination, then in Emerita Augusta under the Romans, then in Toletum, the capital of the kingdom of the Visigoths. As the epochs passed, he would come to Burgos between the years 1050 and 1100, and there, his ear once accustomed to the local dialect, the cultivated Spaniard of today would be able to converse with well-known persons, with the Cid and with men and women of the town. Beyond the slightest doubt the visitor would feel that all in Burgos, between 1050 and 1100, bore a strong resemblance to Spain, in the speech and in the way the people took their stance in life. But the traveler into the past would find no common bond whatsoever if he tried to share the life of the inhabitants of pre-Roman Numantia, or Gades, or Roman Hispalis, or Asturica Augusta, nor would he feel at home in 1050, for that matter, if he visited Toledo, Sevilla, or Elvira-Granada, which at that time were all under Arab domination—even though the traveler could speak their languages.

The cities and persons described above as non-Hispanic were situated on the land where there exists today the *what* that we call Spanish; they were the antecedent and condition which has made that *what* possible, through a concatenation of successive possibilities and impossibilities. But only by means of a crude paralogism could we identify the vital reality of the possibility with the *what* that it makes possible, which is to say, the conditioned with the condition. Yet we do this, and then we think that historical life is something substantial, caused, reducible to psychological and moral essences, given once and for all. For a long time now writers have been trying thus to equate the Spain of today with those who lived in the Peninsula in primitive times. To support this view, one quotes Strabo, yet even Strabo knew that different languages were spoken in Iberia by peoples very different from one another. Those along the Baetis (Guadalquivir) River "are quite transformed, and have acquired the Roman way of living; they are little short of being completely Roman; nor do they even remember their own language" (*Geography*, 3.2.15). "Even the Celtiberians," he adds, "the most savage among the Iberians, have acquired civility." The mountaineers in the north, not Romanized, lived by banditry (3.3.5). We are to suppose, then, that certain inhabitants would appear to be foreigners to the other peoples. Some were gentle and easily dominated; others for almost two centuries resisted the Roman legions, who were permanently established in the region of the northwest. Shall we say that the bellicose Cantabrians were Spaniards, and that the Turdetanians or the Tartessians, or Phoenicians, or Carthaginians, or Romans, successively, were not? Because it is so clearly outlined, the geographic profile of the Peninsula creates the mirage of a fixed and continued unity.

Justinus, author of the abridged *Historiae Philippicae* of the Gaul Trogus Pompeius, in an abstract synthesis, reduces to homogeneity not only the diverse inhabitants of Iberia, but also the land and the climate with all their violent contrasts: "The healthfulness of the air is the same all over Hispania; . . . the rivers are not harmfully torrential, and they irrigate the fields and vineyards." The moderate climate, without the extremes of either Africa or Gaul, "felicis et tempestivis imbribus in omnia frugum genera fecunda est, adeo ut non ipsis tantum incolis, verum etiam Italiae urbique Romanae cunctarum rerum abundantia sufficiat." (XLIV, I, I, 2)[12] And then the well-known passage: "Corpora hominum ad inediam laboremque, animi ad mortem parati. Dura omnibus adstricta parsimonia. Bellum quam otium malunt; si extraneum deest, domi hostem quaerunt."[13] The psycho-biological generalizations prevent us from getting at the functional peculiarity that we are pursuing, and, besides, it would not be difficult to find other peoples, ancient or modern, equally long-suffering and sober. Concerning the Scythians, the same Justinus says that "they scorn gold and silver as much as other peoples crave them. They feed on milk and honey; they know nothing of the use of wool and clothing, even when their teeth are chattering from rigorous cold; yet they wear skins." The Moor too was not exceeded by the Spaniard in getting along with little, as Captain Aldana observed in the sixteenth century:

> It is a common rumor of the common country folk
> That the lack of water from which Spain suffers,
> And the excess of desert land and of aridity,
> Provide her with a defense against whoever
>   approaches;
> And she does not understand the skill
> Whereby the Moor appeased his hunger without food,

[12] "Abundant and opportune rains make her fertile in all kinds of products, so that she can supply not only her own inhabitants, but also Italy and the city of Rome."

[13] "They are made to suffer privations and travails; their spirit defies death; they are all of extreme frugality; they prefer war to peace, and if they have no enemy outside their country, they seek one inside it."

As we clearly saw in earlier centuries,
When we yielded the boundary of the fatherland.[14]

It must be understood, from what Aldana says of the Moors, that other peoples have features that are the same as the Hispanians, but such features by themselves contribute nothing to the understanding of history. Justinus speaks of the inability of the Greeks to form a union almost in the same terms he applies to Iberia: "Under the rule of the Lacedaemonians and Athenians, all Greece was divided in two parts; and from making foreign war she would turn to plunging her weapons into her own entrails" (III, 2, 1). These and other observed qualities are useful to the historian only in the measure that they can be articulated within a particular historico-vital structure. The strict Puritans of New England, for example, scorned the pleasures of the palate for ethico-religious motives, that is to say, after deliberate reflection; at the same time, they cultivated capitalism, social cohesion, and the collective welfare. The insufficiency of the Hispanic diet was the detested result either of not knowing how to make the land more productive or of not importing food from places where it was plentiful. But this insufficiency also could give fecund support to energy or sanctity:

> I am strong like Spain,
> For lack of sustenance.
> (Quevedo)

On the one hand there were the hunger and poverty, poorly dissimulated by Lazarillo and his lordly Squire, and wistfully recalled by those little sisters of Saint Teresa who were saddened by well-being; on the other, heroic fasts that stiffened the Spanish courage whenever a seductive goal beckoned. Abstinence in itself is an abstraction or an anecdote which does not permit life in its totality to be understood. The important thing is what each people does with its abstinence, or with its indulgence.

When we say "Spanish," and try to clarify what it evokes in our consciousness, those evocations will vary with the knowledge and experience of each person, although something unique will be intuited, something difficult to define sharply when we seek to combine the several aspects on which the intuition is based. According to the dictionary, the native of Spain is "Spanish." The definition is elusive, for to say that an ob-

[14] A. Rodríguez-Moñino, *El capitán Francisco de Aldana* (1537-1578), Valladolid, 1943, p. 36.

ject comes from a certain place, that it is produced there, is not to say what the object in question is, or what it is like. To be sure, those who are born in Spain are generally Spanish. But is this all there is to it? Would it be enough to say that an alga is an aquatic plant? In the case of algae it is a matter of little importance, because the curious person will find out all he wants to know about them in a treatise on botany. But where shall we go to find out rigorously what is meant by, what the human object is that is called, "Spanish"? The difficulty is increased by the fact that we have no clear notion of the *what* and the *how* of that Spain of which the Spanish are natives. Shall we apply the idea expressed in the dictionary and say Averroes and Maimonides, born in Spain, are Spanish? Can we, with any rigor, call that Cordova where they were born Spain? Those who, although born in the Spain of today, do not give the impression of being Spanish because they have been brought up in other countries—can they be Spanish? And even granting that, legally speaking, they may be, would being legally Spanish suffice to embrace the total, human reality of being so in fact, authentically? This latter reality can be found in people who, not natives of Spain, still live lives that are structurally ordered in the *way* that we call Spanish.

The static, essentialist criteria fail to capture the fleeting reality that we pursue, the reality that can be grasped by intuition but not defined. If, for example, we take language as a norm, we shall see that in spite of its extraordinary importance, there are those who are Spanish inside Spain, vitally speaking, yet who do not share the community of language, in Galicia, the Basque country, or Catalonia. It will be said that political unity has made up for the difference in language; but it is observed immediately that under a common political allegiance peoples can coexist with different vital structures, for instance, the former Austro-Hungarian Empire. On the other hand, peoples that are politically independent of each other can maintain a common structure that I would call radical. All the peoples of the Iberian Peninsula and of Ibero-America, in spite of their marked differences, coincide in a same basic functioning of life. The historian Gonzalo Fernández de Oviedo (1478-1557) stumbled onto this problem when he saw Galicians, Roussillonians, Biscayans, and Andalusians—all quarreling with each other—as they reached the lands recently discovered by the Spaniards. Their Spanishness, according to Oviedo, consisted in being loyal subjects of the king of Spain. That blind devotion to the king was nothing external, as is well known, but an authentic belief, functional in the life of those people.

Spaniards have never killed their kings. Oviedo's explanation was of a vitalist, not a rationalist, type, and rested on his conscious awareness of the same Spanish existence.[15]

For centuries the answer has been sought by Spaniards to the disturbing question, what is the nature of Spain? This self-questioning about one's own existence has not been, and is not, a scholarly curiosity for many Spaniards. It is, rather, a manifestation of the functional structure of their life, of their problematical history.[16]

[15] If we observe the phenomenon of the monarchical cult more closely, we will see that the royal power did not unite the Hispanic people by acting as a principle external to them; faith in the sovereign was the form in which their inmost yearning for living together, inherent in the human condition, acquired reality. The Spaniards, given their manner of existence, could not unite themselves except in a belief; faith in the monarchy was an anchor of salvation, as was religious faith, neither of them critically analyzed in Spain before the nineteenth century. In the seventeenth century no Spaniard could have written, either in public or in private, as La Bruyère did in his *Caractères*: "Royal courts would be deserted and kings would stand almost alone if men would rid themselves of vanity and mercenary interests. . . ." The courtiers "make the fashions, exaggerate luxuries and extravagance, and teach [the women] ready ways of consuming large sums in clothing. . . . A noble . . . , if he lives at the court, is protected but is a slave: that is the compensation" (*De la Cour*). When the faith in the king collapsed, the vital functioning of the Spaniards led them to group themselves under local, provincial, or national bosses. It would be better to regard these "caudillos" as sought-for chieftains rather than as tyrants. This life structure is a more or less close-fitting garment for all the Hispano-Portuguese people.

[16] Quevedo expressed the strange reality of life in splendid poetry:

How you slip out of my hands!	¡Cómo de entre mis manos te resbalas!
Oh, how you slip away, my life!	¡Oh, cómo te deslizas, vida mía!
. . . .	. . . .
Yesterday has gone, tomorrow not yet arrived;	Ayer se fué, mañana no ha llegado; hoy se está yendo sin parar un punto;
Today is moving away without cease:	soy un fué, y un será, y un es cansado.
I am a has-been, a will-be, a weary is.	

(*Obras completas, verso*, edited by Astrana Marín, 1932, pp. 401, 424.) Further quotations may be found in the article of P. Laín-Entralgo, "La vida del hombre en la poesía de Quevedo," in his book *Vestigios*, pp. 17-46. I find Quevedo's distinctive note, as opposed to the traditional *contemptus mundi* of asceticism, to be the attraction and interest inspired in him by the peculiar nature of human life. He is more concerned with reflecting his awareness of it, with feeling it as it is, than with disdaining it for its claim to value and its claim to comparison with the future life. A disillusioned ascetic would not have written this:

It does not trouble me to die; I have not refused	No me aflige morir; no he rehusado acabar de vivir, ni he pretendido
To stop living, nor have I pretended	halagar esta muerte, que ha nacido
To flatter this death, which was born	a un tiempo con la vida y el cuidado.
At the same time as life and care.	Siento haber de dejar deshabitado
I regret to have to leave uninhabited	cuerpo que amante espíritu ha ceñido. . . .
A body that has clothed a loving spirit. . . .	

On the other hand, the reality of what in man is different from natural reality can be grasped only through autognosis—a sense of failure in success (desvivirse) in Spain, self-confidence among certain other peoples. Proceeding this way in our analysis, we must say a word about the idea of life which began to make headway in nineteenth-century Europe as a step beyond materialism and idealism (Condillac-Kant).[17] As early as 1804 the Frenchman de Gérando was trying to arrive at a knowledge of man through the integral consciousness of one's self. Maine de Biran (1766-1824) is the first one to say, "I am not a thing," and to have a glimmering of "the most strange reality of human life, rebellious against the ruling mental habits." Father Alphonse Gratry (1805-1872) probes more deeply into the idea of life as continual becoming: "Light was from the beginning what it is today. But I shall be what I not yet am. . . . Pursuit, desire, disquietude, hope are the very stuff of our life here below." These thoughts link with Fichte's idea (reality as *Tathandlung*, "feat") and with Kierkegaard's dread: "Because abstract thought is *sub specie aeterni*, it ignores the concrete and the temporal, the existential process, the predicament of the existing individual arising from his being a synthesis of the temporal and the eternal situated in existence. It is impossible to conceive existence without movement. . . . Existence, like movement, is a difficult category to deal with; for if I think it, I abrogate it, and *then I do not think it.*"[18] After this come Nietzsche, Bergson, and Dilthey.

It is surprising that in spite of the fact that these ideas have been in existence in Europe for some time now, history has continued to be written as if history were a transcendence of life, objective culture and nothing else. In spite of the growth of existential, extra-rational expressions of life, history has gone on being either positivistic (man is an excerpt of nature) or abstract and extra-vital (Hegelianism). In the face of this situation it has seemed useful to bring the historical self-consciousness (an experience so familiar to the Hispanic peoples) under the light of the extra-rational (non-physico-naturalistic) thought.

It is not hard to understand why the effort to write a people's history almost as a confession or a biography will be surprising. To professional historians of the past, such a project would have doubtless seemed a

---

[17] The reader should keep in mind the meaning of the term "life" as elaborated in Chapter 1, note 2. See also Julián Marías' introduction to his translation of Dilthey's *Teoría de las concepciones del mundo*, Madrid, 1944.

[18] *Concluding Unscientific Postscript*, S. Kierkegaard, translated by David F. Swenson and Walter Lowrie, Princeton University Press, 1941, pp. 267, 273, 274.

literary frivolity. And on the other hand, the philosophers who have found the matrix of their thought in the idea of life (Kierkegaard's anguished reason; Dilthey's historical reason) would have naturally found it impossible to be interested in the empirical knowledge of history.

Yet the empirical analysis is indispensable. The idea of the abstract universal man has to be broken up into a plurality of men given in historical experience—in this case the man with an Hispanically ordered functional structure, and, furthermore, this man in a form such as would not make him appear as a substantial entity, as a "thing." Every Spaniard preoccupied with what was happening to him and around him could have said with Quevedo, "Oh my life, how you do slip away!" But we historians, instead of observing what there was of movement, of direction, and of insecurity in this "slipping away," try to characterize Hispanic life biologically, racially, or psychologically, as if it were a fixed object and not a "slipping away" between points of departure and goals desired or dreamed of. Much has been said about passion, heroism, indocility, individualism, fanaticism, indolence, ignorance, activism, stoicism, envy, etc., with a view to humbling or exalting a people that has been a source of worries for others. On occasion, writers have had recourse to cause-and-effect chains of explanations, from the scarcity of water (the so-called oligohydric hypothesis) to the prevalence of inquisitionism or of corrupt governments. The constant comparison of Spain with other European countries, which, especially since the seventeenth century, has become a more and more firmly established activity (Quevedo, *España defendida* [Spain Defended], 1609), has provoked the appearance of those characteristically Hispanic works of justification and self-criticism. Menéndez y Pelayo went so far as to try and dig up a hidden Spanish science. By following such paths, however, we get nowhere. On the contrary, it has been necessary to convert the insecure slipping away of life, the "unliving" (desvivirse), into a function of living itself, into a modality of existence, to the end of seeing as a connected whole that which has up to now lacked order or coherence. Neither a heroic and patriotic history nor a history of incapacities and infamies, but a view of the structure, of the lifestream from which overflow both wonders and horrors. There is nothing easier than approaching the history of *any* people as a fabric of monstrosities and stupidities. Robert Briffault has done it with his own country, England, and, as one might expect, indeed, as was to be feared, his historical view appears to be deformed and truncated. All history, like all human action of a certain trajectory, makes its way over ruins, even creating them. The vision of the poet lives at the expense of nonemotive thought, just as the authentic thinker must renounce the nonabstractable; empires and religions—and even the tenderest of these —have their firm foundation in iniquities, the fatal wrong side of their values. Neither glorious nor ignominious history interests me.

In the pursuit of that *what* in which the peculiar existence of the present-day Iberian peoples consists, I start with the evidence (for me) that prior to the Moorish invasion the inhabitants of the Peninsula are not situated in the life structure that has been manifest from the year 1000 till today. The Hispanic vital function cannot be founded on a mysterious racism, not on contact with the land now called Spain. Those who speak of races, if they wish to argue persuasively, will have to describe the life structure of the races they nebulously and dogmatically affirm to have expressed themselves as Spaniards. No one has established a *functional continuity* between the Christians who have lived on the Peninsula since the year 1000 and the inhabitants of the Peninsula prior to the eighth century.

It is suitable for my purpose to insist on the awareness of insecurity as a line which indelibly marks the course of Hispanic existence, and which becomes perceptible in the very process of life rather than in the realizations of that process. The insecure Spaniard does not yearn for a type of actions or conduct *different* from those that motivate his dissatisfaction; he is not like the Roman who, during the Empire,[19] missed the political organization and the customs of the Republic. Hispanic man has not forged a life content which could be referred to as a steady and solid situation; after the 15th century, he misses the *persons* of Ferdinand and Isabella, a very different matter. What I call Spain was made and continues to be made in a web of uncertainties. A corner of the Peninsula, to subsist, had to destroy Islamized Spain, in which even the rivers had changed their thousand-year-old names. Each of the three peoples of the Peninsula (Christians, Moors, Jews) saw itself forced to live for

---

[19] Without speaking of Cicero, Seneca, Tacitus, and other famous writers who have felt a nostalgia for the past, I shall recall a secondary writer, Columella, the author of a treatise on agriculture (*De re rustica*) composed to persuade his contemporaries to go back to the uses of the past: "When I think of so many illustrious captains of pure Roman stock, who ever excelled in the double occupation of defending and cultivating the land (the fatherland as well as conquered land), I understand how it is that our contemporaries, abandoned to luxury and womanish pleasures, do not enjoy the vigorous and manly life of their ancestors" (Preface, 14). Columella then refers to the banquets, the hot baths, the lubricity, and the drunkenness of those who, in Seneca's phrase, "saw neither the rising nor the setting of the sun."

eight centuries together with the other two at the same time it passionately desired their extermination. The wars of the Hispano-Christians, as Don Alonso de Cartagena said, were "divine." All life was placed, was risked, on the gaming table of the faith. No important theme was assigned to the peaceful human-temporal tasks. Thus was developing a structure of life in which the structure prevailing throughout the Visigothic centuries was forgotten, as I shall presently make clear. The principle "cedat curiositas fidei," not functional or totalizing for the Visigoth, became functional and totalizing for those who appear to us today as Spaniards. These—and this is the central point in the conscious awareness of their history—never accepted their existence part and parcel, as the Chinese naturally accepted his "Chinese-ness," or the Hindu his being Hindu. For his existence in a belief, in an orthodoxy, Hispanic man was to struggle first against the Moors, then against the Jews, the Protestants, or the unbelievers. The French and English accepted in the end the compatibility of being French or English and holding a religious belief different from the traditional one, or holding none at all. For the Hispano-Lusitanian people such a situation creates an agonized existence: they know the price they have to pay for their belief, but they cannot help but persist in it. The gaps left by the disappearance of beliefs among the English, French, and Germans have been filled with the cult of certain secular "divinities": science, politico-social institutions, literature, in France; the community of citizens, the protection of women, children, animals, and plants, in Anglo-Saxon countries; etc. Nothing of this sort compensates for the disappearance of belief among the Hispano-Portuguese peoples. For them the alternatives are, and have been, either belief or nonexistence, as anyone sees who is acquainted with life in the Iberian Peninsula, Brazil, or Mexico. For underneath whatever people may wish to explain as a universal phenomenon of "these times," there lies that other thing, each people's perduring "dwelling-place."

This functional structure shows itself in the following ways: (a) the people hope and yearn to rise to heights and destinies prefigured in a belief, be it human or divine; (b) they are insecure over the fulfillment of the promise implied in the belief; (c) they are unable, on their own account, even to try to escape from the condition of credulity and to originally invent new realities, physical or ideal, forged by reason and experience; (d) as a result of this state of mind, they adopt what, by means of experience and reason, has been achieved by other peoples; (e) the irrepressible tendency to express the complex in which the individual's consciousness and his internal and external circumstances are integrated.

The kind of belief I am speaking of here is one that embraces the total vital horizon of the person: he believes in the king, in the dictator, in honor, in tradition, in an imported ideology, in a messianic revolution, in his own importance as a person, and so on.

For manifestation (a)—for instance—we may recall such passages as one from Fray Diego de Valencia (at the end of the fourteenth century): if the Castilians should unite, "I know of no single corner of the world that they could not conquer, including all of Granada." Or this one, from Gómez Manrique, before 1468: "May Christ allow our king to conquer the lands Cismaritime and Outremer held by barbarous nations."[20]

Completely fused with the yearning hope of extending Hispanic life to the ultimate confines of space is the belief that the individual survives in the eternity of time:

> Life that is lasting
> The good men of the cloth
> Win with prayers
> And with weeping;
> Famous knights
> Through travail and trials
> Combatting Moors.
>
> (Jorge Manrique)

Or one might quote Juan Martí, who says (in 1602): "The Spanish Grandees are as stars in the firmament, and *can do what they will to do*." Other manifestations of the Hispanic structure will be found documented elsewhere in the pages of this book.

We must deal with the problem as one might observe a literary or linguistic form of today and connect it with a past of centuries. Instead of handling words, phonemes, topics, or styles, we are interested in that fluid and very real reality, the pulse of which is perceptible in confessions dense with expressive tension:

> Now the softness of peace,
> Now the fury of war hurts us.
> Sad, Spain groans,
> *At the highest summit of fortune;*

[20] For these and other passages expressing Messianic imperialism become a reality in the histories of Spain and Portugal, see my *Aspectos del vivir hispánico*, Cruz del Sur, Santiago de Chile, 1949.

For the weight of her great majesty
Is too much for her and oppresses her;
And structures that *heaven does not support*
Fall under their weight to the ground.

Neither war nor peace brings repose, according to Francisco de Medrano, an ex-Jesuit who died in 1607.[21] Spain was not then groaning, oppressed by any national error, or by her departure from a preceding type of life, as had been seen to happen in imperial Rome. Spain's anguish is the very majesty of feeling herself at the pinnacle of her greatest fortune. The only support that was secure, real, was that of Heaven, and not any conceivable kind of grandiose "structure" (máquina). Long before Medrano wrote, Spain felt that she was nothing but the hollow shell of herself and in a very precarious situation; during the war against the Moriscos of Granada, and even after that, it was feared that the Turks, in alliance with Spain's Christian enemies, would repeat the Mussulman invasion. In verses addressed to Don Juan of Austria, Captain Francisco de Aldana (who died in the debacle at Alcazarquivir in 1578) said:

Receive this tearful prophecy,
Fulfilled in my sad, unseasonable old age:
I tell you that I see the Iberian Monarchy
Falling at the feet of fortune;
Rebellion and heresy are growing;
The Gaul awakens to a moonbeam[22]
And the people most favored by God
Sleeps in the shadow of eternal oblivion.

In the same tone he writes poetically to Philip II:

If at the disaster in the time of Rodrigo
When the world was still such a novice
That the enemy knew neither firearms
Nor any warlike device,
Spain fell in dishonor
Without suspecting the Turks' wickedness,
What can she do now, so unprepared,
Against an enemy so numerous and so well provided?[23]

[21] For the text, see the *Biblioteca de Autores Españoles*, XLI, 351*a*. Concerning the author, see Dámaso Alonso's *Vida y obra de Medrano*, Madrid, 1948, although in it Alonso discusses only the poetic form of this disturbing text.

[22] I.e., the French are uniting with the Turks.

[23] *Epistolario poético completo*, edited by A. Rodríguez-Moñino, 1946, p. 21.

According to this military scientist, who died fighting heroically against the African Moors, Spain offered a superlative void as a front against her centuries-old enemy:

> What must be suspected in such an excessive
> Absence of form and matter,
> As there is between them and us?[24]

These worries might all pass as the isolated voices of fainthearted pessimists, if they did not coincide with the declaration, repeated throughout the sixteenth century, that the conquest of Granada had been a misfortune, because the great heroic stimulus for the Spaniards had thus disappeared. Las Casas and others denied the legitimacy of the Crown's imperial policy in the Indies. Quevedo thought that the more lands Spain conquered, the more enemies she would attract: ". . . ˉambition finally acquires territory that is beyond the reach of the forces necessary to maintain it. . . . America was a rich and beautiful harlot, adulterous to her husbands (the Indians!). . . . The Christians say that Heaven punished the Indies because they worshiped idols; and we Indians say that Heaven is bound to punish the Christians because they worship the Indian women." (*La hora de todos*, 1638.)

I shall return to this subject later, but now it is urgent to relate the consciousness of empty effort in the sixteenth and seventeenth centuries (coincident with a continuous series of splendid creations), with the consciousness of vacuity, of inexistence, which I find in very representative Spaniards of the nineteenth and twentieth centuries. Francisco Giner de los Ríos wrote in 1905: "If, even outside this dark corner—and the darker, the more beloved—there still persists so much vanity and lying, out there in the sunlit empyrean of the proud, resplendent, and glorious nations, how could it be different among a people (such as Spain), *cut off from history*, at least in the more spiritual and more profound respects, *more* than *three centuries* ago."[25] Shortly after, J. Ortega y Gasset says: "*Three centuries* of errors and sorrows weigh upon us. How could we ignore that centuries-old heaviness?"[26] At the opposite extreme the Fascist Phalanx, in 1937, says that for nearly *three centuries*, or since 1637,

[24] A. Rodríguez-Moñino, *El capitán Francisco de Aldana* (1537-1578), Valladolid, 1943, p. 35.

[25] *Problemas urgentes de nuestra educación nacional*, 1905. The text may be read in F. de los Ríos, *El pensamiento vivo de Francisco Giner*, Buenos Aires, 1949, p. 127.

[26] In his essay "La pedagogía social como programa político" (1910), now in the volume *Personas, obras y cosas*, 1922, p. 201.

Spain has not been herself.[27] In 1947 a learned archeologist, Professor Pedro Bosch Gimpera, entitled one of his articles "The Contumacy of Our Historical Deviations"; in this article he affirms that in Spain, "contumacious in her errors . . . , all problems, since Ferdinand and Isabella and *even longer ago*, either have been insoluble or have been poorly solved. . . . In the crucible of Spain, the qualities of her people and of their character are still virginal." (*España Nueva*, Mexico, 20 September 1947.)

The foregoing quotations are only significant samples of very widespread ideas and sentiments. But what can the reality be of a present that is always felt as having its temporal foundations undermined, as being invertebrate? It can be nothing other than a recreating of itself as if the world were beginning anew in every instant, in a continuous process of creating-wasting. And let no one think that the foregoing quotations—the expression of an "autobiographical" conscious awareness —come from nonconformists beclouded with pessimism. We are persuaded of the contrary by the enthusiastic traditionalist Menéndez y Pelayo, who in perfectly good faith forged a Spanish science altogether devoid of scientific content, with the intent of filling the void of the past that afflicted his soul. If such a void had not existed for him, Menéndez y Pelayo would have felt satisfied with Spanish history as it is, with its manifest plenitude, and would not have found it wanting as reality and as value.

The incredible paradox, the irrationality of this history, is that Hispanic observers cannot capture it unless they at least for a while step out of their own living structure and change the negations into some sort of positive reality. The sustained consciousness of existence as a nonexistence, of putting to a test time and again the possibility of the impossibility, is without parallel in either the Occident or the Orient. It is necessary to immerse oneself in this in order to perceive the presence of the functional structure, as constant as it is irreducible to the generic or the abstract. Thanks to this structure we can know when the *what* begins to exist that beyond cavil constitutes the Hispanic reality.

[27] "For nearly three centuries the true being of Spain has been in agony, torn in flesh and spirit by the poisonous darts of a foreign, atheistic, and materialistic conception of life. . . . Now that the tradition of this existence and power of Spain is returning, re-born, by the grace of youthful blood, the arrows of the Phalanx have become sacred flesh." (Decree of 1 October 1937, inaugurating the Grand and Imperial Order of the Red Arrows, from the *Repertorio cronológico de legislación*, Pamplona, 1938, p. 994.)

3

The Vital Structure of the Visigoths

THE MEDIEVAL SPANISH CHRONICLES, in retrospect, called the Moorish invasion of 711 the "destruction" of Spain; and it was perfectly sensible from their point of view to give it such a name. Let us not stop to lament that remote misfortune, nor to imagine what would have been the destiny of the Iberian Peninsula without the eight centuries of warfare that ensued after the invasion. The important thing now is to make clear how from 711 on, history was to be made, not in a Visigothic "dwelling-place" but by other peoples, under different circumstances, and by means of functional activities which it is possible to connect with the succeeding period, but not with the preceding. The form of these new activities, however, was made possible by previous historical situations.

The inhabitants of the northern and northwestern parts of the Peninsula had never served as a support and exemplary guide to the Ibero-Romans or to the Romano-Visigoths. We know very little of them beyond the fact that many of them offered great resistance to the Romans as well as to the Visigoths.[1] The Suevi, a Germanic race, stayed in Galicia for 175 years, until Leovigild subjected them in 585. In the sixth century Saint Martin of Braga composed his treatise *De correctione rusticorum* to depaganize the Galicians and Asturians. Helmut Schlunk wonders whether, in the realm of the fine arts, "there was in these regions a continuous tradition, independent of the so-called Visigothic art, which begins to conquer the northern regions only in the seventh century. . . . That there was in the northwest of Spain a provincial art of individual character, different from that of the center and south of the country, is indicated by the remains of decorations."[2] In the twelfth century the Basque-Navarrese still gave the traveler a strong impression of rusticity.[3] The fact that they were not linguistically Romanized shows by itself their slight participation in the life of the rest of the Peninsula.

[1] "The peoples of the Cantabro-Pyrenean mountains were a perpetual nightmare to the Gothic kings." (R. Menéndez Pidal, *Historia de España*, 1940, III, xlvii.)
[2] *Ars Hispaniae*, Madrid, 1947, II, 342.
[3] *Liber Sancti Jacobi*, transcribed by W. M. Whitehill, Santiago de Compostela, 1944, p. 358.

The Reconquest of Spain from the Moslems was begun in these regions that were only slightly Romanized and not very orthodox in their Catholicism, as the cult of Saint James, at least in its original form, will later show. The greater part of Hispania, the well-Latinized part, yielded to the Moorish pressure, as it had yielded before to the Visigoths, and before that to the Romans, the Carthaginians, and the Phoenicians. When the ten short years of Caesar's conquest of Gaul are compared with two hundred long years that Hispania cost the Romans, up comes the mirage again of a land populated with people united and animated by a national spirit, somewhat like that of the Spain that opposed Napoleon's Frenchmen. But the Numantians and the Cantabrians went on fighting when large zones of the Peninsula were living peacefully under the Roman domination.

The people who started to make war efficaciously against the Moors were not Hispalenses or Tarraconenses, but men from the North of the Peninsula who had no authentic connection with the Visigothic tradition. Although they might regard themselves as the heirs of Visigothic grandeur, it is nonetheless certain that genealogical claims are not enough to build up the structure of a people. The reconquering Christians were not linked with either the Visigoths of Toledo, or Caesar Augusta, or Cartago Nova.[4]

The *Crónica General* of Alphonse the Learned, in the thirteenth century, saw the Visigothic kingdom as something glorious and remote, without similarity to the present: "So great was it that its dominion extended from sea to sea, as well as from the city of Tangier, which is in Africa, to the Rhone river. This kingdom was exalted in its nobility, ample in the abundance of all things, devout in religion, harmonious and united in the love of peace, made illustrious and pure by the teaching of the councils (of Toledo) . . . ; and by the great virtue of the priests that were there . . . and by the holy bishops Leander, Isidore, Helladius, Eugene, Ildefonsus, Julian, Fulgentius, Martin of Braga, Taion of Saragossa; and by the excellent school of high philosophy that was in Cordova."[5]

Yet from all that learning, that existed more as a nostalgic recollection than as a living tradition, there had been no new offshoots. At a distance of more than five hundred years, the Visigothic past was clouded in a mist of legend. The mention of an "excellent school of high philosophy,"

[4] To attribute to material difficulties the absence of culture and thought among the Christians of Northern Spain does not change the nature of this fact.

[5] Edition of Menéndez Pidal, p. 305.

completely unknown except for this single reference to it,[6] reveals the importance attached to the cultural capacities of the Visigoths. The Castilian of the thirteenth century missed that culture, evidently important, but he did not suspect that for his own heroic fortitude as a man, and for the originality of his expression as an artist, he was already worth more than the vague and vacillating Visigoth.

The break between the Hispania of Saint Isidore and the Christian kingdoms of the eleventh century is clearly perceived at precisely that point where there appears to be a link between the one and the others. The basilica of Saint Isidore of Leon, which Ferdinand I ordered to be built in 1063,[7] would seem to reveal, at first glance, that the monarch had some recollection of the great Sevillan scholar. But if we consult the *Crónica Silense*,[8] we see that King Ferdinand of Leon sent the Bishops Alvitus and Ordoño to Seville to get not the body of Saint Isidore but that of a martyr, Saint Justa. When the latter was not to be found, it occurred to them to take back the remains of Isidore as a substitute. According to the Chronicle, the soul of the saint appeared to Alvitus and asked that his body be moved to Leon. It turns out then, if the testimony of the Chronicle is not invalid, that the basilica of Leon owes to a happy accident the fact that it is under the patronage of Saint Isidore.

Visigoths and Spaniards differ above all in the way they are "dwelling" in their religious belief. It is especially surprising that the Peninsula was dominated in the fifth and sixth centuries by Arian heretics who denied the Catholic dogma of the Trinity; for them Christ was a prophet, not a divine person consubstantial with the Father. Menéndez y Pelayo had trouble with this problem for the very reason that he approached Spanish history as a continuity of orthodox Catholic believers. Granted his initial assumption, the following statement of his is logical: "Spain has never been Arian, because the Visigoths were not Spaniards."[9] But then the same historian adds, with passionate arbitrariness, that the Hispano-Romans were the "true and *only* Spanish race" (p. 135). And lost and trapped in this forest of fantasy, he continues: "The race that rose up to reclaim the native soil inch by inch was Hispano-Roman; the good Visigoths (!) had completely blended with it" (pp. 185, 187, 189).

[6] Sidonius Apollinaris (430-488) alludes to a famous Cordovan school about which I possess no further information: "Corduba praepotens alumnis." (See E. Pérez Pujol, *Historia de las instituciones sociales de la España goda*, 1896, III, 490-491.)

[7] R. Menéndez Pidal, *La España del Cid*, 1947, I, 136.

[8] Edition of Santos Coco, 1919, pp. 81-82.

[9] *Historia de los heterodoxos españoles*, 1917, II, 94.

What really happened was quite different. When the Catholic prince Hermenegild rebelled against his father, the Arian King Leovigild, illustrious Catholics like the Abbot Johannes Biclarensis and Archbishop Isidore of Seville took the part of the father against the son. Those prelates, like the Gallo-Roman bishop Gregory of Tours, did not see in Hermenegild a martyr but a rebel against the authority of the State.[10] Even though the attitude of the Catholic Spaniards might be due to the fact that there was "little of the fanatical" (Menéndez y Pelayo, op.cit., p. 171) about them, or to "Gothic nationalism" (Menéndez Pidal, loc.cit., p. xxvii), it is evident that the conduct of such prelates would have been inconceivable among Spaniards, in the tenth century as well as in the twentieth. As Menéndez Pidal rightly says, Catholics and Arians coincided in their esteem and respect for something higher than their respective beliefs—precisely, I add, because they had a structure of life that was not Spanish, and their "dwelling-place" was organized according to a hierarchy of values that was later unthinkable. A Spanish bishop has never admitted, publicly and solemnly, his agreement with a heretic, nor have a heretic and a bishop ever found common shelter under a supreme principle secular in character. The authentic Spaniards, who emerged later, no longer understood the motives of these Goths, and made a martyr out of Hermenegild and a monster out of his father: "Leovigild, King of the Spains, holding his son Hermenegild prisoner in the jail, as we said, killed him while he was lying therein, on the Eve of Easter, because he would not turn to the evil sect of the Arians in which the king believed; and in this way the son was made a martyr of God" (Crónica General, ed. cit., p. 262). But Hermenegild was not canonized until 1586, because it was not until then that Philip II requested it of Pope Sixtus V, a thousand years after what the Visigoths vituperatively considered a rebellion and the Spaniards of much later a glorious martyrdom.

Nor does it strike me as Spanish the way King Recared was converted to Catholicism in 589. It reminds one of the conversion of the Frank King Clovis in 486 and of the Emperor Constantine, which may have served him as a model. To speak of a Spanish king who is not a Catholic implies a contradiction in terms; but even imagining such an absurdity,

---

[10] "The contemporaries Johannes Biclarensis, Isidore, and Gregory of Tours, even though they were prelates full of Catholic fervor, unanimously condemned the prince as a rebel [tyrannus in the ancient sense] against his father and against the kingdom." (Franz Görres, "Die byzantinischen Besitzungen an den Küsten des Spanischen-westgotischen Reiches [554-624]," in Byzantinische Zeitschrift, 1907, XVI, 515-538.)

a heretical king would never have been converted the way Recared was. Here are his words before the famous Third Council of Toledo: "I do not believe that it is unknown to you, very reverend priests, that my object in calling you before the presence of Our Serenity is the re-establishing of the form of ecclesiastic discipline. Since the heresy which threatened the whole Catholic Church has prevented the celebration of councils, God (Whom it has pleased to remove the obstacle of that heresy *by means of Us*) has admonished Us that we should restore the rule of the ecclesiastical custom. May you be filled with joy and gladness to know that, through the providence of God, the canonical custom has returned to the paternal precinct, *to Our glory*." He then exhorts the fathers of the council to fast and pray to the end that "the canonical order so remote from the priests because of long and prolonged oblivion that our generation confesses to not even knowing it," be made manifest to them.[11]

First of all, the king speaks as if he were doing a great service to God and to his Church, threatened by the danger of Arianism. None of this was a fact. Recared expresses himself as if his own person had not participated in the Arian heresy; instead of humble repentance, he arrogantly flaunts his self-sufficiency, for he is converted "so that in the future our glory may shine, honored by the testimony of the Catholic faith" (per omne successivum tempus gloria nostra ejusdem fidei decorata clarescat). The enormous sin of not having believed God to be as He is did not enter the King's mind; he treated the whole question as a matter of custom, ecclesiastical law, and liturgy. Instead of saying, as had been the practice among the Visigoths, "Gloria Patri per Filium in Spiritu Sancto," now the priests were required to say "Gloria Patri et Filio et Spiritui Sancto." A dative instead of the accusative, and all was in order.

Whoever reads the minutes of the famous council without preconceptions will get the impression that political interests, reasons of state, take precedence over religious sentiment and worries about the after life. The king says, "Non credimus vestram latere sanctitatem, quanto tempore in errore Arrianorum laborasset Hispania," which does not mean exactly what Menéndez y Pelayo says in his translation ("for all the time that the error of the Arians has prevailed in Spain") but rather "for all the time that Hispania has suffered (for all the travails she has suffered)

[11] *Collectio maxima conciliorum omnium Hispaniae et Novi Orbis*, by José S. de Aguirre, Madrid, 1781, Vol. II. I have here translated more precisely the passage which may be found in Menéndez y Pelayo, *Historia de los heterodoxos españoles*, 1917, II, 180.

for being in the error of the Arians." These travails were the civil war between King Leovigild and his son Hermenegild, and the occupation of the south of Hispania by the Byzantines, aided by the Catholics. Isidore of Seville writes: "Gothi per Hermenegildum divisi multa caede vastantur" (the Goths—he does not say the Hispano-Romans and the Goths! —divided into two bands because of Hermenegild, destroy and kill one another.)[12] The conversion of Recared and the condemnation of Hermenegild by Saint Isidore are integrated in the proposal to unify and enlarge the Visigothic kingdom. "After the conversion of Recared," says the Catholic writer Görres, "the Byzantines offered no further attraction to the Hispano-Romans." The decision taken by the king might be likened (though only to a certain extent, of course) to that of Henry IV of France, which was also inspired more by political than sentimental motives. With the Byzantines occupying a broad and rich zone in Hispania, the kingdom was being drawn away from the Roman world, which was beginning to order its vital structure under the spiritual guidance of Catholic Rome. To recover sovereignty over a kingdom undivided and in harmony with the tradition of Catholic Rome, it was well worth renouncing the dogma of the nondivinity of Christ.

Let us accept with Menéndez y Pelayo the fact that the Visigoths were not Spaniards,[13] with, however, the inescapable consequence of extending the same negative judgment to the other inhabitants of that kingdom. The Hispania of the Goths was a condition for the Christian kingdoms that came later, as Germano-Byzantine Italy was for the future Italian cities, which, in the twelfth century, were no longer either Germano-Byzantine or Roman, but something else, that is, Italian. The historical strata in such cases bring to mind certain cities of Antiquity, successively razed and "rebuilt," one on top of the other. The excavations at Ephesus have disclosed the ruins of the pre-Egyptian, Egyptian, Greek, and Roman city. Each utilized the materials of the preceding one to the end of building the new city; but not one of them could have lived

[12] Franz Görres, op.cit., p. 522.

[13] In his discourse before the Council of Basel (1434), Don Alonso de Cartagena realized that it was necessary to make his idea of Spain coincide with the continuity of the Catholic faith: "After the Spaniards, in the time of Saint James, received the faith, they did not depart from it," although it is true that "in the time of the King Leovigild . . . *some people* were infected with the Arian heresy. . . . In the third Council of Toledo, the Arian heresy was *completely* destroyed; but the Spaniards as a whole never strayed from the faith, for even during the time when that heresy was most prevalent, there flourished in Spain Saint Isidore, Saint Leander," etc. (*La Ciudad de Dios*, 1894, xxxv, 537). We have already seen that the problem is rather more complicated.

together with one of the older ones, nor did any one of them represent a moment in the "evolution" of those successive cities.

The Goths did not write, or there have not been preserved, poetic works in which they expressed the intimacy of their existence. But enough is known about them that we may affirm that their life was neither Roman nor Germanic, although both elements may have been a condition for their existence. Isidore of Seville, of Roman ancestry, felt that he was a Visigoth, even though, for lack of sufficient testimonies, I may be unable to say what the Visigothic life structure consisted in. I suspect, moreover, that in the undergrowth of history there must be something to correspond to the category of a *vital structure incompletely realized* (a vital "dwelling-place" poorly furnished) that is, peoples who moved through the past (or through the present—a terrible situation) without ever recognizing themselves as completely existing, within themselves and in their achievements. Perhaps they dreamed, or dream, of some magic force which might give completeness to their existence. There are peoples who have lived like those linguistic dialects that have never served as the expression for important and universalizable works. Our imperfect set of historical instruments does not permit us to capture the histories that I would call "half-finished." Perhaps these peoples have combined a yearning existence with the awareness, or with the belief, that they do exist completely. To be sure, there must be a certain structural completeness in such cases: a dwarf is completely a dwarf, although, seen in another perspective, he seems incomplete in his physical corporeity.

If we should look at the Visigothic kingdom in the perspective of the Rome of Augustus, or the Spain of Charles V, or the England of Victoria, we would get the impression that the Visigoths were in the position of a people of small significance as inhabitants of a Roman province; nor were they now, in the fifth, sixth, and seventh centuries, really preparing themselves to be very important. The Visigoths themselves seem to have been aware of their difficult vital situation. Like the rest of the provinces of what was once the Empire, the Hispano-Romano-Visigoths believed that Rome had not disappeared. In the fifth century, Paulus Orosius, a Hispano-Roman, writes: "Rome, after so many years, continues to preserve herself and her authority intact; the Goths and Alaric have invaded her and despoiled her of her wealth, not of her empire." As an intelligent person preoccupied with the transcendent meaning of human events, Orosius had to feel himself as living within the vital orbit of Rome, because the barbarian invaders still lacked a collective form in which one could be included; and the land of Hispania without the awareness of being Roman was something amorphous and deprived of stability. If it was necessary for Orosius to take refuge in the vital notion of Rome in order to escape the anguish of having no place in which to be vitally "stationed," the enlightened Visigoths of that time felt the same way: they felt that they did not exist as an individuality, and in desperation they embraced the illusion of a still existent Rome, in spite of all they were doing to destroy it. A fine anecdote has been preserved by Orosius, who picked it up when he was in Bethlehem with the future Saint Jerome, from a knight from Narbonne, who had heard the King Ataulf expound his political plans. This Visigothic chieftain intended to do away with even the name of Roman (obliterato Romano nomine), and to replace it with that of Gothic. *Gothia* was to succeed *Romania*.[14] Ataulf changed his mind when it occurred to him that the barbarianism of his Goths would keep them from obeying the laws, "without which the state is not a state" (sine quibus respublica non est respublica). He preferred then to utilize the power of his people to restore its former grandeur to the name Roman, for, having been unable to transform Rome (postquam esse non potuerat immutator), he aspired to restore her past.[15] Thanks to this flash of awareness, of Visigothic autognosis, which Orosius noted with human sympathy,[16] we observe the Visigoths entering into history sustained by the purpose of slipping into a life structure that was not their own; these Germanic people were going to live from then on rather like those émigrés who neither fully preserve the life of their country of origin nor acquire that of the country of their adoption. The Goths wanted to be Romans;[17]

[14] This is the procedure that was followed by other Germanic peoples, who created states with ethnic names: Lombardy, France, Anglia, Normandy, Burgundy. It is significant that nothing like this was produced in the Iberian Peninsula.

[15] This important passage has already been noted by Gaston Boissier in *La Fin du paganisme*, 1891, II, 409. See Paulus Orosius, *Historiarum adversum paganos libri VII*, edition of C. Zangemeister, pp. 86 and 560.

[16] I do not share the view that Orosius was a Spaniard. In his *Histoire de la littérature latine* (1912, p. 914) René Pichon says that Prudentius and Orosius differ from Saint Paulinus only in that the first two are Spaniards and the third is French: "It is always the contrast between the French spirit compounded of clear good sense and easy grace, and the Spanish spirit, harsher and more passionate." Seduced by the idea that historical realities are eternal, unchangeable substances, Pichon did not realize that a story such as Orosius' could not be written by a Spaniard; in the one thousand five hundred years that intervene between Orosius and the present time, no Hispanic person has tried to write a universal history to demonstrate a thesis. The modern person who resembles Orosius is Bossuet—or Spengler.

[17] C. Sánchez-Albornoz speaks of the "taste for imitating Roman models in the Visigothic court." (*Cuadernos de Historia de España*, V, 47.)

they occupied the Peninsula in the name of Rome, they issued laws based on the Roman tradition, and they spoke and wrote in Latin. They went so far as to continue the bad Imperial custom of seeking foreign assistance in the settlement of their internal quarrels: the Byzantine invasion is an antecedent of the coming of the Arabs, whose decisive entrance in 711 was preceded by three other attempts at foreign occupation.

Yet I am not trying to present a picture of Visigothic life, or to probe into their deficiencies and incapabilities. I am interested, on the contrary, in bringing out some of their more valuable aspects, to show, by these, how radical the difference is between their life structure and that of the Spaniards. It has already been seen that the conversion of Recared and the conduct of the Catholic prelates are actions incompatible with the religious life of the Spaniards. It is now suitable to consider the supposed theocracy of the Visigoths, regarded by many as a logical antecedent of the Spain of Philip II, even though the major Spanish historians may not think so.[18] The Church and the monarchy supported each other. The kings, especially starting with Recared, preferred having the Church, united under a discipline, as their support, rather than rely on a divided, hereditary nobility, powerful and inclined to sedition. The king customarily named the bishops. The bishops (and future saints) Braulius and Isidore on a certain occasion recommended a candidate for archbishop of Tarraco (Tarragona today), and the king named a person of his own choice.[19]

But there is a more important way in which the Visigoths are distinguished from Spaniards, and this brings us to the intimacy of their life structure, to that "dwelling-place" from which life is projected, and to the area of its possibilities. The learned ecclesiastics of the Visigothic epoch are remembered by posterity as men of learning and not as ec-

[18] "The Church always bent before the power of the princes, and served them without flinching and without regard for the basest humiliations. One cannot speak of Visigothic theocracy. . . . The Church did not live over, but within, Visigothic society." (C. Sánchez-Albornoz, *Cuadernos de Historia de España*, v, 86-92.) "The Visigothic Church of the seventh century cannot be called national, in the sense of being a church directed and governed by the monarch, nor can the Visigothic state be called theocratic, if by this is meant a state in which . . . the bishops and councils hold the reins of government. . . . The Visigothic king manifestly exercised no few rights in matters purely ecclesiastical." (*Historia de España*, directed by R. Menéndez Pidal, III, 286-287.)

[19] In a letter to Braulius, Isidore says: "De constituendo autem episcopo Tarraconensi non eam quan petistis sensi sententiam regis." (*Epistolario de San Braulio*, edition of J. Madoz, pp. 87-88.) The king's action seems normal to Isidore, and he says nothing more about it.

clesiastics. Since them there has never been in Spain any saint who was at the same time learned, in the age-old meaning of wisdom, like Saint Anselm, Saint Bonaventure, or Saint Thomas. The Spaniards did not canonize Father Francisco Suárez, the greatest metaphysician they had; nor even Raymond Lully, who never got above the category of blessed. And canonizations in the past are a valid chart, I think, of the hierarchies of values in the Christian peoples.

The figure of Isidore of Seville (570?-636) clearly illustrates the split between the Hispania prior to 711 and the Spain which slowly and laboriously forged itself into existence through centuries of conflict. He reflected the last flashes of Roman learning, now fragmentary and lacking any connection with the life structure that made it possible. In the works left by Isidore are compilations and systematic reductions of the Roman notions about man and nature, and the theological doctrines of some of the fathers of the Church. For the present purpose, the originality of those writings, or their possible value for modern science, are of no importance. I bring up Isidore at this juncture to put into relief the life structure which made possible his preoccupation with human-divine learning, conceived from and directed towards a horizon of international culture. After the Visigoths, 800 years were to pass before a Castilian Christian would be interested in secular culture, in investigating the nature of things. Isidore, Braulius, Ildefonsus, Eugene and other Visigoths are known for their culture as well as for their virtues.

Issuing out of Roman antiquity, Isidore's work feeds medieval Western Europe's desire for knowledge. In it and in the works of other Visigoths there is a glimmering of what the life "dwelling-place" might have been in the Iberian Peninsula without the Moslems,[20] an observation offered not as an elegy but as an illustration. Isidore is neither profound nor original in his thought. He stops with Roman learning, for he knows nothing of that of Greece, now severed from the West and lying dormant even in Byzantium. The natural science of the Romans had very little of the scientific about it.[21]

Isidore's *Etymologies* (or *Origins*), in spite of what I have already said about him, is not an incoherent melange devoid of internal unity. A simple idea, not perceptible at first glance, dominates the whole: The

[20] C. Sánchez-Albornoz shares with the Belgian Henri Pirenne the idea that "Spain was a part of Europe at the beginning of the eighth century, and that, without Islam, the Iberian Peninsula would have continued along paths analogous to those followed by the other occidental nations." (*Revista de Occidente*, 1929, XXIV, 4.)

[21] See Ernest Brehaut, *An Encyclopedist of the Dark Ages: Isidore of Seville*, New York, Columbia University Press, 1912, p. 40.

line of descent starts from God and goes to angels, then to men, and then to nature. "The fact that the work was left unfinished does not keep us from recognizing that it contains thought ordered as a systematic whole."[22] Isidore's writings were in phase with the occidental mind and continued to be so for centuries. Charles H. Beeson says: "The rapid and truly gigantic diffusion of the manuscripts of Isidore is a notable event in the history of the cultural tradition. To observe the diffusion of those works and the use to which they were put is a profitable task, inasmuch as it reveals the extraordinary favor Isidore enjoyed. By emphasizing the zeal with which this diligent compiler's works were read, we get an idea of the literary activities and theological preoccupations of the darkest period of the Middle Ages. The powerful influence exerted by Spain over that world looms as the background of the picture, an influence to which Isidore contributed more than anyone."[23]

This evident reality is accepted by scholars, whatever their nationality, and it would be idle to adduce further testimony. One of them has gone so far as to try to correct the idea that Isidore knew no Greek, merely because passages can be found in his work that are translated literally from Cyril of Alexandria, at that time accessible only in the Greek.[24]

And for all that he might seem so, Isidore was not a random monolith standing in desert sands. For certain Hispano-Goths it was possible to be interested in the knowledge of things. Ildefonsus of Toledo, another future saint, writes that Eugene (a bishop, d. 646) was well versed in the observation of the phases of the moon; those who heard him talk of this were left astonished and felt attracted to the study of astronomical science.[25] This and other facts reveal the presence of an atmosphere of intellectual curiosity, the density of which it is not incumbent upon us to determine, nor could we. The fact remains that it existed. From the city of Caesar Augusta (which, but for the Arabs, would not be called Zaragoza today), Braulius wrote Isidore an epistle demanding that he

[22] A. Schmekel, *Isidorus von Sevilla. Sein System, seine Quellen*, Berlin, 1914, pp. 1-2.

[23] *Isidor-Studien*, Munich, 1913, p. 3. For the influence of the Visigothic writers on the European liturgy, see Bishop, in the *Journal of Theological Studies*, 1907, VIII, 278.

[24] See Patrick J. Mullins, *The Spiritual Life According to Saint Isidore of Seville*, The Catholic University of America, 1940, pp. 75ff.

[25] "Idem Eugenius moribus incessuque gravis, ingenio callens. Nam numerus, statum, incrementa, decrementa, cursus, recursusque lunarum tanta peritia novit, ut considerationes disputationis ejus auditorem et in stuporem verterent, et desiderabilem doctrinam inducerent." ("Episcopi Toletani," in Migne, *Patrologia*, S. L., XCVI, col. 204.)

remit a copy of his *Etymologies*, the great encyclopedia of knowledge of that time: "Do you think, perhaps, that the gift of your science was granted you for yourself alone? Indeed it is as much ours as yours; it is common property, and not private."[26]

Let us forego a comparison of Isidore with other Europeans (the Venerable Bede, the Irish humanists, etc.) on an absolute scale of values. The only thing pertinent to the present problem is the will to know the natural world and the world of men, the "origin" of things, the rational—not the fabulous—history of the then inhabitants of Hispania (Isidore's *History of the Goths*); or the principles according to which the sons of the nobility ought to be educated. All this was the personal task of Isidore, who was preoccupied with certain questions and with answering them adequately. It will occur to some, perhaps, that Alphonse the Learned, a Spaniard, was also filled with scientific curiosity and composed voluminous works. And in a way this is true. But between Alphonse and Isidore there is a cleaving difference, because their functional life structures were different. The King of Castile, like an oriental caliph, ordered the wise men of his court to undertake long pilgrimages through books Arabic and Christian, to the end of storing up huge masses of knowledge about man as a social being and about his future destiny. Alphonse, with a life already hammered out on the Christian-Islamic-Judaic anvil, had an appetite for being taught what man had been like from the remote depths of time, how he was supposed to be governed morally and legally, what his future might be, according to the predictions of the stars. Rational curiosity, pure and simple, was not a necessity for the wise sovereign, "al-ḥakim," of Castile. He was showered with works of wisdom which in his zeal for wisdom he had requested. Yet the gigantic work he sponsored and fostered remained, like an eccentric recluse, in its own land, because it was not expressed in the international language of Europe. Alphonse was not interested in including contemporary Europe in the panorama of his culture. His work was meaningful and efficacious for those in Spain who shared his life structure. The highly praised *Alphonsine Astronomical Tables*, a product of rational curiosity and thus a possible exception, are the work of Arabic and Jewish astronomers and bear the name of Alphonse only from the time-honored practice of flattery. In order to find a Castilian comparable to Isidore, we would have to come down to the humanist Antonio de Nebrija, a direct and original disciple of the science of Italy of the end of

[26] *Epistolario de San Braulio,* edition of J. Madoz, 1940, pp. 80-82.

the fifteenth century. In the period between Isidore and Nebrija (eight hundred years) we find nothing that we can connect with the scientific trends of the Visigothic vital structure.

The Visigothic ecclesiastics, as is evident from what I have said, did not scorn secular knowledge, nor did they think that this world was a vale of tears that excluded every earthly good. A reading of the works of certain subsequently canonized Visigoths leaves the impression of serenity and peace. Let us read for example the treatise of Isidore of Seville on the education of the children of the nobility, based on principles fundamentally more worldly than ascetic.[27] In the human ideal of Isidore, the Greco-Roman and the Germano-Christian tradition are harmonized; virtue is conceived with human amplitude and not limited to the religious or seignioral life. The treatise of Isidore presupposes the existence of a monarchico-elective regime, within which any knight excelling in gifts can ascend to the throne. A sentence from Plato summarizes the sense of those brief pages: "The kingdom is well governed when the philosophers rule and the rulers philosophize" (p. 559). The sentence is to be found in many places: Boethius quotes it (*De consolatione*, 1, 4, 5), and it is still recalled by La Bruyère. But the fact that it was picked out by Isidore makes us see not so much the perdurability of Plato's idea as it makes us see how Isidore felt in a certain vital situation.

The stoic-Christian spirit can be discerned in the insistent recommendation of chastity; wet nurses and teachers are to avoid all lewd obscenity: "The condition of the well-born is to show itself not only in their high rank but in their good habits of mind." But at the same time the youth is to possess "apta et uirilis figura membrorum, duritia corporis, robur lacertorum" (p. 558)—"a well-proportioned, manly figure, a hard body, and strong muscles"; for this, mountain and sea sports are to be recommended. The pupil must be versed in Holy Scripture, and also in philosophy, medicine, arithmetic, geometry, and astrology; he is to be pure, wise, and of good counsel, a lover of religion, and the defender of the fatherland. The great lord will also have to restrain his greed, so as not to harm the humble: "His fields must not be immoderately extended at the expense of the poor"—"Neque rura sua, exclusis pauperibus, latius porrigentur" (p. 559).[28]

[27] "Isidori Hispalensis 'Institutionum Disciplinae,' " edition of A. E. Anspach, in *Rheinisches Museum*, Neue Folge, 1912, LVII, 556-563.
[28] Petrus Hispanus, since he was the author of thirteenth-century works on philosophy and medicine that were not only read and admired in the Middle Ages but

This brief treatise allows us to see something of the possible human horizon for the best Visigoths in the seventh century, not so dark as it is usually said to be. If Isidore's was a period of darkness, how much light can be granted to the reconquering Christians of the four subsequent centuries?

Isidore's Hispania felt itself firmly seated in this world and sure of itself. The *De laude Hispaniae* at the beginning of Isidore's *Historia Gothorum*[29] begins thus: "Of all the lands that extend from the west to India, thou are the fairest, Oh sacred Hispania, ever-fecund mother of princes and peoples, rightful queen of all the provinces, from whom west and east draw their light. Thou art the honor and ornament of the world, and the most illustrious part of the earth; in thee the glorious fecundity of the Visigothic people takes much delight and flourishes abundantly." And the praise of Spain concludes: "With good reason in another time golden Rome, chief of the peoples, desired to possess thee; but even though Roman valor, victorious, might first take thee as a bride, the driving race of the Goths came later and carried thee off to love thee,

---

were in part even translated into Hebrew, might be thought by some readers to be comparable to Saint Isidore. The Germans K. Prantl in 1866 and M. Grabman in 1928 drew attention to the importance of his commentaries on Aristotle. G. Sarton, *Introduction to the History of Science*, 1931, II, 889-892, mentions his writings on medicine. Subsequently, the Spaniards have treated of this encyclopedist: T. and J. Carreras y Artau, *Historia de la filosofía española*, 1939, I, 101-144. M. Alonso has edited the book *De Anima* (Madrid, 1941) and has published the *Comentario al "De anima" de Aristóteles* (Madrid, 1944). It seems that Petrus Hispanus and Pope John XXI are the same person; Dante mentions Pietro *Ispano* among the major men of learning (*Paradiso*, XII, 134-135). The figure of such an important personage is surrounded by legends, and the reader can see for himself what there is of fact and fancy in the works cited above. It is enough for my purposes to point out that this philosopher, physician, and pope was born in Portugal, presumably in Lisbon, in the thirteenth century; he studied in Paris, and spent the rest of his life in France and Italy. Even though he was born biologically of parents who lived in Portugal, the functional structure of his life was not Portuguese; for, if he had remained in Portugal, he would not have done what he did. There is no reason why an intelligent person born in the Iberian Peninsula today or in the thirteenth century should not become a good scientist, if he incorporates into his life, either totally or partially, alien ways of life. The same thing happened to Petrus Hispanus, or Lusitanus, as he might better be called. The Hispanic person has no *racial* incapacity for theoretical or experimental science. What distinguishes Petrus Hispanus from Isidore of Seville is that the latter was educated in Visigothic Hispania, there he produced his achievements, and from there his work was projected into the international world. The work of Petrus Hispanus, on the contrary, became possible and was achieved outside of Spain. The Spanish scholars have become aware of the existence of their compatriot only in recent years.

[29] In *Chronica minora saec.* IV, V, VI, VII, edition of Theodor Mommsen, II, 267.

after many victorious wars fought over the vastness of the earth. That race delights in thee even today, secure in the happiness of its domain, with regal dignity and greatness of wealth."

It is beside the point to recall the "laudes" of other countries (in Pliny, Vergil, and other writers of antiquity): what counts here is the fact that Isidore exalts the grandeur of the Visigothic people, the strength of their arms, before which the power of Rome had to yield. The pagan image of the rape of the bride gives to the praise of Hispania a quite earthly perspective, devoid of both anguish and uncertainty. The wise archbishop magnifies the military glory of his kings, who do not fight for "divine" motives, as, according to Don Alonso de Cartagena, the Spanish kings had done: "In the year 620, in the tenth year of the reign of the Emperor Heraclius, the most glorious Suintila, by divine grace,[30] received the sceptre. As a duke—a title conferred on him by the king Sisebut—he reduced to complete submission the Byzantine armies (in the south), and he conquered the Rucones[31] (in the north of Hispania). After ascending to the peak of royal dignity, he conquered the cities still under the dominion of the Byzantines. . . . Suintila was the first to possess the whole of Spain even to beyond the Straits of the South (Gibraltar), something his predecessors had not accomplished."

The world, according to Isidore, can be encompassed and dominated by courage in warfare, and also through knowledge and intellectual reflection. Religious faith is not the only leading motive in this optimistic and, at times, worldly approach to life. The Hispano-Goth, insofar as the initial thrust of his life was concerned, was in line with the other peoples of Western Europe: the Franco-Gauls, the Anglo-Britons, the Ostrogoth-Romans. Among them, the other-worldly was articulated with the this-worldly, without the exclusion of the one by the other. That is why the Germanicized Hispanian, Isidore, a Catholic bishop, could align himself with Leovigild, a heretical king and a sure victim of hell, against the latter's son, the rebellious and Catholic Hermenegild; and other Germanicized Hispanians, as Catholic as they were learned, behaved in the same fashion. In the *Historia Gothorum*, Isidore's enthusiasm for the Gothic abductors of Hispania is not veiled in the kind of grief that a "Spaniard" would have felt over the fact that Spain had been sub-

---

[30] The belief that the kings receive divine grace comes from the Roman emperors, who got it in turn from the religions of the Orient, where the monarchs had a sacred character. See the previously cited work of Franz Cumont, *Les religions orientales dans le paganisme romain*, 1929.

[31] A people about whom little is known beyond what Isidore himself says about them.

jected by barbarians to whom Jesus Christ was not God but a prophet, or something of the sort.

When, in the thirteenth century, the *Crónica General* of Alphonse the Learned takes up and elaborates on the theme of Isidore's "praise of Spain," the feeling is quite different, because the Spaniards were no longer Hispano-Romano-Goths. Notice how far away we are from Isidore:

"Everyone must therefore learn that he should not place great value upon himself: neither the rich man for his riches, nor the powerful for his power, nor the strong for his strength, nor the learned for his learning, nor the exalted man for his high station or his goods; but he who seeks to place great value upon himself, let him do so for his service to God, for it is He who strikes and gives ointment, who wounds and heals, for all the earth is His; and all the nations and all people, kingdoms, languages, *all move about and change*, but God, the Creator of everything, *endures forever* and remains in the same state." (p. 311)

This prose shows more Oriental stylistic overtones than does that of Isidore. Six hundred years after him, Spain is submerged in the theological metaphysics of Islam: "For only God is, and has being." Whoever it may have been who composed this part of the *Crónica General*, he could no longer end the praise of Spain with the lucid, chiseled words of Isidore: "Imperii felicitate secura." Rather must he use these terms of trembling and anguish:

"This kingdom, so noble, so rich, so powerful, so honored, was overthrown and brought down in an outburst of discord among the inhabitants of the land, who turned their swords against one another, as if they were lacking in enemies; and in this they all lost, for all the cities of Spain were captured by the Moors, and were ruined and destroyed at the hands of her enemies. . . . Wretched Spain! her death was so hastened that there was no one left to mourn it; they call her the afflicted one, more dead than alive." (p. 312)

This complaint refers to the invasion of 711. Thereafter, one way or another, underneath the most elevated dithyrambs will always be perceived the undertone of insecurity, dissatisfaction, and complaint. The meaning and direction of life in the times of Isidore vanished to make way for something quite different. The dying Goth was reborn, as it were, in the nascent Spaniard with a new emergent life structure which, as he gradually created it, was to be both his glory and his misery—as is the case with all histories, for purposes known only to God.

From Visigothic Hispania to the Authentic Spain

The memory of the Goths remained alive among the Leonese and Castilian kings as an image of past grandeur which they aspired to restore. The people did preserve a few juridical customs of Germanic origin, customs which persisted in spite of the fact that Visigothic legislation had itself tried to get rid of them because they were contrary to the spirit of Roman law. It was a Germanic custom for a creditor to attach the goods of his debtor without the intervention of a judge; or for a family of a murdered person to be allowed to take vengeance by homicide.[32]

The survival of those customs did not imply that the Leonese and Castilians were living according to an inner life structure analogous to that of certain Germanic peoples who had preserved similar legal usages. The Roman laws were in effect at the same time as the legal tradition of the Visigoths, and it would not occur to anyone to think for this reason that the Spaniards were Romans. For everything that is left as a residue of the past takes its meaning from the total life disposition of a people.

The nostalgia for the idealized Visigothic monarchy nourished the belief that Christian Spain had an illustrious past, a belief not lacking in foundation. When Alphonse II (791-835) installed his court in Oviedo (Asturias), he thought he was re-establishing the "Gothic order" of Toledo, and down into the seventeenth century, "to have Gothic ancestry" (ser de los godos) was a seal of glory for Spaniards. This seems most pleasing to certain Swedish scholars,[33] who regard the history of Spain as an expansion of their race, also Gothic. Notice, however, that this very animating aspiration to be like the Goths reveals that the Spaniards of the late Middle Ages were not Goths; nor was the land that they were in process of reconquering and repopulating any longer Gothic. That which inspires and fascinates and the authentic life of those who are inspired and fascinated are different realities; just as we have previously seen that historical condition and possibility on the one hand, and on the other that which is conditioned and made possible are not the same realities. Ferdinand I, as has already been pointed out, did not order his two bishops to bring to his court the body of Saint Isidore, a man

[32] See Eduardo de Hinojosa, *El elemento germano en el derecho español*, Madrid, 1915.

[33] See the article of Johan Nordström, "Goter och Spanjoren. Till den spanska goticismen historia I," in *Lychnos*, Upsala, 1944, pp. 257-280, which is known to me only through the analysis of Carlos Clavería, "Godos y Españoles," in *Insula*, Madrid, August 15, 1946.

great in learning, but rather that of the martyr, Saint Justa, of especial interest to him.

The Visigothic forms of life and language had vanished; the bishops no longer subordinated the ecclesiastical power to the secular interests of the state. The cultural zeal of Alphonse the Learned is not like that of Saint Isidore. The worldly imperialism of the Visigoths is succeeded by "godly" war directed toward restoring Christian beliefs. Whereas the Jews were violently mistreated by the Visigothic kings, they will now be protected and sheltered by the kings of Spain for the eight centuries of Reconquest.

Christian Hispania was left bleeding and in a state of collapse under the Moorish tidal wave.[34] In the region of the northwest, where the resistance against the infidels was born, the perspective of life was not Visigothic.[35] The tasks were different and very difficult on account of the loss of all the large cities and the resources of the civilization of that time. The only cities of any importance in Gallaecia were Bracara (now Braga), Asturica (Astorga), and Lucus Augusti (Lugo); the Asturian towns of the Visigothic period must have been poor and small. Both provinces were rich only in forests, mines, and cattle, whereas the lands agriculturally productive had stayed in the hands of the Mussulmans. To compensate for such poverty, the northern strip of the Peninsula had a long tradition of human fortitude, of stubborn rebellion, which had shown itself in the fight against the Romans and the Visigoths, and in the assumption, or the preservation, of discrepant attitudes in the spiritual realm. The Suevian occupation in Galicia must have contributed to increasing the distance even more from the rest of the country. Actually, the Astures and Gallaici had lived as subject peoples without any feeling of self-determination or direction. This being the case, the catastrophe on the Guadalete in 711 suddenly conferred on them the unexpected power to act, in response to external solicitation, on their own energetic initiative. These people forgotten by history commenced to create a history for themselves starting in the middle of the eighth cen-

[34] In 754 a Mozarabe chronicler, despairing completely, writes: "Quis dinumerare tam importuna naufragia? . . . Spania, quondam deliciosa, et nunc misera effecta. . . . In eadem infelici Spania, Cordoba, in sede dudum patricia, quae semper exstitit, prae ceteras civitates adiacentes, opulentissima, et regno Wisigotorum primitivas inferebat delicias, regnum efferum collocant." (Anonyme de Cordoue, *Chronique rimée des derniers rois de Tolède et de la conquête de l'Espagne par les Arabes*, edited by Father J. Tailhan, 1885, pp. 25-26.)

[35] Sánchez-Albornoz speaks of "the protracted hiatus of the eighth century, during which many of the courtly practices of Gothic Spain were forgotten in Asturias" (*op.cit.*, v, 106).

tury, parallel with the other beginning histories of Castile, Navarre, Aragon, and Catalonia. The accords, the discords, and the discrepancies among these histories were to fill the future of the Peninsula from that day till this. The Hispania of the Visigoths was left broken up into regions with names that had never been heard before: Castilla, Navarra, Aragón, and Cataluña. Leon had been the name of the encampment-city of the Legio Septima Gemina. Only Galicia retained her traditional name of Gallaecia.

The Visigothic nation sank from sight just at the moment when it was apparently on the way to establishing political, linguistic, and religious unity throughout the Peninsula.[36] When its destruction was brought about, the northern strip, from Galicia to the Mediterranean, split into segments that were to remain separate for centuries, and whose forms of speech were to be Galician, Asturian-Leonese, Castilian, Basque, Aragonese, Catalonian. Even though the Basque language may have existed since prehistoric times, what really was bound to weaken and retard the Romanization (Latinization) of those who spoke it was the fall of the Visigothic monarchy.[37] Each of those languages was now going to represent to a greater or lesser degree a project of historical life, a projection based on the situation in which each people found itself, on the needs of war, and on the cultural contacts with the Moors and French. The Visigothic past, as an effective reality, was being left in the remote distance. From now on history was going to resemble the independent movement toward the south of six groups of people—Galicians, Leonese, Castilians, Basques, Aragonese, and Catalonians, who were starting on their course, each of them equipped with its own language and plan of life. From the crossing of their peculiarities would emerge the Spaniards' "dwelling-place" of existence.

For the first few centuries it was Galicia that offered the most original

[36] For a treatment of linguistic questions, see R. Menéndez Pidal, *Orígenes del español*, 1929, and Amado Alonso, "Partición de las lenguas románicas de Occidente," in *Miscellania Fabra*, Buenos Aires, 1943.

[37] And not only this: The new circumstances conferred on the Basques and their language an active and constructive role: they gave a few pronunciations to the Castilians, amongst others, the disappearance of Latin initial *f*, so that Castilians say *hacer*, not *facer*. The impetus of a people without a perceptible tradition of culture thus left its mark on a language of Roman ancestry. I am of the opinion that the Basques had the same kind of effect, but in small degree, on Castilian as the Franks had, on a large scale, on Gallo-Romanic, the French of today. The presence and importance of Basque fighters left its imprint on certain phonetic characteristics of Castilian, which did not take over from the Basques the names of culturally attractive objects, because the Basques did not possess any such. This was to be reserved for the Arabs and the French.

and productive program for Hispanic Christendom: the militant cult of Saint James the Apostle, conqueror of the Moors, future patron of Spain and the axis of her history, as I will demonstrate later. This event of such enormous collective and historical scope is interesting to us at this point for the way in which it can be connected with previous circumstances that may have made it possible—circumstances given in the Roman and Germanic tradition of the Peninsula—and chiefly as an expression of something characteristically Spanish.

A good many Galicians of today would have it that the mortal remains preserved in the tomb of Saint James the Apostle in Compostela are those of the famous heresiarch Priscillian and not those of the Apostle of Christ—a claim that is not without some point. Without getting into an argument about a suspicion that can never be confirmed by means of authentic documents, I am of the opinion that the relation between Santiago, as Saint James is called in Spanish, and Priscillian is not corporal, but of quite a different order. Priscillian, the highest representative of an important heresy or Christian dissidence, was executed in Trier in 385, by order of imperial authority.[38] Priscillianist beliefs took root especially in Galicia. Thus, when the Arian Suevi occupied that territory, they met with beliefs that bore some resemblance to their own in so far as the Suevi themselves did not accept the dogma of the Trinity of God One and Indivisible. The Council of Braga (567) anathematized those who said that "the Son of God and Our Lord did not exist before he was born of the Virgin," as well as those who introduced "other divine persons outside the Most Holy Trinity," errors committed by the Priscillianists. The latter believed in "the Procession of Aeons, emanating from the divine essence, and inferior to it in dignity." One of these Aeons was the Son, wherefore Saint Leo calls the Priscillianists "Arians."[39]

The Priscillianism of the fourth century, the Arianism of the fifth and sixth, the adoptionism of the eighth (which maintained that Christ was the adopted son of God), and other beliefs not very far from these, will be better understood when they can be seen in relation to certain oriental religions spread throughout the Roman Empire, whose legions were often filled with Asiatics, as Franz Cumont and others have shown. The anti-Trinitarian, or incorrectly Trinitarian, belief of many Christians in the Iberian Peninsula, a belief which, as we have seen, had preceded the

---

[38] Information sufficient for my purposes is to be found in what is said by Menéndez y Pelayo in his *Historia de los heterodoxos españoles*, 1917, II, Chapter II.

[39] *Ibid.*, p. 123.

arrival of the Arian Germans, was not altered overnight by the conversion of Recared. The absence in the Iberian Peninsula of firm ideas concerning the dual (human-divine) nature of Christ during the Visigothic epoch and the traditional rooting of such ideas in distant and eccentric Galicia (very much paganized even in the time of Saint Martin of Braga, later Priscillianist, and later Arian)—all these circumstances will make understandable the possibility of Santiago, a fine example of religious syncretism.

Contemplated in the perspective of the Toledo of the Visigoths, these heretical dissidences would figure with only a negative value, as a shrinking of the universal spirit in so far as they drew Hispania away from the totality of the Europe that was Rome's heir. On the positive side, the conversion of Recared, the campaigns against the Byzantines and against the rebellious peoples of the north traced a broad and firm national horizon. Similarly, and again, regarded within the Visigothic perspective, the partisans of the King Witiza who opened the ports of the Straits of Gibraltar to the Africans must have been quite sure of the stability of the monarchy, and they must have thought themselves powerful enough to cope with the claims of their foreign auxiliaries and to preserve the structure of a kingdom full of imperial hopes.

On the other hand, the perspective of the incipient Asturian-Galician-Leonese kingdom is bound to have been narrow and limited. We do not have access to the intimate life of these people between 711 and the end of the tenth century; there was no Orosius to collect such words as those Ataulf directed to the knight from Narbonne. Still, there are a large number of facts which I shall analyze later and which will reveal how the passage from the Visigothic Hispania to the future Spain took place.

Islam and Hispania

THE MOORS came to Hispania sustained by two highly efficacious forces: political unity and the impetus of a newly born religion, the expression of everything that the body and soul of the Bedouin could long for. They did not come like the barbarians of the fifth century, who had not left even so much as a center of government behind them in Germania as a base for spiritual and military operations; the Moors progressed elastically, with the feeling that they were moved by a central mainspring of religion and politics; they had even begun to absorb what there was left alive of Greek culture, now Christianized, in Syria and Egypt. Moreover, Arabic literature of the seventh century, although poor in ideas and devoid of highly significant motives, was already capable of expressing the conscious awareness of the most intimate feelings. In testimony of this, a grammarian says of a poet, Farazdaq (d. 732), that without him "one third of the Arabic language would have been lost."[1]

If the Straits of Gibraltar had been opposite Marseilles, France would have had a very different history, even though she was ruled by Franks and not by Visigoths. But this observation is idle. What is certain is that Visigothic Hispania succumbed, and what remained of nonsubject Christendom in the north was to initiate a course of history different from that of the other western countries. Christian resistance made itself felt very soon, and Islam saw itself forced to start a frontier war that did not terminate until the end of the fifteenth century. Islam was incapable of creating stable and durable political systems; the totally religious character of her vital structure kept her from surrounding her leaders with people capable of creating secular forms of communal life.[2] The strength of Islam lasted so long as there were leaders who could electrify the oddly composed masses of Al-Andalus (as Moorish Spain was called) with victories and dazzle them with wealth. Great masses of Christians became subject to the ruling Arabs, while retaining the liberty to practice

[1] See Farazdaq, *Divan*, French translation by R. Boucher, Paris, 1870.
[2] The reader is again reminded of the meaning of the word "life" and related words as used in this book.

the Christian religion, and these Christians—called Mozárabes—went on living under the protection of Moorish tolerance for four centuries, until the influx in 1090 of the Murābiṭs (Almorávides) and in 1146 of the Muwaḥḥidūn (Almohades)—fanatical tribes from Africa—did away with them.[3]

The struggle between Moors and Christians completely occupied Peninsular history till the middle of the thirteenth century; Cordova was reconquered in 1236, Valencia in 1238, and Seville in 1248. From then on, the impetus of the Christians weakened, consumed as they were by internal struggles similar to those experienced by the Moors. Prior to the petty Moorish kings ("taifas") of the eleventh century, there were the much earlier "taifas" of the Christians (Catalonia, Aragon, Navarre, Leon, Galicia; and the county of Castile). The Reconquest dragged on slowly during the thirteenth, fourteenth, and fifteenth centuries, until Ferdinand and Isabella unified the Peninsula (except for Portugal), and launched the people of Spain on enterprises now known to everyone.

It lies outside the scope of my plan to recount events that are well known and which the reader will find treated in the books of R. Dozy, E. Lévi-Provençal, R. Menéndez Pidal, Ph. K. Hitti, or in the *Encyclopedia of Islam*. My interest is focused on those aspects of medieval life in which Islamic contacts are made evident, less to follow the footprints of Islam in Christian Spain, than to attain to such a point of view as will make patent the structure of Spanish history. Until 1936 I had had more or less the same ideas about this subject as everyone else. We had all thought at one time that Christian Spain had been a given and fixed entity upon which fell the cloak of Moorish language, literature, and institutions. Only after I approached the Spanish Middle Ages in terms of "vital situations" did I begin to perceive the meaning of the Islamic in Spanish history. The Christian Middle Ages then appeared to me as the dynamic action of groups of northern folk (especially the Castilians) to subsist in the face of a world that was superior in technology and thought but not in personal fortitude, thrust, commanding ability, and epic literary expressiveness. The Christians took over a host of things—material and human—created by the Moors, but they did not assimilate the activities that could produce these things precisely because they had to take a new and extremely peculiar course of life in order to oppose, and finally to conquer, the Moors. It seems to me that what the Christians did not do—cut off as they were from their Visigothic tradition—is also

---

[3] See R. Menéndez Pidal, *Orígenes del español*, pp. 445-449.

an effect of Islam, and to the same degree as are the words imported from Arabic. In the same way, the system of values which the Christians had to develop (or conversely could not develop) in order to oppose their enemies effectively, is again something structural that falls within the same circle of life. Medieval Spain is the result of the combination of an attitude of submission and wonder in the face of a culturally superior enemy and of the effort to overcome this very position of inferiority. On this score certain verses from the *Poem of the Cid* (1140) are highly significant:

> Hear me, Albar Fáñez and all knights!
> We have imprisoned great wealth in this castle;
> The Moors lie dead; few live ones do I see.
> Moorish men and Moorish maids we cannot sell,
> Nor by chopping off their heads will we gain
>   anything;
> Let us keep them inside, *for we have the*
>   *seigniory;*
> We shall dwell in their houses, and *we shall*
>   *make use of them.*[4] (616-622)

To exercise seigniory and to utilize the services of the Moors, such was the program, not to imitate them in any way whatever in their technological or intellectual activities; for the vital situation out of which the resistance and effective advance were initiated was founded on religious belief and personal drive, and on the habits of rustic poverty. Let us look at such a delicate historical problem from the inside.

The first thing we shall do is try not to lose sight of its temporal dimension. When we contemplate the past from the present moment, a hundred years, two hundred years strike us as a long period, sufficient for the birth and rooting of new customs, basic for the situation and way of life of the today in which we find ourselves included. But we are not used to proceeding in this fashion when we contemplate a long period of the past from another point in time, also past. The centuries of semi-

---

[4] The Spanish of this text is as follows:
> ¡Oíd a mí, Albar Fáñez e todos los cavalleros!
> En este castiello grand aver avemos preso;
> los moros yazen muertos, de bivos pocos veo.
> Los moros e las moras vender non los podremos,
> que los descabeçemos nada non ganaremos;
> cojámoslos de dentro, *ca el señorío tenemos;*
> posaremos en sus casas, e *dellos nos serviremos.* (616-622)

Moorish history in Spain (711-1492) are regarded by many as a long and annoying interval, as nothing but a protracted military enterprise, slow and laborious, after which Spain returned to normality, albeit scarred and retarded here and there. The question, however, was not to end here, because all the Moors did not leave Spain in 1492; certain of them remained—those called Moriscos, ostensibly and officially subjects of the king, and Christians, but in reality Moors who retained their religion and customs, and whose presence, as we shall see, was not negligible in matters of literature and religion. So Moorish they were that the pious King Philip III decided to expel them from his realm in 1609. But even as a consequence of this, did they all leave? It seems not, for there are those who are sure they discern traces of Moorish tradition in the garden region of Murcia, in Valencia, and in Aragon.[5] Thus, the presence of Moors and Moriscos in Spain actually covers a period of more than nine centuries. Any average scholar knows that the hand of Islam can still be seen in the monuments of Cordova, Granada, Seville, Toledo, and other less important cities, as well as in Iberoamerica.

In the language there exists, in either current or archaic usage, a host of Arabic words. Works of literature have been inspired by Arabic sources from the twelfth-century *Disciplina clericalis*, which diffused thirty-three stories of oriental provenance throughout the Spain and Europe of the period, to the seventeenth-century *El Criticón*, of Baltasar Gracián, the germ of which is to be found in a story preserved among the Moriscos of Aragon. Yet, for all the importance this subject has and for all the vast bibliography that has grown up around it, still, no sort of "vital" study of it had been undertaken until M. Asín Palacios began to probe about under the surface of the history of religious sensibility, and to prove—as I think he did—at least that the form of the mysticism of the most exquisite of mystics, Saint John of the Cross, is not to be explained outside the ascetic and mystic tradition preserved by the Castilian Moriscos. Nor do I think that Saint Teresa's corpo-spiritual mysticism can be accounted for by Christian tradition only. When we think about the historical reality of Spain, we cannot get along without those nine hundred years of Christian-Islamic interrelationship.

As we emphasize the necessity for maintaining a lively awareness of

[5] In the absence of more precise information, see F. Fernández y González, "De los moriscos que permanecieron en España después de la expulsión decretada por Felipe III," in *Revista de España*, 1871, xix and xx. Also, "Manifestación de los hijos de moriscos que quedaron en Onteniente, 1611," published by V. Castañeda, in *Boletín de la Academia de la Historia*, 1923, pp. 421-427.

historical time, let us not forget that 429 years separate the arrival of the Moors and the appearance of the first Spanish literary work in the vernacular known to us, the *Poem of the Cid*, 429 years during which the task, the inescapable obsession, of the Christians was the compulsion to have it out with the Moors. The Roman and Visigothic past was useful in keeping alive the awareness that they were not Moors and the idea of a future of national unity, but with memories and longings it was not easy to conquer the Moslem lords of the larger part of the country. Poor, divided, with a life whose horizon was limited to military action, down to the eleventh century the Christians had regarded the Moors as an extremely powerful enemy whom circumstances had forced them to get along with. In the tenth century, and the third century of the occupation, Cordova oppressed in every possible way the weak states of the north. In 980, seeing how Almanzor's continuous victories were bringing him far into Castile, "the king of Navarre, Sancho Garcés," came out to meet him, "and offered him his daughter; Almanzor accepted her with pleasure, he took her to wife, and she embraced Mohammedanism, becoming one of the most beautiful and most religious women Almanzor had." In 993 King Vermudo II of Leon "sent his daughter Teresa to the Moslem leader, who received her as a slave and later freed her so that he might marry her."[6] Before this, 'Abd-al-Raḥmān III (d. 961) received a Christian embassy in his palace of Medina al-Zahra, a wonderful prodigy of art and grandeur. The road from Cordova to the palace (some three miles) had been covered with mats; alongside the road stretched a double file of soldiers, under whose crossed sabres the terrified ambassadors had to move. As they reached the palace, high dignitaries dressed in silk and brocade came out to meet them. The ambassadors greeted these people respectfully, thinking that one of them was the caliph. But the caliph was found sitting in the middle of a courtyard covered with sand, wearing rude clothing, the symbol of his ascetic customs. In the midst of terrible threats, the Christians signed the peace treaty imposed by the sovereign.[7]

Events of this sort are not surprising in the first three centuries of the Moorish domination. Moreover, the Moors and the Arabianized Jews were the exclusive repositories of science. The opulent Christians went to Cordova to have their ailments treated, just as the wealthy Europeans and Americans went to Germany in the nineteenth century. So, then, if existence was Christian, subsistence and prosperity in the degree to which

[6] R. Menéndez Pidal, *Historia y epopeya*, p. 19.
[7] E. Lévi-Provençal, *L'Espagne musulmane au X⁰ siècle*, p. 49.

it was possible were achieved by submitting to the benefits of the dominant civilization, superior not only by force of arms.

The advances of the Reconquest owed a great deal, on the other hand, to the radical insecurity of the Moorish domination. The caliph 'Umar (717-720) had already thought of having the Moors leave Spain "because, being on the other side of the sea, they were too far removed from the Moorish countries."[8] In 891 the Cordovan emir 'Abd-Allāh thought that the destined term of Arabic domination was up, because of the prolonged uprising of the rebel 'Umar ibn-Ḥafṣūn, fortified in the impregnable fortress of Bobastro. 'Abd-al-Raḥmān III (912-961), the most powerful of the Cordovan caliphs, kept Bobastro as a refuge, against the time when the prophecy of the downfall of Al-Andalus should be fulfilled.[9] If this kind of thing happened in the centuries when the Arabs in Spain were at their strongest and most splendid, one can imagine what the anguish of that people must have been from the eleventh century on. Offsetting their faith in the certain eternity of what they were promised by God was their doubt as to the stability, and durability, and tangibility of earthly things. Let us not think, then, that the question of what happened in the first centuries of the Reconquest can be answered by saying that a weak "culture" submitted to a stronger one, and nothing more. As the Christian acquired Arabic things and ways of living (both external and internal), he also absorbed Arabic doubt and uncertainty with respect to earthly life and to the validity and stability of everything that exists. It would not do to say that such an approach to life was characteristic of medieval Christianity in general, because neither Italy, nor France, nor England lacked a sense of security, and they were thoroughly Christian.

Even if, starting in the eleventh century, the military prestige of the Moors did begin slowly to decay and even if Christian life, thanks to its energy and dynamism, did begin to increase its dimensions, not for this reason did the values of Al-Andalus decline or was there any lessening of the esteem which its Christian enemy professed for it. Valor, stimulated by faith in the institution of royalty (not simply in a leader or, as the Spaniards call him, "caudillo") and in religious belief, established more and more firmly the only superiority effective in drawing out the thousand thorns that the Spaniards had picked up in their centuries of

[8] C. Sánchez-Albornoz, *La España musulmana*, Buenos Aires, 1946, I, 58.

[9] R. Dozy, *Histoire des Musulmans d'Espagne*, 1932, II, 63-66, 273; R. Dozy, *Recherches*, 1881, I, 29. M. Gómez-Moreno, "Las primeras crónicas de la Reconquista," in *Boletín de la Academia de la Historia*, Madrid, 1932, c, 580.

vassalage. It was not only the enthusiasm for Christ that decided the victories in favor of the Christians; stronger than any evangelical impulse was, after all, the trust in Saint James the Moorslayer—Santiago Matamoros—who lent magical aid in the destruction of the Moslems. But in the last analysis, the decisive thing was the interaction of religious faith and the Castilian's faith in his own person, as such capable of acquiring seigniory of wealth, authority, nobility, and liberty—all thanks to impulse and bravery. The affirmative awareness of valor, as it was deliberately cultivated by the individual person, permitted him to rise from serfdom to power, a power whose goal was more to assert one's rights and prestige than to create an extrapersonal, rational, and useful culture—a sense of cultural security.

Hence, in spite of the great victories over Islam, the Castilian had, in a certain sense, to surrender, and to accept the superiority of his enemy as far as the ability to make rational use of this world's possibilities was concerned. In 1248 the armies of King Ferdinand III conquered Seville after a struggle that gave definitive proof of the military incapability of the already decadent Moors. But these victorious armies could not repress their astonishment upon beholding the grandeur of Seville. The Christians had never possessed anything similar in art, economic splendor, civil organization, technology, and scientific and literary productivity:

"How great is the beauty and the loftiness and the nobility [of the Giralda]. . . . And it has many other great and noble features besides those of which we have spoken." To Seville came goods from all parts: "from Tangier, Ceuta, Tunis, Bougie, Alexandria, Genoa, Portugal, England, Bordeaux, Bayonne, Sicily, Gascony, Catalonia, Aragon, and even from [Northern] France."[10]

Even in the fourteenth century, the Cortes (Parliament) lamented over the poverty of the Castilian land: "The earth is very sterile and very poor" (1307). "The land was very poor and needy of attention and depopulated" (1367). "Our kingdoms are poor in cattle and other foods" (1371). "Our kingdoms are very needy" (1388).[11] Besides

[10] *Crónica general*, pp. 768-769.
[11] Quoted by Ramón Carande, in *Anuario de Historia del Derecho*, 1925, II, 267. Life in Seville a century before that city was conquered is familiar to us, thanks to the curious book *Sevilla a comienzos del siglo XII*, by Ibn 'Abdūn, translated into Spanish by E. Lévi-Provençal and E. García Gómez, Madrid, 1948. The book is at once a collection of municipal ordinances, a catechism of public morality and hygiene, and a description of abuses and corruptions. It seems at times as if the city were confessing its faults. The tone, both intelligent and intimately familiar (a native characteristic of the Moors), reveals the high level attained by civic culture

literature and art, the only positive asset, at least until well into the fifteenth century, had been the vital impulse to make war, and this by now had been spent among the Moors. The fact that in the Mediterranean strip comprising Catalonia and Valencia things were somewhat different does not essentially alter the picture.

It is a good idea to emphasize the fact, well-known as it is, that during the Middle Ages there was not a complete separation between Christians and Moors. We have already mentioned the Mozárabes, those bilingual Christians who continued to live their established lives in the midst of the Moors, and who, starting in the first centuries of the occupation, would emigrate from time to time to Christian lands, and who moved en masse during the incursions of the Almorávides and Almohades in the twelfth century. The Mozárabes of Valencia emigrated to Castile in 1102. In 1125, 10,000 Mozárabes expatriated themselves from Granada with the withdrawing Aragonese troops of Alphonse I, who had invaded that kingdom. In 1146 there was another Mozárabe exodus from Seville to the lands of Castile,[12] and it is certain that such displacements must have taken place in other instances not registered by the chronicles. Besides this social class, there was that of the so-called *mudéjares*, the Moors who lived as vassals of the Christian kings—kings who were influenced by the tolerance of the first four centuries of Islamism, as we shall see later. To these *mudéjares* we are indebted for such beautiful monuments as the Alcázar in Seville, and the Puerta del Sol in Toledo, to name only two out of many.[13] Besides there were fugitives from one

---

in Al-Andalus. Here are some samples: "The prince must require that the greatest effort be spent on agriculture, which must be encouraged, even as the farmers are to be treated benevolently and protected in their labors" (p. 42). "Books of science must not be sold to either Jews or Christians, save such books as treat of their laws, because they then *translate the scientific books* and attribute them to their own people and to their bishops, as if these works were not Islamic" (p. 173). "Lawyers ought to be suppressed, for their activities cause the people to spend their money in vain. . . . But if we must have them, let them be as few as possible" (p. 61). "Garden vegetables such as lettuce, chicory, carrots, etc., ought not to be washed in the pools or garden tanks, for there is no surety that these are clean, but in the river where the water is clearest and purest" (p. 132). Etc. As is evident, the translation of scientific books was not limited to the so-called "School of Translators of Toledo." There were Christian churches in Seville, which the author presents as places of immorality (p. 150); Mussulmans and Christians reproached each other for the same vices.

[12] See R. Menéndez Pidal, *Orígenes del español*, pp. 445-446.

[13] See F. Fernández y González, *Estado social y político de los mudéjares de Castilla*, 1866; N. Estenaga, "Condición social de los mudéjares en Toledo," in *Boletín de la Real Academia de Bellas Artes de Toledo*, 1924, VI, 5-27.

religion to the other: *muladíes*, Christians who turned Islamic, and *tornadizos*, Moors who turned Christian. The *Partidas*, or laws, of Alphonse the Learned, say (VII, 25, 8) that at times men "ill-fated and despairing of every blessing, renounce the faith of Our Lord Jesus Christ and become Moors ... either to live free of restraint, or to be relieved of the troubles that may have beset them as Christians." Such renegades were deprived of their property and their life if they were apprehended. The same legal code speaks of the hard life of the *tornadizos* (VII, 25, 3), which discourages those who wanted to become Christians; many would have done so "if it were not for the abuse and dishonor that they see the others receive who turn Christian and are called turncoats [*tornadizos*] and many other evil and insulting names." It is evident, then, that the two religions lived together easily, but that apostasy was not easy in either of them.

To end this list of such classes, there was a fifth, the *enaciados*, who moved back and forth between both religions, and who capitalized on their bilingualism by serving as spies. They lived in border towns, and sometimes they formed complete communities, just as today on all the borders in the world there exist towns that specialize in smuggling. In Estremadura there is still a town called "Puebla de Naciados."

After the political domination of the Moors came to an end, a considerable number of Mudéjares (now called Moriscos) stayed in Spain. There was more than one uprising of them, and the armies of Philip II had to fight strenuously to reduce the Alpujarra rebellion, in Southern Granada.[14] As everyone knows, except for those who were priests, monks, or nuns, the Morisco population was expelled by Philip III in 1609. That unhappy breed survived the spirit that had made living together possible for Christians, Moors, and Jews; once the model of Islamic tolerance, with all its prestige, disappeared, there was no ideal vertex at which Christians and Moors could converge. Like many other problems in Spanish life, this one was insoluble, and it is idle to argue the point whether the Moriscos ought or ought not to have been thrown out of

---

[14] In the *Guerra de Granada* of Diego Hurtado de Mendoza, the fight that went on from 1568 to 1571 is described with a full awareness that it was a civil war of "Spaniards against Spaniards" (*Biblioteca de Autores Españoles*, XXI, 73). The Moriscos were dispersed to remote places: "It was a most pitiable departure for those who had known them well off and established in their homes; many died along the roads, from labor, from weariness, from grief, from hunger; killed by the very ones who were supposed to guard them; robbed, sold as captives" (*ibid.*, p. 92). Luis del Mármol recounts the revolt in Granada in detail in *Rebelión y castigo de los Moriscos de Granada*.

their native land. They doubtless were a political danger, and they did have intelligence with foreign enemies of Spain, who herself was beginning to feel frightened and weak,[15] so weak that it was necessary to bring home the regiments in Italy, because the forces available in the kingdom were not enough to guarantee security against the risks of the expulsion. The war in Granada in 1568 "revealed that our Spaniards are not worth so much on their own soil as they are when transplanted to the soil of other peoples."[16]

The Moriscos were hard and skillful workers, and it is commonplace to lament the disaster that their removal brought on agriculture and industry. This was expressed once and for all by Hurtado de Mendoza, in words of polished steel, when he spoke of the Alpujarra as being "naturally sterile and hard, save where there are valleys; yet under the diligence of the Moriscos—who allowed no piece of ground to be wasted —usable and cultivated" (p. 75). The Moor excelled at manual labor, scorned by the Christians,[17] and for this he became as useful as he was contemptible. The most human description of his skills and aptitudes is the one found in the *Historia de Plasencia* by Friar Alonso Fernández: "They were diligent in the cultivation of gardens, and lived apart from the society of Old Christians, preferring that their own life not be the object of gazing. Others were occupied in trade. They sold foods at the best stands in the cities and villages, most of them living by the work of their own hands. Others were employed at manual trades such as tinkers, smiths, shoemakers, soap-makers, and muleteers. They all paid their taxes and assessments willingly, and were moderate in their food and dress. . . . They had no use for begging among their own people; and all had a trade and were busy at some employment" (Janer, p. 162).[18] They propagated abundantly, "because none of them took up

[15] See above, p. 57.

[16] Marco de Guadalajara y Xavier, *Memorable expulsión . . . de los moriscos*, Pamplona, 1613, fol. 79 v.

[17] But sometimes the *hidalgos* married Morisco women, attracted by their money or by their beauty. Melchor de Santa Cruz (*Floresta*, I, p. 53) has an anecdote about a gentleman who was the "son of a Morisco mother."

[18] Books about the Moriscos were numerous and passionate at the time of the expulsion, and even the scholars who discussed it in the nineteenth century took sides in the matter. For example: Florencio Janer, *Condición social de los moriscos*, 1857, a mediocre book, but containing important quotations; it is favorable to the Moriscos. P. Boronat y Barrachina, *Los moriscos españoles y su expulsión*, 1901, two volumes of polemic documented to justify the expulsion. Señor Boronat thinks that the grandeur of the Arabs (not very evident to him) was due to Spain: "What did the eighth-century invaders bring from Africa? How did they prosper in Africa

the sterile calling of monk, cleric, or nun. . . . All married—poor and rich, sound and lame. . . . And the worst that can be said of all this is that some Old Christians even while they claimed some trace of hidalgo blood, because they had nothing of their own, married Morisco women and thus spotted their already tarnished coats of arms."[19] So far as their customs and character were concerned, "they were quite fond of burlesques, tales, and boasts, and they were inordinately fond of dances and songs (so that they usually had bagpipes, timbrels, and tambourines). . . . They preferred work that required skill rather than brawn; they were weavers, tailors, rope-makers, sandal-makers, potters, shoemakers, veterinaries, mattress-makers, gardeners, muleteers, olive-oil peddlers" (Janer, p. 159).[20]

In sum, the relation between Moriscos and Christians still recalled that of the Middle Ages, with the difference that the literary and scientific culture of the Moriscos now boasted no Averroes or Ibn Ḥazm, and that their writings (preserved in Spanish as spoken in Aragon and written in Arabic characters—that is, aljamía, as this written language is called) are lacking in any special value. By this time the Christians naturally were

---

when they returned from here [Spain]?" (II, 350.) This is a historical sophism. In Spain (and naturally in connection with Spanish circumstances) the Arabs attained a high point in their history at the same time that Islam was flourishing elsewhere; they fell into decay later, just as they did in Syria, Egypt, etc. The Morisco form of life had been integrated within the life lived together by Mohammedans and Christians, and in 1600 the Moriscos were doing about the same thing as before. In Africa, lacking the soil of Spain and Christian markets, they were no longer themselves. Moriscos and Christians complemented each other when it pleased God and Allah; they were rent asunder in the seventeenth century to live lives no better than they would have lived if they had stayed together.

[19] Thus, Pedro Aznar de Cardona, *Expulsión justificada de los moriscos españoles*, 1612 (quoted by Janer, p. 160). This must be the basis for what Cervantes says of the Moriscos in *Persiles y Segismunda*: "They are not plucked off in their prime by any religion . . . they all marry, all, or almost all, beget children." (See my *El Pensamiento de Cervantes*, p. 294.)

[20] The words of Janer's original text are very significant: "Eran muy amigos de burlerías, cuentos, berlandinas, y sobre todo amicísimos (y asi tenían comunmente gaitas, sonajas, adufes) de bailas, danzas, solaces, cantarcillos, albadas. . . . Eran dados a oficios de poco trabajo: tejedores, sastres, sogueros, esparteñeros, olleros, zapateros, albéitares, colchoneros, hortelanos, recueros y revendedores de aceite, etc." *Adufe* "tambourine," *albéitar* "veterinary," *recua* "mule train," and *aceite* "olive oil" are Arabic. *Sastre* "tailor" and *ollero* "potter" were formerly, and to some extent still are, called by their Arabic names of *alfayate* and *alcaller* or *alfarero*. Again, *burlería* "droll tale" is the original of *bulería*, which the dictionaries do not give, although it is a well-known form of *cante flamenco*. The Moriscos were, as we see, very fond of singing and dancing, and the words *zambra* (a festival with dancing and merrymaking) and *zarabanda* (the dance) are also oriental.

dominant over them with respect both to seigniory and to literary ability.[21] In any case, the number of books written between 1610 and 1613
on the subject of their expulsion (some twenty, counting both those in
print and those in manuscript) demonstrates the great importance such
an event had in public opinion. It had proved impossible to assimilate
the Moriscos through either persuasion or violence. These people felt
themselves to be as Spanish as the Old Christians, and their consciousness
of nationality had its roots in a glorious past.[22] Their virtues as diligent
workers and the wealth that was the sign of those virtues were sacrificed
by the Spanish monarchy, which considered wealth and welfare to be
nothing as compared with the national honor, with its foundation in
religious unity and the indisputable seigniory of the royal power. Pacts
and agreements with infidels were medieval practices. In the last analysis, the Moriscos themselves had become an anachronism—even though,
on the other hand, the pattern of national life might have to go on being
that of the Middle Ages: the Moor could work and produce in 1600
as in 1100, and the Christian would be the lord in an ecstasy of personal magnificence. But there was a historical cleavage between 1600 and
1100. The persons behind the noble and mystic figures to be seen in the
pictures of El Greco could no longer get along with a pack of peasants
and craftsmen who occasionally boasted of grandeur and conspired
against the security of the State.

In the time of Charles V, Spain felt very strong, and a residue of
flexibility still permitted her to carry the burdensome legacy of tradition.
In the time of Philip II, everything tightens and stiffens, intolerance
towards the Moriscos grows stronger, and the Moriscos themselves rise
up in arms when the first whiff of the decay of the Spanish empire
reaches their nostrils. Aben Humeya, in the harangue that I have quoted
previously (note 22), expresses himself thus: "The broad Empire of
Spain is nothing to me, because, believe me, when states reach the pinnacle of their grandeur, they must decline. Powerful forces destroy the
refinement, voluptuousness, and pleasure that accompany their prosperity. . . . We are no band of thieves, but a kingdom; nor is Spain less
abandoned to vices than was Rome." In truth, Philip II needed all the
strength he could muster to put down the Moriscos in the mountains of

[21] For lovely manifestations of Mudéjar art in the architecture of Iberoamerica,
see Manuel Toussaint, *Arte mudéjar en América*, Mexico, 1946.

[22] "Don't you know that we are in Spain, and that we have owned this land for
900 years?" Thus spoke Don Fernando de Válor (Aben Humeya) before he un-
leashed the rebellion of 1568. (See Don Antonio de Fuenmayor, *Vida y hechos de
Pío V*, 1595, quoted in Janer, *op.cit.*, p. 144.)

Granada, and to reduce their poorly armed bands he finally had to call on no less a military expert than Don Juan of Austria, after other distinguished generals had failed in three years of fighting. It is therefore not surprising that some Spaniards were afraid lest the Moors, the Turks, and certain enemy Christians should once again destroy Spain (see page 57).

That civil war and the final expulsion of the race which could not be subdued were what had to be, given the terms of the problem up for solution, is self-evident. The breach came about—and with very painful and serious injuries to both sides—because, although the two parties were "rationally" incompatible, at the same time they were "vitally" sympathetic. This sympathy was based on a community of moral experience, yet it was irreconcilable with the *raison d'Etat* of a theocratic empire. Christian and Moor no longer could live together under the belief that had sheltered both of them during the Middle Ages. Yet the Morisco continued to feel that he was Spanish: "Wherever we are, we weep for Spain, for, after all, there were we born, and it is our natural fatherland. Now do I know and feel what is usually called the sweet love of the fatherland." Thus speaks the exiled Morisco in the *Quijote* (II, 54). Which complements what was felt by Christian souls of delicate temper. Hernando de Talavera, the first archbishop of Granada, was of the opinion that if the Moriscos and other Spaniards were to be good Christians the Moriscos "would have to have some of our faith, and we would have to do some of *their good works*."[23] This was not occasional and political sentimentalism, for in 1638 the historian Bermúdez de la Pedraza observed that if "faith was lacking and baptism abundant" among the Moriscos, it was equally certain that "they practised *good moral works*; they showed much truth in their dealings and contracts and great charity toward their poor; they were little given to idleness; all worked hard" (Longás, p. lii).

Here is one more conflict in a time that has its very roots in conflict, an epoch that will find its expression, finally, in the so-called baroque literature. It will not do to oversimplify the question and say that Spanish intolerance overwhelmed Moorish obstinacy, rebellious against the iron-clad unity of Philip II's Spain, when the decisive thing was really the clash between reason and life, a clash of which some of those were aware who dreamed of ideally harmonizing the "faith without works"

[23] According to F. Bermúdez de la Pedraza, in *Antigüedades y excelencias de Granada*, folio 91, quoted by P. Longás, *Vida religiosa de los moriscos*, Madrid, 1915, p. lxxv.

of the Old Christians and the "works without faith" of their adversaries. So long as faith and works remained separate from each other, the social catastrophe was inevitable. In 1614, the Jesuit Pedro de Guzmán observed that certain protestant "heretics" owed the "happiness" of their states to diligence in labor—to works—as a constructive social virtue.[24] Always, some way or other, some Spaniards *felt* what would be good to do in Spain, unrealizable though it might be. *And this polemical dualism between consciousness and conduct is precisely the premise from which derives the permanent and universal quality of Spanish civilization*—"vivir desviviéndose"—*one* of whose expressions is the literature of the Golden Age.

During the sixteenth century certain Aragonese lords accepted with some irritation the Inquisitorial pressure against the Moriscos,[25] who were the main tillers of the soil: "Since the lords have no other more appreciable incomes on which they can live and maintain their houses and estates, they deeply regret that the Inquisition punishes their vassals; whence many unjust complaints against the Holy Office and against those who are in it." Thus writes an inquisitor in Zaragoza to the Supreme Council in Madrid in 1553. Later, in 1569, no less a personage than the Admiral of Aragon, Don Sancho de Cardona, was tried by the Holy Office for his excessive tolerance toward the Moriscos, for whom he had gone so far as to have a mosque rebuilt. To him was imputed the intention of going to the Pope and even to the Sultan of Turkey in protest over the forced baptism imposed on the Valencian

---

[24] "In many kingdoms, not only of the faithful but of infidels and of heretics (such as those of La Rochelle), the rulers thereof take especial care that there be in their cities no idle people; and in this consists a large part of *the happiness of those people*." (*Bienes del honesto trabajo*, Madrid, 1614, pp. 119-120.)

[25] In 1508 Ferdinand the Catholic had already forbidden the forced conversion of the Moors of Catalonia. The protest against the violent acts of the Inquisition had originated with the viceroy (the Duke of Cardona) and other lords whose lands were worked by Moorish vassals. The ideas of tolerance which I analyze in Chapter 7 are here voiced, I believe, for one of the last times: "No one is to be compelled to be converted to our Holy Catholic Faith and to be baptized, for only when conversion comes freely and from a pure heart is it service to God" (Archivo de Simancas, Inquisición, Libro 926, fol. 76, quoted by Henry Charles Lea in his *The Moriscos of Spain: Their Conversion and Expulsion*, London, 1901, p. 407). There persisted in the policy of the Catholic sovereigns a remnant of the tradition of the Moorish, Jewish, and Christian life together, notwithstanding the fact that the people compelled those sovereigns to expel the Jews. (I shall treat of this idea at greater length in subsequent pages.) In 1498 the Moors who had been expelled from Portugal were authorized to come and live in Castile "for as long as you may wish to" (Lea, *op.cit.*, p. 404).

Moriscos.[26] But just as it was not possible to bring together faith without works and works without faith, neither was harmony possible on the plane of economic interests, since the "things" of this world, tangible and interchangeable, were never decisive within the Hispanic "dwelling-place." The leaders of public life could not at the time see anything in the Morisco except a rebellious will; no common field of activities and interests existed, in which the Morisco's love for Spain could be linked with the esteem which a few spirits of delicate temper felt for the Moriscos. The conflict was converted into a clash of wills, naked, in severance from the things and interests of the external, neutral world that belongs to all but all of which belongs to no one. The result of this clash of naked wills could be nothing but the annihilation of one of the groups; compromise was impossible. The lords of Aragon were overwhelmed, and their fields fell into a wretched state.

I am inclined to see a residue of Aragonese animosity toward the central authority of Castile in the fact that during the seventeenth century the Aragonese printing presses were a refuge for bitter, satirical books, in which the existing order did not come off too well. The first editions of Quevedo's most mordant and caustic works appear in the kingdom of Aragon, not in Castile. True, the unifying policy of Philip II, which contravened the provincial prerogatives of Aragon, would itself incline the Aragonese to regard with favor any attack on society; but in addition to this, I think, the expulsion of the Moriscos did its part to disturb the precarious solidarity of the various kingdoms of Spain.

Now, it seems to me, the distance can be calculated that separates the expulsion of the Moriscos in 1609 from that of the Jews in 1493. The Moriscos, in their totality, constituted a portion of Spain and a prolongation, as it were, of its people, and this explains the aforementioned attacks and praises; the Jews were felt to be a thorn in the flesh, the common people never esteemed them highly, and no one, really, ever had the courage to defend them openly after their expulsion. Only the kings and the uppermost classes yielded to them, before their expulsion, in intellectual, technical and administrative superiority.[27] Their social function was different from that of the Moriscos, who in the worst case were highly useful and even amusing pariahs, encased for centuries in the national life. In spite of their suspect faith, the Moriscos challenged the severities of the Inquisition for more than a century, they enjoyed strong protection, they seduced more than one Old Christian with their enticing sensu-

---

[26] See Longás, op.cit., p. 57.
[27] See Chapter 13.

ality, as well as their cleverness in making money; they even insinuated into Spanish Catholicism, along with illuminism, some subtle forms of mysticism, and they funneled the themes and styles of the Arabic tradition into the literature of the sixteenth and seventeenth centuries. A centuries-old tradition protected them, because important zones in the Hispanic soul had been conquered by Islam, as we shall presently be seeing. The cycle which begins in the eighth century with the Mozárabe Christians subject to the Moors closes in the seventeenth with the Moriscos subjugated and finally expelled by the theocrats of a weary Spain.

With those 900 years unfolded before our eyes, why should we find anything strange in the fact that the language, the customs, the religion, the art, the letters, and even the living structure itself of the Spaniard require, for understanding, that we bear in mind this interaction that continued for centuries? And we shall try to keep it in mind as something that gives a structure to history, rather than as the content of a national life. Let me repeat that Christian Spain was not something that preexisted in a fixed reality of her own, upon which fell the occasional influence of Islam, as a "mode" or a result of the life of "those times." Christian Spain "became"—emerged into being—as she incorporated and grafted into her living process what she was compelled to by her interaction with the Moslem world.

I do not intend for a moment to analyze in detail the Moorish and Christian civilizations in medieval Spain, a task that has been in large part already accomplished, albeit with factual lacunae—which I could not fill. I aspire to do no more than explain to myself how the peculiarity of the great Hispanic values was formed. Willing to run the risk of being mistaken, I wish to submit that that which is most original and universal in the Hispanic genius has its origin in a living disposition forged in the nine centuries of Christian-Jewish-Moorish interaction.

Arabic Life in Spanish Language

Nothing is more revealing than language. Numerous Arabic words are found in Spanish and Portuguese as a reflection of inescapable necessity, just as Latin likewise had to accept thousands of Greek words.[28] Many Arabisms have persisted in both the literary and the dialectal language.[29] The Romanic structure of Spanish and Portuguese was not af-

[28] The term *préstamo, borrowed word, emprunt, Lehnwort,* used in linguistics, is inexact, because these words are acquisitions that are never returned. They ought to be called linguistic adoptions or importations.
[29] There is no complete list of Ibero-Romanic words of oriental origin. See Dozy

fected by Arabic, because the Latino-Romanic written tradition was never lost; indeed, it was strengthened in the measure that the Christian states progressively intensified their national consciousness. If all Spain had been inundated by the Moslem domination, as happened in England under the Normans, then the structure of the language would have been altered profoundly; but the Romanic Spaniard took the Arabic words from within his own national life, as things imposed by his circumstances and not by the authority of the conquerors. The case of Norman words in the English language is not parallel. The English had to say *veal* and *beef* because the lords who had authority in the cities spoke thus, and it was to the lords that such commodities were to be sold. The Norman element in English was to a large extent the result of an imposition; the Arabic element in Iberian Romance was the result of the necessity for importing things that belonged to people who persuaded by their superiority. These lexical adoptions in Iberian Romance refer to extremely diverse zones of life: agriculture, the construction of buildings, arts and trades, commerce, public administration, sciences, and warfare. It is significant right off that *tarea* (Portuguese, tarefa), meaning "task," is Arabic. The *alarifes* (architects) planned the houses and the *albañiles* (masons) built them;[30] wherefore the Arabisms *alcázar* (castle), *alcoba*

---

et Engelmann, *Glossaire des mots espagnols et portugais, dérivés de l'arabe*, 1869; L. Eguílaz, *Glosario etimológico de palabras españolas de origen oriental*, 1886; P. Ravaise, "Les mots arabes et hispano-morisques du 'Don Quichotte,'" *Revue de Linguistique*, 1907-1914; J. Coromines, "Mots catalans d'origen aràbic," in *Butlletí de Dialectologia Catalana*, 1936, xxiv, 1-81, xx; A. Steiger, *Fonética del hispano-árabe*, 1932 (important work with extensive bibliography); Jose Pedro Machado, "Alguns vocabulos de origem arabe e comentarios a alguns arabismos" [in the *Diccionario* of A. Nascentes], in *Boletim de Filologia*, Lisboa, 1940, vi, 1-33, 225-238; E. K. Neuvonen, *Los arabismos del español en el siglo XIII*, Helsinki, 1941; R. Lapesa, *Historia de la lengua española*, Madrid [1951], pp. 95-109. M. L. Wagner, "Sôbre alguns arabismos do português," in *Biblos*, 1934, pp. 1-31.

[30] In the records of the town hall of Seville, a century and a half after the city was conquered, we read that in 1393 "two *moros albañies* [Moorish masons] undertook to start and finish this piece of *albañeria* [masonry—it is a question here of a water distribution system], and they made the aforesaid *alcantarilla* [water conduit]. . . . And besides, these two master craftsmen undertook to start and finish all the superarches that were to be made over again." In their work they used *aceite* (olive oil) and *azulaca* (plaster)—two Arabic words. (Text published by R. Carande in *Archivo de Historia del Derecho Español*, 1925, ii, 399.) They needed master craftsmen in Burgos still in the fifteenth century. Here are some data that I find in L. Serrano, *Los conversos D. Pablo de Santa María y D. Alonso de Cartagena*, Madrid, 1942: Three Moorish artisans report, in 1429, on the poor quality of the "machinery and arms deposited in the Castle of Burgos" (p. 73). In the same year some Moors are recorded as supplying the royal army with flour; they also furnished carpenters (p. 95). Houses for the cathedral chapter are contracted for with

(bedroom), *azulejo* (tile), *azotea* (roof terrace), *baldosa* (fine paving tile), *zaguán* (vestibule), *aldaba* (door-knocker), *alféizar* (window sill), *falleba* (bolt lock for doors and windows). The excellent technique for the control and supply of water is evident in *acequia* (irrigation ditch), *alberca* (artificial pool), *aljibe* (cistern—adopted in French in the form *ogive*); and in a multitude of other words. Because the tailors were Moors, they were called *alfayates*, Portuguese *alfaiate*;[31] the barbers were the *alfajemes*; goods were transported by *arrieros* (muleteers) and *recueros* (tenders of the *recua* or caravan); they were sold in *zocos* and *azoguejos* (market squares), in *almacenes* (warehouses), *alhóndigas* (granary-markets), and *almonedas* (public sales, originally, in Arabic, public cries); taxes were paid in the *aduana* (customs house, originally, in Arabic, a book of accounts), weights and measures were in *arrobas* (quarters, that is, fourth parts of a *quintal*, an Arabic hundredweight), *arreldes* (weight units equivalent to four pounds), *quilate* "carat," *adarme* (weight units equivalent to 179 centigrams), *fanegas* (volumetric units equivalent to 55.5 liters, originally, in Arabic, sacks), *almudes* (units of dry measure, varying in equivalence), *celemines* (the name of various dry and area measures, derived from the Arabic word for eight), *cahices* (the name of various units of dry measure), *azumbres* (units of liquid measure equivalent to 2.006 liters, originally, in Arabic, the eighth part of a certain jug); these weights and measures were inspected by the *zabazoque* (originally, in Arabic, the chief of the market) and the *almotacén*; the *almojarife* (originally, in Arabic, the inspector) collected the taxes, which were paid in *maravedís* (originally, in Arabic, of or pertaining to the *Almorávides*; see page 82). Cities and fortresses were governed by *alcaldes* (mayors, originally, in Arabic, judges), *alcaides* (defense officers of castles or fortresses, originally, in Arabic, chiefs), *zalmedinas* (magistrates with criminal and civil jurisdiction, originally, in Arabic, chiefs of cities), and *alguaciles* (lieutenants of police). Accounts were kept by means of *cifras* and *guarismos* (numbers, Arabic, of course), or by means of *álgebra* (which meant *reduction* in Arabic); the *alquimistas* (practitioners of *alquimia*, or alchemy) distilled *alcohol* in their *alambiques* (alembics) and *alquitaras* (stills), or they prepared *álcalis*

Moorish architects and workers in 1397, 1398, 1435, 1436, etc. (p. 257). "We shall dwell in their houses, and we shall make use of them." The execution of the program formulated in the *Poema del Cid* went on. (See above, p. 83).

[31] Since the Portuguese clings even more than the Spaniard to tradition, Arabic words persist in his language that have been replaced by Romance words in Spanish. In Portuguese one still says *alfaiate*, as well as *alface* (lettuce), *ceroulas* (underdrawers, called in Old Spanish by the Arabic word *zaragüelles*), etc.

(soda ash), *elixires*, and *jarabes* (sweetened and fruit-flavored or medicinal potions, originally, in Arabic, beverages), which they put into *redomas* (flasks). The cities were divided into *barrios* (originally, in Arabic, exteriors) and *arrabales* (suburbs), and the people ate *azúcar* (sugar), *arroz* (rice), *naranjas* (oranges), *limones* (lemons), *berenjenas* (eggplants), *zanahorias* (carrots), *albaricoques* (apricots), *sandías* (watermelons), *altramuces* (lupines), *toronjas* (grapefruit), *alcachofas* (artichokes), *alcauciles* (wild artichokes), *albérchigos* (clingstone peaches), *alfóncigos* (pistachio nuts), *albóndigas* (meat-balls), *escabeche* (souse), *alfajores* (pastes of almonds, walnuts, honey, and pulverized toast), and many other things with Arabic names. The plants mentioned above grow on irrigated land, and since the rainfall in Spain is light (except in the northern part), irrigation requires a great deal of work and skill to channel and distribute the water, a skill in which the Moors excelled, for they needed water to keep their bodies religiously clean and to fertilize the soil. I have previously cited *alberca, aljibe, acequia*; but the vocabulary relating to irrigation is very rich; here is a sampling: *noria* (irrigating wheel or draw well), *arcaduz* (water conduit or bucket), *azuda* (Persian wheel, to raise water out of a stream), *almatriche* (canal), *alcantarilla* (bridge, sewer), *atarjea* (a small drain), *atanor* (water pipe), *alcorque* (hollow to hold water around the base of a tree), etc.

Let it be observed that I have not mentioned the military vocabulary (*adalid, algarada, rebato*, etc.), nor the vocabulary of industry and the crafts (*almazara, alfiler, ajorca, adarga, azagaya, azafate*, etc.). On the basis of our knowledge, it turns out to be an inadequate description to say that the Christians adopted the names of things, or that they underwent "influences," for what these words reveal is the area in the Christian life that was occupied not only by Moorish things but by the interest in Moorish skills. It is a question of the projection of a certain type of Moslem life in which the cultivation and the cult of the earth-mother, the taste for physical and aesthetic pleasures, and the practice of warfare were important. The Christian of the first centuries of the Reconquest (a very long period) allowed himself to be dragged along, as far as he could, through that mode of life; his great task was to repopulate the no-man's-land between the two frontiers, and to press his advance as much as possible. The Christian lived inside his Christianity, and he never employed Arabic religious words except to refer to the religion of the Moors (*alquibla*, the point on the horizon toward which they turned to pray; *azala*, prayer; *almuédano*, Muezzin). With respect to science, Alphonse the Learned adopted many names of stars (e.g., *Alde-*

barán).[32] There are, moreover, adjectives such as *jarifo* (showy), *zaha-reño* (wild and incorrigible), *gandul* (foppish), *rahez* (cheap), *mezquino* (wretched), *garrido* (elegant), and many others.

The account of the aforementioned words will give an idea of the scope and depth of the Arabic penetration into Spanish life, even if the reader does not know the Spanish language. Now it should be added that in some cases a Spanish word combines its meaning with an Arabic one, a phenomenon which shows, once more, the effects of the Mozár-abes' bilingualism on their own dialect as well as on the common language. An instance of this kind of phenomenon is *sombra* ("shadow," which occasionally meant also: "the form and aspect of the body, the image of a person as reflected in a mirror."[33] The explanation of this strange meaning is to be found in Arabic *khayāla* "the form and aspect of the body as seen from a distance" (Lane's Dictionary). Comparable to this is Old Spanish *poridad* "secret," with a meaning which cannot be related to Latin *puritas* "purity" in such expressions as "secretary of the *poridad* of the king." But in Arabic, *khalaṣa*, "was pure," has meanings and derivatives that signify "sincerity, friendship" (*kholūṣ*). So the Spanish *poridad* was identified with the purity of friendship, which is at once very Islamic and very Spanish.

Other instances of similar phenomena are discussed in the second Spanish edition of this book. I shall limit myself here to a few words concerning the usage of *hijo de* . . . , "son of . . . ," without any reference to the idea of physical paternity: *hi de malicias*, "son of malice, malicious"; *fill de caritat* (in Catalan), "charitable"; *fi de nemiga* "enemy," etc. It is known that in the Semitic languages *ibn* "son" may carry the idea that the nature of a person or object comes from the nature of something else, it is—as it were—built or begotten by another being. So a tear may be the "daughter of the eye," a rich man the son of richness, etc. *Hijodalgo, hidalgo*, "nobleman," was built according to the same pattern (cf. *bint bayt*, "daughter of a good house," see Dozy, *Suppl.*, s.v. *bayt*).[34]

[32] See O. J. Tallgren, "Los nombres árabes de las estrellas y la transcripción alfon-sina," in *Homenaje a Menéndez Pidal*, ii, 633-718.

[33] E. W. Lane, *An Arabic-English Lexicon*, i, 835. The image in a mirror is called "sombra" (shadow) in sixteenth- and seventeenth-century Spanish. For instance: "Tal es el engaño respecto de la verdad, . . . como la *sombra del espejo* [the image in the mirror] y lo natural que la representa" (Mateo Alemán, *Guzmán de Alfarache*, ii, i, 3). *Sombra* "aspect, image of a person" occurs in Portuguese also: Bernardim Ribeiro, *Menina e Moça* (1554), edit. D. E. Grokenberger, Lisbon, 1947, pp. 10-11; Camoens, *Lusiadas*, vii, 51.

[34] For a detailed discussion of this matter see *Romance Philology*, 1950, pp. 47-53; *Nueva Revista de Filología Hispánica*, 1951, pp. 69-71. The Semitism of the

An Expression from the Koran

There is one Spanish expression which is Koranic in origin, and surely anyone who carefully compares the holy book of Islam with Spanish sayings and proverbs will find others. To express about a person the idea that, however much he knows, his intellectual and human value is of the slightest, one says that "he is an ass burdened with knowledge" (es un burro cargado de ciencia). Here once more is a reflection of the longing for "integration," the ideal condition in which there is a perfect coincidence between the person's existence and his action, his character and his deeds, the inward and the outward. In the seventeenth century Alonso Nuñez de Castro writes: "they confirmed it in Madrid by calling him an ass loaded with letters." The dictionary defines "burro o asno cargado de letras" as a "scholar with a limited grasp" (erudito de cortos alcances). There is no apparent justification for such an extravagant metaphor, nor is it clear how an immaterial reality (letters or knowledge) can be loaded upon the rude and tangible materiality of a donkey. But if we move into an archaic zone of the language, we begin to see more clearly. In Portuguese there is a quip that goes "a donkey loaded with books is a scholar" (um burro carregado de livros e um doutor), and the matter now begins to take on meaning. The meaning becomes perfectly clear from a passage in the Koran (62, 5):[35] "The likeness of those who were charged with the observance of the law, and then observed it not, is as the likeness of an ass laden with books." Mahomet censures the Jews here for not carrying out the precepts of the Bible even though they know them; this incongruity, which destroys the integrality of knowledge and conduct, is expressed in an image that

---

construction fijo-de-algo, "son of algo," has been accepted by some linguists. There is controversy around the origin of algo. This algo may be related to the Islamic institution of the Fifth (al-khoms), "that portion of the spoils of war assigned to the commander." One way of saying "I headed the army" was "I took the fifth part of the spoil in the time of El-Islam" (Lane's Dictionary, s.v. khoms). It is almost impossible to produce documentary evidence about an oral process which took place in Spain between the 8th and 10th centuries. The Christians adopted the institution of the Fifth. The kings took the quinto (fifth) of the spoils. The ways in which this institution developed nobility among the fighting Christians can only be imagined. Normally, algo (Lat. aliquod), means "something"; but algo meant "bounty, good service" also. The thirteenth-century Bible translates "Ut faciam eum misericordiam Dei" (II Reg. 9:13) "a quien fiziesse yo algo." I do not believe that this algo can be Lat. aliquod, or that this algo could have "sons" within the grammatical system of a Romance language.

[35] Professor G. L. Della Vida has kindly supplied me with this reference.

was meaningful in a land where the donkey was a means of transportation. Later, the books in this metaphor (started on its worldly career by someone who must have known the text in the Koran) were replaced by letters or knowledge, and thus it was converted into something barely intelligible.[36]

With this we will leave off for the time being with the analysis of the Arabic background in the Spanish language. Since these facts are interesting as an index of life style rather than as a linguistic investigation, it has consequently not been a question of accumulating anecdotic curios but rather of contemplating the birth of certain expressions. Out of this process I have sought to construct a historical silhouette. What I have tried to underline is, not the fact, but what the fact reveals; the phenomena could be either the ones I have chosen or some others, and I have grouped a few together only to make it clear that the aforementioned words and expressions are not present in Spanish by chance; they all are aspects of the Spanish historical preferences. Other linguistic data will be utilized in successive chapters, so that their testimony will be present where it is most needed, or where it can be best understood.

Digression on Catalonia

Castilian and Portuguese underwent the effects of Arabic or Mozarabic contact at the same time; in some instances Catalan might be added to them, as in the case of *ojo de agua* "spring," Port. *olho de agua*, Cat. *ull d'un rio*, just like Arabic *'ayn* "eye" and "spring." What usually happens, nevertheless, is that Catalan takes a different path, for it lacks many of the lexical and syntactical pseudomorphoses to which I refer here and there throughout this book; and this corresponds to the general direction taken by the history of this section of Hispania. A people (Castile or Catalonia) is identical with what it has done and with what has been done to it; it is not itself plus its history; it is not a human "substance" modified by superimposed events or psychological features. Some historians of Catalonia work with great zeal to trace out Catalonian singularity to the remotest point possible. When he gets to the period with which we here are concerned at present, F. Soldevila[37] says, for

---

[36] There are other references of the same kind in Arabic literature: "Those who collect books without profiting from what they contain have by a certain poet been called Mules loaded for a trip, who know as much about the usefulness of the cargo as a camel does" (Masudi, *Les Prairies d'Or*, translation of C. Barbier de Meynard, III, 138).

[37] *Historia de Catalunya*, I, 34.

example, that the fact that Catalonia formed a part of the Carolingian Empire permitted her to enjoy "an organization different from that of the rest of the Peninsula, *freeing her* from the influence of Mozarabic culture, dominant in Spain." This is certainly true, but it must be understood together with all its consequences. There was nothing intrinsic in Catalonia to make her different from the rest of the Peninsula; for populated lands are not "things" or metaphysical essences; they are history, that is, what is done in connection with, and made *real* in, a human "dwelling-place." Catalonia did not play a primary part in the Reconquest, because her northern region was included within the energetic expansion of the Franks; thus, as an initiator of the Reconquest like Galicia-Leon, Castile, Navarre, and even Aragon, Catalonia had no role of her own. The Franks were stopped in the Navarrese mountains (Roncevaux), whereas they found easy ingress into the Spanish northeast, which became a Frankish frontier, the Spanish March. This province gravitated toward the lands of the north. It was an ecclesiastical dependency of Narbonne until 1091, when the diocese of Tarragona was restored. As early as the ninth century, Visigothic script was replaced by French script, a change that did not become general in Castile till sometime between the twelfth and thirteenth centuries. Documents were dated according to the reigns of the kings of France up to 1180, and then Catolonia adopted the calendar of the Era of the Incarnation, not the Spanish one, which started with 38 B.C. Spanish Christians and Moors still called the Catalonians Franks in the twelfth century. And the result of all this was that while the Galaico-Portuguese and the Castilians were interweaving their life and their language with those of the Mozárabes (or Arabs), the Catalans were moving along within a different horizon. Political relations were very close with the south of France, for instance, with the County of Foix.[38]

From the twelfth century on, the political vitality of the rest of Christian Spain attracted the Catalonians toward its sphere of influence, just as the Carolingian Empire had formerly dominated them. The county of Barcelona was thus converted into a political appendage of Aragon, even though Barcelona had an aptitude for work and for commerce, and, consequently, greater wealth. The Catalan language, in its oldest strata, was connected with that of the rest of the Peninsula, and shows many coincidences with Galician-Portuguese. Its vocabulary links with that of

---

[38] See Charles Baudon de Mony, *Relations politiques des comtes de Foix avec la Catalogne jusqu'au commencement du XIVᵉ siècle,* 1896.

Peninsular languages,[39] and, had it not been for the intervention of the Franks, Catalonia and her language would have followed a development analogous to that of Aragon. When, after the twelfth century, Catalonia began to gravitate toward the Castilian-Aragonese zone, the Islamic-Mozarabic apogee had passed. In view of such historical circumstances, it is easily understandable that the northeastern region of the Peninsula never developed a complete political personality. Between the eighth and twelfth centuries—a long period of 400 years—Catalonia, one way or another, had as the lodestar of her life, the peoples who lived beyond the Pyrenees. From the twelfth century on, she found herself obliged to live as a county (the "condado de Barcelona"), subordinate to the political headship of a rather Castilianized Aragon. The language reflects these alternations, which in turn explain the vacillations of the linguists, divided in their opinions: some connect Catalan with Provençal, others with the Peninsular languages; others, finally, attribute to it the character of an independent language. Each of these ideas contains a part of the truth. As the result of its history, Catalonian has very few Mozarabisms like *ull d'un rio*, and fewer Arabisms than Spanish; amongst the Arabisms, many are peculiar to it.[40] Catalan poetry of the Middle Ages is strongly influenced by that of Provence, and the learned prose of present-day Catalan is in reality Castilian syntax with Catalan words, which would be much fewer, were it not for the deliberate effort to avoid Castilianisms, already very abundant in the *Chronicle* of James the Conqueror (Jaime el Conquistador, thirteenth century). The lack of lively contact with Arabic prevented Catalan from acquiring such expressions as *"amanecí bueno"* and *"anochecí enfermo"*[41] (see Chapter 8), or many other Spanish and Portuguese linguistic phenomena, among them the word *fijodalgo*.

[39] See Amado Alonso, "La subagrupación románica del catalán," in the *Revista de Filología Española*, 1926, XIII.

[40] See J. Coromines, *Mots catalans d'origen aràbic*, in the *Butlletí de Dialectologia Catalana*, 1936, XXIV. In the index of words at the end of A. Steiger's book, *Contribución a la fonética del hispano-árabe*, Catalonian takes up eight pages, Spanish, twenty-two. Although this index does not pretend to be a complete list of Arabisms, the difference in figures is significant.

[41] It would seem advisable to point out to the reader unfamiliar with Spanish that the verbs *amanecer* and *anochecer* mean respectively "to dawn" and "to nightfall." A peculiar feature of their use in Spanish (discussed in Chapter 8) is that they may be used personally, as the examples in the text show. Hence, "Amanecí en Toledo"—literally, "I dawned in Toledo"—the sort of thing a traveler might say if he meant that he arrived at Toledo just as dawn was breaking. Cf. English *benight*, now obsolete in any save the past participial usage, and there used only figuratively, as a rule:

The Spanish structure of the Peninsula makes itself recognizable toward the tenth century. While the northwest of Spain was grafting Santiago into its structure (see Chapter 6) and the Castilian people were rebelling politically, linguistically, and epically (see Chapter 8), Catalonia was living with her back turned to all this, and without developing a powerful and daring initiative. Not even the circumstances (foreign pressure) that determined the independence of Portugal could be given in Catalonia: Her lands were not crossed by the road to Santiago. In a word, Catalonia has never belonged totally to Spain, nor has she ceased to belong to her; this is a rending drama that can be wholly understood only by experiencing Spain from within her history. Spain as a whole lived and lives by a continuous process of self-undoing ("desviviéndose"); Catalonia likewise follows this orbit, although she has also been condemned to turn upon her own axis—condemned, so long as she is Catalonia, to pose the problem of her existence. This is the historical meaning of her paucity of Arabisms.

We have an opinion concerning Catalonian life which is interesting not for its accuracy or inaccuracy, but as an expression of anguished autognosis in the time of the civil war that broke out in 1640:

"Catalonia cannot accomplish anything good for herself, because she is established between two powerful kings whose forces oppress her on both sides. . . . The Catalonian is limited by nature, and so little inclined to expansiveness that his reserve may sometimes seem either rudeness or lack of ability; and he gains so much clarity of mind by contact with Castilians that, when such dealings are established on the foundation of the solid timber of his native character, on the integrity of his temper and on the staunch firmness of his unswerving friendship, they serve him as an excellent embellishment. I desire no further proof of this fact than the difference which has always been recognized in Catalonia between those gentlemen who have been in Castile, or have made it their business in Barcelona to deal with foreigners, and those unsociable creatures who have lived so narrowly according to the custom of their own country that they have scorned contact with strangers. Search your memory for examples, and you will see that there is the same difference as between a log which has still to be trimmed and another which has been squared with the blade of the plane. If they do not 'bathe' in Castile, Catalonian preachers, whose art demands so much eloquence and grace, will only with difficulty achieve great stature in their profession, because our language is limited, and our neglect has allowed it to grow old in poverty, having no author who today deserves to be called classic;

for even though the Catalonian loves the things of his country tenaciously, the failure to fill in the deficiencies of his language only makes it
seem that he has lost his love for it." (Don Alexandro Ros, *Cataluña
desengañada*, Naples, 1646, pp. 60 and 240.)

Here is a Catalonian voice speaking from outside of Spain, and at the
same time, from within, and expressing the same uncomfortable feeling
of incompleteness that, in a way or another, we also find in Castilian and
Portuguese life. My statement could be confirmed by what another
distinguished Catalonian writes in our time:

"Catalonia has been a *potentiality* but not a *reality*. This is the ultimate and deepest root of all her misfortunes as a nation and people.
When Catalonians start to meditate on their history, they ask themselves this question: What would have happened *if*, at a particular moment, events had taken a different course? What would have been our
fortune, *if*, by chance, the things that did not happen had happened?
Let us not deceive ourselves. In this *if*, in this apparently insignificant
but infinitely treacherous conditional proposition, lie some of the deepest
secrets of our people. For if this or that had not happened—this peace
or that conflict—Catalonia could have been something quite different
from what she has been up to now. . . . This irrepressible tendency and
this understandable melancholy have caused all our actions to be failures
in certain respects. . . . In history, that which has been done takes on,
paradoxically, a decisive importance. Historical reality is not the realization of a possibility as is the reality conceived by traditional metaphysics;
historical reality is the pure present which continually unfolds. . . . No
lamentation can change the course of history. Our future will never
open up if we do not henceforth consider it as actually a future and not
simply a reflection of a kind of nostalgic longing. To put it another way:
Catalonia is sick with the past, and not with all the past but rather especially with certain moments of the past, which she and all of us consider
to have been very propitious and especially desirable. Catalonia is sick
with the past, and it is high time for her to begin to cure herself of this
treacherous ailment." (J. Ferrater Mora, *El llibre del sentit*, Santiago
de Chile, 1948, pp. 95-96.) This "ailment," this feeling of incompleteness, is just an aspect of the historical reality, of its way of functioning
and existing in every corner of the Iberian Peninsula.

Islamic Tradition and Spanish Life

MUCH LESS EXPLORED than the Arabisms in Ibero-Romance are certain traditional ways of life and expression that have no meaning outside the Islamic frame. For my purpose it makes no difference that such practices are also found in other countries likewise touched by oriental civilization (Byzantium, India, Russia, etc.), since I am not interested in folklore but merely in the lines left on the face of the Peninsula by 900 years of Christian-Islamic interaction. For this purpose it likewise makes no difference whether the Spanish Moslems owe some of their customs to Byzantium, to Persia, or to any other country. The customs preserved by the Spanish Christians are a vivid reflection of the Moorish prestige which at times "depressed and humiliated" (Menéndez Pidal), but which, in spite of this, forced an unconscious imitation, even after the political and military splendor of Islam had vanished.

Moorish habit probably accounts for the fact that in little towns in Castile where today very few people are addicted to hot-water baths there were *public baths* in the thirteenth century. Municipal ordinances provide us with our information: The ordinances of Zorita (Guadalajara) require that "viri eant ad communem balneum in die martis, et in die jovis, et in die sabbati. Mulieres eant in die lune, et in die mercuri. Iudei eant in die veneris, et in die dominica. Et nemo det sive sit mulier, sive vir, pro introitu balnei nisi obolum tantum."[1] "The keeper of the bath shall provide the bathers with those things which they may need, be they water or other necessaries. . . . Any person who takes anything from the bathing pools will be punished by having an ear cut off" (*ibid.,* p. 69). The same text is to be found in the ordinances of Cuenca. The ordinances of Brihuega (Guadalajara) make the observation that "neither the man-servant nor the maid-servant that are brought to the

---

[1] *Fuero de Zorita de los Canes* (Ordinances of . . .), edited by R. de Ureña, pp. 67-68. For a more complete record of references to public baths in the municipal ordinances, see A. Ruiz-Moreno, *Cuadernos de Historia de España,* Buenos Aires, 1945, III, 152-157.

bath will pay anything."[2] Even an insignificant town like Usagre (Badajoz) had its bath: "The women will go to the bath on Sundays, Tuesdays, and Thursdays; and the men on the other days." Whoever went to the baths was allowed to bring as many as three servants, including "one to bathe the master."[3] In these ordinances the keeper of the bath was usually required to provide the bathers with hot water, soap, and towels. The baths gradually fell into disuse amongst the Christians, who in 1526 started trying to suppress those of the Moriscos. This measure was not put into effect until 1576, when the Moriscos were punished for the rebellion of 1568 by being prohibited from practicing their customs. One of the Moriscos, a gentleman named Francisco Núñez Muley, replied thus to the royal mandate: "The baths were built for the cleanliness of the body; and to say that couples get together there is not to be believed; for where so many people go, there can be no secret. . . . There have always been baths *throughout all the provinces*; and if at one time they were taken away in Castile, it was because the baths *weakened the flesh and the spirit of the men for war*. The men who were born in this kingdom of Granada have no need to fight, nor do the women need to have strength, but rather to be clean; if they do not wash in the baths (and since it is forbidden them to bathe in brooks, springs, and rivers, and in their houses), where then are they to go and bathe?" In 1567 a solemn ceremony took place, and "all the artificial baths" that there were in Granada were destroyed.[4] The people forgot the custom of washing themselves frequently, in Spain as in Europe, until well into the nineteenth century.[5]

[2] *Fuero de Brihuega*, edited by J. Catalina, p. 162.

[3] *Fuero de Usagre*, edited by A. Bonilla, p. 48.

[4] Luis del Mármol, "Rebelión y castigo de los moriscos," in *Biblioteca de Autores Españoles*, XXI, 161, 162, 164.

[5] It is true that baths existed in Hispania as a part of the Romano-Visigothic tradition before the arrival of the Moors, and Don José M. Lacarra is quite right in reminding me of this. I believe, nevertheless, that the habit of bathing was experienced by the Christians as a convenience and luxury that belonged to the Moors. When Prince Sancho lost his life in the battle of Zalaca in 1086, his father, Alphonse VI, inquired of his wise men why the ability to fight had grown weaker in his knights; "they answered him that it was because many went frequently to the baths, and gave themselves too much to vices. The king then had all the baths in his kingdom destroyed" (*Crónica general*, p. 555). Very likely all the baths were not destroyed, and this anecdote is probably apocryphal. But even so, the idea remains that the baths, to which the Moors were much addicted, were regarded in this particular instance as a cause of weakness and vice; if it had been thought that the baths were a traditionally Christian custom, they would not have been thought of in this way. C. Sánchez-Albornoz thinks that in the tenth century the baths in

Also, I think that the *ritual washing of the dead* was very likely an imitation of the Moslems. In the *Poema de Fernán González* (c. 1240), the Castilian count had the corpse of his enemy the Count of Tolosa solemnly washed before it was dressed in a rich silk cloth.[6] The *Crónica general* relates that the count Fernán González "himself disarmed with his own hands the Count of Tolosa, there where he lay dead; and he caused him to be bathed" (p. 399a).[7]

In a version of the Joseph story recorded in Hebrew characters, we read that before Joseph had his father Jacob embalmed, he had him bathed.[8] And the same thing is in the *General Estoria* of Alphonse the Learned: "And they bathed him very, very well, and then they embalmed him" (p. 256). Petrus Comestor thought this usage to be a "mos ethnicorum"; and Sr. González Llubera thinks that the custom is rab-

---

Leon and Galicia were a Mozarabic or Hispano-Moorish institution (*Estampas de la vida en León*, pp. 122-123). This idea and Sr. Lacarra's can be brought into harmony if we compare the baths of those times with words like *albaricoque* (apricot) and *albérchigo* (peach, strictly, *amygdalus persica*) that are derived ultimately from the Latin adjectives *praecox* and *Persicus*, which denoted a quality of those fruits—precocity and coming from Persia respectively. But both words were taken into Spanish in the *form* in which they were pronounced by the Spanish Arabs, good cultivators of the soil; they were *experienced in life* as Arabic, not as Latin. Nothing in history is ever a fixed and durable substance, be it a question of a social institution like the bath, or the name of a fruit. What is durable is the disposition of the historical "dwelling-place."

[6] "Lavól e vestiól de un iamete preçiado" (373).

[7] There are many references to ritual washing among the Moslems in El-Bokhari, *Les traditions islamiques,* translated into French by O. Houdas and W. Marçais, 1900, I, 405ff.: "The one sent from God came into our house while we were washing the body of his daughter. He said to us: 'Wash her three times or five times. . . . Begin with members on the right side and with the parts of the body that are washed in the ablution.' "

[8]
    "Yoçef su mandamiento fizo muy priado,
    Fizo vannar al muerto, luego fue pimentado."

See I. González Llubera, *Coplas de Yoçef*, pp. 19 and 42. Antonio de Guevara, bishop of Mondoñedo, was quite familiar with the customs of the Moriscos and the Jews. He mentions some of them in the *Constituciones sinodales*, which he gave to his Galician diocese in 1541 (in R. Costes, *Antonio de Guevara: Sa vie*, Bordeaux, 1925, pp. 57ff.). "When a man expires and dies, certain persons who do not feel secure in their faith, wash his whole body, thinking that they are washing away his sins; more than this, they shave off the hairs of his beard, which they then keep to make charms; and since this is a Jewish, and even a Morisco rite, we do excommunicate all those persons who henceforth do this. . . . Many men and women also have the custom in time of lightning and thunder of holding up their skillets and tripods to heaven, thinking it certain that thus the thunder and lightning are mitigated. And since this is a Morisco superstition, we do order and command that from henceforth no one dare to perform such an action."

binical. To be sure, many of the customs that I am analyzing might also be found among the Spanish Jews, highly infused with Moslem life.

The custom of having *women cover their faces* was still practiced not long ago in Tarifa (Cádiz), and still today in some Peruvian cities; and in the Argentine a woman's overcoat is called a *tapado* (past participle of *tapar*, "to cover up"), a word which comes from the *manto tapado* (a kind of cloak), mentioned by Tirso de Molina in *El burlador de Sevilla* (II, 101), with which the women covered their head and face.[9] Dozens of seventeenth-century plays contain situations based on the woman's custom of covering her face when she went about town (Tirso, *La celosa de sí misma*; Calderón, *El escondido y la tapada*; etc.). Thus Christian women were permitted to go on doing what had been prohibited to Morisco women in the sixteenth century: "For to want women to go about with their faces uncovered, what is this but to give men occasion to fall into sin by looking upon the beauty which they usually cannot resist?"[10]

The custom of having *women sit on the floor*, as they are said to have done down to the eighteenth century, was a Moorish reminiscence. The proper place for women to sit had been a low dais—a *tarima* just slightly raised from the floor and covered with a rug and cushions. In an early fourteenth-century text we read: "the lady realized that he was the king, and she rose up, and went forward to kiss his hands. The king refused, and went to sit with her on her dais."[11] The family of Don Domingo Sarmiento still lived this way at the beginning of the nineteenth century in San Juan (Argentina), according to his account in *Recuerdos de provincia*. Cervantes knew from his own experience that the dais on which the ladies sat was an oriental institution: "a dais with more velvet cushions than any Moor ever had" (*Quijote*, II, 5). Sancho Panza aspires to have his wife sit in church on *alcatifas* (carpets), *almohadas* (cushions) and *arambeles* (cloth hangings) (*ibid.*), three Arabic words to which must be added *alfombra* (rug). This is why the sofa and armchairs in a drawing room are still called an *estrado* in Spanish (translated here above as *dais*), and for the same reason, to the grandee's ceremony known as "covering oneself" (cubrirse) before the king there corresponded a ceremony for the ladies of the court known as "taking the cushion" (tomar la almohada) from the queen.[12]

[9] See L. Pfandl, *Introducción al Siglo de Oro*, p. 273.
[10] Luis del Mármol, *loc.cit.*, p. 165.
[11] *El libro del Caballero Cifar*, edited by Ch. Ph. Wagner, p. 100.
[12] The reader not intimately acquainted with Spanish custom and tradition will

A great many of the forms of courtesy acquire meaning only when we examine them under the Islamic light. If you are a Spaniard, and you show a friend something of value, if he praises the object, you must, to be correct, say: "It is at your disposal" (Está a su disposición). It has happened once in a while that a foreigner, not knowing that these words are no more than a rite, has asked whether the valuable object was really being offered to him, and this has created more than one embarrassing situation. In the *Poema del Cid* it is told that King Alphonse VI praised the Cid's horse as well as the one who rode it: "this horse of which I have heard such good report . . . ; in all our lands there is no man so valorous" (3,510). To this the Cid replied with a Moslem courtesy that had by then become thoroughly Hispanic: "I give him to you as a gift; have him taken away, my lord" (3,115). As was *de rigueur* in the twelfth century—just as it is today—the king did not accept the gift:

"For this I have no liking;
If I took the horse away from you, it would not have
so good a master." (3,517)

The same courtesy is also exemplified in the legend of the origins of the independence of Castile. Count Fernán González presented himself before the king of Leon, his sovereign, "with a very fine molting goshawk and a very noble horse." The king asked the count to sell him the magnificent animals; but in conformity with the ritual of courtesy, the count told the king to "take them as a gift." The king did not accept, but instead promised to pay a thousand marks for the horse and goshawk on a certain date; if he failed to pay for them, it was agreed that the quantity would be doubled for each day of delay. At the end of three years the king had not paid the by that time incalculable debt, and he ended up by granting Castile its independence.[13]

---

perhaps need a further explanation here. When noblemen were invested by the king with the *grandeza*, or grandeur, of Spain, they were granted the privilege of keeping their hats on in the presence of the king. The queen for her part invested noble ladies with the same dignity by allowing them to sit on cushions in the royal presence.

[13] See the *Crónica general*, p. 410. The Moslems still use today these formulas of purely ritual offering of what they possess, formulas which they have had to repress at times when the interlocutor is a foreigner; this at least is what happened in Morocco.

As a consequence of the long Spanish domination of Italy, some of these Hispano-Islamic customs were eventually adopted there too, especially in the ancient Kingdom of Naples, which was Spanish for more than two centuries. When King Victor Emanuel visited the newly annexed Kingdom of Naples in 1860, it is told that the Neapolitan mothers showed their children to the new sovereign, who could

The custom of saying "This is your house" (Esta es su casa) to one who is visiting it for the first time, is Moslem. When the visitor departs, you say to him: "Please know that you have taken possession of your house" (Ya sabe que ha tomado posesión de su casa). In Portuguese you say: "Disponha da casa como se fosse sua, é uma casa a sua disposição." In Catalan: "Ha press possessió de casa seva." All this belongs to the Arabic heritage: "Al-bayt baytak" (this house is thy house), and foreigners are left astonished when they hear in Lisbon, Madrid, or Barcelona that the house they are visiting for the first time belongs to them.

When you are about to eat or drink in front of someone who for some reason or other is not going to participate in either the eating or the drinking, you must say to him, "Would you care for some?" (¿Usted gusta?) In Andalusian towns people who are eating will say to a passerby: "Come and eat!" (¡Venga usted a comer!) No one accepts, of course. In Portuguese you say, "You are served" (Você é servido), or "Will you keep me company?" (Quer fazer-me companhia?). In Galicia: "Stay with us" (Quédese con nosco). In Catalonia, "Are you pleased [to join me?]" (Sou servit?). The answers are: "May it profit you" (Que aproveche), or "May it aid your health" (De salud sirva), depending on the region, the social class, etc. In Portuguese you answer: "May it be good for you" (Bom proveito).

In the large cities, or amongst those who have picked up foreign customs, such uses do not persist with the same intensity as among the village folk. In Italy, for reasons previously mentioned, one also finds a reflection of the Spanish epoch in the expression "Will you favor me?" (Vuol favorire?), which is heard, for example, on the train when you sit down to eat in front of other travelers. And thus it happens in the Moslem world from Morocco to Syria.

One frequently hears "if God wills" (si Dios quiere, or si quiere Dios): "Hasta mañana, si Dios quiere," "A ver si quiere Dios que llueva," etc. At first glance it would seem that such a phrase is the outgrowth of Catholic piety or religiosity, so deeply rooted in Spain. But when we recall the presence of Spanish "ojalá," Arabic "wa shā'a-l-lāh" (Might God will that . . .), we are getting at the true origin of our phrase. It is a

---

not say enough in praise of the beauty of his little subjects; this caused the mothers, in a transport of enthusiasm, to say, "They are yours, My Lord!" The Arabic origin of some of the usages that I mention has already been noted, although in anecdotic way. For "besar manos y pies," see G. Rittwagen, De filología hispano-arábiga, 1909, p. 57. "Está a su disposición" and "venga a hacer penitencia con nosotros" have been commented on, by M. L. Wagner, in Volkstum u. Kultur der Romanen, 1930, III, 115-116. "A la paz de Dios!" in W. Beinhauer, Spanische Umgangsprache, p. 88.

matter of another pseudomorphosis (like *almogávar-corredor*—raider), which appears now with a Christian meaning.[14] The purely Christian invocation to God may be found, of course, in medieval Latin expressions such as "Deo volente," or English "God willing." We must keep in mind, however, what has been said before concerning the habit of bathing. It seems to me that the Spaniards use, or have used, the name of God more than the other Romanic peoples: the reader who compares the noun "God" in the Dictionary of the Spanish Academy with the corresponding noun in Littré's French Dictionary will understand what I mean. And I believe that in many instances behind the Christian God vibrates the echo of Allah, present even in the interjection ¡olé! (*wa-l-lāh*, "for God's sake") with which audiences shout their encouragement to dancers and bullfighters.

Connected with all this is the existence of greetings and formulas of respect that include the name of God. In the thirteenth century the Mozárabes said, "May God defend, may God preserve," and Menéndez Pidal comments: "To be sure, this custom may be more general than the influence of the Mozárabes, for even today we preserve some trace of it in the phrase 'may God protect him' (que Dios guarde) in official mentions of the king."[15] It seems as if the great linguist did not find enough Moslem motivations to explain both the modern *and* the Mozarabic custom. The question is clarified when it is realized that "Dios guarde" was a general formula of Moslem origin, and that there are relics of this sort of thing in the royal chancery, and in the greeting of Andalusian peasants, "May God protect you, gentlemen" (Dios guarde a ustedes, caballeros), which I have heard in the province of Granada, where the language is very archaic. The same people used "God preserve" (Dios mantenga), which was already regarded as rustic usage in the sixteenth century, and therefore was so annoying to the punctilious Squire in *Laza-*

---

[14] This linguistic pseudomorphosis is confirmed by the Morisco account of the peoples of Gog and Magog as given by F. Guillén Robles, *Leyendas de José, hijo de Jacob, y de Alejandro Magno, sacadas de dos manuscritos moriscos de la Biblioteca Nacional de Madrid*, Zaragoza, 1888, p. liii. Those cursed people, shut up by Alexander behind walls of iron, "unceasingly lick the wall with their tongues that are coarser than files; at times only a thin layer remains to be punctured; and they leave it till the next day, saying: 'Tomorrow we shall penetrate this dike.' But since they do not add, 'If God wills,' when they start to work on it again at dawn, they find the wall of the same thickness as when they began; only on the day appointed by Allah, when, recognizing their error, they add 'If God wills,' will they break down the iron barrier. . . ."

[15] *Orígenes del español*, p. 460.

rillo de Tormes.[16] The Andalusian peasants still say today, "To the peace of God," which sounds, to be sure, like the ecclesiastical "Pax Domini sit vobiscum," but whose existence as a popular form cannot be understood except as a tracing of the Arabic "al-salām 'alayk" (peace be with thee).

Only in Spain has "besar la mano, besar los pies" (to kiss the hand, the feet—the latter in the case of ladies) been preserved as an epistolary formula. In the nineteenth century ladies still took leave of gentlemen by saying, "I kiss your hand"; and the gentlemen answered with "I your feet, señora." In the provinces, where tradition persists more stubbornly than in Madrid, there are still people who say this. Mariano José de Larra (1807-1837) still knew the tradition of the child's kissing the father's hand: "The father, who was not called *papá* then, went about with his hand more kissed than an ancient relic" (*El casarse pronto y mal*). And it will also be found that among the Moslems a son will end a letter to his father with the formula "after having kissed your respectable hand."[17]

The Hispanic Society of New York has on exhibit a letter from Don Luis de Requesens to Philip II, in 1566, which the writer signs thus: "Your Majesty's creature, vassal, and servant who kisses Your Majesty's very royal feet and hands" (De V. M. hechura, vasallo y criado que sus muy reales pies y manos besa). In the Spanish theater of the seventeenth century, a usual formula is "Give me your feet" (Dadme los pies), when an inferior wishes to show reverent gratitude to the king: "Dadme, gran señor, los pies." In the *Quijote* (II, 16), Sancho Panza "again and again *kissed* the feet" of Don Diego de Miranda, a statement that has seemed so normal to the commentators that they have let it pass without explanation. Yet earlier, in the *Poema del Cid* (1140), the hero tries on one occasion to kiss the feet of King Alphonse VI, and the king will not permit it: "Kiss my hands, not my feet."[18] In Raymond Lully's celebrated book, when Blanquerna takes leave of his father to go and live as an

---

[16] See my "Perspectiva de la novela picaresca," in *Revista de la Biblioteca, Archivo y Museo*, Madrid, 1935, II, 138ff.

[17] "Ba 'da taqbīli aydīkum al-kirām." E. W. Lane states: "It is a common custom for a man to kiss the hand of a superior. . . . To testify abject submission, in craving pardon for an offence, or begging any favor of a superior, not infrequently the feet are kissed instead of the hand. The son kisses the hand of the father." (*Manners and Customs of the Modern Egyptians*, London, 1836, I, 252.)

[18] "Besad las manos, ca los pies no" (2,028). In his *Cantar de Mio Cid*, R. Menéndez Pidal cites (pp. 507-508) numerous examples of such usage, but he does not refer to its Moorish origin.

anchorite, "on his knees, he kisses the hands and feet of his father."[19] The fact that the Moslems had acquired this custom through contact with Byzantium or some other civilization, is irrelevant here. What is important is to observe that the Spanish Christians took it from the Spanish Moslems. The formula of vassalage—I kiss your hand—is not connected with European feudalism but with oriental life.[20] How normal it was among the Arabs for one to kiss the hand of another as a sign of submission and homage is seen in the following passage from Ibn Darrāj (d. 1030): "Thou makest me fear the length of the journey; but the journey is worthy of being made only in order to kiss the hand of the 'Āmirī" (in Al-Šaqundī, *Elogio del Andalus*, translated by E. García Gómez, p. 61).[21]

I do not know whether *kissing the bread* that is picked up from the ground or floor is a Christian influence in Islam, or the reverse. In Andalusia when a piece of bread falls to the ground, one picks it up and kisses it, saying that "it is God's bread" (es pan de Dios). The Moors do and say the same thing: " 'āysh Allāh" (God's bread).

What is evidently Moorish, though, is the practice of excusing oneself from giving alms to a beggar by saying, "Forgive me for God's sake, God protect you, succor you, help you," etc., which is the same as the Arabic "God give you alms, help you, sustain you, make you content."[22]

It is hard not to relate the clamorous, spectacular forms of alms-begging—still observable, and especially in the South, in Spain—to the Christian-Moslem life of the Middle Ages: "God preserve your sight!" the blind man will say; frequently the beggars will refer to the holiness of the particular day, especially on Maundy Thursday and Good Friday

---

[19] "De agenollons, besà les mans el·s peus a son pare" (*Evast e Blanquerna*, Barcelona, 1935, p. 84).

[20] At the beginning of the fifteenth century, Rabbi Arragel says: "Rabbi Abraham [Ben Ezra] says that it was the custom in those days for the subject to put out his hand and for the lord to put his on top of it, the one signifying subjection, and the other, seigniory; and he even says that it is still customary to do this in the lands of India." (*Biblia de Arragel*, Alba edition, I, 133.)

[21] Kissing the hand as a sign of respect was also practiced by the Spanish Jews. The *Coplas de Yoçef*, written in Spanish with Hebrew characters, say:

> He went out to receive his honored father,
> He asked for his hand, then he kissed it.

> (A recebir saliera a su padre honrado,
> La mano le pidiera, luego la ovo besado.)
> —(Edition of I. González Llubera, p. 7)

[22] "Allāh yu 'tīka" (in Vulgar Arabic, "Allāh ya 'tīk"). See J. Østrup, *Orientalske Hoflighedsformer*, Copenhagen, 1927, p. 76. Cf. further E. W. Lane, *op.cit.*, II, 23.

and on the patronal festival of the town, and the like. In the *Buscón* (1608) Quevedo speaks of prayers invented to stimulate charity; the beggars allude to the "ill wind" (aire corruto) and the "fatal hour" (hora menguada) in which they suffered the mischance that deprived them of their health. The Archpriest of Hita (fourteenth century) composed songs "such as those the blind beggars recite" (de los que dicen los ciegos), stanza 1,514. These beggars comprised an important social institution, just as they did in the nineteenth-century Egypt described by Lane, who quotes many beggars' cries similar in form to those we have heard in Spain: "O Exciter of compassion! O Lord! For the sake of God! O ye charitable! I am seeking from my Lord a cake of bread!" Or they will say: "The night (eve) of the excellent Friday," etc. (Lane, II, 23).

The *blessings* and *curses*, so numerous and expressive, must also be rooted largely in oriental life. I recall no Romance language outside the Iberian group in which one speaks, with either good or evil intention, of "the mother that bore you" (la madre que te parió); other things, perhaps similar, can be said in Italian or French, but without the phrase "that bore you." And yet I find that the caliph Al-Manṣūr (in Bagdad) said to someone: "May the mother who bore you be for God," that is, may she be blessed.[23] And today in Spain, 1200 years later, some may say to a pretty woman, "Blessed be the mother who bore you!"

He who proposes to lengthen the list of similar facts will find the task easy, for there is much to be added. It suffices for my purpose simply to call attention to this new and fertile aspect of Hispanic history. But since the picture is getting a little monochromatic, we will add color to it with a few references to the *Morisco literary themes* during the declining Middle Ages, a period in which the Islamic imprint on life and customs is accentuated, and in which blossom the Mudéjar decoration of the interior architecture of the castles as well as the Morisco border ballads, like the charming one that has become so popular:

> Yo me era mora Moraima,
> morilla de un bel catar . . .
> (I am Moraima, a pretty Moorish girl . . .)

The ballad goes on telling the girl's misfortune for having arisen, almost nude, and opened her door to a Christian who, in perfect Arabic, pretended to be her uncle.

[23] See Gerardo Meloni, *Saggi di Filologia Semitica*, Roma, 1913, p. 145; he refers to Ṭabarī, III, 413, 1.

The poet Alonso Álvarez de Villasandino (d. *c.* 1427) sings the pleasure of love affairs with Morisco girls, the ancestors of those other Morisco maidens who at the beginning of the seventeenth century were still seducing certain Old Christians. Villasandino says:

> Quien de linda se enamora,
> atender deve perdón
> en caso que sea mora . . .
> Linda rosa muy suave
> vi plantada en un vergel,
> puesta so secreta llave
> de la linia de Ismael . . .
> Mahomad el atrevido
> ordenó que fuese tal,
> de aseo noble, complido,
> albos pechos de cristal:
> de alabasto muy broñido
> debíe ser con grant razón
> lo que cubre su alcandora . . .
> Por aver tal gasajado
> yo pornía en condición
> la mi alma pecadora.[24]

In other words, the poet says that he would risk his sinful soul for the perfect body of a certain Moorish woman—"A most delicate rose planted in a secluded garden." Mohammed, daringly, bestowed all graces on her, graces hardly concealed under her "alcandora." The Christian who loves such a beauty deserves to be pardoned.

Villasandino combines here the theme of the *Roman de la Rose* (13th century) with the sensuousness of Arabic poetry. Although it would be more correct to think perhaps that a Moorish setting has been used as a cloak, or as an excuse, to render in Castilian poetry some of the lightly veiled and well-calculated lewdness of the French poem, since this was incompatible with the Castilian idea of morality. Arabic poets, on the other hand, speak of sex with as much naturalness and innocence as they speak of divine love. But as we will see later, the approach to these "natural" things proved a difficult problem for Castilians.

In this century of the birth of great lyric poetry in Castilian, anonymous songs sprang up with Morisco themes; and there is no reason not

[24] See *Poesía española (Edad Media)*, edited by Dámaso Alonso, Buenos Aires, Editorial Losada, 1942, pp. 175-176.

to believe that some of them were composed by Moriscos. Many of the latter had so forgotten their own language that in 1462 the chief lawyer, or *alfaquí*, of Seville had to issue a Castilian version of the *Summation of the Principal Commandments* (Suma de los principales mandamientos) of the Koranic law.[25] Some of these songs offer that kind of exquisite tenderness which, being intimate, can be felt universally:

> Tres morillas me enamoran
> en Jaén:
> Axa y Fátima y Marién.
> Tres morillas tan garridas
> iban a coger olivas,
> y hallábanlas cogidas,
> en Jaén:
> y hallábanlas cogidas,
> y tornaban desmaídas
> y las colores perdidas,
> en Jaén . . .

> It all happened in Jaén
> that the three enchanting Moorish maids
> Axa, Fátima, and Marién,
> joyfully went to pluck olives.
> But alas, there was nothing to pluck,
> and they returned much dismayed,
> and the radiant glow on their cheeks had faded.
> And all that happened in Jaén.

During the reign of Henry IV (1454-1474) there were Moriscos at the court, and some persons connected their presence there with the unbelief of certain Christians. A few noblemen directed an insolent protest to the king: "It is very notorious that in your court there are persons, in your palace and near your person, who are infidels, enemies of our Holy Catholic Faith; and others who, although Christian in name, are very suspect in their faith, especially those who *believe and say and affirm that there is no other world*."[26]

A Czech traveler, the Baron of Rozmithal, visited Castile towards the

---

[25] See *Memorial histórico español*, 1853, v.

[26] See A. Paz y Melia, *El cronista Alonso de Palencia*, p. 61. I do not know what the basis was for the accusation, nor do I know of any other writer who speaks of Spanish unbelievers before the end of the eighteenth century.

middle of the fifteenth century, and he recorded in his diary certain curious notes on the life he observed. The modes of Morisco existence had infiltrated private life; or better, these modes had been existing as Spanish for centuries, but in the fifteenth century people wrote about the matter, because that was the time when writers were beginning to be interested in what was going on around them—they were conscious of themselves as human beings in a vital situation, in a given time and space. Let us then have a look at the Baron of Rozmithal's diary: "There now resides in Burgos a powerful count, who took my lord and his company to his palace," as one of the baron's secretaries writes; "there also came beautiful damsels and ladies richly adorned in the Morisco fashion, who, *in all their attire and in their eating and drinking followed that fashion.* Some of them danced very lovely dances in the Morisco style, and all were dark, with black eyes. They ate and drank very little, they greeted my lord gaily, and they were very friendly with the Germans."[27]

If this happened in Burgos, where there had been no Moors since the tenth century, one can imagine how in vogue Morisco fashion must have been in zones more recently reconquered. It is obvious, for that matter, that in the first half of the fifteenth century there was increase of wealth in Castile; and the luxury in dress and customs promoted Morisco practices, which, for more than 500 years, had been representing an ideal of wealth and distinction. Henry IV's favorite, Miguel Lucas de Iranzo, rode horseback "a la jineta" (what would in America, oddly enough, be called English style, that is, with the leg from hip to knee horizontal and from knee to foot vertical) "with a Morisco *aljuba*" (jubbah, a long garment with short, close-fitting sleeves) "of multi-colored silk."[28]

But I do not claim to be tracing out a picture of private life in the fifteenth century. I have wished only to make the picture complete enough to show that the Moslem customs were not a fad, something superimposed on Christian life, accepted as an elegant concession which

[27] Edition published in *Libros de antaño*, VIII, 162.

[28] *Memorial histórico español*, VIII, 262. *Jineta* is a style of riding taken from the Moors, with short stirrups and drawn-up legs; the word is Arabic, just as is *jinete* (see A. Steiger, *Fonética del hispano-árabe*, p. 146). The African tribe of the Zanata provided the Moorish kings with their best horsemen, *jinetes*, a word which imposed itself on Castilian, Portuguese, and Catalan, thanks to the fact that *caballero*, originally "horseman," came to mean "a member of the noble class." French resolved the problem with *cavalier* doubling *chevalier*, but Spanish was confronted with the vital fact that those who rode most and best were the Moorish horsemen or *jinetes*, and the Spaniards continued to use the word as their own. *Aljuba* is also Arabic.

the conquerors made to the conquered. A concession of the sort mentioned explains the favor enjoyed by the Spanish colonial style in architecture and other forms of civilization in the North American West. But it is not what happened in Spain.

The Impact of Islamic Religion

In no Catholic country does religion displace a greater social volume than in Spain and in the Hispano-Portuguese nations; and the truth is that religious belief has never been replaced by anything that is equivalent to it in extension and force. This is not to say that the majority of Hispanic people think that they must live according to Christian norms, or that literature and culture as a whole are affected now by religion as they were in 1700. The domes of transcendence under which everyone felt that he had his place and was protected, have disappeared; and with this transcendence has also been lost the pure prestige of the values incarnate in it. But in spite of all this, but with all this, the religion of the Spaniard, the Portuguese, and the Ibero-American is something which is everpresent, as a permanent and infrangible reality, although it may become noticeable and although we may realize the tremendous dimensions of its existence only when someone tries to suppress it. The fact is that the Hispanic people in their great majority are convinced that the Hispanic Church no longer incarnates values comparable to the artistic creations of two centuries ago. The proof that religion is there, whatever its form, is that every effort to combat or silence it unleashes catastrophes of the farthest-reaching kind. Mexicans, Spaniards, and other Hispanic peoples have written this chapter of their history with torrents of blood. The Hispano-Lusitanian people still live in a nonrational world, without earthly autonomy, without a foundation in objectivities *originally created* by Hispanic man. And this must be recognized, without acrimony and without melancholy, today more than ever.

Some of the more important creations of Spanish civilization during the sixteenth and seventeenth centuries, and even during the eighteenth, are nothing but aspects of the most singular religiosity of this people. The most visible part of this creation consists in extremely beautiful churches and religious works of art in Spain and in what was once her empire, enough by themselves to make a culture worthy of existing. Besides the "visible" arts, there were Spanish men of letters; many of these universal figures were monks, nuns, and clerics: Fernando de Herrera, Juan de la Cruz (Saint John of the Cross), Teresa de Jesús, Luis de Granada, Luis de León, Francisco de Vitoria, Francisco Suárez, Juan de Mariana, Lope de Vega, Calderón, Tirso de Molina, Gracián, Feijóo, and others. Hispanic history is essentially the history of a belief and of a religious sensibility, and, at the same time, of the grandeur, the misery, and the paralysis provoked by them.

Spain lived her religion with all its consequences, knowing at every moment what she was risking in such a gamble with destiny, and playing this game with a greater seriousness than some of the Roman Popes showed at times. Some Popes were willing to go to war to defend their temporal interests, and they did not ruin or depopulate their states by fighting against heretics and infidels, as Spain did. For many of the Popes, religion was a mundane, political business, an intelligent bureaucracy, a subtle dogmatism without heart warmth, and a marvelous theatricalism—and these things are not said here in a tone of criticism and contempt, which are entirely absent from my motives.[29] Rome fought at Lepanto (1571) under the leadership of a Spanish prince, Don Juan of Austria. But in 1611, the Duke of Osuna, Spanish viceroy in Sicily, heaped reproaches upon the Pope, whose galleys would come to load silk at Messina but would refuse to fight the Turk at the same time that the Spanish fleet was rushing into battle (see my *Santa Teresa*, pp. 245-246). That man of genius, Machiavelli, had already written that "the closer people are to the Roman Church, which is the head of our religion, the less religion they have" (*Discourses on the First Ten Books of Titus Livius*, 1, 12). The Reformation deflected religious interest toward the social conduct and efficacy of man; and with this, the way was eventually closed to the emotional soliloquy of the soul with God. The religion of the Reformation ended up by being converted into a theology applied

[29] When I take intelligence and a feeling for spectacle as bases of pontifical Italian life, I use these terms without any derogatory accent whatsoever. I use them to make a simple affirmation. Precisely because such was her nature, Italy was able to humanize the coarse Europe of the sixteenth century, which, without Italy, would have gone on as unrefined as it was. Neither the intellectualist skepticism of Jean de Meun nor the lyricism of Provence had the requisite strength to displace the axis of the "vital situation" of the so-called Middle Ages. Italy alone manufactured the serum that made the Europeans change their course completely: she did this by humanizing, "secularizing," the divine without breaking away from it. Rome found the common denominator for man and modern man, bridged the gap between the until then "illegal" instincts and faith, and left the "heretics" with the illusion that they were the ones who were changing the course of history. But without the secular "life" of Catholic Italy in the fifteenth century, the heresies (actually as old as Christianity itself) would have been reduced to sterile efforts, rather like the anarchism of the nineteenth, with many adepts, with many martyrs, but without effective transcendence.

to practical life with a view to restraining any attitude of the individual that tended to break his interconnections in society. France is without doubt a Catholic country, although she has caused her Catholicism to infiltrate itself with whatever substance it has found useful in the rationalism of its enemies; thus it was possible for enlightened Catholicism to emerge in the "Institut Catholique" of Paris, alongside the traditional Catholicism of the rural masses. From the end of the sixteenth century, French Catholicism placed itself at the service of the national state that its kings personified,[30] and on the margin of that Catholicism there was emerging more and more a rationalized world, eccentric to religion. By the sixteenth century, cultivated France regarded the religious theater as an intolerable anachronism, and it was finally suppressed by the Parliament in 1548. In Spain the same variety of spectacle lasted until 1765, when the foreign intellectualist pressure of the period forced a reaction against the traditional tendencies.

Spanish religion, we may then conclude, is based on a Catholicism very different from that of Rome and France—not to mention the Catholicism of the United States. It is a form of belief characteristic of Spain, intelligible only within the peculiar structure of her history. Spanish religion—like her language, her institutions, her very limited capacity for objective science, her prodigality of expressiveness, and her integral personalism—must be referred to the 900 years of Christian-Islamic-Jewish interaction. The Hispanic theocracy, the impossibility of organizing Spain or Hispanic-America as a purely civil state, founded

[30] The splendid funeral oration of Saint Francis of Sales in honor of the Duc de Mercoeur (1602) is the discourse of a politician and courtier, who is more concerned with human compromises than with the divine at any cost, who no longer believes that earthly values are to be scorned and forgotten as the meanest dust: "Je connais bien que mon office n'est pas maintenant (et je vous supplie, *Messieurs*, de ne le pas desirer de moi), de vous representer les raysons que nous avons eu de regretter et plaindre. . . . Soit donq que je jette les yeux sur son bien pour nous consoler ou sur notre mal pour nous affliger, je ne puys eschapper de l'abisme de ses vertues infinies, dont la grandeur et l'esclat est insupportable a la foiblesse de mes yeux. . . . En ceste occasion, que j'estime aussi digne d'une grande eloquence qu'aucune autre qui se soit presente en ce siecle; en ceste assemblee, qui est presque toute la fleur de ce grand royaume; [he is preaching in Notre Dame, to the Court of France] et en ce lieu, auquel *mille beaux esprits* eussent ambitieusement recherche de faire paroistre tout leur art et leur science de bien dire, etc." (*Oeuvres de Saint François de Sales*, Annecy, VII, 401-402.) The whole sermon is a canticle to the glory of the deceased nobleman as the hero of France's imperial cause. How different from another funeral oration, one delivered on the death of Philip II (1598), to which I shall refer elsewhere, in which the preacher presents the king as one put to death for the crime of being mortal and a sinner, and points to the catafalque as if it were a symbolical scaffold.

on objective interests and not on the magical power of individuals, are just an expression of the possibilities and limitations of their living disposition.

As a social institution, the Spanish Church is something that nobody and nothing have succeeded in suppressing or replacing. This failure is, after all, probably quite normal: other religions likewise continue to exist in other countries, and there is no point in regretting it. But the peculiar thing about Spain is not this, but rather that the Church continues to be a power there set up against the State, in a form which is not known to either France or Italy, the other great Catholic countries.[31] As a nation included in the circle of occidental culture, Spain has possessed a State; this State, however, has existed even in recent times as a co-power alongside the Church, which still preserves the memory of the time when Spain was governed Inquisitorially. The efforts to dispense with ecclesiastical power have had only a passing and superficial effect. Deprived of her properties in 1836, the Church succeeded, through the religious orders, in acquiring again a considerable economic power and in exercising a very broad influence through her educational centers. It is useless to resort to explanations of an external kind to account for a fact of such scope. What happens in reality is that the masses continue to find inspiration in a static and immutable belief, and not in objective realities governed by the play of human actions and interests. Spanish capitalists very often preferred to keep their money in bank accounts or

[31] The extra-national character which the Spanish Church presented at the beginning of this century is observable in a criticism of the Library of the Cathedral of Toledo made in a purely scholarly work by an author who subsequently figured in what might be termed Spanish pre-fascism: "At the present time (and it is to the shame of the Chapter of the Cathedral of Toledo and of Spanish ecclesiastical culture that I say so), it is all but impossible to get into the aforementioned Chapter Library, which, acting like the dog in the manger, neither does any work itself nor allows anyone else to do any. . . . Thanks to the well-intentioned orders of the revolutionary government of 1868, Sr. Octavio de Toledo went to that place and in a few days, amidst grave dangers, compiled that part of the *Catalogue* which has recently been published by the *Revista de Archivos*. It is certain that among the valuable codices that belong to that Library (whose contents ought to be moved, *legally or illegally*, in the interests of culture, to the Biblioteca Nacional in Madrid), there are many that include works of the Toledan translators" (A. Bonilla y San Martin, *Historia de la filosofía española*, 1908, p. 322). I have omitted part of Sr. Bonilla's violent attack, which, as is evident, proposed that the State, although it might not have the right to do so, should take possession of a valuable property of the Church—because the Church did not know how important the property was and was incapable of administering it. This is one of the innumerable examples of what I call "reciprocal illegality" in the relations between Church and State, of which the tragic denouement was the Civil War of 1936.

to invest it in government bonds instead of risking it in industrial enterprises. The great industries, the richest mines, and many railroads belonged to foreign concerns. In 1935 there were 17,000 foreign technicians in Spain. Attitudes of quietistic apathy have been frequent there. Earlier (p. 112) I cited the expression of Islamic origin "if God wills" (si Dios quiere), to which should be added at this point, "it is the will of God, it was the will of God" (está de Dios, estaba de Dios), rooted in the bowels of the people, and used at every turn.[32]

Over against the quietistic apathy—old and deeply rooted—of the ruling classes rose up the Messianic hope of the mass of the people, founded on a belief opposite in sign but analogous in root. Among the popular beliefs, anarchism, as great an enemy of the State as religious fanaticism in its own way, has been the most widespread. Several old forms of anarchism, under the disguise of foreign ideologies, have recently rent the soul of Spain in the atrocious conflict that went on from 1936 to 1939. The Spaniard does not think that he is a member of the national collectivity, or that the march and destiny of this collectivity, which he is in but not of, depend on the actions of the people in concert and as individuals; he waits for things to happen, or for some leader with thaumaturgic gifts to rise up. The people who fought against fascism thought, and in good faith in many cases, that they were offering their lives for a sublime and universal cause, and that the sacrifice of the poor Spanish masses would bring about a change in the course of history. This is not new: at the end of the fifteenth century the Spanish masses believed that Ferdinand and Isabella had been sent by God to establish happiness on the earth and to put an end to the tyranny of all the powerful. A few Renaissance thinkers *wrote* utopias, but the Spaniards *have shed their blood* for such dreams on more than one occasion, thus erasing the boundary between the possible and the impossible, the real and the imagined.

It will be said that something similar has happened in every human society; but the chief difference between the Iberic world and the other western peoples is that the history of the latter is integrated not only by persons who fire with their ideals and disenchant with their failures

---

[32] A folksong goes:

You'd live without troubles?	¿Quieres vivir sin afanes?
Let the ball roll;	Deja la bola rodar;
Whatever God wills	que lo que fuere de Dios,
Will fall into your hands.	a las manos se vendrá.

(F. Rodríguez Marín, *Cantos populares*, IV, 143)

(Cromwell, Napoleon, etc.), but also by extra-personal realities (economics, original political concepts, scientific and industrial changes, etc.). Phenomena of this kind are scarce in Hispanic history, and when they have been present—always as an importation from the outside, not as an innovation emergent from within—their influence has been slight. The "personal" in Spanish history is more important than any objective cultural achievement. History thus turns into an alternating process of illusions and disenchantments, the products of faith or disillusion with reference to the leaders of the nation, of the Messianic hope and "anti-Christism," of the exaltation of an idol or of the vituperation of the guilty. From the depths of the Middle Ages till the nineteenth century, literature continued to occupy itself with Rodrigo, the last king of the Goths, and with the traitor Julián, who opened the gates of Spain to Islam to avenge the outrage of his daughter by the lewd king. Both were the "culprits" in the ruination of Spain, and the legend of the wicked king was expanded with exquisite stories of revenge. Some centuries later another "personal" cause was forged to alter the course of history. In 1497 the crown prince Don Juan died, the only male child of Ferdinand and Isabella, and to this misfortune has been traditionally attributed the tortuous course of subsequent history, a course for which, it is said, the House of Austria is responsible. In another sense, an example of transcendent personalism can be found in the enthusiasm of the Spanish people for King Ferdinand VII, who was called nothing less than "the longed for," albeit out of pure pleasure of Messiah-seeking, since he was the most villainous and perverse monarch conceivable. Yet in spite of this, Ferdinand VII served as an incentive for the Spanish masses to throw out the armies of Napoleon (1808-1814). The cultural splendor of Spain during the eighteenth century is attributed to Charles III, whose only merit was that he did not disturb the constructive work of a group of aristocrats won to the cause of intellectualism.

In what Catholic country is there anything like the processions in Seville during Holy Week? The images vie with one another in luxury and splendor, and the rival confraternities in charge of the different ones carry on psychological and sentimental warfare with each other. Among those who carry the images in such spectacular and dramatic processions there are men of the people who, as people, may very well be anarchists (indeed, sometimes they are) who dream of razing the social structure and with it the Church; they are capable of killing each other in defense of the honor and supremacy of "their" image, the image (such as the "Jesús del Gran Poder," the "Virgen de la Macarena," etc.), of which they are the bearers. It is customary to explain such behavior frivolously by referring to the "superstition" of the people, an explanation which clarifies nothing, for there is as much superstition in England (belief in ghosts), in southern Italy, and in Poland as there is in Spain, and there may be more, yet nothing comparable takes place in those countries. A person is superstitious when he is motivated by the harm or good that may come to him through unknowable and indomitable forces; the man who helps to carry a religious image in Seville becomes one with his "superstition," converting it into the substance of his own existence and suffering trials and tribulations for it. I do not think, needless to say, that many of the "Catholics" who participate in the processions in Seville believe in and approve of everything that the Church commands to be believed—among other reasons, because they do not even know what these things are. What is important is that the person includes himself in a halo, in something that is "his" but which, being his, transcends him. He lives trusting in something that is located outside him and that operates outside what he himself does. He lives off what the earth, like a generous "alma mater," gives him. When her fruits are not easily produced, he has recourse to foreign capital and technology. Therefore in the Hispanic countries the mines and oil wells are usually in foreign hands. Or, he lives off the magical munificence of the State, which distributes jobs in abundance, also like a generous "almus pater," without too much concern over the efficiency of the functions that are performed. He floats on the belief in the State, just as he does on the previously mentioned religious belief. In either case he remains shut up within himself—which has little to do with what popular, superficial thinkers have called individualism.[33] Shut up in himself, with his eyes on each of these transcendent objects (Church and State), he lives by expressing himself, presenting and representing his existence, like a theater of his own life, in gestures, in words, in attitudes—at times in prodigious works of art, or in acts of beautiful and unselfish morality. That part of his life which is not this—I repeat—is or has been imported from other peoples, which is not to say that the Spaniards may not occasionally excel in one or another of these imported activities. But the permanent, the basic, is the other.

A way of life with this kind of structure is bound to defend its special form of religious transcendence with tooth and nail, and is bound to oppose every effort to create political forms to be imposed on it as an objective and extra-personal thing. This is why the Hispanic states are

[33] I discuss the special form of Spanish individualism in the last chapter.

shot through with inefficiency and immorality, and it has been impossible for them to be penetrated by an objectified religious consciousness that is the same for everyone. The Hispanic religion is a personalized belief, not a guide for conduct. But the Hispanic man is capable of killing and of being killed in the defense of "his" religion, of that world of his in which reign his will, his dream, and his caprice. He would feel lost in a world governed by norms which he could not inflect according to his will. To keep such a world from eventuating, he can commit the most horrendous crimes and atrocities, incompatible with the most elemental Christianity. Seen in this light, the Civil War (1936-1939) was a struggle between the old Hispanic religiosity, petrified by the centuries, and an effort towards a new religiosity, towards the creation of another transcendent orbit, vague and misty, in which the Spanish "I want to" (me da la gana) was to be combined with a utopian project for universal happiness. The rest—fascism, communism—amount to frivolous sideshows, in servile imitation of foreign models.

I suspect that Spaniards engendered and developed such a way of confronting life in the conquest of the Islamic people, and in having to let themselves be conquered through the Islamic people, as it were, by a way of life based on submission to one belief which in turn begat others. Even though in orthodox Mohammedanism Mohammed was the last prophet inspired by God, it is known that since shortly after his death and up to the present time, the Moslem has quickened his vital quietism with the hopeful dream of a Messiah, a Mahdi.[34] If we add to this the actual presence of the Hispanic Jews and the Jewish converts to Christianity in the upper classes of society, we will be on our way to understanding important aspects of Spanish religion and its dramatic impact on Spanish history (see Chapter 13).

It is, of course, very difficult to present in a visible and comprehensible form the process by which the quality of Islamic religion penetrated into the Spanish-Christian religiosity, because we are not manipulating "things" but considering vital points of view, the feelings of a people as they faced the world around them. These ways of facing the world, as they came to predominate over others, came to constitute a habit, and finally a manner of existing. To be sure, the wide and deep presence of all these manifestations of Islamism in Hispanic life, reflected in the language and customs, was an unconscious effect of the prestige always radiated by a powerful enemy. Islamic life imposed itself on the life of its neighbors, on a life which it opposed; wherefore the neighbors took

[34] See E. Bloch, *Le messianisme dans l'hétérodoxie musulmane*, Paris, 1903.

over whatever attracted them and was materially and spiritually necessary to them, from cosmetics to forms of miracles, as we shall see later.
But if we limited ourselves to cataloguing "influences," the result would
be a presentation of the Spanish Christians as colonists of the Moors,
and there would be no possibility of understanding how they succeeded
in leaving behind their colonial condition, nor of articulating the history
of Spain. The only way to write this history that would adapt itself to
my theme must take as its starting point the following assumption: The
Saracens imposed themselves on and opposed themselves to the Christians. The Christians imitated the enemy and at the same time defended
themselves, using the same approach to life which the Moors had imposed on them, that is, from within a "belief," a belief in extra-rational
power. The Christians opposed and finally conquered the Moslems,
thanks to their own faith in the efficacy of an anti-Mohammed in warfare,
who not only won battles but also provided the first expression of the
singular form of Hispanic life. The Spaniards did not live their beliefs
after the fashion of the Italians, the French, or the Germans, and therefore the Spanish religion was very different from that of the others: outside of Spain there was an "other world" (más allá) and also a "this
world" (más acá). The stimulus for the Italian life structure has been
essentially this-worldly—commerce, luxury, naval science, inquiring
thought, heroism of the mind (Campanella, Giordano Bruno), scant
enthusiasm for war, sensuality, absence of national spirit and, consequently, of epic poetry, etc.; religion was not an essential ingredient for
her history, which was often a theater of war for foreigners covetous of
the fine fruits of Italian intelligence and art. France's structure grew
out of the centripetal force of the capital city of her kings, whose dynasty
(injected with divine powers, as we shall presently see) served as the
country's spinal column. England, Germany, and the other nations of
western Europe, in one way or another built their existence on earthly
foundations; but Spain rests on "godly" foundations, as we have heard
Don Alonso de Cartagena put it so well (p. 13) when he distinguished
motives behind the Castilian wars from those "other interests" which impelled the English to make war. The history of Spain is indeed *godly*,
and only by accepting this evidence without reservation will we attain to
an understanding of it. From the ninth century to the seventeenth, the
axis of Hispanic history, of what there was in it of the affirmative, the
original, and the grandiose, was an ultra-mundane belief that emerged
as a heroic reply to another, hostile belief, under which the remnants

of what had been the Hispania of the Visigoths went through the agony of death. A unique case and charged with extraordinary drama. The Spain of the ninth century remade itself and succeeded in keeping alive, thanks to its faith in Santiago (Saint James)—in what lies entombed in the city of Santiago de Compostela.

6

Christianity Faces Islam

The Belief in Saint James of Galicia

Por quien son las Españas
del yugo desatadas
del bárbaro furor, y libertadas.
(Luis de León)

THE HISTORY OF SPAIN cannot be understood without a knowledge and understanding of the veneration paid to Saint James the Apostle and of the pilgrimages to Santiago de Compostela. That is to say, the history of Spain would have been entirely different without the belief that in that city reposes the body of one of Christ's disciples and companions, beheaded in Palestine and translated to Spain by miraculous means; thus he returned to the land formerly Christianized by him, according to a tradition about which there would be no point in arguing, a tradition which had existed since before the arrival of the Arabs. Faith in the physical presence of the Apostle gave spiritual support to those who fought against the Moors; the extraordinary veneration in which he was held led to the erection of marvelous buildings in Santiago and along the routes of the pilgrims, and it had literary consequences both inside and outside of Spain. The order of Cluny and others of no less importance were established in the north of the Peninsula, attracted by the success of the pilgrimages; between the ninth and the seventeenth centuries millions of people moved along the *via francigena*, or the French Highway, and these people kept up the connection between Christian Spain of the Middle Ages and the rest of Europe. Art, literature, institutions, customs, and forms of linguistic expression interacted with religious belief in that prodigious historical event. The place was the northwestern corner of Spain, the *finis terrae* of Christian Europe, where the outlines of the countryside are blurred by mists in which the land itself appears to be suspended.

In spite of all—and there is much—that has been written about Santiago of Galicia, we continue to wonder how such an event was possible. It is understandable that Rome, the head of an empire, should be continued by Christian Rome, and that Jerusalem should take on a new prominence. Galicia, on the other hand, had been completely lacking in importance; she was not perceptibly significant either under the Romans or in the Visigothic period (see Chapter 3). We would expect, then, that such a miracle as took place there would have only local authority, and that it would have even been rejected as illegitimate when it came to be known outside of Spain. This did not happen. So, we must reconsider this event of such huge proportions and try to remove it from the category of arbitrary and puzzling chance happenings.

At the beginning of the ninth century, near the ancient city of Iria Flavia, a sepulcher was venerated which was said to contain the body of Saint James the Apostle. Orthodox opinion always admitted that the apostle was Saint James the Greater, the son of Zebedee. Berceo and the *Poema de Fernán González* both speak of him as such in the thirteenth century, in agreement with ecclesiastical tradition; but popular belief, in defiance of the Doctors, adored a Saint James who included the Greater (Matt. 4:21) and the one called the brother of Christ in the Gospel (Matt. 13:55), a description taken literally, as we shall see, by those who venerated the sepulcher. For centuries this fraternal relationship, forgotten by orthodoxy, formed the core of that belief, which acquired considerable dimensions, especially because it concerned a brother of the Saviour. Such a belief rested upon pre-Christian cults of twin divinities such as Castor and Pollux—the Dioscuri or sons of Jupiter—one of which ascended to heaven while the other remained on earth (at least for some time) as a protector of man.

If Spain had not been submerged by Islam, the cult of Santiago of Galicia would not have prospered. But the anxiety of the eighth and ninth centuries fortified the faith in a Santiago the brother of the Christ. This Santiago had, in a previous manifestation—as Castor—already achieved magnificent victories, riding his shining white charger. Other circumstances would later cause what was in other places an occasional and dissociated miracle to be the expression of a type of life that would be oblivious of the boundaries between heaven and earth, between miracle and the reality of experience. Indeed, out of the belief in Santiago grows a most original type of existence, something which I shall call integral "theobiosis," without an exact parallel in Christian Europe. The cult of Santiago was not a simple manifestation of piety eventually useful in the struggle against the Moor. The truth is, on the contrary, that the belief emerged out of the humble plane of folklore and assumed immeasurable dimensions as an answer to what was happening on the Moslem side:

one war was sustained and won by religious faith, to be opposed (not rationally, of course) by another fighting faith, grandly spectacular, strong enough in turn to sustain the Christian and carry him to victory. In the same way that the Moors had been unconsciously imitated in many aspects of their existence, a correlation was also established with respect to the military use of religious beliefs.

At the beginning of the ninth century, some hundred years after the Saracen invasion, the Christians in the northwest of Spain must have felt themselves very weak materially and spiritually. They were already seriously isolated from the rest of Christendom in the Visigothic period. Now this isolation must have been almost complete. Probably very few thought it possible to restore the ancient monarchy of Toledo on Spanish soil. But, behold, at the beginning of the tenth century the Christians began to raise their heads, and under Alphonse III (866-910) they considerably extended the boundaries of the Asturian-Leonese kingdom. Alphonse's sons and subjects speak of him in 917 as "magnus imperator."[1] No longer did the Christians belittle themselves in the face of the Moors: their monarchs, once simply *principes* or *reges*, they now called *imperatores*. What justification could be found for such an elevation in rank? I dare to say that the title of *imperator* is inseparable from the title of *pontifex* (pontiff), given to the bishop of Santiago with great verbal pomp. The first indication of this that I know of is in a document from the year 954, most likely not the first one: "I, Ordoño, prince and humble servant of the servants of the Lord, desire for you, illustrious and venerable father and Lord Sisnandus, bishop of the see of our patron Santiago and *pontiff of the whole world*, eternal health in God Our Lord."[2] The person who wrote after such a fashion was King Ordoño III of Leon, who must have had powerful motives, and not only political ones, for giving the papal title to the bishop of Santiago, and consequently not recognizing the hierarchy of the Roman pontiff.[3] The king

[1] R. Menéndez Pidal, *La España del Cid*, pp. 74, 77, 710.

[2] *España sagrada*, XIX, 366. A. López Ferreiro, *Historia de la Iglesia de Santiago*, II, 319. R. Menéndez Pidal, *loc.cit.* The Latin text says: "totius orbis antistiti."

[3] If we bear in mind what the Roman pontiffs were like in the tenth century, and how they must have looked from the point of view of Leon and Santiago, we will be in a better position to understand the claim of the Compostellan prelates. "In that epoch popes appeared and disappeared according to the whims of the feudal factions. There were some who died at the hands of assassins, or ended their days in prison. Demoralization went hand in hand with brutality. More than once, feminine intrigues decided who should wear the tiara, for Marozia and Theodora, taking advantage of their lovers or of their successive husbands, had their sons named pope" (H. Pirenne, *Histoire de l'Europe*, 1936, p. 115). Marozia, who enjoyed

could permit himself such magnification because the bishops of Santiago believed themselves to be pontiffs. And they believed it because Santiago was a higher ranking apostle than Saint Peter: he was a protomartyr, a favorite of God, the brother of Christ, and the "son of the thunder," according to the gospel; popular belief (which was subsequently to be reflected in the liturgy) had indeed converted him into the twin brother of the Lord.[4] And if I may only suppose that Bishop Sisnandus was not the first to believe that he had a right to the universal pontificate, there are documents to prove that he was not the last. In 1049 Bishop Cresconius was excommunicated by the Council of Rheims, "because against Divine law he arrogated to himself the highest apostolic title."[5] During the episcopate or pontificate of Diego Gelmírez

the title of *senatrix* and who was the real power in Rome, had one son who governed the capital of Christianity from 932 to 954. While this son, Alberich, exercised his tyranny, another son was occupying Saint Peter's chair (931-946), which Alberich watched over closely. In his lifetime Alberich named the following popes: Leo VII (936-939), Stephen VIII (939-942), Marinus II (942-946), Agapetus II (946-955). For a few short years Agapetus II restored to some extent the fallen prestige of the pontiffs, but his predecessors obeyed the Tyrant in silence and they had no relations with the outside (F. Gregorovius, *History of the City of Rome in the Middle Ages*, London, 1895, III, 321; Luigi Salvatorelli, *L'Italia Medioevale*, Milan, pp. 530-42). When Alberich died in 954 he was succeeded by his son Octavian, who, on the death of Agapetus II, occupied the pontifical see as John XII, and brought together in his hands the two powers. His pontificate was characterized by chaotic license. The pope, only eighteen years old, abandoned himself to sensuality and to emulation of the Rome of the emperors, in company with boys and girls as young as himself. During one of his orgies he ordained a deacon in a stable (Gregorovius, *loc.cit.*, p. 336). There were not many moral obstacles, therefore, to keep Santiago from strengthening its apostolic pretensions. The Rome of Saint Peter (an apostle of less importance than Santiago, as we shall see, for the Leonese and the Galicians) appeared to be weak, isolated, and depraved, lacking in the moral force necessary to arrest the advances being made by the See of the Son of Thunder. Santiago and Rome were two islands of Christianity, which, during the tenth century knew little about one another. The eleventh century brought a change in that state of affairs.
[4] Thus it is evident that an effort was being made in Spain to duplicate the correlation between pontificate and empire. The decisive effect of Santiago upon the ecclesiastical and political life of old Spain has been recognized by R. Menéndez Pidal in his new edition of *La España del Cid*: "The discovery of the sepulcher of Santiago and the empire [of the kings of Leon] are two correlated facts" (p. 69). In another recent book of the same author we read: "With the discovery of Santiago's sepulcher the small Asturian kingdom did not feel, as it did before, in a condition of oppressive inferiority; they already possessed something very great to outdo the old Visigothic court in dignity" (*El imperio hispánico y los cinco reinos*, Madrid, 1950, p. 22). My idea of the outstanding part played by the belief in Santiago could not find better or higher recognition.
[5] López Ferreiro, *Historia de la Iglesia de Santiago*, II, 483. (Quia contra fas sibi vendicaret culmen apostolici nominis.)

(1100-1140), a period of maximum splendor for Santiago, that magnificent personage established pontifical pomp and honors in his court. He was censured for this by many, who reminded him that some of his predecessors "had claimed nothing less for their church than its equality with the Church of Rome" (L. Ferreiro, iii, 274). Gelmírez named cardinals, and his cardinals wore the purple; he received the pilgrims *Apostolico more*, as if he were indeed the pope.

The foregoing data, which encompass a period of three centuries, will suffice to prove the constant, zealous longing on the part of the prelates of Compostela to establish themselves as heads of a universal hierarchy. I am aware that not only Santiago disputed Rome's supremacy during the Middle Ages, and that at one time Milan thought her own title superior. Moreover, the legend of the Grail presupposes that the axis of Christianity did not pass through Rome alone. But none of these ideas took concrete shape in a claim so thoroughly sustained as that of Santiago nor so closely bound up with a popular state of feeling and with forms of liturgy and worship. Those who believed that Santiago was the center of Catholicism felt that truth and justice were on their side. Such a sentiment must already have been strong around Alphonse III (866-910), who is precisely the one who had the first proper church built in honor of the Apostle: "And he caused the church of Saint James to be built, all of carved stone, with pillars of marble; for the one before this had been made of earth."[6] The increased luster and dignity of the most ancient forms of worship coincided with the intense military activity of Alphonse III.

The presence of the body of Santiago in Iria Flavia is not mentioned before the ninth century, although the coming of the Apostle to Spain for the purpose of christianizing the Peninsula had been spoken of; even then the two Santiagos[7] were being confused, as they continued to be subsequently.

In documents prior to the year 1000 the passion of Saint James is dated the 25th of March, although in these terms: "passio sancti Iacobi Iusti, fratris Domini, sicut in Actibus Apostolorum continetur" (the passion

---

[6] *Crónica general*, p. 369*b*. This king was a great builder of churches. As the Chronicle says (p. 379*a*) "he also built a church, well-wrought, over the bodies of Saint Facundus and Saint Primitivus, on the bank of the river Cea." This was the shrine of that pair of twin saints on the route of Santiago.

[7] The *De ortu et obitu Patrum*, an apparently spurious work of Saint Isidore, already demonstrates this confusion, which is also to be found in the Byzantine text on which it is based. Msgr. Duchesne (*Annales du Midi*, 1900, xii, 156-157) describes such an error as enormous.

of Saint James the Just, brother of the Lord, as it is contained in the Acts of the Apostles).[8] But the passion spoken of in the Acts (12:2) is that of Saint James the Greater, whereas the brother of the Lord (Matt. 13:55) is Saint James the Just, that is, the Less. The juxtaposition of the two apostles was nothing unique: the same thing happened with almost all the rest.[9] In the present case, however, it happens that this third Santiago, the result of the fusion of the two, suffered his passion on the 25th of March, on the same day as the commemoration of the Passion of Christ (L. Ferreiro, I, 311-312), a circumstance that accentuated the brotherhood of the two. The so-called *Codex Calixtinus*, falsely attributed to Pope Calixtus II, and composed in the twelfth century, still had both passions coinciding on the 25th of March. Later, when it was no longer urgent to emphasize the divine brotherhood of Santiago, and when such equality was in fact perceived to be inadmissible, the Feast of Saint James was transferred to the 25th of July.

If Santiago of Galicia was a fusion of the two Jameses of the Gospels, the military and equestrian activity of "Santiago Matamoros," Saint James Moorslayer, as he might be called in English, presupposed in the Christian apostle certain characteristics entirely foreign to everything that is said about either James in the Gospels, the Acts of the Apostles, the Ecclesiastical History of Eusebius of Caesarea, and other hagiographical sources. The Santiago in whom the ninth-century Spaniards believed is the one who later appears in the description in the *Crónica general* of Alphonse the Learned in the narration of the miraculous apparition of the Apostle at the battle of Clavijo (822), in terms corresponding to what was believed by the people, accustomed by tradition to imagine Santiago, and before that the Dioscuri, as riding a white horse and fighting furiously in behalf of his protégés. The Apostle appeared to King Ramiro I and said: "Our Lord Jesus Christ divided between all the other apostles, *my brothers*, and me, all the other provinces of the earth, and to me alone he gave Spain for me to watch over her and protect her from the hands of the enemies of the Faith. . . ."[10] And so that you may doubt nothing of this that I tell you, tomorrow will you

[8] According to López Ferreiro, *Historia de la Iglesia de Santiago*, I, 63, which refers to martyrologies of the eighth century and later.

[9] Rendel Harris, *The Twelve Apostles*, Cambridge, 1927, *passim*.

[10] The chronicle translates the Latin text of the so-called Vows of Santiago, which may be found in E. Flórez, *España sagrada*, XIX, 331. From the Latin text it is evident that the sending of Santiago was felt as a militant action related to the mission of the Reconquest. But Jesus did not send forth his apostles to take up arms and fight, but rather to teach the people with gentle words: "Go, and teach all nations."

see me go into battle, *on a white horse, with a white standard and a great shining sword in my hand*" (p. 360). Then the Christians, "trusting in God's help and the help of Santiago," conquered the Moors.

In 449 B.C. the twins Castor and Pollux had also appeared on their white horses and in the same way decided the victory in favor of the dictator Postumius Albinus at Lake Regillus.[11] Strabo (VI, 261) speaks of an altar erected on the bank of the river Sagra to commemorate the victory won with the help of the Dioscuri in a battle in which 10,000 Locrians conquered 130,000 Crotonians.

The most obvious case of a Dioscuri apparition in Spain is found in the *Vida de San Millán* of Gonzalo de Berceo in the first half of the thirteenth century. Count Fernán González won the battle of Simancas (939), according to the poet, thanks to the help of Santiago and San Millan; the Christians feared the numerical superiority of the Moors.

> While the good people were in this doubt,
> they turned their gaze and thoughts to heaven:
> they saw two persons fair and shining,
> much whiter were they than the recent snows.
> They rode *two horses whiter than crystal.* . . .
> their faces were angelic, their forms celestial,
> they came down through the air in great haste,
> they looked at the Moors with fierce glance,
> the swords in their hands were frightful to see. (437-439)

The defeat of the Moors was complete: with God and the saints the battle was won. (452)[12]

[11] "The gods have appeared to us, to Postumius on the lake Regillus, and to Vacienus on the Salarian way. . . . Do you think that they were riding white horses when they appeared to Vacienus?" (Cicero, *De natura deorum*, III, 5; II, 6). *De natura deorum*, II, 6, states that in the battle of Lake Regillus, Castor and Pollux "ex equis pugnare visi sunt"—were seen fighting on horseback. For these and many other references, see the excellent article on the "Dioskuroi" in Pauly-Wissowa, *Real-Encyclopädie*, IX, col. 1091: "Since early times the appearances of the primitive pair of gods have been connected with horses, especially white ones." Euripides calls them λευκοπώλω . . . ἐκγόνω Διός (*Heracles furens*, 11. 29-30). They were even conceived of as two white horses, although later the horses were converted into their attribute. In Sparta they were the models and protectors of every kind of equestrian or military exercise. There was an altar dedicated to them at the entrance of the hippodrome in Olympia (*Pausanias*, V, 15, 5), etc.

[12] The dioscuric character of this apparition has already been mentioned by A. H. Krappe, *Spanish Twin Cults*, in *Studi e materiali de storia delle religioni*, 1932, VIII, 13. In this article will be found some additional facts about pairs of saints in Spain, as well as other interesting observations, which I do not cite here. My purpose

We are confronted, then, with a mixture of beliefs, the sort of thing that was so frequent in the first centuries of the Christian era, when paganism and Christianity infiltrated each other. This cross-breeding takes place already in the Gospel. In Mark 3:17 we read: "and James the son of Zebedee, and John the brother of James; and he surnamed them Boanerges, which is, The sons of thunder." Rendel Harris has demonstrated that *Boanerges* is a word of Semitic origin which contains in its first part the stem *bn* (son).[13] *Boanerges* says the same thing as *Dios-kuroi* (sons of thundering Zeus), or as Bana-ba Tilo (sons of Heaven), in Portuguese East Africa. I think there can be no doubt about the meaning of *Boanerges* in the Gospel, if Mark 3:17 is considered in relation with Luke 9:54, in which James and John offer to help Jesus by causing fire to come down from heaven and annihilate certain Samaritans, help which the Lord, being pure spirit, rejects: "Ye know not what manner of Spirit ye are of." The belief in the thundering power of Santiago (as one of the brothers "Boanerges") is perceptible even in the office which was sung in the Church of Santiago in the eleventh century, in which is continually the phrase repeated, "Boanerges, filii tonitrui":

"Sicut enim tonitrui uoces faciunt terram tremere, sic omnis mundus contremuit uocibus illorum" (just as the voices of the thunder cause the earth to tremble, so the whole world shook at the sound of their voices). Physical thunder was replaced by the thunder of the word; but it is obvious that without the former, the latter would not have existed.

The son of thunder sends the lightning across the sky; he gives battle like a shining god on a horse of dazzling whiteness, and brandishing his shining sword. To Georgiana G. King belongs the merit of having called attention to the syncretism of such a figure, in which are to be found aspects of other Ibero-Roman divinities.[14] J. R. Mélida has already noticed the relation between the horseman so frequently represented on Iberian coins and the cult of Castor as an equestrian divinity; at times the horseman wields a lance, and on two coins there appear bolts of lightning (Georgiana G. King, *op.cit.* pp. 298 and 289). The connection between all this and the Dioscuri is evident; Toutain[15] finds two inscriptions referring to Pollux in southern Spain, to which another in Tortosa

---

is to make the reader feel the live fact of the belief in Santiago, so that I must deliberately dispense with the folkloric scheme of which this fact is a part.

[13] R. Harris, *Boanerges*, 1913, pp. 2-4.

[14] *The Way of St. James*, 1920, III, 294ff.

[15] *Les cultes païens dans l'Empire Romain*, I, i, 411.

can be added.[16] The cult of the Dioscuri was merged with the cult of Mars, Serapis, and other divinities.

As a study of the belief itself, Georgiana G. King's book is excellent. But I am not interested here in the abstract history of religions. I am seeking the human agent of a belief, concrete and unique, which belongs to a specific time and place. The Spanish problem of Santiago is more than an instance of religious syncretism. Santiago fights like one of the Dioscuri on his white horse, but what essentially mattered for the cornered Christians was the religious sentiment that Santiago was a brother of the Lord Jesus. Under the influence of the cult of the Dioscuri, so deeply rooted in Syria and Palestine, the belief grew up that more than one apostle was the twin brother of Jesus. The Church fathers interpreted this brotherhood spiritually, but the people (whose points of view are reflected in the apocryphal writings) took the statements to be literally true in their physical sense. The name of the apostle Thomas means twin brother in Syriac. In the previously quoted *de ortu et obitu Patrum* (see p. 134) we read: "Thomas, Christ's apostle, called Didymus which means [in Greek] *twin brother of Christ* and like unto the Savior."[17] The famous Galician heresiarch Priscillian, a great reader of apocryphal writings, identified the apostle Judas of the canonical epistles with the Thomas of the fourth Gospel, and thus converted him into the twin brother of the Lord: "Judas the Apostle, the twin brother of the Lord [didymus Domini], who had a stronger belief in Christ after he touched the wounds he had suffered."[18]

Both these passages taken together prove that the belief that Christ had twin brothers had spread over Spain, and that, although the belief was heretical, apparently some, and perhaps many, accepted it in the atmosphere of religious syncretism of the end of the Roman Empire. Some texts make the twin brother one apostle, others another. Saint Matthew had already said (13:55): "Is not this the carpenter's son? Is not his mother called Mary, and his brethren James, Joses, Simon and Judas?" We are not concerned here with the scriptural problem of what

[16] "Castori et Polluci M. Valerius Anthus Votum Solvit Libens" (*Corpus Inscriptionum Latinarum*, II, Suppl. 6070).

[17] "Thomas apostolus Christi, Didymus nominatus, et juxta Latinam linguam Christi geminus, ac similis Salvatoris" (in R. Harris, *The Twelve Apostles*, p. 55).

[18] Edit. Shepss, p. 44. R. Harris, *Boanerges*, p. 408, observes that Priscillian found no difficulty in harmonizing the fact of Christ's divinity with the fact that he had a twin brother. In Chapter 3 we have already seen the importance of Galician Priscillianism and Arianism as prior conditions that made possible the belief in Santiago.

"brother" means, but with what the popular opinion of the meaning was —that popular opinion that fused the two Jameses. What was understood by "brother" is what we read in an apocryphal epistle of the pseudo-Ignatius, addressed to John. After he expresses his desire to see the Virgin in Jerusalem, he adds that he would also like to know Saint James, "the venerable Saint James, called the Just, who, I have heard, is as like Christ Jesus in his life and his way of conversing with peoples *as if he were a twin brother born from the same womb*; they say that if I see him, I shall see Jesus himself, without finding any difference in any feature of his body."[19]

This apostle, the Lord's twin brother, suffered his martyrdom in a form parallel to the passion of Christ, according to the account in the *Historia Ecclesiastica* of Eusebius of Caesarea (II, 23). Bishop J. B. Lightfoot (*op.cit.*, I, 596) says that parallel to the history of the Church, from its earliest times, there was the tendency to find in the lives of the saints and martyrs a literal conformity with the sufferings of the Lord. In the case of Saint James the Just his enemies are the scribes and pharisees; he dies during the passover; for his executioners he prays: "Father, forgive them for they know not what they do"; the destruction of Jerusalem is punishment for having killed him. The same story has been told of other martyrs, and we shall presently see the reflection of the same tradition in the case of Santiago of Galicia.

In other apocryphal writings there is a continued insistence on the brotherhood of Jesus and James: "Is this not the carpenter's son, and is not Mary his mother, and are not his brothers James and Simon?" Here the four brothers mentioned in Matthew 13:55 are reduced to two.[20] For those who venerated the sepulcher in Galicia in the first centuries of the cult of Santiago, the apostle was both "the son of thunder" and the brother of Jesus. Thus there were relics of Santiago, the brother of the Lord—"Sancti Jacobi, Germani Domini"[21]—which we may assign to Santiago of Galicia and not to Saint James the Less, not only because

[19] "Similiter et illum venerabilem Jacobum qui cognominatur Justus; quem referunt Christo Jesu simillimum vita et modo conversationis, ac si ejusdem uteri frater esset gemellus; quem, dicunt, si videro, video ipsum Jesum secundum omnia corporis ejus lineamenta" (in J. B. Lightfoot, *The Apostolic Fathers*, part II, vol. II, p. 655).

[20] "The Acts of Andrew and Mathias," in A. Walker, *Apocryphal Gospels*, 1873, p. 354.

[21] Part of a text written in Visigothic script, and therefore earlier than the twelfth century, found in the Cathedral of Leon (see J. E. Díaz-Jiménez, *Boletín de la Academia de la Historia*, 1892, XX, 126).

of all that we have seen up to now, but also because of the testimony of Arabic historians who write—only, in their case, because it is what they have heard—that the Saint James venerated in Galicia was "the son of the carpenter."

The belief that Jesus and Saint James (of Compostela—Santiago, as he is called, even in this English translation, to keep him distinct from one James or another, including himself in his universal, non-Galician aspect) were twins is reflected in painting. Karl Künstle (*Ikonographie der Heiligen*, Freiburg im Breisgau, 1926, II, 318) says: "The portrait of Saint James by Giovanni Sancti in the sacristy of the Cathedral of Urbino is distinguishable from the figure of Christ only by the long pilgrim's staff. Martin Schäffer represented him with the features of Christ in the Germanic Museum in Nuremberg." As an illustration of this important similarity, I include among the plates that follow in this book a fourteenth-century crucifixion (taken from the journal *Dedalo*, Milan, 1930, XI, 1284) in which the Saint James at the foot of the cross has the same face as Christ, and a painting of Saint James which, as in the case to which Künstle refers, is distinguishable from the Christ in the same painting only by the pilgrim's staff (*Florentine Painting*, III, 2, pt. I, folder 33 [3], by R. Öffner, to whom I am grateful for the permission to reproduce this photograph).

The Arabs felt a lively curiosity about everything religious, and the first historian of religious beliefs was a Hispano-Arab: the Cordovan Ibn Ḥazm (994-1063). In his famous work whose Arabic title reads in English *The decisive word on sects, heterodoxies and denominations*, translated into Spanish by M. Asín as *Historia crítica de las ideas religiosas*, Ibn Ḥazm speaks of certain Spanish Christians who attributed brothers to Jesus. He cannot understand this, "unless they say that Mary engendered them by Joseph the Carpenter, for this is what is affirmed by a certain sect of ancient Christians, one of whom was Julian, Metropolitan of Toledo."[22] Ibn Ḥazm mentions Saint James the Less as the son of Joseph the Carpenter (III, 109), but I have not found in his work

[22] III, 58. Asín notes that no such opinion is to be found in the writings of Saint Julian of Toledo, but that it was held by Apollinaris, who had a pupil named Julian, and that this is the root of Ibn Ḥazm's confusion. According to A. Harnack, no other western church had to contend with as many heresies as the Church in Spain did (*History of Dogma*, London, 1898, V, 282). The belief that Jesus had brothers was held by Helvidius and by the so-called Comarianites. Saint Ambrose and other fathers of the Church avoided the difficulty which the Gospel presented by explaining the brothers of Jesus as Saint Joseph's children by a first marriage (cf. *The Catholic Encyclopedia*, "The Brethren of the Lord").

any concrete reference to the shrine at Compostela. Other writers, on the other hand, give very important references to it. Ibn 'Idhāri wrote a history of Africa and Spain in the thirteenth century, in which, according to the Arabic custom, he gathered up fragments of the most ancient writers. According to him, "Santiago is the *most important Christian shrine* not only in Spain but in all Europe. The church in this city is for them *what the Kaaba is for us*; they invoke Santiago in their oaths, and Christians come on pilgrimage to his shrine from the most remote countries. . . . *Some Christians say that Santiago was the son of Joseph the Carpenter.* . . . The devout come to his temple even from Nubia, the land of the Copts."[23]

Even more important is the testimony of Ibn Ḥayyān, the Cordovan historian (987-1076), recorded by Al-Maqqarī, at the beginning of the seventeenth century, in his famous *Analects*:

"Santiago is a city in the most remote part of Galicia, and one of the shrines most frequently visited, not only by Christians from Spain but also from Europe; for them Santiago is as venerable as the Kaaba in Mecca is for the Moslems, for in the center of their Kaaba is also to be found the object of their supreme adoration [*al-mathal*]. They swear in his name, and they go there on pilgrimages from the most distant parts of Christendom. They claim that the tomb located in that church is that of Saint James, one of the twelve apostles and the one most beloved of Jesus. *The Christians call him the brother of Jesus,* because he never forsook Him.[24] They say that he was bishop of Jerusalem, and that he went about preaching the gospel and making converts until he reached that remote corner of Spain. Then he returned to Syria, where he died at the age of 120 solar years. They also claim that after his death, his disciples brought him and buried him in that church because it was the most distant place in which he had left the imprint of his preaching. Never did any Moorish king think of penetrating that far or in subjecting the city to Islam, because of the inaccessibility of its location and the perils of the road. This undertaking was reserved for Almanzor."[25]

Ibn Ḥayyān was the son of one of Almanzor's secretaries, so that he

---

[23] *Histoire de l'Afrique et de l'Espagne*, translated by E. Fagnan, 1904, II, 491, 494.

[24] The Arabic text uses the word *lazūm*, which means, according to Lane's *Lexicon*, "one who keeps, cleaves, clings or holds fast much, or habitually to a thing."

[25] I have followed the translation of P. de Gayangos, *The History of the Mohammedan Dynasties*, II, 193, but correcting it somewhat (with the help of Professors Hitti and Ziadeh), on the basis of the Arabic text as found in Al-Maqqarī, *Analectes sur l'histoire et la littérature des Arabes d'Espagne*, Leyden, 1855, I, 270.

must have heard a great deal about Santiago, both from Moors and from captive Christians, after the famous expedition that no one had dared to undertake before that military thunderbolt Almanzor. Being there, Ibn Ḥayyān gathered the impression that Jesus and Santiago were considered as brothers because they formed an inseparable pair. This was the belief and feeling of the Christian people around the year 1000, and they had been believing this at least for two centuries. Ibn 'Idhārī knew that Santiago was the son of Joseph the Carpenter, and Ibn Ḥazm was surprised that Christian peoples should accept the belief that Christ had brothers. From different directions, the three Arabic writers confirm our supposition as to what the Spaniards really felt in the ninth and tenth centuries.

In the sermons falsely attributed to Pope Calixtus II, forged by twelfth-century ecclesiastics in Compostela to add still more importance to the cult of the Apostle, we find allusions to his brotherhood with Jesus, although translated now into allegorical language: "It is more important to be the brother of the Lord in the spirit than in the flesh. Consequently, whoever calls Saint James the son of Zebedee the Greater or Saint James the son of Alpheus (the Less) the brother of the Lord speaks the truth."[26] The two beliefs kept alive then, the one in the brotherhood of Santiago and Christ, and the one in the identity or equality of the two Santiagos—and this fits in perfectly with Arabic testimony. Moreover, the sermons of the pseudo-Calixtus are important for the form in which they express what survived of the belief in a Dioscuric Santiago. Carolina Michaëlis de Vasconcellos, who did not suspect any connection between Santiago and the Dioscuri, shrewdly mentions "the great inclination of the coastal peoples in the Northwest of Spain to sidereal superstitions."[27] But Santiago's being a "son of thunder" and his presence at the Transfiguration on Mount Tabor had already established the connection not with superstitions but with astral beliefs, of which there is an echo in the style of the forged sermons: "He shone in

[26] "Majus est esse fratrem Domini spiritualiter quam carnaliter. Quisquis ergo aut Jacobum Zebedaei aut Jacobum Alphaei *fratrem Domini*, verum dicit" (*Sermones quatuor de Sancto Jacobo Apostolo in Gallaecia habiti*, in Migne, *Patrologia*, S. L., vol. 163, col. 1387). Another proof of the confusion between the two Jameses is given us by the *Historia Compostellana*. Mauritius, bishop of Coimbra, discovered the head of Saint James the Less in Jerusalem and brought it to Spain (*España sagrada*, XIX, 252); but the *Historia Compostellana* (*España sagrada*, XX, 222) believes that that head belongs to the body entombed in Compostela. This proves that there was no difficulty in attributing to the patron saint of Spain the head of Jesus' brother, that is, Saint James the Son of Alphaeus (Saint James the Less).
[27] *Cancioneiro da Ajuda*, II, 842.

his conversation like the bright star of the morning amidst the other stars, like a great sanctuary lamp."[28] With the same spiritual and allegorical meaning Santiago "thundered, by command of the Lord, in all Judea and Samaria, and even to the farthest limit of the earth, which is to say, in Galicia; he hurls thunderbolts of terrifying sound, he waters the earth with his rain, and he emits great flashes of light." Both Boanerges "watered the earth with their rain at the same time that they communicated the rain of divine grace to the faithful with their preaching" (col. 1,383). Still today the Portuguese peasant speaks of the thunder as if it were produced by Santiago.

Each of these beliefs had traveled a different road: they belonged to different epochs. There was no rational connection of any kind between them. The ambivalent Santiago of Galicia might be for some the brother of Jesus; for others a half-brother, the son, that is, of Joseph by a previous marriage, an idea rejected by Saint Jerome (346-420) and replaced by another more in accord with his love for virginity; for others, the so-called brothers of Jesus were only his cousins, Joseph had no other wife save the Virgin, and he always remained a virgin himself. But in the fourth and fifth century a *History of Joseph the Carpenter* was current in Arabic according to which Joseph lived for forty-nine years with his first wife, who bore him Judas, Just, James, and Simon.[29] In this enumeration Saint James the Just splits into two persons; whereas in the epistle of the pseudo-Ignatius he is converted into a twin brother of the Lord, a relationship which certain Christians believed in. The thousand-year-old theme of the Dioscuri infiltrated into Christian beliefs,[30]

---

[28] *Patrologia, loc.cit.*, col. 1398.

[29] Cf. E. Amann, *Le protévangile de Jacques*, 1910, pp. 216-217; P. Santyves, *Deux Mythes évangéliques*, 1938, p. 89.

[30] How the substance of the apocryphal writings of the New Testament infiltrated into Spain and what life it had there have never been studied, so far as I know, although, as we have seen, those writings were known and utilized by Priscillian, and they must have persisted in the Mozarabic rite. There is a *Hymnus in diem Sancti Thome Apostoli*, based on the *Acts of Thomas*—that is, Thomas called Didymus, the twin brother of Christ. In these *Acts*, Jesus has the same characteristics as Thomas. Those who confuse him with the Apostle have to be enlightened: "And the Lord said to him, 'I am not Judas, who is the same one as Thomas; I am his brother' " (*The Ante-Nicene Fathers*, New York, 1925, VIII, 537). Thomas, consistent with his Dioscuric ancestry, is a skilled builder of buildings, and it is as such that he figures in the Mozarabic hymn. From India came those asking the Lord for an architect, and the Lord designated Thomas as "aptum artificem." The hymn does not, naturally, say that the two were interchangeable, as it were; it simply calls Thomas "Didimus apostolus" (cf. *The Mozarabic Psalter*, J. P. Gilson, ed., London, 1905, p. 199). Notice how the pseudo-Calixtus reflects this in his sermons when he

and flourished with new intensity and feeling, and this, in the last analysis, interests us more than the actual content of the belief and its origins.

The divine office as sung in the cathedral of Compostela in the eleventh century, and presumably for many years before that, exalted the merits of the Apostle to a degree that was later judged excessive, for the office was changed in the twelfth century. With Mark 3:17 and Matthew 20:21ff. as their inspiration, the offices said:

"Jesus called Santiago Zebedee, and gave him Boanerges for a name. *He called the blessed Santiago aside* in the high mountain, and He was transfigured before him. Santiago and John said to Jesus: Grant us to sit in thy glory, one upon thy right hand and the other upon thy left. Can ye drink of the cup whereof I must drink? But they answered: "We can."[31]

In the sermons of the pseudo-Calixtus an effort was also made to enlarge the role of Santiago in the scene of the Transfiguration, but there is at least a mention of the fact that Peter and John were witnesses of the occasion ("testibus astantibus Petro et Joanne cum eo," *op.cit.*, col. 1,393). The pseudo-Calixtus, although forgetful of the sweet words of the Saviour, "but to sit on my right hand, and on my left, is not mine to give," likewise corrects the exorbitant claim to be seated on the right hand and left hand of Christ. The sermon says, in fact, "that it seems impossible for anyone to sit between the Father and the Son, seeing that the Son himself is at the right hand of the Father, and the Father at the left hand of the Son" (col. 1,394).

But everything seemed justified to the worshipers of the Apostle when the bishop of Compostela raised himself to be the pontiff of Christendom and the pilgrims came to Compostela in increasing number.[32]

---

analyzes the qualifying term *geminus* (twin) as it is applied to Thomas: "Geminus quia duplex in fide fuit." "Thomas dicitur et Didimus, hoc est Christo similis, quia regali statura fuit Domino consimilis" (he was also called didymus, that is, resembling Christ, because in his regal bearing he was altogether like the Lord) (Migne, *Patrologia*, S. L., 163, col. 1,386).

[31] "Ihesus uocauit Iacobum Zebedei et imposuit eis [*sic*] nomina Boanerges. Eduxit Ihesus beatum Iacobum in montem excelsum seorsum, et transfiguratum est ante eum" (A. López Ferreiro, *Historia de la Iglesia de Santiago*, i, 427). The *eis* (to them) betrays the fact that in an earlier version John was also mentioned, since John was present with Peter and James on Mount Tabor (Matthew, 17). But the author of these antiphons was disturbed by the presence of Peter and John along with James, and he converted the Transfiguration and the privilege of contemplating it into a grace granted exclusively to Saint James.

[32] The pilgrimage to Santiago is described in *Las peregrinaciones a Santiago de Compostela* by L. Vázquez de Parga, José M. Lacarra, and J. Uría Ríu, Madrid,

Dazzled by the marvelous halo which had surrounded their Apostle for centuries, his adorers did not limit themselves to singing the foregoing antiphons on the day of his feast—originally the 25th of March, later the 25th of July. There was also a "Passio Sancti Jacobi," in which the parallel with the passion of Christ was accentuated in the manner previously alluded to. The brotherhood was thus complete:

"The Passion of Santiago . . . which he suffered under Herod the king," in a style which recalls that of many apocryphal gospels: "In those days, the Apostle of Our Lord Jesus Christ, Santiago, brother of John, apostle and evangelist, would visit all the land of Judea and of Samaria and would enter into the synagogues." The Apostle works great miracles. Before he is beheaded, he asks his executioner for water just as Christ did (John 19:28). The awareness of the importance of his own person is evident in his reminder to Christ in the form of the prayer he says before his torture: "Thou didst deign to show us the mysteries of the marvelous works. . . . Whilst thou wast on Mount Tabor, and wast transfigured in the divinity of thy Father, to no other apostle didst thou grant to contemplate such prodigious, *save to me*, to Peter, and to John, my brother, etc." When Santiago died, "a great earthquake was produced, the heavens did open, the sea arose, and intolerable thunder was heard; when the earth did open, the larger part of the condemned people were swallowed up, and a brilliant light shone upon that place." His body was taken by his disciples: "they put his body and his head in a bag made of the skin of a fawn, with exquisite perfumes; they carried it from Jerusalem to Galicia, and they buried it in the place where it has been venerated from that day until this."[33]

Consequently, it was not merely a question of the devout enthusiasm of those who adored a certain saint or virgin, and trusted in that saint's extraordinary power. What characterizes the cult of Santiago down to the twelfth century is the intent to bring him as close to Jesus Christ as possible.

Eminent Catholics have cast doubt upon the existence of the body of an apostle of Christ in the shrine in Galicia. The reaction against the cult of Santiago acquired supporters in the seventeenth century, when there were no longer any Moorish enemies against which to make holy war, and when Spanish religiosity was certainly not what it had been in the tenth and eleventh centuries. In 1601 the great Jesuit historian Juan

---

1949, 3 vols. (The origin of the belief in Santiago and its historical meaning are not discussed.)

[33] Latin text in López Ferreiro, *Historia de la Iglesia de Santiago*, I, 392-405.

de Mariana doubted the authenticity of the tomb of Santiago: "Certain grave and learned persons in recent years have found it difficult to believe in the coming of James the Apostle to Spain; other persons, if not the same ones, have found it difficult to believe in the discovery of his sacred body, for *reasons* and writings that move them to hold their opinions."[34] Years later another Jesuit, Father Pimentel, adjudged it more advisable for Spain to put her trust in the protection of Saint Teresa: "He who invokes Saint Teresa will often obtain better favors than he who invokes Santiago."[35] A few years ago the Jesuit Father Z. García Villada insisted on the slight probatory value of the documents that relate to the discovery of the body of Santiago, because the most ancient ones are from the eleventh century, and the suspicion is inevitable that they were forged to provide *a posteriori* justification for a popular and very ancient belief; these texts "indicate the motive which gave some basis for the formation of the tradition that in that tomb were enclosed the remains of the Apostle. This motive is the testimony of the angels and the lights which were seen on certain nights over the place where the tomb is. We cannot certify the degree of veracity in the marvelous account."[36] A Catholic, Monsignor L. Duchesne, thus sums up his disappointing search for rational proofs for the great miracle of Santiago: "In the first third of the ninth century veneration is given to a tomb dating from Roman times, which at that time was believed to be the tomb of Santiago. Why was this believed? We do not know at all."[37]

I cannot share the views of these doctors of the Church, since miracles are believed or they are not believed, but their validity cannot be demonstrated by proofs analogous to those which are legally unimpeachable. This is no place for sworn testimony. Rationalism has been growing more and more characteristic of the most learned history ever since the seventeenth century, and it is only at the cost of some effort that one is able to escape its clutches. Still, we must try, for the simple reason that it is impossible to encompass a vital reality with "rationalist" reason. The efforts to find proofs for the miracle of Santiago did not take into account what would be the meaning of the mere possibility of demonstrating "scientifically" that the body of an Apostle was brought from Haifa to Galicia in the year A.D. 44, in the custody of angels, and that some eight hundred years later it gave signs of its presence. History, that is to say,

[34] *Historia de España*, VII, 5.
[35] *Biblioteca de Autores Españoles*, XLVIII, 445*b*.
[36] *Historia eclesiástica de España*, I, 93.
[37] *Annales du Midi*, 1900, XII, 179.

Giovanni del Biondo's *Crucifixion*, 14th Century. Christ's features and those of St. James are similar. (See p. 140.)

In this representation of St. James, with his traditional staff, the features are unmistakably those of Christ. (See p. 140.)

the integral life of peoples, is not a sequence of "events," isolable by means of logical abstractions (see Chapter 2). The important thing in the present case is the vitality of the belief in Santiago and its fabulous consequences; for it is conceivable that a prodigious event might be "authentic" in the way in which the aforementioned ecclesiastics demand, and at the same time insignificant and sterile as an event connected with human actions and the creation of human values.

There are two realities involved. One is the truth of science, objectifiable and isolable, and the other the truth of any aspect or process of human existence. The boundaries between the real and the imaginary vanish when the imagined is incorporated into the very process of existence, for Shakespeare, anticipating the modern philosophers, has already said that "we are such stuff as dreams are made of." When the substance of one of these dreams integrates the total existence of millions of peoples, then the dream is real, and reality is a dream. The Christian martyrs lived in the reality of Christ as they smiled beatifically while their flesh was torn apart by the wild beasts. Peoples incapable of dying for a faith have never attained a complete reality. Even the most "positive" and materialistic forms of collective life have ultimately been resolved in the devotion to intangible deities, albeit these have the exterior form of a tractor or a skyscraper.

Santiago's shrine arose to face the Mohammedan Kaaba as a display of spiritual force, in a grandiose "mythomachia" or struggle between myths. The city of Santiago aspired to rival Rome and Jerusalem, and not only as the goal of a major pilgrimage. If Rome possessed the bodies of Saint Peter and Saint Paul, if the Islam that had submerged Christian Spain fought under the banner of her prophet-apostle, ninth-century Spain unfurled the ensign of a most ancient belief, magnified in an outburst of defensive anguish, and unmeasurable in any rational way. The presence of a powerful race of infidels over almost the whole face of Spain would necessarily enliven the zeal to be protected by divine powers in the Galicia of the year 800. There is no way of reconstructing today the map of religious beliefs and cults diffused among the Christians at the time the country was invaded by the Saracens (see Chapter 3). In the book of Saint Martin of Braga, *De correctione rusticorum*, some of the beliefs of the Galician peasants of the sixth century are described, and these attest to the predominance of ancient pagan divinities: "Many of the devils expelled from heaven hold sway in the sea, in the rivers, in the springs, and in the woods, and they cause themselves to be adored like gods by the ignorant. The people make sacrifices to them: on the sea they invoke Neptune, on the rivers, the Lamiae, at the springs, the Nymphs, in the woods, Diana."[38] It is undeniable, however, that these and other circumstances only served as a condition for future situations and for the values which made them important and historically real. Santiago, as an expression of Galician life, was not a *necessary* product of any Pagan background, of Priscillian[39] or of the Suevi. The existence of a human event, Santiago or something else, does not consist in elements which the historian separates with his method of dissection, for what happens then is dissection indeed, which is to say, work on a cadaver. We must begin by not calling the belief in Santiago belief in a legend. The term "legend" is simply the epitaph inscribed over what was once a belief, and the belief is intelligible only if we intuit it while it still is a part of human reality and feeling. The history of Santiago of Compostela would consist in reliving what people do with him from the time when he first appears as a belief until he is converted into a legend, into a subject of rational analysis, into the skeleton of history.

No study of comparative religion permits one to see the veneration given to the tomb of the Apostle for what it is, as a case of the opposition and struggle of beliefs. Beliefs are not born and do not prosper because of the caprice of fantasy, because of the malice of priests, or because of the mixture and crossing of various themes or sources, but as something that grows out of the longings, necessities, and limitations of man. The medium in which they live is the masses, infantile or adult, rustic or polished, national or universal. It is not infrequent that what are called legends today were born as a reaction to other, rival beliefs. Monsignor Duchesne, educated in French positivism and rationalism, did not know how it was possible for a Roman tomb to be changed into the tomb of Saint James the Apostle. But if we now approach the question by think-

[38] See M. Menéndez y Pelayo, *Historia de los heterodoxos*, ii, 261. This valuable text should be read in the edition of C. P. Caspari, *Martin von Bracara's Schrift De correctione rusticorum*, Christiania, 1883. The work was written between 572 and 574 for the peasants of the northwest region (diocese of Astorga and Braga). Besides the passage transcribed by Menéndez y Pelayo from the old edition of *España sagrada*, xv, the following should be noted: "It is great madness for a man baptized in the faith of Christ not to celebrate the Lord's day (Sunday), on which Christ was raised from the dead, and for him to celebrate on the other hand the days of Jupiter, Mercury, Venus, and Saturn, who have no proper days, and who were adulterers, magicians, and evil creatures, and died an evil death in their own land" (p. 12). Leaping from the sixth century to the nineteenth, Senhora Michaëlis de Vasconcellos mentions the Portuguese custom of putting a piece of money in the coffin, so that the deceased will be able to pay for his passage on Santiago's ship (*Cancioneiro da Ajuda*, ii, 806).

[39] E. Ch. Babut, *Priscillien et le priscillianisme*, 1909, pp. 120, 233.

ing of life processes, the answer seems simple. The Moslems, moved by a militant faith that had its inspiration in Mahomet, the apostle of God, had extended their dominions from Lisbon to India. The Christians of the northwest had little strength with which to oppose such an irresistible landslide, and thousands of voices must have clamored for celestial help that would sustain their hearts and increase their strength. In the time when wars were made more with valor and singleness of decision than with complicated armaments, the temper of the morale of the combatant was a decisive factor. It was indispensable to have confidence in a tangible, nearby power, that could be opposed to the mortifying shout of "Mahomet" uttered by the enemy. It was urgent to fortify the courage of a people cornered and in constant agony, and whom the collapse of the Visigothic kingdom had left in the first line of defense. For centuries it had been a current belief in Spain that Saint James the Greater had come to preach the Christian faith there. Saint Julian, archbishop of Toledo, was familiar with this tradition and did not accept it; according to him, Saint James preached in Palestine and not in Spain,[40] which reveals that in 686, before the Saracen invasion, the Spanish Church did not feel any special interest in fomenting certain popular beliefs. But in the ninth century, not only was the preaching of a living Santiago urgent; equally urgent was the presence of his sacred body. There was no ecclesiastical guile in this, but rather the historical development of very old beliefs, both pagan and Christian, that had existed for centuries in a form that we shall never know. If people believed that Saint James had come to Spain during his mortal life, they could the more readily conceive that he should return there after his death, although on this second journey his apostolic mission was crossed with Castor and Mars.

This case in which a belief owes its origin to polemical motives is not unique. Everyone knows that the fabled personage Bernardo del Carpio emerged in opposition to Roland and Charlemagne, who were glorified in poems humiliating to Spain. About 1110 the monk of Silos protested, in his Chronicle, against the French epic stories that tried to convert Charlemagne into the liberator of Spain: the Emperor did not conquer the Moors, nor did he rescue the road to Santiago from their control; the Spaniards owed nothing to Roland and his lord. Towards the end of the twelfth century a Spanish minstrel launched Bernardo del Carpio against the arrogant French, in a battle of Roncevaux conceived from

---

[40] Cf. L. Duchesne, in *Annales du Midi*, 1900, XII, 153.

the Spanish point of view—Roland perishes and Charlemagne flees.[41]
A ballad derived from the ancient, lost poem was later to put it thus:

> A bad time you had of it, you Frenchman,
> In the battle of Roncesvaux.

But since it was not a vital matter to believe wholeheartedly in the
deeds of Bernardo del Carpio, King Alphonse the Learned casts doubt
upon the accuracy of the accounts: "Some say that the battle of Ronces-
vaux was in the time of this king Don Alphonse [III, the Great], and
that it was not with Charles the Great but with Charles whom they
called the Bald. . . . And if anyone knows how to explain this better,
and can state it more truthfully, he must be heeded, for we say only
what we find among the Latin writers, in the ancient books."[42] The
learned king washes his hands of the matter, because annihilating Frenchmen was not a topic of the first order for Spain. The people always
regarded the French with special antipathy, while the governing classes
were rather, one way or another, under their enlightening guidance.
Even though Alphonse the Learned's vassals might take the songs of
Bernardo literally, the monarch did not find it urgent to make them feel
that they were right in doing so.[43]

Another example of the legend-belief is that of King Arthur of England. Chronicles prior to the twelfth century spoke of that fabulous
monarch, but they did not make him out to be a personage of major
importance. Yet suddenly between 1136 and 1138 Geoffrey of Monmouth issues his *Historia regum Britanniae*, destined to immortalize
the (rationally) nonexistent king and to influence the poetic sensibility
of Europe profoundly. The motive behind this event was the fact that
the Norman dynasty felt itself humiliated before the kings of France,
who were rich in prestige because they could count Charlemagne as
their antecessor. The subject Britons had little to put against the French
until Geoffrey of Monmouth provided them with a sovereign more

---

[41] Cf. R. Menéndez Pidal, in the *Revista de filología española*, 1917, IV, 151-
152; Th. Heinerman, *Bernardo del Carpio*, 1927.

[42] *Crónica general*, p. 376a.

[43] This was true to such an extent that a Navarrese minstrel-poet of the thirteenth
century could allow Charlemagne, in the Spanish *Roncesvalles*, to say: "I repaired
the roads of the Apostle Santiago." The same poet recognized the French Roland
theme as legitimate for a Spanish poem (cf. R. Menéndez Pidal, in the *Revista de
filología española*, 1917, IV, 151ff.). The author of this *cantar de gesta* very likely
had some sort of connection with French monasteries, which were more interested
in the success of the pilgrimages than in the rehabilitation of the good name of
Castile.

ancient and more illustrious than the great Emperor.[44] The Britannic people thus appeared to be rehabilitated and glorified, and showed for the first time its clear will not to let itself be humiliated by the continent.

Long before this in Spain a Saint James, who was a peaceful apostle, had been converted, thanks to circumstances more dramatic than those that determined the diffusion of the belief in King Arthur, into a martial and invincible Santiago. The militant Santiago had probably not yet penetrated into ecclesiastical literature in the eighth century; a hymn of the time of King Mauregatus (783-788) makes no reference to the tomb, but it does refer to the preaching in Spain: "eiusque [i.e. Saint John's] frater potitus Ispania."[45]

In this hymn the Apostle is still called "Spain's golden and shining head," and he is implored to spare Spain from the pest and from all manner of evils.[46] A half century later he will be implored to exterminate the Saracens, and he will be converted into a counter-Mohammed, and his sanctuary into the counter-Kaaba. Against this background the meaning of such an enormous belief, and its reflections inside and outside Spain, can be understood. The torrent of that faith burst forth from remote, popular springs; its canalization was an ecclesiastical and political task, at once national and international. Down to the twelfth century we can perceive the equivocal interplay between the unrestrained and heretical cult of a multiple Saint James and the orthodox idea that was gradually confining him within his role of Saint James the Great, who retained even so the additional title of the Moorslayer (Matamoros). An analogous equivocation appears in the claim made by the bishops of Compostela to the universal pontificate between the tenth and twelfth centuries, a claim that never reached the critical point of a schism from Rome; nor did the bishops of Santiago even rebel violently against the

[44] Cf. G. H. Gerould, "King Arthur and Politics," in *Speculum*, 1927, II, 37. It had been known for more than a century that King Arthur was the English counterpart of Charlemagne: cf. W. A. Nitze, *ibid.*, p. 318.

[45] *The Mozarabic Psalter*, J. P. Gilson, ed., 1905, pp. 208-209.

[46]
O uere digne sanctior apostole,
caput refulgens aureum Ispanie,
tutorque nobis et patronus uernulus,
uitando pestem esto salus celitus,
omnino pelle morbum, ulcus, facinus. (p. 210)

The reason for dating this hymn between 783 and 788 is the following acrostic: "O rex regum, regem pium Mavrecatum [an Asturian king who reigned from 783 to 788] exaudi cui probe hoc tuo amore prebe."

primacy of Toledo, her not very beloved rival. The extravagant aspirations of the Santiago prelates were above all a spectacular gesture, altogether fitting and proper to the cause of the holy war and for attracting innumerable pilgrims, but they never amounted to a serious effort toward the establishment of a schismatic hierarchy (as far as we know, at any rate). The belief in the invincible warrior was something that the Moor understood and at the same time an effective shield for the Christian. Thus it was that fantasy ran away with those who saw in the Apostle a divine force, a rider on the white horse of the Dioscuri, a protector of agriculture,[47] and a consummate thaumaturge.

But this belief was characterized essentially by the fact that the religious and the militant were integrated in it and that this harmonic contrast should also be present in both its priesthood and its laity. Santiago was a projection of the Moslem holy war, and a support for the holy war which the Christians were to wage against it. At this point the Dioscuric Apostle was converted into the ex-officio master of the military orders, long before such orders had any kind of legalized existence. The ancient refrain went: "Bishop of Santiago, now the sword, now the crosier,"[48] because those prelates fought against either the Norman invaders, or the Moors, or the rebellious members of their own flock when they held the crosier, the symbol of their spiritual authority. In 942 Bishop Rudesindus (later Saint Rosendo) conquered the Norman invaders by invoking the name of the Lord.[49] In 968 Bishop Sisnandus died fighting against the same Nordic peoples, *sagitta percussus*[50] (wounded by an arrow). Such behavior was frequent, and it came to be normal for bishops and abbots to fight like undaunted soldiers, to intervene in politics as counselors of the kings or to direct military campaigns. The ecclesiastical element predominated over the civil just as, in characteristically Spanish fashion, the inspiration and assistance of heaven were more valuable than were such abetments when they were of a purely earthly sort. In the rest of Europe the feudal nobility and the temporal interests operated in history prior to the twelfth century with a vigor equal or superior to that of the ecclesiastics.

The conquest of Coimbra from the Moors by Ferdinand I in 1064 is

---

[47] See C. Michaëlis de Vasconcellos, *Cancioneiro da Ajuda*, ii, 834, for the question of the protection given by Santiago to plants and cattle.

[48] In Spanish: "Obispo de Santiago, ora la espada, ora el blago." In Portuguese: "Bispo de Santiago, ballista e bago." (Cf. C. M. de Vasconcellos, *Cancioneiro da Ajuda*, ii, 816.)

[49] *España sagrada*, xviii, Appendix xxxii.

[50] *Ibid.*, xx, 13.

an excellent example of this peculiar disposition of life, of what I call "theobiosis," something different from theocracy. As a preparation for the difficult conquest of the city, strongly walled and situated on an eminence, the king spent three days before the tomb of the Apostle, who, it was believed, would obtain the much desired victory from God. The offerings were made and the army marched to war, sure of divine protection.[51] The siege began in January of 1064 and in July of the same year hunger forced Coimbra to surrender. The *Chronicle of Alcalá* (*Cronicon Complutense*) says that the king was accompanied by the queen, Doña Sancha, and by the following prelates: Cresconius, of the Apostolic see of Santiago (the one who was excommunicated in 1049 for using the title he was still using in 1064); Vestruarius, of Lugo; Sisnandus, of Viseo; Suarius, of Mondoñedo; the abbots Peter of Guimarães and Arrianus of Celanova. After these a large number of noblemen are mentioned, but as a group and without the citing of any names. Not even one secular name attracted the chronicler's attention.

The city surrendered in the month of July. The royal-episcopal army had passed through serious difficulties because its food supplies were exhausted; but this shortage was relieved by the monks of Lorvão, a Mozarabic monastery enclaved in Moslem territory, thanks to the well-known tolerance of the Saracens. These monks had hidden reserves of cereals in their great silos, and at the opportune moment they were able to supply the Christian army. Thus, combat operations were in charge of bishops and abbots while the services of supply were in the hands of a monastery. Where could we find an event that would be more illuminating for the understanding of such a special way of life? We may relegate to the background the fact that Santiago was a survival of, or reincarnation of, age-old beliefs. The essential thing is rather that the very conditions of Spanish life had made possible a mode of existence by virtue of a belief in which the dividing line between the human and the divine was erased. From the historical and the human point of view, Santiago's Dioscurism and the religious syncretism that his figure represents have here the same value that the chronicle of Saxo Grammaticus has with respect to Shakespeare's *Hamlet*, or Letizia Ramolino with respect to her son Napoleon Bonaparte. Life—the life of art or any other kind of human life—has its foundation in circumstances that are no more indispensable than they are dispensable.

[51] The texts are to be found in A. López Ferreiro, *Historia de la Iglesia de Santiago*, II, 486-489.

The Chronicle of the monk of Silos[52] completes our description of the conquest of Coimbra with a stroke of inestimable value: while the seven months of the siege passed, the people of Santiago were also besieging the Apostle with petitions for prompt and efficacious aid. A Greek pilgrim who was praying day and night by the sacred relic heard people imploring Santiago to fight like a good soldier. He could not conceive how one of Christ's Apostles, a fisherman by trade and a pedestrian who had never been on a horse, could be transformed into an equestrian soldier. This story seems truthful; the pious Greek was probably not the only one to be surprised by a cult that had so little scriptural foundation. The chronicler adds that the Apostle hastened to set aside the doubts of the pilgrim. By the time the account of the Monk of Silos appears in the translated and ornamented version of Alphonse the Learned's *Crónica general*, the pilgrim has been converted into a bishop and is called Estianus:

"While he was there, watching and praying, one day he heard the village folk and the pilgrims who came there say that Saint James appeared as a horseman in the midst of the Christian battles. And the bishop, when he heard this, was troubled, and said to them: 'friends, call him not a horseman but a fisherman.' Forasmuch as he persisted in his obstinacy, it pleased God that he should fall asleep; and Saint James appeared to him in a dream, with keys in his hand, joyful of countenance, and said to him: 'Estianus, you regard it as unseemly for the pilgrims to call me a horseman, and you say that I am not one, wherefore I have come to you now to show myself to you, so that you may never doubt that I am one of Christ's Knights and a helper of the Christians against the Moors.' And the Apostle having thus said, a *very white* horse was brought to him, and he mounted it as well-armed knights do, with all manner of arms, shining and beautiful, and in that dream told him how he wished to go to the aid of the King Don Fernando, who for seven years had been encamped above Coimbra: and 'so that you may be more certain of this, I tell you that with these keys that I have in my hand, I will open tomorrow the city of Coimbra. . . .' And it was found that it truly happened thus later, just as he had said." (p. 487*b*)

When he had won Coimbra, the King Don Fernando "went to Santiago, and there offered his gifts and kept his vigil" (488*a*). The account of this magnificent feat included thus the event itself and its Spanish perspective, its full historical and unique reality. The "fact" that a king

[52] *Crónica Silense*, edit. by F. Santos Coco, 1919, pp. 74-76.

succeeded in capturing a city is in itself an abstraction, that is: something "historically" insufficient.

If a medieval bishop was physically apt, he went into battle like any other *hijodalgo*. If Santiago, to whom Spain had vowed eternal service, was a warrior-apostle, why should the priests in charge of his cult not be soldiers? And if the bishops and abbots were men of war, it seems obvious that the lower clergy would be too. The latter did not customarily wear their long cassocks and cloaks or habits; rather they wore beards and went about armed. This we know because these practices were censured and prohibited by the Councils of Compostela in 1060 and 1063: "Bishops and clergy will wear long outer garments [usque ad talos induantur] . . . they will be tonsured, and they will cut off their beards . . . they will not bear arms."[53]

In the tenth and eleventh centuries the clergy of Santiago already have the air of knights of the military orders, whose character and origin I treat of elsewhere. To be sure, the discipline in Santiago was less rigid than in the cloisters of the primitive orders of the twelfth century, because of the excessive confidence in the power of the Apostle and the copious income from the pilgrimages. The essential thing, however, was the interconnection between the military and the divine, which led to a scorn of contemplation. The belief in the "son of thunder" was developed during years of anguish and oppression, which grew less and less as the Reconquest progressed in the eleventh and twelfth centuries. What had once given courage to the faithful later turned into laxity and an excess of confidence. The most exalted of Apostles brought security, well-being, and an international prestige almost magically won, in a way, just as Peter's Pence converted Rome into a center of irreligion and spiritual indifference—at least until the Council of Trent. The Archbishop of Santiago, Diego Gelmírez (1100-1140), had to forbid his clerics to appear in the choir dressed like secular folk, ill-kempt, wearing beards, or colored clothing, and spurs, and giving the appearance that the Church of the Apostle was manned not by clergy but by knights.[54] It would be a pure and naïve abstraction to speak only of the "relaxation of customs." The reality was that an essentially military saint brought forth fighting prelates and clergy armed and mounted. Diego Gelmírez would first of all have had to change the character of his magical Apostle, thanks to whom he could be surrounded with pontifical pomp and rank.

[53] A. López Ferreiro, *Historia de la Iglesia de Santiago*, II, Appendices, pp. 229, 231, 239.
[54] "Historia compostellana," II, 3, in *España sagrada*, XX, 256.

But the historical trend of Spain already was bound to her destiny. Four hundred years fix the course of the preferences of a people, and by the twelfth century the disposition of the Spanish "dwelling-place" appears clearly outlined.

The Spain of the eleventh and twelfth centuries was the land of Saint James, "Jakobsland," as it was called by the pilgrims from the North of Europe. One can imagine what the faith of the people was like and how much they trusted in their patron saint, when, in 1072, the king of Leon, Alphonse VI, granted certain charter privileges to the city of Valcárcel, near Santiago, because of its love for "the Apostle on whose power the land and the *government of all Spain* are founded."[55] In 1087 his sister, Princess Elvira, as she lies dying, makes an offering to Santiago: "to thee, Apostle Santiago, my most invincible lord and glorious victor."[56] In 1170 King Ferdinand II promises to endow the church of Merida, a dependency of the see of Compostela, as soon as it is reconquered, and thus to continue the good works done by his royal ancestors for the Apostle, "confiding in whose protection, we will conquer the Moors."[57] In his last will and testament Alphonse the Learned (d. 1284) prays to Santiago, "who is our lord and father, whose Alphonse we are."[58]

It would be useless to adduce further testimony to the vital connection between Leon and Castile and the Apostle, the one adored in Santiago ever since the ninth century not only as a pious relic but as a reality present in Spanish life, a reality which guided the direction of national policy. For those monarchs "non erat potestas nisi a Jacobo," and on him were founded the power, the prestige, and the hope of the kingdom. The importance of Santiago as the brother of Christ and as a supernatural force, "invincible and victorious," served as a point of support for the impetus of the Reconquest. The course of life intensified the belief, which was intertwined with innumerable interests, not only political but also ecclesiastical and economic, and it even gave rise to forms of worship which today would be adjudged heterodox.

But history cannot be understood if it is approached from the position of present-day orthodoxy or heterodoxy, or from the point of view of the pedantry of rationalism, which imposes upon life the labels of "myth, superstition, and legend." History does not take place in a vacuum but

---

[55] "Sancto Jacobo Apostolo in cuius ditione terra vel regimen consistit totius Hispaniae" (C. M. Vasconcellos, *Cancioneiro da Ajuda*, II, 797).

[56] A. López Ferreiro, *Historia de la Iglesia de Santiago*, III, Appendix, p. 25.

[57] *Ibid.*, IV, Appendix, p. 108.

[58] Echoed by Quevedo in his *Su espada por Santiago*, in the *Biblioteca de Autores Españoles*, XLVIII, 443*b*.

in the life of the people. Between the eighth and the tenth centuries certain poor masses of people with a strong longing to exist, to subsist, were cornered in the northwest of the Peninsula. Their faith in Santiago was an inseparable element in this longing. Kings and prelates seized upon that faith just as the people did; and this was a coincidence that was to have incalculable consequences, for the people felt themselves to be on the same level with their leaders before the shining sword of the Apostle who made them all equal. The notion of hierarchy was weakened, because the value of the king and the lowliest serf was based rather on the astral power that embraced them both than on the consciousness of their human differences. It was not a question of doing—well or badly—the work of this world, but of a belief and hope in something that floated above the visible world. Assiduous prayer was preferred to efficient action: the greater the gifts to the Holy Apostle, the greater the favors that would be obtained from heaven. In this way, we can understand the laxity of social discipline, the constant disturbances that took place in the city of the Apostle, in which Archbishop Gelmírez at times appeared surrounded with pontifical splendor, in the midst of a dazzling luxury of ornaments and precious jewels, and at others had to hide like a fugitive criminal or leap from roof to roof to escape the fury of the unbridled crowds.

We have lost the key to the understanding of such a strange form of religiosity and its anomalous mixture of motives. The body of one of Christ's companions was adored with such enthusiasm that the disciple left the gentle doctrine of his Master in the shadows. We can understand how medieval Spanish Christianity was more productive of holy wars, propaganda, and thaumaturgy than of reposeful contemplation and of mystic emotion.[59] In the ambit of such religiosity scarcely any room was left for a Saint Bernard, a Saint Francis, a Saint Thomas, or a Meister Eckhardt. The Spanish saints with an international dimension were Saint Domingo (Dominic) de Guzmán in the thirteenth century and Saint Vincent Ferrer in the fifteenth, the scourge of heretics and infidels, who foreshadow Saint Ignatius in the sixteenth century—and let this be said without subtracting from their own greatness, for without them the history of Europe would not have been quite the way it was.

The Spanish Santiago is inseparable from the sustained longing of

[59] I do not believe that Santiago has been the only reason for this most permanent and decisive aspect of Spanish life. What actually has happened is that this special form of religiosity and the meager thinking activity have been two moments of life within the same dwelling-place.

those who sought and found in it a support and meaning for their existence; it is inseparable from the lives of those who lived their belief, a
defensive faith, worked and reworked by the continual need of the people to keep it tenaciously in their grip. The Moors in Spain felt this so
acutely that when Almanzor, at the height of his power, judged it necessary to strike the *coup-de-grâce* against the Christianity of the North, he
destroyed and dispersed the religious communities of Leon and Castile
and finally destroyed the temple of the Apostle (997). He respected
only the clearly defined area in which the holy relic was kept—this in an
extreme gesture of respectful tolerance; the Moslem knew that the power
of sacred objects was not limited by the confines of Islam. He had the
bells of the shrine brought to Cordova as a trophy, on the shoulders of
captives, and there he had them melted and turned into lamps for the
great mosque of Cordova. The damage wrought by this Islamic thunderbolt increased the faith in the holy relic, so holy that not even Almanzor
himself had succeeded in destroying it.

The diffuse and vaguely defined belief in Santiago, extremely ancient
albeit not highly regarded by the Visigothic Church, as we have seen,
acquired volume and structure as a faith opposed and, in a certain way,
similar, to the faith of the Moslems. Unlike the shrines of the Virgin in
Guadalupe, Zaragoza, Montserrat, and many other places, it cannot be
disposed of as a pious fable. Santiago was a positive creed launched
against Mohammedanism; there was nothing illusory about the battles
won under his banner. His name was converted into the national war cry,
in opposition to the cry of the Saracens. In 1140, in the *Poem of Cid*, the
peerless hero of Hispanic Christianity, it is reported that "the Moors call
on Mohammed, and the Christians upon Santiago."[60a]

Santiago, an International Attraction

The shrine of Galicia stood out in various perspectives. To the Saracens
it seemed to be a Christian Mecca, whose efficacy they sensed and sought
to destroy. For the Spanish Christians we now know what it was. Those
in foreign lands converted it into a place of pilgrimage—as venerable
as Rome. In the struggle against the infidel, one of the Lord's apostles
was making war in behalf of the good cause, and this miracle was taking
place in the land of Galicia, a place that was hospitable to miracles and
that also provided an opportunity for the improvement of material fortunes. When the monks of Cluny, in furthering the secular interests of

[60a] "Los moros llaman Mafómat, e los cristianos Santi Yagüe." (l. 73)

the Dukes of Burgundy, undertook the task of restoring scourged Christianity, they must have quickly seen the value of the pilgrims' route as a means of international expansion for the order. Through the diplomacy of the spirit, France got more effective results than she did by fighting the Moors. The crusade into Spain never won the hearts of the French people.

The Spanish Christian Kingdoms found in France the magnet they needed if they were to pull away as much as possible from the attraction of Islam. The kings knew that their power rested only on belief and pure personal courage, and beyond this, their single objective and the limit of their impulses was the conquest of Moslem territory. But now, thanks to Cluny's imperialism, the Christian kings were going to gravitate toward France, whose civilization was to lend its distinctive color to the Christian aspects of the eleventh, twelfth, and thirteenth centuries.[60b] Those Spanish kings used Santiago as a source of international prestige, which they were badly in need of. Since the tenth century, Europe had known of the immensely valuable material and intellectual achievements of Moslem Cordova, and it was to this city that European eyes turned when they were looking for things of this world. Islam made enormous contributions to Europe in mathematics, philosophy, medicine, poetry, and various crafts, and presented, besides, the lovely spectacle of cities like Seville, Cordova, and Almeria, which were in commercial contact with the North of Europe. But the Spanish kings could boast of almost nothing at all save the extraordinary favor that God had shown them in the gift of the body of Santiago.

We can no longer understand clearly what a relic of such great spiritual volume meant in those centuries, when the tokens of divine favor were worth more than any conquest by human effort. God was an effective power in society. He may be on the lips and in the hearts of many today, but war and peace are now determined by other motives, and faith in God does not lead to the meetings of chiefs of state. But in 1010, Alduin, abbot of Saint-Jean-d'Angély (Charente-Inférieure), announced the discovery of the head of John the Baptist, and called several sovereigns together for the purpose of showing it to the faithful. There were Robert II the Pious, of France; Sancho the Great of Navarre; William V, Duke of Aquitaine; as well as princes, counts, and prelates, among whom the most conspicuous were Odon of Champagne and Lan-

[60b] But it did not modify the living disposition of the Spaniards. France brought in a great number of things without changing the least the main course of Spanish life.

dulf of Turin.[61] So dazzling was the assemblage that it ought to have given strong support to the authenticity of the relic and won respect for it with the ignorant as well as with the learned. But such was not the case. The head of John the Baptist begot only a limited cult, and this caused the inestimable merit of the Sepulcher of Compostela to stand out all the more sharply. It was useless to try to compete with it, and to try to launch a new belief dowered with catholicity. The *Acta Sanctorum* call the account of the discovery a fable; but even without this condemnation, how was a relic to gain universal belief for itself if it was already considered an imposture by its French contemporaries? Ademar de Chabannes (988-1034), a monk of Saint Cibar of Angoulême, observes that "it does not appear at all clear who brought the head to this place, nor when, nor whence it was brought, nor whether it belongs to the forerunner of Jesus Christ."[62]

Let us observe first of all the facility with which French monks wrote about subjects of this nature in the eleventh century. Still close to the year 1000—when the Millennium fears were at their strongest—a French monk was already reasoning in terms of clear and incisive ideas in a way that would confirm—if it were not a waste of time to do so— that it is no mere accident that Descartes's philosophy is French. If a Father Ademar or a Monsignor Duchesne had lived next door to the tomb of Santiago in the ninth century, the belief in the Son of Thunder would not have passed beyond the boundaries of Iria Flavia. But the history of each people is the realization of a different disposition of life.

Very likely the basic motive behind the appearance of the Baptist's head in Saint-Jean-d'Angély was the fact that that abbey was located on the road which brought the pilgrims to Santiago. It is well known that since the eleventh century miracles had been blossoming along the *via francigena*, whose starting point was St. James Street, *rue Saint-Jacques*, in Paris. The celestial route of Santiago traced in the milky way had its terrestrial counterpart in a *via miraculosa*, on which one set out in Paris and ended at the tomb of the invincible Apostle. This is the explanation I find for the sudden appearance of the Head of Saint John the Baptist and for the fact that William V of Aquitaine, with such close ancestral ties to Cluny, should immediately call upon the Abbot Odilon to introduce the Cluniac observance in Saint-Jean-d'Angély, which was raised

---

[61] E. Sackur, *Die Cluniacenser*, II, 68.

[62] "A quo tamen vel quo tempore vel unde huc delatum, vel si praecursoris Domini sit, haudquaquam fideliter patet" ("Historiarum libri tres," in *Patrologia*, 141, col. 67).

overnight to the rank of an Apostolic church; that is, its efficiency and rank were increased because of its strategic location.

At this point the presence of Sancho the Great of Navarre at that meeting of sovereigns in France becomes especially interesting, because, as is well known, shortly after that, the Navarrese monarch gave to the monks of Cluny the monasteries of San Juan de la Peña and of San Salvador de Leire (1022).[63] The pilgrims came upon these monasteries soon after crossing the Pyrenees, as they went along the route that joined the main road in Puente la Reina. The Benedictine order of Cluny had been founded in 910 through the initiative of William the Pious, Duke of Aquitaine. Soon it was very widespread, thanks to the support of great lords who, in their turn, abetted by the Cluniacensians, attained to a power in matters spiritual and political that, although recognized by Rome, was at the same time parallel with the authority of the Pope. The interests of the Duchy of Burgundy and the monks of Cluny went hand in hand.

There were already Cluniac monasteries in Catalonia, near the Pyrenees,[64] in 962, which should cause no surprise in view of the fact that primitive Catalonia was a prolongation of France, the Hispanic March of the Carolingians. But the fact that there were French monasteries in tenth-century Catalonia does not explain why they should also have been in the rest of Spain; there were Carthusians in Catalonia as early as the twelfth century, but this order did not appear in Castile until the end of the fourteenth. If we are to discover the beginnings of the movement of the monks of Cluny into Navarre, we must look into the relations between Sancho the Great and William V of Aquitaine, the two who met in 1010, as we have seen, over the relic of Saint John the Baptist. If King Sancho of Navarre, who reigned from 1000 to 1033, was the first—as Menéndez Pidal (*op.cit.*, p. 118) rightly says—to be concerned with "bringing Spain out of the isolation into which she had fallen with respect to Europe," the truth is that this fact is inseparable from the contact with Europe already established by means of the road to Santiago. Although Sancho the Great was at that time the most important of the Hispanic kings, it was the pilgrimage that raised him to a position of international eminence—because he ruled the zone through which those increasing numbers of people going to Compostela entered Spain at the beginning of the eleventh century. The Duke of Aquitaine (c. 959-1030) was among these: "Since the days of his youth he had been in the habit

[63] R. Menéndez Pidal, *La España del Cid*, p. 119.
[64] J. Pérez de Úrbel, *Los monjes españoles en la Edad Media*, 1933, II, 416ff.

of visiting the resting place of the apostles in Rome every year, and if he happened not to go to Rome then he substituted for that holy pilgrimage the one to Santiago of Galicia instead."[65] William lived and traveled more with the dignity of a king than of a duke, and his pilgrimage was therefore an event that attracted attention. The pilgrimage led him to establish friendly contact with Sancho of Navarre and with Alphonse V of Leon (999-1028): "He had captured the sympathy of those kings to the point of annually receiving their ambassadors, who brought him precious gifts, to which he responded with even more valuable gifts."[66]

In these gifts to the Duke of Aquitaine, I see the foreshadowing of the contributions which Sancho the Great, his son Ferdinand I, and his grandson Alphonse VI later pay to Cluny. It was the pilgrimage that caused Leon and Navarre to turn their eyes to France, even though Leon, devastated by Almanzor and his successors, may not have possessed the means of Navarre, at that time full of impetus, to realize advantages out of such contacts. In any case, in these frequent visits of the Duke of Aquitaine, so closely allied with Cluny, are to be found the motives immediately behind the introduction of the French order into the Christian kingdoms of Spain.

For the Hispanic monarchs the pilgrimage was a source of holiness, prestige, power, and wealth, which the national monasticism was not in condition to take sufficient advantage of. It was necessary to bring in "engineers" from the outside to organize an adequate system of *do ut des* between Spain and the rest of Christianity; in this way the importance of the Peninsular kingdoms both with respect to Islam and with respect to Europe would be increased. The razing of the city of Santiago by Almanzor, who at the same time left the holy relic untouched, propagated the fame of the Apostle and provided a unique excuse for bringing in clergy well instructed in matters pertaining to God. When Sancho the Great gave the Monastery of Oña to Cluny in 1033, he said that "at that time the monastic order, the most excellent of the orders of the Church, was unknown in all our fatherland,"[67] an opinion shared generally by kings and great lords in the eleventh century. The fact that many of the monasteries were "double," that is, for both monks and nuns, had given rise to disorders that, if they were not exclusively Spanish, justified the monastic policy of the sovereigns, whose basic idea was

[65] Ademar de Chabannes, in *Patrologia*, 141, col. 56.

[66] The biography of William of Aquitaine can be found in the *Histoire littéraire de la France*, VII, 284, or in Migne's *Patrologia*, 141, col. 823.

[67] A. de Yepes, *Crónica general de la orden de San Benito*, 1615, folio 467.

to attract distinguished people and the wealth and culture of Europe. In anticipation of enlightened despotism, Spain for the first time and through the energetic action of her kings revealed her intention of "Europeanizing" herself, of assuaging the pains of isolation and self-deprecation. The Monk of San Pedro de Arlanza, who composed the *Poem of Fernán González* around 1240, said then what had been felt for centuries and what may easily be sensed in everything that I have written here on this subject: God favored Spain with the body of the Apostle, for

> *He wished to raise her over England and France:*
> See how not one apostle lies in all those lands.[68]

It is indeed worth noting the extent to which Santiago was felt to be a remedy for the national sense of insecurity.

The prestige had come from God himself, and now the monks of Cluny were bidden to organize it from the point of view of human interests. As the eleventh century went on, the French infusion became more perceptible. The first bishop of reconquered Toledo (1085) was French, as were the monks and canons. An echo of this religious colonization is heard in the considerable number of French words that entered the language earlier than the thirteenth century.[69] The introduc-

---

[68] *De Inglaterra y Francia, quísola mejorar,*
[ved] que non yaz apóstol en tod aquel
  logar.   (155)

[69] Instances of adopted French words similar to the Arabic ones which I quote on p. 96 could be mentioned here. The projection of French life on medieval Spain has not sufficiently been investigated. I have studied some aspects of the vocabulary in *Lengua, enseñanza y literatura,* 1924, pp. 102-139. More technical are the several papers I devoted to this topic in *Revista de Filología Española,* Madrid, between 1921 and 1923: "Aranceles de aduanas del siglo XIII" (Spanish tariffs of the 13th century). Waves of immigrants, especially from Southern France, came to Christian Spain during the twelfth century. The French colony had its own justice in Oviedo (Asturias); there was a "Robert, judice de illos francos" in 1114 (R. Lapesa, *Asturiano y provenzal en el Fuero de Avilés,* Salamanca, 1948, p. 10). Professor Lapesa has shown that the strangeness of the language of this *fuero* (municipal law) is due to the fact that it was written by a Provençal who tried to use the local Spanish dialect. Words of French provenience were numerous in Old Spanish and refer to many zones of life: food (*jamón,* ham; *manjar,* dish); church (*deán,* head of the chapter; *monje,* monk; *fraile,* friar; *vinajeras,* altar-cruet); public institutions (*chanceller,* chancelor; *barnaje,* baronage, feat; *duque,* duke); housing (*jardín,* garden; *chimenea,* fireplace; *colcha,* bed, and bedspread); etc. These few Gallicisms in Old Spanish are mentioned here just to emphasize the difference in the adoption of French and Arabic words by the Spanish-speaking people. French words were practically nonexistent before the eleventh century, when the Moors already had left deep imprints in Spanish life. Most of the adopted French words came through the channel of churchmen, of people invested with some sort of authority or prestige, or

tion of French words into Spanish and Portuguese is not comparable to what happened in England, where French and Anglo-Saxon were mixed to produce a third language; Spanish went on being essentially what it had been, although augmented by words (things) which in the eleventh and twelfth centuries corresponded to what had been taken from Arabic in the three hundred years preceding.

The Cluniac invasion and what came after it began to modify the Mozarabe-Islamic aspect of the Christian zone of the Peninsula. The Roman rite, used in Cluny, replaced the Mozarabic rite; the script and the style of architecture were changed; literature, highly original as it was (the *Poema del Cid*, 1140, was among the greatest literary works of its epoch), turned to French sources and forms (the religious theater; the poetic stanza of four fourteen-syllable verses in monorhyme, called *cuaderna vía*;[70] international themes of both religious and profane nature). But whether the Spaniard slept on an Arabic *almadraque* (mattress), or on a French *colchón*, his heroic and personal tension was always the same. He did not become Arab or French.

The Cluniac monasteries marked the way of the pilgrims from San Juan de la Peña to Galicia. Although they practiced charity with the needy, the essential thing was that there should be "no lack of rich travelers and pilgrims who would pay generously for the hospitality that was extended to them."[71] Monasteries like Sahagún came to own immense properties, gifts from people who hoped to attain eternal salvation through the prayers of the monks. This demonstrates that if the people in general looked askance at the monks, the wealthy folk did not feel the same way. Countess Teresa de Carrión, the great-granddaughter

---

simply through reading French literature. At times the vocabulary reflects the very presence of French rogues and rascals with which the road to Santiago was teeming (see Spanish text p. 168). The Arabization of some zones of the Old Spanish language depended, as it were, on a horizontal process; the Gallicization (generally speaking) was rather the result of a vertical process. Such symbiotic phenomena in Spanish as *amanecí, hidalgo, poridad*, etc., could not be produced from Spanish intercourse with French. The vital situation of Spaniards in their relationship was with French monks, clerks, court officers, wealthy merchants, literary texts or—with hosts of French cads. A living and not abstract study of Spanish Gallicisms should take this complex historical reality into account. French words in Old Spanish along with the presence of Arabisms enable us to envision Spanish life between the eighth and the thirteenth centuries as a sort of pendulum oscillating between East and West —and without a consciousness of firm security within Spain herself.

[70] The *cuaderna vía* was used in religious and learned poems (lives of saints, *Poem of Alexander*, etc.). French origin of this form of poetry has been proved by R. Menéndez Pidal, *Poesía juglaresca*, pp. 353-354.

[71] J. Pérez de Úrbel, *Los monjes españoles en la Edad Media*, II, 446-448.

of the Leonese king, Vermudo II, and a widow of the powerful Gómez Díaz,[72] made a gift to Cluny in 1076 of the magnificent monastery of San Zoil de Carrión, on the road "qui discurrit ad Sanctum Jacobum": "dwelling in Spain, we heard of the fame of the town of Cluny and of the lord abbot Hugh, a holy man of that community, whose monks live in the service of God, under the discipline of his rule and turning their steps toward heaven without flagging." In 1077 the countess confirmed her donation, which was signed by the bishop of Santiago, Diego Peláez,[73] to prove, if it were necessary, that the whole matter of Cluny and the pilgrimage to Santiago are one and the same thing.

The aristocracy followed the example of the kings. Ferdinand I (d. 1065) paid Cluny an annual tribute of a thousand gold dirhems. In phrases of sweet submission, his son Alphonse VI duplicated the sum, in testimony of even firmer spiritual vassalage: "to Hugh, Abbot of Cluny, torch quickened by the divine fire, river of honey and sweetness." The motives behind such vassalage are already familiar to us. But it must be borne in mind that there was no sense of self-deprecation in this attitude, since the sincere feeling of catholicity erased any notion of frontiers in the kingdom of God. In any case, the submission to Cluny implied a cession of what we would today call areas of sovereignty, because the monks formed a completely autonomous institution. But it was necessary to fortify the Christian kingdoms, which had scarcely any defense save what their kings themselves provided; that is, they had nothing like the feudalism of the French states. One of the essential reasons for the absence of feudalism was the fact that the royal power was articulated with the people through Jewish and Moorish functionaries (see Chapters 12 and 13). There were no centers of economic and cultural wealth around which public life could be organized. The production of human values was scant, whereas there was a torrent of divine miracles. Santiago was the supreme thaumaturge, and after him, in each region there existed other promoters of miracles: Saints Facundus and Primitivus, in Sahagún; Saint Aemilianus, in La Rioja; and a hundred others. There were also miracle-workers of flesh and blood; in 1083, Alphonse VI gave "the chapel of Saint John and a lodging place in the east gate of Burgos,"[74] a place where the pilgrims passed, to a French hermit who worked miracles in front of the monarch while riding on his little

---

[72] A relative of the famous *Infantes* of Carrión in the *Poema del Cid*; cf. R. Menéndez Pidal, *Cantar de Mío Cid*, pp. 540ff.

[73] *Recueil des chartes de l'abbaye de Cluny*, 1888, IV, 604, 622.

[74] R. Menéndez Pidal, *La España del Cid*, p. 273.

donkey. Spaniards were intoxicated with divinity, quite as much as her Islamic neighbors. It is not, then, the religiosity of the Middle Ages, more or less uniform throughout Western Europe, that determined the peculiarity of Spain. The concept of the Middle Ages is an abstraction that is of little use when we confront the immediate reality of a human group at a given moment in time. What characterized Spanish life at that time was not an abstract medievalism but an immense disproportion between longing for the supernatural and interest in thought and its objective results, a disproportion which has affected Spanish life down to the present moment. In the eleventh century there was predominance of belief over human deeds (even over theological thought), just as literature and art were predominant over science during the seventeenth century. In any historical unity (that of a people), each particular manifestation of life depends on what coexists around it. In this respect, the religion of eleventh-century Spain is not identical with that of the same period in France; nor was seventeenth-century Spanish literature produced and lived like its contemporaries in Europe. We have seen the effort to establish in France a cult around the head of Saint John, an effort which at first glance seems to be a generic medieval trait. But following hard upon this came the monk Ademar with his demolishing criticism. At the beginning of the twelfth century the monastery of Saint Médard (Soissons) exhibited one of the child Jesus's milk teeth, and in the face of this exhibition up rose the Abbot of Nogent-sous-Coucy and treated the other monks as the perpetrators of imposture: "Attendite, falsarii. . . ."[75] Rivalries among the monks, say the positivists. But did not such rivalries go on in Spain too, and fierce ones at that? Accuracy requires us to think that the French monks of the eleventh and twelfth centuries already existed in the same life disposition that was later to manifest itself in Jean de Meun, Descartes, and the Encyclopedia. The French disposition of life (i.e., the French historical reality) existed in the eleventh century as well as in the eighteenth, with no more difference in contents than the space of seven hundred years implies. Because France was like this, the *Chanson de Roland* is not the *Poema del Cid*; nor is there in France a national hero of flesh and blood like Rodrigo Díaz, or writers like Saint Teresa and Cervantes; but there is indeed a Descartes, a Racine, and also a Bossuet and a Voltaire.

But we must sharpen our focus yet a little more to see quite clearly that religion in Spain and in France did not "function" in the same way,

---

[75] Migne, *Patrologia*, 156, col. 652. Cf. M. Bloch, *Les rois thaumaturges*, p. 29.

in spite of the uniformity imposed by the not very exact concept of the Middle Ages. In 987 Robert II, called the Pious, was anointed king of France, and this monarch is the first to appear gifted with the virtue of curing scrofula, by the laying on of hands and the making of the sign of the cross. This miraculous faculty continued to be an adjunct of the French monarchy, and it was exercised in the eleventh century just as it was in the nineteenth. Robert II, who was the son of the usurper Hugh Capet, did not feel very secure on his throne. Fearing lest the legitimacy of the new dynasty should be disputed, his more faithful partisans thought it advisable to attribute to the new monarch the power to cure scrofula. If the monarch had been a usurper, God would not have granted him the miraculous gift of healing the sick.[76] I cannot attempt to discuss how that surprising innovation originated; what interests me here is its possible connection with the French life structure, what the meaning is of the fact that the Capetian kings should arrogate to themselves the power to cure scrofula.

Toward the year 1000, when the people were transfixed with terror and awaiting the end of time, and trusted in everything except themselves, certain Frenchmen deemed it useful and possible to incorporate divine powers in a human being and cause him to work miracles reserved only for the chosen of God. This decision to endow the kings of France with thaumaturgic power implied a sanctification en bloc and a priori of a whole dynasty, of a national cause anchored in human time and space. A divine transfusion was given to purely earthly realities. If the miraculous faculty of curing scrofula seems at first glance to be more thaumaturgic than the intervention of Santiago, a little thought will lead to exactly the opposite conclusions. With the practice of such a rite *a supernatural power was secularized* and regularized in a way impossible even for a pope.

The Norman dynasty in England saw at once how useful it would be to possess the same divine virtues, and Henry I Beauclerc initiated the miraculous cure of scrofula in the twelfth century with the same success as his continental colleague. His only precaution was to invent the fiction that the last Anglo-Saxon king, Edward the Confessor, had already cured scrofula. With this, and with the opportune resurrection in myth of the fabulous king Arthur, the Norman dynasty sent its roots down deep into English soil, without seeking support from heavenly divinities. France and England started their modern life anchored in human interests, in the extraordinary power and prestige of their monarchs.

[76] Bloch, *op.cit.*, pp. 79-81.

The French kings dispensed their therapeutic grace liberally. There even were Spaniards who went to be touched by the king. We have testimony of this as late as 1602.[77] In the 321st *cantiga* of Alphonse the Learned there is an excellent example of the skeptical and ironic reaction of the Spaniards who had no need of such aid. A certain child in Cordova was suffering from

> A very grave illness
> That she had in her neck;
> It was called *lamparones* [scrofula].

The physicians did not succeed in curing her, and a "good man" advised her mother to take her to the king, because

> All the Christian kings
> Have that as one of their powers.

But here is the monarch's reply:

> To what you say to me
> I answer thus and say
> That what you counsel me
> Is not worth one rotten fig.
> Your tongue is too loose
> And you talk as lightly as a swallow.
> For you say I have that power,
> And you speak nonsense.

The "good man" was speaking as lightly and stupidly as a swallow. Instead of the nonsense of claiming that the king would cure her, the king himself ordered the child be taken to "her majesty the Virgin,"

> who is clothed
> in a mantle of scarlet.

They wash the holy image and the child Jesus with water; they pour the water into a chalice "in which God's blood is made from the wine of the grape," and they let the little sick girl drink of it for as many days as the word *Maria* has letters; on the fourth day, the scrofula disappears.

It is an excellent anecdote. To believe that a human being, just because he is a king, can work miracles, is nonsense; but it is wisdom to cast a real spell with Christian ingredients, handled in the manner of the best Judaico-Islamic magic. Let us observe that the whole process takes place as a play of forces and actions exterior to the person. The very language

[77] *Ibid.*, p. 312.

of the *cantiga* expresses this: The Virgin appears "clothed" (*envolta*) in a scarlet mantle, and she expends her powers through the water which touches her, the water receiving in turn the powers of the chalice, which is the crucible of divine transmutation. Nor do the letters of the name of Maria have as such any power of their own to work a miracle, but only by the fact that they are five in number. Things, then, are not things as such but, rather, detached aspects—ghosts—that float about as forms without matter, shadows without substance. Each of these forms glides over the other, for, as in Islam, the only substantial reality is God.[78] The reality of nature is nothing but the flux of aspects, and each thing is cast in an "exterior" so that it can have contact with the "exterior" of other things, and so, to the infinity of the decorative arabesque, which has no content except its own flux. Such was the structure of the natural world for the Learned king, as far as notions about reality were concerned. What matters is that the spell I have described here is part of a royal deed, and not a tale such as old women tell by the fireplace, because there was no line that absolutely divided the learned from the popular, either then or later. Now it is understandable why the effort of the French kings to cure the scrofula was treated as nonsense. Those kings departed from the magical construction of the world, they absorbed and simplified the supernatural, and converted it into an attribute of royalty (like the crown and the scepter), not into a play of appearances floating over man. In Spain, there was to be no humanizing or regulating of the divine, because that would have destroyed the whole Spanish system, beginning with Santiago, a belief to which no one had openly attributed a taint of falsity before 1600. The kings of Spain depended not on themselves, but on supernatural powers.

It was easy to bring pilgrims to Santiago, and it was possible to conquer the Moors with naked energy and heroic exaltation. It was a more arduous task to bring the powers that came down like rain from heaven into articulation with everyday existence, and it was in order to accomplish this task that the Cluniac monks were brought in, those monks who "ad caelestia sine taedio tendunt." On the other hand it would have been unjust to expect the Spanish monks to organize kingdoms with depopulated frontiers and lands milked dry by an endemic war and lacking in productive ability other than the common skills of the Moors and Jews of that time. The Christian wealth usually came from booty captured from the Saracens, or from the pilgrimage. Alphonse VI believed that

[78] A more ample treatment of this will be found in the chapter on the Archpriest of Hita.

in the same impulse the Cluniac monks would resolve both the problems of heaven and those of earth,[79] and he was deceived. An individual monk can be a saint or an original thinker; but a religious order is an institution tied to the interests of the times, and the Cluniac monks were first and foremost at the service of the political interests of the Duchy of Burgundy. History cannot be constructed out of sighs of lamentation and hymns of joy, but the truth is that the most important consequences of the coming of Cluny to Spain were regrettably political. The abbot of Cluny promoted the marriage of Alphonse VI with Constanza, the daughter of the Duke of Burgundy; later the daughters of the king, Urraca and Teresa, married the Counts Raymond and Henry of Burgundy. Leon and Castile escaped from the provincialism (with an Islamic accent) of the Mozarabic tradition to fall into the net of Burgundy and Cluny. While the Spaniards, under the protection of Santiago, were fighting against the Almorávides the dioceses were being populated with French bishops, most of them of Cluniac origin, and the crown of Alphonse VI was about to pass to the head of a foreigner, Raymond of Burgundy. For Cluny, Spain was a second Holy Land in which she could create a kingdom like that of Jerusalem, only very near to the Pyrenees. The French Imperial designs in 1100, so far as designs are concerned, were analogous to those of 1800; the Napoleon of that time was that abbot of abbots, Hugh of Cluny.

Portugal Is Made Independent

Such was the course of the Spanish life with which we are now concerned, and whose total quality we should not lose light of. Santiago, once he was born into the life of belief, unfolded his religio-political virtues; the great dimensions of his personality caused him to be accepted in parts far from Spain with the same faith as in his own land. So inimita-

---

[79] One cannot accept the explanation that Cluny was called upon because the campaigns of Almanzor and his immediate followers left the Spanish monasteries in ruins. In the first place, the great monasteries were still occupied by their own communities when they were turned over to the Burgundian monks, and it was for this reason even difficult at times to install the foreigners in the monastic properties. Moreover, the destruction wrought by Almanzor has been exaggerated: for instance, life went on uninterrupted for a long time in the monastery of Abellar, near Leon; Abbot Tehodus received donations in 994, 997, and 1001, the year in which he was replaced by Abbot Fredenandus. It was not Almanzor but the Navarrese who destroyed Abellar in 1034 and 1035. (Cf. J. E. Díaz-Jiménez, in the *Boletín de la Academia de la Historia*, 1892, xx, 149-150. I have not been able to consult Rafael Alcocer's article, "Relaciones económicas entre los reyes de España y Cluny" in the *Revista Histórica de Valladolid*, 1918, i, 161-168; 201-209.)

ble was his originality that all attempts to replace him failed, as happened in the case of Saint-Jean-d'Angély. The pilgrimage was the result of his international validity, and within its broad stream flowed the elements of piety, prestige, corruption, and material wealth. Aquitaine and Burgundy used the pilgrimage for their own benefit, with a view to the domination of Christian Spain.[80] The weakness of Alphonse VI, and the urgency he felt for exalting his own position and that of his kingdom, made him a docile instrument of the policy of Cluny, which was also the policy of the Duchy of Burgundy. He first married Inez of Aquitaine (a reminder of the activities of Cluny as carried on by the Duchy of Aquitaine and the kingdom of Navarre); then he married Constance, the daughter of the Duke of Burgundy. His sons-in-law, Henry and Raymond, belonged to the ducal house of Burgundy, just as did their relative, Abbot Hugh of Cluny. The death of Count Raymond, heir to Alphonse's throne, disturbed the Cluny's plans with respect to Leon and Castile, plans which at that time were being concentrated on Portugal, a fief granted by Alphonse VI to his son-in-law Count Henry. Thus, the independence of Portugal, arrived at by indirect but very clear routes, is inseparable from the belief in Santiago.

With great acumen, Senhora Michaëlis de Vasconcellos and Teófilo Braga wrote that "only *events* made an independent state out of Portugal, and created little by little in her inhabitants the sense of being a separate people."[81] But now these events must be regarded in the indirect light shed upon them by the Apostle Santiago and Burgundian

[80] The international interventions of the eleventh century must not be confused in kind with those of our own times, aimed merely at bringing about military and economic advantages. The people of the eleventh century lived in God and felt his power, just as today we feel the action of physical forces and are conscious of them. In the eleventh century there was no separation of the spiritual and the temporal; and the proportion in which values were assigned to each of those aspects of life, and the greater or lesser accent on each of them, introduced decisive differences among the peoples of Europe. It would be a mistake, then, to interpret the policy of the French religious orders as insincere maneuvering with the sole end of improving their financial situation. In the tenth, eleventh, and twelfth centuries everything human was included in the sphere of the divine.

[81] *Geschichte der portugiesischen Literatur*, in Gröber's *Grundriss*, ii, 2, p. 129. I think that what I say holds true in spite of Pierre David's book *Etudes historiques sur la Galice et le Portugal du VIe au XIIe siècle*, Lisbon, 1947. The conquest of Lisbon in 1147 was chiefly an international enterprise; the army included more Germans, Flemish, French, and English soldiers than Portuguese (see Alfredo Pimenta, *Fontes medievais da História de Portugal*, 1948, pp. 124-130). The same applies to the conquest of the important stronghold of Silves (pp. 159-189). Many other facts could be quoted to support my idea, which I try to make compatible with the current patriotic interpretation of Portuguese history in Appendix I.

imperialism. The same motives that brought the Cluniac monks to establish their monasteries at strategic places along the route of the pilgrimage also brought Count Henry to Spain; for these same reasons he married Teresa, an illegitimate daughter of Alphonse VI, and thus he also received in fief the lands to the south of Galicia. Henry was annoyed to see the better luck of his cousin Raymond, married to the first-born and legitimate daughter Urraca, and there was serious friction between them, very harmful to the Cluniac policy. Abbot Hugh sent an emissary who obtained an agreement from both counts: upon the death of the king, the rich treasure of Toledo would be divided, two parts to go to Raymond and the rest to Henry, who would also receive the land of Toledo in fief, and if not Toledo, then Galicia. The death of Raymond of Burgundy disarranged everything; the king died in 1109, and his widow, Urraca, occupied the throne for so long as it would take the child Alphonse VII to reach his majority. Many of the nobles feared lest a woman would not be able to face the dangers which beset Leon and Castile, and perhaps because they wanted to counter the French influences, they advised Urraca to marry King Alphonse I of Aragon—an excellent idea in theory, in which was already to be discerned the intention of uniting all Spain into a single kingdom. But the time for Ferdinand and Isabella had not yet arrived, and the marriage begot great disasters, for Alphonse I did not take possession of the kingdom; he devastated it like a cruel invader. The Church of Santiago, the Cluniac Monks, and the County of Portugal opposed the Aragonese. We still know nothing of what lay beneath these events; but it is permissible to think that the chaos created by that intestine war was due to the impossibility of harmonizing the interests of the French clergy, the personality of Leon and Castile, and the violence of Alphonse I, who went so far as to kill with his own hands a Galician nobleman who was holding onto the skirts of Queen Urraca, a refuge considered inviolable. Such chaos was used to good advantage by Count Henry (d. 1112) and his widow Teresa, who had already assumed the title of queen in 1115 and thus soothed her feeling of inferiority in birth and rank, to Queen Urraca, her half-sister.[82] The French interests gained more supporters in the Portuguese County with the arrival of the Knights Templar and the Cistercian monks, just as closely allied with Burgundy as Cluny was. Then, what decided the matter was that Henry and Teresa had as an heir Alphonse Henriques, who from his youth showed excellent gifts as

[82] P. B. Gams, *Kirchengeschichte von Spanien*, 1876, III, 64ff.

both a soldier and a ruler, gifts that were enhanced by the atmosphere of rebellion built up by his father and so well described in the Chronicle of the archbishop Rodrigo Jiménez de Rada at the beginning of the thirteenth century: "Already in the lifetime of Alphonse VI Count Henry of Burgundy began to rebel a little, although so long as the king lived, Henry did not withdraw his homage; he continued to do his best in throwing the Moors back from the border, but in the lands he retook, he kept the sovereignty for himself. In spite of this, he came with all his people when he was called to the aid of the royal army, or to attend at court. Alphonse VI, out of kindness, or rather out of weakness, tolerated Henry's moves toward independence because Henry was his son-in-law; and in this Alphonse showed great lack of foresight."[83]

Such were the "events" that were at the roots of the independence of Portugal, and little by little they produced motives for her separation from Castile and Leon.[84] Portugal was born as the result of the ambition of Count Henry, supported by Burgundy and Cluny, and by the weakness of Alphonse VI, this kind of thing being the very food of civil wars. Portugal was born and grew out of her will not to be Castile; to this fact she indubitably owes great accomplishments as well as certain wretched experiences.

Burgundy tried to bring about in Castile what the Normans had done in England some years before; that is, she tried to install a foreign dynasty. The struggles with Islam and Castilian vitality caused the project to miscarry, but they did not prevent the birth of a kingdom on the west side of the Peninsula. That kingdom did not arise out of its own existence —as happened in the Castile of Count Fernán González—but out of exterior ambitions. The proof of this is that the Hispano-Galician tradition of Portugal remained intact; the eloquent sign of this is the total lack of epic poetry. If Portuguese bellicosity had proceeded from the inner will of the people, as in Castile, Count Henry, or his son Alphonse Henriques, would have been converted into epic themes. But the foreigners who came to populate the land were unable to create any kind of national epic, and the Galicians who came from the north went on being lyrical dreamers. Their will to fight came to them from the outside. The only poetic aureole surrounding Alphonse Henriques is fitted to a model

[83] *De rebus Hispaniae*, VII, 5, edition of the *Hispaniae Illustratae*, II, 114.

[84] It would be senseless to explain the separation of Portugal as the consequence of certain hidden peculiarities of its region, when this region is next to Galicia, which did not separate from Spain. National communities do not exist unless they express their consciousness of being as they are. Without the Burgundian counts and their will to be independent, Portugal would not have existed as a nation apart.

drawn from Galicia and Santiago: the victory of Ourique (1139), after which Alphonse was proclaimed king, took place on the 25th of June, the feast of the Apostle; Christ himself appeared in the course of the battle, and left the imprint of his five wounds in the form of the five *quinas*[85] of the Portuguese coat-of-arms. Portugal came into being by struggling against Islam on her southern border (led and helped by Northern European people) and against Castile with her rear guard. That little detached piece of Galicia developed the spirit of a besieged city which the weak Castilian monarchy of the Middle Ages could not dominate and which the Spain of Philip II with its grandeur among the clouds could not assimilate. The suspicion and resentment with which she regarded Castile were the emotional fires in which Portugal was forged; thus, she was the child of the energetic impulse of Burgundy in the eleventh and twelfth centuries. Lisbon was captured in 1147 by an army chiefly integrated by foreigners.

Galicia, the older sister, remained the while in a state of passive receptivity, enjoying the wealth attracted by the Apostle, benefiting from the reflected homage paid by the masses of pilgrims to the relic enshrined in Santiago. With such fury did the pilgrims dispute the privilege of praying beside the sacred tomb that they would sometimes kill each other, so that it would be necessary to reconsecrate the Church, a complicated ceremony which the Pope authorized to be simplified on account of the frequency of such disturbances. Galicia immobilized herself: doing nothing, she obtained everything—visits from kings and magnates, luxury, the poetry of troubadours, active trade, endless donations. The star-clouds of the Milky Way, through which galloped Santiago's charger, came down and entered into the depths of the Galician soul. Missing the ferment provided by the Templars and the Burgundians and not forced to go outside of himself to extend his land at the price of his blood, the Galician did not become a conqueror like his Portuguese brother. This is not to say that the Galician, beginning with his arch-

[85] *Quinas* or "fives" is the popular designation of the Portuguese shield, so called because it consists of five shields arranged in the shape of a cross, with a cross made of five coins on each of the five shields. Father Juan de Mariana says, in his history (x, 17), that some people believe "stulte scilicet et inaniter" (no doubt foolishly and vainly) that the five small shields are the five wounds of Christ and not an allusion to the five banners of the five Moorish chieftains conquered at Ourique. In the Spanish version of his history, Mariana writes with more caution, and, instead of "stulte scilicet et inaniter" he says "no sé si con fundamento bastante" (I doubt whether with sufficient foundation). Thus, in 1600, Father Mariana's critical reason expressed itself candidly in Latin, which few read, and not in the language of everyone.

bishops, did not fight bravely in the army of the kings of Leon and Castile, as he had once done against the Norman invaders. Clerics and knights were present, and to their honor, in the major battles: Almeria, Cordova, Seville, Tarifa. But they always participated as *auxiliary* troops of the king. Nor did the Galician language conquer new dominions as Portuguese was doing, because Galician imperialism was receptive and not aggressive, or, one might say, it consisted in irradiating the prestige of the Apostle throughout all Christendom.[86]

When the springs of foreign piety were exhausted, the Galician limited himself to spreading out over other lands, with gentle melancholy, the excess of his amorous and fecund population. For centuries Compostela, the lovely recluse, received flattery and homage worthy of Rome; yet such glory did not permit her to exercise an imperial catholicity beyond her own walls, in spite of the fact that she possessed great dominions in the south of France, in Italy, and in other parts of Europe. The *antistes totius orbis* had no orb. He could not even gain for himself the primacy of *Las Españas*.

A vital situation, prolonged from the ninth century to the seventeenth, must perforce leave indelible traces on the forms of life. The constant proximity to the mysteries of the shrine gave rise to skepticism and irony; under the vault of the cathedral were heard songs that accentuated the "human, clever, licentious element."[87] Machiavelli noticed the contrast between the irreligiosity of Rome and the continued presence of the pontiff in the capital of the Christian world, and something like this happened in Galicia. To take the best advantages of the pilgrim, it was necessary to be shrewd and to sharpen the wits; in the end an antiheroic skepticism and a rare talent for political intrigue came to be dominant. The finest gifts of the Galician soul were concentrated in its prodigious lyric poetry always a-tremble with disappointed melancholy; on the other hand, Galicia felt quite disinclined to cultivate the heroic epic, or, later, the drama, genres in which Italy too showed no particular eminence. It is no accident, then, that Father Feijóo (1676-1764), was a Galician; his ironic spirit and his critical mind enabled him to go into battle against false miracles and popular superstitions with an energy proportional to the paralysis into which Galicia had fallen. The Galician

[86] The apostolic prestige of Galicia did, however, lead to a wider use of Galician, which was the language used in notarial documents in Zamora and Salamanca as late as the beginning of the thirteenth century, and in the lyric poetry written by Alphonse the Learned and others.

[87] A. López Ferreiro, *Historia de la Iglesia de Santiago*, v, 369.

connections with Santiago were much more essential for that region than the often claimed Celtic or Suevian character, both quite dubious. This looking back to remote Celtic or Suevian origins is just another aspect of the Spanish "vivir desviviéndose."

Literature and Disorder

The primary stimulus for the monastic invasion of Spain was the holy war against Islam, of which the news reached France at the beginning of the eleventh century in a nimbus of mystic splendor. Rudolph Glaber (d. 1050) says that in the time of King Sancho of Navarre "the army was so scant that the monks of that region found themselves forced to take up arms."[88] The chronicler did not know that the motive for the monastic readiness to fight was not so much the reduced state of the army as the example of the Moslems, for among them the struggle with the infidel was very often associated with monasticism (see p. 202). In any case, the former statement is the first testimony concerning activities which two centuries later were to be organized within the Spanish military orders. It was already known in France that death incurred while fighting the Saracens opened the gates of paradise, as may be inferred from the vision of a holy monk described by Rudolph Glaber: "His church was invaded by a multitude that filled it completely; all were wearing white albs and red stoles. The bishop who led them said the mass and then explained that all had perished while fighting the sons of Hagar in Spain, and how, in the march to glory, they had stopped in that monastery" (*op.cit.* col. 641). Without such visions, Archbishop Turpin would not have fought against the Saracens in the *Chanson de Roland*:

Li arcevesque i fiert de sun aspiet. (1,682)

Nor would he have sent the souls of all who died around him to heaven:

Tutes vos anmes ait Deus li Glorius!
En pareïs les metet en sentes flurs. (2,196-97)

Thus an air of wonder was built up around the land of the Apostle, to which, when all was said and done, came many more pilgrims than crusaders. Christian Europe lent feeble assistance to Spain, because Christ's sepulcher was not in Seville, and the road to Santiago's was cleared of the enemy. Only in poetry did Charlemagne fight to free it. The liberality of the kings and of the lesser folk towards the Bur-

[88] "Historiarum libri quinque," in *Patrologia*, 142, col. 640.

gundian monasteries reached its maximum in the eleventh century with 375 gifts of land and populated places; in the thirteenth century the number of gifts went down to 138,[89] even though the influence of France continued to be intense; but Cluny was falling into decay, and the Cistercians, newly established, still had not made so much of an impression on the owners of land. The Abbey of Cîteaux, near Dijon, sprang up in 1098 under the protection of the Duke of Burgundy, and great was the success of the ascetic mysticism there, magnified by the glorious figure of Bernard de Clairvaux. Alphonse VII, forgetful of Cluny, concentrated his affections on the new white friars, whose monasteries spread profusely in the course of the twelfth century. The architectural marvels of Poblet in Catalonia, Las Huelgas in Burgos, and Alcobaça in Portugal stand out among them. Spain continued to be incapable of finding national forms in which to express her religious feeling, and she came out from under one Burgundian pressure only to go under another, very broad in its scope but only slightly connected with the route of the pilgrims. Cluny was decaying along the road to Santiago, and thus I find an explanation for the clamorous propaganda initiated by those monks and centered in the falsification of the so-called *Codex Calistinus*, attributed to Pope Calixtus II. One part of the famous manuscript refers directly to the Apostle and to the pilgrimage—sermons about Santiago, offices, liturgy, and a description of the road to Compostela, which is valuable as the first tourist's guide written in Europe.[90] This first part is really a *Book of Santiago*, less important in a literary way than its continuation, the *Chronicle of the Pseudo-Turpin*, containing a supposed history of Charlemagne and Roland. The fabulous account glorifies the emperor for his conquest of Spain, and Roland as the hero of Roncevaux; it scarcely mentions Santiago, although the entire subject is related to places along the route of the pilgrims. I think that Bédier is right in connecting this chronicle with the road to Santiago; whereas C. Meredith-Jones has the idea that its object was to incite a crusade. But calling people to a crusade by glorifying events that took place along the *via francigena*—was this not the most effective propaganda? For if those to whom the crusade was being preached were not attracted to the final goal of the crusade—that is, the fight against the infidel—they would at least go and visit the holy places that preserved the imprint of such glorious events. The

---

[89] J. Pérez de Úrbel, *Los monjes españoles en la Edad Media*, II, 450.

[90] Cf. C. Meredith-Jones, *Historia Karoli Magni et Rotholandi, ou Chronique du pseudo-Turpin*, Paris, 1936. See p. 43 of this work for the contents of the codex, and the abundant bibliography on pp. 353-357.

Chronicle of the Pseudo-Turpin made use of the epic accounts of the battle of Roncevaux, a place situated on the road to Santiago.

But we would not exhaust the meaning of the eleventh and twelfth centuries in Spain if we presented them only as centuries under the yoke of Burgundian monasticism. This intervention was solicited by very Christian kings who were seeking a better relationship with God for their peoples, through the free institution of monasticism rather than through the centralized hierarchy of the Church. There was no feeling of inferiority in this, for in the Kingdom of God there were no frontiers. On the contrary, Alphonse VI yielded unwillingly to the pressures of Pope Gregory VII, who forced him to institute the use of the Roman in place of the Mozarabic rite, finally suppressed only through the combined action of the pope and the Cluniac monks. Towards the monks themselves there was no resistance. Their mission, though taking a different direction, was analogous to that of the emigrant Mozarabes: the filling of the voids in Spanish life through help from the outside, a tendency always visible to a greater or lesser degree in later centuries and with especially pronounced manifestations in the Erasmism of the sixteenth century, the enlightenment of the eighteenth century, and the effort to re-Europeanize Spain at the beginning of the twentieth century. As early as the eleventh century Spain felt that she was suffering from initial deficiency in constructive ability, a deficiency never made up in later years; for in spite of it and also because of it, Spain succeeded in creating a life of her own with its own values, although she continued to feel, alongside the plenitude of her existence, the anguish of not existing fully.

This situation was due mainly to circumstances created by the Arabic occupation. Before the Arabs came, Visigothic Spain enjoyed a normal relationship with what was left of culture in the Mediterranean world; trade with Byzantine ships even went up the Spanish rivers as far as Merida, Cordova, and Zaragoza. Spaniards who had fled from the Saracen invasion evangelized important regions of Europe, and it was Saint Pirminius who founded the monasteries of Reichenau and Murbach, whither they carried many codices which they had rescued from Spain.[91] The land of Saint Isidore and Saint Eugenius of Toledo played no mean role alongside the other fragments of the Roman Empire. But the "Spanishness" of Spanish history was to begin in the northwestern zone of the Peninsula, as we have seen in Chapter 3. The Kingdom of Leon

[91] J. Pérez de Úrbel, *op.cit.*, I, 352, 527.

and then Castile put their faith in Santiago, and thanks to them Navarre, Aragon, and Catalonia were not an extension of France, as Catalonia had been at the beginning of the Reconquest. Moslem writers called the Catalans "Franks" (as they were also called in the *Poema del Cid* in 1140), whereas the Christians of the north were "Galicians" to the same writers, a fact that is explainable by the great significance of the Christian "Mecca." Behind the Catalans stood the prestige of the Frank Charlemagne, behind the rest of the Christians that of the Galician Santiago. The number of Galicians in Arabic Spain was not enough to blanket the memory of the Asturians and Leonese; but the Asturians and Leonese had no distinguishing feature that made them stand out, and the Galicians did have. Spanish Navarre, for its part, was dangerously exposed to annexation by France, and did not belong entirely to Spain until Ferdinand the Catholic incorporated it into the kingdom.[92]

The Christians to the south of the Pyrenees gravitated toward France and were slow in opposing the Moslems although the sub-Pyrenean area of the Peninsula possessed a higher "occidental" civilization than Galicia and Asturias.[93] Nevertheless, it was among the Galicians and Asturians that the cohesive force arose with the necessary aptitude to give some sort of organization to the Christians of the ninth century, rude and divided. With that force, the kingdom of Leon began to acquire the outlines of a nation and an inciting ideal strong enough to oppose a similar ideal possessed by the enemy. Through the monks from outside, the country joined hands with the rest of Europe. This coming out of itself and then folding back upon its own self was the shuttle-like process of Spanish history. This process made Spain's submission to the foreign compatible with the awareness of her own independent existence, good or bad. Such surrender was opposed by the unconquered soul of Castile, an ultimate *quid* that must remain beyond the grasp of the historian. I am, on the other hand, more interested in understanding the Spanish form of life as a "dwelling-place," in determining what is, and what is not, Spanish, than in seeking a genetic explanation of a given historical process.

This process is already evident in the eleventh and twelfth centuries.

---

[92] Exaggerating a good deal, J. A. Brutails says: "The Navarre of the Middle Ages belongs perhaps more to France than to Spain" (*Documents des archives de la chambre des comptes de Navarre*, 1890, p. ii).

[93] "The tenth century in the Asturian-Leonese kingdom was a century of rudeness such as to be incompatible with a flourishing life of the spirit" (C. Sánchez-Albornoz, "Notas sobre los libros leídos en el reino de León," in *Cuadernos de Historia de España*, Buenos Aires, I and II, 1944, p. 227).

Cluny and the Cistercians did not modify Spain's religiosity, nor did they produce in Spain figures of international dimension. Almost from their beginnings, the monasteries of Cluny abounded in sterile controversies among the monks, the vassals, and the royal house, sterile in that no party came out of them with an advantage. Of all the foundations of the foreign orders, the abbey at Sahagún, chosen by Alphonse VI for his burial place, was perhaps the richest. Around the abbeys, towns grew up composed of people from everywhere, attracted by the wealth of the road to Santiago: Gascons, Bretons, Germans, Englishmen, Burgundians, Normans, Tolosans, Provençals, Lombards, and many other tradesmen of divers nations and foreign tongues.[94] Such a list helps us to imagine something of the social conditions and the type of life that went on along the road to Santiago. The Abbot of Sahagún was lord over that amorphous multitude, which showed frequent disrespect toward the authority of the monastery. On the death of Alphonse VI (1109), the townspeople revolted tumultuously, and for a long time anarchy dominated that seigniory. Alphonse I of Aragon invaded Leon and Castile, and the religious community suffered a great many indignities. The rebellion broke out again later on, and this continued like an endemic disease until the thirteenth century. We are not interested here in the details but simply in observing how the original purpose of the coming of the monks—the organization of life around a spiritual principle—turned into a struggle between greedy parties, in which each band aspired to take advantage of the wealth that had fallen into the lap of the other. "The townsmen of Sahagún made peaceful use of their trades, and carried on their business in great tranquillity; thus, they came and *brought with them from everywhere* goods of gold as well as silver and even many cloths of divers weaves, so that the townsmen and the dwellers there were very rich, and were provided with many pleasant things. But since offensive and harmful change and great arrogance and pride are likely to rule in the abundance and multiplication of temporal things, the hearts of the said townsmen began to swell up with pride, as usually happens when people of low birth and humble condition are given an excess of temporal things" (*op.cit.*, p. 33). The throng of enriched merchants attacked the monastery, which by the mere fact that it was the target of such an attack showed that it had lost prestige and authority and that it was very much mixed up in "temporal things." The townsmen were joined by the peasants, who called their conspiracy a "brother-

[94] *Las crónicas anónimas de Sahagún*, ed. J. Puyol, p. 32.

hood," a brotherhood which is one of the germs of what would one day be the armed populace, disciplined into an army by Ferdinand and Isabella. The brotherhood of Sahagún refused to pay its taxes, and killed the Jews who were to be found in the neighborhood of the monastery— another antecedent of the massacres at the end of the fourteenth century. Whenever the Spanish people has ceased to be bound together by the nimbus of a common faith, it has confused its rights with chaos and anarchy. In the frequent disturbances in Sahagún, the dominant spirit was demagoguery, a corollary of the excess of the supernatural, Messianic spirit so effectively initiated by Santiago. In those slaughters there was no discernible outline of the organization of a class of craftsmen, because the whole thing revolved around wealth "brought in," not produced, and it fell prey to the greed of monks, merchants, bourgeois, and the peasants. But a strong monarchy was not forged out of this either, nor even the splendor of a mystical theology. There remained the artistic beauty of the magnificent Abbey, which later fell into ruin.

The internal situation of other Cluniac monasteries between 1259 and 1480 is well known, thanks to the documents published by Ulysse Robert.[95] In some of them, the abbots and friars lived with their mistresses and reared their children in the monastery; kings, great lords, and bishops, for their part, confiscated the monastic properties to increase their own wealth. All coveted the already existing wealth, but none was able to turn it into lasting benefits—and this, in turn, anticipates the futile confiscation of ecclesiastical properties in the nineteenth century, easy to justify, no doubt, but disastrous; for the State did not succeed in taking advantage of that wealth either in Spain or in Mexico, and many of the architectural and artistic treasures of the military orders and the Church fell into ruin or were dispersed. The aura of faith that surrounded the monks of Cluny under Alphonse VI had vanished forever.

Apogee and Decline of the Belief in Santiago

Enthusiasm and tradition kept the belief in the Apostle alive and beyond dispute for the whole of the Middle Ages. It is outside my purpose here to relate the details of its vicissitudes, a task which, in any case, has already been performed admirably by A. López Ferreiro in the eleven volumes of his History. The point to be made here is that the

[95] "Etat des monastères espagnols de l'ordre de Cluny aux XIIIᵉ et XVᵉ siècles," in the *Boletín de la Academia de la Historia*, 1892, xx, 321-431.

faith in Santiago served the historical disposition of Spain as a creative impulse. It is for this reason that I emphasize so strongly what the monarchs felt and said about it. Alphonse VII said that he had conquered Coria in 1147 with the help of Santiago: before he took Baeza, the Apostle's hand, grasping a fiery sword, appeared to him. The Apostle's efficacious zeal was repaid with offerings and solemn acts of homage; when Louis VII of France came to Castile because evil rumors were spreading that his wife (the daughter of Alphonse VII) was not a legitimate child, the best way to dissipate those doubts and put a seal upon the good accord existing between the two kings was to organize a pilgrimage to Compostela. Alphonse VII "and the kings Don Sancho and Don Fernando, his sons, and the king of [Spanish] Navarre" accompanied the French king; "the king and his sons showed such courtesies and such marvelous honors to the pilgrim king at each of the stations and vigils that he had to keep," that Louis VII returned to his own country filled with joy.[96]

In 1228 Alphonse IX of Leon says that on account of the "singular watch of the Apostle our kingdom and all of Spain still lives." In 1482 Isabel the Catholic calls Santiago the "light and patron and guide of the kingdom of Spain."[97]

The masses of the people continued to trust in their patron saint even in the sixteenth and seventeenth centuries,[98] even though they were not

[96] *Crónica general*, p. 657a.

[97] *Historia de la Iglesia de Santiago*, v, Appendix, p. 44; vii, 407. Santiago sometimes intervened in French victories, although in a different form. Philip Augustus told the prisoners captured at the battle of Bouvines (1214) that not he but Saint James, the patron of Liège, had conquered them (v, 80). The French king, like a good believer, thought that his victory was a punishment visited by God on the enemy because they had offended the patron of Liège. There may be an influence of the Spanish Santiago here, albeit reduced to purely spiritual limits. There is no visible miracle during the battle; the white charger does not gallop through the air above the armies; and, most important of all, Philip Augustus had not entrusted the direct administration of his nation to any saint.

[98] In 1535 Santiago appeared "visibly to the Spaniards, for they and the Indians saw him, riding on a beautiful white horse," according to Garcilaso the Inca in his *Comentarios reales*, ii, ii, 24. In 1626 the general Don Diego Flores de León made a public deposition telling how he conquered seven thousand Chilean Indians with only two hundred and sixty Spaniards, thanks to the Apostle. In 1639 the Marquis of Flores-Dávila vanquished the whole army of Abdelcader in Oran with five hundred Spaniards, thanks to the help of "a horseman dressed in a white waistcoat, armed with lance and shield, and riding on a horse" (*Historia de la Iglesia de Santiago*, ix, 319-321). Friar Vicente Palatino, to prove that the war against the American Indians was just, says that during one of Hernán Cortés's battles in Mexico "a man on a white horse appeared, and slaughtered the Indians mightily, and his horse

always followed in their faith by a new social class unknown in the preceding centuries, the writers, or men of learning who expressed opinions concerning the life around them and whose effect on belief will be examined later in this book. But for the moment we must dwell a little longer on what was happening in Compostela in the Middle Ages.

Beneath the splendors of the inspiring and solemn belief stood the ecclesiastics of Santiago, no less bound down to earthly interests than the monks of Cluny. Religious experience was for them neither ascetic nor mystic; it was external to the person, and could not unify the faith and the conduct of the believer, that is, faith did not operate within the believer as a determinant of his ethical behavior.[99] Santiago was not expected to reward with the graces of sanctity but with favors that would resolve the urgent problems of each individual: victories in battle, health, good crops.

Belief in the *ex machina* power of the Apostle permitted Castile and Leon to exist, and sustained them against the Moors and the Europeans. The kings of Spain, working at that arduous task, knew this very well, better, indeed, than we historians know it. To Santiago Spain owes both the slow and tortuous effort of the Reconquest and the lasting grandeur of what was created in the Iberian Peninsula. From him also comes, and at the same time, the constructive feeling of those who experienced this form of existing as a nonexisting, and expressed this feeling in works of anguished beauty (from Cervantes to Unamuno), in which life appears as it is, as a problem.

Today these works are a haven and a refuge for sensitive souls alarmed at the turn—also "thaumaturgic"—taken by the material civilization of our own time, which has converted into ends the material means of a culture sterile in meaning and liable to become an empty and anonymous shell. For this reason the history of Spain seems today to be paradoxically modern, even though many perceive only Spain's failure and her arrogance; her exemplary virtue has its roots in her matchless art of living in nothingness without being annihilated in it, for after the night of this nothingness has always dawned the firm awareness of continuing to exist.

---

likewise destroyed them by biting and kicking them." If the war had been unjust, God would not have sent Santiago to fight on the side of the Spaniards ("Tratado de derecho y justicia de la guerra . . . ," 1559, in L. Hanke and A. Millares, *Cuerpo de documentos del siglo XVI*, Mexico, 1943, p. 24).

[99] The belief in Santiago was dependent on the longing of the person; it did not consist in an objective order independent of the person. The belief was shaped to the person, not the person to the belief.

Kings, clergy, and people could not realize that they had to do something with themselves while they were trusting in the invincible sword of the patron of Spain. When need for his help was not urgent, attention was directed toward the treasures which were collected through international piety, and which the kings exploited by having recourse now to cleverness and now to violence. Alphonse X was given what he demanded, although he was forced to declare that he demanded it "as a favor and not by right."[100] To be sure, the Learned King never went on a pilgrimage to Compostela; he was more interested in the cult of the Virgin—whom he exalts in his *Cantigas*—in accord with the new European sensibility of the thirteenth century.

In the Apostolic city there was a continual buzz of foreign tongues, and the multicolored spectacle of the milling crowd. Inside the church it was necessary to impose order on the mob of pilgrims who struggled violently to install themselves near the sacred tomb. The different national groups at times fought among themselves to enjoy the passionately coveted privilege, and it was not unusual for them to leave behind them the germs of plagues that decimated the population. Princes, great lords, merchants, beggars, and sharpers,[101] in a milling jumble, adored the

---

[100] *Historia de la Iglesia de Santiago*, v, 220. Alphonse VII subjected Archbishop Gelmírez to continued harassment (IV, 208, 214).

[101] I think a large number of words having to do with the life of the rabble were introduced into Spanish through the pilgrimage: *arlote* (idler), *belitre* (low, mean), *bufón* (buffoon), *gallofero* (vagabond), *jaque* (braggart), *jerigonza* (argot), *ribaldo* (ribald), *pícaro*, *titerero* (one who operates a puppet-show), *truhán* (scoundrel), and many others, from French or its dialects. Don Cristóbal Pérez de Herrera writes in 1598: "Eight or ten thousand Frenchmen and Gascons, who come [into Spain] to make pilgrimages through these realms, pass by the Hospice in Burgos every year and are given lodging and food there without pay, for two or three days. . . . It is said that in France eligible daughters are promised in dowery as much as can be amassed on a journey to Santiago and back, as if the men were going to the Indies instead of coming to Spain *with their gadgets and trinkets*" ("Discurso del amparo de los legítimos pobres," in Diego Clemencín, *Notas al Quijote*, II, 54). An echo of the beggars from Southern France can still be heard in the Portuguese expression *andar a moina* (beg alms), from Gascon *moina*, Lat. *eleemosyna* (H. and R. Kahane, in *Language*, 1944, XX, 83-84). *Moina*, I would guess, exists, or must have existed, in Galician, coming in by way of the pilgrimages. Moreover, ne'er-do-well outlaws were not the only foreigners for whom Galicia was a popular place of visitation. In 1541 Antonio de Guevara, the bishop of Mondoñedo, can still say "that many French clerics and others from other lands, and many monks from diverse orders pass through our bishopric, saying masses, and even being rectors of many churches. . . . Oftentimes the French clergy cannot be understood . . . and many of the native clerics of the dioceses do not have enough to eat because there are so many foreign ones" ("Constituciones sinodales," in R. Costes, *Antonio de Guevara, Sa vie*, 1925, p. 62).

Apostle and offered gifts, the protection and use of which became a great problem for the cardinal-canons. Each pilgrim received written testimony of his visit, and each bought the shell (*venera*), a symbol of the Apostle, whose sale constituted an important business for some five-score merchants. Lodging for that unsettled mass of people, and the control of the riches that came in, kept clerics and laymen busy, and produced frequent conflicts between the Church and the townspeople. Then, too, there was the military activity of the clergy, who were forced to ride with the army when the king needed them, since the priest was at the same time a man of arms. Religious sentiment dissolved thus in bureaucracy, military service, liturgy, law suits, and financial activities.

The archbishops tried to impose good customs by force of sanctions and external rules, but one can easily imagine how ineffective these were. For centuries the diocesan councils ordered the priests to use the tonsure, to dress as priests, and not to bear arms. In 1289[102] these orders were still without effect. The council of 1289 forbade the clergy to wear beards, even—curiously enough—if they were young, or to wear clothing that was striped, green, or red; or to walk about the city at night under arms; or to drink in the taverns; or to gamble with dice in public; or to participate with their arms in fights between soldiers and citizens; or to keep concubines publicly, either in their own houses or in those of other people. In addition, the priests were forbidden to practice sorcery, spells, prophecies, and divinations.

Although none of these practices was limited exclusively to the clergy of Compostela, one cannot help contrasting the divinity of the Apostle with conduct of his nearest servants, conduct not attributable, as López Ferreiro so innocently puts it, to the "turbulence of the times"; for virtue has always been surrounded by turbulence.

Resistance to the law was connected with the excessive predominance of a very special form of religion that was not interested in creating social bonds in the kingdom of this world. When conduct is not supported by internal-external forms, those who are not saints are anarchists. That quality which is so inexactly called Spanish individualism is what was left of a history that was almost solely supported by the belief in the incalculable and unpredictable power of God and of human will. The principles from which authority emanated were too sublime and could not reach down to the point of shaping the prosaic task of hour-to-hour existence. But, returning to my central idea, if the Hispanic people had

[102] *Historia de la Iglesia de Santiago*, v, Appendix pp. 116, 235.

not been inspired by the unifying stimuli of illusionism and passion, the Reconquest of the Peninsula would have been carried out by foreigners, not by Spaniards.

The pendulum oscillated in Santiago between submission to the procurers of heavenly favor, and chaotic and even criminal rebelliousness. During the civil quarrels between Peter the Cruel (d. 1369) and his brother Henry Count of Trastámara, the Archbishop Don Suero Gómez de Toledo rather inclined toward the latter; Henry was already lord of almost the entire kingdom, and his fief of Trastámara was located in Galicia. Fleeing from his brother, King Peter passed through Santiago in 1365, and he gave the county of Trastámara, as a fief, to his friend and faithful vassal Don Fernando de Castro; Don Fernando and the king being uncertain of the loyalty of the archbishop, they decided to eliminate him. The king summoned the prelate, who had taken refuge in the castle of Rocha, and had him assassinated[103] as he approached the cathedral. The dean suffered the same fate, except that his ebbing strength allowed him to commend his soul to God at the altar of the Apostle.

After King Peter was assassinated by his brother Henry (1369), Don Fernando de Castro continued to be powerful. The bourgeois, taking his part against the Church of Santiago, drove out the new archbishop, Don Rodrigo de Moscoso, who in turn placed the rebellious city under interdict. The spiritual sanction did not frighten the enraged citizens; they rioted in the cathedral (Tuesday in Holy Week, April 1, 1371), and they barred the doors of the cathedral treasury hall with iron, imprisoning the cardinal-canons who had taken refuge there and forbidding them to have anything to eat or drink. The canons stayed there for nine days, and they came out alive only because their relatives got food to them behind the backs of their jailers.[104]

---

[103] Apart from any other consideration, the see of Compostela had to lean towards France in international politics: Henry was supported by the king of France, Peter by the king of England. When King Peter assassinated the archbishop, he committed one more cruel deed, but he did eliminate a serious enemy, albeit too late for any advantage. The policy of Santiago, as I say, never changed.

[104] One of the victims has left a poignant account in Galician of what happened: "E de mais foron buscar todos los outros coengos e personas que eran enna villa, a sus casas. E por forza trouxeron a o cardeal dom Afonso Pérez e a o cardeal dom Afonso González . . . e ensarraronnos con os outros enno dito Tesouro, e mandaron dar pregón por toda a villa que nihum non fose ousado de les dar pan nen vino, nen outra cousa ninhua . . . E alguus seus parentes e criados ascundudamente les davan vino e vianda por que se manteveron. E os vellos a fracos que non podian sair, ouveron de fazer enno dito Tesoura aquelo que e necessario e se non pode escussar" (*Historia de la Iglesia de Santiago*, VI, Appendix p. 142).

When Henry II had made himself secure on the throne, he bestowed his love and gifts on the ill-treated Church of Compostela with prodigality. López Ferreiro says that "it seems that Don Enrique [i.e., Henry II] sincerely believed that he owed a large part of his good fortune to the Apostle" (vi, 198). The Apostolic Church fared well or badly according as it was blown upon by the winds of belief or the gales of capital sins. The castle of Rocha, built in 1223, was an imitation of the Castle of Santangelo in Rome, and the so-called cardinals were parish priests of the churches of the city, just like the cardinals of Rome. But even such pontifical pomp afforded no protection against trouble.

The receipts of Santiago provided for everything, and the pilgrimages did not diminish until well into the seventeenth century. The kings, to be sure, no longer went to Santiago as they had done in the twelfth century, because the monarchy no longer needed the Apostle to conquer the Saracens, and the religious horizon had been displaced. The forms of belief went on being the same, but their perspective was different. There was still the *plus ultra* but now it was the Spanish Empire, where one could be magnified as a churchman or as a conqueror; the feverish desire to become an *hidalgo* was a longing which bound the country together in unity, because in the long run to wait for graces rained down from heaven or to wait for the favors of fortune from all the utopias amounted to the same thing.

Until the fifteenth century, roughly, belief was chiefly attached to Santiago, at whose side, however, other guiding stars had already appeared: the Virgin of Guadalupe (province of Cáceres), for example, worshiped later in Mexico as the patron and protector of the Mexican people.[105] For all that, belief, as the animating force of Spanish living structure, showed itself under manifold aspects; for instance, as faith in the monarchy, which, especially from Ferdinand and Isabella on, appears sur-

---

[105] In the sixteenth century, Saint Joseph intervened in the public and official life of Mexico, just as Santiago had done before and as the Virgin of Guadalupe was to do later, according to a ruling from a Mexican council: "Because the entire Commonwealth, in both its ecclesiastical and its secular constituency has with great persistence begged us to order the keeping and celebrating of the feast of the glorious Saint Joseph, and the receiving of him as the advocate and patron of this new Church, and especially for him to be the advocate and intercessor against tempests, thunder, lightning, and hail, with which this land is much afflicted," the Council of 1555 decided that Saint Joseph should be the patron of the Mexican ecclesiastical province (*Concilios provinciales celebrados en la ciudad de México en 1555 y 1565*, Mexico, 1769, p. 67). The singular thing about the case is not the matter of belief, which can exist in any place and at any time, but rather the high importance attached to it, and the fact that it is treated as a physical principle.

rounded with Messianic prestige. From the sixteenth century on, moreover, there is discernible a faith in the projection by the individual of his own personal valor (that valor which in Quevedo and Gracián reached the status of almost divine myth). A man like Alvar Núñez Cabeza de Vaca must have felt himself to be some sort of divine force after having crossed the North American continent from Sarasota Bay to the rim of the Gulf of California and having subdued savage Indians from Florida to the Pacific Coast. It was the epoch of the cult of heroic leaders, *caudillos*, from Gonzalo de Córdoba to Don Juan of Austria. The halo of prestige that once shone from the heavenly captain, Santiago, now rested over the human hero, who had been rare in the Middle Ages (Fernán González, the Cid). Spain in her own way, in the sixteenth century, began to dignify some purely human values.

The nationalization of the religious orders, already oblivious of their French connections with Cluny and the Cistercians, contributed to the displacement of the horizon, once outlined by the rays from Santiago. Once the wars within Spain were at an end, with neither Moors nor Jews to convert or expel, religion permeated the whole of social life, and overflowed its former banks in the substance of hundreds of thousands of monks and nuns, swarming in cities, fields, and villages. The Middle Ages had had recourse to religion according as each individual had needed it; now religion was encountered around every corner, because it had been converted from an end in life to a means of livelihood. More than half the national wealth ended up in the hands of the Church's secular or regular clergy, and it was in the Church that careers were sought by such as did not go to the New World, or to fight in the wars of Europe. It was the epoch in which religious hypocrisy, as a source of wealth, became a subject for literature in the works of Quevedo and others.

The innumerable monasteries and nunneries created a second Spain inside Spain, and each order fought continually to spread its popularity at the expense of others. Their founders (Saint Augustine, Saint Dominic, Saint Ignatius, etc.) came to be like spiritual monarchs who bestowed the honors of nobility on each professing novice, and these were indeed *hidalgos* in a divine fashion, an aspect which has to be emphasized, because public opinion was shaped much more by religious orders than by laymen, who were lacking a definite social structure and especially lacking an organ of expression comparable to the pulpits, very similar in function to today's press and political forum. There was none but sacred oratory. The pride of the orders in their "nobility" was translated into a parochialism of the spirit which split even further the already precarious unity of the inhabitants of the Peninsula, who had no civil bond save the common reverence for the person of the king, a reverence which, however, was not strong enough to prevent the definitive separation of Portugal from Spain, or to keep Catalonia from trying the same thing, or even to forestall the signs of rebellion in Aragon in the seventeenth century.

In such a brittle, fragile society it was to be expected that the faith in the invincible Apostle would not remain incorruptible. To understand this fact we have taken the preceding detour, in which I anticipate certain ideas that I will treat more amply elsewhere in this book. By this time Madrid was the center of Spain. Santiago was now far away and without any kind of economic tie with the kingdom. Writers of the first order, like the historian Father Juan de Mariana, denied his authenticity; Cervantes, who spoke with trembling emotion of Saint Paul the Apostle: "In life he was a knight errant; in death the Saint never rode again" (*Don Quijote*, II, 58), could speak ironically of Santiago's "knight errantry." So weak did Santiago's dominion become that one religious order rose up against him and tried to dethrone him; failing to accomplish so much, it confronted him with a rival power, to share his already diminished sovereignty. This is the significance of the fact that the discalced, or reformed, Carmelites succeeded in persuading King Philip III and the Pope to establish Saint Teresa, in a new and unheard of arrangement, as a co-patron of Spain.

The country rose up as if it were a question that affected the existence of the whole kingdom. Pulpits trembled and tracts issued forth in torrents.[106] The only one of these that has been reprinted is Quevedo's *Su espada por Santiago* (His Sword for Santiago), addressed to Philip IV in 1628.[107] The disposition of Spanish life went on functioning in the seventeenth century as in the tenth. Life was grounded in religion, and religion was the station from which, directly or indirectly, every activity emerged. This did not preclude the possibilities of changes in the position of the believer with respect to his belief. There was no more land in Spain to be reconquered to the cry "Santiago!" The gigantic bulk of Spanish political institutions during the seventeenth century caused the

[106] Some of these are to be found in the library of the Hispanic Society of America. Cf. Clara L. Penney, *A List of Books Printed 1601-1700*, pp. 624-626.

[107] In the *Biblioteca de Autores Españoles*, XLVIII. In the case of the subsequent quotations from this work, the numbers in parenthesis refer to the pages of this edition.

country to assume more of a bureaucratic than a military appearance. Even more impressive than the offices in charge of public affairs were the innumerable churches, monasteries, convents, and other religious establishments occupied with spiritual matters (see pp. 645-646).

The dispute between the partisans of Santiago and Saint Teresa looked at times like the arguing of two legal adversaries. Although the opponents of the exclusive patronage of Santiago may not have been rationalist skeptics (or even men who reasoned scientifically as Feijóo did in the eighteenth century), their criticism of the powers and efficacy of the Patron of Spain showed a tendency towards rationalism: if the belief that Santiago fought on his horse about the clouds had to be rejected, and if private judgment should be preferred to traditional faith, then the way was open for other pious traditions to be exploded by reason. The Spaniards of the seventeenth century were neither willing nor able to run such a frightful risk. This is why the vacuum that resulted when a belief was brought into question was not filled (as was beginning to happen outside of Spain) by rational judgments concerning men and nature without paying any attention to ecclesiastical consideration. In Spain, when a belief grew weak there were many others ready to replace it. It is a corollary of this that the Spain of the seventeenth century should seem more like the Middle Ages than does the fifteenth, although it would be meaningless to think of a seventeenth century more "reactionary" than the Middle Ages, for the essential thing is not the age, but the people that are living each moment as they can and as it is given them to live. In Spain it was impossible to advance with no weapons save those of reason.

In 1550 the Spaniard had attained a zenith of glory, by being what he was, with his naked personality suffused by the magical nimbus of belief. For centuries he had been the master of Moors and Jews who had discovered and learned whatever could then be known. He had benefited from European technical skills and their products, for which he exchanged the magical powers of his Santiago. Then he had discovered and taken possession of an immense empire, which yielded incalculable riches. Was he now going to admit with Miguel Servet that the dogma of the most Holy Trinity was not acceptable, merely because there were rational obstacles to believing in it? If Calvin, a Frenchman, had Servet's writings burned, what good could the Spaniards have found in his thought? Dilthey may very well call Servet a thinker of genius today; but for Spain to follow in his path in the sixteenth century would have meant something inconceivable. Just as a sedentary philosopher cannot at the age of fifty become an Olympic champion so Spain could not cease living in her "dwelling-place."

Beliefs got out of control in the seventeenth century, in a counter-charge against the gesture to combat them, feeble as this may have been; they were no longer expressed with that innocent simplicity of the eleventh and twelfth centuries, when even the possibility of disputing them was not suspected. But in the seventeenth century you do not breathe a "normal" air of belief but rather something like an oxygen of faith; and this excessively tense situation has inconvenienced many observers. Moreover (as we shall see in Chapters 12 and 13), by the time Christians, Moors, and Jews had ceased to live together in Spain, Spanish Catholicism had already absorbed the totalitarian religiosity of the Moors, and, especially, of the Jews.

The same thing that happened to religious belief happened to everything else—the monarchy, love, virtue, honor—all were galvanized in the seventeenth century with a view to self-defense. In a vital situation of this kind, belief and thought, desire and duty, illusion and disappointment, appear in a conflict which in Spain presents singular characteristics and values. In the seventeenth century life expresses itself in binary formulas, each of whose terms increases or decreases in an inverse function of the other. Thus it happens that the Carmelite friar, Gaspar de Santa María, a native of Granada, can say that if the body of Santiago is interred in Galicia, he could not have ridden into battle on horseback.[108] More than this, he laughs at those who believe that Santiago's horse causes the thunder with his hoofbeats; and since those who believe this are mostly common folk, he casts his ridicule in the mold of the popular speech of Granada:

> The thunder of the cloud,
> Says Johnny,
> Is made by our Santiago's horsey
> > (*Ibid.*, 456)

[108]   El cuerpo de Santiago está en Galicia,
que el orbe nos codicia;
de donde *cierto infiero*,
que no anduvo en las lides caballero.

(The body of Santiago is in Galicia,
which is the envy of the world;
wherefore *I infer with certainty*
that he did not go riding his horse into battles.)
(*Biblioteca de Autores Españoles*, XLVIII, 453)

(El ruido que al tronar la nube suena,
Como dice *Juanico*,
lo hace de Santiago el *caballico*.)

The grotesque poem in which these lines occur was written by Fray
Gaspar in reply to another poem also written by Fray Gaspar but maliciously attributed by him to Quevedo, directed against the co-patronage
of Saint Teresa. The poem by the Carmelite consists of a first part falsely
attributed to Quevedo and of an answer to it. With perverse intention
(full-fledged literary war scarcely existed in Spain before the seventeenth
century), Quevedo is made to say:

Teresa, we know well
Owes to Santiago the Spanish light she drinks
For it is Santiago that brought Spain to light.

The rebuttal reads:

But we should not say that she drinks light.
Light that is drunk—I'll pay you with a gongorism,
Is owed to Saint-Gin, and not to Saint-Jim.

Or as the passage goes in Spanish:

Así Teresa, es cosa conocida
Que a Santiago le debe,
Pues que a España dió luz, la luz que bebe. . . .
Mas decir no se debe
Jamás que bebe luz: luz que se bebe
(Con Góngora te pago),
A *San-Trago* se debe, y no a *San-Tiago*. (451, 453)[109]

The moment rational criticism is brought into a matter of faith, faith
is shattered. This is what happens to Santiago, whose name, symbolically,
splits in two. The first part retains as it were a fragment of sanctity while
the second merges grotesquely with the atmosphere of the tavern. Every-

[109] The original Spanish poem turns upon a malicious pun, untranslatable, the
purport of which may be grasped in the following literal version, only slightly worse
in English than in Spanish.
    "Since Santiago brought the light (of the Gospel) to Spain, it is manifest
    that Teresa owes to him the light she drinks."
The Carmelite replies:
    "But we should never say that Teresa drinks light: should she have drunk
    light, the light would come from a holy draught of wine (San—Trago)
    and not from Santiago (I take my cue from Góngora)."

thing in life goes to pieces both in life and in the mediocre poetry of the monk from Granada: He has faith in Santa Teresa and he destroys Santiago with his reason; his true name is Gaspar de Santa María and he uses the pseudonym Valerio Villavicencio; he divides his poem into two parts, of which he falsely attributes the first to Quevedo; and to cap it all, he cracks open the very name of Santiago so that he may split it into a *San* and a *Trago*. This radical duality in both art and life in the seventeenth century—a characteristic I have been discussing for many years now—has as its base the breaking up of the compact unity of certain beliefs—ranging from Santiago to personal honor—which had hitherto never been questioned in Spain. In this century the awareness of the process I call *vivir desviviéndose*—in a sense a kind of construction by destruction—reaches a maximum intensity, and all literature is impregnated with it. In the sixteenth century, many things were censured, and especially practices and customs, but nothing was attacked at its roots, and institutional values remained positive. But Spain, founded and made possible by Santiago, renounced him in the seventeenth century, not through its scientists but through its clerics and theologians. Reacting against this, Quevedo writes things hard to believe, things I have before called ultramedieval:

"In the ancient annals and histories you will find that four thousand seven hundred open and decisive battles were fought in Spain against the Moors, counting the battles in Castile, Aragon, Portugal, and Navarre; you will find that eleven million fifteen thousand and some odd Moors died in these battles; you will find that the holy Apostle, fighting personally and visibly, gave us victories, and death to such numberless enemies." (439)

Santiago's adversaries used their skepticism to try to destroy him, but not to build any kind of truth founded on rational thought; they limited themselves to killing one belief and replacing it with another of an equally "Spanish" kind. But once the advocates of the patronage of Saint Teresa had found out how to destroy the rival belief by rational criticism they could not forget what they had learned, and the new belief had to live in uncomfortably close quarters with something of the reasons used to combat its enemy. The patronage of Saint Teresa rose out of the dying embers of the belief in Santiago, in what appeared to be a patronal duality, and as such, highly characteristic of the seventeenth-century style of life, for it integrated the *no* and the *yes* of the rejection of Santiago and the affirmation of Teresa. In the same way, the conglomeration of political medicine men that devised one fantastic scheme after another to solve the problems of the kingdom believed in the schemes because they had lost faith in the efficacy of the king and his government. And once started, this process continued. A symbol and expression of that life that was simultaneously possible and impossible was the play on words, the pun, the rejection of words that expressed the elementary experience of everyone (table—*mesa*), in favor of metaphors (squared pine—*cuadrado pino*) that would endow the ordinary references with a new and striking content—as Góngora does. Or else, the writer destroys belief in the reality of things, suffocating them under the shroud of nothingness—as the nihilist Quevedo prefers to do.

The conflict which at its inception was a tension between the worldliness of the cathedral chapter at Compostela and the splendid beginning of the warrior-Apostle—an earth unmanageable and a heaven unattainable—now unfolds in the broader terms of the life that is impossible and possible at one and the same time. To explain the fracture of Spain in the seventeenth century only in terms of contemporary European circumstances seems to me insufficient and abstract. Those things we call the Renaissance, the Counter-Reformation, or the Baroque were lived by the Spaniards from within their own existence, and this existence was established on a base of extremely peculiar habits, tasks, and interests. If we forget this, we shall reduce the history of the Spanisth seventeenth century to an abstract international pattern.

Quevedo, a Knight of Santiago, felt that he was being reduced to the status of a commoner when he saw how Spain's great patron was being snatched away from him only to be sacrificed to the ideal of the Carmelites, who, in Quevedo's opinion, were weak and effeminate. "How can the fathers of the Reformed Order [the Discalced Carmelites] expect Santiago to give you arms [he is addressing the king], and then beg you to turn them against him; how can they beseech you to find your own sword at his altar, and then ask you to take the sword he holds in his hand and give it to Saint Teresa, whose very children have had her depicted with a spinning-wheel?" (443). Quevedo had turned all values upside down; the world around him seemed like a tapestry turned wrongside out; but he clung to his cult of bravery and boldness, the only railings his unsteady soul[110] could lean upon as it looked into the abyss

---

[110] "Not missing on the road [to hell] were *many* ecclesiastics, *many* theologians. I saw *some* soldiers, but *few*; for along the other path [the one leading to paradise], *infinite numbers* were going in ordered file, *glorious in their triumphant honor*" (*El sueño del infierno*). For Quevedo all is chaos, save the order created by valor, which stimulates him to literary expression of exalted nobility in which he ceases

of nothingness. He disposed of institutions, persons, and things with one gigantic, sarcastic epitaph, but he sprang up like a tiger when anyone probed at the foundations of his own nobility as a Spaniard, the foundations of the ultimate reason for his existence. Thus it was that he defended the prestige of the Apostle with absurd statistics about battles and deaths in a way that would have been inconceivable in the twelfth and thirteenth centuries, when the Spaniard's every act was supported by absolute confidence in his unquestioned belief. With this contrast in mind one can sense very distinctly the situation of the Spaniard of the seventeenth century: he could not overcome his belief by means of rational analysis and confidence in the useful efficacy of that process, and yet he could not go on living within the belief with the same security as before, because critical thought had begun to triumph in other European countries. Wherefore the frenetic efforts to "rationalize" the belief and make it tangible through the search for relics and miracles, efforts that were more abundant than ever in the seventeenth century; wherefore also the extreme styles—Quevedo, Góngora, Gracián—the beautiful projection of existences, without inner repose and lacking ideas or "things" on which they might rest. Nothing could change the Hispanic condition and the immense interests created by it. By the time Cervantes appeared, it was useless for him to prefer Saint Paul and to treat Santiago ironically, just as it was for Father Mariana to label as old wives' tales the accounts of the hoofbeats of Santiago's white charger or the stories of Christ's wounds on the Portuguese shield. All this was a trifling gesture without consequences: people tenaciously went on believing that the issues of life were decided in heaven, where, indeed, there was to be found a special secretary for Hispanic affairs: "She is a good sister [Saint Teresa], and, as such, in payment of her wages, she asks for the honor of being the patron saint" (437). The Saint required that her services be paid for with the honor of being the patroness of Spain, as Quevedo puts it in a sentence that displays in the then modern phrase *librar gajes* (to pay wages), imported from the world of business, a notable admixture with the imperturbable Spanish tradition. The whole affair was debated as in a case at law. The partisans of Saint Teresa say: "So long as she cease not her intercessions, the kingdom cannot fail to reserve for her the name of patroness" (435). To this Quevedo replies: "Christ wished that only his *cousin* should be the patron" (435), wherein

---

to present a skeptical grimace. The two words "ordered file" reveal the only thing that had real structure for him, the only thing he believed in, and in which his anguished existence could find repose.

there is still a residue of the faith in the Apostle on account of his relationship with Jesus. Now he is a cousin; formerly he was a brother. In the face of such a claim, the Carmelites brought up strong arguments: No one could say how long King Philip II would have remained in purgatory if Teresa of Avila had not gotten him out of there on the eighth day, "because it would not have taken a fantastic imagination to think that he was supposed to have a long sojourn in purgatory" (438). This was written thirty years after Philip II's death, by a Carmelite from an aristocratic family—so that we can add here one more voice to the chorus of those dissatisfied with the person and policy of the Prudent King. But this is to digress. What is interesting is that the intimate details of purgatory should be dealt with here so fully, as if communications between the other world and this one were quite normal. (It is not surprising that Baltasar Gracián read from the pulpit a letter that came from Hell itself.) Certain clergy, moreover, were of the opinion that Saint Teresa ought to be preferred because she was a woman and God would have to grant her petitions, "or Christ himself would blush with shame to see her denied" (445). At the time when Santiago was the true star by which Spain guided her fortunes, the visible and operative society was in all respects masculine. In the seventeenth century, society had turned secular, had become a social environment, had become conscious of itself as human, and the individual was conscious of being something different from his social environment. Woman's presence then came to be felt and to manifest itself as an active theme in life and art. Gallantry as a literary motive in the novel and the theater is a sign of the social character love had acquired. In the divine scheme of things, nunneries were the counterpart of the European salons, and nuns on earth or Saints in glory (María de Ágreda, Juana Inés de la Cruz, Saint Teresa), were to Spain or to Mexico what Madame de Rambouillet and Madame de Sévigné were to France. It made no difference whether the ladies dwelt in glory or on earth: "If there is any saint—man or woman —known today who has won the hearts through the power to charm, it is Saint Teresa" (436). She was on the point of officially sharing the supervision of Hispanic affairs in the other world with Santiago. Pope Paul V, at the instance of the Carmelites and King Philip III, had declared Saint Teresa co-patron of Spain in 1618, but the majority persisted in their devotion to Santiago: there was a greater sympathy for the attitude of the soldier than for the attitude of mystic contemplation. In spite of popular feeling, Philip IV, more a man of letters than of arms, joined the partisans of Teresa, and brought about the pope's confirmation of the co-patronage. One might say, without the slightest intention of impropriety, that the salons favored Teresa and the people favored the Apostle. The force of popular tradition prevailed against the king. In 1629 Pope Urban VIII revised the earlier brief and left the clergy and the people free to accept the co-patronage of Teresa or not, with the result that her equality of status with Santiago became a reality in the Carmelite convents and virtually nowhere else. As late as 1812, the Cortes (Parliament) of Cádiz incorporated the co-patronage of the two saints into their legislation, and their decree was still legally in force during the reign of Isabel II, dethroned in 1868. Whatever the reason, there still subsisted in nineteenth-century Spain, and I imagine there still subsist in the Spain of today, habits and echoes of the Spain that came into existence in the ninth century.

Although Santiago ceased to attract attention, Saint Teresa did not replace him as a national figure; and the conflict between the ideal of the soldier incarnate in the Apostle and the longing for feminine tenderness were eventually harmonized in the cult of the Virgin of the Column (Virgen del Pilar), in which are to be found reminiscences of the militant divinity of the Son of Thunder.[111] In 1808 there were appearances of this Saragossan Virgin leading the Aragonese troops against the French invaders, and in the twentieth century her image was granted the "honors of a captain-general"—a feeble and belated spark from the warrior cults, of which the antecedents are by now familiar to the reader.[112] To these cults Spain owes the essential features of her personality, features that must be seen in a long and broad perspective and not through the eyes of parochial progressivism. The paths that man may take are infinite, and the knowledge of which ones are just and preferable is in the mind of God alone.

[111] The Virgin of Guadalupe (in Extremadura) was also a center from which Hispanic vitality (life) radiated. Cortés and Pizarro, also from Extremadura, were much indebted to her. Mexico has a replica of the shrine of Guadalupe, although many Mexicans, in their zeal for attributing only the evils of Mexican life to its Hispanic past, prefer to ignore this. The priest Hidalgo began his rebellion against the Spaniards in 1810 by carrying as his standard an image of the Virgin of Guadalupe, a militant divinity that affirmed the Hispanic structure of the country, a structure which is also affirmed in the effort to deny the evidence that the Virgin of Guadalupe, whose very name comes from a river in Extremadura, is not Extremaduran. The Mexicans, too, "viven desviviéndose"—affirm themselves by denying themselves.

[112] Saint Vincent, Saint Anthony, and other Portuguese saints reflect an analogous situation in Portugal with respect to belief, in accord with the basic unity of forms of life on the Peninsula.

It is pertinent at this point to make one further observation concerning Quevedo's little treatise *His Sword for Santiago*. Quevedo was the first Spanish chronicler of current events, and the currency of the events derived in this case from the fact that feelings previously locked in the subconscious had emerged into public discussion. This happened because Spanish life had acquired a social dimension. Material circumstances, such as the absence of war against the Moors, did not provide the only basis for the Santiago crisis. It was also a consequence of the change of direction that took place in religion in the second half of the sixteenth century, thanks to the mysticism of Saint Teresa and Saint John of the Cross, who pointed out for the first time, or at least for the first time in the supreme form that was theirs, the way of religious intimacy. Remote and hidden currents of Islamic spirituality came to the surface of life, and these currents were enriched by those who had been in contact with other kinds of foreign mysticism. This was the process of Spanish history which the reader may not grasp as a whole if he does not keep in mind the totality of the present book in his approach to each of the historical details. Valor—that quality which gives the human metal its temper—was the foundation-stone of success for this people who had but a scant culture of their own; and their existence from the ninth century to the fourteenth consisted first of all in their will to be a separate and distinct people, yet a people of intrinsic dignity—not Moorish, not Jewish—because only by being "another" people could they be themselves. Unconsciously, and out of the necessity imposed by fate, the Christians took much from the Arabs, going even so far as to adopt their capacity for comprehending in a single grasp both the basely material and sublimely spiritual. This vital situation had its effect in the internal experience of the person, without being expressed in exterior forms. The Spaniards' integralistic and realistic way of being (popularism, adherence to tradition, the predominance of belief over rational thought, etc.) did not in itself constitute an objectifiable religion, art, or science, nor did it give the impression of being an imitation of the Arabs. But the Leonese-Castilian would have felt that he was imitating his fearsome rival if, in the five hundred years between the ninth and the fourteenth century, he had expressed his sensuality in lyric verses, or if he had cultivated idle speculation, or if he had abandoned his soul to mystic transports after the Sufistic manner. The Castilian did not begin to devote himself to lyric poetry or to religious intimacy until he felt that he was far removed from the people who had been his neighbors for centuries—which is not to deny that other reasons may have entered. It was not until the fourteenth century that the first lyrical impulses were expressed in Castilian verse, and these early lyric poems were intimately related to Arabic and Jewish models. Shortly after this, the Order of Saint Jerome appeared, the first instance of a kind of spirituality that could be properly called Spanish, even though it was not yet expressed in religious writings. The popular mysticism of the *Illuminati* made a timid appearance a century later. And not until the second half of the sixteenth century did the great development in mysticism take place. The medieval Castilian, who in the end was the one who set the tone of the Reconquest and of Spain, rejected the Arabic orgy of the senses and the sensual display of lyric poetry, and he felt an equal repugnance toward speaking shamelessly of the adventures of the soul in its relations with God. This sort of thing, in Spain, would have sounded Moorish. Even though the works of Saint Bernard may have been read in the Cistercian monasteries, there did not appear in the Iberian Peninsula a single Christian mystic worth mentioning. What mystics there were of any distinction were Moslems.

Extraordinary as it was, the mysticism of the sixteenth century was ephemeral and, in volume, meager, and not only because it had to submit to the repressions of the Church and the Inquisition. In this as in other cases it is undoubtedly more fruitful to look for the explanations of history in the life of the people, rather than in motives superimposed on that life. Not only Quevedo but also the religious orders disliked the reforms of the Carmelites, who cultivated solitude with God and practiced manual labor, as the Hieronymites had done in the fourteenth century.[113] These Carmelites, opposed to mendicancy, were the people who advanced the cause of Saint Teresa as co-patron. Their mysticism provoked the disdain of Quevedo. Before Teresa "this kind of prayer had been treated of in Spain" by Gómez García in his book *Carro de dos vidas* (Sevilla, 1500). "There is nothing at all in this book except discussions of theology, mysticism, rapture, ecstasy, visions, internal unions, in a compilation of everything written by those grave and holy authors, Richard of Saint Victor and Saint Bonaventure" (448). His polemical intent and the frequent aridity of his soul concealed the values in Teresa's mysticism from Quevedo; but such would not be the motives behind the similar attitude of the Franciscan Order, which should have had a greater regard for the love of God, whatever the form in which it might be expressed. However, the order's tradition of mendicancy and its popular roots turned it against the Carmelites. The Franciscans scornfully

[113] It was Portuguese Hieronymites who handprinted the translation of the mystic Henry Herpius, *Espelho de perfeiçao*, Coimbra, 1535.

referred to the Carmelites' claim that they worked diligently and they were reviving the rigorous life "without any burden to the community, but rather with much benefit to it, because *they must work and earn their bread with their hands.* . . . Since this appeared to have the blessing of heaven, they were allowed to establish foundations; and looms and other tools for doing honest work that would earn bread were installed in the convents." The project failed, as the superior-general of the Franciscans happily affirms: "If some part of it was carried out, that lasted but a few days; look now at the multitude of convents that have been founded by this reformed order, and see whether they are only in the desert places, and whether they live from the labor of their hands, and whether they beg for alms and have income from rents" (447).

Around the year 1600 the Carmelites were trying to do what the Brethren of the Common Life, in Flanders, and then the Spanish Hieronymites had been doing since the fourteenth century, that is, to give themselves over to divine contemplation and the cultivation of honest craftsmanship, for social ends. The superior-general of the Franciscans indicated the failure of the Carmelites, and in my *Aspectos del vivir hispánico* (Santiago, Chile, 1949) I have pointed out that the Hieronymites also failed to produce lasting results. The Hispanic disposition of life rejected serene contemplation as well as manual labor, both of which, I repeat, were practiced by the Sufistic Moslems in their own way, with visible results. The Carmelites had been reformed by Saint John of the Cross, whose mystic vocabulary translates in certain essential respects the vocabulary of Ibn 'Abbād of Ronda, as has been shown by M. Asín Palacios. (In a later chapter I shall point out how a Carmelite friar translates, directly or indirectly, portions of a book by Ibn Ḥazm on an erotico-religious theme.) About the same time, Saint John's order sought to integrate physical with spiritual enterprises, and it is precisely his order that reacts against Santiago's militant spirit and makes a plea for the loving, "charming" protection of the Saint of Avila. But the effect of this plea on Spanish sensibilities was slight. Like the other efforts that have run counter to deeply rooted inclinations, this one amounted to nothing more than a gesture. In repressing the progress of spirituality of the intimate kind, the Inquisition was in harmony with inveterate tendencies.

The violent polemic (a far cry from the *pax christiana*) over the question of a single or dual patronage for Spain confirms the idea that Santiago is an essential ingredient for the history of Hispania. Quevedo felt this with a lively intensity: "God made him patron of Spain, *which no longer existed,* against the time when, through his intercession, his teaching, and his sword, *Spain should once again exist*" (445). Everything is owed to Santiago. To the bellico-political conception, the Carmelites opposed the claim that "before Teresa very little had been known" about God (449). Thus, a pragmatic and activist conception of the divine clashed with the experience of God in pure contemplation that was not interested in bellicose activism. Thus, no room was left for diligent labor, for the intellectual concern with "things," as much the works of God as were the words of Holy Writ.[114]

I have not sought to write a history of Santiago but rather to point out how Leon and Castile, and, later, Spain, have revealed themselves through this peculiar belief. This belief strengthened the fighting impulse and made it efficacious, whereas both intellectual and practical work were made difficult. When the belief fell into decay in the seventeenth century, no kind of earthly impulse could replace it. Ever since then the Spaniard has been torn between a tradition that is as indispensable as it is unpractical and a present that is dominated by the constructive zeal of other nations. For example, Cadalso, at the end of the eighteenth century, is still longing for a magical return of the spirit of the Catholic Sovereigns. In the seventeenth century was begun the immense task of changing the course that had been determined by centuries of collective existence, removed from the "progressive" march of the rest of Europe. In a noble and heroic tension, many great Spaniards of the eighteenth and nineteenth centuries made an effort to initiate a new history, a new type of life. And to their efforts are owed many valuable creations, evident not only in works but also in men too well-known to need mention. But with all this, the result was nothing but an intensification of the functioning of the Hispanic structure, the *vivir desviviéndose*.

To make the great fact of Hispanic belief intelligible, I have had to go beyond the limits of the Middle Ages. Once this task is finished, it will be necessary to return to the point from which we started, so that we may examine other results of Hispanic-Islamic living together during the centuries which at this point are of especial interest to us.

[114] When the city of Santiago was in its most splendid period, under the archbishop Diego Gelmírez (1100-1140), there was no one in the maritime province of Galicia who knew how to build ships: "in partibus Gallaeciae homines nauticae artis periti non habebantur." And for shipbuilders it was necessary to send to Arles, Genoa, and Pisa where there were "optimi navium artifices, nautaeque peritissimi" (*España sagrada*, xx, 301, 198). Gelmírez obtained their services with the promise of great recompense (plurimorum munerum). With the help of Genoese ships, Alphonse VII conquered Almeria—"cum auxilio Ianuesium ceperat" (*Historia de la Iglesia de Santiago*, iv, 235).

Three Christian-Islamic Institutions

Military Orders

BETWEEN THE TWELFTH AND FIFTEENTH CENTURIES, the powerful Orders of Calatrava, Santiago, and Alcántara occupy the foreground of history as a military and political force. In them we can perceive the first indications of the future permanent army of Ferdinand and Isabella. They had their origin in a religiosity that was at once spiritual and warlike. In the fourteenth century their character already was more political than religious, and their extensive properties gave them a power that at times dwarfed that of the king and served to foment intestine wars that retarded the progress of the Reconquest. In some cases the knight-commanders of the orders tyrannized the towns of their commanderies, and thus fostered not only hatred between the people and the nobility but also a kind of negative particularism. In the fifteenth century—perhaps the only period in which the nobility fully sensed its mission of guidance—a few of the grand masters of the orders took an interest in lofty enterprises and enjoyed an influence in the spiritual side of religion, in general culture, and in literature. Their economic hegemony lasted till the dawn of the nineteenth century, and even in our own day their colorful uniforms have ornamented the ceremonies of both church and palace, as the decorative feature of an aristocracy that has long since turned into nothing but an external and illusory spectacle. Spain's noble class, which was the depository of the glorious tradition of the Orders, was both unwilling and unable to preserve from ruin the marvellous shrines of Calatrava and Uclés, seats of the ancient grand masters. Like many other reflections of the past the Orders, to use the words of Quevedo, had for a long time been nothing more than "a word and an empty form."[1]

[1] Calatrava—church, monastery, and castle—was demolished in 1804. M. Danvila writes in 1888: "The outcries of good citizens have not kept neglect and bad weather from bringing about the disappearance of the last remains of Calatrava" (*Boletín de la Academia de la Historia*, 1888, XII, 125). The monastery and the

We have no adequate history of the military Orders and of their meaning, in spite of the fact that there are many documents extant pertaining to them. Not having access to these materials, I am interested at present only in what may have a bearing on the relations between Islam and Christendom. The dominant notion today is that the Spanish orders grew up as a replica of the Hospitalers and Templars of France, established in Spain in the twelfth century.[2] In face of this assertion, a few Spanish orientalists have thought that the beginnings of the Spanish orders are to be sought in Islam.[3] For my part, I think that the problem would be badly posed if we thought that we had to choose between the European and the Moslem origin, since the orders of the Hospitalers and the Templars would be incomprehensible without the oriental model, a matter to which the most recent books on the Templars make no reference.[4] One must keep clearly in view the fact that only in the Moslem world is the life of rigorous asceticism fused with the life of combat against the infidel. On this point the thesis of the Spanish orientalists is irrefutable. It is no matter of chance, then, that the Orders in question were born in the twelfth century in lands that were Christian outposts against Islam—Palestine and Spain—and not someplace else. The Templars, "pauperi commilitones Christi," started out by protecting the pilgrims from the attacks of the infidels along the routes to Jerusalem, and before them the Hospitalers had busied themselves with the care of the poor and sick who got to the Holy City. But amongst the Moslems

---

best parts of the town of Uclés were deserted and fell into decay in the middle of the nineteenth century. The archives and the library almost disappeared. In 1860 a commission of archivists was sent "literally to disinter the books and papers from the midst of saltpeter and filth of every kind" (J. M. Escudero de la Peña, in the *Boletín de la Academia de la Historia*, 1889, xv, 308-309).

[2] See, for example, H. Prutz, *Entwicklung und Untergang des Tempelsherrenordens*, 1888, p. 8: "Ein Seitenstück bietet der Ritterorden von S. Jago." The same thing comes up in J. Piquet, *Les Templiers*, 1939: "Les Ordres du Temple et de l'Hôpital excitaient une grande jalousie en Espagne, car la plupart des Frères étaient des étrangers; aussi la tendence fut-elle à la création d'Ordres militaires nationaux" (p. 234).

[3] J. Oliver Asín, *Origen árabe de "rebato, arrobda" y sus homónimos*, 1927. According to M. Asín Palacios, "the *ribāṭ* is the exact model of the military orders" (*Islam cristianizado*, pp. 137, 141). But long before either of these writers, José Antonio Conde, in his *Historia de la dominación de los árabes en España* (Madrid, 1820, I, p. 619), had said: "The military orders both in Spain as well as among the oriental Christians came out of these *morabitos*." How surprising that neither the Spanish orientalists nor anyone else in Europe paid any attention to Conde's discovery!

[4] G. A. Campbell, *The Knights Templars*, 1937.

[203]

"charitable and beneficent works (caring for the poor, the sick, and the leprous, acting as servants to the spiritual leaders, etc.) had occupied the lives of not a few ascetics [for centuries], although these people were not given a distinguishing name based on their profession; on the other hand, those who practiced jointly the devout and the military life, defending the frontiers in convents that were at the same time barracks [ribāts, rápitas], were called 'almorávides' " (Asín, *Islam cristianizado*, p. 141).[5]

One cannot, by taking an exclusively Christian point of view, understand how the practice of ascetic discipline and the impetus of the warrior can be reconciled in the same person—just as Christian Europe provides no key to the understanding of Santiago *Matamoros*. The Church, it is well known, has always frowned on the idea that persons who have taken up the holy life should bear arms in battle. The Moslems, on the other hand, and centuries before the military orders appeared, had the institution of the *ribāṭ* (plural, *rābiṭa*), "a hermitage in which the 'almorávides,' that is, the holy men who alternated between asceticism and the defense of the borders, lived in retirement." Thus it is that *ribāṭ* also means "holy war, especially defensive holy war," and that in Spain and Portugal there are so many places named *Rábida*, *Rápita*, etc. From *ribāṭ*, as J. Oliver Asín has shown, come the words *rebato* (sudden, unexpected attack; alarm; fit of passion), and *arrebatar* (to snatch away, etc.), and the old *arrobda* (advanced guard). The adoption of such words presupposes the prior existence of the things they signify.[6] If, then, we look at the matter from the other side of the borders of Christendom, the birth of the military orders seems extremely natural, just as it

---

[5] M. Asín, *Vidas de santones andaluces*, p. 157, translates the biography of Abū-l-'Abbās Aḥmad b. Hammām as it is related by Ibn 'Arabī in his "Epistle of Holiness": "He was very fervent. He continually bewailed the health of his soul, like a mother who has lost her only son. . . ." One day he said to Ibn 'Arabī: "What I shall do is betake me to the frontiers of Islam, to the front lines of the enemy, and in some one of the *rábidas* there I shall consecrate myself to the holy war till I die." He did in fact go away to one of the frontiers, to a place called Juromenha (in Portugal), where he took up his residence until, sometime later, he returned to Seville, gathered up the things he needed for his new way of life, and returned once more to the frontier to devote himself to the life of a warrior-monk. This happened at the end of the twelfth century, although similar cases had been common in Islam for centuries before.

[6] "The multiplication of *rābiṭas* in Spain, and their possible confusion with *ribāṭs*, are connected with the great movement of mystic piety which, starting in Persia, had brought about the substitution of monasteries—khānaka in the east, *zāwia* in Barbary—for the foundations more military than religious, of the heroic age of Islam" (G. Marçais, in the *Encyclopedia of Islam*, "ribāṭ").

should seem in the highly Islamized Spain of the twelfth century. Nor, by the same token, should it be surprising to find that in the *Poema del Cid* (1140) Bishop Jerome—not a legendary figure like Turpin in the *Chanson de Roland*, but a historical personage—fights fiercely in the advanced guard of the Christians. Furthermore, the type of the warrior-bishop which appears in the medieval French epic probably has to be included in the same oriental current which it would be absurd to try to limit to Spain in those centuries. In *Le Jeu de Saint Nicolas*, by Jean Bodel (end of the twelfth century), an angel appears to the Christians in the battle and says: "You will be destroyed fighting in the service of God, but you will receive the crown of glory." In France the feeling for holy war most certainly disappeared with the crusades, whereas in Spain it was still alive in the sixteenth century. When it was believed that there was an uprising of the Moors in Granada in 1568, "even the friars in the Monastery of Saint Francis left their cells and came out into the square armed." Later, at a critical moment for the village of Dúrcal (in the Alpujarras), "there appeared eight religious, four Franciscan friars and four Jesuits, saying that they wished to die for Jesus Christ, for the soldiers do not dare to do so; but the captain, Gonzalo de Alcántara, did not consent to this" (Luis del Mármol, *Rebelión y castigo de los moriscos*, Book v, Chap. 2).

Now let us see how those at the pinnacle of spiritual Christianity—the circle around Bernard de Clairvaux—reacted to this Islamic innovation in the twelfth century. The first master of the Order of the Knights Templar, Hugh of Paynes, came from Jerusalem to France to obtain the approval of the new order, and with this objective he went to his friend, the future Saint Bernard, Abbot of Clairvaux, the most influential person in Christendom—who named popes and yet renounced the office for himself. Hugh sought to persuade the Abbot of Clairvaux to lend the support of his pen to the creation of that strange institution, whose rule was finally approved by the Council of Troyes (1128). This was the motive behind Saint Bernard's celebrated sermon "De laude novae militiae," in response to repeated requests from the new Master: "Semel, et secundo, et tertio, ni fallor, petiisti a me, Hugo charissime, ut tibi tuisque commilitonibus scriberem exhortationis sermonem."[7] Hugh had to beg the abbot three times, then, to write about the Templars, and Saint Bernard remained undecided, waiting for someone to do it better than he, for fear that his support of the new institution would be ad-

---

[7] Migne, *Patrologia*, S. L., 182, col. 921ff.

judged an ill-considered act of temerity ("sed ne levis praecepsque culpa-retur assensio"). Ultimately he decided to write the sermon because the new order needed to be defended and explained. All this reveals that crusaders returning to Europe from Palestine were bringing back a novelty that was discordant with the Christian tradition: "Novum in-quam militiae genus, et saeculis inexpertum."[8] Saint Bernard lets himself be carried away by the enthusiasm for the holy war, which Christendom had received from Islam by injection, as it were: "Quam gloriosi re-vertuntur victores de proelio! quam beati moriuntur martyres in proe-lio!" His enthusiasm was strange indeed, for according to Saint Bernard it was not even lawful to kill another man in self-defense: "de duobus malis, in corpore quam in anima levius sit." But in the case of the new knights, the defense of God was authority for everything: "proeliantur proelia Domini sui, nequaquam metuentes aut de hostium caede pec-catum, aut de sua nece periculum."

This is the way European Christendom was penetrated by a doctrine and certain habits that had been familiar to Islam for centuries although they were novel and unheard of for the French monks of Cîteaux and Cluny. To give oneself over to mystic ascesis and to spill the blood of the enemy were compatible activities for the Moslem, because in him the distance between the corporeal and the spiritual, between the mundane and the divine, was obliterated. The most contradictory attitudes are in-tegrated in the vital unity of the person. And just as there could be a harmony between the strictest piety and bloody warfare, so there were mystic sects that abandoned themselves to the love of God by means of contemplating a "présence charnelle," feeling an ecstatic pleasure in the presence of "la beauté d'un jeune visage admiré."[9] This harmonious dual-ity within the sphere of the human, something contradictory according to Christian principles, became accessible in Jerusalem to all who re-sponded to the impression of a strange and splendid culture, whose modes of strange spirituality were adopted, just as its ways of living were imi-tated. King Baldwin I dressed like an oriental, and in his customs, cere-monies, and pomp he resembled a Moslem monarch. In so far as the fact is a question of a visible and tangible phenomenon, it is well known; but there has been an unwillingness to see that the mixture of religious

---

[8] Apropos of this, the editors of the *Patrologia* quote a passage from a letter of Peter the Venerable, Abbot of Cluny (1156): "Quis non laetetur, quis non exsultet, processisse vos, non ad simplicem, sed ad *duplicem* conflictum. Estis monachi virtuti-bus, milites actibus."

[9] L. Massignon, *La passion d'Al-Hallaj*, p. 798. M. Asín, *Islam cristianizado*, p. 327.

piety and bloody violence was like an oriental garment of the spirit. Although he ended by being enthusiastic, Bernard de Clairvaux's astonishment nevertheless gives a measure of the great distance that separated the new military orders from the Christian conception of life. If the Templars were accepted and if they subsequently accumulated incalculable riches, this was because only those knights were devoted to a continuous and regular struggle for the possession of the Holy Places, where the dominion of the Christians was more than insecure. So insecure was it that with the fall of Saint John of Acre towards the end of the thirteenth century, the entire undertaking of the crusades collapsed, and with it, the *raison d'être* of the Templars. They had begun as a pseudomorphosis of the *almorávides*, the holy warriors of Islam. In spite of such an origin, they soon came under the influence of that aspect of French life that was more mundane than mystical, and the order was transformed into a banking society which for nearly two centuries made commercial traffic possible between Europe and the orient.[10] History is a web of life structures, and not an abstract event. The Templars were converted into the bankers of the kings and were almost completely "desanctified." When Christian rule disappeared from Palestine, King Philip the Handsome of France got the Pope to dissolve the order, appropriated its immense riches, and, to secure his title to the property, ordered the Grand Master and many of his knights, first to be subjected to exquisite tortures and then to be burned at the stake (1310-1314).

This means that at the beginning of the fourteenth century the French monarchy was already able to rid itself of an annoying competitor, in this case an organization whose main power resided in its religious character rather than its military strength, estimated at some 15,000 men. Alongside these material and immediate causes, there must be kept in mind a strange quality in the Templars' religiosity. This religiosity in no way resembled that of the other orders, against which the power and envy of the civil authority still remained ineffectual. There was something in the Templars that was incompatible with French life, and a sign of this is the legend about their incontinence and their heresies. Their bellicose piety was tolerated so long as they lived in Palestine. But when they were forced to live once more in the country of their origin, the conflict became patent between church and war, between spirituality and profane business transactions—opposites which could no longer be integrated in the rationalized life of France, where a

[10] Cf. J. Piquet, *Les Templiers. Etude de leurs opérations financières,* 1939.

banker was a banker and a religious was a religious. They had lost their mythic halo and showed only their naked reality, open to the cupidity of the great and the resentment and disrespect of the lowly. They could not keep from disappearing, even though as the victims of a sadistic and covetous Inquisition they may inspire our pity.

The incompatibility of the Order of the Templars with the neat separation of heaven and earth, faith and reason, characteristic of French life, serves as a reference point for understanding by contrast the prolonged splendor of the military orders in Spain. There, as in Palestine, the *almorávides* of the *rábidas* made converts. The Orders of Calatrava, Santiago, and Alcántara were constituted in the middle of the twelfth century, during the reigns of Sancho III and Alphonse VIII of Castile, and, indeed, it is more than likely that before that time there had been Christian ascetics who included the slaying of Moors among their pious duties. Thus we can see why it is that the origin of these Spanish orders is concealed in a certain chronological vagueness, a fact which in no way contradicts the idea that the Templars furnished an example for the organization of the Spanish warrior-ascetics into regular communities.[11] Let us recall briefly the known facts. The Orders of the Hospitalers and the Templars spread over Spain in the first third of the twelfth century, especially in Aragon and Catalonia. They were given castles, towns, vassals, and lands, in recognition of the services they had rendered in the war against the infidels. Their prestige reached its highest point when, in 1134, Alphonse I of Aragon named them the heirs of his kingdom, an event without parallel in the Europe of that time. To be sure, the unbridled will of the testator did not have the effect he had desired, for he was succeeded on the throne by Ramiro II, called the Monk. Alphonse I had beclouded the boundaries between heaven and earth in his testament, seeing utopia as materially real, forgetting the notion of the personal and of the national frontier (those orders were foreign), and converting the government of a kingdom into a pure theocracy, thinking it possible to climb Jacob's ladder with the feet of a body terrestrial.

The Templars also benefited from the munificence of the kings of Castile, although to a lesser degree. When Alphonse VII captured the town of Calatrava (Ciudad Real), he charged the Order of the Knights

---

[11] This suggests a comparison with what happened in the fourteenth century to the religious of the Spanish order of the Hieronymites, who for a period of time impossible to determine, lived dispersed, as hermits, until their rule was approved by the pope in 1373.

Templar with its defense—proof that there still did not exist in Castile any organized militia of that character.[12] Ten years later the Templars declared themselves unable to hold that key position on the frontier against the Moors, and they informed King Sancho III that "they could not stand against the great power of the Arabs, . . . for they were not adequately equipped to stop them. Moreover, the king himself had not found any among the great men of Castile that would dare to face the danger of that place" (*Crónica general*, p. 666). Two monks from Calatrava, Raimundo de Fitero and Diego Velázquez, offered themselves to the king for the defense of Calatrava, and raised a large army for that purpose. Out of this crusade came the Order of Calatrava. But let us note rather the example that its two founders presented: one a monk to begin with, Raimundo de Fitero, who threw himself into the fight against the infidel; the other Diego Velázquez, a former knight who became a monk and as such entered the same struggle. This was probably not the first case in which this happened, even though documents may be lacking to prove that it had happened before.[13]

The Orders of Santiago and Alcántara appear to have been organized about this same time, a fact that lends support to the idea that their institutional model was the Franco-Islamic Order of the Templars. In the face of such a complicated set of circumstances, I would venture to suggest that if the Spanish orders did indeed owe the manner in which they were organized to the example of the Templars, their substance and spirit were Hispano-Islamic. What would have otherwise been the sporadic action of guerrilla fighters for the faith, crystallized into a regular force, recognized by the civil authority. I do not believe that the Knights Templar could have inspired the asceticism and heroism displayed by the first knights of Calatrava at precisely the moment when the Templars were abandoning their difficult position on the frontier in 1158, whatever the reasons may have been for their withdrawal. I insist again that the fight against the Moor in Spain did not need to be espe-

---

[12] At the same time, the king entrusted the government of the conquered fortress to Rabbi Juda, son of the illustrious Rabbi Josef aben Ezra. F. Fita conjectured that the Templars accepted this authority because of their Masonry and certain Jewish rites performed in the course of their initiation (*Boletín de la Academia de la Historia*, 1889, XIV, 267). Be that as it may, this fact proves how naturally towns and castles were entrusted to Jews and Moors (see p. 500).

[13] The date of the first mention of the order is 1158, when Sancho III gives Calatrava to Raimundo de Fitero, "ut defendatis eam a paganis inimicis crucis Christi," and to whom in the future might be "vestri ordinis et ibi Deo servire voluerint" (*España sagrada*, L, 413).

cially organized in order to present the combination of heroic warfare
and an extreme devotion to the faith, a phenomenon which must have
occurred in a disorganized way at every turn. It might be presumed, then,
that the primitive organization of the knights of Calatrava, far from
arising as a jealous emulation of the Templars' enterprise, may have been
rather the reaction of ascetic warriors against an instance of faintheartedness on the part of the foreign institution. This in no way denies that the
economico-political structure of the Spanish orders had as its model the
precedent of the Templars—beginning with the name of the head, *maestre* (master), which is a gallicism. An Islamico-Christian tradition was
shaped in French molds.

Moslem tradition and the immediate example of the Templars took
on a peculiarly Castilian meaning in the military orders. Belief, the warrior spirit, and the prestige of the monarchy are expressed conjointly
in a single passage of *De rebus Hispaniae,* a chronicle penned by the archbishop Rodrigo Jiménez de Rada (1180?-1247), and in the version of
this Latin text incorporated in the *Crónica general.* The poetic style and
meaning of these passages have hitherto passed unnoticed. In Jiménez
de Rada we can see clearly the most authentic dimensions of Castilian
existence and of its cultural possibilities. He wrote decent Latin, he knew
Arabic and took advantage of this knowledge in his historical works, he
was educated in Bologna and Paris, he ruled the Spanish church from
the primatial see in Toledo, and in his best days he fought for his faith
and his king on the greatest occasion to mark the centuries-old struggle
between the Christians and the Moors, that is, in the decisive battle of
Las Navas de Tolosa (1212), won by Alphonse VIII. The archbishop
was a Castilian with a more than parochial turn of mind.[14]

Through almost the entirety of *De rebus Hispaniae* the style is simply
narrative and devoid of poetic intention. But in the treatment of the
great deeds of Alphonse VIII, the king most admired by Jiménez de
Rada, the prose becomes consciously artistic; parallelism and a kind of
rhyme become features of the sentences:

> In manu robusta vastavit eos [the Moors],
> et in cordis magnificentia coegit eos;
> succendit ignibus civitates,

[14] To help Alphonse VIII in his war against the *almohades,* people came to Toledo
"from many lands and different in their customs, their ways of dressing, and their
tongues; and *because it pleased the king,* the archbishop of Toledo [i.e., Don Rodrigo Jiménez de Rada], resided there in those days, so that through his wisdom the
discord among the differing peoples might be eased" (*Crónica general,* p. 689a).

The humanist Antonio de Nebrija represented teaching the Grand Master of Alcántara, Don Juan de Zúñiga, and his family. (See p. 218.)

Mudéjar 15th-century door (see p. 403), formerly at the high altar of
the cathedral of Baeza, Spain, in which the Christian Gothic and
the Islamic arabesque are harmoniously combined

et succidit viridia deliciarum;
replevit terram timore suo,
conclusit Arabes adventu suo.

Once Cuenca, the city situated amongst jagged rocks, was taken,

rupes eius factae sunt perviae,
et aspera eius in planicies.[15]

The same kind of prose continues to the end of the chapter. The version in the *Crónica general* reads thus:

And he destroyed them with strong hand,
and he reduced them with the magnitude of his heart;
he burned their cities and their other dwellings,
he cut down their orchards and the places where they found
their delights and took their pleasures.[16]

The Latin text recalls the parallelism of certain passages in the Bible:

Halitus eius prunas ardere facit,
et flamma de ore eius egreditur (Job 41:12).

And English readers will recognize verbal echoes of the passage made familiar by Handel's *Messiah*: "Prepare ye the way of the Lord, make straight in the desert a highway for our God. Every valley shall be exalted, and every mountain and hill shall be made low: and the crooked shall be made straight, and the rough places plain" (Isaiah 40:3-4). In the Vulgate, however, the rhythmic correspondence between the beginnings of the phrases as well as between their endings is lacking.

But what is of special interest is the heightening of the poetic tension in the chapter that follows in *De rebus Hispaniae* (VII, 27), the title of which is "Item de magnalibus et piis operibus Aldephonsi." It has as its theme, albeit in prose, a real piece of poetry, a canticle to the military orders and to the foundation of the commandery of the Order of Santiago by King Alphonse. Here are the finest sentences in this rather inaccessible text:

[15] "De rebus Hispaniae," VII, 26, in *Hispaniae Illustratae . . . Scriptores Varii*, Francoforti, 1603, vol. I, p. 124. I have broken the prose down into verselike lines so as to render its rhythmic structure more perceptible.

[16] In Spanish:

Et destrúxolos con rezia mano,
et encogiólos con la grandeza de su coraçón;
quemóles las çipdades et las otras pueblas,
cortóles las huertas et los logares de sus annazaes, o fazí-
an sus deleytes et tomavan sus solazes. . . .

Cepit Alarconem in rupibus sempiternis,
et firmavit seras defensionis;
aldeis multis dotavit illud,
ut abundaret in eo incola fidei;
constituit fortis in munimine,
ut esset Arabibus via necis; . . .
alcarias rupium domuit populis,
et duritiam ilicis convertit in vias.
In Uclesio statuit caput ordinis,
et opus eorum ensis defensionis;
persecutor Arabum moratur ibi,
et incola eius defensor fidei;
vox laudantium auditur ibi,
et iubilus desiderii hilarescit ibi;
rubet ensis sanguine Arabum,
et ardet fides charitate;
mentium execratio est cultori daemonum,
et vita honoris credentium in Deum . . .
Rex Aldephonsus educavit eos [the knights of the orders],
et possessionibus pluribus ditavit eos; . . .
et sustulit sarcinam paupertatis,
et superaddidit divitias competentes,
multiplicatio eorum corona principis;
qui laudabant in Psalmis, accinti sunt ense,
et qui gemebant orantes, ad defensionem patriae;
victus tenui[s] pastus eorum,
et asperitas lanae tegumentum eorum;
disciplina assidua probat eos,
et cultus silentii comitatur eos;
frequens genuflexio humiliat eos,
et nocturna vigilia macerat eos;
devota oratio erudit illos,
et continuus labor excercet eos.
Alter alterius observat semitas,
et frater fratrem ad disciplinam.[17]

Against the general poverty of Latin literature in Castile, the text transcribed above stands out in sharp relief as an authentic fragment of Castilian autobiography, a genuine vibration of the disposition of Cas-

[17] *Ed.cit.*, p. 125.

tilian life. According to Jiménez de Rada it was Alphonse VIII (1158-1214) who organized the knights of Santiago and of Calatrava, both spiritually and economically: "educavit eos." He praises no other king so extensively and so warmly: the conquest of Cordova by Ferdinand III (1236) was an accomplishment of capital importance for the progress of the Reconquest, yet it is recounted by Jiménez de Rada in a simple and prosaic style. But the memory of the battle of Las Navas de Tolosa and of the leader who made such a splendid victory possible lived in the heart of the spirited archbishop just as Lepanto and Don Juan of Austria were to live in the heart of Cervantes centuries later. Alphonse VIII's achievement in warfare on the frontier had as its counterpart in the interior of the kingdom the great feat of organizing those holy armies. It is perfectly consistent with the Castilian life structure that this battling archbishop should employ an exceptionally poetic style to exalt the monarch he personally preferred, *his* king, and to magnify the half-religious half-military orders in a style Biblical in its rhythm and, in its metaphors, close to Arabic literature, with which Jiménez de Rada was well acquainted. The chronicler does not find his inspiration in the literature of classical Antiquity; his art is limited indeed, if we measure him against such a religious writer as Prudentius. His grave and austere morality is Castilian, and his purpose is not to cultivate exuberant and ornate expression, but to pay reverent homage to the king, to the military orders, and to his own conscience—an exemplary instance of Castilian personalism and integralism.

This is the way the *Crónica general* (pp. 679-80) turns the foregoing Latin passage into Castilian:

"Este rey don Alfonso preso a Alarcón . . . que está en peñas que nunca fallesçrán . . . Las alcarias de las peñas domólas con pueblos, et tornó en uvas sabrosas la dureza de la enzina," etc.

That is: "This king Don Alfonso seized Alarcón . . . which is built on everlasting rocks. . . . The lonely settlements in the stony wilds were tamed by the king through the building of towns. The hardness of the oak he turned into sweet-tasting grapes.[18] The king won the town of

---

[18] The misunderstanding of the Latin original (let me here thank R. Menéndez Pidal for calling my attention to the Latin source of this passage) has produced a curious yet pretty expression. The Latin says: "et duritiam ilicis convertit in vias" (the hardness of the oak was made into roads) just as Jiménez de Rada says earlier, referring to Cuenca, "rupes eius factae sunt perviae, et aspera eius in planicies" (her stony places were made passable and her rough places were made into plains). For *vias* the Castilian translator read *uvas*, and then came out with the phrase "the hardness of the oak he turned into sweet-tasting grapes."

Uclés, and established therein the Grand Master of the Order of Santiago, whose duty it is to fight with the sword in defense of the land. The fighters against the Arabs and defenders of our faith dwell there. Voices are heard there of those praising God; their songs, full of the hope for victory, rise in joy. Their sword reddens with Arabian blood. The faith which springs from their hearts is kindled in love and charity, and their wrath falls upon those who honor and worship the spirit of evil; life and honor are for those who believe in God. The monarch made an offering to God of that land, and consecrated it with the Order of Santiago, so that the Order might occupy the first place in the Christian religion. The increase in the number of its knights is the glory of the king; the virtuous teaching of its friars is a crown for the prince. Those who [in the monasteries] sang psalms in praise of God, today gird on the knight's sword. Those who once groaned in prayer have risen up in defense of the land. Their food is meager, their clothing of rough wool. They keep the rule of silence; humility they learn from frequent genuflexion. The night watch makes them thin in body. The prayer of humility teaches them wisdom. Daily toil makes them used to daily toil; and one brother keeps watch over the discipline of another."[19]

Thanks to Rodrigo Jiménez de Rada, then, thirteenth-century Castilian possesses a small piece of ascetic literature marked by high feeling and the authentic projection of a historical moment and of the personality of the man who experienced it. Such, in effect, was the meaning of the military orders during the reign of Alphonse VIII, when the rugged ground of Cuenca was incorporated into Christendom. The lyric tension of the chronicler makes him allude to the "everlasting rocks" and the "hard oaks" growing among them. The result is a bit of incipient landscape poetry. This rude solidity was a fitting background for those monk-warriors, the hope and support of the crown of Castile, when, following the defeat of Alarcos, the victory at Las Navas de Tolosa (1212) estab-

---

[19] The *Crónica general* translates the two last sentences: "El trabajo cutiano los da usados a ello; ell una de éstas guarda las carreras de la otra, et el frayre al frayre, a las disciplinas" (p. 680). But the Latin original asys: "Each brother of the orders observes the path [i.e. the conduct] of the other; each gives the other an example of discipline." The Castilian translator was not always accurate. Hence the obscurity of the sentence which begins "ell una de éstas guarda. . . ." A thorough understanding of the *Crónica general* would require a detailed comparison with its sources, a gigantic task that no one is likely to undertake, although it would reveal a great deal of the inner quality of Castilian culture. It is curious, for instance, that "erudit" (in the sentence "devota oratio erudit illos") is translated by "los enseña et los faze enseñados": knowledge which is not authentically incorporated into the life of the learner is no knowledge at all.

lished for ever the superiority of the Christians. The archbishop's joyous optimism is mirrored in his well-sung Latin and through it in the text
of the *Crónica general*. It would be hard to find in the Castilian prose
and poetry of the thirteenth century a passage like this one, so dense with
strong metaphor and with biblical inspiration. I do not exclude the possibility that Jiménez de Rada enlivened his expressive impulse with reminiscences from Arabic literature. Thus, Christian-Oriental convergence
once more is evident in this manifestation of Castilian existence at a
decisive moment of her history.

Consistent with the method that governs the structure of the present
book, I should now remind the reader that more important than demonstrating the analogy between the military orders and the Moslem *ribāṭ*,
is to include this fact within the perspective of the Christian whose perspective was limited by a Moslem horizon, a horizon that was a part of
his vital experience in two ways: first, he was circumstantially compelled
to face it, and second, he was psychologically compelled to try to displace
it. It is this perspective that is exemplified in the institution of the hermit-
warrior and in the literary expression of a life so oriented. The fact that
the institution of the hermit-warrior was subsequently converted into
something different must have its explanation in the displacement of the
historical horizon to which it was born. Once the hazardous border watch
ceased to be urgently needed, once it was realized that the Moslems were
no longer capable of winning a decisive battle, the military orders began
to forget their asceticism, and oriented themselves anew, now in terms
of the wealth of their lands and political and social prestige. The military
orders created an illusory halo for themselves—they had a claim to distinction and prestige just because they did, and the knights of the orders
became nothing but the instruments of human passion, as will happen
when a powerful person has no purpose. This accounts for the monstrous
knights-commanders immortalized by Lope de Vega in *Fuenteovejuna*
and in *El comendador de Ocaña*, who are related in name only to those
of the twelfth and thirteenth centuries. Lope could never have said of his
comendadores what was said of the medieval ones: "and of rough wool
was their vesture."[20]

This negative aspect of the orders is what was perceived by the popular
feeling starting in the fifteenth century, when the foreground of history
was beginning to be occupied by the masses, who were destined to annihilate the Jews and conquer America. For the common folk, the power-

---

[20] Like the ascetic Sufis, so called because of the *ṣūf* (wool) of their garments.

ful knights personified what is called in the Spanish language of today *señoritismo*—idleness, sensuality, and the misuse of the privileges that come with the possession of riches. The beautiful dirge, *Los Comendadores de Córdoba*[21]—two Andalusian *señoritos* who found their death in a hapless amorous adventure—already shows (fifteenth century) the light in which the knights-commanders of the orders appeared to the common people. Lope de Vega was eventually to become the interpreter of that sentiment, precisely because it was traditional.

On the other hand, many bright points in the history of the orders sank into oblivion. In the realm of chronicles and local histories, we have nothing to give us insight into the intimate life of the orders in those zones where they exercised their authority; and we especially feel the lack of such works relating to the fifteenth century, a period in which the doctrine of *noblesse oblige* came nearer to being a reality than at any other time in Spanish history. One would like to have some intimate acquaintance with Luis de Guzmán, a Grand Master of Calatrava, who, under the influence of little-known currents of religious thought, was seized with the desire to read an accurate version of the Old Testament, and, to be able to do this, paid large sums of money to Rabbi Arragel of Guadalajara. For ten years that Hebrew scholar worked in the town of Maqueda, a fief of the Order of Calatrava near Toledo, and at the end of this period the Grand Master received from him a handsome manuscript, illustrated with miniatures of the finest workmanship and con-

---

[21] Oh Knights commanders,
   To my sorrow I saw you!
   I saw you;
   You, me!

Los Comendadores,
¡por mi mal os vi!
¡Yo vi a vosotros,
vosotros a mí!

* * * * *   * * * * *

The Knights Commanders
Of Calatrava
Left from Seville
At an ill-starred hour,
For the city
Of Cordova in the plain,
With rich steeds
And golden spurs.
Handsome pages they bring
Preceding them.

Los Comendadores
de Calatrava
partieron de Sevilla
en hora menguada,
para la ciudad
de Córdoba la llana,
con ricos trotones
y espuelas doradas.
Lindos pajes llevan
delante de sí.

(Cf. *Biblioteca de Autores Españoles*, XVI, 697)

taining besides the text a scholarly gloss, prepared, it would seem, in collaboration with the Grand Master himself.[22]

There is another episode of great importance, yet known to us only in its most general, external lines. Don Juan de Zúñiga, the last Grand Master of the Order of Calatrava, at the close of the fifteenth century, attended the classes of Antonio de Nebrija, who brought the new humanistic spirit from Italy to Spain. The pupil became the Maecenas of the teacher, whom he took to his Zalamea palace (Cáceres), where he established a scientific academy in which figured the two Hebrew astronomers Abraham Zacuto and Abasurto.[23] The illustration reproduced

[22] Cf. A. Paz y Melia, "La Biblia de Arragel," in *Homenaje a Menéndez y Pelayo*. The magnificent text was published in 1922, at the expense of the Duke of Alba. The transcription was made by Messrs. A. Paz y Melia and J. Paz. This was not the first time, moreover, that a grand master of the orders had taken advantage of the talents of a Jew to further the ends of culture. Don Lorenzo Suárez de Figueroa, Grand Master of Santiago, ordered Don Jacob Çadique of Uclés to translate the *Libro de sabios e philosophos e de otros ejemplos e doctrinas muy buenas* from Catalan to Castilian, a task that was finished in 1402 (J. Rodriguez de Castro, *Biblioteca española de los escritores rabínicos*, Madrid, 1781, i, 263). Jacob Çadique had been baptized, a consequence, no doubt, of the massacres of 1391. The book he translated must be something like the *Libro de la saviesa* of the Catalonian Jew Jafuda. It is evident, then, that the great lords of the orders were interested in didactico-moral literature, that birthright of the Arabs and Jews for which the Christians had such a highly cultivated taste. In Chapter 13 I shall treat of a translation of Maimónides made at the instance of a son of one of the grand masters of Santiago.

[23] Cf. F. Cantera, *El judío salmantino Abraham Zacut*, 1935. Zacuto was not a Portuguese but a Salamancan, and very much the protégé of the learned bishop Gonzalo de Vivero (d. 1480), who heaped honors on him in life and left him an inheritance in his will. After the bishop's death, Zacuto found patronage in the palace of the Grand Master of Calatrava, whom he describes as "a lover of all the sciences and learned in them, so that, attracted by his fame, all wise and lettered men leave their lands and their birthplaces to seek [at his side] true peace and full perfection"; at his side, "men of letters have refreshment and reward." The most detailed account of the academy created around Don Juan de Zúñiga is to be found in the *Crónica de la Orden de Alcántara*, by Alonso de Torres Tapia, 1763, ii, 569: "The Grand Master was a friend of all good letters; and besides the religious that he kept there [in Zalamea] with him, he brought from without some distinguished humanists: the bachelor [of law] Friar Gutierre de Trijo; the master Friar Domingo, a theologian of the order of preachers; the doctor De la Parra [subsequently a physician at the court of the Catholic Sovereigns]; *Abasurto*, a Jew by birth and an astrologer; the *master Antonio de Lebrija*; and the choirmaster Solórzano, the best musician known to those centuries. Master Antonio taught him Latin, and he [the Grand Master] had given the habit and the commandery of the town to Master Antonio's son, Friar Marcelo de Lebrija. The Jewish astrologer explained the *Esfera* [probably the books on astronomy translated by the order of Alphonse the Learned] to him, and everything that it was permissible to know about his art. And he was such an enthusiast that in one of the upper rooms of his house he caused to be painted the heavens with all their planets, stars, and signs of the zodiac. Today the painting is

here²⁴ shows Nebrija dressed in the habit of a Knight of Alcántara and giving instruction in humane letters to the grand master and his family. I have no idea how extensive or how profound the learning was that he imparted, or what repercussions the Grand Master's cultural initiative may have had within the order. It is noteworthy, in any case, that Extremadura, where the order had its landholdings, could claim a certain literary and humanistic culture in the first half of the sixteenth century. An accident? Perhaps. I would nevertheless venture the opinion that there was some connection between the Order of Alcántara and this flowering of art and human distinction. The Spanish theatre was born towards the end of the fifteenth century with Juan del Encina. It was thus a humanistic offshoot of the University of Salamanca, located in the territory just to the north of Extremadura, and served to satisfy the artistic appetite of the courts of the prince Don Juan and the Duke of Alba, in Alba de Tormes (Salamanca). After this the new art turned southward for further propagation, and the result is found in the works of the Extremadurans Torres Naharro, Miguel de Carvajal, Sánchez de Badajoz, Díaz Tanco, and others. The University of Salamanca, in Leon, the clergy, and the Order of Alcántara in Extremadura were in close contact with one another, although research in Spanish archives would be necessary before one would have an adequate foundation for a discussion of this matter. It may be possible one day to prove that the University of Salamanca, the Hieronymite Monastery of Guadalupe (in Extremadura, and in the past a dynamic center that gave spiritual energy to a variety of developments), and the Order of Alcántara were the instruments that shaped the finest of the conquistadors, a dramatic art of unsuspected daring, and the aristocratic refinement of Zalamea, Plasencia, and Alba de Tormes.

---

faded from age." Zacuto wrote a *Brief Treatise on Celestial Influences* (*Tratado breve de las influencias del cielo*, 1486) "for the help of the Grand Master's physicians" (Cantera, *op.cit.*, p. 87). Concerning Abasurto, cf. Professor J. Gillet, *Torres Naharro's Propalladia*, III, 630. This is what might be called a Renaissance court, in which, very much in the Spanish fashion, Dominican theologians mingled with Jewish astronomers, and humanists educated in Italy. Yet for the meaning of this "Renaissance" we must not turn to Italy but to the ancient tradition of the Spanish Peninsula, a tradition maintained by the great lords of the orders like an echo of that most splendid of courts presided over by Alphonse the Learned in the thirteenth century. At the end of the fifteenth century the courts of the grand masters disappear, and so do the Jewish men of learning: Spain was creating and destroying herself.
²⁴ Taken from an article by A. Paz y Melia in *Revista da Archivos*, 1898, p. 8.

Holy War

Now that we have seen the military orders take on meaning by relating them to Islam, we are also led to see a more profound aspect of the problem, the adoption by the Christians of the idea and the feeling of holy war as a means of attaining eternal glory in paradise. Karl Heisig's excellent study of the *Chanson de Roland*[25] confirmed ideas that I had been entertaining along these lines for some time. Mr. Heisig cites texts left by the Mozarabic writers Eulogius and Albar. In the *Memoriale sanctorum*, composed in 851, Eulogius speaks in exalted language of the "bellum parare incredulis," and of the remission of sins that awaits those who die as martyrs fighting the infidel. According to Eulogius, the apostles were commanded to attack the enemies of God, and he therefore bewails the fact that the will to fight is absent "in pastoribus Christi" —in the popes. Holy war existed neither as an idea nor as even a vague feeling in ninth-century France: two monks, Usuard and Odilard, came to Cordova in 858, and they did not realize what the inflamed preachments of Eulogius meant. It was the Cluniacs in the eleventh century who adopted the Spanish idea of the crusade later to be reflected in the *chansons de geste*. In the battle of Las Navas de Tolosa (1212) there was a moment of serious danger in which King Alphonse VIII feared for victory and his life. Archbishop Rodrigo, who fought at his side and later wrote an account of his deeds, said these words: "Sire, if you go to your death, all [who die with you] will go up with you into paradise."[26] The Chronicle of Alphonse the Learned has the archbishop say, "Sire, if it please God, the crown of victory will come to us" (p. 701). The same Chronicle recounts that the fortified town of Martos was about to be reconquered by the Moors, who were pressing their siege against it. A large number of knights came forth to raise the siege, and before the assault, which took the lives of many of them, Diego Pérez de Vargas harangued them thus: "Those of us who do not succeed in getting through and who die today, *shall save our souls and shall go to our glory in paradise*" (p. 738). Some years later Prince Juan Manuel writes, in his *Libro de los Estados*: "And the good Christians take it that the reason why God consented that Christians should suffer such wickedness from the Moors was so that there might be a reason for a just war with the Moors, and so that those who should die in it, having fulfilled the

[25] "Geschichtsmetaphysik des Rolandsliedes" in the *Zeitschrift für romanische Philologie*, 1935, LV, 1-87.
[26] Cf. J. Amador de los Ríos, *Historia de la literatura española*, III, 426.

commandments of Holy Church, might be martyrs, or *so that their souls might be cleared of the sin that they committed*" (p. 294). "Those sinners who die and who are slain by the Moors—*much greater hope must there be for their salvation* than for the salvation of those other sinners who do not die in the war with the Moors . . . provided they die in defense and exaltation of the Holy Catholic faith; and those who die thus are holy, without doubt, and are true martyrs, and have no other pain to bear save that death which they take upon themselves" (p. 324).

These texts of Don Juan Manuel do not mean what an eminent historian suggests that they mean, that is, that the Christians "carried out their reconquest in fulfillment of an obligation to occidental Christianity," as "martyrs" or victims of the abandonment of the rest of Europe. I emphasize my different interpretation only to point out how far we have been from perceiving the meaning of the spiritual life of the "two" Spains during the Middle Ages.[27] The foregoing passages are a simple reflection of Islamic ideas and emotions. To be convinced of this one has only to read any Moslem writer who speaks of wars against the infidel: "Thus it happens that there are not to be seen in Spain any eyes save those that keep watch to satisfy God, any fighters save those who fight in the way established by God, any warriors save those who make war in obedience to God. Anyone who dies in this state *dies a martyr*; anyone who lives is blessed, for the holy war and those who make it are pillars of heaven."[28] It is well known, moreover, that in the Koran (IV, 97-99) God promises great reward, pardon and mercy, to those who fight zealously, showing preference over those who do not fight; which is exactly what is said in the Christian texts transcribed above. It is evident that in the uppermost circles of Spanish culture in the thirteenth century, the war, which had already been going on for centuries, was given a meaning parallel to the meaning that it had for the Moslems; and this belief, purely Islamic in inspiration, overflowed in the words of Archbishop

[27] One can understand the scholars' resistance against accepting the penetration of Spanish history by Moorish life as a defense against the romantic idea that Spain was a part of the East, a country that was not similar in any important ways to the rest of Europe.

[28] "Description of Spain" by the writer called the "Anonymous, of Almeria," translated by René Basset in *Homenaje a don Francisco Codera*, p. 641. Here is another passage, reproduced by Dozy, of the battle between the *almohades* and the Portuguese at Santarem in 1184: "A large number of the most important *almohades*, of Andalusian chieftains, and of other persons died *as martyrs* on this expedition" (*Recherches*, II, 457).

Rodrigo, Alphonse the Learned, and his nephew Juan Manuel.[29] In a word, the imitative parallelism begun in the ninth century with the Santiago-Mohammed opposition, is prolonged by the pseudomorphosis of the *rābiṭa* in the military orders and in the adoption of the doctrine of the holy war. But with this we are not at the end of the parallel.

Tolerance

According to our inexhaustible source, Don Juan Manuel, the Moors were to be fought, not because they professed a false religion, but because they wrongfully occupied lands which belonged to the Christians: "There is war between the Christians and the Moors, and there will be, until the Christians have got back the lands which the Moors took from them by force; for *neither because of the law nor because of the sect that they hold to*, would there be war between them; for Jesus Christ never commanded us to kill or to reward people in order that they should embrace his law; for He has no desire for forced service but only for that which is done readily and freely" (*Libro de los Estados, ed. cit.*, p. 294).

Menéndez Pidal mentions this passage, and rightly notes that the religiosity of the Middle Ages loses "a certain racial intolerance which it displays earlier in the Christian-barbarian epoch."[30] But we can no longer limit ourselves to observing the "fact," because human facts taken by themselves are unreal abstractions. They must be supported by the "meaning" which is imparted to them from the life in which they are "dwelling." Since the existence of the Spanish Christians necessarily went on within the horizon of tolerance traced by Islam, they created their existence as a function of that horizon. The Koran says: "Fight therefore against them [the unbelievers], until there be no more civil discord, and the only worship be that of God: but if they desist, then let there be no hostility, save against the wicked" (ii, 189). "Let there be no compulsion in religion. Now is the right way made distinct from error" (ii, 257). "But if thy Lord had pleased, verily all who are in the earth would have believed together. What? Wilt thou compel men to become believers? No soul can believe but by the permission of God" (x, 99-100).

The Koran, itself a product of religious syncretism, was a monument

[29] The same idea appears in the glosses to Arragel's Bible (1420): "Whoever in the service of God receives death from the hand of a heretic for the true and Catholic faith . . . not only does not suffer [in the other life] but rather will have a reward for his deed: for without doubt, *martyrs do not die*" (i, 116a). This gloss must have been the work of one of Rabbi Arragel's Christian collaborators.

[30] *La España del Cid*, p. 675.

of tolerance to begin with, since it fused the Islamic beliefs with those of Judaism and Christianity. An anticipatory suggestion of the Sufistic idea that all paths lead to God is to be found in the Koran, and the Koran itself is founded (I venture to think) on the belief that nothing outside the divine essence is substantial or certain. Indifference toward any exclusiveness in religious faith is visible in such notions as this: "The roads that lead to God are as numerous as the souls of men."[31] This basic attitude of tolerance, occasionally forgotten (there is no religion that is absolutely faithful to its creed), was strengthened during the expansion of Islam, which rapidly brought one people after another, with divers beliefs, under its political dominion. Religious tolerance and the harmonious life together of Mohammedanism and other faiths facilitated the exploitation of the conquered countries, and offered the Moslem the possibility of expanding his interests in the changing aspects of life from the Euphrates to the Ebro. But besides this pragmatic consideration, Moslem asceticism and mysticism (Sufism) were bound to make tolerance (or indifference to dogma) the very center of their religious experience, which was based on the love of God, on the rapture of the soul, and not on knowledge. Thus, the Murcian Ibn 'Arabī could say:

> My heart can take on any form: it is a pasture for
> gazelles and a monastery for Christian monks.
> A temple for idols, and for the Kaaba of the
> pilgrims, and for the tables of the Torah, and
> for the book of the Koran.
> I follow the religion of love: whatever the
> direction of the camels of my love, my religion
> and my faith are there.[32]

The Moslem—always something of a bedouin—moves, be it under the sun or within himself, towards remote and changeable horizons, but the intensity of his feeling remains constant. It does not surprise him

[31] I. Goldzieher, *Le dogme et la loi de l'Islam*, p. 143.

[32] *The Tarjumān Al-Ashwāq*, translated by R. A. Nicholson, London, 1911, p. 67. In the commentary the author makes on his own poem we read: " 'My heart has become capable of every form,' as another has said, 'The heart is so called from its changing,' for it varies according to the various influences by which it is affected in consequence of the variety of its states of feeling; and the variety of its feelings is due to the variety of the Divine manifestations that appear to its inmost ground" (*ibid.*, p. 69). For the true Mohammedan, the heart—and everything else—must have been like a weathervane, having no other meaning save that which it is given by the breath of God.

to find entities foreign to each other existing side by side or living together harmoniously. Jews and Christians swarmed about in Cordova, intermingling with Slavic slaves, brought to Spain by Venetian tradesmen. Towards the end of the eleventh century, except for isolated instances of violence, those who did not disturb the peace of the Saracens were allowed to enjoy their own peace in the Saracen cities.

After that time, the *Almorávides* and *Almohades* from Africa struggled to replace the prevailing laxity with a new rigidity, and life for the non-Mohammedans, however peaceful they were, ceased to be pleasant. But during the first four hundred years of Moslem domination, there was more than enough of time and opportunity for Islamic ways of tolerance to prevail in the Peninsula. Tolerance of belief was in turn not separable from the magico-rational syncretism of the Hispano-Arabic culture within which the mathematics of Euclid lived alongside the stories of wizards and fortune-tellers. And with that enormous body of exact knowledge available, it occurred to no one to use it for instilling "clear and distinct" ideas into the disordered, confused minds of the average or common people. Inherently hostile elements continued to exist in a harmonious life together in an atmosphere of tolerance until finally Iblis or destiny turned it all into the golden dust of migrant grandeur, the most splendid caravan in the history of Spain.

Juan Manuel's statement that I quoted above, in which he insists that only service readily and freely given is acceptable to God, was anticipated by his uncle, Alphonse the Learned, who simply translates and amplifies the doctrine expressed in the Koran:

"By good words and appropriate preaching should the Christians seek to convert the Moors and make them believe our faith . . . , not by force or through rewards [*Koran*: Let there be no compulsion in Religion], for if it were the will of our Lord to lead them to it and to make them believe it by force, he would reward them if he wished to [*Koran*: But if the Lord had pleased, verily all who are in the earth would have believed together]; but He is not rewarded by the service that men do out of fear, but by that which is done freely and without any recompense." (*Partidas*, VII, XXV, 2).[33]

It is understandable that Raymond Lully (d. 1315) should have written his *Libro del gentil y los tres sabios* in Arabic rather than in his own

[33] The Moorish jurists were inspired by the same doctrine: "The profession of the Moorish faith, when it is forced, has no validity in religious law" (I. Goldzieher, *Le dogme et la loi de l'Islam*, p. 257, in which is cited a similar decision at the end of the seventeenth century).

Catalan. In this book a Christian, a Moor, and a Jew talk amiably, expounding the contents of their respective faiths without a trace of acrimony. Without doubting Lully's Christianity, one may still be quite sure that here he let himself be carried away by his enthusiasm for a kind of religious Deism in which the three great faiths of the Hispanic peoples might be contained. Just as the three religions live together side by side juridically in the legislation of Alphonse X's *Partidas*,[34] so they also dwell together harmoniously in the intellectual dreaming of Raymond Lully, after the model of Yehuda ha-Leví in the *Cuzari*.[35] What first appears in the Mallorcan mystic as lyrical enthusiasm centered in the heart is converted, in Alfonse X, into a very Castilian juridical objectivity—because the one was a Mallorcan, the other a Castilian: such was the historical reality. Lully's sympathetic feelings for the infidel break out in sentences such as these: "Let our soul in prayer not forget the infidels, who are of our flesh and blood, being like us in species and form. The ignorance of faith and of science that there is in them comes from the lack of masters to teach them."[36] This was the same thing that Erasmus was to preach in the sixteenth century, and we who are attune to the same spirit, can only lament the fact that there is still, in the twentieth century, no study of Lully's work worthy of it, a body of writing as liberal in attitude as Lully's own three wise men were in their religious discussion. Here, however, I must confine myself to indicating the problem and to showing something of what would be revealed by an analysis of medieval Spanish tolerance in its connection with Islam,[37] a connection that must

[34] Among other humane laws pertaining to the Jews, we find this one: "And because the synagogue is a house where the name of God is praised, we forbid that any Christian should dare to break into it or to take from it any thing by force" (VII, xxv, 4).

[35] As we have seen before, Sufism made a positive effort to becloud the frontiers that separated the different religious confessions. Some Sufists went so far as to argue that "with the knowledge of divine unity an element of union was given to humanity, whereas the different religious laws were the cause of the separation." These ideas are plainly present in the works of Raymond Lully, where they are in perfect harmony with the exalted illuminism of his lyric soul. Rationalist Deism was preceded in Europe by the Deism of mystic emotion. Guillaume Postel, with his *Alcorani, seu legis Mahometi, et Evangelistarum Concordiae liber* (Paris, 1543), was trying to bring the Koran and the Gospel into agreement not in order to enrich "the ancient dream of unity *of the Middle Ages*," as some think, but because he was an Arabist who had been in the orient, who had written an Arabic grammar, etc. As is always true in history, here too we are dealing with a problem of life, and not only of ideas.

[36] *Evast y Blanquerna*, Chap. XL, in Ramon Llull, *Obras literarias*, edited by M. Batllori and M. Caldentey, Madrid, 1948, p. 255.

[37] Tolerance had reached down to the deep layers of the Spanish people, to judge by certain local laws, based on the law of custom: "And the Jews shall have rights

not be forgotten: The vital and legal harmony between the Spanish believers and the Moors and Jews was not an aspect of the theological and metaphysical order of the so-called Middle Ages, of which the spirit was most perfectly incarnate in Dante and Thomas Aquinas. The period in Spain that was contemporary with the Middle Ages was something quite singular, as we can see when we examine Spanish history in its totality. Spanish tolerance was the result of a *modus vivendi*, not of a theology.

To Alphonse the Learned and his follower Don Juan Manuel, the Moor was a political rival to be conquered and not a religious enemy to be exterminated. Yet the Spanish Christian was at the same time implacable toward the heretic who divided the faith. The infidel—Moor or Jew—had a "book" just as the Christian did (as the Koran says), and was worthy of respect for this reason. Moreover, the doctrine of tolerance reflected the high favor enjoyed by the Jews with the great lords until the Jews were expelled in 1492. The ideas of the wise and learned Jewish counselors found expression in the *Partidas* and in the works of Juan Manuel. The conception of tolerance lost its power when the Moslems ceased to inspire fear and admiration, and when the masses of the people began subjecting the Jews to a relentless persecution, at the end of the fourteenth century. It was no longer possible for Christians, Moors, and Jews to live under the same roof, because the Christian now felt himself strong enough to break down the traditional custom of Spain whereby the Christian population made war and tilled the soil, the Moor built the houses, and the Jew presided over the enterprise as a fiscal agent and a skillful technician. As late as the fourteenth century the Spaniards were mentioned as believers in three religions, and not as an aggregate of different social classes, or as inhabitants of different regions. The Archpriest of Hita says that Sir Carnal sent his letter of challenge to Dame Lent in these terms:

> The letter came addressed *to all of us*:
> "Powerful Sir Carnal, by the grace of God,
> To all Christians, Moors, and Jews,
> Greetings with all kinds of meat." (1193)

In the twelfth century, the mention of Moors and Christian together took on a locative, spatial meaning: "en moros ni en cristianos"—"no-

---

as Christians do; for whoever shall wound or kill a Jew, shall pay the same fine as if the victim were a Christian, or as if he had killed a citizen of Salamanca" (*Fuero de Salamanca*, edited by Américo Castro and Federico de Onís, p. 202).

where" (*Poema del Cid*, 3514). "Moros e cristianos" meant "everyone" and "moros ni cristianos" meant "no one" (Cf. R. Menéndez Pidal, *Cantar de Mio Cid*, p. 338). What today is felt as a nation or *patria* was then felt as an aggregate of believers, different in faith yet living together, because this was the way things were, and the way they had to be. It was upon the foundation of this odd complex that the power of the kings and the nobility was raised, and their power kept those heterogeneous elements in a state of harmonious interaction and interdependence, of life together, without excessive strains, a state which the Church made every effort to destroy from the thirteenth century on. The popular drive, as it gained momentum at the end of the fourteenth century, pushed the Moor to one side and fell upon the Jew. At the end of the fifteenth century, Spain was ruled by a single belief, which had absorbed the totalitarian character of the other two. It was no longer believed that the Moors ought to live "among the Christians, keeping their own law, and not contemning ours" (*Partida*, VII, xxv, 1). It is thus that I conceive the creation and ruination of Hispanic tolerance, entirely outside the framework of the European Middle Ages. Between the savage Visigothic laws of the *Fuero Juzgo* against the Jews (seventh century) and Alphonse the Learned's mild laws relating to them there are five hundred years of Islam.[38]

During those five hundred years one belief was opposed to the other and at the same time considerable interconnection developed between them. The fourteenth-century Castilians, for instance, were affected by

---

[38] "Let them not keep their Passover, let them not be married under their own law, let them not be circumcised." Let the Jew that does not have his children baptized "receive a hundred lashes, and let his head be shorn, and let him be cast out of the land, and let his goods come into the hands of the king," etc. (*Fuero Juzgo*, Book XII, titles ii and iii.) The situation of the Jews during the Visigothic period has been studied by Solomon Katz, *The Jews in the Visigothic and Frankish Kingdoms of Spain and Gaul*, 1937. The Visigothic monarchs had serious difficulty carrying out their rigorous laws against the Jews, because the Jews bribed the clergy (Katz, *op.cit.*, p. 13) and were protected by the nobles (p. 19). Thus it can be seen that the tolerance which I have been trying to make understandable is a long parenthesis extending from the eighth century to the fifteenth.

On the other hand, the powerful Jews, their anger aroused, contributed to the overthrow of the State at the end of the seventh century by facilitating the arrival of the African Moors (Katz, *op.cit.*, p. 21). This is what the Moriscos tried to do in the sixteenth century, in a world that was by that time different and in which therefore their success was impossible. Speaking of racial conflicts in Spain, the Catholic historian M. Menéndez y Pelayo says: "There is nothing more repugnant than this struggle, the principal cause of the decadence of the Peninsula. . . . Conflicts of race explain many events and resolve many of the enigmas of our history" (*Historia de los heterodoxos españoles*, III, 398; V, 108).

the widespread Islamic Deism as I shall point out in Appendix II, below. Ibn Ḥazm made a detailed study of the skepticism that suspended all judgment concerning the truth or falsity of any philosophic system or religion: "every demonstration in support of a thesis or dogma is offset by another demonstration against it." This, as M. Asín Palacios observes, had already been said by the thinkers of Alexandria.[39] There was this difference however: In eleventh-century Spain there were Moslems who defended the existence of a universal religion. In his *Critical History of Religions* Ibn Ḥazm refers to those who think that "there must be amongst all the religions one that is authentic, but it has not manifested itself clearly and evidently to anyone, and therefore God has imposed on no one the obligation to profess it" (Asín, *loc.cit.*, p. 302).

How it got there I do not know, but there is a spark of the idea of a universal religion in Franciscanism. When asked why he collected the writings of pagans with the same solicitude as those of Christians, Saint Francis replied that it was "because in them he found the letters of which the name of God is composed. What there is of good in those writings belongs neither to paganism nor to humanity, but only to God, who is the author of all goodness."[40] Long before Saint Francis, the Spanish Jew Ibn Paquda had written (in the eleventh century): "The rabbis say that whoever utters a wise word, even if he belongs to the Gentiles, is called a sage."[41]

Poetic reflections of the religious breadth of medieval Spain are to be found in the *Cantigas* of Alphonse the Learned: the Virgin saves a Moorish woman with her infant daughter (No. 205); a king of Morocco defeats his enemy with the help of a banner of the Virgin (No. 181); the Moors bring back from the sea into which they had cast it an image of the Virgin, so that they may catch fish once more (No. 183); etc. Concerning inverse cases, I recall only the Jewish supplications for relief from drought or pestilence, one of them authorized by the cathedral chapter of Seville (see Chapter 13).

During the years of Christian-Islamic-Judaic intermingling, the spiritual communication among the three beliefs made it possible for Alphonse the Learned to base his doctrine of tolerance on the Koran without feel-

---

[39] *Cultura Española*, 1907, v, 299.

[40] A. F. Ozanam, "Les poètes franciscains en Italie," quoted by Father Michel-Ange, in *Etudes Franciscaines*, 1909, xxii, 610. Duns Scotus finds the imprint of God in everything, for "In commendando enim Christum, malo excedere quam deficere a laude" (3, Dist. xiii, qua est, 4, no. 9) (*ibid.*)

[41] *Duties of the Heart*, edited by M. Hyamson, 1925, p. 16.

ing that he was offending the Church of which he was a faithful son. But this passed, and Spanish life took other directions. True, as late as the beginning of the sixteenth century Bishop Antonio de Guevara could say: "To call a person a Moorish dog, or to call him an unbelieving Jew . . . is to use words of great temerity and even of little Christianity. . . . To call a convert a 'dog of a Moor' or 'pig of a Jew' is to call him a perjurer, a false witness, a heretic."[42] And we have already seen other humane remarks with reference to the Moriscos (p. 93). But as time went on, the Spaniard became more and more intolerant, because the motives had disappeared that had created common interests and reciprocal respect. And when this happened the people forced the expulsion of the Jews or their entrance into the Christian community. The Aragonese Count of Sástago, Don Artal de Alagón, wrote in 1593: "Do not mix with any other family. The Christian family follows this rule by neither admitting nor hearing the errors of the infamous nations that are removed from God. . . . Although [Jesus Christ] came to redeem everyone, we see that he told the gentile Canaanite woman that it was not reasonable to give the children's bread to the dogs, meaning to say by this that so long as the gentiles did not change their opinions and recognize and receive his law, they were to be treated as dogs."[43] With the adversaries of the Catholic faith eliminated (by expulsion or by forced conversion), the Spanish Catholics followed the same procedure in the sixteenth century that the Moors and Jews had followed within their own religions. That is, it was not tolerated within Judaism or Mohammedanism that a man should depart from his belief: "The inquisition is a popular institution which functions constantly in Islam, and for searching out and denunciation it is independent of the ordinary tribunals." At the end of the tenth century, Almanzor won the sympathy of the Mohammedan masses as well as the doctors of law (*faqīhs*) "by organizing a true, official inquisition, or purge of all the libraries of

---

[42] "Epistola XIV" in the second part, in *Biblioteca de Autores Españoles*, XIII, 213*b*.

[43] *Concordia de las leyes divinas y humanas*, Madrid, 1593, fol. 104*r*. The crisis in the sentiment of tolerance, and the basing of war against the infidel on purely religious motives are inseparable phenomena revealing a change in the historical horizon. But in the last analysis, the quest for "just causes" on which to base the wars against the American Indians derives from those same medieval circumstances. Before the discovery of America, the king of Portugal, Don Duarte, wrote concerning the justification of the war against the Moors: "The Holy Father admonishes us to wage such a war, and none of the faithful, unless he disobey the Pope, must have any doubt about its justice" (*Leal Conselheiro*, edited by J. M. Piel, 1942, Chap. XVIII).

the realm, not excepting even the royal library of Al-Ḥakam II" (M. Asín, *Abenmasarra*, 1914, p. 24, 91). Presently I shall prove that the Spanish Jews had a genuine inquisition for the purpose of prosecuting those of their co-religionists who departed from their orthodoxy.

Moslem tolerance towards other religions was due chiefly to political motives. At the same time, what I call totalitarianism of belief (the absence of distinction between the religious and the secular) eventually forced the Moors and Jews to be fanatically intolerant. The Spaniards, molded in their structure by the historical impulse of three beliefs, were tolerant because of the exigencies of politics, and intolerant because of the totalitarian, omnipresent character of their belief.

It remains quite evident, then, that the enlargement of the religious consciousness in Spain during the Middle Ages is inseparable from certain forms of Islamic spirituality, and from the fact that peoples with contrary beliefs saw themselves forced to live together.

8

Islam and the Spanish Form of Life

Islam and the Vital Structure of the
Hispano-Christian

I HAVE BEEN CONCERNED thus far with words, customs, beliefs, and institutions directly or indirectly connected with the fact that Moor and Christian lived together. Now I must ask the reader to move with me into more obscure zones, in which evidence of the kind I have been able to adduce up to this point will not easily illumine the lines etched by Islam in the very depths of the Spanish psyche, in certain habits of the inner self. Still, it is natural to presume that structural tendencies very similar to Islamic forms of intimate experience would have developed out of the important contacts previously examined.[1] This class of phenomena corresponds to what the natural scientists call pseudomorphosis,[2] although I make the comparison, to be sure, only to illuminate my meaning, for the human being and crystallizable minerals are altogether different. But something like this we have already observed in the word *hijodalgo*, Romanic in aspect and Islamic in its semantic background.

Certain gestures and movements are made by the inner person just as they are by the physical body, wherefore the popular Spanish expression "his soul is meandering in his body" (se le pasea el alma por el cuerpo), that is, the soul is idle. Sometimes the soul and the ego drag out a languid existence; in other cases they strain to the breaking point. Between one another they maintain harmonious or discordant relations, either with the body's consent or in spite of its rebellion. Once when the Count of Cabra was being armed before going into battle, his attendants, noticing that he was trembling, asked him how it was that a man of such courage could tremble so; and he replied: "The flesh fears the test to

---

[1] I emphasize that I make no claim whatsoever to having exhausted the chapter of Islamic imitations and adoption because my interest is concentrated in the structure of life and not in the quantity of events and facts. I am persuaded that many more facts will be found that can be included in the historical panorama that I am trying to outline.

[2] This term is not used here or elsewhere in this book in Spengler's pejorative sense.

which the spirit is determined to put it."[3] The Prince of Condé (and before him Ignatius of Loyola) said something like this later; and phenomena comparable to these occur continually. The dedicated sage, the hero, the rigid moralist can shut themselves up in their ego and give no heed to the demands of the soul or the sensations of the body. The problem is as familiar as it is arduous to solve, and I must give it only a side-glance, for my concern here is but to remind the reader that in contrast to the vital structure of those people who have the desire and the power to isolate themselves in their rational operations, there is the vital structure of those who do not isolate their ego from the body and the soul.[4]

The idea of the conflict between the psychosomatic inclinations and the regulating authority of the ego is ancient. It has inspired asceticism in all ages, Stoic-Christian, and, at times, Sufistic morality. Literature has referred to this phenomenon as early as the time of Homer (at the beginning of Book xx of the *Odyssey*). The Spanish are not peculiar in having known or mentioned this universal idea, but they are peculiar in that they exist without any possible outlet, within the complex created by the contrary terms of that duality—the psychosomatic and the purely rational. The French structure of life, on the other hand, since the eleventh century, when we first begin to perceive it, rests on the dominance of the rational (the "calculating") ego over the psychosomatic reactions. The Spanish, on the contrary, have experienced existentially the process of this opposition as a vital dialectic. Thus it is understandable, perhaps, that the Jesuits (shaped by Spanish Catholicism) rejected the religious logic of the Jansenists, and opposed it with casuistry. Casuistry is not an absurdity, as Pascal would have it, but an attempted adaptation to the vital complexity of the believer. Each sinner constitutes a unique and living case; there is no rational norm by which it can be totally accounted for. The logical path of Jansenism, if rigorously followed, would lead to the Goddess of Reason (la déesse Raison).

[3] Melchor de Santa Cruz, *Floresta general*, 1574, No. 174. Of one of his spiritual masters ibn-'Arabī says: "He was strong of heart, but weak of body and pale of color. *Severe towards his own soul*, if someone said to him 'Be more indulgent with it!' he would reply, 'To be more indulgent with it, I punish it.' He would rise from his bed to pass part of the night in vigil, and he would stand praying until he collapsed from fatigue" (*Vidas de santones andaluces*, tr. by Asín, p. 103).

[4] Cf. J. Ortega y Gasset, "Vitalidad, alma, espíritu," in *Obras completas* 1936, pp. 489ff.; Francisco Romero, *Filosofía de la persona*, Buenos Aires, 1944. The claimed presence of Seneca's stoicism in the depths of Spanish life seems most doubtful to me (see my book *La realidad histórica de España*, 1954, Appendix I).

The purpose of the act of thought is to find something true and verifiable which is depersonalized the moment it acquires reality; this reality will then be possessed in common by all persons who come to know it, as well as by the person whose thought it was originally. Ratiocinations are universal and supraindividual, and do not necessarily require a knowledge of the body and soul of the person who formulates them. To put it another way, the one who accepts the truth and what there is of reality in it recognizes the existence of something in which his life is not involved. Thus it is, then, that the thinker who objectifies himself in thought dispossesses himself of something that has been his own. To recognize, in turn, the existence of something objective (ideas or things) presupposes the admission that one has no part in their existence. This is an aspect of what generally passes for the "European" Weltanschauung. There are peoples, nevertheless, who have found it more urgent to express the participation of their souls in the world around them than to isolate themselves from the world in order to meditate upon the difficulties or problems that it creates. The results of these meditations are realities that retain nothing of the soul of the one who has brought them forth, nor do they speak to the soul of one who comes in contact with them (a theorem, a dike, an industrial artifact). The Spaniard has never been much attracted by such activities because he is not much given to reasoning—as we have already been told by Alonso de Palencia in the fifteenth century. That is to say, however much rational thinking the Spaniard might engage in, he would not submit completely to the requirement that he abstract himself totally from his soul, and perhaps even from his body. Antonio de Nebrija, Spain's most learned humanist, composed a set of tables for calculating the hours astronomically and for knowing the time in the various cities of Europe. But in his prefatory remarks he explains that he undertook this task only to keep a monk who was a friend of his from annoying him with questions every time the monk's clock broke down. For the Spaniard, then, thought must be integrated in the total life of the person, and this leaves little room for pure theorizing. This explains why there are scarcely any Spanish philosophers who have made completely original contributions to the general corpus of human thought. Let us recall that for Miguel de Unamuno the idea of immortality implied the immortality of his body, including, perhaps, even the very garments that covered it.

As opposed to the absolute and cold communication of thought, the Spaniard prefers the warm expression of his individual soul. For this reason he has an addiction to gesture and metaphor, sensitively relating them to what he is expressing. If gesture and external attitudes have a special value for the Hispanic man, as I have said elsewhere,[5] it is because his life has consisted more in the cultivation of his soul than in shutting himself up in his reason. For the Spaniard, almost nothing has been a purely rational problem, not even the existence of God. Yet on the other hand, everything relating to the way the person expresses and represents himself has been a problem for the Spaniard, and a grave one. A magnificent sentence has been handed down to us by Antonio Pérez from the great Duke of Alba concerning "the bearing that men should have in public places." The Duke says that "for a man to put his cape about his shoulders when he was going out of his house was simply an announcement that in public he was supposed to conceal and control his passions; just as it was permissible on entering the house to take off the cape, so that there the person might take his ease and reveal his feelings, *even as the cord is loosened so that the bow may rest.*"[6] Tense or loose, the passions are always present.

Let us go still deeper into the inwardness of this form of existence. In the *Rimado de Palacio*, the Chancellor Ayala (fourteenth century) says: "A man goes to bed healthy and *amanesce* cold (dead)" (270).[7] Neither in Latin nor in any other literary language of the occident do we find the verb *amanecer* conjugated personally: "I always *amanezco* in a good humor. Have you *amanecido* yet?. God *amanecerá* and we shall prosper." Etc. The same is true of *anochecer* (to dusk), and the phenomenon is common to both Spanish and Portuguese.[8]

It is to Alf Lombard that we owe the discovery that this verbal usage in Spanish is Arabic. The verb *ṣabaḥa* in fourth form *aṣbaḥa* means "to

---

[5] *Aspectos del vivir hispánico*, 1949.

[6] *Biblioteca de Autores Españoles*, XIII, 505a. Antonio Pérez, who recalls the Duke's remark, adds: "Because the soul and the mind are more sensitive to spontaneous language than to elaborate language."

[7] The problem of translation here is insoluble. *Amanecer* is an inchoative verb meaning *to dawn*, and when it means only this it is easily enough translated. But since it has the peculiarity of admitting of a personal conjugation, one can say in Spanish, without any poetical intent, "I dawn" (amanezco) or "I dawned" (amanecí). The meaning varies according to the context. Thus, *amanecí frío* may mean "I woke up at dawn, cold," or "Dawn came and I was cold"; *amanecí en Córdoba*, "I got to Cordova at dawn"; etc. Since the argument in the text here depends on the fact of such verbs as *amanecer*, they cannot be translated by circumlocutions, and are therefore left in Spanish. Admittedly, the resultant mixture of Spanish and English is as ugly as it is unavoidable.

[8] "A tropa amanhecera na formatura de batalha. Amanheceste hoje, sabe Deus se anoitecerás" (cf. F. Fernandes, *Diccionario de verbos e regimes*, Rio de Janeiro, 1941).

experience in the morning in this or that fashion," as if we should say, "live the morning." In the case of *anochecer* conjugated personally, the model is *amsā*, "he entered into the night," the fourth form of *massā*, "to say good night,"[9] another case of pseudomorphosis, or grafting: the use of a Romance form to express a phenomenon of the inner life of the Arab. This is of great importance for my interpretation of Hispanic history, for the Arabic is grafted not only on objective notions (*hidalgo*, etc.) but also on inner experience, on the manner of behaving inwardly while expressing the existence of an objective reality. Instead of limiting himself to perceiving the existence of a natural phenomenon (it becomes day, it becomes night), the soul of the person transforms what he perceives into its own creation, into something which happens not only outside, but inside, the person: *anochecí*, the night met me, and I met the night.

The adoption of the personal conjugation of *amanecer* was not an accident that can be approached abstractly as a case of Arabic "influence." It is without any doubt whatsoever the use of *amanecer* in the first person that separates Spanish from any other Romance language: *yo amanezco*. The adoption of this Arabic way of speaking was possible because the inner form of the Spanish Christian's life entailed acute feeling of the value of his own person. It was the daring, the lack of limits, of the Spaniard's impetus that continually motivated the growing personalism of the Hispanic life. From the Arabic was taken that which fitted in with the Spaniard's vital situation. Situations, tasks, and possibilities built up the dwelling place of life, and this in turn continually built up situations, and possibilities. Wherefore the stubborn persistence of functional structures, simultaneously motivated by and being the motivators of circumstances. It is significant, moreover, that Bartolomé de Argensola (1562-1631) could still feel in his days the pulse of vital consciousness in *amanecer* conjugated in the first person, which he used for the supremely proud Lucifer to express himself:

> "I the noblest of creatures,"
> Said the Ancient Proud one, "who *amanezco*
> The origin of my vivid splendors."[10]

As I shall point out later when I speak of the Archpriest of Hita, the Arab passes with perfect ease from the notion of what a thing is inwardly

[9] *Zeitschrift für romanische Philologie*, 1936, LVI, 641-643.
[10] "Canción a San Miguel," in *Rimas de Lupercio i del dotor Bartolomé Leonardo de Argensola*, Saragossa, 1634, p. 378.

to what it is outwardly, and in the same way he glides from the subjective to the objective, or vice versa: the two aspects of reality are interchangeable. Thus it is conceivable that the morning and the night are what they objectively are and at the same time what I experience of and in them. The reality of that which is object and that which is experienced are perceived as intertwined in an endless arabesque, through an experience that is both affective and sensory, never rational and discriminatory. Reality is "endowed with soul" and the person does not "dispossess" himself entirely of that which is non-person, since the latter is not isolated in depersonalized concepts. *Amanecer* is thus a vital phenomenon, an objective-subjective phenomenon into which one's sentiments and sensations are insinuated (*amanezco* happy, or with a headache), in an experience that I would call "centauric." Such a process means that when in his inner life he felt it congenial to do so, the Hispano-Christian adopted Moslem habits just as he imitated external usages and customs (the kissing of the hands, the washing of the dead, sitting on the floor, etc.).

A Hispano-Moslem poet can say: "I charge against the squadron, taking no account of whether *my* death is *within it* or *outside* it." For another poet, "the villages of Seville excel all others for the charm of their buildings and for the zeal with which they are cared for by their inhabitants both *inside and outside*."[11] The Arabic expression reveals at once a radical instability and the intent to embrace the world and the one who experiences it in a single whole. Reality is then the reality that is lived by the total person, and not the reality objectified by reason. For the occidental, a day is a certain quantity of time that flows outside the person; but in Arabic one says "he journeyed *his* entire day, I came back *my* night (that is, in the course of *my* night), he found himself in the night of *his* day (that is, of the same day)."[12] Thus we can see how the man gifted with learning and understanding can be called "son of the days" (ibn al-ayyām) since man can be the son of whatever surrounds him (e.g., hijodalgo). Or he can be the father, because one of the names for bread in Arabic is "father of the restoration of forces," *abū-jābir*. Such phenomena are normal in Arabic.[13]

[11] Al-Šaqundī, *Elogio del Islam español*, tr. by E. García Gómez, 1934, pp. 96-97.

[12] G. Meloni, "Alcuni studi sul tempo presso i semiti," in *Saggi di Filologia Semitica*, Rome, 1913, p. 132.

[13] Certain passages from the *Chronica do descobrimento e conquista de Guiné*, by Gomes Eannes de Azurara (fifteenth century) provide us incidentally with another instance of personalization. The author is describing the brave deeds of Antam Gonçalvez, and at the end of Chapter XII he writes: "and let us thus bring this chap-

Turning to something far removed from linguistics, we can observe similar phenomena in the field of art. I pointed out some years ago that, on occasion, the Spanish writer or painter has no wish to mark off the circumstance or scene in which he finds his theme from the theme itself and even from the creative process. All three are expressed in the work, which brings with it an accompaniment of reflections and remnants of everything that was present to the artist. In *The Maids in Waiting* (Las Meninas), Velasquez includes his easel, his pallet, the act of painting, and, with all this, the curious spectators who appear in the studio.[14] In my earlier consideration of this matter I saw here a kind of primitivism in which "the gods, the mortals, and the elements do not yet keep their proper distance." But then I noticed the same fusion of literary myth and immediate experience in the *Poema del Cid*, and I connected this phenomenon with the novelistic process whose most complete fulfillment is represented by Cervantes: "far away, the *Cid* yet shows a faint glimmering of the modern novel."[15]

Speaking of my study of Saint Teresa, Aubrey F. G. Bell gave the very apt name of "integralism" to this essential characteristic of the Hispanic genius. The humanist Alonso López Pinciano said as early as 1596 that for a work "to be actually a book, *the whole man is necessary*." This sentence, Bell justly remarks, "might be taken as the motto of Spanish literature and art."[16] Karl Vossler had made similar remarks on his own account, but the fact remains that we had all been content with noting the phenomenon, and with expressing favorable or adverse judgments on the literature and art that has this integralism or realism as its

---

ter to an end, leaving Antam Gonçalves to rest here, until *we honorably make him a knight* in the chapter that follows." Then: "And then may Antam Gonçalvez receive *his* knighthood, as we intended to recount in this chapter, and then *we shall give him* a commandery in the order of Christ" (Chapter XIII). The passages are found on pp. 76 and 77 of the edition of the Viscount da Carreira, Paris, 1841. Notice how the author personalizes his account. It is not Antam Gonçalvez who is made a knight, or to whom the commandery in the order of Christ is given; it is the author who interposes himself in this objective action, living it as his own experience, and who thus says *façamos, daremos* (let us make, we shall give) and puts what ought to be in the third person into the first. Rhetoricians of today would call this enlivened style, but it is clear, I think, that this is something different, and not so easily labeled.

[14] *Santa Teresa y otros ensayos*, 1929, p. 11.

[15] "Poesía y realidad en el Poema del Cid," in *Tierra Firme*, Madrid, 1935, I, 22.

[16] *Revue Hispanique*, 1930, LXXX, 372.

basis.[17] But literature and art, though important, are only aspects of a life disposition, that is to say, of the same reality of Spain that I am trying to make visible.

The extent to which Hispanic integralism may be properly related to the presence of Moors and Jews in the Peninsula for centuries will become more and more apparent the more we penetrate the inner life of history. This is a task which we must seek to achieve without excessive haste and without neglecting by-paths. The preceding chapters, especially the one treating of the belief in Santiago, have made it possible to see how the founders of Spain were compelled to fit their life to the Moorish pattern in order to subsist and to struggle against it. They managed to subsist by virtue of their energy, exalted by their belief, not by overcoming their difficulties through acts based on rational thought, that is, not through taking refuge in reason in order to think out adequate solutions. If the frenzy of that special religious faith had diminished to give place to reflection, Santiago and everything that was dependent on him would have suffered dangerous blows; for Santiago was not a pious belief of the naïve common people, as is usually thought to have been the case, but rather the keystone of the monarchy. There is nothing better for understanding the function of that belief than to recall something that is both contrary and analogous to it, that is, the "raison d'État" of the kings of France in the seventeenth century, who rationalized everything and made everything static, from religion to language. So that France would not go to pieces in social and religious anarchy, the monarchs and their mentors decided to drown the passionate instincts of the French soul in a sea of reason and its objective norms, and to this end they sacrificed everything from poetry to the spontaneity of language. They dressed France in a strait jacket that had the outward appearance of a very elegant garment. The main tendencies of the French living structure got the better of any attempt at escape from the rules of "sagesse" such as is represented by Rabelais, unbridled instinct, or by any spontaneous tendency.

Just as the freedom of the heart was repressed in France, in the same way, allowing for isolated and fleeting exceptions, every effort towards the invention of ideas was restrained among the Hispano-Christians. The very life which created and saved itself in belief was at the same time creating a structure to shield that belief from any mishap. The important thing was conduct and not inquisitive thought; therefore morality and law

[17] Vossler's essay, "Realismus in der spanischen Dichtung der Blütezeit" (1926), can now be read in *Algunos caracteres de la civilización española*, 1942.

were splendidly cultivated disciplines in the court of Alphonse the Learned and in many other places. The University of Salamanca was, from the thirteenth century on, distinguished for its studies in jurisprudence, whereas there is no record of any theologian or philosopher of major importance who taught at Salamanca in the Middle Ages. It was rather the Toledo school of Islamic culture that was well known in the rational fields: "Inter Parisienses ubi floret scientia trivii, inter *Tholetanos*, ubi scientia quadrivii, inter Salernitanos, ubi scientia medicorum, inter Bononienses, ubi scientia legis."[18] Thus, we can see that in the second half of the twelfth century Toledo was a leader in disciplines as important as mathematics, geometry, astrology, and music. A little later, when Alphonse VIII considered organizing a center of learning, it was impossible for him to call upon Moorish scholars, because Castile was not Al-Andalus; but he could not have recourse to Hispano-Christians either, because apparently there was none capable. Hence, around 1185, he sent "to France and Lombardy for scholars, so as to have instruction in his kingdom that learning might never wane there, for through schools of learning God sets forth the course to be followed in the Kingdom where such schools are established, and in this way knighthood is improved."[19]

The Difference between Hispanic Integralism and Moorish Integralism

It is evident that the Hispano-Christians did not follow the Moorish example where intellectual and technological activities were concerned. Perhaps it would suffice to say that the relation between the one people and the other was not that of pupil to master. Moreover, even though I may point out certain structural coincidences in the lives of the two peoples, there was no reason why the results of such coincidental structures should be similar. No law of causality operates here. And in any case, the content of Spanish culture as such is, in the present case, of less interest than the light that such content can shed on the functioning of the life structure—of something that I metaphorically, and insistently, call the dwelling place of life. It is not a question of the image of a static figure; it is a question of the idea of a functional process fraught with multiple possibilities (and impossibilities), whose realization in time and space constitutes the history of a people (see Chapter 2).

[18] Geoffroi de Vinsauf, "Documentum de arte versificandi," in E. Faral, *Les arts poétiques*, p. 283.
[19] *Crónica general*, p. 686. The studies carried on in Palencia were the creation of Alphonse VIII and, of course, the antecedents of the University of Salamanca.

If I give the name "integralism" to certain features that are common to Spanish and Moorish existence, this does not mean that the integralism works out in the same way in the two life structures. Let two lines from *Hamlet* (III, 3) express my thought:

> "Try what *repentance* can: what can it not?
> Yet what can it when *one* can not repent?"

Here is the difference between any generic concept and its vital realization, that is, its realization in life. All the Latin or Romanic peoples are Catholic, yet each of them lives its Catholicism in a different way. Saint Francis of Sales could not have been Spanish, nor Saint Ignatius, French. Descartes and Hegel were both philosophers, but before they were philosophers, the one had to be French, the other German. Both Spaniards and Arabs conjugate the verb "to dawn" personally, and say "I dawn"; yet the Spaniards do not connect personal consciousness with this natural phenomenon the way the Arabs do (p. 234). Arabs and Spaniards alike include the world around them in their consciousness of being persons; they do not cast off their impressions, feelings, and beliefs; wherefore the slow cadence of their inner life, their resistance to innovation, and their traditional quietism. Today even as yesterday, tomorrow even as today.

In spite of the similarities between Spaniards and Moslems, the two peoples were differently situated—inside the vital whole wherein are integrated the activity of the mind and the awareness of the objective and the subjective—the "dwelling-places" of their lives were different. When the Moor expressed his awareness of his existence, he appeared as in a state of flux and as borne along by a world also in a state of flux, lacking in fixed stability. Here is one example among many: A person hears a song being sung, is moved by it, pauses to listen, and expresses his experience:

"Do not accuse me of being inconsistent because my heart has been captured by a singing voice.

"At certain times one must be serious, at others, one lets one's self be moved; like the wood, from which comes the warrior's bow as well as the singer's lute."[20]

According to this, the Moslem's existence is unstable and "inconsistent." With the word *al-taqallub* the poet expresses the change in the direction of his interest, his inconsistency. The word is formed on *qalaba*

---

[20] *El libro de las banderas de los campeones*, by Ibn Saʿīd al-Magribī (thirteenth century), tr. by E. García Gómez, Madrid, 1942, p. 187.

(to turn upside down, to change), which might be related to *qalb* (heart, mind; see page 222, note 32). In this case, as in a great many others, the Arabic language expresses a fluctuating structure of life. If I am not mistaken, then, the Moslem's integralism must have consisted in his feeling himself in flux and changing with the human-natural world in which his life was being created, constantly becoming. I imagine that existence as a river which feels itself being constantly *realized* in the sea into which it pours as well as in the channel through which it flows in a simultaneous integration of existence as both sea and river at the same time.

It is understandable that the Moslem should have been interested in alchemy, or the transmutation of metals, in the effect of the stars on the lives of people, in the progression of neoplatonic ideas, in the transformation of visible forms into open, stylized designs. He must have felt more than a utilitarian satisfaction as he made the fleeting waters move through the arabesque of his irrigation ditches—the *acequias* and *almatriches* of the Spanish lexicon—or as he strove to maintain the cycle of growth from seed to fruit and fruit to seed.[21] The water ran through *arcaduces* and *atanores* (trenches) just as the spirits and essences slipped through tubes of the still; or as the traveler moved over the spaces of the earth. Over the earth in turn flowed peoples and customs in infinite variety.[22]

The authentic mode of Spanish life has been quite different, as will become more and more evident to the reader. First, however, it is desirable to speak a little more of the Moslems.

In the seventh century, when the Moslems came into contact with

[21] "Praise be to God who has brought the earth under the subjection of His servants that they might walk through spacious ways (*Koran*, LXXI, 19); who has put on this earth and caused to exist on it the three vicissitudes of the fate of man: germination, the return to the earth, and the issuing forth from its bowels" (*Koran*, XX, 57) (*Voyages de Ibn Batoutah*, tr. by C. Defrémery and B. R. Sanguinetti, 1893, 1, 2). The *Koran* (XX, 57) says literally: "From the earth I have made thee, to it I shall return thee, and from it I will draw thee forth to life a second time."

[22] The translators of ibn-Baṭṭūṭah (1304-1377) referred to above say: "Few peoples went as far as the Arabs in their fondness for journeys to distant places" (p. ii). Ibn-Baṭṭūṭah himself says of Cairo: "There you can find everything you want, men of learning and ignorant folk, diligent men and those fond of trifles, the meek and the violent, noblemen and plebeians, the unknown and the celebrated. So many are her inhabitants that their surging makes of Cairo a turbulent sea. . . . Although founded long ago, she enjoys a *continually renewed* youth" (1, 67-68). The person feels his existence as a moving in a current; this is what I wish to point out. He does not travel "to see," like Herodotus, but to match the movement of his own life with the progressive movement of the roads and the changes of place.

the complicated existence of Hellenized Egypt, Syria, and Persia, they began to develop activities that fitted the possibilities of the Moslem vital structure. In a few instances the example of Persian science aroused a scientific and technical curiosity that seemed to exceed the possibilities of the Moslem life structure. As Bagdad had once done, Cordova too attained a very high level of civilization. But if the Moors could thus assimilate a foreign element in their own life structure, the disturbing question arises, how could the Hispano-Christians in turn, fully aware of what they were doing, reject the example of the Moors in the latter's diligent and zealous concern with matters of the mind? The question is delicate, and strikes at the heart of my problem.

Let us listen to a voice which for more than one reason can speak with authority for the Hispano-Christians, Prince Juan Manuel, a nephew of King Alphonse the Learned. In his *Conde Lucanor* the prince says:

"In this book I shall speak of things that I understand can be of profit to men as well for the salvation of their souls as for the improvement of their bodies and the upholding of their honor and their estate. And although these things *are in themselves not very subtle*, as would be the case should I speak of the science of theology, or geometry, or metaphysics, or natural and even moral philosophy, and other very subtle sciences, *it is more befitting to me*, and more profitable with respect to my estate, to speak of this matter than of any other art or science."[23]

The authentic Spaniard was always sharply aware of what he was doing and of the motives behind his actions, and he realized that there were other intellectual zones in the world which he had no interest in penetrating. From Juan Manuel's remarks, it is evident that thought is inseparable from the person's consciousness of his station inside his "dwelling-place." Either unwilling or unable to isolate itself from such circumstances, Spanish thought did not succeed in rising above the level of the most immediate preoccupations. If there is no oil in the house in which to fry an egg, it is necessary to *think* of a way to get some. Very different from this is the desire to know *what oil is*, to be aware of the lack of this knowledge, and, with the problem established, to try to bridge the gap in knowledge with a chain of thought. Genuine thought isolates itself from its motives and from its possible consequences; the thinking activity is consistently problematic from beginning to end. The thinking person puts into parenthesis everything that does not pertain to his thinking, and, first of all, his own existence. This is what Juan

[23] *Biblioteca de Autores Españoles*, LI, 426.

Manuel is unwilling to do. He aspires to have the activity of his mind serve him for the preservation of his *estate*, that is, his existence as Don Juan Manuel.

But the curious reader will repeat his question. How was it possible that there were physicians, botanists, and philosophers among the Iberian Moslems, and yet, that in this respect the Moslems were not imitated by their Christian enemies, who, between the tenth and the thirteenth centuries, showed scarcely any inclination to cultivate either the liberal or the mechanical arts? The question becomes more complicated and more serious when we recall that the Aragonese, Catalonians, and Castilians in one way or another dominated large zones in Italy, and even in Greece, from the end of the thirteenth century to the beginning of the eighteenth; and, should this seem of little account, add to it the Spanish rule in the Franche-Comté from 1519 to 1678 and in Belgium until 1713. If, as a consequence of their dominion over the Hellenized lands of Syria, Egypt, and Persia, the Bedouins of Arabia came to assimilate much of Greek learning, how is it that the Spaniards did not imitate the intellectual habits of Italy, Burgundy, and Flanders? The first answer that comes to mind is that historical problems—problems of human life, that is—are not clarified by means of argument from analogy. Moreover, a people does not vary the direction which its disposition imposes upon it, nor can it do, as a people, anything that is not compatible with that disposition stretched to the limits of elasticity. The movements of Moslem history that are connected with the elastic functioning of the Moslem structure must not be confused with the modification or disappearance of that structure. The Moor who came out of Arabia in the seventh century went on living without changing his written language, through the splendors of Bagdad and Cordova. "In our own time, some Arabian tribes still preserve the names which they bore in the sixth Christian century. . . . The modern nomadic tribes of Arabia, notwithstanding the tremendous shift produced by Islam and the Western technical achievements, do not differ substantially from the pre-Islamic tribes."[24]

The cultivation of the sciences by the Arabs was accidental, it did not modify the disposition of their "dwelling-place." Their beliefs did not articulate structurally with rational activities. They produced no such "progress" as did the peoples with structures made possible by the Greco-Romano-Germanic tradition. C. H. Becker pondered this problem in his book *Das Erbe der Antike im Orient und Okzident* (1931), and asked

[24] G. Levi Della Vida, "Pre-Islamic Arabia," in *The Arab Heritage*, ed. by N. A. Faris, p. 49.

himself with great cogency how it happened that the Greek spirit, so imperfectly known in the West, produced the miracle of Humanism, whereas in the East it did not have the same effect (pp. 32-33). Becker answers his question this way: "The historical, geographical, and ethical situation of the East led it to be interested in the Greek writings only for what they had of general validity that at the same time could be fitted to the Eastern mentality—above all, dialectical rationalism." But perhaps we can achieve greater precision if we approach this problem from the point of view of the Islamic structure of existence. The Arabs knew Greece better in the ninth and tenth centuries than the Italians did in the fourteenth; nevertheless, the Islamic view of the world continued fundamentally unchanged, because *it is neither learning nor culture that constitutes the life of a people, but the way in which learning and culture function within their "dwelling-place."*

Certain Moslems adopted the modes of thought and the techniques of the peoples they had subjugated—the Egyptians, Syrians, Persians, all profoundly Hellenized. Yet it did not occur to them to revive Homer, Sophocles, Pindar, or Aristophanes,[25] for the simple reason that to do so would have presupposed escaping from the structure of their personal existence, their human reality. Likewise, the Italian writers of the Middle Ages were perfectly acquainted with the French *chansons de geste*; indeed, some of the Italians even wrote in French, but *they were unable* to compose an Italian epic, save in the form of a skeptical burlesque.

At first glance the caliph Abbasside Al-Ma'mūn (813-833) resembles an enlightened despot of the eighteenth century. One of his courtiers called him "Prince of the Unbelievers."[26] The son of a Persian mother and married to a Persian wife, he seems to depart from the orthodox line and to favor certain heretical doctrines. In 827 he decreed punishments for those who believed that the Koran was uncreated and co-eternal with Allah. Under the caliphate of Al-Ma'mūn the arc of the curvature of the earth was measured, and progress was made in astronomy and medicine, both of which had been cultivated prior to the Arab domination. Yet this caliph furthered the translation of Aristotle, not out of a disin-

[25] It is not an established fact, as it is sometimes assumed to be, that the Greek tradition was unknown by the time the Arabs occupied Egypt. Texts have been discovered indicating that Homer, the dramatists, the orators, and the lyric poets were still studied, even though such studies did not give rise to new creation. Cf. C. H. Idris Bell, *Egypt from Alexander the Great to the Arab Conquest*, Oxford, 1948, p. 61.

[26] De Lacy O'Leary, *How Greek Science Passed to the Arabs*, London, 1948, p. 162.

terested enthusiasm for learning, but in order to bring the Greek *logos* to the defense of Islamic orthodoxy,[27] threatened by gnosis. Greek philosophy helped to build up a religious dialectic similar to the scholastic philosophy of the Western Christian, as a defense against the mystical license of gnosticism.

Thus, Arabic learning either answered to needs of a practical character[28] or it was a resurgence of ancient Greek and Iranian wisdom insofar as this wisdom might be compatible with the Moslem's existence, that is, insofar as it would not mean a variation in the inner form of his life. Furthermore, the brilliant triumph of Islam, together with the extraordinary power of the caliph over his people and the immeasurable distance that separated him from them, made possible an occasional indulgence in intellectual luxury, without the risk that this might affect the existence and thinking of the masses of believers. Thus the Cordovan caliph al-Ḥakam II (961-976) could collect a fabulous library and encourage every kind of learning. The "unauthenticity" of his philosophizing can be seen in this: two years before he died, afflicted with a serious complaint, he sought to prepare himself for the judgment of God by repenting of his fondness for philosophy and recommending to his heir the study of religious books.[29] What had gone before had been no more than a frivolous game, a conscious sin which at any moment the caliph in his omnipotence could forsake for the fold of rigorous orthodoxy.[30]

For the Hispano-Christians, science and critical thought had as little

[27] C. H. Becker, *op.cit.*, p. 14. *Gnosis* (knowledge conceived as attainable only through divine revelation by mystical means) was as dangerous for Christianity as for Islam. What came from the orient returned to the orient in the form of popular philosophy; in the last analysis spells, astrology, love philtres, amulets, etc., are gnostic.

[28] The first mathematical treatise in which the word "algebra" appears is in large part a collection of rules and problems relating to the division of inheritances and to commercial questions.

[29] Julián Ribera, *La enseñanza entre los musulmanes españoles*, pp. 14-15.

[30] This is what happened to various Spanish aristocrats of the eighteenth century. The Count of Aranda wrote to Voltaire and sent him presents. Voltaire replied with verses in which he called the count "un Alcide nouveau, / Vainqueur d'une hydre plus fatale, / Des superstitions déchirant le bandeau" (*Poésies de Voltaire*, IV, 1821, pp. 172-173). Charles III forced the pope to dissolve the Society of Jesus; but, as d'Alembert wrote to Voltaire, he heaped attentions on the other priests and monks "qui ne sont, à ce que je crois, moins dangereux que les jésuites." Olavide fled from the Spanish Inquisition, but he went back to publish his book *The Triumphant Gospel, or the Converted Philosopher* (El Evangelio triunfante, o el filósofo convertido) in 1798. (Cf. François Rousseau, *Règne de Charles III d'Espagne*, I, 196, 232; II, 54.) The Duke of Alba wrote to Rousseau and sent him valuable presents. Yet all those aristocrats died in the bosom of the Church, repented of their sins like al-Ḥakam II.

authenticity and functional pertinence as for the Moslems. The Moslems, however, occasionally found themselves in situations which the Christians never faced. The capital of the Moslem empire was not in Medina or Mecca but in Damascus or Bagdad, that is, in conquered lands, the majority of whose inhabitants accepted the new religion of Islam. On the other hand, the capital of the Spanish empire was not Naples, Milan, Besançon, or Brussels, but Madrid. From another point of view, one can compare the rapid occupation of Egypt, Syria, and Iran, completed twenty years after the death of Mohammed (632), with the slow reconquest of the Islamicized land of Spain by politically disunited Christians. The Hispano-Christians did not fall like an avalanche on the Moslems in the eleventh century, and impose their religion on the vanquished. Far from it; the Christians had to preserve the horizon which the war imposed on them. There was nothing on their side like the secure and all-encompassing rule of the caliphs of Bagdad.

The kingdoms of Spain, as political entities, always kept themselves separate and aloof from the other peoples with different types of culture over whom they had dominion. They did not Hispanize Italy and Flanders,[31] but they did Hispanize—somewhat in the same way the Arabs Islamicized Egypt, Syria, Persia, and part of India—the American

---

[31] That is, they did not assimilate them linguistically, nor did they attract them to the Hispanic life structure. But the Spaniards did somewhat modify the inner form of the Neapolitans' existence: "With the new sentiment of loyalty to the Spanish monarchs, with the code of honor of devoted subjects, the Neapolitan barons, at once subdued and inspired by Spanish power, defended the king of Naples and Spain with a solidarity and continuity unknown among their forebears; they had never fought thus when their kings had been only kings of Naples" (Benedetto Croce, *Storia del regno di Napoli*, 1944, pp. 114-121). In the seventeenth century the Neapolitan infantry became noted for its bravery in combat; the celebrated victory of Prague (1620), which saved the cause of the Hapsburgs, was largely due to a corps of Neapolitan militiamen. But that heroic spirit as seen from my historical point of view was accidental, not structural. A century after Spanish domination in Italy had ended, the Italians recoiled into their own authentic vital structure; they were intelligent (Vico), and they possessed artistic talents (Vivaldi); but their temper was not the same (cf. Croce, *op.cit.*, pp. 224-225). As far as Belgium is concerned, in spite of everything that has been written about the evils of the Spanish domination, the country went on being "inébranlablement fidèle" to the kings of Spain, even in the epoch of the weak and degenerate Charles II. The title "Catholic" gave the Spanish monarchs incomparable prestige. Spain maintained her dominion in Belgium until 1713, thanks to the "aversion inspired in the Belgians by Calvinist Holland and Gallican France" (H. Pirenne, *Histoire de Belgique*, 1926, v, p. 50). Let us add that the boundaries of Belgium today are those she had under the Spanish domination in 1713. Without that domination, Holland would have annexed the Flemish provinces, France those where French is spoken. That is, without Spain, Belgium would not exist as a nation.

Indians. The difference is that among the Indians there was nothing comparable to the Hellenic tradition. In the last analysis, the differences and similarities between the Moslems and the Hispano-Christians become intelligible when we observe the functioning, the direction, and the perspective of the impulses that give structure to their respective existences. Logically speaking (that is, according to the Greek *logos*), the reality of the world was, prior to Mohammed, already evanescent for the Arab: "What is the passing of days but change on change?" And a poet of the ninth century says: "O Time, how do I behold thee run To spoil me? Thine own gift thou tak'st away!"[32] But that very world, fleeting and fragile, was saved from its intrinsic inanity by the continuous heart-beat of divine creation, without which the instants and aspects of reality would dissolve in the nothing which they intrinsically are. So that, if the reality of the world was deprived of ontological substance, that same world none the less had sensorial value. It was the senses, not the reason, that could capture the succession of fleeting instants, the saving spark of a watchful God taking care that things should persist beneath their appearances. Allah made the fleeting eternal, and therefore he preserved the ever reborn virginity of the Huries (*Koran*, XLV, 35). In a half-philosophical half-theological treatise falsely attributed to Emped-ocles we read:

"The individual souls, seduced by the deceptive world of *Nature*, in which they live, imitated Nature in their rebellion against the Spirit and the *Intellect*, and they lent themselves to sensual pleasures in fine-tasting foods, in pleasing drink, in soft clothing, in beholding physical beauty, and in erotic delight, forgetting splendor, forgetting beauty, and forgetting spiritual, psychic, and intellectual perfection—properties of essence itself."[33]

This Arabic philosopher censures precisely what the generality of Moslems did, because they thought it just, good, and pleasing to God. The anonymous philosopher was reasoning with neo-Platonic, Greek ideas that had no authentic efficacy amongst Moslems. The things of this world were appetizing, and for this reason the Arab learned and cultivated the art of doing them. When sensual appetite was made legitimate, this broadened the area of necessities, justified luxury, and led to the invention of means for satisfying luxury's requirements—commerce, industrial arts, alchemy, and many other kinds of knowledge. The very duty of

[32] Quoted by G. E. von Grunebaum in *Growth and Structure of Arabic Poetry*, in *The Arabic Heritage*, ed. by N. A. Faris, pp. 136, 140.
[33] In M. Asín, *Abenmassarra y su escuela*, 1914, p. 52.

making a pilgrimage to Mecca meant a fruitful complication of life. In this way the Mohammedan religion multiplied the possibilities of the Bedouins' simple existence. But that religion had in turn been made possible by the peculiar structure in which the Arab existed, a structure to which his pre-Islamic language remained bound. The difference is that after Mohammed, the Moslem felt himself as heaven-sent to possess everything, to see, to smell, to taste all the pleasant things of this world, and to make them appear as beautiful as possible in his poetry: A walnut "is a shell formed of two pieces so united that it is lovely to see; they are like the eyelids when they close in sleep." Of a dove we read that "Its necklace was the color of pistachio, its breast of lapis lazuli, its neck iridescent, its back and the tips of its wing-feathers of brown." "Drink wine beside the fragrant lily that has bloomed, and have your gatherings in the morning when the rose opens."[34] And so, for thousands upon thousands of instances throughout Moslem history.

The life of the person is diffused through the world around him, and has sensory connection with everything that is visible or tangible. A witness writes of the visit of the mystic philosopher ibn-Masarrah in Medina to the house of Mary, the concubine of the Prophet: "I saw how ibn-Masarrah . . . measured with his hand one of the two chambers." Following these measurements ibn-Masarrah built his hermitage in the Sierra of Cordova.[35] *The Moslem feels himself in things, the Hispano-Christian feels things in himself, in his person.* When the prince Don Juan Manuel met his father-in-law, King James II of Aragon, in 1306, the king told him "that one of the worst faults a man could have was *not to be conscious* (non se sentir)."[36] The Spaniard was not interested in having his gatherings "when the rose opens." The peculiar function of his life structure consists in bringing the world to his person, not in dissolving his person in his contacts with the world. The difference in the vital movements carried Moslems and Hispano-Christians in opposite directions.

I hope that the reader has by now understood my motive in rejecting the idea of "influence" in trying to reveal and understand the reality of this and any other history. The fact that the integralism of the Moslem made possible the integralism of the Spaniard does not mean that that quality of Moslem existence was inserted mechanically, like a wedge, into

[34] *El libro de las banderas de los campeones, de Ibn Saʿīd al-Magribī,* tr. by E. García Gómez, Madrid, 1942, pp. 133-135.

[35] M. Asín, *Abenmassarra y su escuela,* p. 36.

[36] *Libro infinido,* ed. by J. M. Blecua, p. 61.

the existence of Spaniards. The very functioning of Spanish existence, its lack of limits, was what made possible the adoption of inner vital attitudes that were originally Moslem. The integralism of the ego, the soul, and the body was experienced by Christians and Moslems from different positions and in different perspectives. The same thing is true for the welding of the external world with that of the person. It has already been seen how Bartolomé Leonardo de Argensola had Satan say "I dawn" (yo amanezco); the Spaniard is not carried away by the *amanecer* or the *anochecer*; he incorporates them into himself: "Night comes over me (*me anochece*) when I speak to you within myself . . . Dawn comes over me (*me amanece*) when I discourse with you. You fill my night, you fill my day."[37] It is not a question of looking for sources or influences, but of bringing to light the perspective in which history, life, moves. Having reached this point, I would say that the Spaniard *felt* the world personally, that he *thought* it supernaturally from his station in his belief. Thus, we have already observed (p. 168) that when Alphonse the Learned set to thinking about how to cure a disease, he had recourse to a spell: It was necessary to think of ways to make the supernatural forces efficacious, not out of ignorance or superstition, but because of a greater faith in the wisdom of God than in the wisdom of man, and because the authentic reality of thought consisted in this for the Spaniard. Out of humility and subordination to God the Spaniard abstained from plunging himself into the examination of the laws of nature to the end of mastering them. But for the same reason, he rarely believed in the witches that were so abundant outside of Spain. To be a witch is to endow man, rationally, diabolically, with the power of working miracles. The French kings practised witchcraft in the treatment of scrofula because the French predicated their thought on their faith in their reason and not on their faith in their faith. Jean de Joinville, a good Christian *à la française*, did not believe that letting the Saracens chop off his head would get him into heaven. His steward suggested it to him: "Je m'acort que nous nous lessons touz tuer; si nous en irons en paradis." To which Saint Louis' chronicler replied: "Mais nous ne le creumes pas."[38] The authentic history of France abounds in similar confessions. A few of them are noted in the present work to bring out by contrast the history of Spain.

For the Moslem everything was reduced to letting one's self live in

[37] Quevedo, *Obras en verso*, ed. by Astrana, 1932, p. 16.
[38] *Histoire de Saint Louis*, ed. by N. de Waillys, 319.

the will of Allah; and there is no doubt that the Spaniard attached the highest importance to "whatever God wills" (lo que Dios quiera), an importance which the Moor taught him to feel with greater intensity; but almost as important as the will of God for the Spaniards was "what *my* person wills" (lo que mi persona quiere). With the worship of God the Spaniard combined homage to his own person, yet not as egoistic self-complacency. To maintain this self-esteem properly (what was called in Spain "upholding one's honor"—mantener honra), many sacrificed their own lives, or suffered grave hardships. Other people's labor and the cultural wealth created by Moors, Jews, or outlanders were made to serve the purposes of seigniory. The meaning of the words of *Mío Cid*, "we shall make use of them" (p. 83), was not accidental; it was structural. In that life structure the world could not be captured through knowledge but through the will, through the will to live for the magnification of the person himself, or the magnification of God. The authentic history of Spain has had, as two poles, the two extremes—alongside the paralysis of rational inquiry, the dynamism of willing, wishing, to exist for one's self and for God.

The irregular and intermittent adoption of cultural products created by other peoples has to be understood as an attempt at overcoming the limitations imposed by the Spanish life structure. Alphonse VIII *wanted* to have a university, and for this purpose he called in foreign scholars (p. 238); foreign religious orders and gothic and romanesque architecture were brought in to honor God. Incompletely or partially, the objects of Western (or Eastern) culture have always been present in Spain. The churches reflected the interest in God; the epic, the novel, and the drama showed the importance granted everything that pertains to the person. In these respects, as well as in the pictorial representation of the human person, there have been Spanish geniuses of the highest order. The Moslem, on the other hand, has never had, nor has he felt the need to create for himself, anything in the nature of the epic, or the novel of Cervantes, or the drama of Lope de Vega, or the portraiture of Velázquez or Goya— since he has existed in the will of God and his own person has not faced the person of God. The notion that one person, a character, fashions his own personality in interactions with the personalities of other men, that is, novelistically, is inconceivable to the Arab. His narrative literature is limited to "telling," narrating, the flux of events in the midst of which the lives of the persons stream along.

The importance that the Spaniard attaches to the person as one of the poles of his existence has led him to make it a center of attraction and reference for everything that exists in and around him. Out of this condition arises a kind of imperialism of the person: The Spaniard speaks of himself, of his body, of his pleasures, and of his afflictions. Everything is justified and takes on value the moment it is referred to the person. When this point is reached, the difference between the clean and the dirty, the spiritual and the material, the pathetic and the comic evaporates. Examples of this are to be found throughout the present work, although it will be convenient from now on to say that in such matters the Spaniard imitated the Arab, just as he imitated the personal conjugation of the verbs *amanecer* and *anochecer*. It must be kept in mind, however, that for the Moslem the point of departure was his belief that the greatest as well as the least was the constant work of God; the Spaniard, on the other hand, mixed the noble with the base in order to embrace as much as possible of what lay within reach of his person. For this the Arabic style of expression served him as a magnificent model.

As a lesson in modesty to the powerful, ibn-Ḥazm (994-1064) tells a story about the caliph Hārūn al-Rashīd. The caliph asked for a glass of water because he was very thirsty. The ascetic Ibn al-Samak, who was at his side, asked him how much he would have given for the glass of water if they had not been able to bring it to him. "All my empire!" answered the caliph. Ibn al-Samak persisted: "And if you should not be able to pass this water from your body after you have drunk it, what would you give to be free of such an affliction?" "The whole of my kingdom," answered the caliph. And the ascetic commented: "And are you so proud of possessing a realm that is worth less than a urination and less than one sip of water?"[39] The most basic necessities of the human body are spoken of, ritually, in the *hadīth*, or traditions of Mohammed.[40]

---

[39] *Los caracteres y la conducta*, tr. by M. Asín, Madrid, 1916, p. 115. The same anecdote appears in Raymond Lully (*Evast y Blanquerna*, Barcelona, 1935, p. 238), although in a somewhat more prudish version. Blanquerna says to the Emperor: "How slight is the value of an empire that is not as much to its lord as the bread he has eaten."

[40] "Le Prophète étant sorti pour satisfaire un besoin naturel, je le suivis. Il marchait sans tourner la tête. Je m'approchai de lui et il me dit: 'Cherche-moi des pierres pour me torcher,' " etc. On another occasion the Prophet asks for three stones: "Je trouvai bien deux pierres, mais impossible d'en trouver une troisième. Alors je pris une boule de crottin et je l'apportai avec les pierres. Le Prophète prit les deux pierres et jeta le crottin en distant: 'Ça, c'est une ordure' " (El-Bokhari, *Les traditions islamiques*, tr. by O. Houdas and W. Marçais, Paris, 1903, p. 72). I cite this example as a single and time-saving demonstration that everything can be integrated in a vital unity, even the One sent from God and his dirtiest physiological acts. Similar cases are frequent and normal.

The Spaniard blurred the distinction between the clean and the dirty when he wished to integrate them both under the sovereignty of his person, when both aspects of existence were important for him. Don Diego Hurtado de Mendoza, the ambassador of Emperor Charles V in Venice, was not only a great lord; he was also a humanist interested in collecting Greek manuscripts. These manuscripts later became the Greek collection of the library of the Escorial, under Philip II. Yet in the letters from Don Diego to the Emperor's Secretary of State we can read such things as this:

"The truth is, my lord, that I ruined a testicle in a jolt I got against a chair, and beyond remedy; your lordship may well be sorry along with the Jewess, for I had her so well trained that I would not have found it too hard to dig up the bones of my grandparents."[41]

What is notable about these explosions of intimacy is that they take place in letters which in the same breath treat of official matters, letters which were to be filed in the archives of the king. In a later chapter I shall have occasion to point out other cases of integralism of expression. Cervantes, Quevedo, Lope de Vega, Tirso de Molina, and many others had no compunction about mixing the noblest and the basest aspects of man together. Without the example of the Moslems they would not have done this. But it must also be borne in mind that, along with great similarities, in the two cases there are differences both in points of departure and in meaning.

I think we can understand now the curious fact that although Spaniards have traveled and lived in other countries as much as other European peoples—if indeed not more—their travel literature remains meager. The Spaniard who resides in England or France will write about himself, about whatever happens to him in those places. It will not occur to him to compose a geography, a geology, or a history of the foreign land. Bernal Díaz del Castillo wrote his admirable *History of the Conquest of Mexico* by way of presenting to the king something on the order of a soldier's record of service, as Ramón Iglesia has shown. The *Crónicas de*

[41] A. González Palencia and E. Mele, *Vida y obras de Don Diego Hurtado de Mendoza*, Madrid, 1943, iii, 302. Don Diego is referring to his affair with a Jewish courtesan: "For three months here I made love to one of the prettiest wenches in Italy; and just when we had come to an understanding she told me to stop, that she was a Jewess, and that she could do nothing for me if I didn't become a Jew. Since I was close to that already, I told her to go ahead" (iii, 285). Cf. also pp. 284, 288, 291, 293, 297, 298. Either in jest or in earnest—one cannot be sure which—Don Diego alludes to his Jewish descent. In one satirical poem he was called "arch-jew" (archimarrano) (*op.cit.*, i, 70).

Indias are really acts of homage paid to God, to the king, to some hero, or to the person of the chronicler. The Arabs, on the other hand, were interested in the descriptions of both their own and foreign lands, and they have produced an abundant travel literature of great merit.

In sum: Although the Hispano-Christian and the Moslem were alike in maintaining the consciousness of their persons and of the external world in a compact union, there was yet a decisive difference between the two peoples. The direction of the Arab's vital interest impelled him to express himself in the objects exterior to him, thus making possible Averroes, ibn-Khaldūn, alchemy, industrial arts, etc. In the Spaniard the direction of vital dynamism was from the object to the person, since this was the nature of the reality of his "dwelling-place," of that basic *quid* which makes history intelligible.

The Castilian Epic

THE MOST CONFUSING THING in the history of the Iberian Peninsula in the Middle Ages is the crossing of two very different ways (namely, the Islamic and the Christian-European) of behaving towards the outer and the inner world. Germanic institutions introduced by the Visigoths, such as private pawn and revenge,[1] lived on in Castile and Leon. In cases dealing with these matters, the judge had no function beyond directing the proof, inasmuch as it was the offended party who imposed the penalty. Thus there were coincidences in certain legal customs between Spain and Scandinavia. It seems, moreover, that since the tenth century the social forces on which Castile had been seeking to base its organization had been characterized by a greater interest in earthly ambitions than was the case in Leon and Galicia. We have already seen how the latter regions, the initiators of the Reconquest, found for their shield the grandiose belief in Santiago. A pontifical and imperial aureole forced the other kings of the Peninsula to pay homage to the Galaico-Leonese monarchy.[2] The northeastern region of the Peninsula, on the contrary, from the eighth century on, had the appearance of an extension of the Franco-Carolingian monarchy. As late as the twelfth century, the inhabitants of that region, never bound securely to the rest of the Peninsula, were called Franks, not Catalonians, by Moors and Christians alike. Just as the independence of Portugal came about primarily as a result of foreign pressures and interests in the twelfth century, so Catalonia (the Spanish Mark of the Franks) was already the object of extra-Peninsular envy in the eighth century. If the pilgrims' route to Santiago

---

[1] Cf. Eduardo de Hinojosa, *El elemento germánico en el derecho español*, Madrid, 1915.

[2] As late as 1029, when Sancho the Great was at the height of his grandeur as king of Navarre, he recognized the imperial dignity of the young king of Leon, Vermudo III: "Ego Sancius rex, tenens culmen postestatis mee in Aragone, et in Pampilonia. . . . Belengarius comes in Barcelonia, et imperator domnus Vermudus in Gallecia" (Menéndez Pidal, *España del Cid*, p. 118). It seems evident to me that the reason for such an exalted title was Santiago. Note that King Sancho does not call Vermudo emperor of Leon but of Galicia.

[253]

had entered Spain through Catalonia, and not through Navarre and Aragon, Catalonia would have had motives for turning towards the center of the Peninsula, and not only towards France and the Mediterranean. This is seen clearly in the case of Navarre, which, although for a considerable time included in the French sphere of influence, always preserved a close *de facto* tie to the rest of Spain. We have already seen the ancient connections that existed between Navarre and Santiago.

Between the extremes of the northwest and the northeast, supported either by supernatural forces or by Frankish imperialism, Castile emerged relying rather upon herself—which is not to say that she felt none of the protection afforded by the Apostle or that she lacked contacts with foreign lands through Navarre and the Way of Saint James. It is a pity that so little is known about the origins of Castile (the eighth, ninth, and tenth centuries);[3] but, be that as it may, the region north of Burgos, that is, Cantabria, already shows a social personality in the tenth century: it was governed by a count who, even though a feudatory of the king of Leon, seems not to have applied that kingdom's laws in the Roman tradition but rather Castilian customs. Although it may be a legend, there is a profound historical meaning in the story of how the citizenry of Burgos publicly burned the *Forum Judicum*, the book of Visigothic law by which Leon was governed. And it is no legend, according to Menéndez Pidal's admirable study of the first manifestations of Castilian in the tenth and eleventh centuries, that Castile had made its language uniform to a much greater degree than the contiguous regions of Leon and Aragon, and perhaps before it had a written literature. In this is revealed a firm will to action, an urgency to create social links and bonds incompatible with an unstable and anarchic language. But whether or not there was any literature to which to attribute the early regularization of the Castilian dialect (while Leon and Aragon are still writing *puerta*, *puorta*, *puarta*, Castile decides in favor of *puerta* in the tenth century, and discards the other two pronunciations), it seems necessary to postulate the existence of a directing class with prestige enough to inspire its imitation by the rest.

From this evident peculiarity of Castile, the future of the Peninsula took its shape. It is hard to imagine the character of the vital stimuli that impelled the Castilian man, but without imagining them, no history is possible. They were doubtless quite different from the ones that operated in the northwest zone, dominated as it was by "theobiotic" and

[3] Cf. Menéndez Pidal, *España del Cid*, p. 102; *Orígenes del español*, 1950, pp. 472-475.

theocratic forms of life. In the region of Castile-Navarre, on the other hand, there early appeared the first outlines of a vital situation oriented in an earthly rather than a divine direction. Only the results permit one to suspect the existence of such a reality, since the inner history of northern Castile between the eighth and tenth centuries is pure mist. But even so, the thought is inescapable that in the northwest the requirements of defense strengthened the other-worldly beliefs so abundant in that region, whereas in Castile certain men endowed with energy and the warrior-spirit were converted into an ideal toward which the will might strive. But this reliance of the Basque-Cantabrians on the power of personal prestige to motivate human action must have found the same support in the Moslem example as the tendency to let oneself be guided by magico-divine forces among the Galaico-Leonese people.

The Basque-Cantabrian people had distinguished themselves by their tenacity in war both in the time of Rome and under the Visigoths,[4] and had held aloof from the dominant culture of the south and the east of the Peninsula. They had nothing comparable to Visigothic Toledo, Seville, or Tarragon. But in spite of this kind of deficiency, the people in the north, speaking old Castilian, showed a firm individuality and initiative from the first; their speech was characterized by certain Ibero-Basque features (as Menéndez Pidal has demonstrated). The silencing of the *f* (*azer*, and not *fazer*) is explained thus, and there are many other phenomena besides (*e.g.*, the change of Latin *-ct-* to *-ch-*) that must come from the same source. The primitive Castilian peoples, then, appear to have been closely connected with the Basques.

The salient feature of Castilian life in the tenth century is the importance attached to the quality of the person and of his social virtues. The structure of such values had its foundation in man's this-worldly conduct and in his ability to become a guide and a model for others. Castile was rich in chieftains, not in bishop-popes or emperors surrounded by the aura of divinity. There was a stronger accent on the person than on his miraculous halo, and thus there emerged a kind of civilization which is not to be explained simply by recourse to the indomitable courage of rude and tribal Vasconia, although this doubtless was a decisive element. Nor would a Visigothic substratum be a sufficient explanation,

---

[4] Soldiers of superior fortitude were still sought in the Basque Country during the War of Granada. Diego de Valera recommended to Ferdinand the Catholic that he recruit from there "the largest possible number of armed soldiers, and as many foot soldiers as can come from Vizcaya, Guipuzcoa, and Asturias" (*Epístolas*, in *Bibliófilos Españoles*, xvi, 56). The Basques are mentioned first and foremost.

however plausible it may seem to connect the Castilian epic with the Germanic. The Castilian epic in its innermost substance is as different from the Germanic as it is from the French, both of which knew nothing of the art of combining belief in the epic myth with the experience of extra-literary existence. The disconcerting "historicity" of the Castilian epic is a unique phenomenon. The understanding of such a fact will be possible if we keep in sight the analogies between the Castilian and the Moslem disposition of life—*in spite of the profound differences of their literatures.* Moors and Castilians tied together the immediate event, the person who is involved in it, his physical appearance, and his moral inwardness. Let me emphasize that just as the Galician reinforced his beliefs with Moslem example in the matter of religion, likewise the Castilian, who felt inclined to value highly the qualities of the person, found stimulating models in figures like Almanzor, or the great caliphs who preceded him. Opposed as the two types of inspiration were, they both nevertheless were encouraged by the fight against the Moslems; for within his own land the Christian lacked distinguished patterns, and in the ninth and tenth centuries he had no effective contact with Carolingian Europe. The creation of the Hispano-Christian perspectives of values was a Peninsular problem (see pp. 344, 348).

There is a luminous page by the historian Ibn-Ḥayyān (987-1070), written as only an Arab could have written it, and motivated as could only have been done by a Castilian in the Spain of that time. From 995 to 1017 the ruler of Castile was Count Sancho García, "a creature of the Arab *caudillo*," Almanzor.[5] The count was "very bold and daring, and very forthright; thus he moved the nobles to greater nobility, and he diminished the servitude of the lesser folk."[6] But when Almanzor died, Sancho García sacked Cordova (1009) and pursued Castile's now ancient policy of rebellion against Leon. The Arabic history has preserved for us a description of his person, thanks to the "open" manner of the Moslem life structure, which allowed every phenomenon of sensuous or moral appeal that impinged upon the life of the person to enter into that life and there to take on value and meaning. On his way to Barcelona with his army to meet with Count Raymond of Barcelona, Sancho García crossed the zone of Tudela. He indicated his desire to talk with some of the city's worthies, and one of these, Abū Omayya, related his personal impressions to Ibn Ḥayyān:

[5] Menéndez Pidal, *La España del Cid*, p. 79. The author refers to the political support given the Castilian count.
[6] *Crónica general*, p. 453.

"The count penetrated our territory with the knowledge of the emir Mondhir, and he had promised that his army would do us no harm. But the inhabitants of Tudela—at that time haughty and powerful— did not approve of that agreement, and communicated their disapproval to the emir. They begged the emir to avoid the shame of allowing that Christian prince to enter his land. When Sancho was near the city, he dispatched a messenger, who made known to the inhabitants the count's desire to speak with certain persons. I was one of the procurators of the city [continues Abū Omayya]. We went out to his camp, where we counted some six thousand horsemen and foot soldiers, although Sancho had far from gathered together all his men. When we reached his tent, we found *him seated on a dais covered with cushions, and dressed in the Moslem fashion.* His head was uncovered, and his thin hair was just beginning to turn grey; the sun had tanned his skin, and his appearance was beautiful. He addressed us with grace and elegance, explained the motive for his journey, and referred to the agreement with our prince. For our part, we informed him of how unwillingly the citizens of Tudela were allowing him to pass near their city, and of their intention of preventing him from doing so by force. He advised us not to do this, and gave us to understand that a battle would turn out badly for us."

In spite of such a prudent warning, the Tudelans attacked the count's rear guard. The count detached five hundred horsemen, who forced the attackers to take refuge in the city. Abū Omayya continues:

"Amongst Christians I have seen no warriors like Sancho's; nor amongst the Christian princes any who equal him in gravity of bearing, in valor, in clarity of mind, in knowledge, in the effectiveness of his words. The only one who might be compared with him is his son-in-law of the same name, Sancho, son of García, the lord of the Basques [Sancho the Great, of Navarre]."[7]

Thus the Castilian-Navarrese appeared to their Moslem enemies, whose testimony in this case is as unique as it is valuable. We are shown the whole person, in his outward appearance and in his inner qualities, as an exemplary figure who dominated his enemies by his distinction, his seignorial spirit, and his effective acts. Such was the Castile of Fernán González, the Castile of the epics, the Castile that in the end overcame the Saracens, and gave a national tonality to the Christian kingdoms. The Moor of Tudela emphasizes the Castilian Count's elegant and effective expression, and it is of no importance here whether the language

[7] R. Dozy, *Recherches sur l'histoire et la littérature de l'Espagne,* I, 1881, p. 203.

of the interview was Castilian or Arabic. What is important is that the one understood the others well, and that their criteria of value were very similar. Sancho García and his son-in-law, the king of Navarre, elicited Moslem respect precisely because they possessed qualities similar to those of the Moslem chieftains, who were models for the Castilians in more than matters of dress and the way to be seated. The archetypal life must have been presented by the great figures of the Cordovan caliphate, among them Almanzor, the purest example of absolutely personal prestige. This Arab chieftain combined the energy that enabled him to undertake fifty-two victorious campaigns with the "courteous bearing and beguiling manners,"[8] that won him the sympathy of the sultana Sobḥa. Thus endowed, he was able to climb to the heights of success. On his numerous expeditions he was accompanied by poets and writers who reflected and glorified his warfare as well as his moral virtues and his wit. Moslem historians saw and recorded details that contemporary Christian chroniclers were unable to describe at that time.

Almanzor once forbade any fires to be lighted in the camp, lest they be discovered by the enemy. And one chronicler observes: "I saw Jafar blowing from time to time on a brazier of charcoal of oak, hidden carefully among his clothing so that the light of the fire might not shine through. And I saw more; I saw Otman, the son of Jafar, bending under the weight of a great bowl filled with flour and water, which he was carrying to his tent because it was the only food that he and his father had." Otman was moved to recite a poem: "I struggled in vain to change my fate; I saw it return as often and as faithful as a free maiden goes to her tryst."

Such was the compass of the Moslem's personal radius; his interior and exterior life meshed with *whatever was present at the moment* and that touched upon the course of his existence. This was the type of the man who was seen, admired, and feared by those who faced either the Moslem of the tenth century or the Christians fighting under his orders, so numerous that Sunday was a holy day for the army (Al-Maqqarī, pp. 214-215). What Ibn Ḥayyān had the genius to bring out earlier in his description of Count Sancho García of Castile was the integral unity of his personal and social values: the appearance, the gesture, the speech, the distinction, and the suggestive effectiveness of his authority.[9] The

[8] Al-Maqqarī, *The History of Mohammedan Dynasties*, tr. by P. de Gayangos, II, 181ff.

[9] Although I say so elsewhere, let me repeat here that this and nothing else is the key to the so-called Spanish "realism." Analyzing the *Generaciones y semblanzas* of

perception and expression of such values by the narrator were part and parcel of the structure of his existence, and to understand this existence and this expression we must project it against the Moslem form of life, which had been acting on the Christians for three centuries, remembering that three centuries is three hundred years. For the Castilian to be a person meant to be heedful of the individual's present reality—his body, his appearance, his gestures—and of the social impact of his moral qualities. The Castilian's inner experience consisted in living as a person and personalizing the life around him. Consequently, he had no special interest in either abstractions or symbols, as the most superficial comparison of the Cid of the *Poema* with the Roland of the *Chanson* will reveal.

Neither caliphs of Cordova nor Almanzor created the stubbornness and pugnacity or the lordly gravity of the primitive Castilian, but they did contribute in large measure to giving a meaning and a value to those qualities. The rude, hard Castilian-Cantabrian developed the habit of esteeming his own personal spirit and of keeping it in high tension, of fortifying it in his consciousness of being "nothing less than a whole man," as Unamuno would have it—able to create human groupings based on nothing but personal prestige, on the simple fact of existing, not on reasons, or, consequently, on things. The contact with the Moslems acted on the Castilian sense of values and, though indirectly, made possible certain features of her epic, unexplainable if we do not situate Castile in her authentic and immediate history. The fact that the forms

---

Fernán Pérez de Guzmán, the historian E. Fueter says: "Italian biographical literature has nothing comparable to the *Generaciones*. No humanistic work equals these biographical sketches in psychological discernment, precise awareness of the world, independence of judgment, and expressive realism" (*Histoire de l'Historiographie moderne*, p. 112). From the same deep Hispanic sources—rather than from classical antiquity—comes F. López de Gómara's impressive style, which the late Ramón Iglesia has so sensitively revealed to us in his *Cronistas e historiadores de Indias*, Mexico, 1942. The justice of Fueter's remarks concerning the style of Fernán Pérez de Guzmán is supported by the Italian biographies of the fifteenth century, for example the *Vite di uomini illustri del secolo XV*, by Vespasiano da Bisticci. These have been studied closely by Alfred von Martin in *Das Kulturbild des Quattrocento nach den Viten des Vespasiano da Bisticci* (in *Festgabe* for Heinrich Finke, Münster, 1925, pp. 316-355): "Many of the lives do not present any kind of individual portrait of the personality represented; they are rather stereotype patterns of the social class to which they belong" (p. 316); "quite after the fashion of the medieval writers, he wished to produce an exemplary, moralizing effect; so he presents primarily examples, models, patterns" (p. 316); etc. Although Vespasiano cites many examples from Antiquity (p. 251), he does not reach the point of using a personal style like Pérez de Guzmán's—a style which reflects a personal situation.

in which the *cantares de gesta* are expressed are Romanic (interwoven with the Latino-Visigothic tradition) is another problem that enters to complicate the historical process, a problem as rich in motives and reflections as the others that we have been analyzing. The Castilian was hardy, brave, and combative; he cultivated the totality of his being by beholding the paradigms that the Moslem world at the pinnacle of its grandeur imposed upon him. He began to compose written literature in the Romance that he spoke, stimulated perhaps by French trends and models, which were brought in profusion to the isolated land of Castile by foreign interest in the Apostle Santiago. Her unique destiny forced Christian Spain to create her life out of the play of inescapable attractions and repulsions.

Castile built herself around the exemplary strength of certain exceptional men. Fernán González and the magnificent procession of figures that came after him must have been the center of something like what Ibn-Ḥayyān describes: "The news of Almanzor's successes filled the inhabitants of Cordova with joy, and won for Almanzor the hearts of his soldiers, who, *when they realized his virtues and his talents*, longed to die in his service" (Al-Maqqarī, II, 189). Unfortunately, Almanzor was the last Hispano-Arab gifted with a genius for politics and warfare in a heterogeneous society whose form of life prevented it from establishing contact with Western Europe and thus from modifying the Moslem tendency to remain static. The course followed by Al-Andalus was like the one Christian Spain would have taken without her links to Christendom and without the emergence on the historical scene of a Castile established around a succession of men who incarnated what we may now recognize as Castilian values and upon the consensus of a people who "believed" in those men. The historical documents, whether they be poetic or prosaic, always emphasize this essential aspect. Fernán González consulted "everyone" (todos) before he made a decision; Count Sancho García, as we have just seen, increased the nobility of the great and diminished the servitude of the small. This type of organization, at once seignorial and democratic, was certainly not oriental.

In the midst of these human circumstances flourished the epic. As Menéndez Pidal shrewdly observes, the *cantares de gesta*, in both Spain and France, appear where common law, and not the traditional law of Rome, predominates. There are no gests in Southern France, nor where the *Forum Judicum* was the law. When he lives within his juridical custom, man rests upon the feeling that he is sufficient to himself, with no need for the intervention of legal written norms superimposed on him.

The institutions of Germanic tradition—private pawning and revenge—
helped to fill out and strengthen the Castilian form of life, more earthly
and autonomous than that of the kingdom of Leon. In perfect congruence with this there appear in the Castilian epic, whereas they do not
appear elsewhere in the Peninsula, flesh-and-blood characters, united
with the poet and his audience in a temporal experience: Fernán González, Sancho II, the Cid, etc. It is not farfetched to think that the
cantar of Fernán González was composed in the tenth century, just as
there are proofs of the existence of the *cantar* of the Infantes de Lara
in that epoch.[10] The poetry of Castile did not develop around remote,
or legendary, heroes like Roland,[11] and King Arthur or the Nibelungs.
The heroes of Castile were within reach.

Nevertheless, both types of poetry—the legendary and the historical
—found expression in both France and Castile in languages spoken by
the people, a fact at first hard to understand, if we believe that languages
do not begin to be written until they have grown old and mature; but
it is not languages, it is the lives of men that "mature." The everyday
spoken language took the upper hand over the Latin of the clerics as a
consequence of the power of the person to transcend his circumstances
through the impulse of the will; just as Castile rebelled against the
political tutelage of the Leonese monarchy, which was shaped under the

[10] Menéndez Pidal, *Poesía juglaresca*, pp. 322-324; *La leyenda de los Infantes de
Lara*, 1934, p. 458.
[11] I mean that the French epics, beginning with the *Chanson de Roland*, were
conceived in connection with supernatural beliefs, to which the poetic life of the
characters was subordinated. Karl Heisig has shown clearly how the Mohammedans
appear in the *Chanson de Roland* as instruments of the Antichrist, heralds of an
approaching end of the world. The emperor Charles agrees with the legendary representation which imagined him seated on his throne after his death, reclothed in
all the magnificence of his imperial insignia. At the end of the eleventh century
it was believed that Charles had risen from the dead. The Charles of the *Chanson*
is imagined as a person both dead and alive (ll. 2,496ff.). At the time of the disaster
at Roncevaux in 778, Charles was 36 years old; the character in the *Chanson* has
come back to life to lead a united Christendom in the war against the Antichrist.
The theme of the work is "the realization of the Kingdom of God in History"
(*Geschichtsmetaphysik des Rolandsliedes u. ihre Vorgeschichte*, in *Zeitschrift für
romanische Philologie*, 1935, LV, pp. 66, 72, 87). It is said, and maybe it is true,
that there were Roland epics in the ninth and tenth centuries (R. Fawtier, *La Chanson de Roland*, Paris, 1933; Luigi Foscolo Benedetto, *L'epopea di Roncisvale*, Florence, 1941), but we know nothing of their content or style, and there is therefore
no way to form any opinion about them. If the French epic had at one time been
historical, like the epic of Castile, something of this would have remained in the
specimens that have been preserved.

myths of Santiago and Saint Isidore and had no link with the pursuits of Castilian life.[12]

The use of the spoken language as a means of expressing in writing the beliefs, the sentiments, and the longings of the people (meaning here *most of the people*) seems to have begun in France and in Castile between the tenth and eleventh centuries. The spoken language had been used to explain religion to the people orally; but the right of the masses to participate in the banquets of fantasy and imagination that the poets had been offering for the exclusive enjoyment of the few who knew the Latin language was established in the eleventh century. Thus was inaugurated something like a new literary regime. Literary democratization preceded other types of democratization by centuries and prepared the way for them. It must be imagined, then, that as early as the eleventh century the people expressed the will to participate more actively in the collective life, and did not limit themselves to a silent and passive support of those who directed them along the journey through this world and prepared them for the next. It is not correct to say that the Middle Ages were always an undisturbed harmony, a tranquil lake whose surface reflected the image of the Augustinian City of God nicely articulated with the earthly city. If it had been so, European history would have been static. We are accustomed to think that the harmony of the Middle Ages was not really broken until the fourteenth century, and we do not emphasize sufficiently the fact that German-Latin-Christian Europe, spiritually united, emerged in history fully charged with the elements that were to bring about its dissolution. This process could be outlined thus: Charlemagne authoritatively pointing out to the pope the limits of the latter's power;[13] the increasing importance given to mundane val-

[12] A clarifying digression is necessary. If Castile had been able to combine her creative and earthly impulse with a system of objective principles—that is, with a culture based on rational thought and on things—she would have paralleled Northern France in her destiny, and her kings would have thrown themselves into the cure of Scrofula. But the "little corner" of Castile had to be content with subsisting and expanding itself over Moorish ground. In the end Castile had to be included in the same system of religio-political beliefs as Leon and Galicia. When it constituted itself a kingdom under Ferdinand I (1038-1065), the ancient county was ruled over by Santiago (the saint, not the city), and thanks to that Apostle, Coimbra was conquered, as we have already seen. Catalonia for her part lacked the redoubtable impetus of Castile, and was unable to create a political organization to realize her material potentialities. But Castile did not spread towards the East in the tenth and eleventh centuries; by an ironic destiny the Castilian-Leonese judged to be European only those things which he perceived through Santiago, toward which he did turn.

[13] "It is Our part to defend Christendom; Yours to implore divine assistance"

ues, albeit without forgetting those of eternal and divine character; the glorification of purely earthly heroes; rebellions against monarchs in spite of their divine rights; the use of the spoken language for writing about profane subjects; the rationalist criticism of miracles (as in France); the particularism of the religious orders (Cluny, Cîteaux), tied as closely to dynastic and earthly interests as to the universal spirit of the Church; nominalism, which made it possible to oppose the immutable generalizations of realism; and so on. In different countries and in different times, the order that was the legacy of the dual tradition, secular and ecclesiastical, came into flower in different ways. (We shall see in Chapter 13 that the birth of learned prose—astronomy—in Castile was an isolated phenomenon.)

But the process alluded to here did not operate fully in Castile, which is quite comprehensible since Castile did not have a philosophical and theological culture synchronized with the philosophical and theological culture of the West.[14] Arabic and Jewish culture weighed too heavily on Hispanic Christendom, where there was nothing comparable to the so-called "Twelfth-Century Renaissance." Spain could take no part in that philosophical and theological uprising, that began in the eleventh century and was followed by the "counter-reformation" of the thirteenth

---

(Nostrum est . . . Vestrum est . . .). Cf. Henry Pirenne, *Mohammed and Charlemagne*, 1939, p. 230. In this haughty exaltation of royal power face to face with religious power is already to be perceived the functional process of French existence. It is connected with the faculty of working miracles, which the French Kings arrogated to themselves, and thus a human institution makes a kind of "imperialistic" invasion of the zone of the divine. In harmony with this also is the fact that Charlemagne, in the *Chanson de Roland*, leads his people in the supreme task of realizing the Kingdom of God in history (see Chap. 9, note 11). Guibert de Nogent (d. 1121) wrote a history of the Crusades in which appears the celebrated phrase of profound historical meaning, "Gesta Dei per Francos." It seems, then, as if the tenth- and eleventh-century Frenchman felt that God was delegating his powers to the sovereigns and people of France. The temporal and earthly character of the Frenchman thus acquired extraordinary relief: his actions, his thoughts, and *his speech* increased in importance. As Gaston Paris pointed out in 1865, "Charlemagne devenait de plus en plus le symbole de la puissance mise au service de la religion" (*Histoire poétique de Charlemagne*, p. 54). The Emperor was, after a fashion, to France what Santiago was to Spain. Charlemagne was called "caput orbis, episcopus episcoporum, rex, rector et decus Ecclesiae" (see L. Olschki, *Der ideale Mittelpunkt Frankreichs im Mittelalter*, p. 12).

[14] In the sixteenth century, when Juan Ginés de Sepúlveda wants to mention Spanish thinkers and scientists of the Middle Ages, he limits himself to saying that "Averroes and Avempace excelled in philosophy, and King Alphonse in astronomy." Alphonse X's astronomical science was Arabic and Jewish, as is well known. (*Sobre la justa causa de la guerra contra los indios*, Mexico, 1941, p. 101.)

century, of which the greatest figure is Thomas Aquinas. The forces of dissolution yielded before a system of hierarchies with its graduated structure from the humblest being up to God. The so-called European Middle Ages consisted in an unceasing struggle between the forces of dissolution and an order founded on divine transcendence.

Castile had a humanism of a peculiar type, not based, as was the humanism of Northern France, on the idea that man could be the instrument of divine intentions to further the earthly interests of the monarchs and their peoples. The Castilian refused to keep at a distance from the divine order in which he felt himself immersed, and he made no problem of what he felt to be evidence. His epics do not presuppose a metaphysical-theological system such as can be observed in the *Chanson de Roland*. The Castilian epic singer faced topics that were mundane, and sometimes atrocious, with the sure knowledge that in the end the providence of God would set the disturbed order aright. This is what happens in the *cantar* of the Infantes de Lara, with its well-known matter of hatred and vengeance, as well as in the *cantares* of Fernán González and of Mio Cid, victims of wicked enemies, yet triumphant over them at the last. The characters were historical and their actions were verisimilar for both the poet and his hearers.

The French *chansons* served as exemplary spectacles for a people aware that they were constituted as a body politic securely established in its own land. In the *chansons* the monarchy had a halo of prestige that was the legacy of a remote and already legendary past. The Castilian *cantares* were born in a region that had no kings of its own until well along in the eleventh century, and no link with an imperial tradition such as Charlemagne's. They were poetic versions of contemporary or remembered events, things that could always happen, and which had an effect on the vicissitudes of the collective life: the struggle between the Castilians and the Leonese, the constant war with the Moor, the hostility between lords and kings. The Castilians cultivated the epic less to draw fruitful conclusions from their past than to construct an ideal for the future in the face of a harsh and problematical present. In the eleventh century every Spanish Christian must have shared the feeling expressed by the Cid:

> We shall better our lot with lances and swords;
> If we don't, we cannot live in this narrow land. (834-835)

Instead of the *Gesta Dei per Francos*, the epic motto of the Castilians might have been *Gesta Castellae per Deum*.

In both countries the interest in the epic affected the collective life and was connected with urges that had been felt as legitimate for centuries. One recounted the *gesta*, gests, deeds already performed, with one's heart set on the *gerenda*, the future tasks of the people; and this could not be done save in the language spoken and understood by everyone. This did not mean a break with the spiritual order of the Church, but it did mean an accentuation of the now ancient particularism of a well-defined people (that is, of the Castilians as opposed to the Leonese). Alongside the uniform and far-flung hierarchy of the City of God—pure spirit—was glorified the just and legitimate sovereignty of a strong-willed and energetic group of human beings. In principle spiritual gradualism *should* have been sufficient for Christian people ruled by the ministers of God. Hence, there is, strictly speaking, a contradiction in terms between "national" and "Christian" epic, a conflict very clearly perceived by Torquato Tasso in the sixteenth century and by Unamuno in the twentieth (*La agonía del cristianismo*). The exemplary character of the Castilian epic hero was a tissue of virtues and sins, of religion and worldliness. Mudarra, the avenger of the seven *Infantes* of Lara, was begotten by his Christian father, Gonzalo Gustioz, upon a Moorish maiden sent by the Moorish king to sweeten the hours of his captivity. There is nothing Christian about the vengeance subsequently wreaked upon those guilty of the death of the Seven Knights. At times it seems as if a blast of Germanic paganism were shaking the Christian-Romanic structure of the *cantares de gesta*.

Sinful worldliness was felt to be as legitimate as virtue and holiness. Alongside the consensus of the devout-faithful with their trust in the word of the God, there was the consensus of these same people in their devotion to the *caudillo* as the lord of the free men of Castile, a leader who promised them triumphs, independence, and good fortune. Beside the prayers of the clergy, who invoked God in Latin, was the sweet song of the minstrel, who, in the language of everyone, recited the heroic deeds of superior men worthy of imitation for their manliness (hombría) and for their daring. The birth of the epic and its use of the everyday language amounted to something more than a chapter in the "evolution of language." It meant above all that certain Europeans at a certain moment believed in the validity of expressing their awareness of their voluntaristic energy, a belief which they held in connection with the ends that their station in this world imposed upon them. That is, each people did this according to the preferences of its peculiar "dwelling-place."

Western Christendom had aspired to be the best possible suburb of the mystical City of God, envisaged as it had been planned by Saint Augustine, the great architect of the other world. The Church organized life theocentrically, and everything that existed aimed toward the center of the eternal, uncreated spirit. Günther Müller has provided a lucid exposition of the idea that the Middle Ages was a process of gradualistic progression from the human to the divine, devoid of the conflict of duality, without opposing principles that excluded one another. Value judgments were entirely moral and were made in terms of extra-subjective norms.[15] Müller is dealing with medieval literature in Germany, but his ideas become meaningful only when they are taken as a total conception of Western Christendom. The best texts he finds in support of his thesis are taken, as is to be expected, from Saint Thomas Aquinas: "Oportuit ad hoc, quod in creaturis esset perfecta Dei imitatio, quod diversi *gradus* in creaturis invenirentur."[16] Let us bear in mind, however, that Saint Thomas represents a reaction in favor of the order of the mind, after a long period of agitation that was destined to be resumed eventually and to end by dethroning theology. To base a global interpretation of the so-called Middle Ages on the Thomist *Summae* would be rather like bringing up the canons enacted at Trent and the theology of Belarmino to explain the meaning of European literature from the fourteenth to the sixteenth centuries.

The Western Christian idea of gradualism actually existed, to be sure, and it expressed in metaphysical terms the theological reality of the Middle Ages. Indeed, Saint Anselm (1035-1109) had already done this when he conceived of God as the maximum of perfection, of a perfection which unifies all things hierarchically: wood, horse, man. . . .[17] Scholastic

---

[15] "Gradualismus," in *Deutsche Vierteljahrschrift für Literaturwissenschaft*, 1924.

[16] *Summa contra gentiles*, II, Chap. 45 (Müller, *op.cit.*, p. 694).

[17] G. Grünwald, *Geschichte der Gottesbeweise*, p. 30. But let it not be forgotten that already in the tenth and eleventh centuries the conflict had been established between earthly experience, supported by the faculty of critical judgment, and the theological order. In the tenth century we find the first proofs of the existence of God. This had not been a problem since Saint Augustine, some five hundred years earlier. The poor efforts at demonstration in the tenth century made way for the great theological constructions of Saint Anselm and Abelard (Grünwald, *op.cit.*, p. 26). The quarrels between the realists and the nominalists present an analogous process in philosophy. In opposition to the belief in the reality of universal concepts, which permitted one to arrive at the divine reality without any effort, nominalism proposed a long and problematic method of cognition based on the individual sensory experience of things. It was Berengarius of Tours (d. 1088) who did not think the Eucharistic reality could be achieved without a change in the accidents of its matter. For this reason he was told: "You have abandoned sacred authority and

philosophy permits us to understand the theological aspect which stood at the core in those centuries; but an abstract formula does not take in the whole of life. Manifestly, the fact that man existed under a divine vault was enough by itself to impose order upon everything that man did or thought. It is no less true, however, that the earthly-divine order modified its structure accordingly as greater or lesser value might be attached to one or the other of the two terms, namely, to God or to the world. The ordained gradualism was accompanied by a pendular movement now toward the human, now toward the divine. When life became dissolute—that is, separated from God—austere reactions like the foundation of Cluny would appear. When the spiritual impetus of the Cluniacensians grew weak, the Cistercians emerged to reestablish the equilibrium. When the latter in turn failed, Saint Francis came on the scene.

Spain, however, took no interest in the doctrinal aspect of religion, but rather in its propagation in epic fashion through the instrumentality of Saint Dominic and his order, a thirteenth-century anticipation of the Society of Jesus of the sixteenth century. When the ecclesiastical order began to totter in the middle of the fourteenth century, Spain shared the uncertainty of other countries. A result of this was the Order of Saint Jerome, founded by anchorites who preferred the life of solitude. But neither the Hieronymites nor the Spanish Dominicans altered the ideological direction taken by Christianity, because religion in Spain, just like the Castilian epic, was experienced personally as a belief in which man felt himself to exist fully. In the tenth and eleventh centuries the bishops of Santiago claimed to be popes, because they were more interested in their personal interpretation of the divine order than in submitting to the traditional hierarchy. They existed for a long time between the pressures of an "I want to be" and an "I must obey," with more will than judgment. The comparison between Castile and neighboring Europe shows that the Castilians never manifested any critical thought

---

you take refuge in dialectic." His contemporary, Otloh of St. Emmeran (d. 1070), confessed to having doubted the truth of the Bible and even the existence of God, although he later repented and forbade the monks to concern themselves with science, which he judged to be dangerous (Ueberweg-Heinze, *Grundriss der Geschichte der Philosophie*, II, 186). When we add all this to the instances already mentioned of the French resistance to accepting the authenticity of John the Baptist's head and other relics, we perceive how there was already a ferment of tendencies in eleventh-century France that would eventually break down the medieval order. The result of that nominalism was to be the philosophy of William of Ockham (fourteenth century), which, making it impossible to know God through reason, ended up by relegating theology to the exclusive world of the priests.

opposing the ideal structure of the Middle Ages. Nevertheless, the spontaneity of Castile, stimulated by worldly motives, prepared her to assert a peculiarity that set her apart from the Santiago-Leonese regime and made her more like those, in France, who also stressed earthly concerns. In France, awareness of nationality had its foundation in the Carolingian past; in Castile, in the strength, in the rebellion, and in the prestige of leaders like Fernán González, Sancho García, and others equally present and real. The purposes of those rebels were not compatible with the linguistic, juridical, and spiritual tradition of the kingdom of Leon, although they did not make a frontal attack on that tradition, nor did they seek to overthrow it altogether. It was a matter of vital overflowing, not of a calculated plan. But the vitality and the justified rebelliousness of Castile against Leonese rule, and the usage of the spoken language, to exalt Castilian national heroes, are different facets of one and the same phenomenon.[18]

The epic themes caused the emergence of the language, and vice versa. Thinking abstractly, one finds no motive to explain why Latin—the living language of the Church to which all belonged—ceased to be written and spoken. Before the eleventh century, Western people spoke in one fashion and wrote in another in the lands of the former Roman Empire, and the unlettered folk of neighboring regions did not understand each other. Yet, in spite of this, Charlemagne did not encourage the cultivation of spoken Romanic and Germanic languages; rather, he revived as much as he could the study of the traditional Latin. It would be anti-historical to say that the Romanic languages were not yet "formed," for languages are not plants grown in greenhouses waiting to be transplanted into the gardens of literature. It is as conceivable that the spoken language of the eighth century should have been written in its time as that the spoken language of the fifteenth century should not have been written in its time. It is always happening somewhere that there is a divergence between the cultivated language and the vulgar: Basque has never been written till recent times, when it is being done rather artificially; many Italians neither speak nor write Tuscan; in German Switzerland no one speaks at home the German that is written for the public; in many places in Hispano-America, Indian languages are spoken, yet books are written in Spanish. There is no point in saying that medieval Latin was an al-

[18] The use of the spoken language as a means of expression for human feelings in every Romanic country signifies a break in the traditional spirituality, even when the themes of the expressions are religious.

tered language; between the Latin of the twelfth century (spoken and written just as many Germanic-Swiss of today speak and write German) and the Latin of the first century there was no more difference than between the English of a Broadway play and the English of the fifteenth century. A way of speaking is inseparable from the value attached to it by the speaker. If he feels that his speech, however natural it may be for him, sounds crude and plebeian, he is timid in its use and does not write it. The important thing, then, was not that the Romance languages-to-be were but slightly advanced, or that Latin had fallen into ruin.[19] What counted was the impetus and daring to write extensive works of a worldly character in the vulgar tongue, with an uncertain orthography. Contemplated in this light, the late tenth century and the eleventh resemble the transition from Neo-classicism to Romanticism, when languages which till then had had no literature, and dialects which had never been written, began to be used for the composition of literary works, because certain regions of Europe felt their awareness of nationality being reborn.[20] The supra-individual generality of faith and of reason was succeeded by a sense of singularity, together with an intuition of the historical, present reality. In the eleventh century nobody discussed this phenomenon, because the mind of the period lacked both the forms in which to capture the meaning of what man was doing and feeling and the forms in which, once captured, these meanings might be expressed. But just as we guess what a child feels and wants from its gestures and facial expressions, so we perceive the inner situation of people who in the eleventh century took the bold step of saying in a new language things that the language spoken and written by the clergy was unable to communicate. The powerful will of certain groups blasted the armor of the linguistic order. The Castilian people needed to unburden their hearts by expressing in well-articulated linguistic forms their temporal and secular life.

[19] Latin continued to be a means of expression for thought even in the eighteenth century; and in the twelfth century, and later, works of great literary value were written in that language. Luis Vives prefers it to the vulgar languages because its use is widespread "among many peoples and nations, and there is scarcely any art or science that does not have its literary monuments in Latin" ("De disciplinis," 1531, in *Obras completas*, tr. by L. Riber, 1948, II, 574). Latin was felt to be the language of the "ideal" nation created by the learned, the same way that the vulgar languages were the heritage of the concrete, territorially limited nations.

[20] For quite obvious political motives, newspapers are published in Soviet Russia today in languages that have never been written before.

The *"Chanson de Roland"*

A brief comparison of the two gests confirms the idea that runs through the present work, that is, that the Hispano-Christian, revealed as he is in his language, usages, literary forms and art, is closely linked with Europe and takes from Europe everything that his peculiar disposition permits him to take; at the same time, he preserves an irreducible and aggressive singularity, which he owes essentially to the Christian-Islamic contexture of his beliefs. Seen in a certain light, his personality appears as a pseudomorphosis similar to the pseudomorphosis that his language has shown us in bold relief, and it reveals complications and habits acquired in the alternate and sometimes simultaneous struggles with the Moor and the Christian European, both of them superior in that epoch to the Spaniard. The Spaniard succeeded in keeping afloat in his problematical existence by alternately getting support from the south against the north, and vice versa. It is well known that there was rarely a sharp division between Christians and Moors, and that the more usual thing was an opportunistic alliance against the common enemy. The Cid lived in the Moorish kingdom of Saragossa between 1081 and 1087, so that he could protect King Mostain, and therefore he fought against the Moorish king of Lerida, Mostain's enemy. The King of Lerida in turn enjoyed the protection of the Christian Count of Barcelona; but the Cid had to fight the Christian King of Aragon, an ally of the King of Lerida. Years before this, Alphonse VI of Leon found refuge in the court of al-Ma'mūn of Toledo when his brother Sancho dispossessed him of his kingdom. These events and others which the reader may find in Menéndez Pidal's *La España del Cid* were regular occurrences until the fourteenth century. Faced with such a state of affairs, the Spanish Christian was forced to accentuate his Hispano-Islamic peculiarity as a natural defensive measure against the pressure of the numerous monks, priests, knights, tradesmen, and rabble with which foreign lands, especially France, flooded the Peninsula. This was the loom on which the structure of the Spaniard was warped, and on which the fine fabric of his art and literature was woven.

The *Chanson de Roland* was written many years before the *Cantar de Mio Cid*. The meter of the *Chanson* is fairly regular, whereas the Castilian poem alternates between long and short lines,[21] a very significant phenomenon. Simplifying matters a little, one might say that the *Chanson* was written for the people and the *Cantar* from the point of view

[21] Cf. Menéndez Pidal, *Poesía juglaresca*, p. 342.

of the people. The grandiose disaster of Roland and his peers is exhibited for the admiration of everyone, in the popular language, in visual images which serve as vehicles for spiritual doctrines and present in a model form the ideal of monarchy and nobility as being of one substance with France. There are no plebeian characters in the *Chanson* because the intent is to give the people something to admire, not a body of subject matter in which they might imagine themselves as participating. The *Chanson* is like a solemn *reredos* placed at a height suitable for being seen and not for being handled. It is full of shining images that recall the biblical figures of a romanesque portal, whose existence one could share only spiritually:

> Underneath a spruce, beside a wild rose;
> They have raised up a throne of finest gold;
> On it sits the king who rules in sweet France;
> His beard is of snow, his hair like flowers;
> His body is fair, his mien imposing. (114-117)

The people are addressed from a plane that is not their own, and are told of things an infinite distance away from the poor life of everyday. The *Chanson* shows the paradigm of a supreme order that binds the visible and the invisible world together: "Rollant est proz e Oliver est sage" (l. 1,093); Roland incarnates the energy of the paladin and Oliver the moderation, the *mesure*, of the prudent. But the two are excelled by the inestimable figure of the Archbishop, who, as he must, has the virtues of both of them:

> E l'arcevesque, ki fut sages e proz. (3,691)

Just as the paladins are stationed in their order beneath the priest-warrior, so is the military enterprise subsumed under the superior category of holy war against the infidel,[22] so that the war may be brought under the law of salvation, a supreme ideal which the historical Charlemagne could not have felt but which, by the eleventh century, had been communicated to France by Spanish Islam:

> Si recevrat [the Moorish king] la lei que vos tenez. (695)[23]

[22] Cf. Heisig, "Die Geschichtsmetaphysik des Rolandsliedes und ihre Vorge-schichte," in *Zeitschrift für romanische Philologie*, 1935, LV, 1-87.

[23] Other facts are also useful as an indication of the presence of the Arabic life of Spain in the *Chanson*. Speaking of omens, Al-Masʿūdī says (*The Golden Meadows*, III, 333, in the French translation of C. Barbier de Meynard) that such a belief did not belong exclusively to the Arabs: "if it sometimes appears amongst other peoples, as for instance the Franks or other peoples of the Occident, it is very probable that

In this holy war the archbishop takes the initiative in the battle:

Li arcevesque cumencet la bataille (1,487)

and he guarantees entrance into paradise to those who fall as holy martyrs in the fight:

Se vos murez, esteres seinz martirs. (1,134)

The meaning of this is evident now. The reader will recall that multitude of holy martyrs who surrendered their souls to God in the war against the Saracens of Spain, and in glistening white albs and red stoles crossed the land of France on their way to eternal glory. This was happening already at the beginning of the eleventh century, and it makes it possible to understand how naturally the poet of the *Chanson* can speak of the holy war, in which both sides aspire equally to paradise:

Marsile veit de sa gent le *martirie*. (1,467)

Roland himself recognizes that the "paiens" are seeking their martyrdom (l. 1,166). Turpin, the magnificent archbishop, learned to be a "mult bon chevaler" (l. 1,637) from his Spanish compeers, to fight like the Galician bishops of the tenth century and like the future knights of the orders.

The doctrine is insinuated in a dazzling spectacle. Roland flies past on his horse Veillantif, rending the air with the white banner of his lance, which points to heaven and destiny (ll. 1,152-1,157). There is a constant succession of visual effects, because the intention of the poet is to provoke contemplation, not to vitalize the action, which proceeds slowly, like a rite, with its triple formulas: Oliver asks Roland three times to sound his horn; Roland thrice refuses; Charlemagne faints three times before the body of the dead hero.

The *Chanson* was felt and written in a mood of wonder, with a view to exciting and maintaining such a mood in the audience. The figures, the events, and the scene in which the events take place have an immediate effect because of their magnitude—humanity and nature in the superlative degree:

they have taken it from their neighbors the Arabs of Al-Andalus, which forms part of the Greater Land" (p. 335). Let me remark in passing that this "Greater Land" (al-arḍ al-kabīra) is the source of the "Tere Major" of the *Chanson de Roland* (ll. 53, 71), which Bédier has translated as "la Terre des Aïeux." Actually, it is difficult to find an exact equivalent for an expression that designated Europe from the point of view of those outside Europe, as the Spaniards in the Caribbean islands called the American continent *Tierra Firme*. In any case the translation "Terre des Aïeux" is not exact.

Halt sunt li puis, e li val *tenebrus*; (815)
Grant est la plaigne e *large* la cuntree; (3,305)
De l'olifan *haltes* sunt les menees; etc. (3,310)

Menéndez Pidal has observed what he calls the "lack of naturalness" in the *Chanson*. "The sound of Roland's horn is heard for thirty leagues; Turpin with four lance-wounds in his body and Roland with his head split open and his brains coming out around his ears act and fight like men in full possession of their powers. The armies are enormous, with 360,000 and 450,000 knights respectively. Five Frenchmen kill 4,000 Saracens."[24] Today we would call this "propaganda," whose artistic meaning is unintelligible if we do not imagine for ourselves the open-mouthed listeners of the twelfth century standing around the one recounting such wonderful things, things written down essentially to elicit wonderment. The poet felt his subject as hovering over him at an incalculable altitude, and he versifies as a skillful interpreter of a religious and social cause. The minstrel-artist orchestrates, he plays the preexisting melody, as it were on the instrument of his verses, this in harmony with his intent to produce wonder; and not as a "primus inter pares" who puts himself in the place, in the lived or livable experience, of his hearers. In the case of both the French and the Spanish epics, the poet feels that he is an intermediary, a sounding-board for what exists either above or around him. This is why he does not tell us his name: he is not practicing a skill comparable to that of the clerical poet, nor is he inculcating a doctrine derived from books, a task which poets of the Spanish thirteenth century were to deem worthy of being ascribed to an individual name. Pouring into the air a harmony of words that fired the imagination and fortified the religious and moral conduct of the hearer was an art that corresponded to certain theatrical spectacles that delight the public without making anyone wonder who has composed them.

The French gest is a sacred and solemn spectacle rather than a story. If contemplation is the object, visual effects will have to be striven for:

N'unt guarnement que tut ne *reflambeit*. (1,003)
E gunfanuns *blancs* e *vermeilz* e *blois*. (1,800)
Ki pur soleil sa *clartet* n'en muet. (2,990)
Luisent cil elme as perres d'or girunees, etc. (3,306)

The auditory is associated with the visual:

Sunent mil grailles *por ço que plus bel seit* (1,004)

[24] "Poema de Mio Cid," ed. of R. Menéndez Pidal, *Clásicos Castellanos*, 1929, p. 58.

that is, to emphasize still more the splendor of the Saracen army, "a thousand trumpets sound so that it will be more beautiful," and that brilliant procession is beautiful indeed with its helmets from Saragossa, swords of steel from Vienne, javelins from Valencia, and banners white, blue, and crimson, together with armor that glitters under the rays of the sun. The words and their historical atmosphere mutually recreate each other in this sacred representation. The figures of the characters, at once vivid and solemn like those over the doorway of a Romanesque abbey, were carved for the benefit of the faithful and for the spiritual and temporal magnification of those who ruled over them. The *Chanson* is a tissue of theological and chivalric ideals and interests, and of fierce and bloody passions. It was conceived with a downward direction, from the religious point of view, which also included the point of view of the nobility. Its intention was to evoke wonderment in the multitude of the faithful, to incite them to contemplate time after time the places that were sanctified by the blood of the martyrs fallen in a holy war, a war in which Christians and Saracens alike aspired to martyrdom, an idea absorbed by Christian France from Islam, and adopted precisely in order to give Christian meaning and a sense of spiritual order to the pleasure of spilling blood, a pleasure that Roland felt like a beast of the forest, like the hero of a Germanic epic:

> Quant Rollant veit que la bataille serat,
> Plus se feit fiers que leon ne leupart. (1,110)

France knew this idea of the holy war, but she did not experience an existence shared with the Moslems, and the Moslems did not leave their imprint in the inner movements of the French soul, anchored as it was in its Romano-Germanic structure. When the "sage" Oliver feels the entrails of the enemy quivering under his spear, his wild soul cries out with joy: "Gente est nostre bataille" (Beautiful is our battle!) (1. 1,247). The *Chanson* either expresses the spirit of German paganism, or is a symbolical and didactic expression of French Christianity.

The poet rigorously keeps apart the world of his immediate experience and the poetic plane on which his fantasy floats. The characters and places cannot be pinned down historically as they can in the *Poema del Cid*. The *Chanson* gives a structure to the "facts" in the beautiful liturgy of its art, a structure that proceeds in an ascending scale which, starting with bloody prowess, passes through *mesure*, and attains finally to sanctity. Dominating the grandiose construction rises the figure of the venerable Turpin—"preux et sage"—who has to his proud credit the death of the king of Denmark (l. 1,489) and who opens the gates of paradise to the martyred heroes; at his side, Charlemagne, whom time cannot wither, of incalculable age, with his beard of silver and his hair like a tangle of flowers.

"Cantar de Mío Cid"

The literary theme of this *cantar* does not float above the poet and his auditors as is the case in the *Chanson de Roland*. The characters are not stylized forms without an inwardness to make visible, without an inner perspective and an outer perspective. The myth is not seen from afar, to be merely contemplated and venerated. Just as "to dawn" (ama-necer) and "to become night" (anochecer) are phenomena incorporated into the experience of the Spanish speaker, likewise the epic theme is realized in the immediate life of the artist and his audience:

God, what a good vassal! Would that he had a good lord! (20)

The Cid, then, is not only the ideal figure who rides through these verses. He is also the person whom the minstrel-poet perhaps knew, and whom many of the listeners undoubtedly knew or had known. Others had heard of him from their parents, and they knew that the king who had exiled the Cid was the grandfather of their own Alphonse VII. The poet projected his affective longings on the hero because the *Campeador* was something more than a venerable figure standing remote at the summit of the mystical ladder of veneration: he was a literary character and, at the same time, a person within reach of the hearers' experience. As a literary character he appears framed in epithets that he wears like a set of formal robes: "of beauteous beard" (l. 274), "of auspicious birth" (l. 294), "he who girded on his sword at a well-omened hour" (l. 507), etc. But some of the epithets, even so long ago, have a *novelistic* savor: "Much I thank you, *storied* Campeador" (l. 493). This sentence fuses the person-character addressed and the character already celebrated through previous accounts. Thus we have an embryonic cell of what, centuries later, is to be the Quixote,[25] of the

---

[25] Let it be said here that in this scheme of literary life is Cervantes' most original creation. Don Quixote as a character issues from certain books read by Alonso Quijano, and he thus appears as magically transformed into a knight errant in such a way that there is never any clearly defined boundary between reality and fantasy. The Don Quixote of the second part is in turn a magico-human projection of the *storied* character of the first part. The figures emerge from preceding accounts (for instance, when the Duchess sees Don Quixote, she says that she already knows him from having read Cervantes' book).

To prevent misunderstanding, I will mention here the allusions in the French

second part of the Cervantine novel, the Quixote who is himself plus the "storied" Quixote of the first part. This feature is so natural to our sensibilities of today that it does not surprise; yet it should, and very much, because the *Cid* was written in 1140. The person who appears in the poem is the same one who has been told about. The Cid is himself and his "novel," just as is Don Quixote and as is every authentic expression of Hispanic existence. This is the abyss that separates the *Chanson* and the *Cantar*; the former offers matters to be venerated, the latter is a hearty toast to wonderful experiences that can be humanly shared:

> The lion, when he saw him, was ashamed;
> Before my Cid he lowered his head to the ground.
> My Cid Don Rodrigo took him by the neck,
> And led him and put him in the cage.
> *All that were there* had to marvel at it. (2,298-2,301)

The character officiates as a hero, and a lion becomes humbly respectful before him. The scene has an audience—"all that were there"—to which is added the audience around the poet. But this same legendary character discards his mythic halo and sits down to eat like a flesh-and-blood person:

> And for my Cid Don Rodrigo a great meal they cooked (1,017)

and he invites the Count of Barcelona to share it. The count has already been characterized in the line

> The count was most vainglorious, and said a boastful thing. (960)

Downcast to find himself defeated and imprisoned by the Cid, the count refuses to eat. The Cid threatens him with a long captivity if he

---

chansons to the poems for which the heroes have already provided or may yet provide the subject: "Dist l'uns a l'altre: j'ai öi un jougler;/ Oiés con cante de Guillaume au court nés!" ("Le Moniage Guillaume," quoted in Menéndez Pidal, *Poesía juglaresca,* p. 327). In the *Chanson de Roland* the hero spurs his men to battle: "Or guart chascuns que granz colps i empleit,/ Male cançun de nus dite ne seit!" (ll. 1,013-1014). In his admirable edition (Florence, 1936, p. 481) of the *Chanson,* Giulio Bertoni says: "For the preoccupation of the heroes with what will be told about them, see Wilmotte, *Romania,* LIV, 124"; and he calls the reader's attention to Jeremiah, *Lamentations,* III, 14: "Factus sum in derisum omni populo meo, canticum eorum tota die." To this I would add "in fabulas ire." But for all that we may add, the "storied *Campeador*" of the *Cid* will retain its particular meaning; the song (canto), the story (cuento), do not exist here as a reality transcending the person, but as an integral, immanent element of his existence. To provide the occasion for songs and stories is different from existing as sung and storied. The same life structure that made possible the "storied *Campeador*" also made possible the Don Quixote of Part Two, who includes the Don Quixote of the story in Part One.

persists in his refusal, and on another occasion offers him his freedom:

Said my Cid: "Eat something, count,
For if you don't eat, you will never see Christians again." (1,033)

The work is at the same time a poem and a novelized chronicle, and its expressive form is nearer to prose than to verse. The tone of familiar proximity, the ingenuous nakedness of what is expressed, would not fit into elaborate measured and rhymed verses, which imply in themselves a departure into an unaccustomed, inaccessible, solemn reality that could never be successfully expressed in the poor language of everyday. The name "poema," borrowed from the treatises on rhetoric, is really not suitable to this "cantar," which can find no ready-made label in the stocks of literary history. We are dealing here with a "centauric" genre in which are mixed the poetically transcendent and the experience actually lived or livable by the hearer or reader. Compare the description of Charlemagne quoted above with the following lines:

My Cid spurred his horse; he reached the door;
He took his foot out of the stirrup, and struck the door;
It did not open, for it was well locked. (37-39)[26]

Such verses (in Spanish) are neither regular nor irregular. To call them irregular would presuppose that they could have followed some rule or other, and this is inconceivable. If the verse is irregular, it is because the *Cantar*, with its "centauric" structure, answers to no set of preexisting, descriptive rules, or, rather, because it takes its form from the internal requirements of its existence and from nothing else. The chant in which the poet recited the verses, and the assonance, provided the minimum stage necessary to mark the distinction between any sort of relation and this particular one, important and filled with matters of high interest, matters whose factual skeleton the audience was already acquainted with. Now it expected to hear them embroidered, as it were, and embossed. But the audience knew very well that the poet was not going to take them through depths where they would lose their footing. The men and women of Burgos—the "Burgueses e burguesas"—who are at the windows watching the exiled knight enter their city are the same ones who later hear his deeds of prowess recited. The audience wants its hero brought as close as possible. There is not the slightest

[26] Aguijó mio Çid, a la puerta se llegaua,
    sacó el pie del estribera, una ferídal dava;
    non se abre la puerta, ca bien era cerrada.

interest in contemplation for the sake of contemplation, or in imagination for its own sake. "A little girl of nine" gave the Cid the message from the citizens of Burgos in the *Cantar*, and there must have been girls just like her among those who heard it recited. If it was necessary to say later that "the child of nine went back into her house" after reciting her touching message that the Cid's own people had repudiated him, then this had to be expressed in everyday language, unadorned by counted syllables, consciously spaced accents, isochronal caesuras, and rhymes, because the return of children to their own houses was an elemental act that would not tolerate artifice of any kind. The naïveté of what was expressed was matched by a correspondingly slight degree of expressive tension, which it would not be correct to call metrical irregularity.[27] It is true that the little girl is a figure of special interest because she is the only one to address the Cid on this occasion. Yet this does not render it impossible to express her elemental, simple character in the phrase "she went back into her house."

It is well known that poems rhymed according to the scheme of the "fourfold way" (cuaderna vía) constituted a kind of literary camp hostile to the *Cantares de gesta*. But let me add, by way of incidental digression, that the usual concepts "learned" and "popular" do not adequately express the nature of this opposition, for the gests were not rude and artless works. The so-called craft of the clerics (the *mester de clerecía*, found in the works of Berceo, in poems on the heroes of antiquity, etc.) employed a versification imported from France, consisting of symmetrical units in a uniform rhythm. The creative dynamism of the Castilian-epic genre, in which the poet and his audience participated, was replaced in the *mester de clerecía* by the contemplation of events fitting a pre-established pattern, an order that floated in the realm of the spirit over the poetic matter. The significance of the event lay in the fact that it was an exemplary realization of a prior order (religious, institutional, moral). This significance is revealed even in the fact that the event had

[27] To be sure, although the sentence may be naïve in its form, the artistic intention is not. The powerful person of the Cid who kicks against the door of a house with his boot is opposed by the voice of a fragile child who begs him to go away, else the townspeople will lose all that they have and "their eyes in their heads besides." This *cantar* as yet knows little of metaphors, and repetition serves it as a poetic device. The poet tells of a messenger who arrived with a threatening troop of warriors; he brought a letter with the king's seal on it, and this adds force to his threat. The stylistic device here consists in having what has been previously said by the poet in a narrative tone repeated now by the voice of a nine-year-old girl. Herein lies the charm of the sentence, which is hardly verse: "This the little girl said, and went back into her house" (Esto la niña dixo, e tornós pora su casa).

already been narrated in earlier texts ("el escripto," the *written*, the Latin sources, not at all the same as "el contado," the told, the *storied*, as the term was applied to the Cid). The sources of the epic *cantares* (I refer to the more ancient ones) were in oral tradition, adjusted to lives that were lived in a struggle with adverse circumstances felt to be contemporary and immediate:

> Today the kings of Spain are his kinsman,

> we read at the end of the Cid. (1. 3,024)

The style of such works consequently had to be fluid, open, and flexible, and not encased in closed, uniform receptacles. In contrast, the "fourfold way" is like a reflection of the unquestioned, immutable, transcendent order that presides over medieval Christianity and infuses the "spotless craft" (mester sen pecado) with its solemn virtue. Such an order was very different from that of the *Cantares*, based on the demands of existence, that is, on the tasks the Castilians were carrying out and necessarily would continue to carry out, and not on the intention to exhibit ideal models in narrative form. The *Cantar de Mío Cid* and its kind glorify heroes felt as persons of flesh and blood and as the progenitors of great lines of descendants (the Cid, Fernán González, the Sons of Lara, etc.).

It will be said that the *Libro de Alexandre* treats of a personage of antiquity, that it has nothing to do with Christianity. But the real intent of the poet is revealed in many of its didactic features, and especially its ending on the note of "sic transit gloria mundi":

> Alexander, who was a king of such great power
> That neither seas nor land could contain him,
> At last was cabined within a trench
> That could not be more than twelve square feet.
> (Ed. of R. S. Willis, stanza 2,672)

The moralizing intention was one with the very idea of an art with rigorous rules, a human transposition of the spiritual regularity to which all men and things were subject. This is why the popular epics, those sung by the *juglares*, were impugned as sinful, that is, as unruly: they were not subject to a "rhymed course," nor to the "counting of syllables." Their order was the order of life—as was to be the order of Lope de Vega's drama centuries later—and not the order of objectified reason, which in its turn found exact expression in the regular couplets of the drama of France, the drama of a secularized reason.

It is thus instantly understandable how it was possible for the Castilian epic to be historical. The mythic subject approached the real happening, and the form of the verse approached the form of prose. The Castilian epic had to be historical—that is, it could not go beyond the immediate horizon of the hearers—because the stimulus and the inspiration that made it possible were shared by the poet and his audience. The French *Chanson*, on the other hand, was projected over the hearers from the heights of the monarchic institution, and channeled through and by high political interests, which were far above the elemental plane of life. In all its decisive respects, the history of France followed a direction from above downward. The incitement to literary activity came from the court in Paris (one recalls the anecdote about the poet Conon de Béthune, whose provincial speech made the queen's ladies-in-waiting laugh), or from the feudal courts (Marie de Champagne and Chrétien de Troyes), or from the great monasteries (certain *chansons de geste*) or, as it did finally, even from the universities and schools (Latin prose and poetry, the *clerici vagantes*). In Spain the forms of life at the highest social level still maintained contact with the collective source from which they sprang. We have seen this already in the case of the belief in Santiago, which, according to Alphonse VI, was the "regimen totius Hispaniae," the belief under which monarchs and people alike found protection and stood thus on the same footing. Let us remember the profound significance of Alphonse the Learned's scorn for the power of the French kings to work miracles. With the miraculous as the very core of Castilian policy —beyond rational criticism or the power of the kings—the divine was incorporated into immediate experience, and placed itself within arm's reach; and it was not necessary to ascend to God by the way of theological knowledge or through mystic elevation. The divine entered into the flow of everyday history.

If divine patronage of "the Spains" was the form assumed by the zealous clamor of the Spanish people, the direction taken by politics also preserves the imprint of its origins: "Castilian men . . . made her from a poor judgeship [alcaldía] into a county." This sentence is from the *Poema de Fernán González*, itself significant enough for being the only existing sample of the national-clerical epic in Castilian. The author was a monk of the monastery of San Pedro de Arlanza (Burgos). In the *Poema de Fernán González* he dissolved, as it were, an eleventh-century gest, whose echoes are still preserved in the chronicles and the Romancero. By attributing its foundation to Fernán González, the monastery based its own prestige on a hero who belonged to the Castilian land. Through the erudite fabric of the poem can be perceived the popular tone of the original, for instance in the scene where Fernán González appears as incarnating the consensus of his people:

The Castilians came to see their lord;
Great and small *all* delighted in him. (185)
He talked with his vassals about what they might agree on:
He wished to hear from *all* what advice they would give him. (202)

The people that empowered Fernán González as their deputy were as rebellious as their count, who

Always was at war with the kings of Spain:
He wouldn't have given a chestnut for any of them. (177)

The Castilian gests never exalted a king as a central character, and there is nothing in them to correspond to the *chansons* of the Carolingian cycle. Quite the contrary, the great heroes of the Castilian epic had to oppose the kings, or were the victims of their unjust treatment: Bernardo del Carpio, Fernán González, and the Cid.[28] The people at the lower end of the social scale thus gave their breath to artistic creations that were obliged to remain within their grasp. Those who rewarded the poet with wine and money, including those who were not plebeians, saw in the hero of the *cantar* a magnification of their own vital projects, an incarnation of high, remote, but not impossible destinies. Bernardo, Fernán González, and the Cid were splendid superlatives of the people. This explains why the Infantes of Carrión, authentic aristocrats, are shown in the Cid in a very unfavorable light, first mocked for their cowardice and then punished for their infamy.

The predominance of collective forces and inspirations (beliefs, attachment to particular *caudillos*) infused Castilian life with a certain repugnance for discipline. The integration and fusion of the objective and that which is felt personally cause the individual *I* to draw to itself the objective *it* and try to control it, and in reality to control it in the *I*'s own way. The hero, the superior man, can be superior only in so far as every man can feel himself as sharing the superiority. This explains the meaning of the statement that Castile "makes men and wastes them,"

[28] Some of the French *Chansons* present rebels, for instance, *Les quatre fils Aymon* (Renaud de Montauban) and *Girard de Roussillon*; but the rebels all end up by submitting docilely to the king, whose authority overwhelms the rebelliousness of his vassals. These rebellions are different from those of the Castilian heroes; Fernán González and the Cid establish legal authority over the lands where they have dominion. And I emphasize that no Spanish *cantar* glorifies a king in the way this is done in the *Chanson de Roland*.

of the fact that the epic heroes are always on the side of "the people,"
and the fact that the stage of the gests *must be* actual, not fictional, that
is, *it must be adapted to what the people know.* Those listeners would
have had no interest in imaginary geography and happenings such as we
find in the *Chanson de Roland* or *Les Quatres fils Aymon*, remote and
beyond personal participation. Now we can understand in all its implications why the poet of the *Cid* disposes of the hero's greatest deed
in 130 lines ("the long and arduous siege of Valencia, with the taking
of Jérica, Onda, Almenar, Burriana, Murviedro, and Peña Cadiella")
and "on the other hand spends 450 lines telling us of the taking and
abandoning of border villages like Castejón and Alcocer."[29] It was not
the "objectified" Cid who was important to the poet; it was his own Cid,
the one who had fought around Medinaceli, where the poet lived and
wrote. For the same reason, the epic of the Infantes de Lara continually
modified the line of the Moorish frontier in successive versions, so that
each generation of hearers might follow the episodes of the gest as a
contemporary event,[30] because the area of the literary action also had to
be felt as something of immediate concern to them.

Now and then an orientalist has tried to find Arabic models for the
Castilian epic, but such models will of course never be found. The epic
of Castile is not oriental in genre. However unique it may be as a narrative genre, it is clearly related to the Franco-Germanic tradition. Menéndez Pidal has pointed out any number of typical stylistic features that
indicate how the poets had the Northern French *chansons* in mind.
The Castilian gests do not imitate the style of Arabic poetry, which did
not begin to be fully imitated in Castile till the fourteenth century.
The *Cantar de Mio Cid* contains numerous words of French origin, and
its Arabisms do not belong to it alone.[31] But none of this is of essential

[29] Menéndez Pidal, "Poema de Mio Cid," in *Clásicos Castellanos*, p. 29.

[30] In his new edition of *La leyenda de los Infantes de Lara* (1934), Menéndez
Pidal has demonstrated that the tragic expedition in which the seven Infantes lost
their lives is based on such an occurrence that took place in September, 974 (p. 458).

[31] The Cid's belief in omens must have been an Arabic characteristic; and reading
(catando) the future in the flight of birds is another Moslem characteristic. Not only
the Spaniards, but European Christians in general learned magic and divination from
the Moors of Al-Andalus, who had as one of their pupils Pope Silvester II (Gerbert).
(Cf. Menéndez Pidal, *Cantar de Mio Cid*, pp. 486, 596.) The Cid was reproached
for being too much of a believer in omens, and I have already pointed out in another
connection above the lines:

At the departure from Bivar, they
had the crow on the right,
And on entering into Burgos, they had it on the left. (11-12)

importance. What is, is *the form in which the poet experiences his subject* and brings it to life under the pressure of his emotions in language such as to produce a style that in the twelfth century must have sounded noble and refined at the same time that it remained on a plane familiar and accessible to all. (See p. 344).

The speech of the little girl in the *Cid* (ll. 41-48) begins with "you girded on your sword in an auspicious moment" and ends with "the Creator keep you with all his holy virtues." The speech, then, is bounded, first by the belief that the hero was dubbed a knight at an astrologically favorable moment, and second by the belief in divine protection. The same kind of thing happens in *"at the departure* from Bivar, they had the crow on the right, and *entering into Burgos,* they had it on the left" (ll. 11-12). The Cid's troubles stem from the king's failure to be what it was thought he ought to be: "*God,* what a good vassal! would that he had a good *lord!*" (20) The sentence is framed by "God" and the "lord" king, but the latter has failed. The characters or objects are important because their existences are described, expressed, in terms of the halo that surrounds them, in keeping with the repertory of most evident values in which all believe: "Martín Antolínez, the perfect Burgalese" (65); "O Cid, beard so perfect" (26). Sometimes the enhancing epithet refers to the whole of the person: "the *beautiful beard* lowered his hands" (274); "My Cid, *he of Bivar*" (295), from the "heart" of Castile; "Sant Estevan, *a good city*" (397), as everyone knew San Esteban de Gormaz to be; "With Alphonse my lord *I did not wish to fight*" (538), for to do so would have been a breach of loyalty, the foundation stone of that body politic; "Albar Fáñez, *who commanded in Çorita*" (735); "The count *was very vainglorious, and said a boastful thing*" (960) wherewith the Count of Barcelona is fixed in the center of a negative specific value.

The order of the sentence is based on the hierarchy of admitted values. The valued quality (positive or negative) appears in the background as the projection and poetic *raison d'être* of what has been previously mentioned. When the beginning and the end of the verse are both substantives, both individualized, this order is inverted, if possible, and the element of higher rank precedes: "In the name of the Creator and

---

Al-Mas'ūdī of Bagdad, who lived in the first half of the tenth century, devoted a chapter of his book *The Golden Meadows* to the "opinions of the Arabs concerning omens and prophecies based on the flight of birds from right to left and from left to right." He observes that "among the Arabs, the animal that moved from left to right was a good omen," and vice versa.

of the apostle Santiago!" (l. 1,138); "I thank the Creator and lord Saint Isidore" (l. 1,861); "To you Minaya Albar Fáñez and to Pero Vermudoz" (l. 1,870). The order of the sentence depends upon a system of evaluations, on an axiological grammar. The verse generally consists of two parts (not hemistichs), the second of which heightens the meaning or value of the first. That is why the poet is not interested in counting syllables or in melody: the rhythm is axiological, not phonological. Generally speaking, each verse or assonanted line states a complete meaning, with its second part serving as an "axiological" (not a "grammatical") predicate to its first: "On my sons-in-law of Carrion, *may God let me take vengeance*" (l. 2,894); "the king saw them, *and he recognized Muño Gustioz*" (l. 2,932); "there they go *my counts and barons*" (l. 2,964), etc.

The substratum of this poetic order coincides with the idea of Castilian life itself. All persons or things are seen or felt in terms of value that transcends them; they do not appear as the result of the abstract and absolute expression of their being or of their appearance or their actions, as is the case in the French epic: "Roland *est* preux et Olivier *est* sage." The procedure used to express the conscious experience of the values is the unfolding or projecting of the conception in an axiological perspective in which the verb *to be* has a ponderative function: "Peña Cadiella, which is a strong rock" (l. 1,330); "A wonder it is of the Cid, that his renown increases so much" (l. 1,861). It is not a question of cognition, but of justifying everything in a value intuition which, however, excludes the caprice of the speaker's private passions. The Cid's coif "is adorned with gold, made so that no one could pull his hair" (l. 3,095). The poem of the Cid belongs to a very peculiar Middle Ages, and it is permissible to suspect that the lost gests would be similar to it. The Castilian shunned everything that did not exist already objectified as aesthetic or moral value illuminated by a socialized belief. The free and detached "I" was felt to be wicked indulgence, and with it, fantasy, sensuality, rational criticism, and everything else that might lead to atomization and anarchy. The person and his halo of belief formed a compact and indivisible unity, for only what ought to exist existed, and life was, above all, moral conduct. When the Cid is told what has happened to his daughters—how their husbands abandoned them in a woods full of wild beasts after tying them naked to a tree and beating them savagely—

> He thought a long while, and pondered;
> He raised his hand, stroked his beard. (2,828-2,829)

There is no fit of passion, nor action outside the norms respected by everyone. *Think* (pensar) here does not mean to look for new solutions but to ponder (comedir): to find the measures that must be applied in such a monstrous case, that is, recourse to the justice of the king and of the good customs of Castile. We are not confronted here with *individuals*, with idiosyncratic characters, but with *persons* sustained by a faith in themselves which is identified with the belief by which they are all transcended. That is why Castilians of the eleventh and twelfth centuries gave their own names to the towns they founded (see Chapter 15). The names of those towns are to the men who gave them expression as "the worthy Burgalese" is to "Martín Antolínez."

The hierarchy of values on which the jongleur has built the poem is expressed in many ways. The following passage clarifies and sums up what has been said thus far in this connection:

> Seated in his gilded saddle, how marvelously he fights,
> Mio Cid Ruy Diaz the excellent fighter;
> [with him] Minaya Albar Fañez, who ruled over Zorita,
> Martín Antolínez, that most useful knight from Burgos,
> Muño Gustioz, raised to knighthood by the Cid,
> Martin Muñoz, who ruled over Monte Mayor. . . !

In this description of valorous knights, the Cid is the only one whose physical person is made visible through a present tense—*lidia* (fights). His evident grandeur, like that of the gods, does not need to be explained. His knights, on the other hand, owe their distinction to what they have done or been; thus their names are followed by a verb in the past tense: he ruled, he was raised, he possessed some valuable quality. They had been created by their past, whereas the Cid is a creator of past.

The Castilian and the French epics do not fit completely into the same genre. The style of the French *Chanson* does not rest only on intuitive evidence but on analysis: "ço sent Rollanz que la mort le tresprent, / Devers la teste sur le quer li descent" (2,355-2,356). The hero feels that death is descending from his head to his heart, and he gives logical expression to his observations. The audience must have listened with amazement, but it remained outside the spectacle. Spectacle likewise are such gests as *Aliscamps, Loherens,* and the others with their narration in unbroken, logical sequence. In the *Cid,* such phrases as "Sant Estevan, a good city," and hundreds of things of the kind, éstablish an osmosis between the poem and the reader. The account of the happening in the *chanson* was not pitched at the level of the daily experiences of the audience, which was limited to allowing itself to be seduced by the spectacle which the poets offered it.

In the strange genre of our poem are combined poetic melody and prosaic accompaniment. The hero is seen both heroically and at the same time in his anti-heroic intimacy. The Cid of the *Cantar* "shrugged his shoulders and shook his head" with magnificent hauteur; he will force the lion to cower in shame; or he will appear in the royal court in all the splendor of his dignity. But this same hero, like a professional swindler, deceives two Jews who trust his honorable word, or he is presented as a mill owner and with the concerns of a modest bourgeois. The external qualities of his figure we perceive in the detail of his clothing: "breeches of good cloth," shoes of fine workmanship, "shirt of linen" with its buttons of gold and silver, gown with threads of gold . . . ; and, so that his long beard, the symbol of masculine dignity, may not be touched, he keeps it tied with a little cord (ll. 3,085-3,097). But in one rapid stroke the poet alludes to the Cid's innermost being:

Why did you force me to reveal the fibers of my heart? (3,260)

Thus the Cid rebukes the wicked Infantes, the "treacherous dogs," for having flogged and abandoned his daughters in a wood full of wild beasts: they have revealed the fibers of his heart. The Cid's daughters are rescued by their cousin Félez Muñoz; they are consumed with thirst, and beg in anguish for water. But if they cannot go to a place where there is some, how is it to be brought to them? "In a hat that Félez Muñoz has, *new and fresh it was; he got it in Valencia*"—in this hat he brought the water and gave it to the poor victims of the Infantes (l. 2,800). On another occasion, Asur González, the brother of the Infantes of Carrión, appears on the scene ("red-faced he came, for he had just eaten breakfast"), and he covers the Cid with insults in front of the solemn court that is to judge the men who have offended the hero. He accuses the Cid, amongst other things, of being too interested in the mills he has on the Ubierna River:

He had better go to the Ubierna River and roughen up the
    millstones,
And take his shares, as he is wont to do. (3,379-3,380)

Menéndez Pidal has established the fact that the Cid actually did own some mills along the Ubierna. So we find ourselves outside the realm of the poetic, far from the unreal, the fanciful, story, and in presence of concrete notions that give a novelistic cut to the epic myth: a new hat, recently bought in Valencia; a historical personage, who is red-faced after a hearty breakfast; a hero seen as the owner of mills that he actually did own in historical reality; etc. The Cid is the illustrious man whose deeds had been *told* before his *cantar* was written, and at the same time he is the prosaic matter, the reverse of his poetic tapestry. This *mixed* form of both historical and epic characterization has no prototype in the literature of the rest of Europe or in the literature of the Arabs, which is essentially metaphorical and removed from the his-torico-national idea. Furthermore, in Arabic literature the characters are dissolved in the narrated event, they are transformed into metaphorical expression or into moral wisdom; they never stand out "sculpturally" against other characters or against their environment. Neither characters nor things have sharply chiseled existences. To feel the presence of a character presupposes feeling him as present and not as flowing through timeless time, or unwinding in a continuous arabesque from one hap-pening to another. In Arabic literature there are no characters, either novelistic or dramatic, because Islam has no notion of existence in terms of a life that believes itself to be autonomous. There are magnificent narrations of lives in flux, and fine autobiographies, but there are no personalities etched in sharp profile and carrying on conversations with others of their kind. Although this will be seen more clearly in the chapter on the Archpriest of Hita, it would seem advisable to set forth here in precise terms the respects in which the *Cantar de Mio Cid* cannot be oriental. It is evidently not oriental for the characters to construct their own lives on the pedestal of their will: "With Alphonse my lord I did not wish to fight" (538) says the model of perfect vassals. The scene of the Cortes in which the king presides over the judicial debate between the Cid and his offenders, the Infantes of Carrión, has a novelis-tic-dramatic character; the action moves from narrative to dialogue, and each one expresses himself in the first person, in this way bringing out his singularity. The characters here are, as I said before, like talking sculptures, rich in expression and life:

> Peter Vermudoz began to speak;
> His tongue stuck, and he couldn't loosen it,
> But once he got started, know you, that he didn't hesitate
>   any more:
> "I'll tell you, Cid, it is your wont
> Always to call me Peter Mute in the Cortes!
> Well you know that I can't help it." (3,306-3,310)

Here is tongue-tied Pero Vermudoz, who, before making his speech in favor of the Cid, humorously reminds his lord and good friend of the latter's unpleasant custom of calling him Peter Mute (Pero Mudo), because his tongue thickens when he tries to talk in public, although the truth is that once he manages to get started, his oratory acquires great fluency. We can imagine the laughter of the grave assembly, in which the enemies hurl improprieties at each other and friends are prodigal with mutual praise and favors. When the two adversaries finally meet for the trial by combat, "each thinks of the adversary he has in front of him" (3,614).

French and Oriental Styles Are Different from Spanish

It may seem to the reader that what I judge to be peculiar in the Spanish epic is generally characteristic of "primitive" manners of expression, and that phenomena of the same kind are to be found in the French *chansons*. Let me remove this possible cause of confusion and interpretative chaos.

The French epic does have its comical features. In the *Chanson de Guillaume*, for example, Tebbald flees in fright, and leaves traces of his fear on the trappings of his horse:

De la pour en ordead sa hulce.[32]

In the *Pélerinage de Charlemagne*, the emperor quarrels with the empress because she tells him that King Hugo the Strong is his better. Charlemagne then undertakes the pilgrimage to Jerusalem, collects a great quantity of relics, and, on his way back, stops in Constantinople to see Hugo the Strong. He finds the monarch plowing with a plow of gold. Later, Charles and his barons, their heads swimming from the wine they have drunk, boast of their abilities to perform all manner of fantastic deeds, some of them offensive to Hugo's honor. Oliver, on other occasions so "sage," wagers his head that if Hugo will let him sleep with his daughter, he "will have her, and her a witness to it, a hundred times" (489). King Hugo learns of these boasts from a spy, and he forces the Frenchmen to carry them out or give up their lives. Charlemagne has the relics brought out, says a prayer, and is visited by an angel, who orders him in the name of God to refrain from such wagers (gabs). But for this once they will be allowed to carry all of them out. Hugo de-

[32] Maurice Wilmotte, *L'epopée française*, 1939, pp. 152, 168-169.

mands that Oliver make his word good, and he does, with debonair success, as do all the rest.[33]

I do not know whether anyone has observed that the *Pélerinage de Charlemagne* is a French recreation of oriental tales of the type of *The History of the King's Son of Sind and the Lady Fatimah*.[34] The relics have the same abetting function in the *Pélerinage* as the animals and the grateful jinn in the Arabic story. The medieval Frenchman, seeing things from his position in his own life structure, had no qualms about using divine powers for his own purposes, be it to stabilize the national dynasty, to indulge a hundred times, in Rabelaisian fashion, in one sin, or to support any other profitable worldly enterprise. But from the strictly literary point of view, it is very much worth noting that the gravity of the noble *chanson* turned into humor (humor from the Western point of view) when it came into contact with Arabic fantasy, and this even as far back as the first half of the twelfth century.

On another level, the solemn tone of the venerable *Chanson de Roland* is broken when Ganelon says to the emperor:

> Guenes respunt: "De bataille est nient!
> Ja estes vieils e fluriz e blancs;
> Par tels paroles vus resemblez enfant." (1,770-1,772)

But neither in this nor in other examples of the mixture of a grave style and a tone of irreverence, of "fabliau," is there what I have tried to specify as the form of the Castilian gests, or, in any case, of the *Poema del Cid*. In this *cantar* the character is simultaneously a literary figure, *who already has his story*, and a historical person: the Cid appears in Ubierna, a village near Burgos, looking after his mills, mills which he did in fact own, and at the same time as a character of song and story. *Things*, a hat, for example, play a part in a perhaps imaginary episode (the Cid's daughters bound to trees and afflicted with thirst), and yet, at the same time, they escape from the literary frame and appear as extra-literary objects, existing in the time-space of the audience: "a new hat, which I have just bought in Valencia." Persons and objects have half their bodies in the work and half outside it. In the French *chansons* the comic and the serious do not depart from the imaginary field of poetic invention.

The mixture of the humorous and the serious is usual in Arabic literature, and Ibn Ḥazm of Cordova, Ibn 'Arabī of Murcia, and Avicenna of

---

[33] Cf. the analysis of the "Pélerinage" in Bédier, *Les légendes épiques*, IV, 142.
[34] *The Arabian Nights*, tr. by Burton, vol. v of the supplement, p. 1.

Transcaucasia will provide us with adequate examples in later pages. However, this does not mean that there were, or could have been, literary figures in Arabic literature like the Cid or Roland, able to create freely from within themselves decisive actions that constitute their well-delineated individualities. The Cid does not want to fight against his lord and king, he does not want to take angry revenge on his sons-in-law; Roland does not sound his horn, or he does, according to the dictates of his own sense of decorum.

But a figure like Almanzor did not, and could not, give rise to an epic *cantar* because of the structure of Islamic life. (Tragedy and epic were not understandable for Averroes; he felt that Homer excelled in the art of praising and blaming and nothing else.) But although the conception of the Cid's personality as a human "substance" which exists in and of itself and acts with the freedom granted it by the Christian God is Occidental in its roots, the style of its literary life does not fit within the frame of the other European literatures of the twelfth century, in which contact is inconceivable between a Cid who is a literary figure and a Cid who is a visible, tangible, historical person, an integral part of the experience of both the poet and his audience. Each of these Cids separately could be European, Occidental, Christian, or whatever one might want to call it. But combined in an indissoluble unity, they are possible only in a life structure that is Christian and Arabicized at the same time. I repeat once more, because the repetition is necessary to attain the maximum clarity possible, that the remote and objectified Cid of the myth (like the Rolands of any of the *chansons*) is to the Cid represented as a real person, tying down his beard, revealing the fibers of his heart, etc., as the dawning is to the person dawned (amanecida) in the expression "I dawn" (amanezco), traced on the fourth form of an Arabic verb.

The articulation of the solemn with the commonplace, the imagined with the verified, is not conceivable save as the expression of habits contracted in the course of centuries of living together with the Moslems. Pero Vermudoz begins his speech at the perhaps imagined royal court, in which the fate of the Cid and his men is going to be decided, by telling a story with a *personal and factual* tone about how the Cid made fun of his stammering. In the same way we have seen combined in the unity of a single account the splendor of Harūn al-Rashīd, the joke of a courtier, and the physiological necessities of the monarch.[35]

[35] Since it is very important to prove beyond a shadow of a doubt that such contrasts were not contrasts at all for the Moslem spirit, and that we are not dealing here with popular anecdotes or drolleries, I shall turn again to the style of Ibn Ḥazm

None of this will be surprising to those familiar with Moslem literature. This is the key which permits us to understand the style of the
Cantar. Here, as in all art, style includes the aureole that envelops the
bare linguistic expression and illuminates it so that it can be recognized
as an artistic style. In the *Chanson* dawning is an objectified phenomenon:
"Vint al jur cler" (l. 162); in the *Cantar* it is announced by the roosters:
"Suddenly the roosters sing, and the dawn is about to break" (l. 235);
we attend the inchoation, the progressive flow, of the phenomenon here
as well as in a number of other passages in the *Cid* (ll. 456, 1,122, 1,620,
1,699). And just as the dawn forms before our eyes, likewise the courage
to fight is created in the Cid's heart: "My courage increases, because you
are standing before me" (l. 1,655), the hero says to Doña Jimena. The
style is in the same key throughout, and it would be tiresome and useless to accumulate more examples; any reader can do it. It is unnecessary
to say, moreover, that the other Castilian gests fit the same pattern. In
the short fragment of *Roncesvalles*, the Castilian version of the French

---

in his *Critical History of Religions*, accessible through the Spanish translation of M.
Asín. This, as is well known, is the first of its genre, and it is surprising that it
was written in the eleventh century, when nothing like it existed in Christian Europe.
Ibn Ḥazm proceeds like a scholar and a theologian who is acquainted through his
own study and experience with the religions of his time, and he analyzes them in
detail, quoting their texts. Yet this historian of theology introduces into a work of
such serious character passages such as the following, which I take as exactly as possible
from Asín's translation: "This imbecile, wishing to avoid a manure pile, has fallen
into a latrine full of shit" (II, 255); such a dirty impropriety is directed against the
Jews, whom he abuses continually, just as he does the Christians: "The sons of
Israel, who are the most loathsome and the vilest of all peoples" (II, 293). "I have
never seen a more shameless person than the one who wrote these vile books for the
Jews" (II, 314). "This is very funny! It is in truth enough to make even the armpits
blush with shame" (II, 327). Of Saint Peter he says: "To a creature of such qualities
it is not right to give even the keys of a latrine or a dung-heap" (III, 61), etc. Ibn
Ḥazm makes no distinction between his learning and his temper, his reflection and
his passion. The high teaching of his work overshadows such outbursts, shocking to
the reader of today. Asín, thoroughly imbued with Moslem ways, and a Roman
Catholic priest, did very well in translating to take the point of view of a Spanish
Moslem of the eleventh century without any kind of prudery. Once inside such an
environment, we understand how Muño Gustioz can say to Asur González, in the
Cantar de Mio Cid:

> Calla, alevoso, malo e traidor!
> Antes almuerzas que vayas a oración,
> a los que daz paz, fártaslos aderredor. (3,383-3,385)

That is, "You eat before you go to mass, and when you give the kiss of peace there,
the belches from what you have eaten are offensive to the noses of those who are near
you." Using much paler tones, the Hispano-Christian literature imitates the expressive integralism of the Moslems. Inhibition does not exist.

Roland, when Charlemagne sees the dead bodies, he exclaims: "With the rancor I feel on your account, my heart is about to break." When the emperor faints, his knights "take cold water, and dash it on the king." In the *Chanson*, the emperor "se pasmet, tant par est anguissus" (l. 2,880).

In an encyclopedic work which presents a clear expression of the Islamic view of the world, Al-Mas'ūdī (born in Bagdad) writes at the beginning of the tenth century:

"History gets the ear of the wise man and of the ignorant one; the simple and the intelligent are charmed by its accounts, and beg for them. History comprises all kinds of subjects. . . . Its superiority over the other sciences is evident, and all men of understanding concede to it its supremacy. Rightly, the wise men say that the surest friend is a book. . . . It offers you at the same time the *beginning and the ending*, little or much; it combines the far away with what is near you, the past with the present; it combines the most divers forms, the most different species. It is a dead man who speaks to you in the name of the dead, and who makes understandable to you the language of the living. It is a person of intimate sympathies, who rejoices with your rejoicing, who sleeps with your sleeping, and who speaks to you only of what pleases you."[36]

Al-Mas'ūdī speaks of the divine and the human from the point of view of his own life: geography, political and social history, beliefs, languages. Apropos of elephants, he tells an anecdote about a mule that belonged to one of the caliph Almanzor's secretaries, and which got frightened by elephants. He attributes the anecdote to a person who, passing by the Gate of the Arcades one day in Bagdad, encountered a troop of elephants that were going to be used to carry a certain great lord on a journey, and he mentions all the circumstances of the case in great detail; the mule reared, at the same time some camels nearby were frightened and bolted into a blind alley, and the mule huddled in among the camels "as if he had always lived with those animals," etc. (III, 19-20). Al-Mas'ūdī keeps on with his account this way, telling not what he knows about this, that, or the other, but rather what happens to him, what he has heard or observed, his immediate experience. In the city of the king, he has seen oxen harnessed like horses, yet which kneel like camels, and which "move as swiftly as lightly loaded camels" (III, 27). Along with such trifles we find a history of the ancient and the contemporary worlds with a surprising wealth of detail. He knows that "among the states

[36] *Les Prairies d'Or*, tr. by C. Barbier de Meynard, 1866, III, 135-136.

near the Franks, the most powerful of those that have dominion in Spain is Galicia, to such a degree that the Franks always had to make war on her; but the Galicians were the better warriors" (III, 72). He is certain that in the struggles between Christians and Moslems, "the victory has fallen to the latter up to the present moment." He says that at the time in which he wries, Ramiro is king of the Galicians, that is, Ramiro II (930-950).

It is not my intention to analyze a book so accessible, but to point out the mixture of its subject matter, its serious and learned character, occasionally theological, and its anecdotes of the sort that could be found only in Western literature in a "fabliau."[37] Thus there is no distance between the spiritual and the material; everything is unified by entering into one personal experience, unified and dignified. But then the life of the person turns into a flow determined by circumstances. This flux does not trace its course by weaving together the decisions of the will as it operates on knowledge with notions derived from experience, or with the changes which destiny brings on. There is no way, then, to compose epic poems or dramas. Islamic man was submerged in the world; he did not fashion his existence, or oppose it to destiny, since he included the totality of the world external to him, in the expression of his own life, with a richness of content not to be found in contemporary Western literature. The fact that objects are bound to the subject in the way that we have seen doubtless prevents anything in reality from being absolutely objective, because reality is present as floating in the illusion of the account, or as included in the total lyric or autobiographical experience of the person. Among the Arabs, science itself was quite frequently the expression of personal and immediate necessities; geography and astronomy largely answered to the necessity for being oriented in the direction of Mecca, a condition indispensable for prayer.[38] Pure theory seems to have enjoyed scant fa-

[37] A poet seeks to speak one day to the King of Iraq. The chamberlain does not dare bring the poet's request to the sovereign. The poet tells him to transmit his message to Kahled, a courtier who is taking part in the festival that is being celebrated. Fortunately, at this moment "Kahled, urged by one of those necessities that are the result of copious drinking, comes out of the royal saloon," and then he is informed of the case (III, 202).

[38] "Their books remind one of good secondary or university text books. The Arabs were traders, travellers, and lawyers; they had the positive mind; their science therefore had a practical object; arithmetic had to serve the needs of commerce and the divisions of estates; astronomy the requirements of travellers and those who cross the desert, or of religion which has to know the hours of prayer, the azimuth of Mecca and the moment of the first appearance of the month of Ramadan" (Baron Carra de Vaux, in The Legacy of Islam, ed. by Arnold, 1931, pp. 378-379). An

vor among the Moslems, even in the time of their greatest intellectual splendor; and such thought as there was, was a development of Aristotle and Plotinus (general speaking). But without theory, genuine science is impossible, no matter how numerous and extensive the applications of theoretical sciences invented by those who have known how to maintain a rigorous detachment from the world around them. The great tragedy of the human being, today more acute than ever, is rooted in the inescapable option between having to deny the totality of one's self and to dehumanize one's self, and having to renounce seeking through thought the solution of the problems that life presents. When all was said and done, the Moslem chose the latter course and renounced knowledge. The Spaniard has lived undecided, between the two courses—total existence or thought. He resolutely chose the first, but he could not reject the anguish of moving at the same time and only slowly along the second.

Thanks to this struggle within herself, Spain not only escaped from the total paralysis in which Islam was finally to become engulfed, but out of her existence as the buffer between two antagonistic worlds, she was also able to give rise to the finest achievements of her art and her life. Naturally the character of her science and thought preserves a considerable similarity to the "practicality" of Arabic science and thought mentioned before. Science had more connection with practical than with theoretical problems: warfare, navigation, architecture, mining, jurisprudence, medicine, ethics, the propagation of religion, etc. In spite of the brilliance of philosophic culture among the Moslems and the Spanish Jews, Spain produced scarcely anything in the way of entirely original doctrine or system. Much the same thing is true of the Hispanic countries, where one finds brilliant derivatives of the thought of other nations. And these derivatives display their most original aspects in connection with the problems of existence and of deportment. If there is ever to be any great philosophy in the Hispanic world, such is the course it will take, and not that of physical-mathematical science.

Menéndez y Pelayo, who had remarkable insights, speaks (apropos of Ibn Ṭofayl) of the "realistic idealism in which the human personality is saved by consciousness, even though it go astray through logic. . . . This deeply rooted sense of the I . . . saves Ṭofayl . . . from that treacherous languor of contemplation. . . . All sophisms raised against such an Arabic civilization as flourished on our soil melt away in the presence

exception is made in the case of the Persians Al-Battāni and ʿUmar al-Khayyām, who in the tenth and eleventh centuries brought mathematics to heights never attained by the Greeks (p. 392). But the Persians occupy a special place in Islam.

of a work like this." Thinking of the existential psychology, as we would call it, which he believes to be found in Avempace, Ṭofayl, Fox Morcillo, and Gracián, he adds: "One comes to suspect that laws which have not yet been discovered but which someday will be, govern the historical web of our philosophy."[39]

Tradition as Present

If the subject aspires to live in symbiosis with the object, the spiritual with the material, the valuable with the insignificant, the serious with the trivial, the distant with the near, it is not surprising that the boundaries beween past and present should be blurred. I have already discussed (Chap. 1) the significance of the earth, of what I have called the telluric cult, and its possible connections with the Moslem form of life. According to Al-Masʿūdī, an Arabic man affirms that "God has made the nations prosper by inspiring their inhabitants with a love for the land in which they are born." Hippocrates, Galen, and Plato explained the affinities between man and nature as known to him in the place were he is born, in physical terms—medicines, air, food.[40] But Al-Masʿūdī is less interested in physical explanations that in man's love for his own land, a theme he says he has developed in his books *On the Secret of life* and *The Medicine of Souls*, because "the inner power and the force of habit are such that man sacrifices his existence to go back to his fatherland" (III, 134-137).[41] Let it not be said that such a characteristic is universal and "human," because such an explanation is inadequate here. The important thing is the particular value that Al-Masʿūdī attaches to the notion in treating of it the way he does, all the more important because his behavior is repeated by a Morisco (in Don Quixote) seven centuries later. The land here means a physical beyond, a material past-present, with which the spiritual past-present of history is articulated. Different from Western Europe, Spain lived under the vault of a belief and rooted in a land that meant habit and tradition.[42]

[39] Preface to the translation of Ibn Ṭofayl's *El filósofo autodidacto*, by F. Pons Boigues, 1900, pp. xliii, xliv, liv.

[40] Dr. Juan Huarte (*Examen de ingenios*, Chap. xv) takes this doctrine as a basis for his explanation of the proverbial keenness of mind of Jews.

[41] Ricote, the Morisco, says the same thing in *Don Quixote* (II, 54): ". . . the desire that almost all of us have to return to Spain is so great that most of those (and they are many) who know the language, as I do, return there, and leave their women and children helpless: so great is the love they have for her; and now I know and am experiencing what is so often said: that the love of the fatherland is sweet."

[42] There are habits and traditions everywhere, not to mention beliefs. What

In Spain the present was the face of a past always living and contemporary in the archives of belief and of historico-poetic tradition. The
constant renewing of the epic themes infused them with a kind of permanent vitality. From the *cantares de gesta* sprang the *Romancero*, which
in turn inspired the drama of the seventeenth century and still had
enough life in it to stimulate the fantasy of some of the Romantic writers. This kind of tenacious survival is a characteristic of Spanish literature, and a major aspect of the Spanish people's form of life. I have
referred to Al-Mas'ūdī and his ideas of history[43] as the queen of sciences,
and I pointed out that such a conception is inseparable from his love for
the land. If one receives materially what the land produces, tradition is
the spiritual soil through which are transmitted the "sayings of the
wise"; and the mission of history is to "tell the story of their virtues and
skilled accomplishments." Life turns to the past, since everything that
has been is the basis of all science; what has existed in either ideal or
terrestrial soil has value, and man is not a point of departure but a port
of arrival. Thus the "new," the innovations, lost their temporal meaning (see chapter 15).

For a historian as learned as Alphonse X, the *cantares de gesta* were
as believable as the chronicle of Rodrigo Jiménez de Rada. If there was
no dividing wall between poetry and reality for the minstrel-poets,
neither did the historians distinguish between poetic legend and verified
history.[44] The gests and later the *Romancero* were the stream which
carried the historical tradition of the people, and each generation inherited the tradition only to transmit it, enriched, to the next. Tradition
and belief thus comprise the horizon that unified Spanish life, disunited

happens, for example, is that France built her medieval existence on a human and
temporal continuity, the dynasty of her kings, or on the desire for wealth and
welfare (for this reason many Frenchmen came to Santiago, to engage in trade, etc.).
Protestantism even humanized religion. England had earlier attached political value
to wealth. In one and another European country, traditions were utilized in accord
with the interests of the present, and not in the reverse fashion, as in Spain.

[43] In the text in question (III, 135) the word used for "history" is *akhbār*, the
plural of *khabar* "information, account, narration, that comes to one from a person
of whom he asks it" (Lane, *Lexicon*). "History," on the contrary, is derived from
ἰστορία "one who knows, the judge who arbitrates a dispute." In the one case, history is what has been received through tradition; in the other, what has been constructed, found out as true.

[44] The Learned King wants everyone to understand him too; he wants the reader
to transform into his own experience moral, juridical, and historical science. Not
only does he write in Castilian; he also interprets all the learned words that come
up in his work (*cavernas*: means caves, etc.). Alphonse thus made up the first Spanish dictionary.

as it was and with few tangible and present things that it might utilize as a common center of reference. Castile had no fixed capital city, and her peripatetic court wandered from place to place. The sense of a national dynasty was lacking, since Christian Spain was divided into what were really *taifas* (Castile, Portugal, Navarre, Aragon), which often fought among themselves like the Moslem *taifas* of the eleventh century, even though they all felt themselves as parts of Spain. The records of the court of Castile were preserved nowhere, but oral tradition kept alive the memory of the great deeds and the common tasks and dangers of the people. As late as the seventeenth century the people had a surprising knowledge of their history, which they did not learn from books or in schools. The *pícaro* Guzmán de Alfarache tells a good part of the history of his country to one of his masters, an Italian, and when the master asks him where he has learned it all, he answers that "what he had related were very well known matters, which spread by word of mouth from person to person as tradition; and it takes more craft not to know them than to know them; for they were notable matters, albeit they concern *facts that come to pass*, which are no less notable than matters of permanent fact, such as that Rome and Naples are *founded* where they are."[45] In his dithyrambic praise of Spain, Guzmán first expounds his conviction that his fatherland is the best and the greatest in the world, "the one that has no superiors, and of which all are the inferiors," and then he recalls the deeds of Spaniards from the times of the Romans to his own. He does not mention *things*; that is, he mentions nothing "founded," objectified in visible reality (cities, artifacts, discoveries, etc.); he limits himself to expressing his faith dogmatically in the greatness of Spain ("pillar of the Church, defender and fighting proponent of religion"), and to naming persons worthy of eternal fame. For the people, living meant the cult of heaven, the cult of the glorious tradition, and the cult of their own land, which was another form of tradition. Spain has never planned her existence with a view to material realizations in the future, but with her gaze fixed on a heavenly eternity or on the attainment of imperishable fame. Living has been the same as feeling oneself flowing within a tradition that has prejudged what one is to be: "Our lives are rivers going to the sea" (Jorge Manrique). There was a moment when the Spanish people, deeply immersed in Islamic-Judaic Messianism, believed that the hour of salvation had come, and that Ferdinand and Isabella signified the realization of all their dreams, their

---

[45] *Biblioteca de Autores Españoles*, III, 369-370.

freedom from all bondage and tyranny.[46] Disillusionment was not long in setting in, but at the time, the most extraordinary regressive mirage of modern history was produced. Since the form of life was framed on one side by tradition, and on the other by the Messianic dream (both essentially Oriental features), when the Messianic dream failed, there was nothing left but to fall back on tradition. The result of this was what one might call the regressive rhythm of Hispanic history. Thus, we can understand the puzzling fact that for centuries Spain has been trying to unspin her web, as it were, to return to the times of the Catholic Sovereigns.

In spite of the vastness of the Spanish Empire, still envied and feared in the eighteenth century, Spain has habitually longed for the moment of Ferdinand and Isabella, the moment she has deemed unique. One thinks at once of the similar state of mind in Imperial Rome, which expressed with such frequency its nostalgia for the glorious centuries of the Republic. The difference is that the Romans were thinking of an institution, but the Spaniards were thinking of the vital style of two persons. The War of the Municipalities (Guerra de las Comunidades, 1520-1521) was fought mainly over the demand for the restoration of conditions that the people had known under Ferdinand and Isabella, especially with respect to taxes. Charles V never attained the prestige of his grandparents, and no one has ever seriously expressed the wish to return to his reign. Philip II got perhaps more censure than praise; Cervantes wrote verses of biting irony to his memory, and was not surprised that he left the country in poverty, for "they say you kept your treasury hidden in heaven." By indirection Quevedo called him incompetent in warfare: "he was more formidable when treating of matters of state by himself than when he was supported by armies and people." Quevedo must have known, like everyone else, that at the battle of St. Quentin, the king had said he could not understand how his father had found pleasure in such things. Quevedo finishes his sharply etched portrait of the Prudent King with this sentence, tense as an archer's bow: "His fear was very costly; he rarely conquered his suspicions."[47] Let us remember, besides, the Carmelite who thought it natural that Philip II would remain a long time in purgatory, whence he was released, however, after a few days, thanks to Saint Theresa, not to Santiago.

Whatever the case may have been with regard to Philip II, as the

[46] A. Castro, *Aspectos del vivir hispánico*, 1949, pp. 23ff.
[47] "Grandes anales de quince días," in *Biblioteca de Autores Españoles*, XXIII, 216.

situation in Spain grew more and more problematical, the eyes of memory turned to the Catholic Sovereigns, not to Charles V or Philip II. For Quevedo, King Ferdinand "knew how to be a king himself, and knew how to teach others to be kings."[48] During his reign the real value of money equaled its nominal value.[49] Baltasar Gracián enlarges on the thought of Quevedo, and thinks that "a hundred kings could be forged from one Ferdinand the Catholic, and there would still be enough substance left for as many more" (El Criticón, 1657). Gracián had already resorted to hyperbole of this kind at the beginning of El Político (1640): "I oppose one king to all kings of the past; I propose one king to all kings to come: Don Ferdinand the Catholic, that great master of the art of ruling kingdoms, the major oracle of the raison d'état." And similar encomiums appear in El Héroe (1637).[50]

Such praises are not to be taken as the exuberant foliation of the so-called baroque age, for they reappear in a less florid style in the Cartas marruecas (1793) of José Cadalso, from whom we might rather have expected an orientation towards the future, since he was writing at a time when science and reason were inspiring faith in progress and in unlimited perfectability. Cadalso has not so much as a glance for Charles III and his gigantic effort to modernize Spain. He believes simply that "the Spanish monarchy was never happier within Spain nor so respected outside Spain as in the epoch of the death of Ferdinand the Catholic (1516). Let us, then, discover which maxims among those that together made up that excellent policy have declined from their former vigor; let us restore this vigor to them, and we shall have the monarchy on the same footing on which the Hapsburgs found it." Cadalso, combining the re-

---

[48] "Carta del rey don Fernando el Católico (1621)," in Biblioteca de Autores Españoles, XXIII, 171-174.

[49] El chitón de las tarabillas, in which Quevedo has the coins speak: "The silver real says . . . that he was worth four copper reales in the time of Don Ferdinand the Catholic; that the glorious emperor Charles V came along, and emergencies, or uprisings, or disorder (he is not sure which of these things it was) took one real away from him, and he was left with a value of three. Came Philip II, and another was taken away, and he was worth two. . . . Came the lord King Don Philip III, and another real was taken away, and the silver real was worth one copper real." Let it be noted that when Quevedo mentions the Catholic King, he uses the title Don, which he does not use either with the Emperor nor with Philip II. He uses it again with Philip III because he was the reigning monarch when Quevedo was writing. The value of the adjective "glorious" which precedes Charles V is neutralized by the "emergencies, uprisings, disorder" that initiated the ruin of the power of the monarchy, which, for Quevedo as well as for his contemporaries, really dated from Ferdinand and Isabella.

[50] Cf. Angel Ferrari, Fernando el Católico en Baltasar Gracián, Madrid, 1945.

gressive Messianism of the Spaniards with the abstract intellectualism of the eighteenth century, tried to turn back the clock of history. Diego Clemencín, a great scholar who died in 1834, expresses himself with no less faith: "If the succeeding centuries had followed the path indicated to them by the example of Isabel, and had progressively perfected her maxims with the aid of experience and learning," then "Spain would have possessed the naval power of England."[51]

Thus, tradition and Messianism are integral parts of the personal reality of those who live them. Just as the poet of the *Cid* planned what his hero might do if he had a "good lord," so Diego Clemencín planned a history of Spain that might have been, around his belief in Isabel the Catholic. If the Cid had had a good lord, if the Catholic Sovereigns had had good successors. History and reality are thus converted into the surface of a dream on which the will may trace lovely arabesques. One of those arch-Spaniards that populated the novels of Galdós of around 1870 says with the same Messianic hope: "Commercial treaties, railroads, administrative morality, let them all come!" (*Angel Guerra*, I, V, IV).

---

[51] *Elogio de la Reina Católica*, p. 32. I have of course not pretended to gather together numerous texts. I limit myself to those that come to hand and are deeply meaningful. The memory of the Catholic Sovereigns has been damned by those who, thinking as abstractly as Cadalso, attribute to those monarchs the expulsion of the Jews, the Inquisition, and the so-called backwardness of Spain. The Spaniards and Hispanic-Americans who curse their past—which is to say, themselves—are examples of what I call *vivir desviviéndose*.

Thought and Religious Sensibility

WE HAVE NO ADEQUATE HISTORY of the philosophical ideas and, especially of the religious sentiments of Christian Spain during the Middle Ages, and I do not propose here to fill so considerable a gap. Whatever the detailed content of such a history might be, the only Spanish thinker whom one could qualify as of high rank is the archdeacon of Segovia, Dominicus Gundisalvus, who lived in Toledo and was the most eminent figure of the so-called school of translators of Toledo[1] organized under the patronage of Raymond, archbishop from 1126 to 1152. Dominicus Gundisalvus translated into Latin what John Hispalensis (a converted Jew called Ben Dāwūd) translated from Arabic. But besides this unoriginal work, Gundisalvus was the author of writings completely his own, in which he tried to harmonize Aristotelian, neo-Platonic, and Moslem thought. The resulting philosophy was what one would expect, given the circumstances of Spanish life; that is, it was a synthesis of East and West. It is conceivable that if Christian Spain had possessed a systematically formulated philosophy, it would have found its embryonic outline sketched by the Archdeacon of Segovia, who, let us note, is regarded as heterodox by Menéndez y Pelayo. His most important works are: *De unitate, De processione mundi, De anima, De immortalitate animae,* and *De divisione philosophiae.* God does not create souls directly, but through the instrumentality of angels, who do not create them from nothing, but from the "spiritual matter," a paradoxical concept which would doubtless have enjoyed Unamuno's sympathy. The corporeal and spiritual substances, in as much as they proceed from God, are in-

[1] Actually nothing like an organized school existed. What there was was a group of translators who made their translations by way of satisfying the demands of European philosophers and scientists. This kind of work had already been done before the twelfth century, and it was not limited to the group in Toledo, although this may have been the center of such activities. Cf. J. M. Millás Vallicrosa, *Las traducciones orientales de la Biblioteca Catedral de Toledo,* Madrid, 1942, pp. 8-9. Concerning the translators in Moslem Seville in the twelfth century, see Ibn 'Abdūn, *Sevilla a comienzos del siglo XII,* tr. E. Lévi-Provençal and E. García Gómez, 1948, p. 173.

corruptible and infinite: "every body, *qua* body, is perpetual." It is not my purpose here, however, to analyze the thought of Gundisalvus, which had no issue in Spain, although it bore fruit in the works of William of Auvergne, Saint Bonaventure, and Albertus Magnus, and thus is of significance in European Scholasticism.[2] Gundisalvus' mind is a solitary light in twelfth-century Spain, and confirms the idea that in Spain everything was at once possible and impossible. Abreast with the philosophical problems of his time, his thought passed like a meteor, just as was to happen with the philosophy of Luis Vives in the sixteenth century.

A Glance at Catalonia

The extraordinary figure of Raymond Lully (c.1236-1315) stands outside of Castile. He is within the Christian-Islamic framework of Spanish life, although his position in it is in conformity with Catalonian circumstances. Lully does not hesitate to confess his similarities to Sufistic mysticism, which he takes as his model:

"Blanquerna recalled how, when he was an apostle, a Saracen once told him that there are religious men among them. The most esteemed among these religious men are those called Sufis. They speak words of love and make use of parables, stimulating great piety. Their words have to be explained. When one studies them diligently, understanding is increased, and the will multiplies and increases its devotion. When Blanquerna had considered these words, he proposed to write a book after the fashion that we have just described."[3]

What is of interest here is Lully's relationship with the Islamic style of life, and not his own doctrine, which is considered to be Catholic and orthodox by the most exacting, and concerning which there is an abundant bibliography.[4] While the Castilians were still refraining from the conscious literary imitation of the religious and lyric subjectivism of the Arabs, this fiery Majorcan put himself on the level of the enemies he

[2] Cf. J. A. Endres, "Die Nachwirkung von Gundissalinus' De immortalitate animae," in *Philosophisches Jahrbuch*, 1900, XII, 382-392, and the important bibliography on Gundisalvus in B. Geyer. *Die patristische und scholastische Philosophie*, Berlin, 1928, pp. 729-730. The form *Gundissalinus* is the result of a misreading of *Gundisaluus*. See also Manuel Alonso, "Algunas notas sobre los traductores toledanos Dominico Gundisalvo y Juan Hispano," in *Al-Andalus*, 1943, VIII, 155-188. In Mozarabic documents of Toledo, Gundisalvus is called "Dominico Gonzalvo"; he still lived in 1181.

[3] *Libre de Amich e Amat*, ed. by M. Obrador, 1904, p. 47.

[4] M. Menéndez y Pelayo, *Historia de los heterodoxos españoles*, 1918, III, 257-273. B. Geyer, *op.cit.*, p. 759. E. Allison Peers, *Ramón Lull*, 1929, pp. 422-434.

sought to convert, as centuries before Galicians had used Santiago against the enemy they sought to conquer. The result was a style in which matters of exalted spirituality alternated with references to surprising material details. The mixture of the two planes produces an impression of folklike naïveté, of "realism," of unrestrained abandon to whatever one feels and thinks. Along with the abstractions and allegories of *Blanquerna* one can find such things as the following:

"Children must be raised on milk, because if they are not, they get scabs and itches, and they have warts and blisters. . . . From each house a servant would come out, carrying a rain cape and galoshes to her master and mistress who were in the church. . . . In the back of the house he saw two palettes made of vines, on which there was very little straw, and on each one only one blanket."[5]

In Castile of the thirteenth century, cut off from lyric poetry, from mystic writings, and from any such prose as Lully's, there was nothing comparable to this. As is known, the genres cultivated in Castile were the epic, learned poetry (religious, or treating of the heroes of antiquity), history, and the moral or juridical treatise. The inwardness of the writer, either real or imagined, did not constitute in Castile a subject for literary expression,[6] whereas in Catalonia it was already possible in the thirteenth century to have an autobiographical chronicle like that of James the Conqueror (1208-1276), the father-in-law of Alphonse the Learned. It is a question whether this chronicle was actually written by the king, or by someone who either kept up with the smallest details of his life or else wrote down both what James dictated to him and what he observed himself. From the literary point of view, it makes little difference who the author was. The essential thing is that there exists an autobiographical form and a human theme that has meaning only inside that form, because what is expressed is seen and experienced according to the scale of magnification of the writer's own consciousness. The king, or whoever wrote the Chronicle, expressed the things that he discovered by examining the reactions of his soul. He did this because he judged it a normal and worthy thing to do, that is, because he lived in an environment in which it was regarded as natural and worthwhile to tell one's

[5] Pp. 31, 100, 108 of the edition of Barcelona, 1935.
[6] Although Berceo refers to himself, he uses the form that he does, and which I shall examine at a later place, so that he could prove the authenticity of his miracles. The presence of a literary "I" who speaks of himself does not appear till the fourteenth century with the Archpriest of Hita and with Prince Juan Manuel, as I shall also point out later; although the real and complete confession of the inner self of a life does not appear till Saint Teresa.

audience about one's intimate experiences. At a difficult moment in the conquest of Valencia, the king spent a bad night:

"Thereupon we[7] went to bed, and we would not reveal the conversation that had taken place to any of those that were with us. And although we were in January when it is very cold, we tossed in the bed, rolling from one side to the other more than a hundred times; we sweated as if we were in a bath. After much thinking, we went to sleep, exhausted by the fatigue of the long insomnia. Between midnight and dawn we went back to our thought." (Ed. of M. Aguiló, 1874, p. 281)

This is not a description of events through which one passes, but of the intimate situation of the person who experiences them. The distance between this style and that of the Chronicle of Alphonse the Learned is the same as the distance between the vital situations of Catalonia and Castile. James's entire Chronicle is written with the same air of familiar abandon, which is intimately related with the fact that he is using the Catalan language of everyday life, a language which had as yet had hardly any use in poetry. For their poetry the Catalans borrowed the language of the Provençal troubadours.[8] What keeps this style from being utterly vulgar, what gives it its tension, is the feeling that everything is happening to a royal personage, aware of the value and importance of his most trivial actions. For, I shall repeat, here the events objectively matter less than the awareness of them as experience and the interest that consequently attaches to them. This is why James, like Lully, encompasses in his expression the spiritual and the sensual, the beautiful and the ugly, the sweat of one who cannot sleep, in the case of the king; the scabs on the children's skin, in the case of Lully—all this after the fashion of Moslem spirituality. It is to this that we owe, in the last analysis, the elemental beauty of James's Chronicle, its virginal fragrance; in its naïve style are fused the impression of the remote and of the immediate.

This is the way the king and Sir Bernard Guillen d'Entenza converse before undertaking a certain military operation:

" 'What?' we said. 'You have not taken food supplies to Burriana either by sea or by land? Because we have nothing. . . .'

---

[7] King James expresses himself in the first person plural of royalty.

[8] In the conversation with his son, James preserves the latter's regional speech, which was Aragonese, not Catalan: "Se[n]yor, lo que yo feyto he me pesa muyto, e muyto gran dolor n'he en mon coraçon. . . . E viengo aqui a Vostra Merced, e fets de mi e de les mies coses lo que vos queredes," etc. (p. 501). The same thing happens in other cases, when Castilians are the speakers.

"Sir Bernard said, 'In Tortosa I have 300 *cahices* of wheat as it is measured in Aragon, and 50 slabs of bacon; but I have them pawned for 1,500 *sueldos*.'

"We said, '*Por Dios*, Sir Bernard Guillen, you have played both yourself and me a bad trick; trusting you, I made no preparations, and I can't help either you or myself. . . .'

"The next morning when Sir Bernard came, we already thought how we should proceed, and we said to him, 'The only thing I can think of is to march to Burriana, if you will give me all the mules you have here. . . .' I went to Burriana; but before that, when we went to break camp, we saw that a swallow had nested on our tent, and we commanded that she be left there until she should go away with her fledglings for she had come there trusting in Us [pus *en nostra fe* era venguda].'"[9]

The swallow does not figure here as a military event. Nor does it have anything to do with sentimental motives—the traditional tenderness towards birds; nor with religious motives—the traditional Spanish respect for swallows because of the widespread belief that they drew out the thorns from Christ's head. The swallow is included within the halo of royalty, within the radius of the hospitality and the obligations a lord has toward his vassal, in the awareness that James has of the worth of everything that is associated with his royal person. From this royal person comes the light that lets us see the *cahices* of wheat, the slabs of bacon, and the swallow. Generic motives (the moral structure of a society with its typical figures and its scale of ranks) are combined here with motives of individual sensibility: the person who tosses in bed is not *a* king but King James, on whom another very concrete person has played a trick. The events narrated are not disposed of entirely in objective, didactic, supra-personal, generic constructions; they rest ultimately on the exclusive conscious awareness of an individualized person.

No doubt the reader will think at this point of the Chronicle of Saint Louis by Sire Jean de Joinville, a work of greater human and artistic stature, in which the biography of the king is intermingled with the autobiography of the chronicler. But since what is of interest on the present occasion is not a balance sheet of literary merits but rather the understanding of a peculiarity of style, let us place side by side a passage from Joinville and another from King James, in which both bring to the foreground affecting situations in which they are the central figures:

[9] Ed.cit., pp. 257-258.

[As soon as he had conquered the city of Murcia, James had one of the mosques consecrated, and it was converted into a church of Our Lady Saint Mary . . .] "E quan vench al segon dia e fo aguizat l'altar, nos lo faem guarnir gran matí ab la roba de nostra capela. E ab nostres creus e ab ymage de nostra dona sancta Maria moguem de la albergada on nos estavem en la ost, e a peu venguem e entram per la vila entro en la esglesia. . . . E quan vim l'altar ens acostam a ell, pres nos tan gran devoció de la gracia e de la misericordia que Deus nos havia feyta per prechs de la sua Mare. . . . E nos abraçats ab l'altar, ploram tant fort e tant de cor, que per anadura d'una gran milla nons poguem partir d'aquel plorar ni del altar. E faem cantar *Veni, creator spiritus*, e puys la missa de *Salve, sancta parens*. E aço feyt, entram nosen en l'al-

cacer albergar ab gran alegria." (Ed. M. Aguiló, p. 452)[10]

"Or avint ainsi que contenue me prist, et toute ma mesnie aussi. Ne onques un jour toute jour je n'oy onques qui me peust aidier ne lever: ne j'atendeoie que la mort, par un signe qui m'estoit delez l'oreille: car il n'estoit nus jours que l'on n'aportast bien vingt mors ou plus ou moustier; et de mon lit, toutes les fois que on les aportait, je ouoie chanter, *Libera me, Domine*. Lors je plorai et rendi graces à Dieu, et li dis ainsi: 'Sire, aourez soies-tu de ceste soufraite que tu me fais; car mains bobans ai eus à moy couchier et à mon lever. Et te pri, Sire, que tu m'aides, et me delivres de ceste maladie.' E aussi fist-il, moy et ma gent." (Ed. of N. de Waillys, §415)[11]

There are some similarities between the two texts—the weeping and the giving thanks to God—but the differences are more important. Joinville directs the expression of his life through the channel of reflection: He knows that he may die, because he hears how they are bringing victims of the epidemic to the church; he understands that God may have sent him his illness as a punishment for his life of dissipation; his tears

10 "When after two days the altar was set up, we had it adorned early in the morning with the ornaments of our chapel. . . . And with our crosses and with the image of Our Lady Saint Mary, we left our royal lodging place in the camp, and we came on foot and entered through the city into the church. . . . And when we saw the altar we fell upon it and felt ourselves filled with great devotion for the grace and mercy which God had bestowed upon us through the intercession of His Mother. . . . And clinging to the altar, we wept so much and from the heart, that for the time it takes to walk a good mile we could not abandon that weeping or that altar. And we caused to be sung the *Veni, creator spiritus*, and after that, the mass *Salve, sancta parens*. This done, we went and took our place in the alcazar with great rejoicing."

11 "It happened then that a continuous fever overtook me and all my people, on account of which I had to go to bed. During all this time, there was not a single day when someone could help me and lift me up; and I was only waiting for death, because of something I could hear very clearly: there was not a day on which they did not bring to the church some twenty-odd dead, and whenever they came I could hear them, from my bed, singing *Libera me, Domine*. Then I wept and gave thanks to God, and spoke to him thus: 'Lord, be Thou adored through the suffering thou has sent me, for I have shown much pomp on going to bed and on rising up. And I beg Thee, O Lord, to help me and to deliver me from this illness.' And He did this for me and my people."

proceed from physical misery and the fear of death, and he prays to God
with the object of obtaining benefit to his own health. Joinville's religion
is not effusive or lyrical. It rests on the idea of an objective order, which
has as one aspect the spiritual vassalage of man with respect to God.
He relates the misfortunes that happened to him at Acre so that his
readers "will trust in God in their persecutions and tribulations; and
God will help them as He has helped me" (§406). Joinville believes and
thinks more than he feels. There is no place for a holy war in his system,
as we have seen. When his steward suggests that if they all let themselves be beheaded, they will certainly go to paradise, Joinville says
bluntly "We did not believe him" (§319). When all are confessing,
Joinville does not remember having committed any sin, "and *I reflected*
that the more I defended myself and the more evasive I was, the worse
it would go with me" (§354). This good seneschal of Champagne felt
himself perfectly adjusted in a social structure in which the divine and
the human elements existed in an ordained harmony. While he was
experiencing brilliant deeds of prowess, he was thinking about recounting
them: "You and I," he says to the Count of Soissons, "must talk about
this day's happenings in *les chambres des dames*" (§242).

Joinville connects everything he sees and everything that happens to
him with an objective and justified order, but he does not integrate it
in the "irrationality" of his own experience. For James, the importance
of what he tells derives from the fact that he is the one who is experiencing it. Nothing like the anecdote of the swallow can be found in
Joinville, incapable of the emotional luxury of weeping like King James,
who clung to the Virgin's altar for a period of time that had its measure
in existential, not objective, terms—the time it would take to walk a good
mile. Thus the king reveals his basic Spanishness—spontaneity, and lack
of restraint. James planned a crusade as "his" affair, as a great gest.
Elegant bearing and presence are characteristic traits of King James'
personality. He proudly refuses to declare himself a tributary of the
pope. When he leaves the pontifical court, the old king makes his horse
curvet—"faem li fer una gran parada"—and the chronicler notes the
comment of the Frenchmen who are watching: "The king is not as old
as they said he was." And on leaving, the king says to his barons: "Today
all Spain has been honored" (p. 353).

King James has more faith in himself than in the ruling order; his
real religion rests on his faith in the Virgin, in his love for Mary. The
Virgin is for him what Santiago had been for the Leonese and the Castilians, although there is a tinge of lyricism and emotion missing in the

cult of the Apostle.[12] The intensity of personal feelings here is in inverse proportion to the value assigned to the objective order, whether this order be divine or human. King James moves in not altogether coherent society, and he trusts himself more than his nobles. When a message from the Moorish king of Valencia is brought to him, he writes that "I did not communicate those words to anyone in my army, nobleman or not, because there were many to whom the conquest of the city was not pleasing; they preferred that it belong to the Moors" (p. 271). When he informed his nobles of the surrender of Valencia, "they paled as if they had been wounded in the center of their hearts; only the archbishop and a few bishops said they were grateful to God for the favor and grace that He granted us; of the rest, none praised or gave thanks to Our Lord, and they limited themselves to asking us how and in what manner that thing had happened" (p. 281). On another occasion he tells his nobles: "Confound you! We shall carry out our wishes without you" (p. 519). Among other things, James advised his son-in-law Alphonse X of Castile that "if he could not keep with him all the people of his kingdom, he should at least keep two classes, the Church and the commoners of the villages and cities of his realm, because God loves those people more than the knights; the knights rise up against the king sooner than the others, and if one can count on the churchmen and the people, it is possible to destroy the knights" (p. 498).

There is an evident connection, then, between the familiar and at times even utterly informal style of the Chronicle and the slight respect that the king has for the society around him. More important than the objective order is the feeling that his strength is in his own life. Reality is captured by keeping in mind one's own interest, and within the realm of one's own interest the distinction between high and low, superior and ordinary, is blurred. This pattern of life did not find the resistance amongst the Catalonians that it found amongst the Castilians, who felt compelled to fashion, in so far as they could, a life with an objective structure, Castilian in type and quite distinct from the Islamic. Thus it was that the Castilians turned their backs on lyricism and the unrestrained expression of their inwardness, and were able to produce the book of laws known as the *Siete Partidas*, in which Alphonse the Learned gave a moral and juridical form to the society of his kingdom. Even though Alphonse suffered the rebellion of his nobles (led by his own son, San-

---

[12] "All the good that God does for you and for us, we have through the One who prays to her Son for us" (§453).

cho), he continued to see the moral world as an order in the form of a graduated hierarchy.

Let us examine, as a significant illustration of the peculiar quality of Catalonia, King James' description of the death of his father, Peter II of Aragon, who fell in the battle of Muret (1213): "The day of the battle, he had slept with a woman, and had spent himself so with her (according to what I heard afterwards from one of his butlers named Gil, who later became a friar in the Hospitalers, and from others who saw it with their own eyes) that he could not stand during the Gospel of the mass that was said before the battle, and had to sit down in his chair" (p. 9). Such complete lack of reserve is unthinkable in the Castilian chronicles, which, besides, are never autobiographical in form. In comparison with Joinville, the difference is evident. King James relates how he has experienced the events that affect him personally; whereas the Frenchman describes the events of which he has been the witness, arranging them in a hierarchy of objectified values—the saintliness of King Louis, the knightliness of Sire Jean de Joinville, trials and tribulations as the result of the will of God, the ladies who eventually listened to the accounts of the great deeds, etc. Behind Joinville, we perceive the courtly tradition of Marie de Champagne and Chrétien de Troyes.[13] Opposed to all this, the prancing of James' horse to provoke wonder in the French, and James' awareness that in such a way he had saved the honor of Spain, are vital phenomena with an essentially aesthetic and existential value.

The Book of the Lover and the Beloved

Lully gives us the first key to the understanding of certain forms of Catalonian style when he says in the Book of the Lover and the Beloved (in Catalan, Libre de Amich e Amat) that he is following the example of the Sufis (see pages 302 and 311-314). He declares that "among the Moslems devoted to the religious life, the most esteemed are the Sufis," and that Blanquerna (of which the Book of the Lover and the Beloved is a fragment) is inspired by Sufistic models. To imagine that Lully was forsaking the truth would hardly make sense. He was writing for read-

---

[13] A detailed and intimate study of the Chronicle of Joinville might make one wonder whether contact with the orient has left traces in that magnificent account. We find there Baudoin d'Ibelin, "who knew the Saracens well" (§354); his brother Gui d'Ibelin, Constable of Cyprus, "who liked the people of this [Saracen] country very much" (§339); "Master Nicholas of Acre, who knew the Saracens" (§361), etc.

ers who knew very well what a Sufi was—they swarmed about the roads and cities no more nor less than Christian friars. Lully felt no scruple in declaring his Moslem inspiration precisely because he had made his own the Islamic idea of tolerance, as is manifest in his *Book of the Gentile and the Three Wise Men*. Asín Palacios has clearly pointed out the traces of the orient in Lully's works,[14] yet there are readers who still do not know what to make of the case. I do not believe that Asín troubled to make a detailed analysis of the *Book of the Lover and the Beloved*, although to realize the presence of Islam in Lully one has only to read what Lully himself has written. His work cannot be broken down, as some have done, into "manner" and "matter," or into "expression" and "content." Lully's book is equal to the total of what it expresses plus the way in which this is expressed, and for this reason it has artistic meaning and value.

The delightful *Book of the Lover and the Beloved* is one more example of literary mudejarism.[15] It is a mingling of the neo-Platonic-Christian tradition of divine love and Moslem mysticism. (In a later chapter we shall see how, similarly, the Archpriest of Hita gave a Christian slant to Islamic works with erotic themes.) It is not simply a question here of whether the "ideas" (few and frail in Lully's little book) proceed from Saint Augustine or from Islam, or whether this kind of divine love can be fitted entirely into the Christian tradition:

"The lover was lying on the couch of love: the sheets were made of pleasures; the coverlet, of languors; the pillow, of tears. One might wonder whether the cloth of the pillow was like that of the sheet and that of the coverlet.

"The beloved dressed his lover—gown, coat of mail, and kilt; he made him a hat of love, a shirt of thoughts, hose of tribulations, and a garland of weeping."[16]

One foresees the plastic integralism of seventeenth-century sculpture with its interlacing of spirit and matter, divinity and humanity—the sculptures of Alonso Cano or Pedro de Mena. Neither in Saint Augustine nor in Saint Bernard is there anything comparable to the style

---

[14] *Abenmasarra y su escuela*, 1914, pp. 125-126, where Asín refers to others of Lully's writings.

[15] *Mudéjar* is the Spanish adjective to describe those Mohammedans who, without changing their religion, became vassals of the Christian kings in the course of the reconquest of the Peninsula. They developed a characteristic art and architecture, in which the mixture of Moslem and Christian motives was clearly perceptible. Hence, *mudejarism*.

[16] Obrador's edition, §§127, 128.

of Lully, nor even in the *Song of Solomon*. The most commonplace reality (sheets, coverlets, pillows) is infused with poetic and symbolic intention. Nor is it Christian to connect amorous enjoyment with the sufferings caused by the enmity of the beloved, a familiar theme in Arabic erotic literature, be it religious or profane. As one example among many, compare the following passages:

The lover found himself hung up, tied, beaten, and being killed for the love of his beloved; and those who tormented him asked him: "where is your beloved?" He answered: "you see him in the multiplication of my loves, and in the way in which he nourishes my torments" (*Libre de Amich e Amat* (§52). The lover complained of the beloved when the beloved caused him trials and pains. The beloved excused himself saying that the trials and pains of which he was accused by love were the multiplication of loves (§71, etc.).

My suffering in love is my health; and my life, when I am in a transport of passion, no longer is my life. The torment which is death to you is sweeter in my mouth than happiness. . . . Such delight did his tribulation cause him as was like what other men experience in well-being. . . . Have you heard perchance of a love so ardent that it makes the well heart so ill that it feels itself favored by punishment and by favor? [17]

Other themes characteristic of the Islamic erotic tradition are also to be found, such themes as I shall consider in greater detail in the discussion of the Archpriest of Hita and Ibn Ḥazm. Let the following passage serve as an example: "The first *signs of the loves* which the lover makes to his beloved are tears. . . . The lover would look for solitude, and his thoughts would go with him to his heart. . . . When the lover returned to the society of people . . . he found himself alone among them" (*Libre de Amich e Amat*, §§227, 228). We also find the gossip or informer (the *lauzengier* of Provençal poetry, where it is also a theme of Arabic origin): "False flatterers one day spoke ill of the lover in the presence of the beloved" (§247). This is meaningless if we do not remember Lully's literary models. There is also a connection between these models and the lover's submissive resignation to the will of the beloved, the *tawakkol* of the Sufis. For example:

The beloved purchased for his own honor a man enslaved and subjected to thoughts, languors, sighs, and weepings. He asked him what he ate and drank, and he answered, whatever he wished him to. He asked him with what he

clothed himself, and he answered, with whatever he give him. He asked what he desired, and he answered, whatever he wished him to desire. And the beloved said: "Have you any will?" And he answered that the serf and subject

[17] These passages come from Ibn Al-'Arīf (1088-1141), a Sufi of Almería. Cf. his *Maḥāsin al-Majālis*, tr. by M. Asín, Paris Geuthner, 1933, pp. 37-40. The notion in question here is a widespread commonplace.

has no wish but to obey his lord and his beloved." (*Libre de Amich e Amat*, §214)

Where is humble submission, where tears, vigils, sleeplessness? . . . I have

reflected on the gifts God grants to his servant when the servant obeys him and subjects himself to God's service, and continues in this path all his life. (Ibn Al-'Arīf, *op.cit.*, pp. 61, 64)[18]

The following parallel is also noteworthy:

The lover praised his beloved and said that the beloved had gone beyond *where*, because he is there where no *where* can reach. And therefore, when they asked the lover where his beloved was, he answered: "He is," but he knew not where; he knew nevertheless that his beloved was in his memory. (§213)

I have seen my Lord with the eye of my heart, and I have said: There is no doubt that Thou art Thou.
Thou occupiest the boundary of nearness and farness, and the *where* knows not where Thou art.

The text on the right is a poem by Al-Ḥallāj (858-922), quoted by Ibn Al-Arīf (*op.cit.*, p. 48). On another occasion that celebrated martyr had said that "he who seeks God in the consonant *ya*, between *alif* and *nun*, loses him."[19] To understand this we must know that *ayn* (a word formed by the letters *alif* or *a*, *ya* or *y*, and *nun* or *n*) means "where"; that is, God cannot be located at the center of any *where*. According to Al-Ḥallāj one can reach God only through an act of supernatural communication with Him, in which first of all the divine *fiat*, the becoming in some way divine, must be produced in the person (Massignon, p. 542). According to Lully, the Beloved, that is, God, is "in the memory" of the Lover. Lully's mysticism ought to be carefully studied in relation to Sufism, and especially to the doctrines of Al-Ḥallāj, a task I cannot undertake. But let us note, in any case, the central role of love in the dogmatic theology of Al-Ḥallāj. God is contemplated in the totality of love, because "in His essence, Love is the essence of the essence, for Him love is his attributes, in all His ideas." This explains the verse of the Persian poet Abū-l-Khayr: "God says: 'I am Love, the Lover and the Beloved'" (Massignon, p. 604). And it is difficult not to associate

[18] Concerning total self-abnegation—essentially connected with the enjoyment of suffering—cf. Ibn Ḥazm, *The Dove's Neck-Ring* (tr. by A. R. Nykl, pp. 60-65), which treats only of human love. Concerning the *tawakkol*, or total abandonment to God, as a mystic state, cf. L. Massignon, *Lexique technique de la mystique musulmane*, p. 228, where he points out the quietistic aspect of this virtue. But it is Ibn 'Arabī who devotes more discussion to this than anyone else. Christian in its roots, the total renunciation of will achieved peculiar developments in Islamic mysticism. Cf. M. Asín, *El Islam cristianizado*, pp. 56, 146, and *passim*.

[19] L. Massignon, *Al-Ḥallāj, martyr mystique de l'Islam*, p. 130.

with it—since Lully openly states that he follows Sufistic models—the following passages from the *Libre de Amich e Amat*:

"On the right of love is the beloved, and the lover is on the left; and therefore, unless the lover pass through love, he cannot reach his beloved. And in front of love is the beloved, and behind the beloved is the lover; and therefore the lover *cannot reach love until his thoughts and desires have passed through the beloved* (§250). Tell me, mad one, what did your beloved do before the world was? He answered: He co-existed as essence [covenia a ésser] through divers eternal qualities, personal and infinite, there where are lover and beloved [on son amich e amat]." (§252).

According to Al-Ḥallāj God made his own attributes visible in the creation: "He created an image; this image was His image, the image of the essence, and He, God, when he beholds a thing, creates in it an image for all future eternity [in which] are to be found science, power, motion, will, and all the attributes. When God radiates through an individuality, this individuality becomes *he, He*" (Massignon, pp. 605-606). Here we have the "eternal qualities" in which, according to Lully, "lover and beloved" coincide, and which, according to Al-Ḥallāj, existed before the creation, in the pre-eternal anteriority of God.[20]

Another indication of the relationship between Lully and Sufistic mysticism is furnished by the charisms, the miracles that divine favor permits the holy man to work. For example:

The lover was passing through strange lands, and he was attacked on the road by two lions. The lover felt the fear of death, because he desired to live to serve his beloved; and he sent his memory[21] to his beloved, so that love might accompany him in his passing, and that with it he might better endure death. While

[20] It is difficult to determine the extent to which such mystical effusions should be called pantheistic, and it is beyond the scope of my purpose to enter into this question. Suffice it to say that Sufism, like the neo-Platonic speculation that is its basis, is always inclined to blur the boundaries between man and God. P. Pourrat observes that the medieval commentators on Dionysius the Areopagite, "misunderstanding the doctrine of the return of souls to God, fell into pantheistic errors" (*La spiritualité chrétienne*, I, 353). One Sufi says: "In the beginning my soul and thine were but one. . . . I am not I, Thou art not Thou. . . . I am I and Thou at the same time, Thou art Thou and I at the same time" (I. Goldzieher, *Le dogme et la loi de l'Islam*, p. 127, in which are to be found additional texts relating to this matter: "The love of God is the Sufistic formula by which the soul concentrates its effort to absorb the *appearance* of personal existence in the *reality* of the divine Being that embraces everything.")

[21] One does not "think" about God. Rather, the divine quickens in the memory, that is, in recurring to the "eternal qualities, personal and infinite" that Lully mentions (§252).

the lover was remembering the beloved, the two lions came humbly to the lover, licked the tears of his eyes, and kissed his hands and feet. And the lover went in peace to seek his beloved. (§109)

"The submission of the animals, fierce, wild beasts etc. [is one of the charisms granted to the Sufis]. The beasts of the wilderness love him and the lions will wag their tails in testimony of their sympathy for him." (This is the seventeenth charism that God grants to his servants in this world, according to Ibn Al-'Alarīf, op.cit., p. 66. For a description and classification of the charisms in Ibn 'Arabī, see Asín, Islam cristianizado, pp. 397ff.)

Although charisms of this type and others may be found in the lives of the earliest anchorites (as Asín has already noted), it is most probable that Lully was inspired by the Sufis, whom he follows so closely in everything else.[22]

If a summary analysis of Lully's little book has yielded these results, there is no telling what would come out of a minute and methodical comparison of the Majorcan's entire work with Hispano-Arabic literature. One can only imagine how completely Asín's observations on certain concrete aspects of Lully's thought would be confirmed.

Castile's Moral Objectivity till the Fourteenth Century

Raymond Lully's thought and mysticism are not in themselves of interest for my present purposes. What is interesting is the fact that there could exist in the Catalonian part of Spain in the thirteenth century a mysticism colored by Islamism. In the Castile of that time this is unthinkable. But for a Catalonian it was possible to express all the turns of inner personal experience—the weeping of James the Conqueror as he clung to the altar of the Virgin, or the raptures of divine love in

[22] To readers ready to deny the evidence itself, I will even go so far as to say that Lully not only took the Sufis for his models, as he expressly says, but that he proposes that certain Moslem religious practices be imitated: "The lover censured Christians for not beginning their letters with the name of their beloved Jesus Christ, and for not paying Him the honor that the Saracens give to Mohammed, who was an impostor, whom they honor by naming him first of all in their letters" (§149). Lully dedicated his life to converting the Moslems, and at the same time he tried to Christianize, or rather, to adopt and adapt for Christianity certain Islamic customs. This imitation of Islam is noticed even in small details: "I am wearing vile cloth," says the lover, "but love dresses my heart in delightful thoughts" (§144). It should be recalled that Sufi means "of wool," and came to be the designation of the particular species of oriental mystics on account of the clothing they wore (L. Massignon, Le lexique technique de la mystique musulmane, p. 133). I do not believe it would occur to a Christian ascetic to allude to the vileness of his clothing. Moreover, the contrast between the "outer" and the "inner" is a characteristic trait of Islamic style, as I shall point out later.

Lully. Such subjectivism is connected with Islamic forms of existence, in which the spiritual and the sensory blend into one another. We have already seen that the Arabic chroniclers do not confine themselves to recounting facts and actions, but that they also include in their accounts the inner experience of the historical personage.

How is it that the same thing did not happen among Castilians? The problem takes shape for us when we observe the almost total absence of subjective expressiveness (either religious or literary) in Castile before the fourteenth century. To look for an explanation in the myth of race, in inherent qualities, would be futile: from the fourteenth century on Castilian lyric poetry became more and more abundant. After that came the mystical asceticism of the Hieronymites. And in the sixteenth century there was a veritable explosion of mysticism, in the popular manner of the Illuminati and in the exquisite manner of Saint Teresa, Saint John of the Cross, and other lesser figures. The absence of subjective expressiveness before the fourteenth century, then, is the result of a historical situation, not a racial phenomenon.

Prior to the fourteenth century, no religious order interested in mystic contemplation was founded in Spain. In the orders that came from foreign parts—the Cistercians, the Franciscans—there appeared no mystic worthy of mention. The Castilian Saint Dominic created an active militia whose mission was to convert heretics and infidels; but he left no books resembling those of the French Saint Bernard. I suspect that this phenomenon—the absence of emotional expressiveness—is inseparable from the anti-Islamic mission that Castile imposed on herself, that is, from the awareness that she was the firmest foundation of a nationality whose structure and strength drew their very nature and nurture from her persistent effort to escape the pincer of Islam and Christian Europe. Castile was gradually converting herself into the core of Hispanic nationality, thanks to her militant religiosity. Her cohesion was rooted in an anti-Islamic moral sense, in a grave austerity, which found in the prestige of power, consolations for the absence of pleasures and material splendor. Castile sent down her roots in the principles of prudence and of law, which are the promoters of social cohesion. She shielded herself, on the other hand, from individual transport, of whatever kind. This, however, the Catalonians did not fear, precisely because they lacked the consciousness of being a nation always in danger of ceasing to exist as a nation. The matter is put clearly in the *Poema de Fernán González*, a work filled with political doctrine:

Just as she [Castile] is *better* than her neighbors,
So all you who dwell here are better;
You are men *of reflection, you inherit self-restraint* [mesura];
Hence, *throughout all the world you win great esteem.* (155)

The lack of reflection and of self-restraint (mesura) promoted dis-union and national weakness. To avoid this, Castile saw her lesson in the example of the Moslem courts, dazzling in their luxury, sensuality, poetry, and science, and at the same time an easy prey to Castilian energy or to the African hordes, as ignorant and fanatical as they were devastating.

There could be no clearer testimony to Castilian preferences than the Cid as he appears in the epic: brave and daring, but also prudent in his deportment, an expert in law, a good paterfamilias, so loyal to his king that royal injustice does not shake him in his vassalage. In him the Castilian people glorified a hero devoted to chastity and master of his passions, which might very well have broken loose over the heinous mistreatment of his daughters by his sons-in-law. The Cid's social and juridical virtues are the qualities that the twelfth-century poet put into relief in his work of sober and perfect beauty. An episode in the life of the Cid that is celebrated, not in the well-known epic but in another *cantar*, is the Oath in the church of Santa Gadea, where the hero forces Alphonse VI to declare solemnly that he is not implicated in the assassination of his brother, King Sancho. The Castilians admired the Cid especially as a virtuous vassal and chieftain, incapable of disloyalty; on the other hand, they did not regard the impulsive and sensual King Alphonse, incestuous lover of his sister Urraca, as a "good lord." The heroes of the gests were always models of good conduct, not in the fantastic region of myth, but within the type of life favored by the Castilian people. The count Fernán González and the Infantes de Lara embodied in their exemplary lives the virtues that united the people and their lords. Moral objectivity, combined with a religiosity that was also objectified in supernaturally efficacious beliefs, permitted Castile to pass from the state of virtual nonexistence—from the "little corner" of her Count Fernán González' poem—to the state of "winning great esteem throughout all the world," and finally to the state of being the strongest kingdom in the Peninsula, the kingdom that pointed the way to the Reconquest. Her very effectiveness deepened and widened the channel of her history. The cultivation of moral, juridical, and religious norms, which militate against the development of impassioned, uncontrolled individual action, was a grateful task for the Castilian. This was no climate in which the expression of rebellious emotions might flourish —lyric poetry and mysticism. But how propitious it was, on the other hand, for the fruitful growth of that body of work inspired by Alphonse the Learned, the "Summa Pragmatica," as it were—not a "Summa Theologica"—of moral and juridical norms.

Attempts at writing amorous literature, whether treating of divine or profane love, must have been no more than feeble experiments between the eleventh and thirteenth centuries, if indeed there were any such attempts at all in the language of Castile. This was the way I put the matter in the first (Spanish) edition of the present work, when my only support was my belief that the very course of Castilian life could not realize itself in history except within the limits of its historical possibilities. A sensational discovery has, at the very moment of the present revision and translation, confirmed my suspicion. During the eleventh and twelfth centuries there was a lyric poetry written in the Romance dialect spoken by the Spanish Mozarabes, prior, therefore, to the lyric poetry of the Galician-Portuguese, and without the slightest connection with similar writings by the Provençal troubadours.[23]

In Hispano-Arabic poetry there was a type of stanza (muwashshaḥ), whose two last lines, or refrain, must be written in vulgar Arabic, or in the Romance dialect spoken by the Mozarabes. Stanzas with this kind of ending have been discovered. Some are written in Hebrew, some in Arabic. The refrain (kharja), of course, is written either in Hebrew or Arabic characters. Here are some samples:

Des cand meu Cidello vénid   tan buena albishara!
com' rayo de sol éxid   en Wad-al-ḥijara.

That is, "From the moment my Cidiello comes (Oh, what good tidings!), it is like a ray of the rising sun in Guadalajara." The personage celebrated in these lines was a Hebrew in the court of Alphonse VI (d. 1109). Since Guadalajara was conquered in 1086, we may date the verses as between 1086 and 1109. Some of the poems of this kind must

---

[23] See S. M. Stern, "Les vers finaux en espagnol dans les mwaššaḥs hispano-hébraïques," in *Al-Andalus*, 1948, XIII, 299-346. Dámaso Alonso, "Cancioncillas 'de amigo' mozárabes," in the *Revista de Filología Española*, 1949, XXXIII, 297-349, and the bibliography given there, pp. 298-301. E. García Gómez, "Sobre un posible tercer tipo de poesía arábigoandaluza," in *Estudios dedicados a Menéndez Pidal*, 1951, II, 397-408. R. Menéndez Pidal, "Cantos románicos andalusíes continuadores de una lírica latina vulgar," in the *Boletín de la R. Academia Española*, 1951, XXXI, 187-270. E. García Gómez, "Veinticuatro jarŷas romances en muwaššaḥas árabes," in *Al-Andalus*, 1952, XVII, 57-127.

be earlier, and there is no reason why they could not have existed in the tenth century. The language of the poems is Mozarabic, a continuation of the vulgar dialect spoken by the people when the Iberian Peninsula was invaded by the Moslems, and distinct in its phonetics and other features from the dialect that was to become Castilian. The latter, as has already been said, owed its birth and growth to the will of the nascent Castilians to differentiate themselves from the peoples with whom they were in contact. Ramón Menéndez Pidal has a profound treatment of this matter in his book *Orígenes del español*.

Now just as the Castilians did not continue the phonetic tradition of the Mozarabes, it is also important to note that they turned their backs on erotic Mozarabic literature. Opposed to Mozarabic *uello, yed, yermano, yana*, etc., the Castilian said *ojo, es, hermano, puerta* (eye, is, brother, door). Instead of lyric poetry—effusive or amorous, the Castilian cultivated epic and juridico-moral literature. The Mozarabic lyric poetry known to us today was cultivated by Hispano-Arabic and Hispano-Hebrew poets who lived at the end of the eleventh and the beginning of the twelfth centuries. One of them was the great Jehudah Halevy. I quote one of his Hebrew-Mozarabic poems—Hebrew-Mozarabic because the first part of it is in Hebrew, the second in Mozarabic:[24]

> (The Hebrew translated into English)
> My heart leaves me for a roe that thirsts to see it.
> To heaven she raises her pure face full of tears.
> The day when they told her "Your lover is sick," she
>   exclaimed bitterly.

> (The Mozarabic transliterated into Spanish)
> Vayse meu corachón de mib,
> ¡yā, rab! ¿Si se me tornarád?
> ¡Tan mal meu doler li-l-ḥabīb!
> Enfermo yed, ¿cuándo sanarád?

In English the Mozarabic says: "My heart is leaving me, Oh Lord! Will it return to me? How great my grief for my beloved! [My heart] is sick; when will it get well?"

In this poem there are present in a vital unity the following elements: The Romance language, the Arabic language (*li-l-ḥabīb*, "be-

---

[24] The Spanish translation of the Hebrew text is by Messrs. Stern and Cantera, and the transcription of the Mozarabic sections is by Sr. F. Cantera. Cf. p. 311 of the aforementioned article by Dámaso Alonso.

cause of my lover"; *yā rab*, "Oh Lord"), and the inspiration of the Jew who composed it and set it down in his script.

The general theme of the poem is the burning lament of a girl in love who feels that she is dying because of the absence of her lover, or, because he is going away from her. Turned into modern phrasing, one of the couplets would read something like this: "What shall I do, or what will become of me? Do not leave my side, my love." Or another: "What shall I do? How can I live? I await my lover; because of him I shall die."

The discovery of this poetry establishes the direct provenience of Galician lyric poetry. It is no longer necessary to suppose that the latter owed its beginnings to Galician contact with Provençal literature. It suffices to open the *Cancioneiro da Vaticana*, as Dámaso Alonso (*op.cit.*, p. 323) has done, to find compositions exactly like the Mozarabic ones:

> Que farei agor', amigo?
> pois que non querdes migo viver.
> (What shall I do now, beloved?
> For you will not live with me)

Here we see that what the little Mozarabic songs call *habib* in Arabic the Galician-Portuguese *cantigas de amigo* call "amigo," that is *amado* = beloved. The Galicians opened their hearts to that Romanico-Oriental poetry, whereas the Castilians, to whom it was equally accessible, turned a deaf ear to its seductive but enervating sentiments. Mozarabes, Moors, Jews, and Galicians could permit themselves the delights of emotional expressions that the Castilians denied themselves at least until their historical perspective was displaced in the fourteenth century. Before this time, Castile had not written lyric poetry, even though the Mozarabic and Galician traditions in easy reach offered her the possibility of having it.

What I am interested in is the oriental (Arabic and Judaic) tradition of the erotic themes expressed in the Mozarabic lyrics. The beloved's complaint over the absence of her lover is to be found in the Song of Songs, with which the Jews were obviously familiar. If we read the Biblical text as it appears in a thirteenth-century Spanish version, we find it close in style to certain of the *kharjas*:

"Demuéstrame el que ama la mi alma, ó pasces o iazes al medio día ... Torna, *mío amigo*, e sey semeiant a la corça ... Abrí al *mío amigo* el pestiello . . .[25] Coniúrovos, fijas de Iherusalem, si fallardes al *mío amigo*, quel digades que d'amor so enferma."[26]

Recently E. García Gómez has published a number of *muwashshahāt*, in Arabic. Some of these poems have a refrain, or *kharja*, in Mozarabic Romance, but in some of them the language of the refrain is almost entirely Arabic. In one of them (No. IX) the only Romance words are *non, te,* and *con*; the rest of the refrain reads thus in translation: "I shall not love you, unless you join my anklets with my earrings." This, says García Gómez, is a frequent theme in Arabic poetry: "Nothing makes the lover's union so sweet as bringing together the earrings and the anklets" (*Al-Andalus*, 1952, XVII, 92). Some of the *kharjas* contain more Arabic words than others, but the oriental tone of their themes does not change:

> "Si queres como bono mib,
> béŷame idhā al-nadhma dhuk:
> bokella de ḥabb al-mulūk."

Which means: "If you really love me, kiss this string of pearls of mine, my little cherry-mouth" (García Gómez, *loc.cit.*, pp. 95-96). The biblical song has already said in one place: "Let him kiss me with the kisses of his mouth" (1:2); and in another: "Thy teeth are like a flock of sheep that are even shorn, which came up from the washing" (4:2).

For my purpose this discussion can end here. To add further examples would only belabor the point that the themes of the *kharjas* as well as their Romanico-Arabic language are clearly a part of the ambience in which they were produced—a society in which erotic sentiments were

[25] Some of the poems discovered by Stern are plainly related to the biblical tradition:

[Hebrew]   "One day the *young deer* [in the Bible, *roe*]
             knocks at her door . . . and she raises her voice
             and leans upon her mother: 'I can endure no more.' "

[Mozarabic] "Qué faré, mamma?
             Meu-l-ḥabīb está ad yana."
             (What shall I do, mother?
             My beloved is at the door.)
                            (In Dámaso Alonso, *op.cit.*, p. 320)

[26] Text published by J. Cornu in *Festgabe für W. Förster*. The corresponding lines in the Authorized Version read as follows: "Tell me, O thou whom my soul loveth, where thou feedest, where thou makest thy flock to rest at noon [I, 7]. My beloved is like a roe or a young hart [II, 9]. By night on my bed I sought him whom my soul loveth [III, 3]. I rose up to open to my beloved [V, 5]. I charge you, O daughters of Jerusalem, if ye find my beloved, that ye tell him, that I am sick of love [V, 8]."

expressed with natural simplicity. There is no reason to consider the *kharjas* as mysterious survivals of a proto-Hispanic past, unfathomable and unknown. After almost four hundred years of living with Moors and other oriental people, the arabicized Christians we call Mozarabes quite naturally made use of their mixed language to express themes and sentiments which had become as natural to them as their mixed language. The Mozarabes were not Castilians. The poetry they wrote must have struck the Castilians of the eleventh and twelfth centuries as shockingly lascivious and degenerate. Whatever there may have been of this kind of thing in the Castilian dialect, it never was written. We will never discover, in the Castile of the epic period, lyric poetry that deals with sensuous kisses and sexual union. Any effort to express intimate feelings would have drawn the austere soul of Castile toward modes of free-ranging sensibility that would have endangered the stability that soul had developed.

And when I speak of the expression of intimate feelings, I have in mind not only erotic but also mystic poetry. Medieval Castilian mysticism would have been, first of all, rather like Lully's and the mysticism of the Catalonian visionaries, Beghards, and *fraticelli*.[27] When Alphonse the Learned treats the miracles of the Virgin in his Galician *Cantigas*, he does it, as I shall point out, in a half-cultivated, half-vulgar style without parallel in Europe. Mysticism in Castile would have immediately become incompatible with orthodoxy. The equilibrium maintained at such cost through the practice of prudence and objective morality could not have existed.

We can now understand how Castile could let the rhythms and melodies of Mozarabic, Moorish, and Jewish erotic poetry pass over her land in their march to Provence and the rest of Europe without collecting any toll from it before the fourteenth century. What was possible for Provence, Galicia, and Catalonia—where there was no aggressive or constructive plans—was not possible for Castile, whose energetic soul, prudent and chaste, was her best shield,[28] and whose longing for poetry was

---

[27] Cf. *Archivo Ibero-Americano*, 1919-1923, and my *Aspectos del vivir hispánico*, p. 76.

[28] Rodrigo Jiménez de Rada was fully aware that the Castilians were like this: "Castellani quorum constantia audaci consilio semper fulsit" (*De rebus Hispaniae*; cf. B. Sánchez Alonso, *Historia de la historiografía española*, 1941, I, 139). Of King Alphonse VIII, Jiménez de Rada says that he "neglexit delicias seducentes" (*De rebus Hispaniae*, VII, 26), a sentence which the *Crónica general* translates and amplifies: "he scorned the pleasures which corrupt princes" (p. 679a). In the fight against the Moors of Cuenca, Jiménez de Rada says that Alphonse "succendit ignibus civitates,

satisfied by the *cantares de gesta*. There would have been a vital contradiction between her form of life and lyricism, mystic ecstasy, or religious heresy—all related phenomena that might weaken the collective unity and tension. Aragon-Catalonia, without inward national unity and without a directing mission in the struggle against Islam, took the side of the Albigenses, and Peter II of Aragon lost his life in their defense in 1213. A king of Castile would not have done this.

Towards the end of the twelfth century a heresy resembling that of the Albigenses[29] spread over Leon. It is reported by the thirteenth-century historian Lucas of Tuy in a Latin work which I know only through the fragments quoted by Menéndez y Pelayo. Lucas says that the heretics of Leon followed the doctrines of Amalric of Chartres (that is, of Bène) and David of Dinant:

"Under the guise of Philosophy they wish to pervert the Holy Scriptures. They prefer to be called naturalists or philosophers, and quite naturally, since the ancient philosophers are very near to heretics, and many of the modern natural Scientists [modernorum naturalium] are stained with the stain of heresy. They attribute to nature everything that God achieves each day with wonderful order . . . they say that God has conferred on nature the power to do all these things. . . . Their aim is to introduce the sect of the Manicheans, and to show that there are two gods, one of which, evil, has created all visible things.[30]

"Certain heretics say that what is contained in the Old and New Testaments is true if it is understood in a *mystical* way. Taken literally,

---

et succidit viridia deliciarum" (vii, 26), which the *Crónica general* also amplifies: "he burned their cities and other towns; he cut down their gardens and the places of their pleasures [annazaes], where they indulged in their delights [deleytes] and had their relaxation [solazes]" (679a). Where the Latin text uses one word to mention the pleasures to which the Moors were addicted, the *Crónica general* uses three —*annazaes, deleytes, solazes*. To be sure, Alphonse also enjoyed the delights of groves and gardens, but he did not cultivate the pleasures that "corrupt princes." This clarification was necessary in the *Crónica*, for it goes on to say that Alphonse VIII tried to make the stay of the foreigners who came to help him as pleasant as possible: "Outside the city on the bank of the Tagus he gave them gardens and groves and other delightful parks where they might enjoy themselves and take their ease. These places he had made for himself so that his royal majesty might enjoy himself and take his ease when he was in that city and wished to *go for a walk*" (689a). The *Crónica* distinguishes between the corrupting pleasures of the Moors and the virtuous ones in which the Castilians indulged. The two texts confirm what the observation of Castilian literature has already revealed.

[29] Cf. Menéndez y Pelayo, *Historia de los heterodoxos españoles*, iii, pp. 169ff.
[30] *De altera vita fideique controversiis adversus Albigensum errores*, Bk. iii, Chap. ii.

everything they contain is null. . . . Their profane writings, such as the book called *Perpendiculum scientiarum*,[31] are full of these and other errors. In order to attract surreptitiously those that do not openly fall into the error of their fetid infamies, some of these heretics appear as secular priests, friars, or monks, and, with clever cunning, deceive many in the secrecy of confession. . . . Others sometimes circumcise themselves and make themselves pass for Jews, so as to speak with Christians on the pretext of arguing. . . . The synagogues protect them, they ingratiate themselves with princes by giving rich presents, and they attract the judges to their camp with bribes. . . . They blaspheme the virginity of Mary, and thus they go counter to Spanish custom." (Chap. III)

We do not know how true or how exaggerated Lucas of Tuy's description is, because the heretical writings to which he refers are not available to us; nor do we know what portion of Leonese society was affected by such doctrines. What matters, however, is the Bishop of Tuy's comment on the effect those heretical deviations had in Leonese territory: *"That bellicose and Catholic ardor of the Spains* that used to devour the enemies of the Catholic Faith with its flame, *is growing cold"* (Chap. III). The author adds that the heretics corrupted the divine offices by mixing in "erotic songs so as to distract the worshippers from the divine worship. . . . They perform mimes and they tarnish the acts of worship with sacrilegious songs and games."

Even with the little we are told about such important events, we have a basis on which to conclude that naturalistic-pantheistic thought (nature possesses divine powers), the mystical (symbolical or allegorical) interpretation of the sacred texts, and literature of an erotic type (Veneris carmina), that is, lyric poetry, are bound together in the mind of the bishop of Tuy. All this happened, moreover, in Leon and not in Castile, where there is no record that this heretical dissidence had any success. The *Anales Toledanos* (*España sagrada*, vol. XXIII) say that in 1233 Ferdinand III of Castile "hanged many men and boiled many in cauldrons" for heresy, without giving any other details.

But through what Lucas of Tuy does tell us we have a brief glimpse of a sudden burst of religious and literary humanism in Christian Spain of the twelfth century, stifled before it could attain any growth. There is a mention of the names Amalric of Bène and David of Dinant, and this shows that there were the germs of a philosophical culture in Leon at the end of the twelfth century. The thought of those foreigners, who

[31] I do not know whether this book has been preserved.

doubtless came into Spain with the French monks, was very much within the pantheistic tradition of neo-Platonic mysticism as well as in line with the thought developed in the focus of culture at Toledo, mentioned before. The relationship between David of Dinant and Dionysius the Areopagite can be drawn as easily as between him and Avicebron and Gundisalvus.[32] We can perceive dimly and with some confusion the existence of an intellectual, religious, and literary process, strangled with an iron hand by the Church and the royal power of Castile and Leon. This power was very much aware that such efforts caused "that bellicose and Catholic ardor of the Spains" to grow cold, and this at a moment when the Castilians were readying their attack on Cordova and Seville, the greatest centers of Spanish Islam. Even if we discount these immediate objectives of the Castilians, their form of life was already too completely molded for them to abandon "inherited prudence." It was all very well and good to live harmoniously with Moors and Jews, but it was impossible to express oneself *consciously* like them; for if the Castilian had done this he would have ceased to be what he was. The Christian court could not reflect the poetic splendors of the kingdoms of the *taifas* (eleventh century). The latter, be it remembered, were overrun by the ruthless, uncouth *almorávides* while they dozed in religious and moral laxity and listened to the sweet music of fountains and the glossing of young and beautiful bodies in poetry. Such a king as Alphonse VI must have lived like a Moslem; but the collective feeling expressed in literature, or the thought of those who guided that collectivity, could not take the direction of Islamic poetry and intellectual speculation, or of foreign philosophers whose ideas would produce disunity and bad discipline.

It now begins to be clear why Sufism could find a welcome in the Catalonia of Lully and not in Castile. We have already seen that Catalonia was separated from the major enterprises of the Reconquest until the twelfth century, and that her attention was directed more towards France than towards the interior of Spain. Catalonian poetry was not epic but lyric, and it was written not in the language of the Catalonian people but in the language of the troubadours of Provence. Castile, on the other hand, produced epic poetry in the language of her people as early as the eleventh century. The real Catalan language appeared in prose before it did in verse, and even so, it advanced with great hesitation, alternating with Latin. This uncertainty was symptomatic of the

[32] B. Geyer, *Die patristische u. scholastische Philosophie*, 1929, p. 252.

uncertain awareness of national singularity within the international culture of the Middle Ages.[33] Catalonia was in contact with Southern
France, Aragon, Castile, and Islam, and this had important consequences
in Catalonian culture, which, in the Middle Ages, produced Raymond
Lully, the only Hispano-Christian figure of international dimensions in
the fourteenth century. The Aragonese-Catalonian court had more contacts with the outside world than Castile,[34] and more intellectual curiosity. As a single example of this we may recall that the *Dragmaticon Philosophiae* of Guillaume de Conches (1145) was translated in the fourteenth century with the Catalan title *Suma de filosofia.* If this is no great
intellectual undertaking, it becomes a significant one, nonetheless, when
we realize that nothing of the kind happened in the Castile of that time.
Boethius' *Consolatio* was translated into Catalan before it was translated
into Castilian, just as Catalonia and Valencia were ahead of Castile in
their willingness to receive the humanism of Italy. Aragon and Catalonia struck out in international ventures (Sicily, Sardinia, Greece, Italy)
when Castile was still contending with the Spain she hoped to make her
own. For Aragon and Catalonia the Reconquest ended with James II
(1291-1327).

Nothing brings out more clearly the different horizons of the two
kingdoms than the comparison of the following events that took place
virtually at the same time: Peter II of Aragon died in 1213 while fighting for the Albigenses in France, and Alphonse VIII of Castile aided
by other Spanish kings, won the battle of Las Navas de Tolosa in 1212,
which tipped the balance definitively in favor of the Spanish Christians.

[33] One example, among many, may be found in the interesting *Documents per
l'historia de la cultura catalana mig-eval* (1908-1921), of A. Rubió y Lluch. An
examination of all the documents between the dates 1275 and 1356 (that is, a total
of 176), reveals that 139 are in Latin and seven in Castilian-Aragonese. The
documents in Catalan begin in 1310, and they are neither the most extensive nor
the most important ones. Document No. 173 (of the year 1356) is an inventory
that begins and ends in Latin, and uses Catalan only to describe the inventoried objects, thus indicating the distinction between the official, cultivated style and the
everyday style. In 1356 the Aragonese kings who spoke Catalan as their normal
language still felt no indissoluble relationship between the language of the people
and the language of the state, in spite of the fact that Catalan could already boast
of splendid works in prose. Politically and linguistically, Catalonia was still a county.
The king's chancellery in the fourteenth century did not accord full dignity either
to the language of Saragossa (a mixture of Castilian and Aragonese) nor to the
Catalan of Barcelona. This is why Latin persisted.
[34] See, for example, H. Finke, *Acta Aragonensia. Quellen zur deutschen, italieni-
schen, französischen, spanischen, zur Kirchen- u. Kulturgeschichte aus dem diplo-
matischen Korrespondenz Jaymes II (1291-1327),* 1908-1922.

James I of Aragon conquered Valencia in 1239, while Ferdinand III of Castile was taking Cordova (1236) and Seville (1248); the Aragonese was victorious thanks to his personal fortitude and in spite of his nobles, whose conduct we have already observed; the Castilian carried out the more arduous task as a great national mission, in which nobles and people outdid each other in sacrifice and enthusiasm. James I was later to advise his son-in-law Alphonse the Learned to seek support everywhere save in the nobility, because Catalonia felt a sense of interior anarchy; there was a feeling of "seny natural" (common sense) but without "inherited prudence."

In spite of James I's great individual effort and Alphonse X's slight aptitude for warfare, Castile continued to be the hub of the Reconquest. The Moors still presented serious problems, even after the capture of Cordova, Valencia, and Seville. When the Moors of Murcia rose up against Alphonse X, the king of Aragon asked his kingdom for a special tax and raised an army to help his son-in-law for reasons of common sense, of "seny natural," since, as he told his nobles, "if the king of Castile should lose his land, we should find ourselves in bad straits in our own land."[35] The fierce people of the African continent had poured over Spain three times, and a fourth invasion was feared. With these words Aragon admitted that she was a second-rate power with respect to Castile. All this helps us to understand how Moslem mysticism and literature of autobiographical or lyrical character could make their way in Catalonia while they were shut out of Castile and the regions under her immediate influence, Leon and Aragon. Galicia, without any special political mission, could also enjoy the luxury of lyric poetry in the thirteenth century.

The connection that I am trying to establish between the forms of expression of inner experience and the objective structure of society can be corroborated in Hispano-Moslem history itself, if we remember that the *almorávides* and the *almohades* came to Al-Andalus to settle the political disorder caused mainly by religious anarchy. The political revolutions in Islam, as Asín remarks, first took the aspect of politically harmless fanaticism, and this explains the eventual persecution of ascetics and mystics. In Cordova a cadi burned the works of Al-Ghazzālī; the Almerian Sufi Ibn Al-'Arīf (1088-1141) suffered much persecution and it is said that he died from being poisoned; a disciple of his "organized a religious militia in the Algarbes [Portugal], comprised of members

[35] *Chronica del rey En Jacme Primer*, ed. by Aguiló, p. 400.

of Ibn Al-'Arīf's sect, he proclaimed himself a high priest of Islam (imām), won military victories over the *Almohades*, and reigned for ten years as the sovereign of that region."[36] Mysticism led to rebellion and to political particularism. Sufism embraced everything from the highest forms of mysticism to the street-side miracle-mongering of dervishes and vagrants. Its religious sentiment and expression boiled over into the most varied sects and personal attitudes, the esoteric (symbolical or allegorical) or exoteric (literal) interpretation of the sacred writings, pantheism, and heterodox and social anarchy. We do not know what headway this Islamic tendency made in Castilian territory, but from what I have pointed out one can make a reasonable guess as to how drastic the defensive repression must have been.

From the position which I have been gradually building up, I believe that one can understand why first the Mozarabes and then the Castilians tried to explain to themselves the Moslem invasion of Spain, and why this was not attempted by either the Galicians or the Catalonians, whose languages were never used for the expression of an original treatment of the theme of Rodrigo, the last Gothic king. How was the Visigothic monarchy overthrown so suddenly? History does not say, but answers to the question were provided by legends. According to one, Witiza, the next to the last of the Gothic kings, seduced the daughter of Count Julian, or Olian, the Visigothic governor of Ceuta, who opened the gates of Spain to the Saracens in order to get his revenge. Another version attributes the violation of the maiden to Rodrigo.[37] One way or another, the Mozarabes and the Castilians attributed the downfall of an entire kingdom to the lasciviousness of its kings. That fable (whose parallels and links in folklore are as secondary here as such things were in the case of Santiago) took deep root and was incorporated into history because it answered to the needs of a very strong feeling in the soul of the people. The *Crónica general* of Alphonse the Learned not only says that Rodrigo "took by force" the daughter of the count and "coupled with her"; it goes on to present Rodrigo's predecessor, King Witiza, as a lewd monster:

"In his wickedness he gave license and authority to all his clergy, that each one should have many wives and concubines *openly*, either one or many, *as they might wish for themselves.* . . . And he commanded be-

---

[36] Ibn Al-'Arīf, *Maḥāsin al-Maŷālis*, ed. by M. Asín, p. 5.
[37] Cf. Menéndez Pidal, *Floresta de leyendas heroicas españolas*, I.

sides that they should not obey the decrees or injunctions of Rome that forbade such a thing as he was commanding them to do."[38]

Thus, to King Witiza was attributed the same sensuality and religious anarchy as had been recognized in the Moslems, the open practice of immorality, the inciting of people to do what they pleased and to disobey the Church—irresponsibility, sensuality, and anarchy were one and the same thing. This was the significance of the scandalous polygamy of the clergy, to which Witiza quite possibly never gave a thought. The restoration of Spain consequently drew its inspiration from all that was contrary to the idea expressed in these legends, from the will to be the opposite of everything that was attributed to the last Visigothic kings. The meaning of such tales is to be found not in the tales themselves, but in the spirit of the people whose experience they expressed. It was the direction taken by history that brought them to flower, not the caprice of fantasy or the crossing of themes drawn from abstract folklore. The urgent desire for social cohesion motivated the nascent Castilians to attach social value to chastity and austere deportment. The clerics of the thirteenth century, to be sure, lived with concubines, but what was bad was that Witiza had authorized the clergy to do this "openly." Because Castile for centuries bore the brunt of the struggle against a people judged to be lascivious, a people that spoke of love and orgies in their literature, she imagined that the violation of a maiden and the polygamy of the clergy were the determinants of the triumphant Saracen invasion. The legend served both as a release for feelings and a lesson. The redemption of the Spain-to-be demanded in her own deportment a rectification of the moral error of those who had brought about her ruin and of those who continued to oppress her.

Fernán Pérez de Guzmán, a Castilian brimming with national feeling, says that when Cordova was conquered, "all the uncleanliness of Mohammed the Wicked, the womanish prophet, was banished."[39] He also condemns theoretical knowledge that has no practical or moral importance: "Knowledge that is put away without ever coming to fruit we can compare to buried treasure; when the mind disregards practice, it *theorizes* without acting; if my thought does not err, it is called a body without a soul."[40] The eschewing of the Arabs' moral effeminacy and the rejection of theoretical thought are different facets of the same vital phenome-

[38] Edition of Menéndez Pidal, p. 304.
[39] "Claros varones de Castilla," in the *Nueva Biblioteca de Autores Españoles*, XIX, 738, 739.
[40] *Coblas de vicios e virtudes*, ed.cit., p. 576.

non. Pérez de Guzmán parallels Juan Manuel (see Chapter 8) in his scorn of theoretical knowledge, the cultivation of which was, besides, bound up in Europe (France, Italy, England) with the modification of traditional beliefs through the denials of skepticism or through dissident heresy. Spain, the creation of Santiago and Castile, could not permit herself such liberties; and in this situation the absence of a scientific tradition and the lack of necessary will to start a new one were the conjoint result of that historical situation. If we immerse ourselves thus in history, we understand the Castilian inclination to moral didacticism as a profound aspect of her existence, and we understand the abundance of translations of Arabic didactic writings, because in this case the example of Islam was strengthening, just as her masons and all her other artisans and technicians were useful. It was the program already implicit in the *Cantar de Mio Cid*.

If the Spanish Moslems had been as pure as hermits, or if they had not occupied the land of the Peninsula, the Castilians might very likely have written with the same freedom used by other Christian peoples not involved in national, religious wars. James I, free of Castilian scruples, could write that his father was given to women (hom de fempnes), and all the other things mentioned above. But the Castilians did not allude to sensual and erotic matters until later—occasionally in the fourteenth century (the Archpriest of Hita), and especially in the fifteenth, when the Marquis of Santillana no longer felt the slightest timidity in describing his daughters' beautiful bodies:

> Two apples from paradise,
> their equal breasts,

not surprising,

> Because God put aside all his works
> When he decided to make them.[41]

The higher society of Castile no longer feared the Moorish world. It was beginning to turn in a different direction, and, from the days of the Archpriest of Hita on, literature did not conceal the beauty of woman. In the fourteenth century, the Jew Santob was to speak of the sweetness of a feminine mouth; in the fifteenth century, another Jew, Antón

[41] In Spanish:

> Dos pumas de paraíso
> las sus tetas igualadas,
> porque Dios todos sus fechos
> dejó cuando fer las quiso.

de Montoro, was to compose a cynical description of the sexual act. But in the thirteenth century only the moralizing works of the Arabs were imitated or translated: *Calila e Dimna*, the *Engaños y asayamientos de las mujeres*, not to mention others equally well known. It is noteworthy, moreover, that even the learned poetry of the thirteenth century, today regarded as Castilian, comes from the periphery of Castile and not from Castile itself, as is shown by the dialectical forms of its language: *Alexandre, Apolonio, Reys d'Orient, María Egipciaca, Elena y María*.

Related to all this is the fact that before the fourteenth century the Castilians used the Galician language for lyrical expression. Their own language inhibited them when they felt lyrical inclinations. The moral pragmatism of Castile inhibited the soul just as puritanism and rationalism did later in other countries. We cannot say that Alphonse the Learned wrote the *Cantigas* in the tongue of Galicia because of its politico-religious importance and the excellence of its lyrical literature, as if one could disengage human expression from the inner process that determines it. The written language in Castile in the second half of the thirteenth century had a wider variety of expressive possibilities and had been more extensively used than Galician in Spain, thanks precisely to the translators and compilers assembled by Alphonse the Learned, a great promoter of literary activity as a part of his royal program. The Bible and Ovid, to cite obvious examples, had been turned into Castilian in the court of the Learned King. It thus became possible to express sensibilities objectified in the Bible or in Ovid, but when it came to personal sentiments—the love of the king felt for the Virgin Mary—his pen faltered. To break habits of centuries' standing, a high tension is necessary, a revolutionary spirit. Those who lack this must remain silent or have recourse to indirect procedures. The Galician language of the *Cantigas* is an artistic "euphemism." The Castilian poet had recourse to Galician, a closely related language, a somewhat archaic Castilian after all, that discharged the function of a thin disguise, a transformation of the poet's blush over his intimate confession.[42] Two generations later, his grandson Alphonse XI would not hesitate to say in good Castilian:

[42] This is an occurrence on a large scale of what is to be observed on a small scale in other languages. For motives of sexual modesty, the Englishman has recourse to French to say "*liaison*, love *affair*, *gigolo*, etc.," just as he uses expressions like *tour de force*, *de luxe*, etc., and thus reveals a puritan tendency to avoid any display of personal effort or luxury or superfluity, etc. For still other reasons, the Spaniard uses foreign words to signify a person that is converted into a spectacle for others: *payaso, títere, clown*, etc. (See my note on *La palabra "títere"* in *Modern Language Notes*, 1942, LVII, 504-510.)

Once I picked flowers
From the very noble paradise,
Stricken by my love
And by her beautiful smile, etc.[43]

This measures the distance between the Castile of the thirteenth century and the Castile of the fourteenth.

Religion and Inward Existence

The history of man's expression is not complete if it is limited to the orderly presentation of the traditions that it embraces. "Man," Heidegger rightly says, "is the heir and the apprentice of all things." The Castilian man has been no exception to this manner of existing. Like all human beings, he has created with his own energy everything compatible with the main tendencies of his own "dwelling-place." Paraphrasing Spinoza's formula "natura naturans, natura naturata," one might say that all history results from the interaction of "spiritus spirituatus" and "spiritus spirituans." If we fail to perceive the effect of the latter, man's history becomes a corpse for scholars to dissect.

The "centauric" style which I find in Hispanic literature is a symptom of broader forms of life. Something very much like this style is found in Arabic literature and in Islamic inner disposition as well. This analogy is compatible with the fact that the themes, genres, and general orientation are quite different in the two literatures. The problem is complex, and must be examined from various points of view, even at the risk of repetitions. Searching for sources and underscoring similarities between certain themes is only a partial help, because what we need to find is something that lies beneath the themes. The observation of the inwardness of existence is more important than the "history of ideas," which occasionally forgets that ideas are vitally connected with history.[44]

[43] Menéndez y Pelayo, *Antología*, 1, 1890, p. 53.

[44] Loyal to his integralism, to his essential Hispanicity, Unamuno says: "In most of the histories of philosophy that I am acquainted with, we are presented with systems as if they were spawned one from another, and their authors, the philosophers, scarcely appear as anything more than mere pretexts. The intimate biography of the philosophers, of the men who have philosophized, occupies a secondary position" (*Del sentimiento trágico de la vida*, 1912, p. 1). Ortega y Gasset amplifiies this idea in 1944: "There is no 'history of ideas' as such. . . . A doctrine is a series of propositions. The propositions are sentences. The sentence is the verbal expression of a 'meaning'—what we are in the habit of calling an 'idea' or a 'thought.' We hear or read a sentence, but what we understand, if we understand, is its meaning. This is what is understandable. So it is a mistake to suppose that the sentence 'has *its*

It is not enough, therefore, to establish contacts between a work and its sources. The fact that a Spanish work, the *Libro de buen amor*, for example, has Arabic sources, does not mean the same thing as the fact that Dante used Arabic models, as Asín has shown, for the *Divine Comedy*, because Italy was not immersed in Moslem life, did not share an existence with Islam, and did not feel Islam as a thorn in the flesh.

The Spanish Christian turned the Moor into his servant, he was seduced by Moorish civilization, and at the same time he took every precaution he could to orient his own life in a different direction. This ternary attitude—service, seduction, precaution—must be remembered if we are not to get lost in the examination of the phenomenon we call Spanish medieval life.

It was in the domain of religious and moral experience that the Christian and the Moor frequently met or avoided each other. We have already seen how Alphonse the Learned included the Koranic doctrine of tolerance in his *Siete Partidas*,[45] and how the warrior-ascetics of Islam became the knights of the Spanish military orders. The latter combined in an integral unity war and holiness in a way that was unknown to Christianity as a whole, but which was nothing more than one aspect of the profound harmony between the spiritual and the material, between contrary values.

The Koran, to begin with, is a personal book, a divine revelation that

---

meaning' in any absolute sense, abstracted from the time when and the person by whom it was said or written. There is nothing that is 'absolutely understandable.' But histories of philosophy are based on the contrary supposition: the doctrines are presented to us as if they had been enunciated by 'the unknown philosopher,' without any date of birth, or any place of habitation, an abstract and anonymous entity who is nothing but the empty agent of the act of saying or writing, and who consequently adds nothing to what has been said or written, who neither qualifies it nor makes it more precise" (*Dos prólogos*, 1944, pp. 157-160).

[45] Or he translates literally from the *Bocados de oro*, a work by the eleventh-century philosopher Abū-l-Wafā Mobāsir:

Franqueza es dar al que lo ha menester e al que lo merece segun poder del dador. . . . El que da al que non ha menester . . . es como el que vierte agua en la mar, etc. (*Bocados de oro*, ed. by Knust, p. 253)	Franqueza es dar al que lo ha menester et al que lo merece segunt el poder del dador. . . . El que da al que non lo ha menester . . . es tal como el que vierte agua en la mar, etc. (*Partida* II, tit. v, law 18)

These passages are from H. Knust's collation of the two texts (in *Mittheilungen aus dem Eskurial*, p. 558). They are a brief indication of how normal it was in Spain to adopt Moslem works treating of morality. It makes no difference that such works owe a great deal to the Greco-Latin tradition and even, as in the case of the *Bocados de oro*, to the Christian tradition.

is part of the existence of one person, the prophet Mohammed. In Christianity the Father is to the Son and to the Word as Allah was later to Mohammed and his Book. The evangelist tells what he has seen and heard, but his own person is not essential; for Christianity does not depend on whether the number of the synoptic gospels is three or more than three. However, "the Koran is only a revelation revealed to *him*" (LIII, 4), the Prophet, the voice of God; for according to certain theologians, there exists an eternal relationship, established by God, between the person of Mohammed and the sacred text, the same relationship as between a lamp and its light.[46] The evangelist's message is more essential than his person, while Mohammed's person is more so than the reality of the Koran. Therefore it was called the supreme reason, the divine emanation, that came to be imprinted in the human reason of individuals.[47] The Book is the Book of God and of Mohammed, and each thing is connected with divinity through the word, the breath of God. Religion is verbalized and personalized. God breathes into things, whose reality, nothing in itself, rests entirely on God. Thus the advent and presence of the divine in the world was felt and enjoyed by the Mohammedan in a way impossible for the Christian, whose interest was in the opposite process, the ascension to God from the finiteness or wretchedness of the world of sensation. The Christian has always suffered from the hammering anguish of original sin, which the Moslem, saved by his faith, has never known. Mohammed made a bridge between the other world and this world, and theology then undertook to give the bridge a foundation in neo-Platonic speculation. The things of this world are also in the other, and vice versa: "For those who have believed and have done the things that are just . . . , for them, the gardens of Eden, in whose shade will run the rivers; they will be covered there with bracelets of gold, they will wear green raiment of silk, and sumptuous brocade, and they will recline upon thrones. Blissful reward and delightful bed!" (XVIII, 30) "And the people on the right hand, Oh, how happy will be the people on the right hand! . . . Of an exquisite creation have we created the houris, and we have made them ever virgins for the people on the right hand" (LVI, 26, 24).

[46] Concerning this theological point, cf. L. Massignon, *La passion d'Al-Hallaj*, pp. 831-832.

[47] According to Massignon, the notion that inspiration of the spirit is a deterministic mechanism whereby the passive souls of those so predestined are impregnated was an idea adopted later by Ibn Masarra and by Ibn 'Arabī, that is, by two Spanish Moslems (one of the ninth, the other of the twelfth century) whose doctrines, as Asín has pointed out, enjoyed a wide degree of acceptance.

There is no essential difference, therefore, between the good things of this world and those of the other, between the reality of the senses and the reality of the spirit, and this will permit an easy interchange and infiltration between the one and the other. Religious belief also leads to the establishment of links between man's existence and the objectivity of what he has lived, and both are fused in the unity of inner, conscious experience and outward expression. When I speak of religion in the Moslem sense, I have in mind the totality of life; for religious belief takes in everything, including what among Christians would be civil institutions of a juridical or political nature. The Bible was read and explained by the priests, and until the thirteenth century it was written in a tongue not understood by the people. The Koran, on the other hand, was a book recited by everyone, it was the language itself, the only language which the Moslems who speak Arabic today still write, a language which precisely because of this circumstance has not broken up into literary dialects.

Now the holy book teaches that man has no freedom: "And it is not possible for the believer, man or woman, to have a choice in his affairs, when God and His apostles have made a decree in a matter" (CIII, 7). "Misfortune did not happen on Earth or in yourselves; we created misfortunes first; *they were in the Book*; for this is easy for God" (XCIC, 22), etc. To be sure, other passages in the Koran, written before the ones quoted, assert the doctrine of the freedom of the will; but I. Goldzieher says very justly that "the sentiment which prevailed in the whole field of the Islamic consciousness was without doubt favorable to the denial of free will."[48] The presence of a God always lurking in nearby ambush, then, was an established belief, and man's freedom was eliminated, and none of the sects that took the part of free will succeeded in altering that indestructible belief. Moslem and fatalist, as everyone knows, amount to the same thing.

What about the derivations from such a faith? If God is the real maker of the small things that we achieve and that happen around us, this means that creation is an eternal present. According to the Moslem, God is doing now the same thing He was doing in the moment of creating this world. There are then no "second causes," for neither nature nor man can be accepted as such. Everything that exists is a point of itself incapable of prolonging itself along a line of continuity. But with the divine impulse the point or instant A can change itself into B—or vice

[48] *Le dogme et la loi de l'Islam*, p. 74.

[334]

versa. That is, the subject can be object, and the object, subject. In such a situation, man renounces the creation of anything with an objective and finished existence, since God is the only one empowered to do this, and man should not aspire to compete with Him. It is only possible and fitting to create realities with "open" or unfinished or extensible lines, figures that may resemble a flower or an animal but which do not imitate them after the Western notion of verisimilitude;[49] or one may draw in the open and undefined manner of the arabesque, or one may fashion the indefinitely reiterated columns of the Mosque of Cordova, or one may tell the "story that never ends" of the *Thousand and One Nights*, or one may write the book that always goes back to its beginning like the Archpriest of Hita's *Libro de Buen Amor*.

Everything in the world, the greatest and the least, has a value, for it is upheld and visited by God at every point and in every moment of its existence, and from these points and moments, as well as from man, any activity can issue. Everything is included in the creative, ceaseless flow of the divine, and everything is a passing moment that leaps toward the moment that succeeds it, all moments being as ephemeral as they are legitimate. Personal consciousness thus includes the inner experience of things and other persons. The Islamic world is a neighborhood of good neighbors, in which the beggar rubs shoulders with the great lord, and what we call the base, the obscene, or the fetid, alternates with the divine as it does in those traditional writings in which we find detailed descriptions of how Mohammed, a man of God, cleans himself after attending to his physiological necessities. For nothing escapes from the perennial flux of divine creation.

But since the stone and the bird do not express themselves, and man does, it happens that man, when he speaks or writes, finds his consciousness filled with an enormous content, for he stuffs it with everything that affects him, near and far. Arabic writers of the tenth century (for example, Mas'ūdī in *The Golden Meadows*) bring a storehouse of things to their works, which bestride zones frequented by no one *simultaneously* in antiquity (Polybius, Pliny, Pausanias, etc.). This is in line with the belief in the intimate and permanent contact that things have with God. The individual consciousness is inflated disproportionately, and then it expands over the life around it—an itinerant consciousness without a fixed headquarters, with changeable seats, as I shall point out in considering Ibn Ḥazm and his disciple the Archpriest of Hita.

[49] L. Massignon, "Les Méthodes de réalisation artistique des peuples de l'Islam," in *Syria*, 1921, II, 47-53, 149-160.

It is quite understandable that the Islamic thinkers, in their reasoning about their special problems, should have turned to the neo-Platonic philosophy of emanation, to the atomism of Democritus, or to anything in Greece or the orient that would fit their inescapable way of looking at life. Simple contact with Greek civilization—in Persia, Syria, and Egypt—would not by itself explain a fact of such magnitude.[50]

One's own consciousness is intensified as a compensatory consequence of the difficulty of arriving at solid and objective structures. In his excellent analysis of the dogmatic theology of Al-Ḥallāj, Massignon says: "The atom is the unique and ultimate element of the reality of every created thing. . . . God, who creates and re-creates atoms every instant, puts them together *according to his whim* to form bodies, *discontinuous, momentary* combinations. Such combinations have no existence of their own; only the atom exists. Everything—from geometrical volumes to human states—*is pure nothing*, subjective and ephemeral accident, superimposed *upon the atom of our hearts.*"[51]

Religion and philosophy are tightly interlaced. The latter does not depend upon an objectified idea or upon intellectual cognition, but on the "atom of the heart." There are other more learned philosophies in Islam, but they are not so close to the religious sentiment of the mass of the people and are less connected with the prevailing ideas and tendencies, which are the ones I am pursuing here precisely because these were the most widespread and the ones that affected the atmosphere in which the Moors and the Spanish Christians came together. Within this style of existence are to be found Sufism, lyricism, autobiography, and the integration of the consciousness with the whole of the person and the circumstances surrounding him—what Ibn 'Arabī calls acting "with one's whole being." The European Christian acted differently; he trusted in the world created by God, made solid by Him and not needing to be recreated at every moment in its tiniest atoms. The Christian rested upon his inner freedom and on the *spiritus spirituatus*—the stabilized

---

[50] See p. 242. Something like this happened in Spain, because each people has the philosophy demanded by its functional structure. The thought of a Descartes or a Kant could fall on deaf ears in Iberia, where neither of these systems bore any kind of fruit. Yet Krause appeared at the beginning of the nineteenth century with his spiritualistic, moralizing, juridical philosophy concerned with the total problem of existence, and the best Spaniards of the age fell upon it and used it to get results that Krause himself could not have thought possible. Something like this is happening today with certain modern philosophies (from Kierkegaard to Dilthey and Heidegger) very popular today in Spain and Latin America.

[51] *La passion d'Al-Ḥallāj*, p. 551.

spirit—of his Church, which said quite distinctly what was good and what was bad, and ordered the world in a graduated hierarchy from the lowest up to God, assigning a different value to every human act. The Moslem, on the other hand, had to carry his life suspended over "the atom of our hearts," with a full and expressed awareness of the *spiritus spirituans* that was acting on the *spiritus spirituatus*. Life and the world were thus inseparable from the process of experiencing them in living and from the awareness of this process—rather like people who can feel the circulation of their own blood.

Medieval literature which is not Islamic or which has no ingrafting of Islamism gives an impression of repose when we compare it with the Islamic—nervous, overflowing its outlines, lacking in reserve, orgiastic. A Western European feels this style as primitivism, vulgarism, and would characterize it as realistic, naturalistic, or shocking. But to do this is to be surprised that fish are good swimmers.

Let us consider for a moment one of the major figures of Islam, Avicenna, or Ibn Sīnā (980-1037), a philosopher and an encyclopedic scholar, who tried to harmonize neo-Platonism with the Koran and thus anticipated Thomas Aquinas' effort to combine Aristotelianism with Catholicism. As in the case of the mystic Al-Ḥallāj, his central problem is God's relationship to the world: "the creative *flux* attests to the essential and constant dependence in which the created being finds itself."[52] Moslem theology was made of genuinely living thought, which penetrated into the remotest corners of individual and collective existence— into the most exalted science and the most naïve faith. Hence, Islamic thought was never secularized, as happened in Christian Europe, which, even in the Middle Ages, was beginning to separate faith and reason, a separation which it finally realized. But I am not going to examine Avicenna's thought; rather I shall take it as an example of how the inner philosophico-theological form is interwoven with the expression of the thought itself.[53] A little treatise of Avicenna's on the "congealing and

[52] Cf. A.-M. Goichon, *La distinction de l'essence et de l'existence d'après Ibn Sīnā (Avicenne)*, 1937, pp. 208ff.; M. Cruz Hernández, *La Metafísica de Avicena*, Granada, 1949; *Sobre metafísica (antología)*, Madrid, 1950.

[53] Perhaps it is not beside the point to recall that according to Medieval Christian theology, God created the world and the world's order, but He is not occupied in the recreation of every specific thing that man makes or does, "the activity sometimes called the 'second creation,' which does not imply a creative act as such" (the article "Creation" in *The Catholic Encyclopedia*, New York, 1908). "The Moslem ideas about creation are naturally far removed from those of a mystic like Eckart: the creature resembles God, his creator, only in that they both possess being. . . . In a unique and simple act God maintains all created things in their being" (*Meister*

agglutination of stones"[54] will serve for this purpose. It is a treatise in which everything is described not as static but *as becoming*. It treats first of mountains, of their formation, of the "formation of stones, of crags, of heights. . . . Many stones are formed from a substance in which dryness predominates. . . . Sometimes the mud dries and changes first into something intermediate between stone and mud, that is, into soft stone and then into real stone." And at this point the author brings his own existence into the work: "*In my childhood I saw*, along the edge of the Oxus, deposits of this mud which the people use to *wash their heads*; later I observed that it had changed into soft stone, and this happened in approximately twenty-three years" (pp. 18-19). The Latin translator rejected this style of existential integralism and changed it into a didactic and objective style: "Scimus quoque quod in terra illa" (p. 46), and provides us thus with an excellent opportunity to measure the distance between two forms of life. The translator found the intrusion of the author's childhood and the washing of heads objectionable, and he abstracted the purely "objective" notions, just as French dramatists were to do centuries later when they translated and adapted the Spanish theatre of Lope de Vega. In Lope things and ideas are habitually mixed together, interwoven, with the existences of the people that experience them. This detail reveals how valuable it would be, from the point of view that I take here, to compare the Latin translations made in Spain with their Arabic originals.

But to continue with Avicenna: "In Arabia there is a stretch of volcanic land that makes everything that lives on it and everything that falls on it change color. *I myself have seen* bread in the form of a loaf—baked, narrow in the middle and with the tooth marks of a bite—which had petrified, but which still preserved its original color, and on one of its sides it still had the marks of oven grooves" (p. 23). The solemn Latin translator confines himself to saying: "Est locus in Arabia qui colorat omnia corpora in eo existencia colore suo. Panis quoque in lapidem conversus est" (p. 47), and thus destroys the tasty slice of life that Avicenna gives us with both more learning and more grace than his heavy-handed interpreter.

Let us now see what happens when an aerolite falls:

Eckehardt: Das System seiner religiösen Lehre, by Otto Karrer, 1926, pp. 72, 77). For what Eckart believes about "being" and the thought of God who creates it, see Käte Oltmans, *Meister Eckehardt*, 1935, p. 117.

[54] *Avicennae de congelatione et conglutinatione lapidum*, published in Arabic, Latin, and English by E. J. Holmyard and D. C. Mandeville, Paris, 1927.

"I consider as authentic, on unimpeachable evidence, an event that happened in Jūzjānān in our own time: A ferrous body, weighing perhaps 150 *mana* [some 300 pounds], fell from the sky, penetrated into the ground, bounced two or three times like a ball thrown against a wall, and then dug itself into the ground again. The people heard a frightful, terrible noise, and when they found the matter out, they took possession of the object and carried it to the governor of Jūzjānān, who wrote about it to the sultan of Khurāsān, a contemporary of ours, the emir Yamīn al-Dawla [whom Avicenna calls by his ten surnames], who commanded that they bring him the object or part of it."

The author goes on, describing the difficulty of handling such a heavy object, and of cutting it, even though they used such and such tools. As a witness to the truth of what he writes, Avicenna mentions a friend of his, a lawyer, who was present at the whole business. A sword was made from the stone of the aerolite:

"I am told that many of the fine swords of Yemen are made from this iron exclusively and that the Arabic poets have described this in their poems" (p. 24).

A natural phenomenon is thus presented in relation to the time in which the author lives, as a human event, stamped with the experience of the people it touches, as a series of developments, each one engendering the next in an open sequence, like a piece of divine creation, and with a final resolution in poetry. Nothing could illustrate better what I have been saying, nor make more evident the deep-lying strata of Hispano-Islamic existence. The Latin translator as a matter of course reduces everything that Avicenna says to an intellectualized abstraction: "Et in Persia cadunt etiam cum coruscatione corpora aerea" (p. 47). Lacking the sensation of the "atom of his heart," he crushes Avicenna, extracts the conceptual juice, and leaves the rest reduced to pulp. If the Spaniards had done the same thing, they would have eventually had a physical-mathematical science, but they would not have produced the art of Lope de Vega or Velázquez or Unamuno, with his poem to the star Aldebaran.

The style of Avicenna insofar as it is a reflection of an inner form of life, is normal in Islamic literature, and is found in works of superior quality as well as in accounts of no special value. And whoever is familiar with the literature and character of the Spaniards is not the least surprised to read such things. This was the style of James the Conqueror, Berceo, Lope de Vega, Gonzalo Fernández de Oviedo, and Saint Teresa, and it is the style of the Andalusian peasant. If I have chosen Avicenna, it is because that great thinker had no contact with Spain, born as he was beyond the Caspian Sea and educated in Ispahan. It is occasionally said that the Spanish Moslems formed their spirit in Spain and absorbed the Hispano-Visigothic culture. These asseverations are always vague, and those who make them never get around to saying clearly and concretely what there is in Spanish Islam that is not to be found in the Islamic civilization of Syria or Egypt. And in any case, it is not possible to cite a single text prior to the advent of the Moslems (Saint Isidore, Saint Braulius, Prudentius, Martial, Seneca, Lucan, Pomponius Mela, etc.) that is conceived in the style of Avicenna's work, where learning is mixed with the tooth marks in a loaf of bread, the washing of heads, "his friend" the lawyer, etc.[55] Whereas this mixture is obvious as soon as we open the earliest major Spanish literary text, the *Poema del Cid*: myth combined with experience, the hero revealing his inwardness and his outwardness, telling jokes, calling Pero Vermudoz mute because he stutters when he talks; another character's crude belching, which makes it possible to guess, from the smell, what the person has eaten; etc. I say this again and again because it is necessary to make it perfectly clear that the so-called historicity of the twelfth-century Spanish epic is only an aspect of its integralism, based, in the last analysis, on five centuries of existence shared with Islam.

Islam endured in spite of sects and dissensions, for the essential thing was the "Book," the declaration of faith ("there is no God but Allah"), and not membership in a church, with a supra-personal structure. What Western Europeans call objective reality was a problem for the Islamic man only when it affected body, soul, and spirit simultaneously. Only in the case of a rare exception, and then for only a limited period of time, was any place left for the luxury of speculative thought as a faculty isolated from sensation and emotion.

Mysticism, quietism, and something like pantheism were frequent in the literature of the Sufis, in a complicated form which the reader may examine in works previously mentioned here. But there is another aspect of Sufism which, although not found exclusively in religious literature, is present there to a more extreme and more evident degree. In this literature, as I have said before, the person appears as the point in which the divine graces (the charisms) converge, and with the divine

---

[55] For Spaniards expressing themselves after the fashion of Avicenna and for the difference between their style and Seneca's, see *La realidad histórica de España*, Mexico, 1954, Appendix 1. In Seneca's philosophy there is a split between one's consciousness and one's body and physical sensations.

graces, that part of the visible and tangible world related to the experience. It is the mystic's special pleasure to recall the circumstances *with* which he has lived until he reaches the moment in which the temporal and accessory fades away. There unfolds then, in his consciousness, as an integral whole, the panorama of the human and the divine. This indeed is what we find in the Murcian mystic Ibn 'Arabī (1165-1240), a tireless narrator of the smallest details of his life, who never forgets time and space. I shall cite an example to show how, at the beginning of the thirteenth century—when Christian literature was incapable of reflecting fully the contemporary reality in which the writer was immersed—a Moslem Sufi tells us perfectly naturally about what happens to him:

"In the year 1201, when I was living in Mecca, I used to frequent the company of certain persons, men and women, all of them excellent people, most cultivated and most virtuous; but among them I saw none to be compared with the learned doctor and teacher Zāhir Benrōstam, a native of Ispahan and a citizen of Mecca, and with a sister of his, the venerable and ancient Bintorōstam, a wise woman of learning from Hedjaz, called 'Glory of Women'. . . . That teacher had a maiden daughter, a slender girl, by whom everyone who contemplated her was ensnared in the chains of love, and whose presence alone was an ornament of gatherings and a wonder to all eyes. Her name was Nizām [Order], and she was also called 'Eye of the Sun.' Virtuous, learned, religious, and modest, *she personified in herself* all the venerable age of the Holy Land and the ingenuous youth of the city faithful to the Prophet. The fascinating magic of her eyes had such charm, and the grace of her conversation (*elegant like that of the natives of Iraq*) was so enchanting, that when she spoke at length, her words were fluent; when she spoke concisely, the result was a wondrous work of art; and when she spoke in figures, she was clear and transparent. If there were not some cowardly spirits, looking for scandal and predisposed to think evil, I would go so far as to ponder here the gifts with which God has endowed her, both in her body and in her soul, which was a garden of generosity. . . .

"During the time I saw her, I carefully observed the gentle gifts that adorned her soul, *and I took them as a constant source of inspiration for the songs that this book contains*, songs that are love poems, made of lovely and gallant phrases, sweet conceits, although I have not succeeded with them in expressing even a part of the emotions that my soul experienced and which the frequent society of the girl excited in my heart, nor a part of the generous love that I felt for her, nor a part of the recollection of her constant friendship left in my memory, nor a part of her kindly spirit, nor a part of the chaste and virtuous countenance of that virginal and pure maiden, *the object of my spiritual longings and desires.* . . . Every name that I mention in this little work refers to her. . . . But in these verses, besides, I allude continually to divine illuminations, to spiritual revelations . . . because the things of the future life are preferable for us to those of the present one, and because, moreover, *she well knew the hidden meaning of my verses.*"[56]

The book inspired by the lovely Niẓām is *The Interpreter of Loves* (Tarjuman al-Ashwāq), edited and translated into English by R. A. Nicholson. The woman as the ideal and stimulus of the creator of spiritual values had been present in Arabic literature since long before 1200 (for example, in the works of the Cordovan Ibn Ḥazm, 994-1063). This was compatible with the common idea that women should confine themselves to the domestic functions of wife and mother. But in Ibn 'Arabī we have an extreme case of an ideal woman, a precursor of Beatrice and Laura, treated not according to a stylistic formula, but, rather, novelistically, that is, by combining the generic and timeless with the experience of the person in a specific time and place. Niẓām spoke like the natives of Iraq. That narrative style, when adopted by the Spaniards, was one day to make possible the novel of Cervantes. Of course Ibn 'Arabī was not attempting, nor would he have been able, to write a novel. He aspired to something different, to enshrining God and Niẓām in his heart. Nor are these books by this great mystic similar to what were later to be called memoirs, for their purpose was not to relate interesting events in which the author had participated, but rather the contrary, to tell everything that had participated in the author's most intimate self. Here the events are pure inner experience. The nearest thing to this form (not a *genre*) of literature would be Saint Teresa's *Life* rather than the *Confessions* of Saint Augustine, in whose consciousness the spectacle of the visible world quickly vanishes. And therefore the recent discovery that Teresa was of Jewish descent has not been a great surprise.

In his urge to capture in his soul reflections of the life around him, Ibn 'Arabī proceeds to give the biographies of fifty spiritual masters, because of the indelible traces those Andalusian mystics left in his existence. One of the holy persons was the Sevillan Nunna Fātima, an old woman past ninety. The feminine influence did not always go hand in hand with the charm of a beautiful young body.

[56] I have used Asín's text in *El Islam cristianizado*, pp. 81-82.

"When I sat down to converse with her, I was ashamed to look at her face, because of the delicacy of her features and the rosiness of her cheeks, even though she was already in her nineties. . . . *With my own hands* I built her a cane hut, in which she dwelt together with two friends of mine. She used to say: 'None of those who come in to speak with me do I like more than so-and-so,' meaning me. They would say to her, 'And why do you say this?' She would answer: 'Because none of them come in to speak with me save with a part of their own beings, leaving outside the rest of their being, that is, their preoccupations with home and family. Only Muḥamad Ibn 'Arabī, my spiritual son and the consolation of my eyes, *when he comes in to speak with me, comes in with his whole being; and likewise, when he gets up as when he sits down, he does it with his whole being, without leaving behind him anything of his own soul.* This should be the course of spiritual life.' "[57]

When the old woman of Seville says "with his whole being" she is describing essentially what I have been calling integralism. The expression of the integralism of Moslem living structure was but an aspect of the functioning of this very structure. The fact that we may find Spanish literary texts paralleling Ibn al-'Arabī's shows how close to each other ran the Spanish and Moslem living structures.

When consciousness of the integralism of one's own life is expressed in writing, the Spaniard portrays his inner self at times as a completed consciousness (con todo su ser) and at times as a part of a larger consciousness or being (Saint Teresa recognizes the Divine presence through physical sensations). Sancho Panza's personality is an outstanding example of the first variety: "existence with all of one's being." Now the point

---

[57] *Vidas de santones andaluces*, tr. by M. Asín, p. 184. Jews found themselves enclosed, of course, in the same integral pattern of life. Ibn Paquda says the following in his *Duties of the Heart*: "The aim and value of the duties of the heart consist in their securing the equal cooperation of body and soul in the service of God, so that the testimony of heart, tongue and the other bodily organs shall be alike, and that they shall support and confirm, not contradict or differ from, each other. . . . On the other hand, the man whose inward thought and outward life are not consistent is condemned in the texts. . . . I have defined the complete recognition of God's Unity as the accord of heart and tongue in the acknowledgment of the Unity of the Creator." Of long standing in Jewish and Oriental tradition is the Spanish habit of having an author question in his book whether or not he should have written it, of entering into personal explanations full of protestations of modesty, either false or authentic, in summary, all that personalist rhetoric to which Spanish and Portuguese-speaking people are so given. Ibn Paquda says: "I saw that a man like myself was not fit to compose such a work. . . . I do not possess an elegant style in Arabic, in which the book would have to be written," etc. But he wrote the book. (Pp. 12, 14, 15, 24 of M. Hyamson's translation, New York, 1925.)

I am trying to make is this: While in Cervantes (and in the aforementioned text of Ibn 'Arabī) we find an awareness of inner existence as unique and complete (consciousness of self *from within* as a totality embracing the exterior world)—in Lope de Vega this same awareness is focussed *from without*. It embraces a pictorial and sensorial vision of the world as an effortless assembly of parts. A foreigner says, for example, in *La ocasión perdida* (The Lost Opportunity):

"I dread nothing in the world save a Spaniard, for he bears the whole world in his soul [tiene en el alma el todo]. If he walks, his whole soul is in his feet. His soul is in his hand when he raises it, or in the grace of his moving body. His spirited speech is surcharged with soul, and so are the glances of his eyes and his raging anger. When horses they ride obey the bit, Spaniards give them their whole soul, and rider and horse are one body. Like Midas, their golden soul turns everything they touch into gold." (Edit. Academia Española, 1930, VIII, p. 215.)

Thus, whatever a Spaniard does (as such a Spaniard) is portrayed by Lope as the expression, on the one hand, of the act itself (perceptible effect, contour of movement) and, on the other, of the life and living impulse behind the act (soul, elan). Like a centaur, these two aspects are always expressed together by Lope—in irretrievable symbiosis. Now it is true that while Cervantes sees this living integralism as emerging from the deepest roots of human life, Lope is hardly so profound. Nevertheless each writer in his own way exemplifies the same thing, the same Hispanic variety of consciousness, at different levels of literary beauty.

If I have spoken of Sufism it has not been to say anything new about its theological content, but simply to reach a point from which to contemplate the present problem. Our Ibn 'Arabī fuses his longing for eternity with his own existence. And in his existence we are shown his person in its most detailed and evanescent aspects: speaking, getting up, sitting down. He gives us his book, *The Interpreter of Loves*, and its genesis in a specific time and place, and he gives us his feeling of the presence of Niẓām within the book—Niẓām, who lived in Mecca in 1201 and spoke with the accent of Iraq. Now we can understand how the Cid, the idealized hero, could bear within himself the Cid the proprietor of some mills on the Ubierna river—mills which historically he really owned, a detail known to the poet and his audience alike. Nothing like this can be found in the style of Lucan's *Pharsalia* whose historicity has an entirely different meaning, being, as it is, a stoic interpretation of Roman life.

This is the vital course on which destiny set the history of Spain, determined to act "with her whole being," in the personalized and peculiarly Hispanic fashion that I have previously analyzed. This course of ambition and anguish has been taken by Spain in her greatest ventures as well as in her most wretched failures, for to live to the utmost—*vivir viviéndose*—is not separable from living in agony—*vivir desviviéndose*. And having adopted this perspective, I find that I have a better understanding of Don Quixote and Sancho Panza, the life of Saint Teresa, and the life of Lope de Vega; and I believe that in general such a perspective makes possible a more accurate perception of the meaning of the phenomena which in modern times have been ineptly called Hispanic realism or individualism. I mentioned before Unamuno's and Ortega y Gasset's objection to the "history of ideas" that have issued from the "unknown philosopher." Behind their objection these writers are postulating ideas "with their whole being," not isolated from the human perspective of which they are integral parts.

Let me return to the Sufis, and to the similarities and differences between Moors and Christians. A consequence of the Islamic form of life as it is presented in paradigm by the Koran was the fact that in the new belief as it followed its triumphal course there was as much room for ascetic renunciation as for sensualism. Among the companions of Mohammed there appeared the type of the very rich and ultra-pious Moslem,[58] thanks to the celestial-terrestrial unity of a belief that was more concerned with the sins of the spirit than the sins of the flesh. Within this framework, it was possible for the Sufis, ascetic as far as creature comforts and the renunciation of wealth were concerned, to combine mystic pursuits with the possession of a beautiful woman and, what is more strange for us, with the languorous contemplation of beautiful young male bodies. 'Abd Allāh of Moron (Seville), "had a most beautiful and very young woman, better than himself and more intense in her spiritual life." Abū 'Alī al-Shakkāz "was a witty man, full of jokes, who liked to joke with the truth"; since his name, *shakkāz*, meant "tanner of flexible and delicate skins" and at the same time "crestfallen," a woman once took the liberty of making fun of the holy man by playing on his name, drawing from Abū 'Alī a very witty reply.[59] Ibn al-'Arabī tells all this as he writes the biographies of the spiritual masters who influenced the course of his life.

In the religious and moral literature of the Christian Middle Ages, the woman symbolized sin. In the Arabic literature of the same type the woman was often an incentive on the journey towards God, and not only

[58] I. Goldzieher, *Le dogme et la loi de l'Islam*, p. 112.
[59] *Vidas de santones andaluces*, pp. 89, 107, 108, 117.

when the woman was as beautiful as Niẓām. The aforementioned Nunna Fātima occupied a high place in mystic life of our Ibn al-ʿArabī, in spite of her ninety years, just as did another old woman, called Sun and Jasmine, of whom he says: "Among the men of God that I have encountered, I have found none to compare with this woman in the fervor with which she mortified her own soul" (*Santones*, p. 180).

The literature of Christian Spain kept silent before such phenomena —the effect of one soul, one life, on another, until Saint Teresa[60] came along to describe the formation of her own spiritual personality, and to tell how her readings and her confessors influenced her. Yet this phenomenon is very frequent in Islamic literature centuries before the Romanic writers had eyes to see such subject matter. We must get rid of the half-true notion that woman was nothing but a piece of physiological reality in Islamic civilization. The important role played by her beauty, her sensibilities, and her spirituality in the art of expression cannot be ignored. Precisely because woman was first and foremost physiological, she led the way to the spiritual, just as from the summits of the realm of the spirit one passed to the plane of sensation. Sometimes, Arabic poetry succeeded in capturing in one expressive impulse the simultaneous anguish of the body and the consciousness—without abstractions and allegorical veils—and in finally reaching a poetic synthesis, just as

[60] Although she is almost a century earlier than Saint Teresa, the nun Doña Teresa de Cartagena could write her *Arboleda de los enfermos* (Garden of the Afflicted, c. 1470) in which we find such passages as the following, motivated by anguish over being totally deaf: "If you look closely, you will find me more alone when I am in the company of many than when I withdraw to my cell. The cause is this: when I am alone, I am accompanied by myself and such poor sense as I have [that is, by her awareness, expressed with false modesty, that she is a very intelligent woman] but when I am with others, I am completely forlorn, for I can neither find pleasure in their company and speech, nor can I find any comfort within myself. My sense leaves me, for it is occupied with feeling the extraordinary affliction which I feel; reason departs with the very explainable torment that I feel afflicting it. . . . Where hearing fails, what good is talking; what good my presence, lifeless and altogether alone?" (edition of M. Serrano y Sanz, in the *Biblioteca de escritoras españolas*, 1, 220). Speaking of women, she says: "The coarse mind of a woman makes what I say of little or no authority" (p. 222). Many years ago I thought this passage an anticipation of "modern" psychology; today I see it as a growth from the Hispano-Islamic trunk, very ancient and at the same time very modern. I have been unwilling to accept the insufficiently founded arguments regarding Doña Teresa de Cartagena's descent, even though I have been much interested in the question they have sought to answer. However, recent investigations have established the fact that the nun was indeed descended from the converted Jew Pablo de Santa María. Thus, the figure of Doña Teresa de Cartagena, with the remarkable awareness and analysis of the innermost self in her autobiographical confessions, anticipates Saint Teresa, likewise of Jewish descent, by a century.

the graceful rose, on opening, gives us the essence and the meaning of the plant from which it takes its life.

Let the reader judge for himself, even though he must remember that he is reading through a translation, and that translations always bruise the delicate candor of the original expression. I take as example some verses of Ibn Faraj, a native of Jaen (Andalusia), who died in 976. The speaker in the poem is a chaste man, influenced, no doubt, by the Sufistic spirit, which gave shelter to the pure as well as to the sensual:

> Although she was ready to give herself to me, I
>   held off from her, and did not obey the tempta-
>   tion that Satan presented to me.
> She appeared without veil in the night, and the
>   nocturnal shadows, lightened by her face,
>   likewise that once lifted their veils.
> There was no look of hers in which there were not
>   powers to make hearts leap.
> But to the divine precept, which
>   condemns lechery, I gave power over the capricious
>   charging of the steed of my passion, so that my
>   instinct might not rebel against chastity.
> And so, I passed the night with her like the thirsty young
>   camel whose muzzle keeps him from sucking.
> Like a flower garden, where for one like me
>   there is nothing to enjoy save sight and smell.
> For I am not like the abandoned beasts who treat gardens
>   as if they were pastures.[61]

If our ears could vibrate as sympathetically to the words of the original Arabic as they can to the familiar words of Dante, so skilled in the affective use of meaningful sounds—

> Amore e 'l cor gentil sono una cosa . . .
> Donna pietosa e di novella etate . . . ,

—then we would grasp the full value of the Ibn Faraj's poetry. But there would always remain considerable differences between the art of the Andalusian and the art of the Florentine. In Dante, the poetry appears to be detached from the poet in a sequence of objective value judgments:

[61] Translated into Spanish by E. García Gómez in *Poemas arábigo-andaluces,* p. 104.

Tanto gentile e tanto onesta pare . . .
La vista sua fa onne cosa umile,

so immediately beautiful and captivating to our Western ears that we
surrender without reserve to its enjoyment, without wondering about
the person who expresses himself in these words that are at once of a
quivering fragility and an eternal solidity. The existence of the speaker
in such poetry is not present as an essential poetic element. But in the
preceding Arabic poetry (leaving aside for the moment questions of
relative merit) the existence of its poetic agent is essential. This agent is
a soul visited by desires so violent that, when they are left unsatisfied,
the poetical agent feels that the substance has gone out of his life. The
void of love is then filled with the totality of the person's feeling: "I
am not like the abandoned beasts," an expression which at first sight is
reasonable and anti-climactic, although the intensity of the metaphor
gives evidence of the high price paid for the moral luxury of renunciation. The idea common to Stoicism, Christianity, and Islam is transformed here into a process of total and poetic life, not into a simple moral
lesson. The woman is at once a sin and a wonder, whose unveiled brightness dispels the shadows of the night. Three centuries before Dante was
born, there was poetry to say that a human being's beauty diffuses its
radiance: "the nocturnal shadows, lightened by her face, likewise that
once lifted their veils" (per che si fa gentil ciò ch'ella mira). The poetry
of Ibn Faraj has nothing to do, then, with the theme of the anchorite
and his temptations, so congenial to the writers of lives of the saints.
The anchorite struggles objectively with temptation, and subjects himself to harsh penances or implores divine help. But in our Arabic poem
the temptation is a perfectly beautiful creature who is esteemed as such.
The resistance to the senses stems from the moral conscience: "But to
the divine precept . . . *I gave power*" (God and myself, not scourges
and prayers); "*I am not* like the abandoned beasts."

In the rather confused arguments about the relation between Romance
and Islamic poetry it has perhaps been forgotten that there is a difference
between the expression of *what the lyrical agent of the poem feels* and
the expression of his feelings *as a vital* process, as a section of becoming in
his own existence, in which the inner and the outer are one and indivisible. In the last analysis, the Hispanic element in the *Poema del Cid*,
the element that is not found in the European epic, or in Lucan, or in
any other writer, is this: "With his eyes weeping violently," my Cid
"turned his head" and looked at his house that he had to leave, that

stayed there with its doors open, without locks, the perches bereft of their falcons. But the hero saddened by the king's injustice reacts quickly:

> My Cid shrugged his shoulders, and shook his head:
> "Good news, Albar Fáñez; we are cast out of the land!
> But with great honor we shall come back to Castile." (13-14)

A saddened soul reacts upon itself and bursts out in a shout of joy and decision. For a first moment he weeps and sighs ("my Cid sighed, for he had very great cares"), but immediately he shakes his head and speaks hopefully. There is an essential difference between this and scenes in the *Chanson de Roland* that are superficially similar to it:

> Li quens Rollant revient de pasmeisuns:
> Sur piez se drecet, mais ad grand dulur.
> Guardet aval e si guardet amunt, etc. (2,233-2,335)

We see Roland inside his sphere of myth, in an intemporal present (drecet, guardet); the Cid is carrying out a continued action in the past (estávalos catando); from within his myth Roland contemplates the dead Turpin, another myth; while the Cid looks at doors, locks, perches and no falcons. Roland is shut off in a mythic narration which immobilizes him. The Cid moves under his own power, as it were. He is sometimes in low spirits, sometimes in high spirits, and the movements of his body and the things that exist around him (an abandoned mansion, the flight of crows, etc.) all figure integrally in the condition of his soul. Such phrases as "with weeping eyes" (llorando de los ojos), the commonplaces of epics, thus have a different function here. But most important is the fact that the Cid (like the Arabic poet quoted above) gives power to "a precept" by the change in his spirit. The precept, although not stated, is perceptible: A leader, a *caudillo*, must inspire confidence in his people, and he must do this with good humor and the opportune use of irony: "Good news, Albar Fáñez; I tell you that they have expelled us from the kingdom!" The rigid frame of narrative objectivity has been broken, and in its place we have a descriptive style. We see life in the present and from the inside.

The Sufis: Ascetics and Mystics

Asceticism and mysticism found ready and abundant expression in Islam.[62] The structure of the new religion made it possible for the Mos-

---

[62] The following is a selective bibliography that does not pretend to be complete: M. Asín, *Abenmasarra y su escuela* (Origins of Hispano-Moslem Philosophy), 1914.

lem to find both Christian neo-Platonism and Buddhism meaningful. Ideas, I repeat, do not travel as baggage in the caravans of history. They are inseparable from the man-world complex in which they have their existence and their meaning. The Moslem believer's relationship with his faith (his God) was both more immediate and more casual than the Christian's. In the Moslem's case, the terms of the relationship were the believer, the sacred book, and God; the religious bond was established through ritual prayer, the pilgrimage to Mecca, fasting, and alms-giving. There was not properly speaking a visible church, or sacraments such as penance and communion to bind the faithful together in a spiritual community. The paths between the Christian and God were traced out and guarded by the spiritual and political authority of the Church, externalized in a strict hierarchy that was formerly patterned after the government of the Roman Empire. To be a Christian consisted first of all in recognizing this hierarchy made up of God's ministers, the only persons authorized to administer the sacraments and perform the rites of the Church, and to supervise their use. In this way the area of external regulation was broader than the area of the free operation of the conscience—the direct contact with the spirit of God. There is a great contrast here with the situation of Islam, which actually had no priests or a church with a hierarchy. Their place was taken by the men learned in the Koranic law—the *faqīhs* and imams who directed the prayer in the mosques. The believers had a direct relationship with God and with his Prophet, through prayer and spiritual works, and this brought with it a more personal, a freer attitude, than that of the average Christian. We find the Sufistic sects already established about the end of the seventh or the beginning of the eighth century, and consisting of ascetics and mystics who wore a garment made of coarse wool (ṣūf). The center of religious life was prayer, the naming of Allah (dhikr):[63a]

R. A. Nicholson, *The Mystics of Islam*, 1914. I. Goldzieher, *Le dogme et la loi de l'Islam*, 1920. R. A. Nicholson, *The Idea of Personality in Sufism*, 1923. Ibn Ḥazm, *Los caracteres y la conducta*, tr. by M. Asín, 1916. Fundamental for the study of Ibn 'Arabī, the great mystic of Murcia, is M. Asín's work, *El Islam cristianizado*, 1931. M. Horten, *Die Philosophie des Islam*, pp. 236. A. E. Affifi, *The Mystical Philosophy of Muhyid Din-Ibnul 'Arabī*, 1939. M. Asín, *Vidas de santones andaluces*, by Ibn 'Arabī, 1933. M. Asín, *Huellas del Islam*, 1941. Also other books previously mentioned.

[63a] This is behind the recurrent mentioning of God in Spanish, where it is more frequent than in the other Romance languages. When Lazarillo says, "God made me encounter a squire," he is talking like Saint Teresa: "God is among the pots and pans." The mention of God is not connected with an inner state of religious tension, nor does it have any of the solemnity of such phrases as "*fate* would have it" that

"Remember Allah frequently" (Koran, XXXIII, 14); with quietistic abandon it rested entirely on the will of God (tawakkol). Sufism immediately found itself with numerous disciples, whose position was actually opposed to the official practice of the Mohammedan ritual of the majority of the faithful. A similar movement within the Christian church would have meant a very serious danger, and would have been contrary to the nature of the Church itself. When the Albigensian heresy broke out in the twelfth century, it had to be suppressed by the combined power of the Church and the State.

The Sufistic spiritual life made it possible, as early as the tenth century, to reach such heights of expression as we find in the poetry of Ibn Faraj's thanks to the absence of distinction between the divine and the earthly, between doctrine and the expression of the person's total existence. This is the way to the understanding of Saint Teresa's Spanish art, which gains little by being broken down and catalogued according to the themes of universal mysticism, timeless, landless, colorless, tasteless.

Gonzalo de Berceo

Here is the first Castilian poet who can be named: Gonzalo de Berceo, whose lifetime bridges the twelfth and thirteenth centuries. His subject matter is religious and international: the lives of saints, the miracles of the Virgin Mary. His versification, the fourfold way, is of French origin. Nevertheless, Berceo produces a characteristic, strange impression, which it is customary to attribute to his ingenuous candor, to his primitivism.[63b] The poet himself tells us all we know about his life in a brief autobiographical stanza:

> Gonzalo was the name of him who wrote this book;
> In San Millán de Suso was he brought up from childhood;
> A native of Berceo, where San Millán was born:
> God keep his soul from the power of Satan.
> (*Vida de San Millán*, stanza 489)

He refers to himself frequently, not out of vanity, but because he is

---

this or that should happen; it is an everyday expression, a reflection of the continuous presence of God, of his influence in both the most exalted and the most trivial. Like many other usages, this one passes as perfectly Christian, and it is, although it is peculiar to Spanish Christianity.

[63b] According to G. Guerrieri Crocetti, *Gonzalo de Berceo*, Brescia, 1947, Berceo's style is both candid and plebeian; "his is a strong and primitive coarseness" (p. 161). The criticism of this most learned Romanist—surprised to find such a kind of literature in Christian Europe—suits my purpose extremely well.

conscious of fulfilling his holy mission as he writes, and he incorporates his own process of writing into his writing.[64] Berceo, who was a priest acquainted with Latin and French, lived an inner life that was shaped like any other Spaniard's, and I have already pointed out what this means. At the beginning of the *Vida de Santo Domingo de Silos*, he announces that he is writing in a language that everyone can understand for the good reason that he is not sufficiently schooled to write in Latin:

> I seek to make a work in plain Romance,
> In which the people customarily speak to their neighbors;
> For I am not so learned as to make one in Latin:
> It will be well worth, *so I believe*, a glass of good wine.
>
> (Stanza 2)

On another occasion he says that he does not know where a certain event took place, because the manuscript in which he read about it was confused and the Latin of the passage in question was difficult:

> The parchment does not identify the town very well,
> For it was in bad handwriting, in obscure Latin;
> *I could not* understand it, by the Lord Saint Martin.
>
> (Stanza 609)

Sometimes he cannot say what he would like to, and blames the inadequacy of his source:

> Whether he was of lineage, or whether he was a peasant,
> The text does not say, and *I do not know*.
>
> (Stanza 338)

His story is chopped off because the manuscript that he is following is missing a section:

> How he got out [of prison] I could not say,
> For the book in which I learned about it failed:

---

[64] He says that Saint Dominic of Silos
> "Built the church, you may well believe . . .
> *I, Gonzalo, who write this* for the love of him,
> *I saw the church*; so may I see the face of the Creator."
> (*Vida de Santo Domingo*, 108-109)

Saint Oria had a vision in which she saw a column:
> "The column had steps in it;
> We often see such built into towers;
> *I have climbed up some of them*, this, many times."
> (*Santa Oria*, 39)

It hardly seems necessary to quote more passages.

A quarto was lost, *but not by my fault*;
To write by guess would be a great folly.

(Stanza 751)

The passages quoted are sufficient to show how the poet includes his own process of writing in his writing.[65] It has been said that Berceo is a candid and primitive artist, but this ignores the fact that there is nothing naïve in the skill of his versification or in the spirit of propaganda in which he promotes the interests of the monasteries with which he was connected. As a narrator of miracles and wonders, Berceo is neither less nor more naïve than the other medieval writers who have treated of such matters. What has happened is that the historians, upon discovering the "integralism" of his style, no doubt surprising, have explained it by calling it candor and primitivism. The truth is that Berceo combines the Hispano-European perspective (Latin sources, Christianity, miracles) and Hispano-Islamic perspective, projected into his time through a vital distance of five hundred years.

Thus Berceo's own personality will reveal itself. If we analyze his work objectively in terms of topics and metrical forms, he shows up as a "typical" medieval writer, lacking in genius and of no significant originality. Why, then, does he delight the reader of today? My own generation was highly entertained by him in school, even before we could understand very well what he was saying. Then came his renascence, and Azorín, Rubén Darío, Antonio Machado, and others have referred to his style, in Azorín's phrase, as "spontaneous, jovial, plastic, informal." For Rubén Darío, his verse

> Has freedom with decorum,
> And returns, like the falcon to the wrist,
> Bringing rhymes of gold from the blue.

Antonio Machado has written that

> His verse is sweet and grave; monotonous rows
> Of winter poplars, in which nothing sparkles;
> Lines like furrows in brown fields,
> And far away, the blue mountains of Castile. . . .
> And he said: "My work is not minstrelsy;
> We have it in writing, it is true history."

[65] When Gautier de Coincy wants to express something that is not in harmony with the objectivity of his miracles of the Virgin (such as criticism of contemporary society), he brings it in at the end of the miracle as an appendix.

There is here something more than the enthusiasm of a generation, or a taste for the antique. Berceo entered into the souls of these exceptional readers and of lesser ones because of his style, "spontaneous, jovial, plastic, informal," not because of his subject matter, but because of how he experienced it, how it exists in him.

Let us look at the story of Saint Dominic, Abbot of Silos in the eleventh century.[66] A monk of that monastery, named Grimaldus, wrote a Latin account of the life of Saint Dominic, who later came to be called "thaumaturge," because he had worked extraordinary miracles both during his life and after his death. In a style that seems "spontaneous" and "plastic" to us, Berceo elaborated the Latin biography poetically. Actually it is a personalized style in which we feel the presence of the author just as we do in the Sufistic texts quoted above. He treats Saint Dominic as a miracle-worker whom God favors with charisms similar to those we found in the lives of the Sufis. Berceo relates the miracles with crude naïveté; the miraculous is surrounded with details of the elemental aspects of life that stand in sharp contrast with the artifice of form, which was imitated from French models by the most cultivated poets in Spain. The miracle ranges from cries uttered by the sick to the manifestation of the divine spirit, brought down to earth by the virtue of the saint. Here, for example, is a blind man, tortured by a terrible earache:

> In the neighborhood of Silos, we do not know what town,
> There was a blind man, of him we will tell you.
> How he became blind, that we have not read;
> What is not written we do not assert.
> John was his name, if you wish to know it . . . ,
> Besides this affliction . . .
> He was so sick in the ears, *that he gnawed the walls.* (336-337)

Then he is taken to Saint Dominic's house:

> The wretched man would not *beg for wine or bread*;
> But he said: "Oh, father, by Saint Millan,
> Be thou distressed by this my longing . . .
> Put thy hand upon me, sign me with thy thumb;
> Could I but kiss thy hand,
> I would be healed of all this affliction. (340-342)

The holy monk then

> With the hyssop sprinkled him with salt water,

[66] Cf. M. Férotin, *Histoire de l'abbaye de Silos*, 1897.

He signed his eyes with the sacred cross,
The pain and the affliction was eased then,
The light that he had lost was all recovered. (348)

The sensory phenomena enter our experience through an elemental language, in an atmosphere of solemnity and wonder. At the end of the twelfth century there lived in Seville a certain Abū-l-Ḥajjaj Yūsuf, one of Ibn ʿArabī's spiritual masters. Ibn al-ʿArabī relates:

"Once when I was in his house with several other people, a man came in to visit him who was afflicted with pain in his eyes so great that it made him *cry out like a woman in childbirth*. The man, then, made his way through the people (who were much distressed to hear his cries). The master *changed color*, and trembling with compassion, stretched out his blessed hand and put it over the eyes of the sick man. At once the pain was calmed, and *he fell to the floor on his side*, as if he had died. But then he got up again, and went away from there together with all the people, and had no pain whatsoever. He then became one of the master's disciples." (Asín, *Vidas de santones*, p. 84.)

A miracle characteristic of peninsular life is the freeing of captives. One of Saint Dominic's followers fell into the hands of the Moors:

They put him irons and in hard chains . . .
They gave him *bad dinner* and *supper that was not good.*
If they would give it to him, he would gladly eat oaten
bread. (355)

His kinfolk went to the saint and begged him to free the man. Saint Dominic implored divine aid, and

The captive escaped from his captivity.
The irons in which he lay enchained fell open,
The enclosure, which was well closed, did not hold him;
He went back to his kinfolk bearing the irons;
He himself marveled at this. (368-369)

The spiritual master Abū Madyan rendered a similar service to Mūsā al-Baydarānī, unjustly condemned to imprisonment by the Sultan of Morocco:

"He was accused before the Sultan, who ordered him seized and put into chains. They were bringing him, laden with chains, into the Sultan's presence; but when they were near Fez, they put him in a room of one of the inns on the road, and they locked it with a key, putting guards there, besides, to watch him during the night. The next day, when it dawned, they opened the door and they found the chains which he had worn, thrown on the floor, but him they did not find." (Asín, *op.cit.*, p. 147.)

Saint Dominic being the abbot of Silos, the steward came to inform him that the monastic pantry was absolutely empty. The abbot spoke to the community thus:

> I see, dearly beloved, that *you are murmuring*,
> Because our refectory is so empty. (447)

He promised to relieve the penury, and he addressed his fervent prayers to God:[67]

> Send Thou us food for our needs,
> So that this convent be not broken up . . .
> You see how this convent *is murmuring*,
> All are turning against me, I am in bad
>   straights. (451, 453)

After a little a messenger appeared with the good news that the king had given the monastery

> Three times twenty measures of fine flour (457)

so that the abbot recovered the confidence of the monks:

> Those that doubted before now repented,
> Because the father's promises came true. (461)

For a similar reason the Sufi mystic Abū Ja'far found himself in difficulties, not with a monastic community but with his family. He had abandoned his labor to devote himself to solitary communion with God. His wife used to abuse him to try and make him give up such an unproductive enterprise and, instead, work to procure the necessities of the family household. The good ascetic called on God in much the same terms as Saint Dominic: "Lord, this woman is going to be an obstacle between me and Thee. . . . If Thou wishest me to devote myself to Thy communion, deliver me from the worries of my wife." The Lord promises him that that very day He will grant him *"twenty sacks of figs, enough to keep thy family for two and a half years, and even more and more. . . . The sun had not yet set, and I already had the twenty sacks.*

[67] The Moslem mystics do the same thing. Compare:

The holy confessor prayed all night to the King of the heavens. (*Santo Domingo*, stanza 345) He spent all that night in solitude praying to God. . . . (*Santones*, p. 150)

My wife and the children were filled with happiness, and besides my wife thanked me, completely satisfied with me" (*Santones*, p. 59). Notice how religious meditation presented the same risks and the same edifying examples both among Moors and Christians.

These miracles have their complement in those worked by various holy men after their death—miracles that were known in Hispania, naturally, before the coming of the Moslems. Saint Braulio of Saragossa, who died in 646, gives a sober and objective account of several miracles performed by the Spanish Saint Emilian: "Sed hoc solum dignum putavi scriptis tradere quod illico post ejus transitum duo oculis orbati redditi sunt lumini" (*Patrologia*, S. L., LXXX, 713). Furthermore, the tomb of Saint Emilian has the power to restore the exhausted oil and extinguished flame of a sanctuary lamp: "plenam oleum ardentemque repererunt" (*ibid.*). At this point there is nothing more than a simple, informative method of writing, for the integralist, vitalized style does not yet exist. Let us see, indeed, what Berceo does with the sentence "duo oculis orbati redditi sunt lumini." He begins by saying that two penniless blind men lived in a certain village. They heard the news of the miracles performed by the saint, and they conceived the hope of having their sight restored. With their guides they left their houses and went along, digging into the ground with their staffs. When they reached the tomb they were still in their unfortunate condition, but they could already feel happiness in their hearts. They began to cry out, because this is what blind men do:

> They gave great cries, *for such is their nature.* (325)

As a result of their clamorous petitions, both blind men got their sight back. The abstract concepts of Saint Braulio have been converted into the sense imagery of the two blind men who walk along digging their staffs in the ground, who have misfortune in their eyes but happiness in their hearts, who call out in piercing cries such as were made by the blind men that Berceo knew. Here is another effort to express an integral portion of life, in which the inner and the outer are well joined together, including the corporal, the affective, and the spiritual. When Berceo later comes to elaborate the bald datum of the miracle of the lamp, he tells us that the lamp

> Never, neither days nor nights, was without oil,
> Save when the minister changed its wick. (331)

The writer feels the compulsion to express the total existence of the lamp, and to do this he must mention the only moment at which the lamp was ever without oil.[68]

From what happened as I have described it we may infer that around the year 1200 a vital connection between the miracle and the person who recounted it had been created. This connection did not exist in accounts belonging to the Visigothic epoch, nor—I add—in the Latin texts contemporary with Berceo, nor in the Frenchman Gautier de Coincy. If we recall Berceo's texts, we see that the account of the miracles includes the person who tells them, the circumstances under which he writes, the circumstances surrounding the miracle, and the vital reactions, be they sublime or base, of those involved in it.

Berceo's miracles, Christian in essence and in tradition, appear to us as experienced within a vital "dwelling-place" that is related to the peculiar Hispano-Islamic tradition. This is the vital meaning of the fact that the author includes within the poem his consciousness of himself making his poem.

The miracles which Ibn 'Arabī attributes to the fifty spiritual masters who had served him as models and supports are all parts of a long tradition of Sufi beliefs deeply rooted in the Islamic world. This is where the presence of Berceo in his own work comes from, and not from naïve and primitive spontaneity:

> I Gonzalo, who make this in his honor,
> *I saw it* [the church of Saint Dominic]:
> A good-sized kitchen, built without thought of cost. (109)
> I, Gonzalo by name, called of Berceo,
> Live, thanks to Saint Emilian's monastery, that brought me up:
> I had a very great desire to do this work.(757)

However fleeting these appearances of Gonzalo himself may be, they are enough to give the flavor of experienced reality to the impersonal theme of his narration. The narration too appears to be coming into existence as it reveals the inner process of its fabrication. The monotony of the account is broken, and the modern reader experiences a pleasure

[68] A miracle with the motif of a lamp but much more vitalized than the one to which Saint Braulius and Berceo refer, was to be found in the Islamic tradition: "When the hour of sunset had come, we prayed the ritual prayer, and, as the master of the house in which we were staying delayed in lighting the lamp, my friend said: 'I would wish that the lamp were already lighted.' Abū 'Abd Allāh said to him: 'Very well.' And taking a handful of dry grass from the room in which we were in one hand, he struck it with his index finger and cried out, while we watched to see what he was going to do: 'Here is the fire.' And indeed, the grass took fire, and with its flame we lighted the lamp" (*Santones*, p. 144).

he has not expected. The condiment that is responsible for this pleasing taste is simply something of the Islamic way of expressing life—though to be sure, no more than a bit of this manner, for not until Saint Teresa did anyone in Spain equal or excel the Sufis in the art of expressing the totality of personal existence. Whereas Ibn 'Arabī, a contemporary of Berceo, was already writing in this fashion:

"Once I went into the house of this master, and he said to me, 'Worry about yourself, Oh my little son!' I said to him, 'Our Master Ahmad, whom I have visited, has told me, "Oh my little son, worry about God!" Whom, then, am I to heed?' He answered me, 'Oh my little son. I am with my own soul and Ahmad is with God; each of us tells you what his own spiritual state demands that he tell you.' "[69]

Here it is appropriate to add that Berceo's autobiographical style is different from that style in certain contemporary French works which to superficial observation appear to be similar to it. In the *Jeu d'Adam*, composed around the end of the twelfth century, the religious subject was seen in a human perspective as something in line with the experience of the audience and without any halo of divine mystery. The sin of the first man was presented as the result of matrimonial disloyalty: Eve promises not to reveal a secret to her husband (Il n'en saura rien); the Devil excites her vanity and her coquetry (À ton beau corps, à ta figure, Conviendrait bien cette aventure); later she will tell Adam that the Devil "m'a parlé de notre honneur." Here then we again find the divine experienced in a secular and earthly perspective, as is characteristic of the functioning of the French history-life. The French writer dislodged the divine transcendence from its supra-human position and brought it within the human framework as an objectified reality: *Gesta Dei per Francos*.

Berceo approaches the divine themes from the opposite direction. In the miracle of the lascivious sacristan (*Milagros*, 75-99) there is a debate between the Virgin and the Devil over who has the right to the soul of the sinful sacristan. The litigating parties have recourse to the procedures of human justice, but the trial itself is seen in a divine perspective, as a lawsuit tried according to the gospel and submitted to Christ for decision. The human theme is given a divine orientation—"vuelto a lo divino," as was to be said of certain literature belonging to the end of the sixteenth century, and as is always the case in Berceo.

This distinction between French and Castilian literature in regard to

[69] *Santones*, p. 94. Cf. also Asín, *El Islam cristianizado*, *passim*.

the treatment of religious themes also applies to the autobiographical aspect, as well as to what is loosely called "realism." Berceo and his French contemporaries are not "realists" of the same kind. Let us consider for example the *Jeu de la feuillée*, by Adam le Bossu (c. 1276), in which the author is also one of the characters and as such talks about his family and about people who lived in Arras, where the *jeu* was played. The author tells coarse jokes, such as that he is going to anoint his body with mustard so as to repel his wife now that she has lost her charms: "grasse, sans taille, triste et grincheuse." He mentions his father's avarice, and makes jokes at the expense of certain citizens of Arras to make the audience laugh. Works of this kind are the antecedents of those which Alphonse the Learned, in the *Siete Partidas*, forbade to be represented by the clergy in the churches: "They must not be performers of plays of mockery [juegos de escarnio] for the people to come and see them . . . , for God's church is made for prayer and not as a place for the performance of mockeries" (1, v, xxxiv). The mention of such *juegos de escarnio* in the thirteenth century is explained by the presence of numerous French clerics in Spain from the eleventh century on. All that remains of these representations is their name and the reference to the fact that they existed. The fact that they bore no fruit in the Spanish tradition suggests that their existence was somewhat marginal, not genuinely related to Castilian life. As opposed to this, we can still perceive today a distant echo of the medieval *jeux* in the art of the French cabaret entertainers, who lash at the spectators with invective or talk about themselves with absolutely shameless candor. (Needless to say, between the representation and the real person speaking, whether today or in the thirteenth century, there is interposed as a kind of heavy insulation the irony and sarcasm of a conventional art, which does not claim to be, and has no reason to be, sincere.)

Adam le Bossu converted his person and the circumstances of his life into the literary matter of his *jeu*, in which the boundary between the extra-literary reality and the artistically constructed reality is blurred. In the *jeu*, Maître Adam speaks as a theatrical character within the play, not as an "I" trying to set off his own existence against the existence represented in the play. Gonzalo de Berceo, quite the contrary, shows himself in the interstices of his work as an extra-literary person, an admixture in the constituent matter of the poetic narration. In this narration, for instance, it is told that Saint Oria saw a staircase in a vision. But Berceo does not leave it at that: There are staircases like that one in the tower of certain churches, he says, and moreover, "I have gone up some of them, and have done this frequently." This *I* is positively heterogeneous to the poetic matter. Such phenomena have one modern counterpart in the motion picture when a portrait is represented as suddenly changing—coming to life, we call it—into a living person. In Berceo this was done without ironic intent. Nor was there any such intent in his Moslem contemporaries and precursors (Ibn 'Arabī, Ibn Ḥazm, etc.) when they insinuated the awareness of their individual selves into their literary constructions. The passages quoted already, and others that will be brought in later, provide examples of what I am saying. The "realism" of which I speak, then, has no connection with French literature, whose presence in Castile is manifested in other ways.

The distinction I have established between Berceo and certain of his French contemporaries who include something of their own life in their work might be understood, if we go into it a little more deeply, as a contrast between two different literary forms—the autobiographical confession and memoirs. In the former, the writer presents himself as existing in the privacy of his own consciousness. In the latter, the interest is focussed on what happens around the life of the author, on that in which the author has participated in some way or other. The autobiographical thread which runs through Berceo's poetry is spun from Islamic wool. In this connection I have in mind the Book of Job, the *Confessions* of Saint Augustine—a Semite, Islamic confessions and autobiographies, Saint Teresa's *Life*, *Lazarillo de Tormes*, *Guzmán de Alfarache*, etc. French classic literature is as rich in memoirs as it is poor in authentic confessions. The autobiography of Guibert de Nogent, *De vita sua*, of the end of the 11th century, which has more than one oriental feature, seems rather exceptional. As for Montaigne's *Essais* it should be kept in mind that his mother was a Spaniard of Jewish extraction.

The Cantigas of Alphonse the Learned

The Castilian language of the thirteenth century had not yet acquired a lyric dimension. Berceo narrated the miracles of the Virgin Mary in a tone of emotion, but his inner feelings were transformed into an objectified account. His *Praises of Our Lady*, when they are not narrative and didactic, are expressed in the style of prayers without any subjective tinge. The uniform and monotonous stanza of the fourfold way is in itself objectified poetry—hieratic, part of a pre-established order of belief, worship, and doctrine.

Alphonse's *Cantigas* are something else again. Their expressive form does not come from French sources, but from the Arabic stanza called the *zajal*.[70] This provenience was in part direct (Alphonse's court was full of Moslem scholars), and in part through Galician literature, where the stanza was already in use. The *zajal* is variable and flexible, and, moreover, those in the *Cantigas* were written to be sung. This is why the modern reader, knowing only their texts, does not always find them artistically satisfying. The poet combined his words with a musical melody addressed to the soul and not to the understanding, and in this way accentuated the lyrical feeling, which was incompatible with the regular beat of the fourfold way:

> Rosa das rosas e fror das frores,
> Dona das donas, Sennor das sennores.
> Rosa de beldad e de parecer,
> e fror d'alegria e de prazer;
> dona en mui pïadosa seer,
> Sennor en toller coitas e dolores.
> Rosa das rosas e fror das frores.[71]

The stanza here is the *zajal*: the expression of inner feelings led the poet in Castile directly or indirectly into the domain of Arabic humanism. The fact that Galician poetry and Alphonse the Learned use the *zajal* is not an external phenomenon: poetic form is not merely the label of poetry. With the Italian hendecasyllable, Petrarchianism and the neo-Platonic idea of love were to come into Spanish poetry three centuries later:

> Yo no nací sino para quereros,
> mi alma os ha cortado a su medida.[72]
> (Garcilaso)

---

[70] For the forms of this stanza and its adoption in Romance literature, see R. Menéndez Pidal, "Poesía árabe y poesía europea," in *Bulletin Hispanique*, 1938, XL, 337-423.

[71] In English:

> Rose of roses, flower of flowers,
> Lady of ladies,
> Rose beautiful in appearance,
> And flower of happiness and delight;
> Your ladyship shows in your mercy,
> Your ladyship shows in your taking away cares and sorrows.
> Rose of roses and flower of flowers.

[72] In English:

> I was born only to love you,
> My soul has cut you out to its measure.

Likewise in the case of Alphonse, the metrical form symbolized a new way of conceiving of man poetically. For if 335 of the 402 *Cantigas* of Alphonse the Learned are in the form of the *zajal*, something of the Islamic conception of life must lie beneath this poetic phenomenon. What it is, is that very outpouring of the "atom of our heart," as Al-Ḥallāj would say, an activity which the Castilians, with their need for intellectual discipline and prudence, had deemed to be dangerous before the fourteenth century. The history of poetry is not to be understood by decomposing it into its formal techniques and its motives or themes, which we convert into prose the moment we objectify them and abstract them from the unity which is the poetical expression of a poetical content. The verse "Rosa das rosas e fror das frores" can be thought of as a little island rising from a land submerged under the waters—its invisible foundation. The moment we give close attention to any of the *cantigas*, we do indeed perceive their Christian-Islamic character.

Amador de los Ríos has already pointed out that the *cantigas* dealing with the history of Spain are especially interesting "because they *give a live picture* of her customs."[73] He thinks that the Learned King proceeds like "the popular singers," but to say that Alphonse X writes in the "popular" manner would mean that he clothed himself in a disguise that was not available in his case, because there is in the *Cantigas* neither comedy nor irony. The problem does not concern a social class but a form of life shared by both high and low. The historic character of many of these poems derives from the same motives that make the Castilian epic historical, motives which furthermore are complicated by the presence of the author at certain moments. There are elements recalling epic narration and, in other instances, the poetry of Berceo and the Chronicle of James the Conqueror. Occasionally the tone of the verse is that of prosaic conversation. But this tone would be instantly more elevated if the verse were heard with its music, which regrettably cannot be made audible here. Take, for example, the account of how the Virgin cured a man of the stone: "El espertou-sse / enton e achou enteira / a pedra sigo na cama, / tan grande, que verdadeira- / mente era come castanna: / esto de certo sabiades" (*Cantiga* CLXXIII).[74]

But let us look at a case of integralism comparable to the many already mentioned. There was a church dedicated to the Virgin in Murcia, apparently built by Italian merchants when the city was Moslem.

[73] *Historia crítica de la literatura española*, III, 508.
[74] In English: "He awoke, and then he found the stone unbroken in his bed. So large was it that it seemed to be a chestnut. Know that this was true."

When Murcia was conquered by the Christians, the Moors asked for the church to be demolished because it was situated in a place sacred to the Mohammedans. James the Conqueror ordered its demolition, but the Moors did not succeed in touching a single nail. Alphonse X subsequently authorized the destruction of the temple in exchange for great gifts, but the Moorish king would not permit it. Later, when Abū-Yūsuf attacked Murcia, he was beaten off, thanks to the help of the Virgin. In other words, according to the *Cantiga*, no power could prevent the building of the church and no power could bring about its destruction. Let us see now how the Learned King interweaves his own life with the miracle performed by the Virgin Mary:

> Et d'aquest'un miragre
> direi, *que vi*
> *desque mi Deus deu Murça,*
> et *oy outrossí*
> dizer a muitos mouros
> que morauan ant'ý,
> et tijnnan a terra
> por nossa pecadilla.[75]

To that church came "Genoese, Pisans, and still others from Sicily," and it was never profaned by the Moors. With the failure of the effort to destroy it as James had commanded,

> Depós aquest'aueo
> *que fui a Murça eu,*
> et o mais d'Arreixaca
> a aljama *mi deu*
> que tolless'a eigreia
> d'ontr'eles; *más mui greu*
> *me foi, ca era toda*
> *de nouo pintadilla.*[76]

Although the Moors gave the king the larger part of the rich district of Arreixaca, it was not easy for him to give them what they wanted, because the church was newly "pintadilla" (endearing diminutive of

[75] In English: "I shall speak of a miracle I saw right after God gave me Murcia; I have also heard it told by many Moors who dwelt there and held that land because of our sins."

[76] In English: "After that it happened that I went to Murcia; the Moors gave me most of Arreixaca on condition that I destroy the church there; but it was hard for me to do this, for the church was freshly painted."

pintada, "painted"). But then it was the Moorish king who opposed, saying:

> Non farei;
> ca os que Mariame[77]
> desama, mal os trilla.[78]

And the king concludes:

> E porend'a eigreia
> Sua quita e iá,
> que nunca Mafomete
> poder ý auerá;
> ca a conquereu ela
> *et demais conquerrá*
> *Espanna et Marrocos*
> *et Ceuta et Arcilla.*[79]

The Virgin becomes part of a national cause as Santiago has done before, and the king treats the miracle in such a way as to incorporate it into the events of his own life. We have here, besides, a valuable indication of the horizon that limited the aspirations of Castile in the Reconquest towards the end of the thirteenth century: Morocco, and in Morocco, the cities of Ceuta and Arcila. It is plainly evident that Spain's future imperialism is a projection of her medieval belief, and that it is an expansion of the Reconquest. The expansive impulse that reappears with intense energy in the fifteenth century suffers some diminution in the fourteenth. The Jewish convert Father Diego de Valencia de León, one of the strangest poets in the *Cancionero de Baena*, says that if the Castilian people

> Were in harmony,
> And were of one heart,
> *I know of no corner of the world*
> *They would not conquer, including all Granada.*

Years later, in a poem addressed to the inept king Henry IV, Gómez Manrique writes that he hopes "the Son of Saint Mary"

[77] The name the Moors gave the Virgin Mary.

[78] In English: "I will not do it, because the Virgin Mary tramples upon those she does not love."

[79] In English: "Therefore the church is here, altogether free; Mohammed will never have any power there, because she won it and will gain, besides, Spain and Morocco, Ceuta and Arcila."

Will make you reign
Peacefully in your own regions;
May he let you conquer
The barbarous nations
Cismaritime and outremer.

In the fifteenth century it was no longer either Santiago or the Virgin Mary who inspired the imperialist predictions: the convert Diego de Valencia trusted in purely human motives (agreement among the Castilians), and Gómez Manrique expected Christ to do everything. It is the epoch of the *moderna pietas*, and the Christians turn their attention to the Gospel, to the imitation of Christ, rather than to the traditional beliefs, even though in Spain this was an aristocratic attitude which did not affect the direction that Spanish religion was to take after the expulsion of the Jews.

Thus it is clear how the *Cantigas* take us along certain central paths of Hispanic history. Their integralism, in a process of concentric circles, includes the environment of things and persons, and everything is "painted in living colors." There is no better way for us to understand the peculiar nature of this process than to compare the same miracle as it is treated by Gautier de Coincy, Berceo, and Alphonse the Learned. Let us take for example the miracle of the Jewish child to whom the Virgin Mary gives the communion:

En lieu de prestre vint l'ymage,	Quand'o moç'esta visión
Desus l'autel prise a l'oublée	viu, *tan muito lle prazia*
Que le prestre avoit sacrée.	que *por fillar seu quinnón*
Si doucement le communie,	*ant'outros se metía;*
Que li cuers l'en rasazie	Santa María entón
(Ed. by Poquet, col. 283)[80]	*a mao lle porregía,*
	e deulle tal comunyón,
	que foi *mas doce cà mel.*[80]
	(*Cantiga* IV)

Coincy's objectified account becomes in Alphonse's poem an action developed from within the person outward. This is the Hispano-Islamic touch. Here is the point of contact between the *zajal* as the form used and the inner form of life. The Jewish boy was so pleased by the vision

[80] In English:

Instead of the priest, the image came and took from the altar the host that the priest had consecrated. She gave him communion so sweetly that his heart is fully satisfied.	When the boy saw this vision, he was so pleased that he jostled his way in among the other children to get his part; then Saint Mary stretched forth her hand and gave him a communion sweeter than honey.

of the Divine Lady that, "to get his share, he shoved and pushed ahead of the other children," and we imagine him making his way with his elbows like any child that wants to get hold of something it likes. The Virgin stretches forth "her hand," and the communion tastes "sweeter than honey" to the boy. That which is materially human and that which is spiritually human are harmonized. There are suggestions of this in Berceo, but in a poorer form:

> Prisol al iudezno de comulgar *gran gana,*
> comulgo con los otros *el cordero sin lana.*[81]
> (*Milagros,* 356)

On another occasion the Virgin raises a boy from the dead, because in life he had sung "Gaude, Virgo Maria" to her: He sang so well that

> A son mengier chascun le maine.[82]
> (G. de Coincy, col. 12)

In *Cantiga* VI this becomes:

> qualquer que o oya
> tan toste o fillava,
> e *por leval-o consigo*
> con os outros barallava,
> *dizend'*: eu dar-ll'-ei que iante,
> demais que merende.[83]

The inviting of the child to eat is enlivened. The children fight with one another, they are persistent, and one of them offers him not only luncheon but the afternoon snack besides.

The natural is described by Coincy without mincing words, and he even has a more refined technique than Alphonse. But he does not go beyond the objective action, and he does not connect the action with the inner experience of the person who performs it. The monk afflicted with sores is healed by the Virgin with her own milk:

La douce Dame, la piteuse,	E deitou-lle *na boca e na cara*
Trait sa mamele savoureuse,	do seu leite, e tornou-ll'a tan crara

[81] In English: "The little Jewish boy longed very much to communicate. This fleece-less lamb communicated with the other children."

[82] In English: "Everybody asked him to eat."

[83] In English: "Whoever heard him would seize him at once and would struggle with others in order to take the child, saying, I will give him food at noonday and in the afternoon too."

Si la boute de denz sa bouche.[84]
(Col. 349)

que semellava que todo mudara
como muda penas a andorinna.[84]
(*Cantiga* LIV)

These quotations allow us to see the originality and at the same time the limitations of the poetry of the Learned King, stammering in his lyricism, too close to his subject, and (he or whoever did write the *Cantigas*) unskilled in handling the language as a purely artistic instrument. When the Virgin causes five roses to bloom from the mouth of the dead monk as a reward for the five psalms he addressed to her, Coincy and Alphonse respectively say:

En sa bouche V fresches roses
Clères, vermeilles et foillues,
Com s'il fussent lors droit coillies.[85]
(Col. 361)

Na boca ll'apareceu
rosal que viron teer
cinque rosas.[85]
(*Cantiga* LVI)

The Learned King and his collaborators were sober Castilians with a highly developed sense of their own existence, who knew nothing about describing roses. But they did know how one moved in and out of a vital action, and therefore the *Cantigas* are our most accurate document for knowing and understanding the customs of the times in their smallest details. This work contains more of the germ of the modern novel than it does of authentic lyricism, although it is beside my point to consider this matter here. My only intention has been to point out the common ground of the *Cantar de Mio Cid*, Gonzalo de Berceo, and the *Cantigas*, and to show how the *zajal*, an Islamic form, takes us into the innermost regions of the artistic life. The fact that such a modest lyric form could be translated into the Galician language and not into Castilian presents, moreover, a problem with profound historical implications.

[84] In English:
The Lady mild and merciful
Took out her sweet-tasting breast
And put it into his mouth.

And she squirted some of her milk in his mouth and face; And his face turned so fair, It seemed he was wholly changed as the swallows change their feathers.

[85] In English:
In his mouth five fresh roses,
Clear, crimson, full-petaled,
As if they had just been picked.

Out of his mouth came a rosebush on which they saw five roses.

11

The End of the Thirteenth Century: A New Direction

AT THE END OF THE THIRTEENTH CENTURY Castilian life took a turn in a new direction—although it did not go beyond its personal limits, which have already been made familiar to the reader. The motives underlying this change of direction are to be found both in the Castilian way of existing, by now traditional, and in fortuitous circumstances. During the reign of Alphonse X (1252-1284) the Christian horizon underwent considerable displacement. Nor did Castile present the same appearance to the Moors and Jews after the victory in Las Navas de Tolosa (1212) and after the conquest of Cordova in 1236 and Seville in 1248, for these non-Castilian elements could now regard the Christians with expectations and fears of actions unthinkable a century earlier. Now Castilian literary supremacy was an evident fact. When we consider the question of the Jews in Spain, we shall see that their presence was decisive in the birth of the Castilian prose into which Arabic didactic and scientific works were beginning to be translated at the middle of the thirteenth century. Into that *Summa Pragmatica*, as I have called it, sponsored by Alphonse X, entered the Bible, universal history, law, astronomy, lapidaries, and even the art of playing chess. The boundaries between East and West were forgotten in this gigantic task, and Castile thus found herself possessed of a literature in the vulgar tongue without equal in Europe at the middle of the thirteenth century,[1] whereupon she drew still farther away from the guild of European scholars, whose medium of expression was Latin. Saint Thomas and the jurists of Bologna did not write in Italian.

The use of the spoken language in important works of learning was a sign of national withdrawal, a kind of isolationism, on the part of Castile, yet it went on during the same period in which Alphonse X was

---

[1] That literature in the vernacular was primarily a product of the court, and corresponded to a systematic cultural plan, not to isolated individual impulses. The French jurist Guillaume Chapu could say as late as 1284 that he read French better in verse than in prose (G. Gröber, *Grundriss*, II, 757). It is curious that Brunetto Latini, the author of the *Livre du Tresor* (c. 1265), had been ambassador to the court of Alphonse the Learned in 1260.

elected Emperor of the Holy Roman Empire. However, to the Pope, who regarded that magnificent monarch from the central see of Christendom, Alphonse's kingdom, I surmise, seemed excessively orientalized, and he withheld his placet by way of vetoing the expressed will of the electors. The immense production of the Alphonsine court was unknown to Europe. In the ensuing years the Spaniards themselves kept nothing of this production alive save the *Siete Partidas*, which were after all the law of the land. Of the other major works, those on astronomy were the first to be published—in the nineteenth century. The *Crónica general* was not published until early in the present century, as was also a part, and only a small part, of the *General estoria*. But the linguistic supremacy of Castile in the Peninsula was left undisputed after that flood of learning, universal in its scope and anonymous in its authorship, expressed in the language of everyone and diffused in abundant manuscripts.

The Moors and the Jews, especially the latter, regarded thirteenth-century Castile as a political power that was taking the place of the vanished caliphate of Cordova. Her superiority was confirmed as indisputable after the Andalusian Moslems failed in their rebellion during the reign of Alphonse X. The capital cities taken from the Moors greatly increased the Moslem population of Castile and the volume of Islamic culture that had to be contained within the Castilian political embrace. At the same time, the power and activity of the Hispano-Hebrews, closely tied to the Arabic tradition, were at their greatest in the thirteenth and fourteenth centuries. A result of this was the large number of didactic and narrative works, from *Calila e Dimna* to the *Caballero Cifar*, and including moral treatises within the intellectual grasp of everyone (*Bocados de oro, Poridad de poridades*, etc.). It was the first time for such a phenomenon to occur in the Christian kingdom, which until then had had no manifestations of scholarship and wisdom that they could esteem and call their own either in Latin or in the vernacular.

As the Islamico-Jewish cultural pressure increased—and it did so in natural consequence of the increased number of non-Christians—the intensity of the Castilian aggressive impulse diminished. The epic tension of both literature and life was easing. When the gests were turned into prose they were despoiled of their distinctive style. They were dissolved, as it were, in the solemn or, at times, enlivened prose of the *Crónica general*, artistic prose of a high order.[2] The power of the *Almohades*

---

[2] Cf., for example, the chapter on ". . . commo Garcí Pérez de Vargas tornó por la cofia a aquel logar o se le cayera" (ed. of Menéndez Pidal, pp. 751-752).

was broken forever in Las Navas de Tolosa; Cordova (cipdat real et commo madre de las otras çipdades del Andalozia) and Seville (complida de todas cosas et de todas noblezas que a abondamiento de toda complida et abondada çipdat pertenescan)[3] were taken; but the Christians did not possess enough reserves of "occidentalism," or enough people to replace or transform the volume of Islamico-Judaic culture they had captured. It was as much as they could do to defend themselves against the tempting blandishments of Arabic lyricism and storytelling, and to accept only Arabic moral wisdom, at once inoffensive and comforting to the spirit.[4] The generation of Alphonse X did not maintain the heroic tension of its predecessor, and it could not finish up once and for all with Moslem sovereignty in the south. Its great effort was in the direction of forming a Castilian culture out of the national history and imported materials (translations of Latino-Roman, Latino-European, Arabic, and Hebrew works). If Alphonse tried to penetrate into Europe politically, the learning and scholarship that he sponsored in the vulgar tongue worked rather in favor of Hispanic singularity. Castile fell into a kind of "Mozarabic rite" of culture, for the manner in which the culture was built up was not such as to force the foreigner to learn Castilian, as he indeed would be forced to do three centuries later.

A fortuitous accident that contributed to the weakening of Castile's not very intense occidentalism was the death of Prince Fernando de la Cerda, heir to Alphonse X's crown. Alphonse's second son, trampling upon the rights of the legal heir—his nephew the son of Fernando de la Cerda—managed to get the crown for himself as Sancho IV. Although the dynasty was not changed by Sancho IV's usurpation, any change at all in the form of succession prescribed by the law left the Castilians with a feeling of chaotic disorder. A rigorous observance of the right of suc-

[3] Cordova is described as a "royal city and the mother, as it were, of the other cities in Andalusia," and Seville (here the style of the Chronicle becomes untranslatably "oriental") as "complete with all things and all excellences that belong to the abundance of every complete and abounding city" (*Crónica general,* 729b, 768a).

[4] It was not a lack of knowledge of the Arabic language that kept the forms of Moslem poetry at a distance, for many Christians knew Arabic. At a difficult moment in the attack of Cordova, "the Christians took counsel together and said, 'What shall we do?' Domingo Muñoz, the leader, said to them: 'My advice is this . . . let us struggle to scale the walls, and let those among us who know Arabic best scale them, and let them go dressed as Moors, so that if they talk with Moors, the Moors will not recognize them.' And the first Arabic-speaking Christians that climbed the walls were Alvar Colodro and Benito of Baños, and afterwards the others that went with them; they wore Moorish clothing and headgear" (*Crónica general,* 730a). These people, with ultra-Castilian names, could pass for Moors if they dressed like them.

cession had been one of the essential differences between Christian-European Spain and Moslem Spain. In the latter the sovereign was also a kind of pontiff—the "prince of the believers"—a mouthpiece of the divine spirit. The Christian kings were earthly rulers, and their right to rule was based on their will to perpetuate their dynasties according to human laws in human time and space. They were not caliphs, which is to say, successors of Mohammed, sons of the sun, etc., as the oriental emperors were. The structure of the European nations was founded on dynastic continuity (without any halo of magic) and on a geographically fixed capital. Spain had lacked the latter to begin with, since her court was nomadic and moved about till 1560, but she did have a monarchy of the European type, and she therefore never knew the kind of calamity that overtook the Saracens.

But Spain lacked the bond of feudalism, at once homogeneous and elastic, in her "national" life, and the cohesive forces in her society were disturbed, besides, by the extraneous intervention of Jews and Moors in a fashion that we have lost sight of and which I shall later try to explain. Under such circumstances, the monarchical institution acquired a disproportionate importance, because its shortcomings could not be compensated from other sources of national energy. The alternatives were monarchy or chaos, because nothing existed comparable to the stabilizing or compensating force of the great feudal estates of Europe (Burgundy, Lorraine, etc.). We shall grant, then, the great significance of the disturbances that weakened the monarchy on the death of Alphonse X. With Sancho "el Bravo" (that is, the violent, the wicked) began a period that culminated in the civil wars of his great-grandson Peter the Cruel, during which the manifestations of Moslem life were very intense. The Christian-Islamic-Jewish contexture had hindered the formation of a dwelling-place with secure occidental foundations, and in the fourteenth century this situation was to become evident in dozens of ways. But among other things, the Castilian art of that century owes to this contexture the *Libro de Buen Amor* and the synagogues of Toledo. History of the usual sort has not been amazed by the appearance of these two extraordinary phenomena, so at variance with the life of European Christendom. But such events are no less surprising than the appearance of scientific prose writings in a Spanish court of the thirteenth century.

Prince Fernando, called "of the Sow," fell ill and died in 1275 at the age of 20, while he was governing Castile in the absence of his father "in such a manner as to please all the kingdoms."[5] The untimely death of the crown prince brings to mind another dynastic catastrophe—the death of Prince John, the only male heir of Ferdinand and Isabella, who was cut down in his youth at a time when all Spain regarded him with the most hopeful tenderness. Prince Sancho, Don Fernando's brother, refused to recognize the law of succession introduced by Alphonse X in the *Siete Partidas*, II, 15, 2, a novelty borrowed from the ideas of contemporary Italian jurists. It had been the custom in Castile to accept the succession of the first-born son, but not that of his subsequent heir as his representative. Sancho, then, reflected the popular, local idea, while his father espoused a learned innovation brought in from the outside. The life of the kingdom, not very well organized as it was, was completely unhinged. Old and tired, Alphonse X had no means with which to quell the family rebellion, and the sons of Don Fernando were too young to fight for their rights.

A single detail will show what chaos resulted from Sancho's uprising. Alphonse X was laying siege to Algeciras in 1278 and was having a hard time of it on account of a shortage of supplies. The army put its hopes in the money that was to come from the Jew named Zag de la Malea, the collector of royal revenues in Leon and Castile. Thus the lifeline of the nation was in Jewish hands. Don Zag and his co-religionists subsisted, thanks to their position as financiers—made doubly secure by royal protection; and they realized that the winds of fortune were blowing in favor of Prince Sancho. Sancho demanded the royal revenues for his political needs while Alphonse X and his armies were languishing at the gates of Algeciras, moneyless and sick. Don Zag delivered the sums he had collected to Don Sancho, whereupon Alphonse's troops and fleet suffered a total defeat. King Alphonse then had Don Zag drawn and quartered, but the damage had been done. Till the last, that wise and irresolute monarch hesitated between his duty and his fear of Sancho's violence. Then, at death's door, he cursed Sancho and disinherited him, whatever the Chronicle of his reign may say. When Sancho IV put his private passions, which would have been quite proper in a Moslem court, above the law and traditional good sense of Castile, the effect was calamitous. It had been bad enough for Alphonse X to have his brother Don Fadrique assassinated. With Sancho IV there began a period of civil disturbances and open disregard for discipline that did not end until Ferdinand and Isabella brought their intelligently directed energies to bear on the resistance of the Spaniards to living harmoniously together.

[5] *Crónica de Alfonso X*, Chap. LX.

The violent king furnished an example for the disorder that spread among the great lords, quick to rise up if royal favor did not measure up to their desires. For the first time, and this is significant, the king shared his authority with a favorite, Don Lope de Haro, Lord of Vizcaya. Uncertain and afraid of Don Lope's disloyalty, the king was humiliated into pawning to his "favorite" certain royal castles. But Don Lope in turn had to lean upon Don Abraham called the Barchilón, who controlled the treasury of the kingdom and authorized royal documents.[6] Thus, the increasing importance of the role played by the Jews in the national life from the reign of Alphonse X on becomes evident, and this is one of the clues to the understanding of the strange course taken by the life of the Castilian Christians, who had neglected the development of wealth[7] and industry as well as the administration of the state. The Jews took charge of this and of much more (see Chapter 13), while the Christian's aversion to productive and well-coordinated labor made him unfit to be the master and competent administrator of his own land. This is why the Spanish disturbances of the fourteenth century are not of the same character as those that went on at the same time in Europe, where quite different circumstances were having their effect.

The powerful Haro and Lara families are the first ones to appear in a long line of great and influential lords—not feudal lords, for they did not base their strength on fixed, politically organized dominions, but on the insecurity of the monarchy and on the intrigues and the money of the Jews. In sum, these families had no institutional force. Nevertheless, the primary importance of the great lords emerged as a new and decisive fact for subsequent history, because these great lords inclined rather to work for their own petty interests than to make war against the Moor. If Castile's structure had formerly been founded on faith in her saints and heroes, now, in 1300, she was to be more attentive to the raptures of souls; and saints and heroes were no longer to be raised up on pedestals of myth. Not that belief was replaced by ideas and doctrines; rather, faith in one's personality had enfeebled collective impulses whose expression had been Santiago and the epic.[8] The weakness of the monarchy

[6] Mercedes Gaibrois, *Historia del reinado de Sancho IV*, III, civ, cv.

[7] Within the Iberian Peninsula there is great potential wealth (mineral, agricultural, and industrial), yet there is no effective way to connect these potentialities with the living potentialities of its inhabitants. The lack of concord between man and his environment can thus have much graver consequences for history than the hardships caused by the environment.

[8] It is currently fashionable to blame the rule of regents during the protracted minorities of Ferdinand IV and Alphonse XI for the disturbances in Castile in the

invited arrogance, the refusal to open the castles to the king, and a chronically undisciplined life. The Castilian was gaining awareness of his personality, and he felt no hesitation in speaking of himself. There was more and more room in the Castilian spirit for the Arabic propensity to autobiography and lyricism. A political and literary figure like Prince Juan Manuel would not have fitted in the court of Alphonse X.

Prince Alfonso de la Cerda renounced his claims to the crown only under Alphonse XI, Sancho IV's grandson. Until then the pretender, supported by the king of Aragon, encouraged the rebellion of his Castilian partisans, and this created hostility between Castile and Aragon. Christian Spain consequently felt herself less compact than in the preceding century, when Alphonse X and James I combined their efforts to defend themselves against the Moors. However, the economic power of the Christian kingdoms had broadened; their needs had increased and they were served by a more active commerce, in the hands of Jews, Moors, and Genoese. Castile's interest was now drawn toward the fertile lands of Cordova, Seville, and Murcia, and she forgot Santiago de Compostela and the times of the Cluniac and Cistercian ascendancy. And at the same time, new cultural elements, Islamic in spirit, were reaching the central plateau, bringing the new ways of Andalusian and Mediterranean life. But at the same time that this was happening, Aragon and Castile each preferred for the Moors to continue in possession of the lands not yet reconquered. Neither of them was willing, that is, for the unconquered Moorish lands to fall into the hands of the other. And, deprived of possibilities of expansion in Spain, Aragon, together with Catalonia, sought compensation in Sicily and Greece in the fourteenth century.

The Reconquest had not returned Christian lands to Castile, but, rather, either large nuclei of Islamic peoples, highly civilized, or deserted areas that urgently demanded repopulation. In the "reconquered" Spain there were no longer any Mozarabes after the twelfth century. These newly recovered territories did not resemble those taken by the Arabs in the eighth century even in their geographical names, which were either completely Arabic or had been given an Arabized pronunciation. What had once been the river *Tago* was now the *Tajo* or *Tejo*; the *Anas*

---

first half of the fourteenth century, and the fratricidal struggles of Peter the Cruel and Henry II for the confusion and weakness of the second half. But the problem takes a different form when we ask ourselves what the Christians, Jews, and Moors were doing in the fourteenth century, and we observe the new direction of literary expression.

had become the *Guadiana*; the *Betis*, the *Guadalquivir*; *Hispalis* had turned into *Sevilla*; *Compluto* into *Alcalá*; *Caesar Augusta* into *Zaragoza*; *Acci* into *Guadix*; and it was the same in many other cases. Other cities had been founded by the Arabs: *Jaén, Granada, Almería, Alcolea, Alhama*, and many more. It is true that some Latin names persisted: *Córdoba, Toledo, Valencia*. But what resemblance could the conquering Christians find between the Visigothic capital of Toledo that they had lost in the eighth century and the Toledo that they recovered in 1085, except the topography and a Roman monument here and there? Alphonse VI did not give the churches of Toledo to the Mozarabic Christians, who represented the Visigothic city, as it were. He gave them to French bishops, monks, and priests. Even the traditional rite of Visigothic Spain was violently discarded in favor of the French rite, which was the same as the Roman.

The Christians entered Seville in 1248, and their sense of astonishment and wonder is reflected in the pages of the *Crónica general*. Their impressions must have been similar in every place they conquered. They were faced by a new world that had no contact at all with Spain's pre-Islamic past, and no analogy with the European world. Here, instead, were novelty and surprises—the architecture, the industry, the skilled craftsmen, the trade, the customs, the science. Ferdinand III reoccupied the place where ancient Hispalis had been, and where, in 1248, there was a city that had nothing in common with the one given up there to the Moslem in 711. Not without reason did the chronicles call the Moslem conquest the "destruction" of Spain. The new settlers amongst whom the kings distributed the conquered lands restarted Christian history on an Islamic foundation which could not be dispensed with. Let us imagine as a fantastic case that after a few centuries the Mexicans should succeed in retaking California—Los Angeles and San Francisco—and let us ask ourselves if this would be a reconquest. The retaking of Toledo, Cordova, Seville, and Granada must be thought of in the same way. We have already seen how Juan Manuel said that there would be war until "the Christians have won back [cobrado] *the lands* that the Moors wrested from them." That is, it was necessary to recover the geographical space of Spain, which formed a unity and had been inhabited by Christians centuries before. In this case I believe that language makes a distinction not generally incorporated into the way of thinking about the matter. "Reconquest" is the term generally applied to the "recovery of the Spanish territory invaded by the Moslems," but one does not in Spanish say that Ferdinand and Isabella "reconquered" Granada. One says rather that they took it, or that they conquered it.[9] The chronicles say that Alphonse X "won Jerez"; the *Crónica general* speaks of the "prisión" —that is "the taking"—of Seville.

This was the historic reality, and this is why the "reoccupation" of Spain by Christians, entirely different from the inhabitants of that land in the eighth century, was such a long and arduous enterprise. It was a struggle against a tough people with Africa and the spiritual empire of Islam behind them. The Christians reached the southern coast of the Peninsula, and they could make no further effective headway against the Moors. In spite of their occasional occupation of certain points here and there in Africa, the Christians did not succeed in conquering and assimilating the territory. The African Moslem was not like the American Indian, conquered by Cortés and Pizarro; or like the south of Italy, won by Gonsalvo de Córdoba in a couple of fortunate battles. All the might that Charles V could assemble collapsed in Algiers, and King Sebastian of Portugal lost his life in Morocco. Europe continued to fail, up to the nineteenth century, in her efforts to dominate Mediterranean Africa. In the end the Crusades were a failure, for that matter, and the Turks managed to preserve their vast dominions until the nineteenth century. Castile almost singlehanded conquered and colonized an immense portion of America, but in the war against the Moslem world she achieved decisive victories only by uniting with the rest of Spain. In the battle of Las Navas de Tolosa (1212), Castilians, Aragonese, and Navarrese fought together; in the battle of the Salado (1340), Castilians and Portuguese; and the war of Granada (1492) was a completely national, that is, Spanish, enterprise. We must remember that when the Moriscos rebelled in the sixteenth century, famous generals gave a sorry account of themselves in the Alpujarras in southern Spain, which were finally subdued only by committing the best troops the kingdom had in Flanders. The Moslem was never an easy foe. Since he was not repelled in the moment of his invasion, the recovery of the land had to be the way it was—a loom on which the history of Spain was warped.

With the most important zones of the Peninsula occupied in the fourteenth century, it is to be expected that the Castilian's attitude toward the Moor would change. Austerity was now less urgent, nor was it so important to eschew Islamic ways openly and consciously. The Castilian knew and felt that the Moor was no longer a serious danger, and that his final defeat now depended on the unity and skill of the Christians

[9] There are seventeenth-century plays entitled *The Taking of Granada, The Conquest of Toledo*, etc.

rather than on the degree of strength of the enemy. From the time of Alphonse X, the Moorish king of Granada had signed all the documents of the kings of Castile as a vassal, and had paid the kings tribute.[10]

The fact is, then, that fourteenth-century Castile found itself facing a horizon different from the one it had faced in the thirteenth century. The Castilian was aware of himself and of the world in which he lived, and he expressed himself in ways he had never used before: "I was born in Escalona," says Juan Manuel, "on Tuesday, the fifth of May, in the year of 1282, and my father died in Peñafiel on Saturday, Christmas day, in the year of 1283" (*Tratado sobre las armas*). Speaking of a later period in his life, he says "At that time I was in the kingdom of Murcia, for the king had sent me there to establish a front against the Moors; although I was very young, not having yet reached my twelfth birthday" (*ibid.*). The incipient autobiographical impulses of such poets as Berceo are now a confident and broad expression of the writer's own life.

And if the nobleman, sure of his power, expressed himself individually, the people likewise took a step forward, and expressed, albeit not altogether in words, what they were feeling. Precisely at the end of the thirteenth century, when the kingdom was falling into the turbulent disorder that followed on the death of the crown prince, Ferdinand, son of Alphonse the Learned, the Castilian brotherhoods[11] began to develop an intense life. In 1282 the municipal councils of Cordova, Jaén, Baeza, Úbeda, Andújar, and Arjona declared themselves in favor of prince Sancho as their protector against any lord "who might come to diminish

[10] Mercedes Gaibrois, *Historia del reinado de Sancho IV*, III, xcvi. By way of confirmation, a document of Ferdinand IV speaks of "Don Nazar, King of Granada, vassal of the king" in 1310 (A. Benavides, *Memorias del rey don Fernando IV*, II, 752). Although it was already a practice fortified by tradition for the Moorish kingdoms to pay tribute and to be in close contact with the Christians, the position of the Moorish kingdom of Granada as a dependency of Castile and Aragon became more firmly established at that time. In 1297 James II of Aragon asked the Moorish king of Granada to help the prince De la Cerda against King Ferdinand IV; in 1300 he requested a loan of 20,000 gold *doblas* against the crown of his father (Benavides, *op.cit.*, II, 124). In 1310 the Moorish king pledged himself to pay James 300 *doblas* a year at the same time that he admitted he was a tributary of Ferdinand IV of Castile. The document is drawn up in Spanish in the manner of the Christian kings: "Don Nazar, by the grace of God, King of Granada, Malaga, Almería, Ronda, Guadiex and Amir-Amuminin" (Benavides, II, 756). From this it is evident that both the Spanish and Moorish kings reigned over different groups of "taifas," and not over a compact nation. The "kingdoms" were united in the magical unity of a crown and not by means of the horizontal ligatures of earthly interests.

[11] The Castilian brotherhoods (hermandades) were a political and military institution comprised of the commons headed by the municipal officials. Their aim was to protect themselves against the abuses of the crown and the nobility.

or destroy our rights and our privileges." The brotherhood was formed by "us *alcaldes* and our burghers."[12]

The brotherhoods became frequent after the death of Sancho IV in 1295. The councils joined together to protect themselves against the designs of the powerful—but in a legal fashion, to be sure: the Castilian people still put their faith in law rather than in blind violence. Here we see reappearing the democratic and disciplined language of the Castilians of the poem of *Fernán González*. In case of an infraction of the law, they agree that "we will join together to inform the king of it, or the kings who come after him; and if they see fit to rectify the matter [very well]; and if not, let us join together to protect ourselves against the injustice, as is said in the privilege granted us by our lord the king Don Sancho, when he rose up in behalf of all the people in the land."[13] But we notice at the same time that Sancho IV, in need of support to oppose the succession decreed by his father, had aroused the commons, thus paving the way for the popular upheavals that characterized the fourteenth century—all kinds of rebellions, the political demagoguery of Peter the Cruel, the uprisings against the Jews—social changes, in sum, of the greatest significance. We see how the death of Prince Fernando de la Cerda was, as I have said, an event that was accidental yet pregnant with consequences, in view of the fact that Spanish history has always oscillated between the firm authority of the kings and the confused power of the lower orders (law as such has never meant very much).

Another of the brotherhoods, when it was constituted, stated that if anyone should bring letters from the king with requests for taxes contrary to the established privileges (fueros), or with any other "illegal" order, and if the person who "brings the letter be a citizen of the place or of the brotherhood, let the council kill him for doing so" (Benavides, *op.cit.*, ii, 6). Similar agreements were reached in Murcia, Lorca, Cuenca, and other cities (ii, 45, 46, 75). Faced with legal uncertainty, the people organized their own will, which had been aroused by those seeking their cooperation. The boundary line between justice and violence was from then on to become more and more unstable.

The conjunction of the interests of the king and those of the commons in the time of Sancho IV ("when he rose up in behalf of all the people in the land") marks the entrance of history's principal character, the people, no longer occupied with the task of fighting against the Moslems.

[12] *Colección de documentos inéditos para la Historia de España*, cxii, 1895, 1-6.
[13] A. Benavides, *Memorias del rey don Fernando IV*, ii, 4.

The empty space left in life by the virtual cessation of warfare against the Moor was not filled by peaceful occupations. There was nothing much the members of the Christian population could do in Spain beyond preparing themselves to step up into the ruling caste by taking advantage of qualities and virtues ingrained in their personalities as individuals. In the thirteenth and fourteenth centuries it was still the Moors and especially the Jews who did almost all the work that was anything more than the mere cultivation of the soil. Don Juan Manuel classifies fourteenth-century society into "those who pray, those who defend the land, and those who till"; and this scheme corresponded to the Spaniard's scheme of social values. It tells nothing, of course, about the actual composition of society, omitting, as it does, craftsmen, public officials, doctors, etc.[14] If we anticipate here the perspective that is to be established in the chapter on the Jews, we will understand the entrance of the people (that is, the Christians of the lower classes) on the stage of history, and we will understand the exasperation that motivated this entrance. The Hispano-Hebrews had control of the money, which they lent at an annual interest rate of 33%, and the "people" were unable to dislodge them from their dominant position.

The Christian population began to show its irritation with the Jews at the end of the thirteenth century, when Sancho IV tore down the

---

[14] This abstract, well-ordered vision of society came from France. Adalbert of Laon (d. 1030), in his *Carmen*, addressed to King Robert II, the Pious, says: "Triplex Dei ergo domus est, quae creditur una: nunc *orant*, alii *pugnant* aliique *laborant*" (Migne, *Patrologia*, S.L., cxli, 782). Alphonse the Learned includes the same idea in the *Siete Partidas* (ii, 21): "Defenders are one of the three estates by which God has wished to maintain the world: for just as those who pray to God for the people are called prayers, and likewise those who till the soil . . . are called tillers, so likewise are those who must defend everyone called defenders." Gregorio López comments thus: "Hipodamus antiquus philosophus in sua *politia* dividebat in tres partes numerum civium uniuscujusque civitatis: bellatores scilicet, artifices, et agricolas, tradit Lucas de Penna in *L. colonos, C. de agric. et censit. lib.* 11." The Lucas de Penna cited here was a "doctor Gallicus" who published a *Super tres libros Codicis X. videlicet XI. et XII.* in Paris in 1509. But the passages from the *Partidas* and from Juan Manuel are connected with the one from Adalbert of Laon and not with the one from the Greek philosopher (fighters, artisans, and farmers) interested rather in earthly than in heavenly labors. This idea of the composition of society was crystallized for the Spaniard. In 1517 the Bachiller de la Pradilla still sees the social panorama within the frame of the *Partidas*: "Just as the clergy with their very dignified capes perform solemn ceremonies . . . so let the *defenders*—dukes, counts, and marquises—enjoy the privilege of making the *peasants* secure with their lances and armor." (*Egloga Real*, in E. Kohler, *Sieben spanische dramatische Eklogen*, 1911, p. 221.) See on this problem G. Dumézil, *L'héritage indoeuropéen à Rome*, p. 95.

fragile foundations on which the structure of the kingdom rested.[15] During the reign that followed Sancho's, the people found a way to organize their vexation. In the Cortes of Toro (1304), the Regent María de Molina said: ". . . you, the Council of Valladolid, showed me, when I was in Valladolid, how the community of Jews in your town won from the king my son [Ferdinand IV] a letter sealed with his lead seal against you in respect to the debts you owe them and many other things, by which letter you were much offended; and you informed me that if this situation should continue, the city and township of Valladolid would form a brotherhood, and that this would be harmful and outrageous and disloyal to the king and to me. . . ."[16] In view of this situation, the Cortes issued certain decrees to bring about more order in the court procedures for dealing with debts between Christians and Jews. To obtain what they could not obtain in any other way, the people threatened to form brotherhoods, that is, popular organizations against the royal authority, and these brotherhoods are the antecedents of the "Communities" that rose up against Charles V.[17] None but Ferdinand and Isabella ever managed to harmonize for a time the interests of the crown and the interests of the people, and they succeeded by converting the brotherhoods into state police with the mission of putting down disorders and banditry. But let it be remembered that temporary alliance between the monarch and the commons had as a condition and a result the exile of the Jews, and could be maintained because Ferdinand the Catholic provided his people with their favorite task: war against the

[15] Fernán Pérez de Guzmán sensed this acutely in the fifteenth century: "According to what is found in the histories, Spain has always been easily agitated and not very stable in what happens to her, and very rarely has she been lacking in troubles and scandals" (*Generaciones e semblanzas*, "Clásicos castellanos," edition, p. 143).

[16] *Cortes de León y Castilla*, I, 172.

[17] The same thing happened in the fifteenth century in a moment of great weakness of the crown. The records of the *Cortes*, meeting in Ocaña in 1469, quote the following statement of the deputies: "For last four years during the disorders and tumults that have been happening in your kingdom [Henry IV, the Impotent, was the monarch] all the people therein have risen up with the cry of 'Brotherhood!' [Hermandad] and held mass-meetings and formed general and special unions undertaking great tasks, especially the pacification of your kingdom and the restoration of the royal power and the reformation of the legal system. And under this pretext they have constituted themselves a body politic . . . , and they have induced the towns to contribute to a treasury for the *hermandad* . . . , and many excises were put on the things that were sold . . . , and great taxes were levied and collected. . . . All this effort fell through, and while it yielded little, and we cannot understand how and on what such great amounts as were collected in the name of *Hermandad* were spent" (*Cortes de León y Castilla*, III, 794-795).

Moor at home and war abroad. Without the undertakings in Europe and beyond the seas in which the Spaniard, out of the possibilities of Spain's living dwelling-place, could express himself in significant achievement, the Spanish people would have gone to pieces in internecine struggles or fallen into lifeless inertia.

The period that ended with Ferdinand and Isabella had been initiated by Sancho IV, who opened the way to all kinds of lawlessness. As a single significant example I will mention that in 1287 the administration of the royal finances was being contested by Samuel of Belorado and Abrahem the Barchilón, protected by King Sancho and his favorite Lope de Haro, respectively. To settle their differences amicably, the two Jews appeared before Martín García, Bishop of Astorga, who was something like a minister of justice. Don Martín decided the case in favor of Don Samuel, and when Lope de Haro heard this he burst out in the tribunal and abused the bishop "with evil and ugly insults," telling him in front of everyone, "I don't know why I don't kick your soul out of your body with my spurs."[18] A year later, in 1288, King Sancho called Don Lope and other nobles together in Haro. He closeted himself with them and demanded the return of the castles they had taken away from him. To this Don Lope replied in rage: "You mean you are going to arrest me? Why? ¡A la merda! Oh, my people!" For the first time history records an insult uttered publicly against a king of Castile. We are here in a period of inaugurations, in which the way is opened for the expressive faculty of Castilians, hitherto incapable of putting in writing the inner experience of a person in a given time and place. Unfortunately for Don Lope, the affair turned out as he least expected. His own men did not respond to his call, and the king's archers first cut off one of his hands with a single slash, and then clubbed him to death (loc.cit., p. 79). Sancho killed one of Lope's knights with his own sword.

The new way in which Castilians expressed themselves made it possible to describe the inwardness of their souls. For example, we shall see the conscience of King Sancho IV reveal itself to us through an anguished confession. An experience so novel does not dawn in rosy tints but shrouded in streaks of grey. It is to the *infante* Don Juan Manuel that we owe the first intimate, throbbing page of a confession written in Castilian, novelistically situated in a given time and space. A man's conscience opens up so that a witness can explore its depths.

In the middle of March 1295 King Sancho IV came to Madrid. He

---

[18] "Crónica de Sancho IV," in the *Biblioteca de Autores Españoles*, LVI, 76*b*.

was very ill—it appears that he had tuberculosis—and he went to a convent of Dominican nuns to stay.[19] But let us hear Juan Manuel: "After a few days I went to see the king, and I found him in Madrid, staying in the house of the Ladies of your order.[20] He was in a very serious condition, and he wanted to have present at the parley certain persons, among them "Don Zag, my physician, who was the elder brother of Don Abraham, physician to both the king and myself. For believe you me that throughout the lives of King Alphonse and my father and King Sancho and myself, our houses were always one, and we had the same officials."

This scene, relived by Don Juan Manuel in his mature years, had taken place when the prince was thirteen. (We should remember that at the age of twelve that lad of exaggerated precocity was sent to Murcia to be the commander of the frontier outpost.) Let us follow the prince-author in his evocation of the episode from his childhood, an account in which he merges what he had seen as a boy and what it behoved him to write as an ambitious prince:

"As soon as all of us were with the king and the other people had left his chamber, the king, miserable in his bed, took my arm and made me sit down by him, and he began his speech in this wise:

" 'Don Juan, although I consider all my people yours, and consider all yours mine, especially those that are here now do I hold to be more evidently yours and mine than all the others. . . .' "

The king, aware that he is dying, is going to speak now from the depths of his soul, and he wishes to draw a circle of intimacy around the tragic revelation that he is going to confide to the nephew of Saint Ferdinand:

" 'Now, Don Juan, I must tell you three things. First I must beg you to share the suffering of my soul, for, alas for my great sin! my affairs have turned out in such a way that my soul is in great shame before God. Second I beg you to grieve for my death. . . . In me you lose a king and lord, your first cousin, who brought you up and who very truly loved you. To no other first cousin in the world will you be able to turn *save to that sinful Prince John who lives in dishonor among the Moors.* [Sancho is referring to the Don Juan who had Guzmán the Good's son murdered in the siege of Tarifa.] You see me before you, dying, and you

[19] Documents relating to the illness and death of the king may be found in Mercedes Gaibrois, *Historia de Sancho IV*, ii, 366-378.

[20] This *Tractado* was written at the instance of Juan Alfonso, a Dominican friar, who asked Don Juan Manuel to tell "how the parley went that the king Don Sancho had with me in Madrid" (cf. *Biblioteca de Autores Españoles*, li, 257).

cannot help me. And I know without doubt that . . . if you should see a hundred lances approaching to strike me, you would put yourself between me and them. . . . Now you see that you are alive and in good health, and that I am being killed before your eyes, and you can neither defend nor help me. *For be sure that this death that I am dying is not a death from sickness, but is a death that my sins have brought on me, and especially because of the curse my father put upon me,* much deserved by me. . . . I trust in God that you will live long, and will see many kings in Castile, but there will never be a king who will love you, will distrust you, *and will fear you as much as I have.*' [Here speaks, not without some perversity, the conscience of Juan Manuel, the turbulent and rebellious prince, whose ambition and scheming created such great difficulties for Ferdinand IV and Alphonse XI.] And having said this, he was seized by a fit of coughing and could not spit out the phlegm that came up from his chest, so that we took him for dead; and that happened twice. And on the one hand because we saw what condition he was in, and on the other because of the words he said to me, you can well understand *how broken-hearted and grieved we were.* . . . 'Now, Don Juan . . . I want to take leave of you and I would give you my blessing, but, alas! I cannot give it to you or to anyone, *for no one can give that which he does not have.*' "

The king goes on to explain scholastically why he does not have benediction in him and why Juan Manuel does have. This prose charged with emotion, in large measure autobiographical, is still governed by the rules of medieval rhetoric, and is fashioned in the mold of the graduated and ordered argument. But we have here anguished speeches uttered between moments of mortal agony and suffocating coughs. A cursed king now feels the noose of his curse growing tighter and choking even more than his cough, like a sinister power weighing over an entire dynasty. The king is immersed in a Judaico-Islamic atmosphere, the belief in the real power of curses and blessings, favorable and hostile sub-deities that chain one generation to the next. The terrible voice of the Old Testament coincides with the Moorish proverb: "If thy mother and thy father curse thee, the saints will not heal thee."[21] All this led to a fatalism that has little of the Christian about it; but such was the belief of Sancho IV and Don Juan Manuel:

"I cannot give you my blessing because I did not receive a blessing from my father. Rather, for the sins I committed against him, I received

---

[21] E. Westermack, *Origin and Development of Moral Ideas,* 1, 622. See also the article "Cursing and Blessing," in J. Hasting, *Encyclopaedia of Religion and Ethics.*

his curse; and he gave me his curse many times in his life when he was alive and well, and he gave it to me as he was dying. Likewise, my mother, who is alive, gave it to me many times, and I know that she curses me now, and I do believe that she will surely do the same thing at her death. And even though they might wish to give me their blessing, they could not, *for neither of them inherited it; they received it neither from their father nor from their mother.*"

King Ferdinand III, as a matter of fact, gave Alphonse X a blessing contingent on certain conditions that his heir did not fulfill. And as for his mother, Sancho IV says:

"I reckon that she did not have her father's blessing, for he hated her because he suspected her of the murder of the *infanta* Doña Constanza, her sister."[22]

Opposing the "cursed" branch of the house of Castile, headed by Alphonse the Learned, according to Juan Manuel's account, Juan Manuel exhibits his own branch, issuing from Prince Manuel, the younger son of Ferdinand III, the Saint, and rich in all possible benedictions. The description of the agony of Sancho IV, with its novelistic touches, was not written, though, as a disinterested experiment in a new kind of literature. It was written rather in a transport of arrogance and in justification of the author's own life, the turbulent ambitions of Don Juan Manuel. The *Treatise* on his coat of arms is an autobiographical fragment, and because of this it includes a portion of the biography of Sancho IV. Juan Manuel's prose grows both from an artistic impulse and from pragmatic necessities which gave form and content to the will to express. When the personal consciousness was converted into an expressible object—thanks to a change in the literary horizon— it was possible for the "literary" character slowly to acquire more and more reality, which, of course, is not a verbal representation of what really happens to a person of flesh and blood, since art is not naïve sincerity.

But before subjectivism of literary expression could exist, the barrier of inhibitions that kept the Castilian inwardness shut off and silent had to disappear. A literary phenomenon, like any other human phenomenon, always takes place in a historical contexture. Juan Manuel wrote the

[22] A. Giménez Soler doubts the accuracy of some of the facts mentioned in the "parley" of Sancho IV. Queen Violante—wife of Alphonse X, mother of Sancho IV, and daughter of James I of Aragon—did not harbor such great hatred for her sister Constanza, who was still living. James could not have cursed his daughter Violante for having murdered a person who was still living. (*Don Juan Manuel*, Saragossa, 1932, p. 692.)

impressive passage transcribed above because he felt the necessity to talk about himself; as a great lord he felt himself strong enough and daring enough to do it. The scene, the mention of the place where it happens, and the persons present, the surprising attribution of absolute truth to the words of the dying king—all this is a foundation block for the asseveration that he, Don Juan Manuel, is descended from a purer and more blessed line than that of the reigning monarch, who has been deprived of the support of ancestral benediction. Indeed, Sancho concluded his conversation with Juan Manuel thus: "Your father gave you the fullest blessing he could; and I am certain that your mother—who had the blessing of her father and her mother—when she died in Escalona—I know for sure that she gave you her blessing."[23]

The fact that in the fourteenth century, prose begins to express the inner reality of a person who himself appears in the prose and speaks for himself is a phenomenon contemporary with the lyricism of the Archpriest of Hita and the poetry of the Jew Santob of Carrión. The same Don Juan Manuel wrote a *Book of Songs* (Libro de Cantares) which was still in existence in the sixteenth century (in the library of Argote de Molina), and the existence of such a book establishes the connection between the novelistic prose and the lyric poetry of that period. All this is inseparable from the totality of Castilian history after 1300. Because Don Juan Manuel gave free rein to his inner self, something that had not gone on before, it was possible for him to go beneath the

[23] No less extraordinary is the *Libro de los Estados* (Book of the Estates), a didactic work which has for its narrative frame the legend of Barlaam and Josafat, and for its content an examination of the norms of society. Into the framework and content, essentially hostile to the display of personal feeling, the author injects himself by means of a naïve expedient (as Maria Rosa Lida de Malkiel pointed out to me). Julio (= Barlaam) is a native of Castile, where he has been in close association with the parents of Don Juan Manuel and has brought the latter up. Julio recalls Don Juan Manuel and his family apropos of the most diverse topics: p. 312 (I refer to the *Biblioteca de Autores Españoles*, vol. 51): Don Juan Manuel's advice to his brother-in-law; 313: attempts to poison Don Juan Manuel; 316, 317: nursing and exemplary education of Don Juan Manuel; 331: reprimand administered to Don Juan Manuel by the bishop of Santiago; 335: opinion of the vocabulary and style of Don Juan Manuel's works; 345: theological debate between the *Infante* and the Moors; etc. Don Juan Manuel's writings are also an excellent example of the predilection for the proverb (see pp. 243, 254, 268, 269, 275, 277, 278, 327, 331, 375, 384, 440) also evident in the contemporary *Libro de Buen Amor*. This predilection for popular sayings is another result of the Islamic-Judaic-Christian contexture, and it presents another contrast with Europe (one thinks of the unique place of the proverbs in works like the *Corbacho*, the *Celestina*, the *Quijote*), as I observed in my *Juan de Mal Lara y su "Filosofía vulgar,"* in *Homenaje ofrecido a Menéndez Pidal*, Madrid, 1925, III, 574.

surface of other lives and tell us what he found there. His stories are an expression of personal life and of the historical circumstances that make it "real."

Such is the style of Don Juan Manuel's book of stories called *El Conde Lucanor*, which is like an epic in which the author has come out of his poetic hiding place and has fixed the narrative in a time and place which he shares with the reader and in which the reader may experience with him the inner vicissitudes of the storied characters. " 'My lord Count Lucanor,' said Patronio, 'Don Lorenzo Xuarez Gallinato used to live with the [Moorish] king of Granada, and he lived a long time with him there; and then it pleased God that he should enter again into favor with King Ferrando. . . .' " In the story of Don Pero Meléndez de Valdés, this much honored knight of the kingdom of Leon breaks his leg, and we hear the people say to him: "Ah, Don Pero Meléndez! You who always say, 'What God does, that is best,' now take this good thing that God has done to you." In the epic the poetic matter was a great event of national or collective dimensions: now the matter of the Castilian story is the anecdote, in which the happening does not extend beyond the dimensions of the person. That which has been public becomes private and personal, and the way is thus prepared for the *Romancero* in the fourteenth century, for lyric poetry and the authentic novel. The presence of the narrator Patronio symbolizes the relation between the story and the mythic atmosphere out of which it comes—between individual vicissitude and transcendent morality. Even Cervantes was to echo this historical process in Cide Hamete Benengeli—the Patronio of the *Quijote*. But the essential point here is that the earliest germs of the novel came into existence in Spain accompanied by the personal expression of an "I." This is what has led me to write elsewhere that the lyrical style of the pastoral novel and even the style of the Spanish mystics played a dominant part in the historico-literary gestation of the *Quijote*. And at the deep center of such complexities one can hear the echo of oriental tradition, the beat of "the atom of my heart" which Al-Ḥallāj has told us about.

The figure of King Sancho, whose anguished confession is brought to our ears by Juan Manuel, casts a sinister shadow over the reigns of all the Castilian kings of the fourteenth century. Under a curse or not, the Castilian dynasty lived in an atmosphere of continual uncertainty and disorder. King Ferdinand IV ordered two knights thrown to their death over a precipice—unjustly, says the *Crónica*; and the knights, before going to their punishment, summoned the king to "appear before God with them for judgment on this death which he wrongfully decreed for them." And as a matter of fact, thirty days later "they found him dead in his bed, and he had died in such a way that none had seen him die." Whether this be legend or not, there is no doubt that Ferdinand IV was called "the Summoned" (el Emplazado). His son Alphonse XI— the best Castilian king of the fourteenth century—fell in love with Leonor de Guzmán, who "was the most conspicuous beauty that there was in the kingdom." She was moreover "very intelligent; and from the moment she came into the king's favor, she worked hard to serve him in every way that she knew she could do him service, so that the king loved her and esteemed her very highly." But the situation was grave, because the king had children by both the legitimate queen and the illegitimate one, and this was the root of future disasters, for the problem of bastard sons took on special seriousness in this century. Peter, the legitimate son, inherited the crown, and he is the one that some called "the Cruel" at the same time that others (the people in conflict with the nobility) called "the Just." The illegitimate son, Henry, stabbed his brother to death after the fratricidal battle of Montiel, in 1369.

Once the people had become aware of their power, they took an active part, through their brotherhoods, in events of historical dimensions, and the chronicles speak of this fact. In the course of certain intrigues involving members of the royal family in 1326, the people in Valladolid who were part of the plot aroused the peasantry and the common people, telling them that an *Infanta* was being taken to marry a Count. "And when the *Infanta*, riding on a mule, came out of the house where she dwelt to go on her way, the people came in great excitement and sought to kill Yusaf and those who were with him. . . . The members of the Council of the City sent for ladders, and wanted to tear down the walls in order to go in and kill that Jew. Etc."[24]

Before this the chronicles do not record facts of this nature because their narrative mesh was much larger and would not hold small, every-day events. Thus the style of the fourteenth-century chronicles is parallel to that of the story and that of poetry: it now includes hitherto unrecorded aspects of Castilian life, which did not consist only in wars and civil strife. In the time of Alphonse XI (1312-1350) there were new triumphs over the Moor as well as solemn public festivals and a chivalric splendor never seen before. The king founded the Order of the Ribbon, and had himself anointed and crowned in dazzling ceremonies. The

---

[24] "Crónica de Alfonso XI," in the *Biblioteca de Autores Españoles*, LXVI, 215a.

Jews, at the height of their power, put large amounts of money into circulation, and everywhere there were signs of bustling vitality. On the occasion of a visit Alphonse XI made to Seville "all those in the city— the nobles, the nights, and the citizens—had great pleasure over the coming of the king, *for they knew that by him they were saved from all the evils from which they had suffered up to then.*" The oriental messianism of the Spaniards flourished extravagantly in the most beautiful city the Christians possessed: "the city is of itself so noble that it well knows how to meet and receive its lord when he comes to it, and they received the king with great delight and much rejoicings." There was dancing and music, and "along the river Guadalquivir there were many armed vessels, which played and engaged in sham battles." The king "found the streets wherever he went all covered with cloths of gold and silk, and the walls along the streets the same way; and in each of the houses along these streets were set out sweet-smelling things, the finest that there could be."[25] This is what happened in 1324 to King Alphonse XI, who "was not very large in stature but of good appearance, strong, fair and white, and fortunate in war" (p. 391). "His speech was very Castilian, and he did not hesitate over what he had to say" (p. 198). He established as much peace and order as possible in his domain, and when the Cortes met in Madrid in 1327, the Chronicle observes that "such was justice at that time in the towns where the king dwelt, that during that meeting of the Cortes, at which very great people were gathered together, all those who brought food to sell lay down at night in the public squares, and much food was without anyone to watch over it save only the fear of the justice the king would mete out to wrongdoers" (p. 223).

During this reign, the person of a knightly sovereign with a gift for show stands out as never before in the Peninsular life, which was centered in Castile, strong and powerful in this period. In 1330 the king managed to pacify the troublesome Don Juan Manuel, who, even though he was the king's vassal and held valuable lands through the king's favor, still "looked for all kinds of ways to be of disservice to him." But the monarch's prestige was beginning to make itself felt against the wayward, "for this king was very noble of body, and he considered it a good thing to receive the honor of coronation and likewise the honor of knighthood." With true Hispanic instinct the king sought to win his subjects by surrounding himself with a halo of wonder, "for he strove mightily to bring honor to the royal crown." The custom of solemnly investing the

[25] *Ibid.*, p. 204*b*.

nobles with the order of chivalry had been lost: "For a long time all had been excusing themselves from receiving knighthood until the time of this king Don Alfonso," who revived ancient and noble customs, even though he gave them a different meaning. Two centuries before, the kings had gone to Santiago to implore the Apostle for a miraculous victory. Alphonse XI went there just to be dubbed a knight. In the course of his journey he made a pilgrimage to Saint James' sacred tomb, and "before he reached the city, he went on foot from a place called Monjoya. As soon as dawn broke, the archbishop, John of Limia, said a mass for him and blessed his arms, and the king armed himself with all his arms—with gambeson, cuirasse, cuisses, jambs, sollerets; and he girded on his sword, himself taking all the arms from the altar of Santiago; no one else gave them to him. And the king went up to the image of Santiago over the altar and caused the image to slap him on the cheek. And in this way did this king Don Alfonso receive knighthood from Santiago" (p. 234).

The prestige of the Apostle is not used here to secure victories over the infidel, but to invigorate the faith in the greatness of the king,[26] to whom the Apostle had physically administered the symbolic dubbing. The human continued in alliance with the divine, and the national war effort with the international rite of chivalry, enlivened in the fantasy of the lords through the reading of chivalric poems, which were very much in vogue, as the Archpriest of Hita tells us, at precisely that time:

> Blancheflur was never so loyal to Floris
> Nor is Tristan *now* with all his loves
> [As I am to my mistress].
> (*Libro de Buen Amor*, stanza 1,703)

It was with such elaborate solemnity, then, that the king had himself crowned in the midst of jousts, tournaments, and merrymaking—a great period, this first half of the fourteenth century in Castile, even if it was incubating the germs of disaster. A knightly king and a good fighter, Alphonse XI was in love with a woman of surpassing beauty. But the plague, the scourge of the epoch, snatched him away prematurely while he was laying siege to Algeciras in 1350, and Castile was left divided between two hostile families whose hatred could be washed away only with blood.

---

[26] One notices the difference between this and what happened in France, where the kings arrogated to themselves divine powers on their own initiative, as if God had delegated his powers to them.

Two figures of great proportions fill the stage of Spanish letters in this period: Don Juan Manuel and the Archpriest of Hita, characteristic representatives of the new, disquieting energy that pulses through Castilian life as it is touched by the culture of Europe and at the same time more deeply anchored than ever in the Hispano-Oriental form of life. Elsewhere, in *Aspectos del vivir hispánico*, I have tried to delineate the spiritual situation of Spain during the second half of the fourteenth century. The most significant events of this period turn out to be the foundation of the Order of Saint Jerome, the birth of the *Romancero*, and the brilliant writings of the Chancellor Pero López de Ayala. Let it suffice here to say that the distance between the first half and the second half of the century can be measured by comparing Ayala's work with that of the Archpriest of Hita, and it is as a preparation for understanding the latter that I have written the chapter ended here. The next chapter, however, has not been written with the purpose of contributing a few more pages to the History of Spanish literature. *The Book of Good Love* by the Archpriest of Hita is going to be in the present case only an aspect, an outstanding one indeed, of the functioning of the Spanish form of life in the fourteenth century, at the moment Castilians began to feel less inhibited in expressing themselves than in the thirteenth century.

The Archpriest of Hita and His "Libro de Buen Amor"

THE *Libro de Buen Amor* is a loosely connected series of poems, a *can-cionero*, one might call it, composed by a certain Juan Ruiz, Archpriest of Hita, about 1330. Concerning the author we know only his name and his work, but he looms, as poetic agent, behind his poem that overflows with love affairs, passions, and sensuality, even while it is enveloped in a cloud of morality and allegory. The book is heterogeneous yet abound-ing in persistent reiterations. Because the *Book of Good Love* is foreign to the spirit of earlier Castilian poetry and, in certain respects, to the spirit of Romanic literature as a whole, it has generally taken readers by surprise. The methods that are used for understanding Romanico-Chris-tian poetry fail with the *Libro de Buen Amor*, because this brilliant manifestation of erotic literature is actually a reflection of Arabic models. If it is seen in the perspective I have tried to establish in the preceding pages, it ceases to be so anomalous.

The book is moralizing yet equivocal. It speaks perfectly naturally of the sexual attraction of woman, but not in the manner of Ovid, or the goliard poets of European Christendom, whose poetry it resembles in certain superficial ways. Juan Ruiz's minstrelsy was Hispano-Arabic, but this did not keep him from treating European and Christian themes, such as the "Debate Between Sir Flesh and Dame Lent," or from making a highly original translation of the metrical dialogue *Pamphilus*. Here for the first time in Castilian we hear a poetic voice expressing personal awareness of an "I"—not to be identified with the historical "I" of the poet. Realities that hitherto could not speak their parts in the realm of art now emerge endowed with poetic values: street cries, dialogues laden with innuendo, a girl speaking in Arabic, kitchen paraphernalia and the tasks in which they are involved, farm chores—"old wives by their fires now tell their tales" (stanza 1,273, Ducamin edition). Fur-thermore, for the first time in Castilian letters, the poet speaks of the living individuality of certain Spaniards: "I mistook a trail for a road, the way the Andalusians do" (116). Such a display of phenomena apprehended through the senses, of lively experience, has no antecedents in Castilian literature.

Here is a poet who can put into rhymes all that takes place in the inner souls of people and in the world in which they live. We feel the presence of wholly Castilian cities, the bustling and jostling of three races and faiths; there is mention of astrologers; go-betweens appear on the scene; there are references to learned books, to peasants and knights in the service of Spain, to ladies, monks, and nuns; there is a riot of tunes and songs, appetizing foods, liturgical feasts, mountain passes in the Guadarrama, exquisite language and plebeian improprieties—all mixed together in an orgy of sensations that is periodically interrupted by a flood of abstract moralizing. But the man who wrote this was an original and powerful artist, not merely a naïve moralist or a cynic making playthings out of vice and morality. Nor was he a mere verse-hawker transmitting the commonplaces of a nameless and timeless tradition. Juan Ruiz lived during the time of Alphonse XI, when Castile was beginning to find an expression for her sensibility and was not ashamed to speak of the matter. In short, his book provides us with a repertory of gay literary themes and in addition it raises for discussion the question of the charms, the complications, and the risks of love. The author, an impresario of public and private pleasures, arouses and admonishes from the abundant experience of what he has seen, heard, and read, appearing alternately as an unbridled rake and as a wise preacher. This artistic play is not to be found in any European work of that epoch, not even in Chaucer.

The author is the first to enjoy his own song book—an open arabesque in which beginning and end are not only lacking but impossible—and he invites his audience to join in the merry game, to toss the volume like a ball from hand to hand, and let him who can, catch it (stanza 1,629). He asks for neither learned commentaries nor interpretations, because neither he nor his book is learned. He wants the artistic merriment to go on, and he foresees that the book is going to be widely read. He even imagines what the reactions of the reader will be, although the reader sometimes feels himself at a loss in his rich tangle. It is indeed extraordinary for an author—Juan Ruiz or whatever his name may be—to experience in his own poetic life the delivery of his book to an anonymous audience with the intent that the book may be continued in the indefinite progression of an arabesque. For this volume is not like the later *Cancionero de Baena* and others of its kind, made up of separate, unconnected poems. Here there is interlacing and continuity, no matter how external and illusory the interlacing and continuity may be; and one even discerns certain lacunae left by the author, as I shall presently point out. None of the figures that appear in these verses is adequately endowed with vitality, with the exception of Trotaconventos, who is on the verge of having a personality full to overflowing. What is beyond a doubt created here in the way an author creates a character, is the book itself: Juan Ruiz gives it a name, debates its meaning, is proud of having put it into poetry of such art, fears that it will be misinterpreted, suggests how it ought to be read, and, finally, bequeath it, on certain conditions, to posterity. A first text is dated 1330; another, 1342.

The artistic individuality of the poet is evident at the outset in his desire that the *Cancionero* be continued by "any man who hears it, *provided he knows how to write good verses*" (1,629), by adding or emending according to his taste. We cannot say whether this occurred or not, for in the book there is no subject matter or happening that lends itself to reworking as in the medieval epic, in the *Celestina*, or in the seventeenth-century theatre, which all, without invitation, were reworked time and again. Only Trotaconventos remained alive in the poetic air and could thus reappear in the *Corbacho* (1438) and the *Celestina* (1499). A few verses of the *Libro de Buen Amor* survived in the fifteenth century, and that is all. But what is important here is that the *Libro de Buen Amor* used Castilian for the first time to give expressive form, in the first person, to sense experiences outside the framework of myth and from within the conscious awareness of a poet expressing himself:

> At the top of the mountain pass
> I thought I was dying
> From the snow and the cold,
> And from the drizzle
> And from the heavy frost. (1,023)

The poetic characters of the *Corbacho*, the *Celestina*, and the *Quijote* were to move down the path of personal expression opened simultaneously by Juan Ruiz and Don Juan Manuel, broadening it as they went along. But Juan Ruiz's own song book, with its kaleidoscopic variety, could not be reworked by anyone: the tone of personal expression dominated the objectivity of fable or happening. Every line gives the impression of personality, of a unique person talking, and it would be childish to argue over whether this person is or is not Juan Ruiz. A century later, when the jongleurs spiced their performances by reciting portions of the famous book, they did not say that they were going to tell this or that story but rather "now let us begin from the Book of the Archpriest."[1] The personal tone of an author welded to his work persisted, and his "copyright" did not dissolve in anonymity.

If we wish to get at such a strange and complex art, we immediately face questions that extend outside the pages of Juan Ruiz's book, which even before it was first printed, in the eighteenth century, was the subject of "interpretations." Overly chaste hands had by that time already torn out a few folios, and there is no doubt that the author's manuscript contained a good deal more than what has been preserved. The first editor, the eighteenth-century Tomás Antonio Sánchez, mutilated the text for reasons of morality. Since then, opinions have been varied and passionate.

Towards an Interpretation of the "Libro de Buen Amor"

Underlying the jests and running counter to the helter-skelter arrangement of so much amusing anecdote, a constant thread of meaning is perceptible. The themes—didactic, parodic, or whatever—are put into order according to a certain idea of the poetic matter itself, existing prior to the poet's work and functioning as its structural principle. This is the distinctive *quid* of the *Libro de Buen Amor* as compared to the *Carmina Burana*, the *fabliaux*, the imitations of Ovid (*Pamphilus, Nuntius sagax*), or any such poetry of the *clerici vagantes*. From all these the Archpriest took what he liked, but he recreated the borrowed material in a poetic form that is the only thing of its kind, without precedent and without sequel. Strictly speaking, one cannot even say that Love is the single vertex at which the other values converge. To be sure, Love is one of the converging points, but it is also a light that illumines other aspects good in themselves: versification, verbal luxury, the sound of musical instruments, the creative dynamism of money, the art of the *alcahueta* in inciting the passions, the conflict—half game, half battle— between the forces of pleasure and the forces of abstinence, the universal rejoicing over whatever is expressed in life. But in spite of all this, the primary and directing subject matter can only be the tense and spirited activity of freely willed life, in which the destination is Love and the fuel is joy. Juan Ruiz is aware that all this happens both *in* and *to* his book, center and *primum mobile*, a complex of multiple overtones

[1] R. Menéndez Pidal, *Poesía juglaresca*, p. 270.

for those who have ears to hear them. Let us see what this happening consists in:

> As Aristotle says, and it is true,
> The world *exerts* itself for two things: the first,
> To have enough victuals; the other,
> To couple with a pleasant female . . .
> Men, birds, beasts of the field, all animals living in caves
> By nature *crave* always a *new mate*,
> And how much more so man who is moved by the call
>   of every thing. (71-73)

The reference to Aristotle is inspired in the *Politics* (Book 1, chapters 1 and 3), as E. Buceta has pointed out (*Revista de Filología Española*, 1925, XII, 56-60). The difference between the Philosopher and Juan Ruiz is not only that the latter speaks humorously, but that Aristotle is explaining the abstract being of nature, whereas our poet makes use of the vital impulse in human existence in order to base the construction of his work on a frenetic and all-embracing dynamism. What is theory in Aristotle appears here as urgent vitality: man *exerts himself*, he *craves*, he is moved by *every thing*. Juan Ruiz is not interested in the nature of man; it fascinates him rather to feel man toiling feverishly away, desiring, or even sinning:

> When a man sins, he realizes he is slipping;
> But he doesn't renounce this, for nature prods him. (75)

Man is goaded and preoccupied by cares and feverish urges. His pursuit of woman derives from the basic fact of his situation in a toilsome existence:

> I got rid of my sadness, of my troublesome cares,
> I sought and found a lady, something I am always
>   craving to do. (580)

Juan Ruiz's book is more than an *Ars amandi*. Its fundamental theme might rather be thought of as the travail and disquietude bound up with the necessity of loving:

> I've never tired while serving ladies . . .
> For what black reason did I fail to get one? (577)

Precisely because other difficulties exist alongside those created by love, such difficulties are intensified:

As the Wise One says, a *hard and unbearable thing* it is
To abandon *custom, fate, lot*;
Custom is a second nature, to be sure.[2] (166)

Nature, custom, and fate are at the same time both urges and obstacles in the course of existence. The awareness that life is like this figures integrally in the complex structure of the Archpriest's poem in spite of the irrepressible humor of his jokes. The book moves forward dialectically —not so much between the notions of virtue and sin as between the conscious experiences of the vital impulse (effort, fleetness, gaiety, etc.) and of the obstacles encountered (rejection, disillusion, sadness, etc.). The interpretation of the book as a ridiculing and salacious work (Goliardism) has hitherto prevented us from grasping what there is of the seriously human behind its gay, playful, youthful style.

The subject of the book fits in with the possibilities of the Spanish vital "dwelling-place" and *vividura*. Those acquainted with the *Roman de la Rose* (completed about 1280 by Jean de Meun) can measure the distance between its deliberate rationalism[3] and Juan Ruiz's vitalism evolved in the constant reversals of an existence fraught with difficulties, in the continual oscillation between longing and frustration. The *Libro de Buen Amor* does not fit within the bounds of didactic poetry, where life is contemplated from the outside, set between parentheses and viewed in the stable, ideal reality of the ought-to-be, not in the problematical reality of its existence. Besides the usual didactic works, there was in Hispano-Arabic letters another kind of literature at once moralizing and vitalized. The finest example of this is the work of Ibn Ḥazm, *Human Character and Conduct*, where morality is presented as a function of living and is illustrated by means of autobiographical experiences:

"I have persistently sought an end for human actions which all men might deem to be good and which all might find appealing, and I have found only one: the end of avoiding *anxiety*. . . . No one *is moved* to act, nor does one decide to say so much as a word, if he does not ex-

[2] Notice how Juan Ruiz vitalizes the idea which, as a well-worn commonplace, had been repeated ever since Aristotle. Cf. "What is demanded by custom is stronger than what is demanded by nature" (*Bocados de oro*, ed. by H. Knust, p. 375).

[3] *Bel Accueil* censures *Raison*'s use of such dirty words as *coilles* "Qui ne sont pas bien renomees / En bouche a courteise pucele" (ed. of E. Langlois, ll. 6,930-6,931). *Raison* answers that "Coilles est beaus nons e si l'ains; / Si sont, par fei, coillon e vit; / Je fis les moz e sui certaine / Qu'onques ne fis chose vilaine / E Deus, qui est sage e fis [to be trusted], / Tient a bien fait quanque je fis" (ll. 7,116-7,122). There is not the spontaneity in the use of these words that there is among the Arabs, or in Juan Ruiz when he wants the woman to have "wet armpits" (445). Jean de Meun thinks out and measures everything he says; he does not plunge into life.

pect to get rid of anxiety and to banish it from his soul by his acts or words. . . . Man goes so far even as to risk his life in order to expel from his soul the anxiety that overwhelms it." (Spanish translation by M. Asín, *Los caracteres y la conducta*, pp. 4, 145.)

One of the major preoccupations present in the texture of Ibn Ḥazm's existence was the correction of those things he regarded as defects, for example, his "irresistible inclination to mocking jests, because to speak seriously always seemed boring to me and the way of proud folk" (*loc.cit.*, p. 44). Ibn Ḥazm, then, does not define man as a rational being, as a divine creature, or in any other conceptual way. For him man is a being endowed with a "troublous life," and as such he is totally contained within this life's boundaries. It is of no interest now to dig out here the antecedents of this way of understanding man (see Chapter 14, footnote 37). It is more important for us to see that Juan Ruiz also approaches man as a totality, from the point of view of his cares and urges. The mentions that he makes of his sources ("Cato said," 44; "Aristotle says," 71; "the Wise One says," 166; "Ptolemy says and Plato says," 124) must not be taken for an abstract feature of medieval anecdotalism. They are manifestations of the Archpriest's way of seeing man as caught between his cares and his labors, by the designs of fate and chance. Something in keeping with this vision of man pre-formed the Archpriest's artistic intent. The work is thus quite explainable in terms of the possibilities and preferences of the Hispanic *vividura*, and is not to be related to the tradition of Christian Europe only. The comic effect of the *Libro de Buen Amor* does not come only from the failure of vice in the face of virtue. Human actions are regarded as either effectual or ineffectual, and their locus is between a vital urge based on a *care* and the end they are expected to achieve. The painter Don Pitas Payas, of whom Juan Ruiz tells, decides to go on a long journey; he takes certain naïve precautions to keep his wife from deceiving him, and, as he should have expected, he does not succeed (474-484): "Women, mills, and gardens always require a lot of use" (472). Don Pitas Payas is deceived by someone "cleverer" than he, who follows the adage "he who flushes the hare, if he doesn't give it chase and catch it, is a bad hunter" (486).

The persons and things that dwell in this book live in tension, committed to the task of attracting and being attracted. If a woman's favor is to be captured, one must say things, one must be both agile and gallant (518), all such activities being as efficacious as money. The role of the "Exemplum of the Properties of Money" (Ensiemplo de la propriedad que el dinero ha, 490-513) is not to emphasize the corrupting force of money, a treatment of the matter that had been as frequent before the *Libro de Buen Amor*[4] as it was to be after it. Money does create and encourage evil, but it also has its part in the creation of important values. One can hardly regard as an evil "the finest dwellings, lofty and very costly, beautiful and painted, castles, lands, and towered cities" (501); or "the noble cloths, guilded garments, precious jewels, noble steeds" (502). Money corrupts the clergy, but "where there is much money, there is much that is noble" (508). Money is one of a number of impelling forces operative in the journey through life. Its function is harmonized with the structure of the book as a whole, for he who has no money to give away can be "generous with words," or he can play a musical instrument, or he can sing beautiful songs (514-515). These are not simply Ovidian formulas for winning the love of a woman. The poet is subject to his vision of the incited and inciting vital process, which is capable of overcoming the obstacles that appear in man's way: "You will not lift a huge beam with a thin cord, . . . / the heavy rock cannot be moved with a single wooden shaft; / with wedges and hammers it can be dislodged little by little" (517). The artistic intention is expressed in these images of sweat-marked, productive fatigue, followed, in elegant contrast, by a rapid and brilliant flash:

Be swift in your moves, daring in action. (518)

in the same key as these lines concerning non-erotic matters:

By serving well, the knights of Spain conquer. (621)

and

You are more proud and more dashing than all Spain together. (304)

The service of the beloved or desired woman is one supreme aspect of man's life, but not the only one, for he *"is moved by every thing"* (73), and if the initial impulses are in his cares and longings, he is kept going by joy, ardor, swiftness, gallantry, cleverness, effort, words, songs, and music.

The motives, modes, and ends of the primary activities of life appear suddenly, rapidly intuited and sketched in a single stroke. The author was without the art and the possibility of channeling that torrent in individual lives. The figures in the book, obedient to a dynamic impulse that impels them and existing outside of time and space, repeatedly demonstrate their vagueness. It is nonetheless true, however, that the impersonalized idea of natural motives and the throbbing of that dyna-

[4] See Felix Lecoy, *Recherches sur le Libro de Buen Amor*, p. 237.

mism in the soul of the poet here take on expressive and highly effective forms in fables and exampla or in intense flashes of poetry. What is most genuinely poetic in the book shows itself in isolated aspects and in discontinuous points, for instance, in the picture of Doña Endrina, as her slender figure moves unattended across a square:

> Oh God, how beautiful is Doña Endrina as she comes
> across the square!
> What a figure, what grace, what a proud heron-neck!
> What hair, how pursed her lips, what color, what a
> fine gait!
> When she raises her eyes she strikes with love's darts. (653)

This is what Juan Ruiz made of the original Latin verse on which he bases this episode—"Quam formosa, Deus! nudis uenit illa capillis" (*Pamphilus*, v. 153). The vague mention of a beautiful woman with her hair uncovered acquires line, grace, color, and movement. Across the square she goes; her graceful figure, discerned in her upright, rhythmic walk, leaves a trail of aroused passions.

Wherefore the paradoxical impression that the atmosphere of forces and motives surrounding the literary figures is more real artistically than the figures themselves, who never are concretized in authentic individuality. Hence the strangeness and heterogeneity of the literary form created by Juan Ruiz. At times we seem to be getting close to a truly personal, novelistic style, free of the slightest abstract and generic slag:

> At the top of the pass the weather was harsh,
> Icy wind, sleet biting cold.
> Since one doesn't feel so much cold if one runs,
> Down the hill I went running. (1,006-1,007)

But the myth reappears immediately:

> At the foot of the pass I came upon a monstrous person,
> The most enormous fantasm I ever have seen . . .
> Saint John the Evangelist in his Apocalypse
> Never saw such a figure. . . . (1,008-1,011)

Such contrasts are repeated time and again:

> One of God's holy seasons is drawing near;
> I set out for my own country to have a good time for a while;
> Seven days from then was Lent. . . . (1,067)

But then Lent is personified in a mythical being: Dame Lent and all the abstractions around her.

So it is that the frame and the tracks that carry the action forward come to view in a literary perspective that is out of harmony with the perspective of the figures in whom the human event takes form and substance. The elements that are not individualized come closer to earthly experience than those that claim to be individualized: The farmer who in January "filled his casks, filled them with a funnel, put ice on them to keep the wine strong" (1,276). Donkeys "don't stop braying till August is past" (1,285). In July "The gadfly makes the beasts bear their noses on the ground" (1,293). Etc.

The world, the earth, as a motive or scene for human actions, seems closer to personal experience than the human beings situated in that scene. The reason for this is obvious: The cold of the mountain, the casks of wine, the braying of asses, or the rhythmic walking of a lovely girl across a square were not established literary categories in the Romanic tradition;[5] these phenomena could either have occurred in the book or not, they could have been what they were or others could have been used in their place, depending on the form and direction of the artistic purpose. On the other hand, a literary character was a structure with its life already made, already existing, that is, in a transcendent tradition—epic, religious, didactic, allegorical, or satyrical. The Archpriest could and did intuit freely the circumstances around personal existence, as well as the motives that make this existence possible. But he could not take literary characters out of the frames in which they were traditionally encased, and individualize them within a system of impulses that were not traditional. For this we shall have to wait for the *Celestina* (1499). In the *Libro de Buen Amor* we find literary strata of uneven extension, density, and meaning. The basic unresolved disharmony of the work keeps it from belonging to or establishing a genre; yet, it cannot for the same reason, be considered as a random grouping of miscellaneous fragments. But herein also lies its powerful originality, its Christian-Islamic ambiguity. The following pages will permit the reader, I believe, to confirm what I have already said in this regard, and to contemplate certain aspects of the book in greater detail.

The author announces what his work is to be: "a Book of Good Love

---

[5] I do not refer to the traditional pattern of the description of the months of the year (Lecoy, *Recherches*, pp. 276ff.), but to what Juan Ruiz adds in terms of his own vital intensity and of concrete detail. The fine description of the months in the *Libro de Alexandre* (Willis edition, pp. 440-442) is approached from another kind of sensibility.

to gladden the body and *serve* the soul" (13). Rather than a gradual ascension from the mundane to the religious, from earthly appetite to the regulation of conduct, there is here a continual interweaving of vital impulse and moral consciousness. We are a long way from the well-known medieval debates between the soul and the body, for the this-wordly and the transcendental converge and become one in the unity of experience reflected in the first person. This is why the fifteenth-century minstrel spoke of the "Book of the Archpriest" and not just of a book. For this author, life is a totality, composed of physical, sensuous, subjective gaiety, and of a moral transcendence. If the Archpriest had been a Moslem, the continual oscillation between the one plane and the other would have taken place with undisturbed ease, and he would have felt no surprise and betrayed no effort. Since he was a Christian (even though imbued with Islamic tradition), he could not help revealing the contrast between the spontaneity of the senses and moral reflection. Not only his writing, but he himself was Christian, and he could not speak in the same breath as both a sinner and a moralist. The mingling of such opposites, of course, the Archpriest had not only observed among the Moslems but had read about in their literature. But for them the life of the flesh did not necessarily mean the forgetting of the spirit, or vice versa.[6] The medieval Christian did not give up the life of the flesh,

[6] As Ibn Ḥazm wrote in 1022: "Love . . . is not condemned by religion nor forbidden by religious law, for *hearts are in the hand of God*, Most High and Exalted, and among those who fell in love were many well directed orthodox Khalifs, and righteous Imāms" (*The Dove's Neck-Ring*, tr. by A. R. Nykl, p. 6). In his *al-Faṣl* the same author says: "The one sent by God . . . has told us that over there in the future life there will be food, drink, clothing, and sexual union. . . . God created our souls in such a way that it is never repugnant or impossible for them to enjoy fine foods, things to drink, pleasing odors, lovely spectacles, the sounds of music, and wonderful clothing, because all these delights agree and harmonize with the nature of our souls. . . . Then, when God comes again at the day of judgment to join our souls to our bodies, in the other life they will be rewarded and delighted with the pleasures that are proper to them. Nevertheless, the food there will not be prepared over fire, nor will it have any defects, nor will it be transformed into excrement and blood, for there will be no death there, nor corruption." Ibn Ḥazm adds that the theologian Ibn 'Abbās, Mohammed's uncle, said: "Of the things that exist in this world, there is nothing in paradise save the names." But Ibn Ḥazm insists that, if there is no form in the world here below that does not exist in the world of the celestial spheres, "it will have to be accepted that in the other life there are also clothing, things to drink, fine foods, and sexual pleasure, trees, etc." (from the Spanish of M. Asín, *Historia crítica de las religiones*, III, 153-155). One sees at once that the boundaries between "good love" and "mad love" are very much blurred.

but he knew that it was sinful even while he persisted in it; and he used it as subject matter for *comic* literature:

> Removere famulas, non levis est tractatus . . .
> Vitae castae regula nimium est dura:
> vita sola angelica est pura.[7]

But neither to the writer of these verses nor to any other would it have occurred to write poems including the gay and the moralizing at the same time. Juan Ruiz, very familiar with Islamic life, was able to do so—by stretching a bridge of humor from sensuality to morality, a humor not Islamic, to be sure, but his own. This "centauric" combination of two modes of life confuses and misleads us when we try to get at the heart of the Archpriest. When Christians spoke in the first person of matters of morality, they did not at the same time express pleasure in the sensual charms of this world. The use of seductive descriptions of evil as a guide toward virtue therefore seems cynical or hypocritical. Juan Ruiz writes "to give example, and for all men to be warned," just as does Ibn Ḥazm, who (according to texts to be quoted presently) excuses himself for treating of certain matters on the grounds that his object is to caution. Seen in his proper perspective, the Archpriest ceases to appear cynical and hypocritical. His art (for art it is, and not abstract didacticism) consists in giving a Christian meaning to Moslem literary forms, and it is thus parallel to the *mudéjar* architecture so widespread in his time. Love can do good to both the senses and the spirit: therefore his book, an interweaving of Islamism and Christianity, amuses and teaches. The beautiful woman appears here as desirable and desired, even though the poet subsequently moralizes on the worldly dangers of love. On the other hand, wine and its consequence, drunkenness, call forth 84 lines of the Archpriest's gravest censure: "Above all, keep yourself from drinking much wine" (528-549); and although he admits that

> Wine is very good by its own nature
> And has many virtues taken *in moderation* (548),

his final advice is that one must eschew it: "wherefore flee from wine" (549), and there is nothing of the goliard about this.[8] For if there is one

[7] Thus speak the priests in the well-known *Consultatio* (see *The Latin Poems Commonly Attributed to Walter Mapes*, ed. by T. Wright, 1841, p. 174).

[8] Don Juan Manuel, likewise deeply imbued with oriental wisdom, gave this advice to his son, that, if he drank wine, "let it be watered, at least let half of it be wine and half water, . . . and except when you eat, drink no wine in any form" (*El libro de los castigos*, Chap. 11). And he treats of the evils that come from wine again in other places in his works.

theme that is popularized by the poetry of the "clerici vagantes" and the goliards, that theme is undoubtedly wine:

> Tertio capitulo memoro tabernam:
> Illam nullo tempore sprevi, neque spernam . . .
> Meum est propositum in taberna mori, . . .[9]

It turns out, then, that the Archpriest describes the charms of the female body in highly provocative terms while the consequences of drunkenness are painted in gloomy colors:

> If you wish to love a lady, keep yourself away from
> wine. (545)[10]

There are to be sure moral exempla in Christian Europe that have as their theme "Ebrietas plura vitia inducit,"[11] and it is from these that Juan Ruiz took his story of the tippling hermit. But his frequent strictures against wine (296c, 303b), not only because of the moral damage it does but also because of its bad effects on the body (544-545), were a familiar theme among Spanish Jews and Moors: "Wine blinds the eyes, blackens the teeth, takes away the memory, and makes the wise man mad. . . . It weakens the power of the body and paralyzes the members in their functions and troubles the nerves that govern them," etc.[12] Juan Ruiz says: "It causes sight to be lost . . . , it exhausts all strength . . . , it causes the members to tremble, it forgets all sense," etc. (544).[13] There is, furthermore, a sermon for the Moslem Ramadām (the Arabic origin of which must have been very old), which, although it does not have

[9] *The Latin Poems Attributed to Walter Mapes*, ed.cit., pp. xxxix and xlv, and also the "Goliae Dialogus inter Aquam et Vinum," p. 87, with its Romance adaptations, p. 299. As is well known, the theme is to be found in many of the "potatoria" songs of the *Carmina Burana* and other medieval poetry.

[10] This is contrary to the pagan tradition: "Sine Bacho et Cerere friget Venus" and to Ovid's *Ars amandi*: "Et Venus in uinis ignis in igne fuit" (1, 244). Such judgments changed their signs in the Arabic tradition: "Wine is the soul's enemy and interferes with its works, and it is like the man who pours fire upon fire" (*Bocados de oro*, ed. by Knust, p. 137).

[11] See F. Lecoy, *Recherches sur le Libro de Buen Amor*, 1938, pp. 150-154.

[12] *The Book of Delight*, by Joseph ben Meir Zabara (a Catalonian Jew of the end of the twelfth century), tr. by Moses Hadas, 1932, p. 49. Rabbi Arragel of Guadalajara was of the same mind: "I wish to tell you some of the evils which, according as I have read, have happened because of wine, as the Scripture of God puts it. . . . Wine killed the first-born of the world: . . . the tree of which Adam ate was the vine; the wine drunk, death therefore came to him and to his generations" (*Biblia de Arragel*, ed. by the Duke of Alba, 1, 117). Rabbi Arragel mentions many other ways that wine harmed the kings of Israel.

[13] In Spanish: "Faze perder la vista . . . tira la fuerça toda . . . faze temblar los miembros, todo seso olvida."

so close a literal correspondence to the work of the Archpriest as the Jewish text quoted above, does resemble it very much in that it is also written in *cuaderna vía* without a fixed number of syllables. This text[14] is in *aljamía* (Spanish in Arabic characters), and its tone strongly recalls the *Libro de Buen Amor*; but it cannot be affirmed that one is taken from the other, in spite of the similarities between them:

> From the drinking of wine be you well guarded.
> ("Above all, keep yourself from drinking much wine,"
> J. Ruiz, 528.)
> From much and from little, be you well guarded,
> For it is a great enemy of both vile man and the man
> of honor,
> It deceives the whole body, even though the body
> be much lettered. . . .
> Because wine causes much evil to be done,
> It makes the good man lose his loyalty,
> It stirs up much strife and hatred. . . .
> To many men it brings death and injuries.
> ("Wherefore come deaths, disputes, and quarrels,"[15]
> J. Ruiz, 547.)

The coincidence of these two texts in their condemnation of wine, and the literal similarities that we find between the Jewish text quoted earlier and certain verses of the Archpriest's make it evident that the criti-

---

[14] Published by M. J. Müller in *Sitzungsberichte der königl. bayerischen Akademie der Wissenschaften*, Munich, 1860, pp. 201ff. The ms. is in the library of the Escorial, having been found in 1795 when a house in Ágreda caved in. It is known that the Moriscos were in the habit of hiding their books in this way at the time of their expulsion, trusting that they would be able to come back and reclaim them. The editor gives no date for the ms., the language of which could be of the fourteenth century, although it must be remembered that the Castilian of the Moriscos contains Aragonesisms and archaisms. The use of Arabic letters makes dating by script impossible in this case.

[15] In Spanish:
Del beber del bino, tú sey bien guardado,
    ("Guárdate sobre todo mucho vino bever," J. Ruiz, 528)
    de lo poco y de lo mucho, tu sey bien bedado,
    qu'es grand enemigo del bil y del onrrado,
    enganna todo cuerpo, aunque sea grand letrado. . . .
porque el bino faz[e] fazer mucha maldat,
    faze al bueno perder su lealtad,
    buelbe mucha pelea y mucha enemistad . . .
a muchos onbres acarrea muertes e lisiones.
    ("por ende vienen muertes, contiendas e barajas," J. Ruiz, 547.)

cism of wine-bibbing is of oriental provenience in the *Libro de Buen Amor*. This criticism I judge to be more Moslem than Christian: the Koran condemns wine as an abomination,[16] the Gospel does not. This is why wine and its dangers constitute a topic for the preaching of the Ramadān. And the Spanish people, especially the Castilians, are well-known for their sobriety in the matter of alcoholic beverages; and drunkenness, as is likewise well-known, has been a much-censured social vice in Spain since the Middle Ages. When King Alphonse XI solemnly entered Seville in 1324, the Chronicle takes the trouble to mention that the king "found there Don Abrahen son of Ozmín, and because he drank wine, they called him Abrahen the drunkard" (p. 204*b*). In Spain drunkenness has not been a matter of either indifference or of comedy; rather it has been something talked about seriously by the people. The Germans in the Swiss guard of the kings in the seventeenth century were noted for their tendency to get drunk, and the language of drinking—*brindis, carauz*—is Germanic: "*Carauz*, a German word introduced into Spain when people toast one another, and meaning the same thing as finishing the glass and drinking it all up."[17] It is not enough, then, to reduce the foregoing passage from Juan Ruiz to the status of an abstract medieval commonplace unrelated to the vital experience of the Castilian people.

The sermon for the Ramadān in *aljamía* has more than one stylistic trait recalling our book:

Understand my words and be alert to my meaning . . .
Do not take the teaching or the learning without its substance,
Else you can count yourself as like the muleteer's ass.
What does this ass do when they try to saddle him?
He lays back his ears and kicks when they load him. (p. 216)[18]

Whether it be found that this text derives from the Archpriest's book or whether it be found that they both go back to the same models, it is still true that in this case Juan Ruiz and the Moriscos treat the same moral theme. This sermon is the versification of an originally Arabic

[16] I. Goldzieher, *Le dogme et la loi de l'Islam*, p. 53.
[17] See Covarrubias, *Tesoro*; cf. R. del Arco, *La sociedad española en las obras de Lope de Vega*, 1942, p. 645.
[18] In Spanish:

Entiendi mis palabras y sey bien abisado . . .
No tomes la dotrina ni'l saber menos el suero,
pues bien te puedes contar como el asno del recuero.
¿Qué faze este asno cuando lo quieren albardar?
Guinna las orejas y coceya al cargar. . . .

text that must have been much older and which, at a date I am unable
to determine but in any case when it became all but incomprehensible
for the Moriscos, was translated into Spanish.[19] The sermon also treats
the theme of death, equally interesting for both Christians and Moors.

So we are getting closer and closer to the reality of this book of songs
that has as its intent the projection of gay and pleasant lives in alternation
with moral reflections that may be taken as background or foreground,
as we prefer. When the author appeared on the public square with this
radically new kind of literature having for its subject matter profane
love, he did not enjoy the liberty of either the Latin-European poets[20]
or the composers of Arabic literature, for reasons already explained. Juan
Ruiz's book was a bold innovation in the austere land of Castile, for
moral inhibitions had not disappeared there. I have already mentioned
that medieval readers tore pages out of the book, and in the Salamanca
manuscript there is more than one instance where the daring language
of the earlier texts (the manuscripts called G and T) has been toned
down. At first, chastity in written expression was an aspect of Castile's
defense against the Moors, and then it became a characteristic feature
of its literary style.[21]

[19] "This is the Ramadān alkhoṭba [sermon], translated from Arabic into Castilian, and it is rhymed in stanzas so as to be sweeter to the hearers and so that
they will have pleasure in listening to it" (p. 201).

[20] Who could write such things as this:

> Abbas qui monachum mittit ad curiam,
> si non vult perdere stulte pecuniam,
> huic prius geminos abscidat, quoniam
> castrati proni sunt ad avaritiam.
>
> (In F. G. E. Raby, *A History of Secular
> Latin Poetry*, II, 224)

[21] The story of *Teodor, la doncella*, is a very significant case. This story, drawn
from the *Thousand and One Nights*, is first found in a manuscript of the fifteenth
century, but this is most certainly a copy of a fourteenth-century text, to judge
by the language. The text was published by H. Knust in *Mittheilungen aus dem
Eskurial*, 1879. There are many editions of the *Historia de la doncella Teodor* from
the sixteenth to the eighteenth century (see Menéndez y Pelayo, *Orígenes de la
novela*, I, LVI), but all of them have changed the ancient translation into a moral
tale. In the fourteenth century (it is not possible to fix the date more precisely),
translations were made from the Arabic that the thirteenth century would have
judged immoral. As is well known, the girl in question (called Tawaddud in Arabic)
is a slave who astonishes with her wisdom, and in this way acquires a large sum
of money with which she is able to relieve the poverty of her master, who finally
marries her. The things this omniscient girl knows are said in Arabic quite as a
matter of course, though they were suppressed in subsequent revisions. The girl
knows that "the revealing of secrets and sleeping with an old woman are mortal
sins" (p. 510), and she knows the techniques of sexual intercourse: "If the woman

The Archpriest's literary framework is quite ample. He has one style for the treatment of patrician love and another for plebeians and rustics in love. Thus, in spite of the fact that his work has been more expurgated than Jean de Meun's, Chaucer's, and others', it is still possible to find him alluding without qualm to sexual intercourse in the broad style of the "song of a mountain girl" (cántica de serrana):

> The mischievous cowgirl said: "Let's wrestle a while;
> Be quick then, get out of those clothes."
> She took me by the wrist, I had to do all that she wanted;
> I think I gave a good account of myself. (971)[22]

The language is shaped to the image of the action, and so it happens that the means of expression are enriched and made flexible. The form here is not closed as it is in the epic or in the works in the learned poetry of the *cuaderna vía*. It does not treat of great figures (heroes, saints) that have an existence prior to the poem. Here the situations and actions of the people are more important than the people themselves. The cowgirl, with rude humor, says "luchemos" (let's wrestle), "desbuélvete" (undress), "hato" (a shepherd's word for clothes), she takes the man "by the wrist," not by the hand, that is, with force and decision; the man does "all that she wanted," because he is an instrument for satisfying elemental appetites; there is nothing ladylike or courtly about it, and he therefore says: "fiz buen barato" (I gave a good account of myself, I gave her plenty), a coarse expression in keeping with the whole scene. The naturalness of the situation is accepted and at the same time that which was felt then and later by the Castilian to be obscene is avoided. Juan Ruiz is not Chaucer or Rabelais; he limits himself to presenting a

---

be the kind whose orgasm comes slowly, or if the man's comes quickly, then her pleasure will be cut off altogether, and it may happen that she will not recover from this" (511). "Lying with a woman is an hour's pleasure" (515). Some features of the Arabic ideal of feminine beauty as expressed by Teodor are also found in Juan Ruiz's perfect woman: "ancha de caderas" (broad of hips) (Teodor, p. 514), "ancheta de caderas" (broadish of hips) (J. Ruiz, pp. 432, 445), a detail not given in the models of rhetoric (see María Rosa Lida, *Revista de Filología Hispánica*, 1940, II, 122), which think of clothed women, whereas Juan Ruiz advises: "fight to have a woman that you can see without her gown" (435), and he wants her to have "her armpits slightly wet" (445). This suggests not only the established models for poetry, but also the intimacies of the brothel.

[22] In Spanish:

> La vaquera traviesa diz: "Luchemos un rato;
> liévate dende apriesa, desbuélvete de aques hato."
> Por la muñeca me priso, ove de hacer cuanto quiso;
> creo que fiz buen barato.

human event—what the cowgirl did—without malice, without winking at the reader. And in the next breath, thinking about the problem of conduct, he preaches and teaches; Islamic literature is also didactic and sermonizing.

The Castilian had all along been fashioning his life in the image of the person as such, who by his success in his own conduct, that is, by the effective use of his intrinsic powers of perseverance, loyalty, faith, etc., had continually been able to blot out ancient humiliations and inferiorities:

> By *serving* well the knights of Spain conquer. (621)[23]

It was possible for Juan Ruiz to cultivate erotic poetry for the additional reason that Europe had for some time been treating of love as a means of perfecting the soul and as a "by-product" of divine love. The traditions of Europe and the Christian-oriental traditions of the Peninsula were harmonized in serene beauty by the Archpriest. In this song book both the beautiful woman and the Virgin Mary are objects of love, but only to the latter are expressions of "direct" love addressed:

> I will follow thee, flower of flowers. (1,678)[24]

The Archpriest did not dare compliment a woman; he did not dare to express himself like the Arabs, who spoke without restraint of the charms of the woman beloved even in the case of a chaste man rejecting them, in which latter instance the poetry aroused the flesh perhaps more than that which was frankly lascivious.[25]

The *Libro de Buen Amor* was the ambiguous offspring of the joy of life and moral restraint. The two themes collide and intermingle in the complex play of its style. To be sure, the author did not conceal his sensuous delight in the immediate and sweet-tasting world. His vehement impulse comes through in his expression, in his contempt for the flaccid and the inert. Sir Love and the Archpriest alike have a high regard for agility:

> Be swift in your moves, daring in action (518),

[23] In Spanish:
  Con buen *servicio* vencen cavalleros de España.
[24] In Spanish:
  Quiero seguir a ti, flor de las flores.
[25] Accessible texts are to be found in the translations of A. R. Nykl, *El Cancionero de Abén Guzmán*, 1933; *Hispano-Arabic Poetry*, 1946; H. Pérès, *La Poésie andalouse en arabe classique au XIe siècle*, 1937; E. García Gómez, *Poemas arábigo-andaluces*, 1940; as well as in the previously cited bibliography.

like
> The good hound, light, and fleet and bold (1,357),[26]

a verse with the thrust and course of an arrow. This is an active, roving poetry, gay and sensual—a literature of going and seeing, or seeing and tasting as much as possible of this world, an aspiration that was eventually to be fulfilled by the boundless sensuality of Lope de Vega.

From the silence in which the epic, religion, and didacticism had left it because it was judged useless for their purposes, Juan Ruiz brought forth the reality of the small and everyday things of life. We have heard an uncouth mountain girl say to her rather hesitant bed-mate, "desbuélvete de aques hato" (971). Now the poet invites us to "sample all things" (950), the great and the small:

> Many people come with the great Emperor [i.e. Sir Love],
> Archpriests and ladies, the former to the fore;
> Then *everyone and everything* I told you before:
> *The valley resounds with the noisy uproar.* (1,245)

And as for going about, traveling: "Passing one morning through the pass of Malangosto" (959); "I went off to Segovia" (972); "Monday before daybreak I got on my way" (993); "I set out for my part of the country" (1,067); "I want to go and *see* Alcalá, I shall linger there at the fair" (1,312), etc. And as for music, songs, and dances: "I wrote many songs for dancers and for *troteras*" (1,512). The latter are songs for women who work as roving messengers, called *troteras* by Juan Ruiz. And in relation with the *trotera* appears the figure of Trotaconventos, a woman who moves adroitly in and out of convents, acting as a panderess. Trotaconventos, I have said, is the character with the most density in the entire book, a symbol of profane traveling and of religion turned worldly. In the goings about and in the flow of gaiety, without perversion or rationalization,[27] everything—"el mundo todo"—gradually emerges. The good world of Islam, pleasing and palatable, opened itself up to Christian Castile with literary dignity, thanks to the personal propensity for the joyous that runs from the beginning to the end of Juan Ruiz's *Book of Good Love.*

[26] In Spanish:

> Prueba fazer ligerezas e fazer valentía . . .
> el buen galgo ligero, corredor y valiente.

[27] Not with the rationalistic joy of Medieval Europe: "Gaudeamus *igitur*, juvenes *dum* sumus."

The Theme of Gladness

From its beginning the work proclaims itself "a Book of Good Love ... to gladden people's bodies and edify their spirits" (13): it is desirable for man to intersperse his troubles with "*pleasures,* and to *gladden his reason,* / for too much sadness brings too much care (44).[28] The blind man begging alms implores the Virgin Mary to look with favor on his benefactor: bring *joy* to his body and salvation to his soul" (1,712). "A woman likes to have a *happy* man for a lover" (626); "*happy* goes the nun from the choir to the parlor, / *happy* goes the monk from tierce to the refectory" (1,399); "*happiness* makes a man elegant and handsome" (627); "love left me with care, but also with joy; / This my lord [love] was always like this" (1,313). "On Low Sunday churches and altars / I found filled with the *joy* of weddings and songs" (1,315). Etc.

This gladness (alegría) is not a convention, a thematic framework, or a commonplace unconsciously borrowed from other texts. Quite apart from considerations of its frequency and the appropriateness with which it is introduced, we find it present in the very conception of certain religious motifs, and this proves that "joy" shapes the poet's poetic intent itself. Thus he sings of the "joys" (gozos) and not the sorrows of the Virgin Mary (21, 28, 34). These joys appear again in stanzas 1,635 and following: "I sing your joys as my offerings in your service." There is nothing here, on the other hand, of the Sorrowful Mother of the "Stabat Mater." The only sorrows are those that occasionally beset the poet, causing him to cry out in his affliction to the Mother of Joy, begging her to deliver him from his tribulation: "From tribulation without delay come and free me now."

He takes poetic pleasure not in griefs and sorrows but rather in the overflow of his mild and anti-dramatic sensibility, which is inclined towards love—both the refined and the coarse varieties—and opposed to the death of pleasure and its consequent effect of oppressing the spirit. He is the first Castilian to delight in pure word-play and the use of "strange" (estraños) verse forms (1,634), the *zajal* (see Chapter 10, footnote 70, for a description of this form) with its internal rhymes that swell his pride as an artist without pretensions of scientific learning. This defines and individualizes the first lyric poet of the Castilian language, zealous to show others the paths of a poetry based on experiences of life

---

[28] To be sure, this idea is found in the Bible, in the Koran, in *The Dove's Neck-Ring* of Ibn Ḥazm, in the distichs of the pseudo-Cato, and many other places, but this has little to do with its value as propulsive element in Juan Ruiz's poetry. Ideas are to genuine poets as marble and chisel are to sculptors.

and not only on the "sinless" models of the clerks' verses. Behind Juan Ruiz resounds the echo of a long tradition of Hispano-Islamic literary pride.[29] He knows that he has composed a "new book" (Ducamin edition, p. 5) using "strange verses," but he also knows that these verses have been much used in "songs in Arabic" very familiar to him. This is the foundation of his half-learned, half-popular minstrelsy.

But to resume the theme of gladness: Juan Ruiz dedicates nine compositions to the Joyful Virgin, and only two to the Passion of Christ (1,049-1,066), in a style, moreover, which confirms his hedonistic preferences. The Passion is described with tenderness and in almost feminine or childlike terms: "They gave something to the one who betrayed Him and sold Him. . . . *Those old dogs* came right up to Him *and grabbed Him*—all those that were around Him" (1,050-1,051). Judas the Wicked stirs the poet's righteous indignation: "You, being with Him at the hour of prime, saw them carrying Him away, striking Him, *what a pity!*" (1,052). "What a great sorrow! Who would say, milady, which of these was the greatest?" (1,054).[30] It is with the sensibility of a *Mater Dolorosa* that the poet grieves over the cruelties committed by the executioners; but the Christ who lives in his poetry does not sweat blood or cry out as He does in the French *Passions*, or in the Catholic baroque works in the seventeenth century.[31] If he says somewhere that "blood and water came forth" from Jesus' side, the image is neutralized in the sequel "it was a comfort to the world" (1,056-1,065). The terrible scene serves the poet as a source of peace and consolation: "Please bring consolation to my sorrows" (1,058).[32]

[29] I shall mention only a single text. Abū Gālib, a writer of the eleventh century, refused to inscribe the name of the Lord of Denia on the title page of his book, in spite of the offer of rich presents: "A book which I have composed so that people will benefit from it and my effort will be of eternal value—am I to head it with the name of another, yielding my glory to him? I shall do no such thing" (p. 49 of the delightful book *In Praise of Spanish Islam*, by Al-Shakundī, translated by E. García Gómez as *Elogio del Islam español*). Literary "wealth" was one of the major bases of pride amongst the Spanish Moslems.

[30] See also stanzas 1,063-1,664.

[31] "Si fort sudor dunques suded, / que cum lo sang a terra curren, / de sa sudor las sanctas gutas." Juan Ruiz does not cry out "Heli, heli, per quem gulpisti?" nor does the Virgin appear at the side of the cross: "De laz la croz estet Marie" (Bartsch, *Chrestomathie*, 1927, pp. 7-9). In the *Passion d'Autun* an old woman brings a nail of fine steel with which to tear open Christ's flesh: "Tenes les cloux, beaulx doulx amys, / Jhesucrist en sera mal mys. / Monlt ['mine'] sera fort sy les desyre, / Point de meilleur n'a ann en la ville: / De fin acier sont" (edition of Grace Frank, *Anciens Textes Français*, p. 104).

[32] An inverse reflection of the concern for gladness is the rejection of all that is

Juan Ruiz's Virgin Mary is neither the *Mater Dolorosa* nor does she work miracles as in the thirteenth century. She exists clearly and fully in the poet's inner soul, and there is no need to establish her cult on the basis of the favors she grants her worshippers. Juan Ruiz is concerned with experiences, with literary *self-consciousness*. Events and random befallings of all kinds take on their perspective from the person who is living them—the one who speaks to us in the first person—as well as the reader whom the Archpriest invites to share them intimately.

The concern of this song book is not the clear-cut, objective distinction between good and evil. It is meaningful behavior of the spirit engaged inwardly in the process of moralizing. The author does not assert bluntly and dogmatically that this is better than that. With nimble irony he shows us the process of emergent values in the movement towards the good or the ill. Fundamentally characteristic of this work is the air of playful gaiety, as I have said. Gaiety, play, emotional naïveté, unceasing movement from place to place, the shifting of points of view in quarrels, the renewal that comes with every spring, the oscillation between indulgence and abstinence—all this is the form and aspect of an open structure rooted in the sensibility of the speaking character, and into this structure the Archpriest fits everything he knows, sees, and understands of the world.

This gladness, then, is not a random and separable feature. Rather it is effective energy of an artistic form that invests this poetic invention with the capacity to realize itself out of its own resources, as it were. Gladness has the advantage of being open to every perspective imaginable. Sadness, on the other hand, must gravitate like a tombstone to the finished and the frustrated. In the dynamic awareness of its hopes, the blithe spirit feels itself more in the process of continual self-realization than it does in the actual satisfaction of its longings; the spirit of a sad person surrenders passively before a motive exterior to it or before something created and finished which controls and paralyzes it. So it is that people of gay disposition and with a sense of humor move more freely and more gracefully within themselves than the sad and the sarcastic. The Archpriest prefers the former. He does not dogmatize on good and evil as closed, objective entities. He invites us to an open and

---

sad and disturbing: "be wise and not outraged, nor sad nor angered" (563). "Sadness and grudge give birth to bad enemies" (626). To the Virgin he says: "You removed our sadness" (1,666); "never sadden those who do not forget you" (1,682). He rebukes death because "you make gladness sad" (1,549). "Let my pain and my anguish not be without comfort" (605); "many pleasures come after sadness" (797), etc.

humorous discussion—necessarily charged with subjectivism—between good things and evil, while the antennae of his fantasy turn now toward the ones, now toward the others.

The Structure as Continuous Inner Transition

In the book of the Archpriest, the alternately hostile or friendly reception accorded to Sir Love (Don Amor) in various parts of Spain is not cast in terms of judgment, that is, in terms of sin or virtue; rather it is presented as a happening. Through the "sighing and seemingly troubled" confidences (1,303) Sir Love makes to the person who speaks in the book, we learn concerning his wanderings that

> In the winter I visited Seville,
> All Andalusia, I didn't miss a town;
> There everyone gladly bowed to me;
> I was so full of life that it was a marvel. (1,304)

Sir Love says, in effect, that the Andalusians were sensual, and earlier we have been told that they are daydreamers: "I mistook a trail for a highway, the way the Andalusians do" (116). The success or failure of Sir Love is not bound up with a moral purpose; it depends on the condition of the people he meets with, that is, on the way the author characterizes them. To make Sir Love suffer the rigors of Lenten austerity, the poet chose the people of Toledo. Few received him; he was beset rather by

> Many a lady, lean from fasting,
> With many pater nosters and much sour praying. (1,306)

The prayers, although they were sour and were pronounced by thin women, succeeded in driving the undesired visitor away: "They drove me out of the city by the gate of Visagra" (1,306).

To console himself for all his rebuffs, Sir Love went to Castro Urdiales (Santander), the seaport from which the redoubtable Dame Lent had begun her offensive (1,073):

> I went to keep Lent in the town of Castro,
> Myself and my sequit were very well received (1,311),

which proves that Lent was not the cause of Sir Love's bad treatment in Toledo. The motive for this must be looked for in the alternating rhythm of everything that happens in the book. Morality, like everything else, is subordinated to the structure of moving and gliding in which the book consists. Life here is drive and cyclic movement, not a succession of fixed and closed units of content. The changing style with its extended figures is a matter not only of certain words but also of reiteration in the narrative, in the change from love to austerity, or from Dame Lent victorious to Dame Lent fugitive.

In the contest between Dame Lent and Sir Flesh, the stag offers his services to the latter:

> Ahevos ado viene muy ligero el *ciervo*:
> "Omíllome"—diz—"señor, yo el tu leal *siervo*,
> Por te fazer servicio, ¿non fui por ende *siervo*?" (1,089)

In stanza 121 the word *cruz* was at the same time the name of a person and the name of the holy symbol before which a Christian knelt and crossed himself (121):[33] "Cuando la *Cruz* veía, yo siempre me omillava." In a passage important for the understanding of the book as a whole, the author plays with the alternation between *miente* and *verdat, pintadas* and *puntos*:

> Las del Buen Amor son razones encubiertas:
> trabaja do fallares las sus señales ciertas.
> Si la razón entiendes, o en el seso aciertas,
> non dirás mal del libro que ahora rehiertas.
> Do coidares que *miente*, dize mayor *verdat*;
> en las coplas *pintadas* yaze la falsedat;
> dicha o buena o mala, por *puntos* la juzgat;
> las coplas con los *puntos*, load o denostat.
> De todos intrumentos yo, libro, so pariente;
> bien o mal, cual *puntares*, tal te dirá ciertamente;
> cual tu dezir quisieres, í faz *punto* y tente;
> si me *puntar* supieres, siempre me avrás en miente. (68-70)[34]

[33] The passage quoted from stanza 1,089 depends for its effect on the homonyms *ciervo* (stag) and *siervo* (serf, servant), an effect that is completely lost in translation: "Look you, / there where comes the *stag* so fleet: / 'My lord,' he says, 'your loyal *servant* at your feet, / Was I not made a *serf* to serve Sir Meat?'" The girl's name, *Cruz Cruzada* (Cross Crossed, stanza 116) has within itself a word-shift, a repetition of itself amplified.

[34] In English:
> The utterances in the Book of Good Love are masked:
> Strive to find its true meanings.
> If you understand what's said, or if you hit upon the meaning,
> You will not speak ill of the Book that you now censure.
> Where you think it *lies*, it is most *true*;
> Its falseness is in the *colored* stanzas.
> Judge the sentence according to the *points* [overtones];
> The stanzas with the *points* you may praise or censure.

Pintadas means "colored, falsified,"[35] and by its form has evoked *puntos*, the "points" used in ancient books of music to indicate the melody and the manner of playing or singing it; from this, the infinitive *puntar* or *puntear* to designate the peculiar way of playing a stringed instrument. The technical meaning of *punto* is less interesting than the comparison of the book with a musical instrument as a consequence of the gliding from *punto* in the music book to the *puntar* of the musical instrument, all this having its beginning in the contrast *miente-verdat*, and in the multiple meanings inherent in *coplas pintadas* (colored stanzas). The meanings of the book will vary as the reactions vary between the peoples of Seville, Toledo, and Castro Urdiales when they confront Sir Love. The author makes of this a delightful game, inviting the reader to play too. Such an acquaintance with this work shows the puerility of attaching a logical meaning to the words *miente* and *verdat*; and of trying to refer them to a fixed, objective content. The verses quoted above do not contain any definite or objectifiable thought. "Señales ciertas" (sure signs) and "mayor verdat" (the greatest truth) float in an intangible poetic atmosphere just as do "miente" (it lies), "pintadas," "cual puntares" (however you "point"). Nor is there any point in assigning a precise meaning to "siempre me avrás en miente" (you will always have *me in mind*). What is there for us to keep in mind? The words and what they say float in an airy ballet as we are again invited to join the dance: "cual tu dezir quisieres, í faz punto y tente." That is, let everyone choose his own truth, a truth of poetry, of a musical instrument. The verbal similarity between "do coidares que *miente*" (where you think *it is lying*) and "siempre me avrás en *miente*" (you will always have *me in mind*) is now significant. The Archpriest was not interested in the kind of truth that the biblical and legal glossarists were looking for.[36]

> I, the book, am akin to all the instruments;
> Good or bad, whichever way you *point* [play it] so will
>   it surely answer you;
> When you think you have the right meaning, *point* there
>   and stop;
> If you know how to *point* me out, you will always
>   remember me.

[35] Cf. Old French *peint*, "feigned, false."
[36] There is no point in comparing Juan Ruiz to the Provençal poets of the *trobar clus* (hermetic poetry, poetry closed to easy comprehension); they ornamented and inverted their art to get away from the easy, light poetry of the *trobar leu*. The enigmas in their obscure poetry were not functional, they were not linked with the inner structure of the work. Moreover, the poet averred that he knew the key to the puzzles he was giving the reader: "If anyone wishes to object to this

What he plainly says is that the book is like an instrument—like those he gives life to with his descriptions in a number of places, like an instrument that produces open melodies in freely flowing repetitions, as much a part of the poet's art as of the reader's interpretive pleasure. Love (moral or immoral?) is therefore more a reiterated incitement than the occasion for moralizing dogmatism, which would be absolutely incompatible with the tone and style of the work. People love or hate; animals run, fight, or swim; instruments send forth their sounds. And the reader in his turn must play upon the book as on an instrument and interpret it. How? Juan Ruiz does not say, for he is only interested in the interpretive movement as such, as a shifting, gliding function:

> Think not that the book is foolish, idle,
> Nor that anything I read in it is a joke. . . .
> The fennel-flower is *blacker* on the outside than
>   a stew pot:
> Inside it is very *white*, more than ermine;
> *White* meal is under a black covering,
> Sugar, *black* and *white*, is in the lowly cane, etc. (16-18)

This admonition, like all the rest, enters into the flow of the book, and is repeated time after time,[37] although the author may never say, "This is good and that is bad," in a plain and decisive manner, seriously, and without contradicting himself a few lines later. The passage quoted has to be understood in concordance with these others:

> She turned the skin on her first speech. (827)
> They make *white* out of *black*, turning its skin inside out. (929)
> Good *grafters* make the white grapevine dark. (1,291)
> He *grafted* the trees with *foreign* bark. (1,291)

Black and white, the tree's own bark and bark foreign to it, do not convey difference in quality but are only mere expressions of the transition and alternation of which they are a sign. The graft, the opposite colors, keep the structure of the book alive by keeping it in effective movement. They are necessary to it, and thus they are artistically valid. The difference between this poetic form and that of the medieval disputes between the body and the soul, water and wine, the cleric and the

---

verse, I will not fail to defend you, verse, and to say why I have put three words with different meanings [tres motz de divers sens] in you" (Alegret, in A. Jeanroy, *Jongleurs et troubadours*, p. 6; cf. Martín de Riquer, *La lírica de los trovadores*, p. 133).

[37] See stanzas 46, 65, 67, 443, 892, 904, 908, 986, 1,390, 1,631.

knight, is obvious, for the terms opposed to one another in the latter works are fixed entities, not accidental qualities or fluid and reversible situations. The Archpriest is attracted by things that move and are changeable—in plants, in skins, or in love affairs. The girl *Cruz* (Cross) turns into a *cruz* (cross) in the same way that she passes from her first to her second lover. The book, with its open, changing flow, projects this structural property into the experience of the person reading it:

> . . . I shall put
> A period to my little book, but *I shall not close it.*
> It has good *properties* everywhere,
> For if a man who has an ugly wife hears it,
> Or if a woman whose husband is no good hears it,
> They feel at once the desire to serve God.
> They want to hear masses and make oblations,
> They want to give bread and meat to the poor. (1,626-1,628)[38]

It would follow that the man in possession of a pretty wife is not encouraged to attend mass; although what matters here is that the reader lacking piety becomes pious and changes his desires by virtue of the same vital rhythm observed before: "Good grafters make the white grapevine intó dark" (1,281)—save that in the present case the "grafter" is the virtue radiated by the book, itself changing as it radiates its power to change others.

It is all this that keeps me from applying the term paronomasia— word-play—to the gliding from the name *Cruz* to the common noun *cruz*; I prefer to see in this a sign of the formal structure of the book, of its inner poetic reality. In the light of such an idea, we can go through the book from cover to cover without getting lost in what at first glance appears to be its formless labyrinth; that is, we will be able to follow the transitions which consist, occasionally, in jumping from a word to an unexpressed image of something related to the word. For example, as the poet has used *liebre* (hare) to designate the animal (1,090) that answers Sir Flesh's tocsin "fast and nimble," he jumps to the image

[38] In Spanish:

> . . . Faré
> punto a mi librete, mas *non lo cerraré.*
> Buena *propiedat* ha do quier que sea,
> que si lo oye alguno que tenga mujer fea,
> o si mujer lo oye que su marido vil sea,
> fazer a Dios servicio en punto lo desea.
> Desea oir misas e fazer oblaciones,
> desea dar a pobres bodigos e raciones.

of an article of clothing lined with hare's fur, which causes an itch and can cause boils on the neck; the hare, then, speaking as both a living animal and as his future hide converted into clothing, promises Sir Flesh to communicate the itch and boils to old Dame Lent. When the boils burst, the old Lady will suffer so much that, as the hare says, "she would rather have my skin" than her own—as if to say, "she would rather let her existence slide into mine." The transition thus forms a progressive-regressive cycle, convertible and reversible. With this we can understand the hitherto baffling passage:

> Vino presta e ligera al alarde la liebre:
> "Señor,"—diz—"a la dueña yo le metré la fiebre;
> darle he sarna e diviesos que de lidiar non se miembre:
> más querría mi pelleja cuando alguno le quiebre." (1,090)[39]

The animal present as a unity in terms of either an *I* or a *he* comes apart in the fantasy, unfolds as it were, into several things, and this unfolding lends a strange vivacity and charm to Juan Ruiz's work, which is very different from the allegorical *Roman de la Rose* of Guillaume de Lorris or from the *Bataille de Caresme et de Charnage*. In our book, the expressed image of the animal must be integrated in the halo of the metaphor, which, although unexpressed, nonetheless illuminates it. The whale attacks Sir Flesh: "He embraced him, and cast him on the sand" (1,120). Does this mean that the whale threw him up on the sand with his *arms* (brazos)? Of course not. There is, to be sure, a metaphorical embrace, but in the poetic reality the whale is on the shore and in the sea at the same time, embracing Sir Flesh and carrying him in his belly like another Jonah, only to cast him later on the shore: "And it vomited out Jonah upon the dry land" (Jonah, II, 11). In cases like this, the *Libro de Buen Amor* is the first manifestation of what was one day to be the poetry of Gongora.

Being simultaneously in the sea and on land—the one expressed, the other not—is repeated in the case of the eels:

> From Valencia came the eels,
> Salted and preserved, in great schools:

---

[39] In English:
> The hare came light and fast to muster. Said he,
> "Lord, I'll put a fever in the lady.
> I'll make her itch with boils, forget the duel;
> She'd rather have my hide when her boils burst."

They attacked Sir Flesh in the middle of the ribs;
Trout from Alberche attacked his cheeks. (1,105)[40]

As in the case of the hare, the eels are both dead and alive, just as
Sir Flesh is on dry land and swimming in the water, as earlier the whale
has been. We find him, moreover, in the Valencian sea and the Alberche
river, dressed and naked; otherwise the eels would not have attacked
him "in the middle of the ribs." The leaping trout strikes him in the
face, which he holds above the water. A little later the dogfish (lixa),
with its "very tough skin, / with lots of hooks, gave them [Sir Flesh
and his crew] a black time in their sides and legs" (1,109). The rough
skin of the dogfish would not have done much harm to a clothed person.

There is a shift from the fish in the sea to the fish on land. The
poet speaks in the first person in the episode of his affair with Doña
Endrina (596-891), and this first person changes into Don Melón
de la Huerta (Sir Melon of the Garden, 738) and subsequently into
Don Melón Ortiz (881). The poet escapes from the fantasy of imagining himself in love with Doña Endrina ("I told it so as to give you
an example, not because it happened to me," 909),[41] only to trans-
mute immediately his own consciousness as a man of flesh and blood
into the consciousness of another fictional entity:

Myself being after this without love and troubled,
I saw an elegant lady sitting on her dais:
She carried off my heart at once. (910)[42]

Care (cuidado—trouble, worry, anxiety) is the force that drives the
transient activity of existence, felt by Juan Ruiz as a going out of in
order to enter into, whatever be the motive or the occasion:

Since I make mention to you of penitence,
I should like to repeat a good lesson to you. (1,131)[43]

[40] In Spanish:
De parte de Valencia veníen las anguillas,
salpresas e trechadas, a grandes manadillas;
davan a Don Carnal por medio de las costillas;
las truchas de Alverche dávanle en las mexillas.

[41] Actually, the poet is following in a general way the dialogue Pamphilus, a piece
of twelfth-century Latin verse. See the edition of Eugène Evesque in La "Comédie"
latine en France au XII⁰ siècle, II, Paris, 1931.

[42] In Spanish:
Siendo yo después de esto sin amor e con cuidado,
vi una apuesta dueña seer en su estrado:
mi coraçón en punto levómelo forçado.

[43] In Spanish:
Pues que de penitencia vos fago mençión,
repetir vos querría una buena lición.

This leads him to think of the person who is to provide the lesson:

> It is a very grave thing to me to speak of such a great
> event. . . .
> I am without skill and without learning,[44] I do not dare. . . .
> I am an uncouth scholar, neither wise nor learned.
> (1,133, 1,135)[45]

From things spiritually and invisibly conceived, one passes to things material and visible. It is not enough to repent inside the conscience, because the Church does not have access there. One must pass, then, from the inwardness of the soul to the outwardness of the body. The penitent

> Must make, through gestures and groaning,
> Signs of penitence . . . ,
> Sighing very sad, piteous sighs,
> Weeping signs of penitence from the eyes,
> Where he can do no more, inclining his head. (1,138-1,139)

There are ignorant clerics who absolve people from their sins who are not their own parishioners. So says the author as if speaking of something general and abstract, like a rule of canon law. But from here he moves in one jump to the vision of a concrete and tangible reality to exemplify what he has just said:

> "In Rome what power can a judge from Cartagena have,
> Or how can the mayor of Requena make judgments that
> are good in France?" (1,146)

[44] Brunetto Latini had already said, at the beginning of the *Livres dou Tresor* (written between 1262 and 1266): "And so I do not say that this book has come from my poor *intelligence* or from my unadorned science." Close to the learned tradition of Toledo, Juan Ruiz is aware of his scant learning: "*I*, with my *very little science* and with *very great rudeness*" (ed.cit., p. 5). "I don't know any astrology, nor am an expert in it, / nor do I know any more about the astrolabe than a *leading ox*, / but because *I see this happen* every day, / I tell about it" (151). And with his tireless arabesque, he ends his book by returning to the same opening theme: "My lords, I have served you *with little learning*" (1,633). Like a good Spaniard, he doubtless got most of his learning from idle conversation and street talk ("every day *I see something*—a little thing *I heard* scholarly dispute of"). He boasts of being a "lay wit," but he rises to the mention of his art: "I also composed it [this book] to *teach a lesson* to some people and *give them a sample* of measure and rhyme . . . *exactly the way that science demands*" (p. 7). Don Juan Manuel also confesses to little learning and to having learned more by listening than by reading (*Libro del Caballero e del Escudero*, xxxi).

[45] In Spanish:

> Esme cosa muy grave en tan grand fecho fablar. . . .
> so rudo e sin ciencia non me oso aventurar. . . .
> escolar so mucho rudo, nin maestro nin doctor.

This sentence, of a humor without precedent in Spain, links in a normal way, even so, with the style of going in and coming out, of going up and coming down, upon which are founded the book's inseparable form and content. The flow and transition are functional; so a rigidly fixed boundary is lacking between holy love and profane love,[46] between the serious and the comic, between the generic-abstract and the concrete-sensible.

Let me make it quite clear that the terms of these contrasts can be found in other works of Christian Europe in which the grave and the comic, virtue and sin, exist side by side, but that in Juan Ruiz the extreme positions that I am pointing out appear as a continuous gliding from the one into the other, as I have shown in the passages quoted above. We shall now be able to understand how it is that, although Juan Ruiz draws his content and motives from the jongleur literature of Europe, these "borrowed" materials present an aspect that does not have its like outside the *Libro de Buen Amor*. This is what happens, for instance, with the subject of a religious parody. In the first place, it had never before occurred to anyone to take as the theme for a parody the canonical hours of prayer.[47] These prayers trace out a cleric's life from dawn to night, and even though the person in question is an abstract character, the content of Juan Ruiz's parody comprises the concrete things any cleric might do, and not a moral evaluation of his acts:

> In the house of your mistress you begin to arise;
> To sing in a loud voice, *Domine, labia mea,*

[46] Juan Ruiz says: "If anyone . . . should wish to practice mad love, he will here find some ways for doing so" (Ducamin edition, p. 6).

[47] "The Archpriest's text [stanzas 374-387], considering its date, is unique in its point of view" (Lecoy, *op.cit.*, p. 219). Some of the *pastourelles* of the thirteenth century had already mingled French and Latin, and one profane song has an admixture of phrases in a religious tone:

> L'autr'ier matin el mois de mai,
> *regis divini munere,*
> que por un matin me levai,
> *mundum proponens fugere. . . .*
> Jo regardai sun duz viz cler *cordis et carnis oculo,* etc.

(See F. J. E. Raby, *A History of Secular Poetry in the Middle Ages,* II, 334, 336.)

Although these *pastourelles* may serve Juan Ruiz as some sort of model, they do not parody the liturgy and they do not present the changing activities of a person throughout the day.

To play musical instruments, *Primo dierum omnium*;
And make them wake up, *Nostras preces ut audiat.* (375)[48]

Bits from the psalms and sacred hymns[49] are mingled with the cleric's awakening and his sensuality. The prayers said aloud are mixed with the noisy dawn-actions of a man who, after he gets up, also stirs from their rest his musical instruments. The awakening spreads to the instruments, in a riot of forms, just as the prayer in Latin slides into life in Spanish. The psalm says: "Thou shalt open my lips, O Lord, [and my mouth shall show thy praise]." But the lips cease to be those of the praying person, giving way to the "loud voice" of the cleric who rises early but in the world. Then comes: "On the first of all days," alluding to the day of the creation, a meaning which teeters in the direction of this other one: "At the beginning of each day the cleric begins to play his instruments." Finally: "So that he may hear our prayers"—God, in the Latin; the beloved, in the context of this verse. So that she may hear the songs of her lover, he wakes the instruments up. The irreverent alternation continues between prayer and sensuality, the inward and the outward. In order to understand stanzas 375 and 376, one must suppose that the cleric and his beloved are dwelling in the same house. In 377 the imagination must shift without transition to the idea that they live in different places. Then the cleric commissions his *xaquima*, or go-between, to go and see her, and, on the pretext of going with her after water, to make her leave her house. Going on in this way the poet combines the everyday, small detail of life with the theme of the canonical hours. But the girl who cannot wander freely through the town's narrow streets (378) must be taken into the garden by the go-between on the pretext of picking "red roses"—if she is stupid enough to believe in the "sayings and counsels" of the old woman.[50] However, it is not

[48] In Spanish:

> Do tu amiga mora, comienza a levantar;
> *Domine, labia mea*, en alta voz cantar;
> *primo dierum omnium*, los estrumentos tocar;
> *nostras preces ut audiat*, a fázelos despertar.

[49] See Lecoy, p. 226. The European parodies are a generic and intellectualistic criticism of ecclesiastical vices: greed, lechery, etc. The texts have been compiled by P. Lehman, *Parodistische Texte. Beispiele zur lateinische Parodie im Mittelalter*, 1923. Here is a sample: "Initium sancti Evangelii secundum marcas argenti. In illo tempore dixit Papa romanis: 'Cum venerit filius hominis ad sedem maiestatis nostre, primum dicite "Amice, ad quid venisti?" At ille si perseveraverit pulsans nihil dans vobis, eicite eum in tenebras exteriores'" (p. 7), etc.

[50] The metaphor *coger rosas bermejas* (to pick red roses) is a "euphemism for defloration," according to J. Gillet (*Hispanic Review*, 1950, XVIII, 179).

part of my plan to explicate the obscure passages in the book. I confine myself here to showing the connection between the abstract praying and the experience of earthly existence, both permutable and reversible. The ice of the Latin meaning melts into the living stream of Romance expression, and we are left under the equivocal impression of fraudulent prayers and sensuousness. The "good love" of the divine office dissolves into sensuality, although the sacred words remain there as a haven of refuge, since the whole passage is presented in the guise of an invective against Sir Love:

> You never think of acts of piety. (373)

All value judgments passed on things as well as human actions have a tremulous, ambiguous appearance, and this ambiguity is not comparable to the opposition of vice and virtue with its eventual resolution in the ideal unity of divine mercy.

Echoes of Arabic Literature

The transitions observed as a feature of the book's style are not a derivative of materials that come to it from the European tradition. Neither in the *Pamphilus* nor in the *Bataille de Caresme et de Charnage*, nor in anything else of the kind, is to be found the fluid, gliding form characteristic of the Archpriest's style. This way, then, that the poet has of entering into his literary reality, and of establishing himself in it, belongs to the Arabic way of being in the world.

It is significant, to begin with, that the basic theme here is the love and erotic experiences of a literary character. Events, moralizations, ideas about life, and lyricism are all subordinated to the autobiographical form in which the work is cast. The preoccupation, the *care* (cuidado) that goes with love, causes a character to feel alternately attracted and repelled by the woman beloved, incarnated in a succession of highly varied figures. Love, a great miracle-worker, alters the condition both of persons and things, and may be the motive for illusion and deceit.

Someone, for example, thinks he can marry three women, whereas the truth, it turns out, is that half a woman is enough for him (189-192). Love leads to sin and to danger, but at the same time it cultivates friendship, not the friendship of "the prisoners and the afflicted, but of strong, young men, unwed and brave" (373). As earlier in the case of money, so good and evil are mingled in love.

Love also appears as an ambiguous sentiment and fraught with risks in *The Dove's Neck-Ring* of Ibn Ḥazm, a book which we will discuss later: "Love . . . is a delightful condition and a disease yearned for. . . . It makes appear beautiful to a man what he has been abstaining from because of shame, and makes appear easy to him what was difficult for him, to the extent of changing inborn characteristics and innate natural traits" (Nykl's translation, p. 13). To abandon oneself to love means to embark upon the sea of human uncertainty: "You will find every opposite upheld in it, / So how can you then limit the dissenting meanings? / O body devoid of [firm] aspect" (*ibid.*). This is the nature of the existence of everything that is not God for the Moslems. Love makes the object of desires to come closer and to move farther away at the same time, and it is not easy to know whether it is the lover or his object that advances or recedes. Al-Ma'arri, a famous ascetic who was Ibn Ḥazm's contemporary, says that "men of acute mind call me an ascetic but they are wrong in their diagnosis. Although I discipline my desires, I only abandoned worldly pleasures because the best of these withdrew themselves from me."[51] And he also says in another place that poetry is essentially false, "because it follows human life and nature, which belong to the vanities of this world and are themselves radically false" (*loc.cit.*, p. 51). Nicholson quotes another poet as follows: "It was said by a man of acute mind that gay poetry raises a laugh, while grave poetry is fiction; therefore the poet has no choice but to tell lies or to make people laugh" (*ibid.*). According to a certain Persian writer, "poetry is that art whereby the poet arranges imaginary propositions, and adopts the deductions, with the result that he can *make a little thing appear great and a great thing small*, or *cause good to appear in the garb of evil and evil in the garb of good*. By acting on the imagination, he excites the faculties of anger and concupiscence in such a way that by his suggestion men's temperaments become affected with exaltation or depression; whereby [the poet] conduces to the accomplishment of great things in the order of the world."[52]

Some two centuries later Juan Ruiz says that "In a small rose is much color . . . , In a small woman lies very great flavor" (1,612). The poet is the artist of the reversible and the ambiguous, of the comic and the evanescent. Ibn Ḥazm relates (p. 12) that a black child was once born to a white mother and father because the mother had

---

[51] R. A. Nicholson, *Studies in Islamic Poetry*, p. 125.

[52] *Chahār Maqāla* (Four Discourses), by Nizamī i 'Arudī i Samarkandī (c. 1150), quoted in E. G. Browne, *A Literary History of Persia*, 1906, p. 32.

been gazing at a black figure on the wall in her bedchamber. Poet-theologians, he adds, "use this motif very much in their poems ad-dressing the visible exterior as if they were addressing the imagined interior." Appearances, consequently, are not appearances of a sub-stance; they are the transferences of other appearances: the black color of the wall slipped into the black color of the child. It is in this way and no other that good love and profane love glide into one another in Juan Ruiz's Book—not because of moral relativism or skepticism but because this is the way his poetic imagination functions.

Christian and Moslem ascetics are alike in the belief that the reality and the value of this world are vain and fleeting. They differ, how-ever, in that the Moslem's poetry, whether he be an ascetic or not, plays with a world of shifting appearances in a way unknown to the Christian who has no contact with oriental literary forms. A good Christian could subscribe to these sentiments expressed by Ibn Ḥazm:

> Now came the time for the heart to wake up from its
> drunkenness
> And to take off the veils which have been covering it. . . .
> He who came to know God with a true knowledge,
> Has renounced, and his heart dwells in God's fear. (p. 211)

But Moslems went as far as to say: "Has a prohibition of love been permanently put down in the positive verse of the Qur'ān?" (p. 52). If we move somewhat further along the path of Moslem lyricism, we find that the Christian has gone a different way, on which he will find nothing like the following disclosure: "Perhaps the jet has un-sheathed a sabre as it leaves the water, in which it was hidden from our view as in a sheath."[53] Or this one: "I saw her take off her tunic, and I embraced that sabre that had just come out of its sheath."[54] This eleventh-century metaphor penetrated the Spanish tradition, and we find Lope de Vega saying of the Duchess Cassandra:

> Here comes
> Naked the sweet sword
> For whom I lost my life.[55]

[53] From a poem by the king of Seville Al-Mu'tamid, in H. Pérès, *Poésie andalouse*, p. 203.
[54] *Ibid.*, p. 403.
[55] In Spanish:

> Ya viene aquí
> desnuda la dulce espada
> por quien la vida perdí.
> (*El castigo sin venganza*, II, 7)

The jet unsheathes itself from the water, the woman from her veils, in an alternation between the outward and the inward which could not have been unknown to the Spaniards of the fourteenth century, with much closer Moslem ties than Lope de Vega or Góngora had in the seventeenth century. The technique of such shifts was well-known to Juan Ruiz, who uses it according to his own spiritual and poetic lights in the following texts (translated in p. 417):

> De prieto fazen blanco, volviéndole la pelleja. (929)

> Vid blanca fazen prieta buenos enxeridores. (1,281)

The utterances in his Book are not obvious in their meaning, and must be unveiled:

> Si la razón entiendes, o en el seso aciertas,
> non dirás mal del libro que ahora rehiertas. (68)

Three centuries earlier Ibn Ḥazm was just as much on his guard against wrong interpretations, and for similar reasons: "I know that some of those who are fanatically against me will find fault with me on account of having written something like this, and will say: 'It is contrary to his religious views,' and: 'It departs from his chosen way': but I do not permit any one to suspect of me something which I did not mean. . . . Do not suspect any evil about a word which came out of the mouth of a Moslem, when you find in it something good to base it on" (pp. 219-220).

Literary texts, like any other reality, have esoteric meanings. This is consistent with the Moslem's total attitude toward the world and toward his own life. Thus one can understand how the ideas of the sect of the bāṭinīya, devoted to the hidden meaning of the sacred texts, penetrated into literature. Al-Mu-'tamid, king of Seville, sprayed the body of a concubine with rose water, and a poet wrote: "Her beautiful features are seductive, and her skin is utmost delicacy: one could almost perceive her inwardness (bāṭin) from her outwardness (ẓāhir)."[56]

In his prologue to Kalīlah wa-Dimnah, Ibn Moqaffaʻ says that the wise men of India and other parts sought means "to reveal their thoughts to the world around them," and therefore they put words in the mouths of wild animals. The advantage of such a procedure was that they said "what they wanted to *in a concealed manner*," and thus they stimulated the general taste for philosophy (that is, wisdom concerning human conduct), accustoming the mind to uncover the in-

[56] H. Pérès, *Poésie andalouse*, p. 405.

ward underneath the outward, without which all knowledge is worthless: "If a man gather good nuts in their shells, he can not have any good of them until he split them and take from them *what lies in them*." By knowledge or wisdom here is not meant the accumulated results of study and learning, but rather, good works, because "knowledge is like a tree, and works are the fruit thereof; and the wise man does not ask for knowledge save to make profitable use of it." The object of such knowledge is not nature but human life and experience; its goal is the establishment of ethical values that at the same time do not depend on absolute, rigid, objectifiable norms. To live is to move among the symbols of symbols; not among the appearances of substances, but among *sesos* or meanings. This is why I say that word-plays in Arabic are something more than rhetorical figures or supplementary adornments—to children games are not a diversion, they are their normal occupation. One word form glides into another, as the black figure on the wall glided into the black color of the child who had a white mother (in the example quoted on p. 425). The title of a certain book goes: "The Book of Wonders (mugrib) concerning the Beauties of the West (Magrib)."[57] Long before Góngora, the Archpriest of Hita was already reflecting the Arabic poetic tradition, of which, to a certain extent, he was a part. Wherefore the word-chase that I have mentioned: *cruz-Cruz, pintadas-puntos, ciervo-siervo*, etc. And this is inseparable from the going in and coming out of the poetic figure that speaks in the book in the character Don Melón de la Huerta, or from the shift that takes place in Ibn Ḥazm's soul in the song of the girl who does not requite his love:

> I was thrilled at the sight of the sun when it set; . . .
> The sun *embodied* in the shape of a slave-girl. (p. 159)

Juan Ruiz may lack Góngora's poetic richness, and he may move on a much more elemental plane, but his way of using metaphor is no less Arabic. Compare these two passages:

> "The standards of the horsemen swirled like birds around thine enemies.
> "The lances punctuated what was written by the swords; the

[57] See Dámaso Alonso, "Poesía arábigo-andaluza y poesía gongorina" in *Al-Andalus*, 1943, VIII, 147; and E. García Gómez, in his Spanish translation entitled *El libro de las banderas de los campeones*, p. 121, for a similar thing: "Verses [Shiʿr] that excell Sirius [al-Shiʿra] in splendor," etc.

dust of the battle was the sand that dried the writing, and the blood perfumed it."[58]

> Slices of beef, suckling pigs, and kids
> Go leaping about there, shouting loudly;
> Then the squires, little fried cheeses,
> That put their spurs to the red, red wines. (1,085)

Juan Ruiz interpreted themes from the Christian-European tradition with a Hispano-Moslem sensibility. The fried cheeses spur the red wines just as the lances punctuate or the swords write. The difference is that Juan Ruiz's metaphors are more practical, less disinterested, than those of the Arabs and of Góngora, because the field of his fancy was more limited. Which is not to deny that some of them are remarkable:

> Before him [Sir Flesh] stood his humble standard-bearer,
> On bended knee, in his hand the wine barrel,
> Which he played on like a trumpet;
> Sir Wine, the chief of all, was greatly talkative. (1,096)

The fund of action available for narration and of sculpturally closed figures is not that of the Arabs' lyric poetry, in which the images—unstrung pearls—are to be contemplated as a discontinuity, in an attitude of ecstasy:

> "The Moon is like a mirror whose silver has been dimmed by the sighs of maidens.
> "And the night clothes itself in the light of the lamp, as the black ink clothes itself with the white paper."

In Juan Ruiz there are no similes in which, as in some Arabic ones, the image of the experiential datum is left almost in the dark: the eggplant "seems a sheep's heart between the claws of a vulture" (*Libro de las banderas*, p. 171). His images are connected with happenings rather than with resemblances, and tend to vitalize the activity of everything he imagines. Other images in the Arabic suppress the bridge between the real and the imagined ("seems," "is like," etc.), and the metaphor thus expresses the activity of an object or, if the object is passive, one of its qualities:[59] "Each of the flowers opened its mouth in the

---

[58] *Libro de las banderas de los campeones*, tr. by E. García Gómez, p. 229.

[59] The tendency to equate the subject and the object is functional in Arabic poetry, and is an authentic aspect of the Arabic life structure:
"The whole heart grows dizzy from the verses, and without asking permission, they gain entrance into the heart."

darkness, looking for each of the udders of the fecund cloud" (p. 183).
"The earth's cheek has been covered with the fuzz of the grasses"
(p. 156). But Juan Ruiz does not take these metaphors as his model
either. Rather, he adopts the metaphor which is integrated with the
activity of an object, and in his preference he reveals his familiarity
with the poetics of his neighbors the Moors:

> The trees receive him [Love] with branches and flowers. . . .
> Ladies and men receive him with love. . . .
> There comes forth the Moorish guitar, crying out. . . .
> The shouting rebec, with its high note . . . ,
> The bowed viol makes sweet scales, etc. (1,126-1,231)

An imaginative verbal frenzy animates Juan Ruiz's style, a perfect
artistic symbiosis of the Christian and Arabic traditions. Persons, animals,
and things live together in a poetically fertile harmony:

> Be like the dove, pure and prudent,
> Be like the peacock, haughty, calm. (563)[60]

The tendency to animate any objects of the fantasy leads to conceiving them as an expression of themselves, as being realizations of
their own existence, not as beings that are narrated or described from
outside themselves:

> The wild goat came up, with roebucks and doves,
> Uttering *his* baas and many threats. (1,091)[61]

"Love is weary of traversing the distance that separates us, and journeying from
itself to me and from me to itself."

"I caused [the wine] to fall into my mouth, and it has caused me to fall down."
(*Ibid.*, pp. 124, 136.)

The theme of love, then, is an expression of that reality of the world in which
man moves; it unifies in an existence what occidental thought unifies as an objectified
essence. In this poem the reality shows itself in the reciprocal leveling of the subject
and the object. But since the science of the Hellenic tradition occasionally enjoyed
favor among the Arabs (see Chapter 8), now and then the verses of some unknown
poet reacted against the habitual belief:

"The eyes regard the star as small; but the fault is in the smallness of the eye
and not of the morning star" (p. 124).

[60] In Spanish:

> Sey como la paloma, limpio e mesurado;
> sey como el pavón, loçano, sosegado.

[61] In Spanish:

> Vino el cabrón montés, con corços e torcazas:
> deziendo *sus* bramuras e muchas amenazas.

The *cabrón* (male goat), the most lecherous of animals, came up uttering his
bramuras (not simply baaing). He says that if Sir Flesh will couple (*enlazar*) Dame

The ox came forth, *his* step by step. (1,091)
The octopus gave the peacocks no rest. . . .
Since *he has* many hands, he can fight with many (1,116).[62]

Each person and each animal exists according to his connatural condition and possibility: the Andalusian daydreams and lets himself be seduced by love; the Toledan is austere, and the octopus fights with his numerous tentacles.[63] As Juan Ruiz gives life to *inner* natures, he is led to present persons and things as realizing themselves in their *outer*, vital activities: Doña Endrina, Sir Flesh, the ox, the octopus, or the musical instruments. And this is the aspect that the book itself presents —it lives while it radiates its lovely and, according to its author, strange verses. Sure of himself as far as his Christian faith is concerned, the author at the same time wanders along the literary roads of the Spanish Moors, who are themselves not so certain of the boundaries between some things and others. This is why "good" (bueno) love and "mad" (loco) or profane love reciprocate their values, and why the book tries to teach the lessons of both. This is why one is never sure when the Archpriest is joking and when he is serious. The "good love" of God becomes thus the love of Trotaconventos, the go-between:

For love of the Old Woman and to tell the truth,
I have called the book *Good Love.* (933)[64]

This both is and is not a joke. We cannot apply to this work the rational criteria of today for deciding what is right, comic, or serious. Whether intentional or not, the effects produced by the transposition of Arabic forms of imagination and sensibility into Romanic Spain were humorous and comical. Yet how else would it have been possible for

---

Lent with him, "she will not be able to hurt you with all her spinach" (1,091), a statement which, as in other cases, must be completed by the image of an unexpressed situation: Dame Lent is a witch capable of carnal intercourse with a goat.
[62] In Spanish:
Vino *su* paso a paso el buey.
El pulpo a los pavones non les dava vagar . . .
como *tiene* muchas manos, con muchos puede lidiar.
[63] "He who is profoundly acquainted with the character or the moral constituency of human habits, both praiseworthy and blameworthy, knows perfectly well that no one is free or capable of doing anything different from what he does, that is, what God creates in him. . . . The man with a fortunate memory cannot help remembering, just as the man with a weak memory cannot help forgetting" (Ibn Ḥazm, *Historia crítica de las religiones*, Asín translation, III, 277).
[64] In Spanish:
Por amor de la Vieja e por dezir razón,
Buen Amor dixe al libro.

a Castilian to write serious poetry about love as a vital impulse, both delightful and dangerous?

The Archpriest's song book is not an Arabic work, but a Christian-Arabic harmony, rather like the fifteenth-century door that stood next to the high altar in the Cathedral of Baeza, to be seen today in the museum of the Hispanic Society of New York. Here is a gothic frame, Christian-European, enclosing ornamentation in arabesque, open designs without beginning, end, or repose, in pursuit of unarrestable being, alternating between "inner" and "outer," leaping from gaiety to deception, and from good love to mad love.

The Archpriest of Hita and Ibn Ḥazm

Love as a moral problem was a frequently treated theme in Hispano-Arabic literature. The Cordovan Ibn 'Abd Rabbihi (860-940) wrote poems of the genre gazal (love) in which he describes the youthful predilections of which he has repented. He composed thereafter a series of pious poems called al-mumaḥḥisāt (the cancelling ones), refuting what he had said in his poems of gazal (A. R. Nykl, Hispano-Arabic Poetry, pp. 35-42). The same man wrote:

> I had rather not see the sun and the moon,
> So that I could see you, who are both the sun and the moon.

and:

> If nothing but death were there to warn you,
> It would suffice to make you beware of pleasures.

The outstanding representative of this ascetic tradition is another Cordovan, Ibn Ḥazm (994-1064). In 1931 A. R. Nykl won the praise of the orientalists with the publication of his version of the Ṭawq al-Ḥamāma (The Dove's Neck-Ring), and made accessible for those who do not read Arabic one of the most delightful books in Arabic literature, a work subsequently translated into German, French, Italian, and Spanish. In 1916 Miguel Asín translated the same author's Kalimāt fī al-Akhlāq into Spanish as Los caracteres y la conducta (Human Nature and Conduct), and in 1927 al-Fiṣal as Historia crítica de las ideas religiosas.

Ṭawq al-Ḥamāma, that is, The Dove's Neck-Ring, belongs to a literary genre that has no counterpart in Romance literature until modern times—the erotic confession or autobiography. An exquisite soul imbued with neo-Platonism and asceticism narrates its surrender to love in prose and verse, and at the same time renounces love, the greatest delight which, according to Ibn Ḥazm, a man can find in this life: "Were this world not an abode of bitterness, trials and troubles, and Paradise the abode of retribution and security from all unpleasant things, we would say that the union with the beloved is an unalloyed joy . . . , the perfection of the feeling of security and fullfillment of hopes" (p. 86).

Ibn Ḥazm speaks of certain lives—his own and others'—immersed in love, and of the final renunciation of its deceptive pleasures. An occidental of today would be concerned above all with *his own* erotic feelings, the expression of his own conscious experiences in the dialogue or in the solitude of love, excluding everything that is not a part of the individual "I" enclosed in itself. But the Arabic "I"—whether pre-Islamic or Islamic—could never have been like a projectile crossing through space in conflict with its atmosphere. Therefore the Arabs had no drama or novel, and not even an epic of the occidental style. But occasionally there were refined spirits who for an instant illuminated their persons vividly, and described the experiences of their lives in an unceasing flow through all that exists. Like everything else in this civilization, lives are also resolved in arabesques, in points or lines, not in planes and volumes of time and space that limit them absolutely.

Ibn Ḥazm analyzes the effects of love in his own soul and in the souls of other people with great subtlety, treating the object of his attention with no greater intimacy in the one case than in the other: his "I" and the others are at the same distance from him, *they are interchangeable.* The feminine figures that are the causes of the divine madness are left vague. Sometimes their states of mind are described in a summary stroke with just a trace of dialogue. As a faithful Moslem, Ibn Ḥazm did not reject the human, which is good inasmuch as it is permitted by God: "the hearts are in the hand of God." The combination of Islamic and neo-Platonic ideas made it possible for eroticism and religion to live peacefully together, a kind of cohabitation that was impossible for the Christian, whose belief did not permit him to abandon himself legitimately to the delights of carnal love. Juan Ruiz, a Christian author, in his turn was to mark carnal love with the stigma of madness, but he lingered over his delight as if this stigma were not there, since

If God, when He formed man, had understood
Woman to be an evil thing, He would not have given her
To man for a mate, nor would He have made her from him;

If she were not for a good purpose, she would not
 have turned out so noble. (109)
However holy a man or a woman may be, I know no one
Who does not desire company if he is alone. (110)

In both our writers the boundaries between the good love and sensuous love is blurred, not precisely because the sinner trusts in God's
mercy, but because woman is at once a source of evil and a source of
good, according to God's will: "For in a gay and beautiful and gracious
woman one finds *all the good* and all the pleasure of the world" (Juan
Ruiz, 108); love "is not condemned by religion" (Ibn Ḥazm, p. 4).
Islam's point of departure is a basic combination, both necessary and
universal, of optimism and indifference. God is the greatest good, and
nothing made by Him is evil. But woman, like everything else "lived"
by man, is deceitful, and the man who is dedicated to God should not
put his real trust in her, nor in anything else. Wherefore the tendency
to mental and artistic wandering, the breadth of the Arab's so-called
realism or naturalism at a time when Christendom did not even have eyes
to see what was going on in everyday life. Everything was felt as a
momentary stop in the journey of life, not as a permanent dwelling.
As early as the ninth century Abū'Aqqāl wrote a treatise *On the Customs of Ill-Bred People*. The cadi of Saymara (d. 888) compiled his
Histories of the Humble Folk (Akhbār al-Sifla). And Al-Jāḥiẓ (d.
869) took special pleasure in describing the social classes, as for instance, in his *Ṭirāz al-Majālis*. Al-Jāḥiẓ wrote on every possible subject
from the schoolmaster to the illustrious Banū Hāshim, from bandits to
lizards, from the attributes of God to the improprieties suggested to
him by the wiles of women. Al-Mas'ūdī says of Al-Jāḥiẓ: "When he is
afraid of boring the reader, *he shifts from the serious to the funny*,
from wisdom to witticism. This tendency leads the writer *to speak of
everything*, like a nocturnal woodman who makes up his bundle at
random."

And one must see all this as related to the mixture of the narrative
with the poetic style, both in works of a spiritual character and in those
that are exclusively artistic in their intention (*The Thousand and One
Nights*, for example). These works in turn cannot be classified according to our occidental criterion, because the religious and the profane are
intimately combined—just as it is not fitting to distinguish between
secular laws and religious laws, both kinds being contained in the Koran
and in the traditions derived from it. For Islam, there is no funda-

mental, basic, ultimate reality such as exists for the West, rooted in the Greek notion of the substantial nature of things. On the contrary, things are somehow transitory in character, just as real in the fantasy of sleep as in the experience of wakefulness. Nothing can be made to live by human actions, nor can anything be relived; for to try to give permanent life to a thing would be the same as trying to compete with God, the only creator. No one but Satan—and he in vain—clings to this fleeting world and tries to convert it into something firm and substantial.[65]

With this in mind, it seems to me that it will now be possible to understand the alternation of prose and verse in Arabic works. The poetry must have been to the prose as the metaphor was to the thing metaphorized, as the moralizing gloss was to the human experience. The writer never stops with the substantial reality of what he is narrating or describing, nor does he regard his product as a clear-cut fragment of the world; he proceeds rather in the style of a "theme and variations," converting his matter into an echo or a memory, dissolving it in poetry, or moral or didactic disquisition. Narration and description, then, become what one would expect, that is, a fleeting and migrant reality.

Massignon, in his justly praised article, mentions two examples that confirm what I have been saying. According to the artistic theory of love, the lover is supposed to withdraw from the beloved and live in the unreality of memory. The legend has it that Mahnū comes upon Leila, his beloved; she speaks to him and wants to have a pleasant conversation. "Be quiet," he says, "for if you don't, you will separate me from the love of Leila." In another instance a painter inquires whether it would be possible to paint animals. "Yes," he is told, "but you should cut their heads off so that they will not look like living beings, and will seek rather to resemble flowers." This, then, is the way that poetry turns the statement of prose into the "flower" of metaphor and memory.

The alternation of prose and verse is ancient in Arabic, being found as early as Farazdaq, a poet of the seventh century.[66] It is common in the *Thousand and One Nights*, in mystic and ascetic works, and, of course, in Ibn Ḥazm. This artistic form has exerted a profound influence on Romance literature and, particularly, on the Archpriest.[67]

[65] I refer again to Louis Massignon's study "Les méthodes des réalisations artistiques des peuples de l'Islam," in *Syria*, 1921, II, 40 and 149.

[66] See *Le divan*, of Farazdaq, tr. by Boucher, pp. 53-54 and *passim*.

[67] The mixture of prose and verse is already to be found in Greek (Menippus of

The only prose in his book is the beginning, but the structure is based on the alternation of narrative verse with lyric poetry or moralistic verses (fables and apologues), so that what is first stated in direct, unadorned style then gives way to a half-metaphoric, half-exemplary development in which the theme itself recurs in the open figure of a tireless arabesque. This stylistic feature alone should bring us to some realization of the poetic world in which the Archpriest moved. Let me give some examples:

A man says he has fallen in love with a woman; he sent a certain messenger to win her for him, but in the end the messenger betrayed him, becoming himself the suitor. On this prosaic event the poet composed the well-known "risqué song" (trova cazurra):

> Mis ojos non verán luz
> pues perdido he a Cruz (115),[68]

in which the mockery he has suffered is converted into mocking poetry:

> ca devríenme dezir neçio e más que bestia burra,
> si de tan grand escarnio yo non trobase bulra. (114)[69]

The line of distinction is left blurred between the girl's name Cruz (Cross) and *cruz* the cross of Christ (permutation of a noun and a person):

Gadara), then in Petronius, and in Boethius' *De consolatione philosophiae*; but as W. von Christ says, "Such a mixture of style, and to such an extent, is not Greek but oriental, recalling the Arabic *maqāmāt*" (*Geschichte der griechischen Literatur*, 1920, p. 89). See also G. E. von Grunebaum, *Journal of the American Oriental Society*, 1947, p. 288. The mixture of prose and verse is normal in Arabic and Jewish authors of Spain (see, for example, the previously mentioned *Book of Delight* by J. ben Meir Zabara, a Catalonian Jew of the twelfth century, translated by M. Hadas, New York, 1932, p. 41). But the style of the *maqāmāt* does not show through in either Petronius or Boethius the same way it does in Ibn Ḥazm: "And on that subject I have a poem, from which I quote. . . ." He quotes a few lines and then continues in prose. The subject is drawn out and developed in a little story in prose, and thus the flow goes on without repose, with an occasional movement from the consciousness of the author who is speaking to the consciousness of another person whose point of view he assumes. This form, of course, left its imprint in *Aucassin et Nicolette*.

[68] In English:
> My eyes will not see light,
> For I have lost my Cross.

[69] In English:
> For I would have to be called foolish and more than
> a beastly ass,
> If, out of such a great piece of mockery, *I didn't*
> *make a mocking verse.*

> Cuando la Cruz [the girl and the thing] veía, yo
> siempre me humillava,
> santiguávame a ella, doquier que la fallava. (121)[70]

This will seem normal to anyone familiar with the free and easy verbal glidings of Arabic poetry.

What is most frequent is for a sententious moral commonplace to be developed in an exemplum in a highly expressive and artistic style. Thus, for example, to the excessively proud man the same thing happens "as to the ass who fought with the armored horse." Juan Ruiz here writes in mock-heroic lines:

> Iva lidiar en campo el cavallo faziente,
> porque forçó la dueña el su señor valiente, etc. (237)[71]

One's attention is drawn here to the oscillation between prosaic simplicity and poetic tension, between what is known and what is imagined. In the last analysis, the essential theme of the book is this play upon verbal ambiguities, this oscillation between morality and fantasy, between good love and carnal love,[72] between rude commonplaces and artistic refinements. Juan Ruiz was acquainted with Islamic art.

There are references in the *Libro de Buen Amor* to songs which the poet says he has composed yet which do not appear in the poem:

> I sent her this *cantiga* which is set down below. (80)
> I made a *cantar* as sad as this sad love:
> The lady sang it, sadly, I believe. (92)
> Out of this I made a *troba* of very great sadness.[73]
> I made these *cantigas*, they were perfectly safe,
> I ordered them given to her, either at night or at dawn. (104)
> [I gave my lady] these *cantigas* that are copied below. (171)

---

[70] In English:
> When I saw my Cross [i.e., Cross the girl and the
> cross], I always knelt down,
> I crossed myself to her [it] wherever I found her [it].

[71] In English:
> A fighting steed went to joust in the field
> Because his brave master had raped a lady, etc.

[72] I do not say that the Archpriest is an amoralist, or that moral values are of no importance to him. I do say that his interest and the stylistic grace of his art are centered in the ceaseless movement from one position to another. This is artistic play, not a code of morals, and as such not easy to apprehend.

[73] The fragment of the Portuguese translation gives a better line: "Desto eu fiz hũa trova: ¡Ay que tristeza tamanha!" (in the *Revista de Filología Española*, 1914, I, 171).

She gave her those *cantigas*, she tied the ribbon around her. (918)
By my old hag I sent her a present,
These *Cantigas* that I have signed and sealed for you here. (1,319)
About the lecherous scholar, my fellow-trickster
I wrote another *trova*, don't let it surprise you. (122)
[Concerning the mountain maid's hideous figure]
I wrote many *cantigas* for dancing and for messengers
For Jewesses and Mooresses and for girls in love. (1,513)

Some of these songs ("set down below, copied below, those *cantigas*, these *cantigas*") we would expect to find in the text; others not ("Later I made many *cantigas*," etc.) But the only independent songs we have are the song of *Cruz Cruzada*, two blind man's songs, and the already analyzed religious poems. This repeated reference to omitted songs as if they actually figured in the poem is inexplicable if we do not keep in sight the author's model. Fresh in the mind of Juan Ruiz is some Arabic literary pattern, in which the writer passes from prose to verse by means of a constantly repeated formula, as Ibn Ḥazm does: "On this subject I have written a poem . . . ,"[74] which recurs with slight variations from the beginning to the end of the book. What explanation can we imagine, then, for the fact that in the passages quoted above Juan Ruiz preserves as an empty frame an important part of the literary schema given him by his literary models? It is hardly a question of lapses of memory or the copyists's systematic excision of the passages of lyric lamentation. The only explanation that occurs to me is the author's Christian Castilianism, which inhibits him when he seeks to write poetry "seriously" and from the depths of his soul on the subject of love as an expressible sentiment, when he tries to speak directly to a beloved. I don't deny that he wanted to do so, but either he could not or he did not dare to, and accordingly we discern valuable evidence of the motives and limits of his artistic activity.

One did not dare treat of the frankly erotic theme save under the disguise of farcical humor (the zajal "Cruz Cruzada, panadera," 116), or in religious songs, or the narration and description of adventures with all those fleeting women who appear and reappear in the continuous play of an arabesque. Among these narratives, the one with the most precise detail is the original adaptation of the story of *Pamphilus*, and in this one the sinful, the "ugly" (feo) part of the tale is attributed to Pamphilus and Ovid (891).

[74] Nykl translation, pp. 50, 51, 57, and *passim*.

It was not easy for Castile to take the first steps along the path of lyric expression or to surrender to the enjoyment of beauties that expressed neither the collective interest of the epic nor exemplary morality. The language was reluctant to give metaphoric form to poetic intuition, and we have already seen how Alphonse the Learned had to turn to Galician when he needed a purely lyrical language:

> Ca Deus que e lua et dia,
> segund'a nossa natura
> non víramos sa figura,
> senon por ti que fust'alva.
>
> (Cantiga cccxl).[75]

Fifty or sixty years later it had become possible for the Archpriest to say:

> Vi estar a la monja en oración, loçana,
> alto cuello de garza, color fresco de grana . . .
> ¿Quien dió a blanca rosa, hábito, velo prieto? (1,499-1,500)[76]

But when it is a matter of speaking of love in the first person, the poet restrains himself even though he knows very well how this was done in the Arabic songs. Precisely in *The Dove's Neck-Ring* by Ibn Ḥazm (p. 90) a poet three hundred and fifty years earlier had said:

> I wish my heart were split by a knife,
> And you were put into it,
> And then my bosom were closed tight again.

It is poems of this kind that Ibn Ḥazm intersperses between one passage of prose and another. Without attaining such expressive violence, Romance poetry had spoken of love in the first person, above all in Provence:

[75] In English:
> Since God is moonlight and daylight,
> By our natural powers
> We would never see his face,
> Except for you who were bright as dawn.

[76] In English:
> I saw the nun while she was at prayer, majestic,
> A high heron-neck, a fresh blush of scarlet . . .
> Who gave a habit, a black veil, to the white rose?

Ja de sos pes nom partira
S'il plagues ni m'o consentis. . . .⁷⁷

And in the twelfth century, Coucy's "Chatelain" can say:

Or me laist Dieus en tel honor monter,
que cele ou j'ai mon cuer et mon penser,
tiegne une foiz entre mez braz nuete,
ainz que voise outre mer.⁷⁸

In this respect Juan Ruiz cannot follow either the examples of the
North or those of the South, for he is a Castilian. No matter how Arabic
some of his models may be, his heart will never open the way Ibn
Ḥazm does in the poem quoted above. Juan Ruiz can say objectively
of Doña Endrina: "When she raises her eyes, she inflicts wounds with
the darts of love" (653), a commonplace as ancient as the little god of
love.⁷⁹ But the inclusion of Doña Endrina's eyes in this metaphor reminds us of other passages, such as: "The arrow from her eyelids pointed
straight at what is in the heart. . . . She sends forth a glance, and her
eyes cleave the mortal man. If she should look at the heart of an indifferent man, she would strike it with deadly arrows."⁸⁰

But even if Juan Ruiz had borrowed his metaphor from an Arabic
author, his own art would not permit him the sequel in the little poem
of *Bayad and Riyad*: "Beauty shines forth in the brightness of her brow,
/ And from her comes an air of musk and camphor." This oriental
feature is internally connected with the very essence of the *maqāma* or
chantefable, because the poetic theme in the verse develops from the
prose poetry just as the arrow comes from the eyes, the brightness from
the brow, and the perfumed breeze from the woman's beauty itself.
Romance poetry took generous advantage of the oriental theme of radiant beauty, but such themes are scarcely present in the Archpriest, with
whose limitations I am concerned here. The theme of radiant beauty is
a manifestation of the perpetual flux of existence:

⁷⁷ Cercamon, twelfth century, ed. by Jeanroy, p. 27. In English:
I shall not leave her feet
Even though it should please her and she allowed me
to do it.
⁷⁸ Bartsch, *Chrestomathie*, 1927, p. 164. In English: "Before I leave for Outremer, I wish God would let me deserve for one single time the honor of having
naked in my arms that lady on whom I have my heart and mind."
⁷⁹ Stanza 597 contains a similar verse, derived from the *Pamphilus, de amore*:
"This lady wounded me with a poisoned arrow."
⁸⁰ *Historia de los amores de Bayad y Riyad*, a pre-thirteenth-century Arabic text,
translated into Spanish by A. R. Nykl, pp. 13, 18.

And she gilded the grove with her gracious sight:
From her radiance the sun taketh increase. . . .[81]

"She appeared without her veil in the night, and the nocturnal shadows [lightened by her face], then likewise raised their veils," says a tenth-century Andalusian poet, Ibn Faraj, quoted earlier. We have to do here with an extremely widespread commonplace, which is also to be found in Hispano-Hebrew poetry, itself based, as is well-known, on Arabic models. Let us look at an example taken from Jehudah Halevi (1086?-1141?), whom I quote in the translation made by Nina Salaman (Philadelphia, 1928):

The sun is on thy face and thou spreadest out the night
Over his radiance with the clouds of thy locks. (p. 48)
Ophra washeth her garments in the waters
Of my tears, and spreadeth them out in the sunshine
    of her radiance. (p. 51)
She was like the sun making red in her rising
The clouds of dawn with the flame of her light. (p. 55) Etc.

Traces of these radiant metaphors remain in Romance poetry:

Quan totz lo segles brunezis.
Delai on ylh es si resplan.[82]
        (*Cercamon*, ed. by Jeanroy, p. 2)

A pilgrim who suffers from dizzy spells is suddenly cured when he

[81] *The Thousand Nights and a Night* (Burton tr.), I, 11. Actually, Spanish poetry did not adopt these Islamic traits without reservation except during the so-called "Golden Age," when there bursts forth what is at first glance nothing but baroque hyperbole:

¿Quién es esta diosa humana	Who is this human goddess divine
a cuyos divinos pies	At whose divine feet
postra el cielo su arrebol?	Heaven lays out its red hues?
. . . Amanecer	. . . Dawn
podéis, y dar alegría	You may, and give joy
al más luciente farol.	To the brightest lamp.

        (Calderón, *La vida es sueño*, II, 5)

In a Toledan poet of the eleventh century, Damaso Alonso finds a description of the cock similar to Góngora's celebrated one: "and, coral-bearded, he girds on not a golden but a purple turban" (*Al-Andalus*, 1943, VIII, 145). The Castilian Christians took centuries to assimilate the asceticism, the methods of narration and of poetic metaphor present in the literature of their Moorish compatriots. One day it will be as natural for us to speak of this as it is for us to say that Virgil and Ovid are present in the literature of the sixteenth century.

[82] In English: "When the whole world grows dark, the place where she is glistens."

sees the beautiful leg of Nicolette, whose beauty has thus been transmuted into a beneficent force:

> Si soulevas ton träin
> et ton peliçon ermin,
> la cemise de blanc lin,
> tant que ta ganbete vit.
> garis fu li pelerins
> et tos sains.
>
> (Bartsch, *Chrestomathie*, p. 193)

Radiations of gentle sweetness emanate from Dante's beloved:

> La vista sua fa onne cosa umile;
> e non fa sola se parer piacente,
> ma ciascuna per lei riceve onore.
>
> (*Vita Nuova*, XXVI, 12)[83]

Juan Ruiz would have written in that tradition of the Spanish Arabs and Jews had he made the decision to fill the poetic gaps in the *Libro de Buen Amor* with erotic expression and not with moral exempla. His art consisted in harmonizing in a Castilian and Christian fashion the two fundamental tendencies in Arabic literature of the preceding centuries, sensuality and moral exemplarity.

It is time to return to Ibn Ḥazm's delightful book, a perfect *maqāma*, with its alternations of prose and verse, sensuality and spirituality, the unrefined love of the sailor who takes his turn with each of the pilgrim women returning from Mecca in his boat and the exquisite love of Ibn

---

[83] Although it may be idle to say so, I shall observe that late Latin poetry has nothing to do with the Arabico-Romanic style of the texts quoted. We read in Petronius:

> Ipse tuos cum ferre velis per lilia gressus,
> Nullos interimes leviori pondere flores. . . .

Or in Venantius Fortunatus:

> O Virgo miranda mihi, placitura jugali,
> clarior aetheria, Brunichildis, lampade fulgens,
> lumina gemmarum superasti lumine vultus. . . .
> Sapphirus, alba, adamans, crystalla, zmaragdus, iaspis
> cedant cuncta: novam genuit Hispania gemma. . . .

The examples are from G. Errante, *Sulla lirica romanza delle origini*, New York, 1943, pp. 210, 223. In these verses the beautiful woman is "like" a shining lamp, "like" a precious stone; her step is so light that lilies do not bend beneath it. It should be noted, however, that in no case does the light's or the gem's own virtue emanate from the woman; in sum, she is not a being that communicates her virtues to the things around her.

Ḥazm, who converts the sentimental experience into a twilight tinged with melancholy. *The Dove's Neck-Ring* was written when its author, still a young man, already preferred religious and moral meditation to the pleasures of the senses. It must have been something like a farewell to women at a time when the memory of their charms and the troubles they caused him had not yet faded. The treatises on love inspired in neo-Platonism and tinged with moralism begin to appear as early as the ninth century,[84] but Ibn Ḥazm's work, according to Goldzieher, "deserves the palm for its great excellence." These treatises are not like the ones we find in Ovidian poetry. They go back rather to Persian and Indian antecedents which it would be beside the point to analyze here. It is to the point, though, that Ibn Ḥazm's work circulated in Christian Spain, whether by oral transmission or in some other way, and that in the *Libro de Buen Amor* we find something of its artistic form (not of its content) along with European literary themes, the combination displaying the stamp of Juan Ruiz's original genius. From the Arabic come not only fables and apologues or moral anecdotes like censure of drunkenness; also Islamic is the central motif of the book, that is, the constant movement back and forth between sensual impulse and ascetic restraint. The moral commentary, the tireless repetition of similar situations, the dual aspect of everything that is said—all is to be found in *The Dove's Neck-Ring* and other Arabic ascetic and mystical treatises. Raymond Lully's work, analyzed earlier in this book, and the Archpriest's work are divergent ramifications from the same trunk. Ibn Ḥazm's book is preserved in a fourteenth-century text made with the liberty that reminds one of the Spanish custom of rewriting the literary works of others without respect for the original author's rights. I do not know whether Juan Ruiz knew it by way of the written or the oral tradition. The latter was certainly alive in the thousands of persons who understood the essentials of both languages. We know that a multitude of texts both Spanish and Arabic have been lost. But even so, we are bound to encounter great surprises as soon as we decide to make a careful exploration of the correspondence between the two literatures. Although I have not made such an exploration, I have by chance come upon echoes of *The Dove's Neck-Ring* in 1601, in a book by the Carmelite monk José de Jesús María, *Excelencias de la virtud de la castidad*:

"The *Arabic physicians* give as *indications of lascivious love* a mellifluous voice, affected language, deep sighs, and frequently a downcast, sad, thoughtful face; the avoidance of the company and conversation of

[84] See A. R. Nykl, *The Dove's Neck-Ring*, p. ciii.

friends, the seeking out of solitary and deserted places (all signs of a vehement imagination); sunken eyes and a very rapid movement of the eyelids, many changes of expression in a short space of time, being sometimes too happy and others noticeably sad; the hastening of the breath with the troubles felt by the heart from the poison; changing color when the name of the beloved is heard, or getting upset if the beloved is suddenly encountered, and getting excited, and the pulse changing. . . . An emaciated face, damp eyes, and much primping and preening."[85]

The "Arabic physicians" referred to here were familiar with the chapter on the "Signs of love" in *The Dove's Neck-Ring*: "Another sign is the surprise which occurs and the thrill that comes over the lover when he sees unexpectedly the person loved, or when that person suddenly appears before him. . . . Another sign of love is predilection for solitude and preference for being alone, etc." (pp. 15ff.). The presence of the Arabic literary tradition is revealed in this and other statements. In literary texts of the fifteenth century and in the *Romancero* we find a woman's beautiful face compared to a shining sword, and the same metaphor is found in *The Dove's Neck-Ring*: "That silvery surface of her face which looked like a polished sword" (*ed.cit.*, p. 161). The Arabic verb for "polish" here is *saqal*, from which is derived Spanish *acicalar*.[86]

Since, whatever may have been the channels, passages from Ibn Ḥazm were turned into Spanish in 1601, and since some of his metaphors had found their way into the *Romancero*, no one should be surprised by the assertion that Juan Ruiz made the acquaintance of *The Dove's Neck-Ring* in the fourteenth century. It is hardly necessary to say that the differences between the two are considerable and that it is more a matter of thematic similarities and general stylistic movement than of literal resemblance. Nevertheless, let us see what a summary comparison of the two texts will yield (the Arab on the left, the Spaniard on the right):

[85] From folio 18, quoted by A. G. de Amezúa in *Lope de Vega y sus cartas*, 1936, p. 349. I am unacquainted with Fray José's work save for the passage quoted by Amezúa. There are some data concerning the author in Nicolás Antonio, *Bibliotheca Nova*, 1, 806.

[86] E.g.: "It shone like a sword, . . . Shining like a sword" (Alfonso Martínez de Toledo, *Corbacho*, Part 11, Chap. 2). "Make your face blush with water from the jug, / until your countenance is like a burnished sword" (P. Bénichou, in the *Revista de Filología Hispánica*, 1944, p. 261). "Maidens burnished like a Genoese sword" (*Romancero General*, 1600, 11, 323).

And were it not for the fact that *I wish to warn against them* [go-betweens] I would not have mentioned them. . . . Happy he who is warned by someone else's experience. (p. 50)

And God knows that my intention was not to do it to show a way of sinning, nor to say evil things, but *it was in order to give an example . . . and so that everyone might be warned*, and so they might better protect themselves against the many wiles used by some in worldly love. (p. 7)

Ibn Ḥazm's book is based on the author's own experiences, the contents and perspectives of which are enclosed in a venerable tradition. In this tradition persons and feelings are more important than ideas or precepts. Love is approached in terms of the people who further or hinder it: the mediator, the slanderer (mesturero), the watcher, which is to say, the Argos interposed between the love and his beloved. Then come other aspects of the amorous relationship: the keeping or revealing of the secret (that is, the question of *poridad*), the delight of union, the sadness of separation. Granted that the treatment of these themes is different in the two works, the important fact remains that they are present in both, accompanied by common stylistic features such as the reiteration of some of the same motives.

One of the unfortunate things in love is the *watcher*. He truly is like hidden fever and recurrent pleurisy etc. (p. 73)

I could not be alone with her
  for an hour;
They *watch* out for men where
  she dwells,
Much more than the Jews
  watch over the Torah. (78)

Divulging the secret . . . is a cause which leads to the estrangement of the beloved. (p. 59)

Then my *secret* [poridad]
  became public,
The much watched parted from
  me. (90)

Another misfortune of love is the slanderer. . . . Slanderers have various ways of talebearing. One of them is to tell the beloved about the lover that *he is not keeping the secret*. (p. 77)

Those who wish to separate
  us, as they have done,
Have gossipped about me to her,
  and have told her
That I boast of her as
  of a good quarry. (93-94; *cf.* 566)[87]

And on that subject I say: Strange that the talebearer should go on disclosing our affairs. (p. 79)

Out of this I made a *troba* of very great sadness. (103)

[87] This theme reappears in a work of Morisco background: "The Moor Tarfe, seeing that Zayda would never stop loving Zaide, resolved to stir them up by sowing seeds of discord between the two, although this effort of his cost him his life . . . ; this is what usually happens to those who break friendship with their friends" (G. Pérez de Hita, *Guerras civiles de Granada*, 1, Chap. 6).

[Separation by death:] For him who has been struck by it there is nothing except lamentation and tears, until one perishes or becomes tired of it. (131)
[One of Ibn Ḥazm's little slave girls whom he adores dies:] After her death I remained seven months without taking off my clothes. (131)

[Old Urraca manages to find the Archpriest (or his literary double) a very young girl, who, however, dies shortly thereafter:]
With sad moaning and
  great grief
I fell upon my bed, and
  thought I was dying;
Indeed two days passed
  during which I could not
  get up. (944; cf. 1,506, 1,517)

Such trivial matters as going to bed are not introduced by Juan Ruiz for comic effect but because his poetic existence is included within the perspective of Islamic art, which did not consider the elemental aspects of life comical.

. . . constantly to be put off by Fate, awaiting blows of God's decree. (220)

. . . it is true, what God has ordained, what is to be according to the course of nature, cannot be distorted. (136)

The passage above is fundamental in the understanding of Juan Ruiz's fatalism: "yo creo los estrólogos verdad naturalmente" (140); that is, "I believe that what the astrologers say is true within the natural order"; "but God, who created nature and accident, / He can change them and make them otherwise than they are, / *according to the Catholic faith*; in this I am a believer" (140). The author moves back and forth between the Islamic faith in fate (fused with God, and for Juan Ruiz the same thing as the ineluctable sequence of events in nature), and Christian faith in divine Providence, or rather, in the divine power to alter the course of natural events through miracle. The inclusion of human events in the area of natural fatality inclines the balance to the Moorish side. Lecoy, in his *Recherches sur le Libro de Buen Amor*, p. 193, says that "this looks like an exception in literature. Juan Ruiz shows himself to be closer *to the common people* than to the learned." But were not the Hispano-Hebrews men of learning? "The fear of God protects man against the ordainment of the heavenly bodies," says Ibn 'Ezra in *The Beginning of Wisdom*.[88]

Now let us see what the effects of love are on the lover:

An ignoramus became clever, . . . a coward became brave, . . . an aged one became youthfully sprightly . . . (p. 16)

Love makes the plain [rudo] man clever [sotil] . . . the man who is a coward it makes very daring . . . and it causes the old man to lose much of his old age. (156-157)

[88] Edition of R. Levy and F. Cantera, p. 152.

In this case the translation is literal. It is not surprising that Lecoy (*Recherches sur le Libro de Buen Amor*, p. 304), was unable to find a source for the following verses of Juan Ruiz in Ovid:

The beloved is telling something and wondering at anything he says, even though it be the very acme of absurdity and unheard of, . . . he believes him, even if he lies. (p. 15)[89]

The lover, no matter how ugly he be, / likewise his beloved, even though she be very ugly, / there is nothing that either the one or the other sees that seems so good or that they so much desire. . . . The dunce seems good to his beloved . . . . Everything he says seems very good. (158, 159, 164)

While both are speaking here of how love blinds the judgment of the lover, Ibn Ḥazm emphasizes the moral, Juan Ruiz rather the aesthetic, error.

The messenger of love may be either a man or a woman, and sometimes the intermediary plucks the fruit reserved for the one who has sent him:

"The base trick in betrayal is when the lover sends a messenger in whom he confides to his beloved with his secrets, and the latter exerts himself until he swings the beloved over to himself, and then he appropriates her exclusively instead of the other; to this subject I say:

"I sent a messenger whose purpose was to find what I wanted:

"Like a fool I put my trust in him, and he excited a strife between us. . . . And so I became a witness after I had brought a witness." (Ibn Ḥazm, p. 120)

This is Juan Ruiz's point of departure for the well-known episode of Ferrán García (113-121), with the same alternation of "prosaic" poetry and "higher" poetic variation. The germ of the comic element is already to be found in the last verses of the passage from Ibn Ḥazm. To be sure, the Spaniard converts the Arab's rather diffuse expression into a piece of delightful humor, preserving only the framework of the original matter. Islamic moralism in Juan Ruiz is infused with exhalations of life, and the wit of the *trova cazurra* finds expression in the form of the Arabic zajal. Lecoy's efforts to find sources for Juan Ruiz in Ovid or in medieval Latin comedy are, it seems to me, beside the mark. The *de Nuncio sagaci*, which offers resemblances, is later than Ibn Ḥazm's work by a century, and its editor, Alphonse Dain, has found "no direct source" for the Latin (*La "comédie" latine en France au XII⁵ siècle*, II, 109, 111). In the *Historia septem sapientum* (ed. of A. Hilka, I, 21-22) there

[89] The beloved appears as masculine. Cf. the Provençal *midons*, Spanish *mi dueño* (the beloved woman).

is a story *Gladius* in which someone sends a messenger to his beloved to announce his arrival; the lady, overcome with impatience, "concubuit cum legato." But it is known that this collection of tales comes from the orient. If we do not remember this, we cannot understand that the relationship between the *Libro de Buen Amor* and those European works that more or less resemble it is the relationship of common origin and not of interdependence. The connection between the anecdote of Ferrán García and Ibn Ḥazm's work is decisively established by the fact that in both cases the betrayal by the messenger is developed in a poem. This does not happen in the aforementioned Latin texts.

The realization that the model after which Juan Ruiz fashions his personal style is Arabic leads to the recognition of the new paths in literature. Without the vital pressure of Moslem literature, the poetic zone of Christian Castile would never have been enriched by the baker-girl Cruz Cruzada and the characteristic imagination of the Andalusian.[90] The naturalness with which the author speaks in the first person of the world about him—both material and spiritual—is also significant. Subject matter is not the only thing he got from Islam. Because the dynamism of Castile blended in a vital relationship with the belief of Islam in the value of *all levels of realities* without any differentiation into categories of propriety that would prevent the association of any one with any other, the Archpriest was also able to give value to a wide area of personal experience:

> At the top of the mountain pass
> I thought I was dying
> From the snow and the cold,
> And from the drizzle,
> And from the heavy frost. (1,023)

Leaving aside the question of whether this actually happened to the Archpriest or not, the new thing we find here is that a person going over a mountain should produce literature out of his own sensation of the cold—at a place in the Guadarrama well-known to his readers—bringing his particular poetic experience into the poetic tradition of the *serranilla*. There was a justification for doing this: Poet-moralists like Ibn Ḥazm had written thus:

"There are people with dry eyes, devoid of tears, and I am one of

[90] The collective life was the object of the same attention as the life of the individual. Ibn 'Arabī says that "the men as well as the women of Seville are very fond of witty jests and repartee" (*Santones andaluces*, tr. by Asín, p. 107).

them. The origin of this was my habit of taking incense for palpitations of the heart from which I suffered in my youth." (p. 23)

Ibn Ḥazm also speaks of how he fell in love (pp. 36, 39); he analyzes two essential features of his character (p. 165); he describes the ruin of his family, his exile, the loss of his fortune (p. 220). And all this is inseparable from the extrapersonal magic of metaphors, didacticism, and religion. The author lives within himself and outside himself at the same time.

The confusion that has grown up around Juan Ruiz's art comes in part from the desire of some to convert the author into something non-existent in the Christian-Moslem world of Castile. Others, noticing that the Archpriest is not a "modern" in our contemporary sense of the concept, make of him a medieval writer without any substance of his own. But the truth does not lie with either of these extreme positions. First of all, we have here an awareness of personality which actually anticipates what we call the Renaissance both in the value attached to the human as well as in the vitalization of *things*. Let us not try, says the Archpriest, for example, to use certain instruments for Arabic songs, "for, when forced to, they sing them *with shame*" (1,517). I doubt whether there is a musical instrument in medieval Romance literature that is "ashamed" to play music for which it is not suited.

Hence the gulf which Lecoy observes between the French "Débat de Caresme et Charnage" and the quarrel of Don Carnal and Doña Cuaresma (Sir Flesh and Dame Lent). Under the surface of each thing, each musical instrument,[91] each animal, every fine dish of food, each woman with sweat-moistened armpits and broad hips, throbs the spirit of the Islamic God, who dignifies the flight toward mystic sublimity without disdaining to speak of the less seemly aspects of the body's functions, regulated as rites in the *ḥadīths* of Mohammed. Thus the Archpriest could play with the exalted and the base, with licit and illicit conduct. In the Islamic tradition, with half of your life you affirm the validity and substantiality of the world, and with the other half you dissolve the world into a poetic mist. The *realism of vital experience* is not accompanied by intellectual realism, because the things are in God and in life, but they are not pure objects defined by the mind. One drifts in

[91] The musical instrument gives the impression of having life because it expresses itself, its own inwardness comes to the surface, it grows out of itself like a plant from a seed, it "writes" its autobiography, so to speak, the way any reality does, be it visible or invisible. Al-Maʿarrī (937-1057) has a wonderful sentence that clarifies my idea: "Time is silent, but its events interpret it aloud, so that *it seems to speak*" (quoted by R. A. Nicholson in *Studies in Arabic Poetry*, p. 59).

the sea of things, in which everything floats, in a variety, an abundance, and contradiction unsuspected by the West. The body is important—with both its beauties and its foul smells (as Sancho Panza well knows)—as are stones, flowers, stews, theological exegesis, and science in so far as it enlightens conduct.[92] The purely theoretical is of scant importance. When the literary vocabulary of European Christendom was still wretchedly poor, that of Islam was already fabulous. This vital "fraternizing" with things was one day to make possible the enormous lexicographical wealth of Lope de Vega's work, fruit of a tradition that accustomed the Spaniards to the elimination of partitions between one thing and another. Whatever one was aware of—in waking hours, in dreams, or in the fantasy—could, without answering any other requirement, be made to play on the plane of literary expression. And this is what happens in mid-fourteenth century in the verses of the Archpriest, a milestone that points the way to subsequent literary generations, to Spanish "realism" and vulgarism.

Juan Ruiz speaks of the *alcahueta*—the go-between—as a type present both in the actual life of the fourteenth century and in the pages of Ibn Ḥazm's work. The *alcahueta* has a corporeality perceptible to the senses:

Ibn Ḥazm: "Those who use prayer beads such as curanderas, . . . peddlers, . . . fortunetellers." (p. 50)

Juan Ruiz: "Great beads around their necks" (438). . . . "Old women who compound herbs" (440). . . . "Peddler" (723). . . . "Such a spell they use" (442).

The description in our poem of the physical characteristics of the woman most to be preferred (444, 445) stems not merely from Latin poetic models but also from Moslem traditions.[93] The observation "They say she has slightly wet armpits" (445) sounds somewhat like perverse salaciousness, but Juan Ruiz does not speak of the matter maliciously.

Juan Ruiz is also imitating the Moslems when he composes blind beggars' verses, a form of *maqāma* (cf. the *Encyclopedia of Islam*), and we have already seen what an important institution begging was among Mohammedans. Writing verses for beggars had been a part of the Islamic literary heritage since the earliest days, a heritage enriched, for

[92] According to the eleventh-century Afghan writer Al-Hujwīrī, one must learn astronomy, medicine, and the sciences in general in so far as they are important for the religious life: "this knowledge is obligatory only in so far as it is necessary in order to do the right things" (*Kashf al-Maḥjūb*, tr. by R. A. Nicholson, p. 11).

[93] See the bibliography given in H. Pérès, *La poésie andalouse au XIᵉ siècle*, p. 401, n. 2, and the text of the *Doncella Teodor*, which I quote on footnote 21. Girls with space between their teeth (*Libro de Buen Amor*, 434) were preferred by the Arabs (see Damaso Alonso, *Insula*, Madrid, July 1952, p. 3).

instance, by the elegantly composed beggars' poems of Al-Hamodhānī, a sort of bohemian litterateur of the tenth century.

Towards the Meaning of Trotaconventos

Trotaconventos as a name reveals immediately something of the Arch-priest's temperament—the shifting urge of a man who slides his glance over all things without letting it settle on any of them, in a continuous passing from one aspect to another, walking along, "trotting," coming and going from the city to the mountains, from the field of Sir Flesh to the sea of Dame Lent. This traffic growing out of vital appetites and the "care" of love, corresponds to the mobility of the surrounding world, lacking in "substantial" repose, without a "portus quietis"; everything is agitation, a flow of sounds, the restless life of a cleric from matins to compline, dances, the going and coming of love messengers, Doña Endrina crossing the square, the messengers (troteras) running here and there from convent to convent, within whose walls there is also a con-tinual movement from the love of God to the love of the archpriests.

A possible perspective opens for us. The going from one place to an-other, from one love to another, has its formal parallel with the move-ment of the *pícaro* from one master to another, each of which appears with his reversible "inner" and "outer" aspects—the *hidalgo* in *Lazarillo* comprises an illusory inwardness of nobility and an imaginary outward-ness of a full stomach. The *pícaros* that scamper about through sixteenth- and seventeenth-century narratives were Spaniards incapable of experi-encing any self-realization by expanding in a heroic dimension. They sought refuge then in the lives of their neighbors or in the things they came across in their wandering through the vast world, and then they found that nothing had a fixed objectivity on which to lean (in Mateo Alemán's *Guzman de Alfarache* nothing is what it seems to be—neither material things nor moral values). The ascetic negation of the value of all things human in sixteenth-century Spain was based on a tradition that put no faith in the substantial and productive reality of things. Every-thing seemed; nothing was:

> In her grief the old woman told me:
> Archpriest, very few walnuts make a lot of noise. (946)[94]

The comings and goings of the "lad of many masters" are, in the last

[94] In Spanish:

> Con su pesar la vieja díxome muchas vezes:
> Acipreste, más es el roido que las nuezes.

analysis, like the amorous adventures of the Archpriest, change for the sake of change, without the possibility of stopping in any one place. The picaresque is one more effort to present life as a gliding over other lives, something which exists as aspects of a fleeting personality. The authors of picaresque works did not aspire to describe customs, or to present lives that were failures, or take ascetic flight from the world. Juan Ruiz, the *pícaros* and the ascetics tried to project themselves in the only form of life that was theirs in the world which was for them mere aspect. The Archpriest turned a happy smile of acceptance on the merry dance of the data of his experience (forms, colors, sounds, movements), which led him from one aspect of things to another. But in the sixteenth century the ascetics were terribly exercised when they faced the pure deception of the world.[95] The sixteenth-century Spaniard felt himself ill at ease in that edifice which was his legacy from the architects and masons of the Islamic spirit, later reinforced by Judaic desperation. But as he was animated besides by impulses and purposes unknown to the orient, he could not resign himself to prostration in that evanescent world which his inescapable history had bequeathed him. His Christianity—and in part his Judaism—made him desire realities and values whose absence did not disturb the Moslem but did disturb the Spaniard, who writhed desperately beneath a burdensome mass of ascetic treatises, or wandered aimlessly along deceptive paths. In those "watchtowers of human conduct" raised by the picaresque novel, the true protagonist is not the *pícaro* but the world around him, which stubbornly affirms its unreality, its mere appearance in the face of the madman who tries to find a solider base in it:

He who looks for more than wheat bread is senseless (950). Using other words, this is Don Juan's cry in Tirso's *El Burlador de Sevilla*:

> But Oh! I wear myself out for nothing,
> Beating against the air.

[95] "Oh, if sinners would only see how fast the world runs by; how quickly kings are finished; how the highest pontiffs and princes and powerful men perish; so that they would not love such an inconstant and variable thing" (Beato Alonso de Orozco, *Victoria de la muerte*, chap. 20). "There is no deceiver like the world; there is no necromancer so subtle, who can thus form towers out of wind in the air, and the loveliest figures. . . . Everything moves with caution and deception; everything is founded on falseness. . . . If there were nothing else in the world save the wild beast death, which goes about so swift, so free and cruel, leaving no green branch or clear, pure spring without cutting off the one and stirring up the other. . . ." (Alonso de Cabrera, "Sermones," in the *Nueva Biblioteca de Autores Españoles*, III, 282.)

I have always found enigmatic such personalities as Tirso de Molina (d. 1648), a good friar no doubt, and the author of plays in which he affirms among other things that in the Madrid of the seventeenth century even the angels were "pregnant," because "virgin and court are things that imply a contradiction." Accustomed as we are to taking the strange phenomena of Hispanic history without surprise, we have accepted as normal the name of "the Spanish Boccaccio," given to Tirso. But what form of life, what historical "category" would serve us as a means of grasping such a strange existence? I think that in its decisive features the same scheme is applicable to Tirso that has emerged through our contemplation of the Archpriest of Hita in his authentic history, fluctuating between mad love and good love. The character of Don Juan, to which Tirso owes his perennial value, can be clearly understood inside the life forms of traditional Spain, of the Archpriest, and of Ibn Ḥazm. The type of Don Juan would have no meaning in the literature of antiquity or the Middle Ages. The folkloric antecedents which have been adduced in this case are at best shadowy anecdotes. Don Juan skips from one love to another like the Archpriest-as-character in his song book, which links together "aspects" of love in a progression of inconclusive arabesque.[96] The prototype of this character, possible only in the Islamic world, appears at the beginning of the eleventh century in *The Dove's Neck-Ring* of Ibn Ḥazm, and I imagine that other treatments of the same theme are to be found before and after him. There always have been and there always will be men who behave like Don Juan, but only Arabic and, later, Spanish literature have given *literary form* to the shapeless commonplace of falling in love with many women and quickly getting bored with all of them. The Arab and the Islamicized Spaniard perceived in this action one more example to corroborate their conviction that the world, for one reason or another, was a procession of transitory and deceptive aspects. The literary ability to treat in a static

[96] The counterproof of this is given at once by Molière's *Don Juan*, who lives in the midst of deceptions but with an assured awareness that they are deceptions: he knows that nothing is known. "SGANARELLE. What, Monsieur, you don't believe in medicine either? DON JUAN. It's one of the great errors current among men. . . . Why do you think I should believe in it?" (III, 1). But there is something in which he does believe and which gives his life a foundation of substantial and earthly reality. When Don Juan demands a few blasphemies as the show for which he is willing to give the beggar a louis d'or, the beggar refuses; but in spite of this, the rationalist Don Juan of the seventeenth century gives him the money: "All right, all right, I'll give it to you *for the love of humanity*" (III, 3). Once more, then, we find the same radical contrast between France and Spain that was to be observed in the eleventh and in the thirteenth century.

fashion the love of a single woman to the exclusion of all others was acquired by the Spaniards through their contact with Italian letters and the neo-Platonism of the Renaissance (Garcilaso, Herrera, etc.). In the Spanish Middle Ages, the love theme either was absent or was treated as a fluid sequence of experiences. This is what happens in Juan Ruiz's book or in the *serranillas* of the Marqués de Santillana. The artistic use of the Don Juan theme came into literature on the strength of the belief that any aspect of reality vanishes away the moment one feels urged to grasp it by an act of the will—that it is a mirage like the one seen by the mastiff while he was carrying the piece of meat in his mouth:

> From the image in the water, they seemed so much like
>   two to him,
> In his greed he seized it, and he dropped the one he was
>   carrying.
> Because of the lying shadow, because of his vain imagining,
> The Mastiff lost the meat that he had. (226, 227)

The conceited young man who begged his parents to marry him to three women ended up by admitting that with one woman he had half again more than he needed, etc. In this atmosphere the reprehensible act of seducing and then abandoning women acquired literary possibilities, since the real victim in the long run was the seducer, who grew weary of "beating the air in vain." The women of the "future Don Juan," Abū'Āmir, passed through his bored existence like the magic-lantern images that succeeded one another on the retina of Ibn Ḥazm's eye.[97a] Ibn Ḥazm writes about both of these facts from the center of his outlook on the world:

"The afore-mentioned Abū 'Āmir when he saw a slave-girl (he liked) could hardly wait (to get her), and he was seized by a desire and pre-occupation to have her that nearly overcame him, until he possessed her, even when there were difficulties in the way harder than the thorn of the tragacanth tree; and when he became certain of her being in his possession, his love became avoidance, and his kind companionship a disinclination, and anxiety to be with her anxiety to be away from her, and he would sell her at the lowest price—this was his habit—until he wasted in what we had mentioned vast sums of tens of thousands of

[97a] In the *Kalimāt fī al-Akhlāq*, made available by M. Asín in 1916 under the title *Los caracteres y la conducta*, Ibn Ḥazm says: "I have not seen anything more like this world than the Chinese shadows of the magic lantern. They are figures mounted on a wooden wheel, which turns rapidly; one group of figures disappears when another group appears" (p. 33).

dinars. And despite that, may God have mercy upon him, he was a cultured man, perspicacious and intelligent, noble-minded, gentle, clever, possessing great distinction, exalted rank, and vast power.

"As regards the beauty of his face and the perfection of his features it is a thing beyond anyone's power to describe, and all imagination is weak to describe the least of it, and no one can engage his powers in describing him: why, streets were abandoned by travelers, and they made their minds purposely to pass by the gate of his house in the street beginning at the small rivulet at the gate of our house on the East Side of Cordoba (leading) toward the road connecting it with the palace of Az-Zāhira. . . . And they did it for no other purpose but to obtain a look from him!

"Many slave-girls died because of their love for him: they fell passionately in love with him and gave themselves completely up to him; and he betrayed them in what they had hoped for from him, and they became hostages of misfortune, and solitude killed them.

"And I know a slave-girl among them whose name was Afrā': I recall that she did not conceal her love for him wherever she was sitting, and her tears never dried up; . . .

"And he himself, may God have mercy upon him, told me about himself that he was tired of his own name, beside other things. And as for his friends, he changed them during his life, though he was a young man, very often; and he did not adhere to one fashion of dress. . . . On that subject I say:

> Do certainly not put any hope on an easily-bored one:
> Such a man is not to be depended upon!
> Leave the love of a man of this kind:
> It is a loan which is to be returned!"
>
> (Nykl translation, pp. 106-107)

Here we have the first literary appearance of what, five centuries later, will be Tirso de Molina's Don Juan (*El Burlador de Sevilla*); he is also a conjunction of moral baseness and noble conduct:

> So long as you don't give him
> A girl or anything like that,
> You can trust him completely;
> For, although cruel in this matter,
> He is of noble estate. (II, 161-165)

The differences between Abū 'Āmir (Almanzor, or his grandson, according to some orientalists) and Don Juan are considerable. There always is a great variation between a given literary motive and its artistic treatment at some unpredictable time in the future.

The connection between *El burlador de Sevilla* and its remote sources might be compared with that between *El condenado por desconfiado* by Tirso de Molina and the story from the *Mahabharata*, its remote source too, even though the hermit Paulo in no way resembles a brahman, nor does the criminal Enrico resemble the hunter Dharmavydha. (See R. Menéndez Pidal, *Estudios literarios*, 1938, pp. 9-80.) Before Tirso de Molina, Ibn Ḥazm is the only writer who has sketched the literary figure of a seducer of women combining noble distinction and erotic perversity.

Tirso de Molina's innovation consisted in articulating the traditional type of seducer into an aesthetic system of problematic responsibilities.[97b] Before him seducers had been morally censured but not punished. About 1500 Juan del Encina wrote:

> MINGO. Be quiet, Pascuala;
> Don't let this betrayer,
> This deceiver from the palaces,
> Deceive you;
> He has already tricked another shepherdess.
> SQUIRE. Coarse, shaggy, uncouth peasant,
> Son-of-a-bitch.
>
> (Edit. Bibliotheca Romanica, p. 67)

Abū 'Āmir was a victim of boredom; one of the characters in *El Burlador* also says that love is a brief pleasure and a long worry:

> Ah, the tyrannical glories of love!
> As light in the passing moment of pleasure
> As heavy to live with thereafter (II, 602-604)

Everything vanishes and changes. Don Juan, like Abū 'Āmir, is both good and bad at the same time, for he is ready to risk his life to save his servant—like Enrico, who is both a criminal and a self-sacrificing son in *El condenado por desconfiado*, also by Tirso. The Comendador turns into a "dead" and a "live" ghost, the bearer of a divine message and, at the same time, a rascal who does not keep his word and deceives Don Juan, who is a better knight, after all, than the man-statue-ghost

---

[97b] In the literary character of the polygamist *grand seigneur* Tirso de Molina merged both the Islamic and the classic tradition. Don Juan (at times a seafarer) and Tisbea (a fisherwoman) were patterned after Aeneas and Dido as I have shown in an article (*El Nacional*, Caracas, August 3, 1953) which I expect to develop.

and celestial body all in one. Tirso de Molina, the great playwright, as well as his characters, was contained within the form of life that we have discovered in the Book of the Archpriest of Hita, in which fiction and experienced reality in some cases seem merged.

When Alfonso de Paradinas finished copying one manuscript of the *Libro de Buen Amor* at the beginning of the fifteenth century, he felt that work to be a personal confession, and at the end of his copy he added that Juan Ruiz composed his book in prison "by order of Cardinal Don Gil, Archbishop of Toledo" (Ducamin edition, p. 327). Paradinas, a very hard-working scholar, took the first-person speaker to be a living person since in the first forty lines he begs God to take "poor me from this bad prison. . . ." "Messiah, save me," he says (1, 4). This imprisonment may be purely spiritual, the imprisonment of the sinful world. But the Salamancan copyist and, along with him, well-qualified readers, have believed something else. Let it be noted that Juan Ruiz attributes this great ordeal not only to his sins but also to the evil offices of "traitors" and "slanderers" (7, 10), who stirred up baseless complaints against him. Thus, from the opening lines of the book, we find ourselves involved in a double game that runs throughout it. Here, between the sinner and the delinquent, between the spiritual man and the man of flesh and blood, it would make no sense to speak of traitors and slanderers if the poet were thinking only of the divine tribunal and not of human judges. God would not listen to gossip.

The poetic character extends his existence downward as it were, and comes out on the plane of the non-poetic. The character Juan Ruiz penetrates the sphere of common knowledge when he says: "Let every punishment fall upon the slanderers" (10); just as he does when he declares that the adventure with Doña Endrina did not happen to him (909). The reader then takes him for a real figure who speaks in the first person. The projection of the poetic work to include the reader reveals its "centauric" ambivalence, and this is much more important than whether the Archpriest was actually a Señor Juan Ruiz, and whether he was thrown into prison or not by the Archbishop of Toledo.

Trotaconventos, Celestina, and their literary kin were later to slip out through the same gap that made it possible for the Archpriest to escape from the realm of poetry and appear as a thick-necked priest, sensuous and turbulent. Nothing is accomplished when rationalist logic dissolves these figures into impersonal themes. Closer to the truth was that crazy woman in the *Corbacho* (1438), who, beside herself because her chicken had disappeared, shouted that she wanted "Trotaconventos, my cousin's old woman, to come and go from house to house looking for my hen." Balzac too, it might be recalled, grasping at the last shreds of hope, cried out in his deathbed delirium for Dr. Bianchon, the physician in his novels.

Later, escaping from the confines of the book, this Trotaconventos was to become trotaconventos: "What I am most sorry for," says Parmeno, referring to Celestina, "is to fall into the hands of that *trotaconventos,* who has been tarred and feathered three times" (Act II). If she hadn't been outshone by her later colleague Celestina, *trotaconventos* would have been the name of the go-between in Spanish.

It is interesting in this connection to analyze the Arabic origin of the Spanish term for go-between, *alcahueta,* Arabic *al-qawwād,* and related words in Romance, *alcabuete, alcabote, alcayuete;* Cat. *arcabot,* Gal. *alcayote,* Prov. *alcaot, alcavot.* The diphthong of *al-qawwād* was treated as was the diphthong of *puarta, puerta* (Lat. *pŏrta*), and was expressed as *o* in Catalan, Provençal, and Galician, which do not diphthongize the Latin *ŏ. Al-qawwād* was first used in Arabic of the person who led a horse with a halter or brought it as a gift on the part of his master. This being a means of winning a husband's sympathy with the ultimate object of gaining access to his wife, the meaning of the word was attracted to the act of seduction.[98]

[98] *qādaho* (he brought him a horse); *qāda* (he acted as a go-between with respect to his own wife, for having received a gift of horses) (Lane, *Lexicon*). Notice the migratory quality here. The same word designates the go-between and the person who is the go-between's victim, that is, the husband, because the latter is infused with the condition of the person who has brought him the gift. Let me say in passing that this makes it possible to understand the full "historical" meaning of the Comendador of Ocaña's act when he gives the pair of handsome mules to Peribáñez in order to conquer the latter's will and then seduce his wife:

LUJÁN. I have never seen
   Better beasts, on your life and mine. . . .
COMEN. Tell me, Luján, how we can
   Give them to Peribáñez, her husband,
   So that he will not find malice in my purpose?
Luján then acts as the *al-qawwād:*
   By calling him to your house, and telling him
   That you are thankful for his love.
   But it makes me smile to see that you make
   Your secretary in matters of your pleasure
   A man of my qualities.
   (Lope de Vega, *Peribáñez,* I, 15)
The go-between's condition is infused into the lackey Luján, who realizes that this new kind of life has come into him. Someday the Islamic perspective of Lope de Vega's art will be considerably widened, for it was no less effectively projected

Consequently one must not look in Latin literature for the type of Trotaconventos, but in the Arabic tradition and in the Spanish life penetrated by it. "Others there are who work at corrupting them [women] through *alcahuetas*, so that with the great pressure that is put on them, there are some among them that come to do wrong" (*Siete Partidas*, VII, VI, 5). Disgrace fell upon anyone engaged "as a truchman with women, as a go-between, or as a seducer of women in behalf of another person" (*ibid.*, 4th law). The death penalty was given to any woman who "procured [alcahotase] another woman who was married, or a virgin, or *a nun*" (VII, XXII, 2). Other legal texts might be cited in which *alcahuetas* were associated with diviners and fortune-tellers who practiced magic arts.

The profession of *alcahueta* was still being written about at the beginning of the seventeenth century as a heritage not of Ovid but of the Islamic tradition. Besides, it is a fact that for many years Lope de Vega busied himself writing the Duke of Sessa's love letters; there were *alcahuetas* in the theater of his life just as there were in the life of his theater by virtue of certain relationships between life and art that recall the world of the *Libro de Buen Amor*.

Returning to Juan Ruiz's poem, we shall see that the theme of the *alcahueta* occurs as a commonplace at home in Arabic literature, and Juan Ruiz refers to it as something of which the readers or listeners share his knowledge. They were familiar with the type of Moriscan woman who went up and down the streets playing on her timbrel and crying her wares so as to gain entrance into houses and deliver and pick up love messages. The alcahueta in *The Dove's Neck-Ring* lived in the work of Ibn Ḥazm and in the streets of Cordova.

> Your messenger is a sword in your right hand, so choose
> A sharp sword and do not strike with it before grinding it:
> He who relies on a blunt sword, the damage (resulting
>   to him therefrom)
> Rebounds upon him who depends upon it because of his
>   stupidity! (p. 49)

"Most of this type are found among women, especially those who use crutches and prayer beads and two red dresses. And I remember that

into Lope than was the literature of the Christian Middle Ages and the Renaissance. S. G. Morley has collected the 53 pseudonyms through which Lope alludes to his own life in his comedies (*University of California Publications in Modern Philology*, Vol. 33, 1951, pp. 421-484).

[459]

in Cordoba chaste young women were warned against women of this description, wherever they might see them" (p. 50). Juan Ruiz must have known this or other literary treatments of the ancient theme, deeply rooted in the orient.[99] The style in which he conceives it continues in the oriental tradition. The Old Woman oscillates between the vague and abstract representation evoked by a name, and a figure described in terms of its appearance, its actions, and its conversation with other people. This character (or character intention) is at the same time both one and several, in the oriental fashion. She is called Urraca (magpie) or Trotaconventos; her name is felt to be now a common noun, now a proper noun:

> These *trotaconventos* make many deals; (441)
> I looked for a *trotaconventos* as love told me to do; (697)
> She was an old peddler, one of those that sell jewels. (699)
> The peddler walks along with her tambourine, ringing its bells,
> Waving her jewels, rings, and pins around;
> Speaking of towels, she would say: "Buy these table
>   cloths!" (723)

In the last quotation, the figure is vague and generic, but it is sharpened at once with the act of crying out the wares. Crying out in this way about the towels for sale is not as indefinite as "one of those that sell jewels."

The character is given much more life in the following passage. In the comedy of *Pamphilus*, utilized by the Archpriest in the episode of Doña Endrina (called Galatea in the original), there is no mother; but here Doña Endrina is the daughter of Doña Rama, who appears in a scene which, for its comic, novelesque quality, is unique in the Spanish Middle Ages. The Old Woman invents a pretext for entering Doña Rama's house; she comes breathless, fleeing from an offensive man who

---

[99] It is idle to speak here of Ovidian "sources." Since I have pointed out the basic orientalism of Juan Ruiz's book, it is obvious that details of the parts harmonize with the structure of the whole. Ovid's Dipsas (*Amores*, 1, 8) is a woman who incites others to prostitution rather than a go-between for lover and beloved; she does not suggest that the girl love anyone, but that she give herself to whoever gives her the most:

> Qui dabit, ille tibi magno sit maior Homero;
> crede mihi, res est ingeniosa dare. (61-62)

Works like Aretino's could derive from this, but nothing like the works of Ibn Hazm and Juan Ruiz. Ovid's old woman advises the girl to show her new lover the gifts of his predecessor:

> munera praecipue uideat quae miserit alter. (99)

has been pursuing her all day to get her to buy a ring for him; the Old Woman does not understand why he is doing this, for he is very rich. Intrigued by the story, Doña Rama goes out into the street out of curiosity to see such an odd person. This is part of the clever plan of the Old Woman, who takes advantage of the moment to speak with the girl alone.

> Fuese a casa de la dueña; dixo: "¿quién mora aquí?"
> Respondió la madre: "¿quién es que llama ý?"
> —"Señora dona Rama, yo, que por mi mal vos vi,
> que las mis fadas negras non se parten de mí."
> Díxole dona Rama:—"¿Cómo venides, amiga?"
> —"¿Cómo vengo, señora? Non sé cómo me lo diga:
> corrida e amarga, que me diz toda enemiga
> uno, non sé quien es, mayor que aquella viga.
> Ándame todo el dia como a cierva corriendo,
> como el diablo al rico ome, asi me anda siguiendo,
> quel lieve la sortija que traía vendiendo:
> está lleno de doblas, fascas que no lo entiendo."
> Desque oyó esto la renzellosa vieja,
> dexóla con la fija, e fuese a la calleja. (824-827)[100]

This comic scene is based on Moriscan cunning, and recalls the tone of the *Engaños y assayamientos de las mujeres* (Tricks and Schemes of Women), of some of the stories in the *Disciplina clericalis*, and of *Kalilah wa-Dimnah*. The novelty is in the true-to-life, agitated style, the chatter with the same formulas that women use today: "¿Cómo vengo, señora? Non sé cómo me lo diga," with the emotional *me* characteristic of feminine style. The Old Woman appears in a "here" and a "now"

[100] The tone of comic banter is lost in English:
She went straight to the lady's house; she said: "Who lives here?"
The mother answered: "Who calls there?"
"Señora doña Rama, I who wish I hadn't seen you,
For my black fairies will not leave me."
Doña Rama said to her: "How do you come, my friend?"
"How do I come, señora? I don't know how to say it:
Run after and bitter, for I am told every kind of insult
By a man, I don't know who he is, bigger than that beam.
He's been chasing me, all day, as if he were running after a deer,
Like the devil after the rich man, so he follows me around,
For me to return the ring that I had been carrying around to sell;
He is so full of doublons that I hardly understand why he does that."
When the grumbling old lady heard this,
She left her with her daughter and went out into the street. (824-827)

as she uses her invisible finger to measure the size of "aquella viga" that has been pursuing her: "He's been chasing me *all day* as if I were a deer." Everyday life that is impatient to express itself is here releasing its first babblings.

But the Old Woman changes roles and types, because her self, her name and her actions, are as changeable and as shifting as the book itself.

> And with this I shall put
> A period to my booklet, but I shall not close it. (1,626)

The book is as open and indefinite as the Old Woman, who is given 42 names: "escofina (rasp), pala (spade), campana (bell), taravilla (clack), escalera (ladder), abejón (drone) . . ." (924-927). The Old Woman is also supposed to be like an instrument that sounds to some like a bell and to others like a clack; she is what each person calls her: "Don't ever call her *trotera*, even if she does run errands for you." The movement from name to name corresponds to the movement from place to place—the successive steps evoke names and aspects that are likewise ambulatory:

> To tell all her names is a hard job for me;
> Of names and tricks she has more than a fox. (927)

The existence of the Old Woman consists in the unfolding of her aspect-names: *vieja* (old), *urraca* (magpie), *picaza* (magpie), *trotera* (love-messenger), *trotaconventos* (convent-trotter). . . . Her life is as open as the character's who speaks all through the book; and the book itself is open to the pen of any poet who feels the urge to add to it. Neither here, nor in Arabic literature, is anything conceived and represented as a portion of absolute existence, marked off by a real or ideal boundary line. The objects of both inward and outward experience are ultimately resolved into the flow of their own "going-on." Ibn Ḥazm had a friend, Ibn aṭ-Ṭubnī, who was "as if beauty had been fashioned according to his model, or had been fashioned according to the soul of anyone who saw him."[101] That is, the belief that a beautiful being realizes or incorporates into itself the preexisting idea of beauty now inverts its

---

[101] Ed.cit., p. 169. The biblical commentaries of Rabbi Arragel of Guadalajara show how this oriental conception of reality succeeded in penetrating Castilian texts. Here is an example: "They say that the waters of the deluge came down very hot. . . . The reason is, some say, that the deluge came because of *lixuria* (lechery), and *lixuria* is hot humidity, and therefore the water of the deluge was hot" (edition of the Duke of Alba, I, 115*a*). The word *lixuria* is a mixture of *luxuria* (lechery) and *lixo* (filth); the matter which comes from the sky has its nature confused with that which proceeds from man. Everything is interpenetrable and interchangeable

terms: it is the beautiful being which now communicates its beauty to
the ideal archetype of beauty, as well as to anyone who sees it, which
person is thus himself converted into the archetype of beauty. Beings,
in their most essential aspect (that is, the idea that makes them possible)
must have been for the Arab rather like images that are reflected from
one mirror to another, indefinitely. This being the case, it is just as valid
to take as reality the terminus (object) of the semantic intent of a word
as, inversely, to take the word as the terminus of the intent of "something" to realize itself and thus be reflected and live in the word. Therefore the greater the appetite for reality, the greater the abundance of
words, because the word is an existence, one of the infinite number of
refractions into which the light of existence passes. Instead of trying to
dwell upon a single, unique, and limited person, object, or word, and
thus establish a firm and consistent reality, Ibn Ḥazm decomposes, re-
fracts the excellence of his aforementioned friend into 29 names of virtues, listed without any principle of order or hierarchy: "beauty, hand-
someness, form of body, moderation, reserve . . . , indulgence, reason,
manliness . . . , knowledge (by heart) of the Koran and Ḥadīths, grammar, calligraphy, eloquence, theology, etc." This man is broken up into
radiations, and depending on our point of view, he will appear as beautiful, as a calligrapher, or as a theologian; and since he has many aspects,
he has to be expressed in many words.

Ibn Ḥazm uses the same procedure to say what a good friend is. Instead of reducing the matter to a central and essential point, he spreads
it out in 48 characteristics or aspects: "agreeable in speech, simple in his
life, sharp in his dealings, of subtle insight . . . ," and this verbal volume
is the container of the good friend. His elusive reality peels off in a litany
of praises, just as the Divine Essence is sought for in the endless enumeration of its names and perfections.[102]

[102] Echoes of Lope de Vega's oriental tradition are to be heard in his dithyrambic
ABC's:

Amar y honrar su marido	To love and honor your husband
es letra de este abece,	Are letters of this ABC;
siendo buena *por* la B,	You will be good *because of* B
que es todo el bien que te pido.	Which is the only wealth I ask of you.
Haráte cuerda la C,	C *will make you* wise,
la D dulce y entendida, etc.	D sweet and understanding, etc.

(*Peribáñez*, 1, 9)

The words radiate vital virtue, just as vital virtue suffuses them. That which the
occident understands as a magical function of the name was for the orient its normal
function. The name expresses the power or virtue of that which is named. A wor-
shipper of a Greco-Egyptian deity says: "I know thy name, . . . thy several mani-

Now just such a verbal litany, though with an inverted purpose, is the string of names which should not be given (and which are given) to the old women called *trotaconventos*. And these names reflect the urge for constant reiteration, which is an expressive procedure inseparable from the nature of this art: "I have likewise told you. . . . I have already told you. . . . My old woman *that you already know about*" (937, 939, 1,317). Author and reader ended up by persuading themselves that an old woman who came and went so much corresponded to a living being, especially because Juan Ruiz, after making her die, gave her a life certificate:

> And I, with my great sorrow, cannot utter a word,
> Because Trotaconventos neither walks nor scuttles about.
> She died serving me, and this leaves me dismayed;
> I don't know how to put it, but many a good door
> Was later closed to me that before was open to me. (1,518-1,519)

However commonplace the lament that follows, it nonetheless is so vivid that listeners and readers took it as something that seemed true:

> O Death! Be you dead, dead and damned!
> You killed my old woman; you should have killed me
>   first. (1,520)[103]

Those who heard the epics and the ballads sung knew that the Cid and King Don Sancho were actual persons, regardless of how the poems presented them. But the Archpriest said:

> O my *real* and loyal Trotaconventos!
> Many followed you alive, you lie dead alone. (1,569)[104]

How could this person not have been a being that had really existed? Death and the comico-mournful accent of the mourner converted Trotaconventos into a live person.[105]

---

festations. . . . I know thee, and thou knowest me. I am thou, and thou art I" (R. Reitzenstein, *Poimandres*, Leipzig, 1904, p. 20). Of fundamental importance is W. Schmidt's work, *Die Bedeutung des Namens*, 1912. Additional bibliography will be found in Charles Guignebert, *Jésus*, tr. by S. H. Hook, New York, 1935, p. 76.

[103] In Spanish:

> ¡Ay, muerte, muerta seas, muerta e mal andante!
> ¡Mataste a mi vieja, matasses a mi antes!

[104] In Spanish:

> ¡Ay, mi Trotaconventos, mi leal *verdadera*!
> Muchos te seguían viva, muerta yazes señera.

[105] The rationalist canon in the *Quijote* denied the existence of non-historical literary personages, just as other ecclesiastics have denied the presence of Santiago

Trotaconventos enjoyed the grace of God for having been a good *trotera*, a "martyr"; for having died fighting on the field of love. Ibn Ḥazm says: " 'He who fell passionately in love and abstained, and died, is a martyr;' and on that subject I composed a poem from which I quote:

If I perish of love I shall perish a martyr"

(*The Dove's Neck-Ring*, p. 167), like those who die in holy war. The Old Woman, *trotera* and martyr, also went to enjoy the sight of God:

Where have they taken her from me? I don't know for sure;
Those who take that road never come back with news.
Surely you have been given your place in paradise;
You must be in the company of the martyrs;
In the world you were always being martyrized for the sake
     of God. (1,569-1,570)

The Islamic-Christian symbiosis permitted the Archpriest and Trotaconventos to go on living outside their book. The Ibn Ḥazm who is borne up on the clouds of lyric metaphors is the one who at the same time writes: "And I shall tell you about Abū Bakr my brother, may God have mercy upon him, who married 'Ātika, daughter of Qand, commander of the Upper Frontier, in the days of Al-Manṣūr" (p. 168). The poetic character and the real character are confused here, just as they are in the case of the Archpriest, ignorant as a "leading ox," ambling through the streets of Hita, Alcalá, or Toledo, as a literary being and also as the reference to a man of flesh and blood. His complex yet delightful art becomes more enjoyable when it is approached within the disposition of life that made it possible.[106]

---

in Galicia. But Don Quixote, firmly entrenched in his own vital logic, replied with this indestructible argument: "I remember that a grandmother of mine on my father's side, when she would see some lady wearing a widow's wimple, would say to me: 'That lady, my grandson, looks like Lady Quintañona,' from which I gather that she must have known her, or at least, must have seen as much as some portrait of her" (i, 49).

[106] The preceding remarks have been amplified in *Comparative Literature*, 1952, iv, pp. 188-189; 211-213. See also my article about Ibn Ḥazm in *Cuadernos Americanos*, 1952 (October), Mexico.

The Spanish Jews

THE HISTORY OF NON-HISPANIC EUROPE can be understood without assigning the Jews a position anywhere in the foreground of the picture. This is not the case with Spain. And the primordial, decisive function of the Hispano-Hebrews is in turn absolutely inseparable from the circumstance of their having lived in close articulation with Hispano-Moslem history. The language used by their greatest figures (Maimonides, for example) was Arabic, although they wrote it in Hebrew characters. Their evident superiority to their European co-religionists is correlative to the superior level of Islam as compared with Christendom from the tenth through the twelfth centuries.[1] Without their contact with Islam, they would never have become interested in religious philosophy.[2] No less significant is the fact that only in Spain did the Jews possess an architecture of their own that showed an artistical distinct quality even though it was closely connected with Islamic art. We hear the lovely voice of the Hispano-Hebraic spirit issuing from the synagogues of Toledo and other towns with a firmness and expressive intensity unequaled elsewhere in Europe, where—and this is the explanation—they never felt themselves at home. But the tone of these architectonic expressions—almost totally destroyed—is Islamic; and the poetry, the thought, and the technology of the Hispano-Hebrews are likewise sequels of Arabic civilization. However, I am not going to write a history of the Jews. I am only interested in showing how they fit into Spanish history and what traces they have left in the disposition of its living dwelling-place.

The Jews ejected from their fatherland, that is, Spain, in 1492, felt themselves—and how rightly we shall soon see—as Spanish as the

---

[1] Benjamin of Tudela describes the situation of the Jews in Constantinople in the twelfth century. In spite of their wealth, they lived apart and in an atmosphere of humiliation. Only the emperor's physician could ride on a horse. The tanners poured out dirty water in front of their doors. "Being so defiled, they became the object of hatred to the Greeks. Their yoke is severely felt by the Jews" (*The Itinerary of Rabbi Benjamin of Tudela*, tr. by A. Asher, London, 1840, pp. 55-56).

[2] See H. Hirschfield, p. 2 of his introduction to the *Kitāb al Khazarī* of Yehudah ha-Levi, London, 1906.

Christians. Let us listen at random to one of them, a certain Francisco de Cáceres, who, like many others, outwardly accepted Christianity and returned to his native land around 1500. The officials of the Inquisition, into whose clutches he happened to fall, asked him why he had gone away. Cáceres answered them with reasons plain and good: "If the king our lord should order the Christians to become Jews or else to leave his realm, some would become Jews and others would leave; and those who left, as soon as they saw their sad plight, would become Jews so they could return to their native place, and they would be Christians and pray like Christians and deceive the world; they would think that they were Jews, and inside, in their hearts and wills, they would be Christians."[3]

Between the tenth and the fifteenth centuries Spanish history was Christian-Islamic-Judaic; and during those centuries the definitive structure of Hispanic life was forged. It is not possible to break up this history into stagnant pools, or to divide it off into parallel, synchronous currents, because each one of the three groups was a part of the circumstances projected by the other two. Nor could we capture this reality merely by gathering together data and events, or by objectifying it as a "cultural phenomenon." We must try to feel the projection of the lives of the ones into the lives of the others. For this and nothing else is what their history was. Facts, ideas, and all the rest are inseparable from the lives with which they are integrated.

Supremacy of the Despised

Against the commonalty of the Hebrew people scattered throughout the medieval world, the Jewish population of Spain stands out with surprising features. Since the days of Egyptian antiquity that people had been enduring attacks aimed at annihilating them. Their monotheistic belief, without any visible symbol of divinity (*Iudaei mente sola unumque numen intellegunt*, Tacitus, *Histories*, v, 5) and an integral part of their consciousness as a people, made them incompatible with the Roman

---

[3] Fritz Baer, *Die Juden im christlichen Spanien*, I, 1929; II, 1936. This work is an excellent registry of documents, some of them unpublished, concerning the Spanish Jews, in large part taken from scattered sources. Such a rich treasure of reliable documents makes it possible to take the first steps in a discussion of the Jewish problem in Spanish life. Hereinafter I shall cite Baer simply by volume and number. M. Vallecillo Avila's article "Los judíos de Castilla en la alta edad media," in *Cuadernos de Historia de España*, Buenos Aires, 1950, XIV, 17-110, is a compendium of data which in no way affects what is said in this book about the meaning and the historical reality of the Spanish Jews.

conception of the state, and attracted hostility and persecution from very early times on. The Jew proudly kept himself apart from other peoples: "they eat and sleep apart from the others . . . , they do not make unions with alien women" (Tacitus, *ibid.*). Their aggressive and exclusivist spirituality was not accompanied by a strong enough military impetus. The Hebrews' radical Messianism took them away from contacts with the present, and deprived them of a rational construction of the world of experience. Rome undid them politically, and the birth of Christianity put them in a position without parallel in history, for they turned out to be an indispensable creed and at the same time an extremely troublesome burden for the triumphant belief.[4] Most of the books of the Old Testament were accepted as the backbone of Christianity, most of them as divinely revealed, and this strengthened the Hebrews' faith, for they saw thus the totality of their faith accepted and revalidated. Greco-Roman paganism, on the other hand, was completely eliminated as a religious system. Under such circumstances, the fate of the Hebrews was bound to be tragic, for they were entombed and alive at the same time. Their deicide turned out to be as much of a *felix culpa* as Adam's, in as much as it was a condition required for the birth of Christianity, which fulfilled and did not abrogate the old law. It is no surprise that Iberian Christianity, squeezed between Islam and Zion, at times got along much better with the Jew than with the Moor,[5] with a sympathy that rose above the disparity in beliefs.

For almost two thousand years the Western world has been suffering from the chronic effects of this anomalous situation, and has been affected by it in a number of ways. The barbarous attempt in old and modern times to eliminate the Jews by violence has had consequences still incalculable. During the Middle Ages, their sojourn in Spain and

[4] For a detailed study of this point, see James Parkes, *The Conflict of the Church and the Synagogue*, London, 1934, pp. 370ff.

[5] Don Juan Manuel, the *Infante*, whom we must consider as the highest type of Spaniard in the fourteenth century, expressed his feelings in his last will and testament as follows: "Although Don Salamón, my physician, is a Jew and can not and ought not be an executor, and yet even so, because I have always found his loyalty so great that it would be hard to describe or believe, I therefore beg Doña Blanca and my sons to keep him in their service and to trust him in their affairs; and I am certain that they will benefit from doing so, *for if he were a Christian, I know what I would bequeath him*" (text published by Mercedes Gaibrois in the *Boletín de la Academia de la Historia*, 1931, xcix, 25). There is also considerable significance in what James II of Aragon wrote in 1321 to his daughter, who was married to Don Juan Manuel: "Daughter, we have received your letter . . . concerning the son you have borne. . . . But, daughter, do not raise him under Jewish tutelage as has been your custom" (A. Giménez Soler, *Don Juan Manuel*, p. 501).

their final exile traced indelible lines upon Iberian history. For many centuries Hispano-Christian life depended upon that alien people, choking and nourishing its history at the same time. If the logic of reason were effective in human affairs, Spain should have been the ideal place for the harmonious cooperation of two such different peoples. But to meditate on this would be idle utopianism. What happened was that the aristocratic spiritual attitude of the Jews and the habit of adapting themselves mimetically to the most difficult of circumstances allowed the persecuted people to transpose its oriental mode of life into the Western key while preserving itself as a religious nation, acephalous and always *in partibus infidelium*. The bitterness of its exile, by dint of necessity almost metaphysical, gave birth to defensive qualities and a rare aptitude for slipping through every crevice and scaling the steepest heights. In entirely different milieus Jews have known how to withdraw into themselves or to rise up and triumph—living like humble pariahs in the mountains of Morocco or giving new directions to physics in contemporary Europe. The Iberian Jews presented one appearance in the Arabic zone and another in the Christian zone. In the latter, the Jews of Castile were different from those of Andalusia and the Spanish Levant.[6]

The history of Israel was interrupted by Rome and by the triumph of Christianity. The exile and the dispersion turned the Jews into appendages of the histories of the various countries into which they were driven by destiny. In Spain the persecutions they suffered under the Visigoths (see Chapter 3) impelled the Jews to help the Saracen invaders. We can guess that they were the ones who best saw the meaning of the Moslem occupation of North Africa while the court of Toledo— the weak capital of a poorly unified land—indulged in the deadly pleasure of civil conflicts. The condition of the Jews improved with the arrival of the Saracens, and in the eighth century they shared with the invaders the domination of Toledo.[7] Once they had adopted and mastered the new customs, many of them excelled in the literary use of the Arabic language. When Spanish Islam reached the summit of its vitality in the tenth century, the great Jewish personalities also began to appear. Ḥasdāy ben-Shaprūṭ (910-970) was a physician, the minister of finance, and the

---

[6] According to the book of the *Alboraique* (c. 1488), the converts in Old Castile, Leon, and Zamora were sincere: "scarcely any of them will be found to be heretics." In Toledo, Extremadura, Andalusia, and Murcia "you will find scarcely any of them faithful Christians, as is well-known in all Spain" (text of I. Loeb, in the *Revue des Etudes Juives*, 1889, XVIII, 241). The false converts were called "alboraiques" after the name of Mohammed's horse, which was neither horse nor mule.

[7] S. Dubnov, *Die Geschichte des jüdischen Volkes in Europa*, 1926, IV, 88.

ambassador of 'Abd al-Raḥmān III; he is celebrated besides for his translation of Dioscorides. Shĕmuel ibn Nagrella—who lived between 982 and 1055—became the vizier of the King of Granada because of the beautiful style of his letters, and he was succeeded in office by his son Yūsuf. A similar post was occupied by Abū-l-Fadhl ibn Ḥasdāy in the kingdom of Saragossa in 1066.[8] But these and various others were eventually eclipsed by Abraham ibn 'Ezra (1093-1167), a native of Tudela; Shĕlomo ibn Gabirol (1021-1052), from Malaga; Yĕhudah ha-Levi (1080-1140), a Toledan; and especially by the Cordovan, Maimonides (1135-1204). Their literary, scientific, and philosophical works occupy a conspicuous place in the history of European civilization, and it falls outside my plan to evaluate them again. Let us say simply that none of these Jews would have been what he was without Spanish Islam. When the latter declined after the twelfth century, the creative genius of the Hispano-Hebrew likewise declined. Among the Jews writing outside of Spain after the expulsion, Abravanel links with fifteenth-century Italian literature in his *Dialogue of Love*; and the thought of Baruch Spinoza is a product of rationalist Europe, in spite of the profound echoes of the Hispano-Hebraic spirit. Luis Vives, however, was still a Spaniard.

The Almoravide and Almohade invasions in the eleventh and twelfth centuries had consequences almost as dire for the Hispano-Hebrews as for the Mozarabic Christians. In 1066 there was a massacre in Granada that cost the lives of thousands of Jews.[9] Many sought refuge in the Christian zone. The Hebrew communities that had existed since the beginning of the Reconquest suddenly swelled, and they became the vehicle for Moslem ways of living just as much as the Mozarabes were. It must be remembered that in reality the Arabs taught the Christians the art of utilizing the Jews as physicians, scientists, tax-collectors, public officials (local judges in Aragon, for example), diplomats, and, in general, as administrators of the wealth of the state and of the nobility. They transmitted the prestige of Islamic life with the advantage of not being Moslems and of having a belief and a morality much closer to the Christians. Kings and lords placed unlimited trust in them—but they punished them fiercely if they were disloyal, just as they did, after all, the Christians. When Alphonse VI sent an embassy to Al-Mu'tamid of Seville to collect the tribute due him, he did not commission a Chris-

---

[8] R. Dozy, *Histoire des musulmans d'Espagne*, 1932, III, 18 and 71. S. Dubnov, *op.cit.*, IV, 220 and 223.

[9] R. Dozy, *op.cit.*, III, 72.

tian knight to receive the money but the Jew Ibn Shālīb (Dozy, *op.cit.*, III, 119).

We know that in the Visigothic epoch the Jews bought off the clergy and enjoyed the protection of the nobles, in spite of the severe laws dictated against them. But the situation under the Christian kings of the early Reconquest was quite different. The Jews were tolerated if not by law at least in practice, and the kings themselves declared time and again that without the sons of Jacob, their finances would go to pieces. The *aljamas*, or Jewish communities, paid a head tax and also the church tithe. But apart from these relatively mild discriminations, they were the collectors of the royal taxes, as well as of the tributes owed to the military orders and the great lords, and it was not unusual for them to perform similar services for church officials.

The *aljamas* were able to pay the high tribute that the kings coveted so hungrily because the Jews were good craftsmen and very clever entrepreneurs. There was no trade they did not practise, no remunerative business in which they did not have a hand. They exported and imported merchandise, and lent money at an interest rate of 33 per cent per annum.[10] The resentment of their debtors and the hatred of the taxpayers had a great influence in their ruination when the common people

[10] During the Middle Ages, the normal rate of interest varied between 33 and 43 per cent; in the sixteenth century, after the expulsion of the Jews from Naples (actively encouraged by Genoese and Florentine usurers), the Christian money-lenders reached the rate of 240 per cent. See S. W. Baron, *A Social and Religious History of the Jews*, Columbia University Press, 1937, II, 16 and 35. The first victim of the medieval economy was the Jew, who was much more extensively and arbitrarily bled of his money than the Christian (Baron, II, 18). Christendom paid no attention to the poor Jew, and in the ghettos the misery of the oppressed must have been terrible (see Béla Szekely, *El antisemitismo*, Buenos Aires, 1940, pp. 162-163, 203). This is so true that it is only thanks to the cultural importance of the Spanish converts that we have specific notice of two indigent Jews: Juan Poeta, of Valladolid, and Antón de Montoro. In the records kept by Christians, whether they were debtors or taxpayers, we find mention of only the rich Jew, the hated royal tax-gatherer whose fortune prospered so long as it did not stir up the king's envy. Was such not the case with Peter the Cruel and his treasurer Don Simuel el Leví? Saint Thomas Aquinas had already set down the rule that the church committed no injustice by levying taxes on the Jews and confiscating their property, and the kings had followed this principle before it was formulated by Saint Thomas. "Since Jews are the slaves of the Church, the Church may take disposition of their property," says the *Summa theologica*, II, 2, 10, 10. Nor had the fact that the income from the ghettos came largely from the exploitation of Christian poverty escaped Saint Thomas, who ingeniously disposed of this problem in his communication to the Duchess of Brabant (Baron, III, 99, n. 6). (I am indebted to Sra. María Rosa Lida de Malkiel for this note.)

acquired a power and initiative in the fourteenth century that they had lacked up to that time.[11]

As the Jew developed his tradition of learning he gave it rather a practical orientation (medicine, prognostic astrology, ethics, law, the making of technical instruments, translation, etc.). He adapted himself to the frame of interests traced out by his Christian lords, and he satisfied them by doing the things that Christianity could not or would not do. This way he could live happily and savor the delights of exercising his power and exhibiting his superiority over the caste of his lords. Thus was born the belief, still very much alive in the sixteenth century, that the Jews were by nature intelligent and sharp-minded. In a trial before the Inquisition in 1572 the opinion came out that "Sebastián Martínez and his brothers . . . were descended from converts, to judge by the sharpness of their mind."[12] This popular idea is found "scientifically" demonstrated by Dr. Juan Huarte in his *Examen de ingenios* (Inquiry into the Nature and Kinds of Intelligence, 1575): "The descendants of the people of Israel have not yet lost the temper and qualities which the manna introduced into their seed, nor will their diligence and sharpness of wit be for this reason soon exhausted" (Chap. xv). So it was that when Francis I of France fell ill and was convinced of the ignorance of Christian doctors, he sent to Charles V begging him "to send him a Jewish physician, the best in his court. . . . Which request was heartily laughed at in Spain. . . . Whereupon the Emperor ordered that such a physician should be sought for . . . , and when one was not found, he sent a *New Christian*." It happened, however, that this physician told the king of France that he was a Christian. Then Francis I "dismissed him . . . and sent to Constantinople for a Jew, and with nothing but asses' milk the Jew cured him" (*ibid.*). The humorous tone of the anecdote possibly does not exhaust its meaning, nor does it reveal clearly what Huarte thought of Jewish physicians. But in any case, what he

[11] The twelfth-century *Cantar de Mío Cid*, in which society is viewed from below, already reflects the popular animosity toward the Jewish money-lender, who is seen rejoicing in his profits: "Raquel and Vidas were together counting the part of their money that was their profit" (ll. 100-101). The hero belongs to the lesser nobility and is supported by the sympathy of the common citizens—"burgueses e burguesas." The Jews Raquel and Vidas had helped the Cid with their money more than once: "Don Raquel and Vidas, you have already forgotten me" (155); and the fraudulent business with the chests witnesses to a joyful revenge of the plundered on the plunderers, an act that may be taken for the *vox populi*. (Note of Sra. María Rosa Lida de Malkiel.)

[12] *Proceso contra el hebraísta salmantino Martín Martínez de Cantalapiedra*, edited by M. de la Pinta Llorente, Madrid, 1946, p. L.

thought about the intelligence of Jews and their natural and biological motivations is not a joke. The agreement on this point between the ignorant populace and a learned scholar shows how deeply rooted the belief in the cleverness and knowledge of the Jews was in Spain.

Admirable and important as were the contributions of the learned Jews in the thirteenth, fourteenth, and fifteenth centuries,[13] there are no longer to be found among them figures such as those of the eleventh and twelfth. Not only is their participation evident in the juridical, historical, and astronomical work of Alphonse the Learned; without them this work is inexplicable. The Jews at Alphonse's court included such personages as "Don Xosse, nuestro alfaquim," which is to say, the astronomer "Don Yuçaf" or Joseph (Baer, II, 51), and others to whom I shall refer later. In the court of Alphonse VIII was to be found the astronomer "Avomar Abenxuxen" (Baer, II, 21). In 1349 Peter III of Aragon commanded that a certain book in Arabic be given to "Maestre Salamó" for him to turn it into "our language." A certain "Maestre Alfonso" translated a "book of figures and astronomy" into Romance in 1351.[14] In 1346 Peter IV of Aragon commissioned his physician, "Maestre Menahem"—"magnus experimentator et nigromanticus"—to work at certain scientific experiments. "Daví Bonjorn" built astrolabes for the same king. John I of Aragon had Cresques de Vivérs who "knew much about horoscopes" as his astrologer in 1391 (Baer, I, 259, 310, 570).

In cities with large Jewish communities there were schools supported by the *aljamas*. We know of one in Cervera (1323) and another in Calatayud. Those who attended these schools (qui addiscerent vel legerent) were exempt from the head tax till they were twenty-three years old. Rich Jews contributed to the maintenance of such institutions. One of them, "Yucef Cohén," founded a school for poor Jews, in Tortosa, and endowed it with a dormitory and a library, as well as a thousand Barcelonan solidi for its support.[15] If disasters and carelessness had not so greatly reduced the number of documents, we would know many more facts of this kind. Let me add only that before the fifteenth cen-

[13] "Among the Jews of Valencia there were no idlers. They were extremely skillful in industry and trade, and in the cultivation of letters and sciences, attaining such success that the noblemen and wealthy bourgeois not only displayed with pride the cloths, furniture, garments, and jewelry that they made but also went to their rabbis and teachers to get their ailments cured or to entrust to them the literary or scientific education of their sons." (Francisco Danvila, "El robo de la judería de Valencia en 1391," in the *Boletín de la R. Academia de la Historia*, 1886, VIII, 366.)

[14] A. Rubió y Lluch, *Documents per l'historia de la cultura mig-eval*, pp. 143, 155.

[15] A. Rubió y Lluch, "Notes sobre la ciencia oriental a Catalunya," in *Estudis Universitaris Catalans*, 1909, III, 390.

tury the type of man that we think of as middle class—not an ecclesiastic —devoted to scholarly endeavors was represented by the Jews. An outstanding example is the Majorcan physician Leon Mosconi, who in 1375 was living in a house with fine, comfortable furniture, and abundantly provided with books on theology, philosophy, medicine, mathematics, and literature.[16]

Alphonse the Learned and the Jews

The sudden appearance in the court of Alphonse X the Learned of great works of history, law, and astronomy, written in Castilian rather than Latin is an inadequately explained phenomenon if we limit ourselves to saying that a learned monarch wished to compose huge works of encyclopedic knowledge in a language understood by all. Such an assertion is really an abstraction, for it does not take into account Alphonse X's vital horizon or the circumstances in which he lived. It would not have occurred to any non-Spanish sovereign to bring out in the common language such works as the *Grande e General Estoria*, the *Libros del saber de astronomía*,[17] or the *Siete Partidas*. Nor is there any instance outside Spain of the translation of the complete text of the Bible in that century (G. Gröber, *Grundriss*, II, 714). This fact goes hand in hand with the scarcity in Spain of important theological, philosophical, scientific, or juridical works composed in Latin. In contrast, let us recall such figures as Siger de Brabant, Roger Bacon, Thomas Aquinas, and many others.

We now possess a valuable bibliographical study of scientific manuscripts of the Spanish Middle Ages,[18] manuscripts which, although not well known up to now, turn out to require no essential modification in the panorama of Castilian science during the Middle Ages. The author of the study, in his minute analysis of the process of translation of Arabic texts, which began in the tenth century and carried on in the twelfth and thirteenth, observes how "that cultural movement first noticed amongst the Spanish Moslems soon radiated outside its own zone and shone like a rising sun *upon the European Christians*, half-asleep in the darkness of the high Middle Ages" (p. 6). The fact is well known, but not enough thought has been given to the question of why it was "European Chris-

---

[16] See *Revue des Etudes Juives*, 1899, XXXI, 242; 1900, XL, 62, 169.

[17] For the fidelity with which the Jews translated this astronomical work from the Arabic, see J. M. Millás Vallicrosa in *Al-Andalus*, 1933, I, 155-187.

[18] José M. Millás Vallicrosa, *Las traducciones orientales en los manuscritos de la Biblioteca Catedral de Toledo*, Madrid, 1942.

tians" and not the Spaniards who opened new ways of thought with means quite within reach of the Hispano-Christians on their own ground.[19] The oldest center of French learning, the School of Chartres, took advantage of Spanish Arabic thought even before the translations of the twelfth century were begun in Toledo. It was the French bishops of Tarazona and Toledo (Michael and Raymond) who served as a bridge to the foreigners curious about oriental learning at the beginning of that century. To Toledo, Seville,[20] and other cities came people avid for knowledge, who employed Spanish Jews to interpret the prized Arabic manuscripts. Famous among these Jews were Moshe Sefardi (that is the convert Petrus Alphonsus); Abraham bar Ḥiyya ben David (that is, Johannes Hispalensis or Hispanensis). By way of them and others less celebrated, the learning of the Moslems (philosophy, astronomy, mathematics, medicine) passed into Europe. We know the names of some of those who, in the twelfth and thirteenth centuries, put into intelligible Latin the things the Jews dictated in Castilian or in defective Latin: Plato Tiburtinus, Gerard of Cremona, Hugo Sanctallensis, Adelard of Bath, Michael Scotus, Hermann the Dalmatian, Rudolph of Bruges, Hermann the German.[21] What were the Spanish Christians doing in the meantime, besides making final conquest of Toledo, Cordova, Seville, and Murcia, and opening the treasure-house of Moslem civilization to the foreigners? The only thinker of originality, as we have seen, was Dominicus Gundisalvus, shaped in the Islamico-Jewish milieu, and whose thought remained isolated and unproductive in Castile. Sr. Millás Vallicrosa has brought two new names to light, Alvaro of Oviedo and the Toledan canon, Marcos; but these are of no great significance: Alvaro of Oviedo (end of the thirteenth century), annotated and corrected translations from the Arabic, in which he became interested with the object of demonstrating "all the errors of the Arabic philosophers," especially of Averroes.[22]

It is evident, then, that Latin original texts of a learned character were

[19] I leave to one side consideration of such Catalonian centers as Vich and Ripoll, whose importance is emphasized by Sr. Millás in his *Assaig d'historia de les idees físiques i matemàtiques a la Catalunya medieval*, 1931. We have already seen that in the tenth and eleventh centuries Catalonian life gravitated more toward centers outside the Peninsula than toward those inside it, and scientific history confirms this view.

[20] See E. Lévi-Provençal and E. García Gómez, *Sevilla a comienzos del siglo XII*, Madrid, 1948, p. 173.

[21] Sr. Millás Vallicrosa (*op.cit.*, pp. 8ff.) gives the necessary bibliography.

[22] *Op.cit.*, p. 165. M.-T. d'Alverny et G. Vajda, "Marc de Tolède," in *Al-Andalus*, 1951, XVI, 99-132. Canon Marc of Toledo was a Mozarabe who lived at the end of the twelfth century. He studied medicine out of Spain and translated Galen.

very scarce in the thirteenth century, in sharp contrast to the abundance and merit of the Castilian translations and adaptations of European and Arabic works during the Alphonsine period. This fact is to be understood as an expression of the Christian-Islamic-Jewish contexture, as a result of the importance achieved by the Hispano-Hebrews and of their interest in placing moral and scientific learning within reach of the courtly and lordly society on which the power and prestige of the unpopular Jews depended. The Castile of Ferdinand III had shown its abilities in warfare against the richest Moslem lands, and its predominance over the crown of Aragon was perceptible. Alphonse X, his successor, enjoyed in peace the fruits of military successes (Las Navas de Tolosa, Cordova, Seville) which he himself might never have achieved, and he had more recourse to diplomatic skill than to military impetus in his efforts to enlarge his kingdom. For the first time science and poetry, under his aegis, took possession of the royal halls, and learning and imperial ambition were both a part of the activities developed under Castilian policy. Knights of the Reconquest now could hear and read in their own language the moralized account of sacred and profane history. Thanks to the linguistic innovation, the law and good learning would be able to give moral unity to all that had been conquered by force of arms. Action was succeeded by aspiration. The king longed to be the lord of Gascony and of the Holy Roman Empire, and thus once obscure and remote Castile now saw her future in an international perspective. The troubadours of Provence repaid Alphonse's generosity with hyperbolic praises;[23] some of the learned humanists of Spain, France, and Italy took care of new cultural needs, while, very much in the foreground, Moors and Jews gathered together their indispensable bodies of knowledge. All this is known to us as an outward event and in terms of its results, but not in the detail of its happening. The king left not so much as a single line about his inner life; he did not confess for posterity as so many Moslem writers did. We know his nephew the *infante* Don Juan Manuel better than we know the magnificent uncle, and this leads to the presumption that the wise king was a praiseworthy "impresario" of culture rather than a profound and original spirit. But to accentuate his character as a great statesman of culture is not to belittle his virtues; it is to make them understandable.

We do not know what his education was like, or the names of those who aroused his insatiable curiosity about jurisprudence, history, and

[23] For the jongleurs at the court of Alphonse X see R. Menéndez Pidal, *Poesía juglaresca y juglares, passim.*

astronomy. The culture of his court reveals an exalted view of human destiny connected with the stellar forces, in historical time and in the totality of social life. The solemn style of the *Partidas* reflects against this broad background. As an authentic Spaniard, Alphonse fused the grandeur of his Christian-Oriental conception of the world with the grandeur of his own existence, and he dreamed of attaining the highest position his times afforded—the throne of the Holy Roman Empire—a dream realized only in the ceremonious formulas of his chancellory. From his early youth he undoubtedly heard tempting voices inciting him to ascend *ad astra*, for a career marked by such high flights could not have been the outcome of casual motivations.

Without trying to reduce a phenomenon of such magnitude to a single motive, we must for the present keep in mind the situation of the His- pano-Hebrews in the middle of the thirteenth century. As late as the twelfth century the language of civilization was still Arabic for a Mai- monides; the orient was the pole toward which he tended. From the middle of the thirteenth century, the horizon of the Hispano-Hebrew was Castile, inspired by designs of empire quite evident to the sharp minds of the Jews, and very much in keeping with the new splendor of the court. We have only to compare the diplomas of Alphonse X with those of his predecessors; we have only to observe his magnificent calligraphy and the long lists of his *confirmantes*, among whom Moslem kings appear as vassals along with a considerable number of prelates and lords. The Jew, who had formerly felt himself attracted by the blazing star of Saladin, at whose court Maimonides took up residence, turns now toward the court of Castile. But there is a difference. The Arabic lan- guage used by the Hispano-Hebrew belonged to a civilization that towered over him from summits of perfection attained without his par- ticipation. In Castile, on the other hand, learning was meager, and a Jew need only to say or write something about Islamico-Jewish culture in Castilian (as much his language as Arabic), and he put himself in a dominant position. If in earlier periods the Jews had no rivals as finan- cial administrators of the kingdom, as tradesmen, and as physicians, they were now going to excel as transmitters of Moslem civilization. For the Castilians of the mid-thirteenth century, subject Moslemry was what Italy, conquered but not subject, was later to be for the kings of Aragon: a fountain of learning and aristocratic distinction. Thus in the thirteenth century the Jews played a role similar to that of the Hispanic humanists educated in Naples, Rome, and Bologna in the fifteenth century. That which was to be sought for in the neo-Senecan morality of Petrarch in the fifteenth century was found in the thirteenth in the treatises on Islamic morality, in all probability, translated into Castilian by Jews.[24] In the twelfth century the group called somewhat inexactly the "school of translators of Toledo" worked in the service of non-Spanish foreigners thirsty for philosophy, mathematics, and physical science. The "school of translators" of the thirteenth century put into the Spanish tongue, not into Latin, those creations of Islamic civilization which served to clarify the Alphonsine view of the "human": what man has been historically, what he should be morally and juridically, what the stars cause him to be. The "theoretical" problem of the nature of reality did not preoccupy the Learned King for a moment—whose trend of thought, moreover, fitted easily in the perspective of the Jew with his interest in morality, law, astrology, and applied science rather than in mathematics and pure philosophy. Let us not forget that Averroes, al-Battānī, and Avicenna had no counterpart among their contemporaries in the Jewish world.

Learned Jews figured in the court of Alphonse X, and their tongues and pens were not idle. Their labor consisted in making available a culture for which the great lords were as hungry as they were ignorant. We do not know what part they played in the intellectual formation of the Learned King. His father-in-law, James I of Aragon, "received the science of Rabbi Moshé ben Nahman."[25] James' daughter, the queen Violante, Alphonse's wife, had as one of her attendants (perhaps as physician) Don Todros ha-Leví Abū-l-'Āfiya, a cabalist and poet,[26] who stayed behind to attend the queen in Perpignan when Don Alfonso went to see Gregory X in Beaucaire (1275) with the object of getting support for his imperial pretensions. Don Todros says in one of his poems: "How good it is to carry out the mandates of the King. Don Alfonso destroys

---

[24] The following are well known: *Calila e Dimna, Poridat de poridades, Libro de los doce sabios, Bocados de oro, Libro de los engaños et assayamientos de las mujeres* (the last named translated in 1253 by order of Don Fadrique, the brother of Alphonse X), etc. In the *Bonium* or *Bocados de oro* we read that the beauty of the buildings constructed in early times by "certain gentiles and kings . . . moved the young men to go to the schools where they could learn. And for this reason today the *Jews* make many carvings in their synagogues, and the *Christians* likewise make many figures in their churches, and the *Moors* many ornaments in their mosques" (H. Knust edition, p. 76). I do not believe that a Christian would have mentioned the three religions in this order, nor would a Moor.

[25] We have testimony to this fact from Yosef ben Ṣaddiq de Arévalo and Abraham ben Shelomo de Torrutiel. See Francisco Cantera, *El Libro de la cábala*, pp. 33 and 56.

[26] His *Diwan* has been published by David Yellin (Jerusalem, 1932). See Baer, I, 52.

all who rebel against him. His orders are always executed. There is no evil in him, and no one is able to sing all his praises, nor could any song contain them all. Who could know how to express fully all the good that the Creator put in him? The task is long, and the day is short."[27]

The exaltation of the monarch's greatness was the work of the Jews. Ishaq ben Cid and Yehudá ben Moshe, the authors of the astronomical *Tablas* which, out of deference toward the king, are called *alfonsíes* (Alphonsine), propose in Chapter 1 that his reign be taken as the starting point for a new era. The Greeks began theirs with Alexander, "the Romans took the year in which Caesar began to reign . . . , the Arabs took for an era the year in which Mohammed said that he was a prophet. . . . *Now again* the Moors are making use of a Persian era, so called because of the victory they had over the King of Persia. . . . And *we see* that *in this our time* there has taken place a notable and honorable event, and as much to *be esteemed* as all the former ones; and this is the reign of the lord king Don Alfonso, who has excelled all the wise kings in learning, wisdom and understanding, law, piety, and nobility. And therefore we have thought it fitting to fix as the beginning of an era the year in which this noble king commenced to reign, so that this era be used and shown forth just as the other eras were used and shown forth before it, and so that the renown of this noble king *last* and remain here *for ever*."[28]

The foregoing passage is pregnant with meaning. Eras based on superhuman beliefs, on "acts of God,"[29] are excluded: the Jewish era of the creation and the Christian era. Mohammed is left with the responsibility of believing himself a prophet ("the year in which Mohammed *said* that he was a prophet"). Their era is based on a historical event like the era of the conquest of Persia. The writers have forgotten the divine halos, have left to one side the *scala caeli*, and have put into play their own experience of time. The conscious experience of time is the staff that has helped modern man in his laborious march toward autonomous being. The absence of the element of divine transcendence in the text in

---

[27] Yellin edition, p. 92. For this translation I am grateful to Mr. Abraham Berger of the New York Public Library.

[28] *Libros del saber de astronomía*, ed. by M. Rico y Sinobas, 1867, IV, 119-120.

[29] Compare this "secularized" style of history with the following purely Christian style: "And they made of this many books, which are called his histories and gests, in which they told of the *acts of God*, and of the prophets, and of the saints, and *likewise* of the kings, and of all the great men, and of the deeds of chivalry, and of the peoples" (*General Estoria*, ed. by Solalinde, p. 3).

question and the expression of time as personal experience are phenomena which converge at the same vertex. The theme of the passage is the glories of the past and the intention of establishing a new glory, starting in "this our time," so that it will last "here for ever." It makes no difference that this effort failed; it is simply a question of seeing what happens in a specific Castilian text of the thirteenth century, in which someone, out of the conscious experience of his present, comprehended the past and the future in delicately graduated terms: "the Romans took . . . , now again they are making use . . . , we see in this our time." This style is inconceivable in a Christian writer of the thirteenth century. In its personal and "extracelestial" character it announces the humanism of the so-called Renaissance and forces us to recognize in Islamico-Jewish Spain the presence of Renaissance germs that never came to fruit in the sciences.

The positive tone of the transcribed passage comes from the authors' feeling of security in their intellectual domination of Castile; therefore the effort to label the new times which the Jew hoped to make his own in some way. One of the means for achieving such an end was the Castilianization of Islamic culture, which could be offered to the king and the great lords as something useful and profitable, without offending the values and inhibitions of the man of Castile. The Jews, not the Christians, knew and revealed the hidden treasures in the language of conquered and already decadent Islam. They were the ones who awakened and stimulated the king's desire to read—in his own language—the whole body of Christian-Islamic-Hebraic knowledge, beginning with the Old Testament, which was incorporated in the *Grande e General Estoria* and also translated several times independently (in certain cases from the Hebrew) along with the New Testament. How could it have occurred to a king with a reputation for learning and wisdom to sponsor works on history, law, and science in the vulgar tongue and not in Latin, when Latin was the only language in which such forms of culture could be expressed in the Western Christendom of the thirteenth century? This is the answer. The living culture of Castile was at once Christian, Islamic, and Jewish, and its common denominator had to be a language understood by those concerned with making a unified whole out of such a strange conglomeration. The forces from Africa that came after 1200 were evidently a failure. They wanted to revive the Islamic Empire in Spain when it was already dying a slow death and incapable of reacting. Castile was affirming itself as a dominant and undisputed power, and over the throne of Alphonse X shone the star of a Peninsular, perhaps

a European, empire. Since every empire has to have a language of culture, the Jews, ever alert to such needs, proposed an *era alfonsí*, and
filled the spoken language with material compatible with the special form
of Castilian existence.[30] The literary triumph of that language was not,
as in Italy, due to the aesthetic prestige of an individual creation, but
to doctrinal works, grave and austere, which spoke to ethical man and
not to sensuous or imaginative man.

In the prologue to the *Libro de las armellas* (The Book of the Armil-
lary Sphere), Alphonse says: "We commanded our learned Rabbi Zag
of Toledo [Isaac ben Cid] to make it thorough and *plain to understand,*
so that *any man* who looks into this book will be able to work with it,"[31]
a sentence which illuminates what the king understood by science—a
clear popularization which would not excite the mind. If Alphonse had
been really interested in astronomy, he would have thought about its
problems and not about how to make other people understand it without
any trouble.

The desire for popularization *ad usum regis* coincided with the Castilian Jew's only slight interest in Latin, the medium of expression which
reflected the Christian unity of the Occident. His language par excellence
was Hebrew; then came Arabic as the expression of the most valuable
culture; and then, from the thirteenth century on, Castilian was imposed on him as the language of his only possible homeland. The Christian population did not use the Castilian text of the Bible for their religious ceremonies, but the Hispano-Hebrews did, and it was considered
one of their peculiarities that they read the Old Testament in Castilian.
As late as 1487 the Inquisition accused a certain Pedro Serrano of reading
"the Bible in the Romance tongue the way the Jews have it, in the
homes of the Jews" (Baer, ii, 476). This must have been going on since
the thirteenth century, the time of the first translations of the Old
Testament, translations which acquired historical meaning as the flowering of culture in the vulgar tongue, due first and above all to the vital
necessities of the Jews. The vulgar tongue, used in the didactic works
already mentioned, allowed the lords and the clergy to become acquainted in a worthy form with aspects of Islamic thought that were compatible with the Castilian form of life. Those treatises on abstract moral

[30] The Cordovan Ibn Ḥazm had already said, in the middle of the eleventh century, that "what fixes and preserves a nation's language, as well as its sciences and its
history, is simply the strength of its political power, accompanied by the happy welfare and leisure of its inhabitants" (see M. Asín in *Al-Andalus,* 1939, iv, 278).

[31] *Libros del saber de astronomía,* ii, i.

doctrine gave comfort to the spirit without touching upon experiences of the senses, which individualize and divide.

It must be emphasized that the literature of thirteenth-century Castile was not a pure luxury of the senses and the fancy.[32] A Castilian poet like Chrétien de Troyes would have found nothing to do at the court of Alphonse VIII or Alphonse X, which in no way resembled the court of Marie de Champagne. We have already observed how Joinville, while he was campaigning in Egypt, would think of the ladies at the court of Saint Louis—hardly a place of dissipation. Those who wrote lyric poetry for the Castilian courts were up to the beginning of the thirteenth century Provençals and after that, Galicians.[33] As early as 1138 the troubadour Marcabru was to be found at the side of Alphonse VII, for whom he had composed a moralizing song exhorting the lords of Southern France to forget the pleasures of idleness and join the fight against the Moors. The jongleur Gavaudan did the same thing in 1211 when Alphonse VIII was preparing for the decisive battle against the Almohades. So that the very art of the troubadours, when it came into Castile, put itself in the service of a political and religious cause, got tinted with Castilian shadings, and was utilized by the kings as a medium for international propaganda. Alphonse VII the Emperor (1127-1157) aspired to annex the Duchy of Aquitaine to his empire.

[32] Poems like the *Alexandre* and the *Libro de Apolonio* not only treated of imported subject matter but also used non-Castilian dialects of Spanish. But even so, their character is primarily exemplary. The author of the *Apolonio* says, toward the end of the poem:

> Commending them all to the spiritual King,
> I leave them to the grace of the heavenly Lord. (638)

One exception would be the *Razón de amor*, at the beginning of the thirteenth century, in which a pretty girl

> Took the mantle off her shoulders,
> Kissed me on the mouth and eyes;
> She was so eager for me,
> She could hardly speak to me.

This author, though, was a man of schooling

> Who always loved ladies;
> But he had been entirely brought up
> In Germany and France;
> He lived a long time in Lombardy
> In order to learn courtly manners.

This jongleur of foreign manner wrote in a language full of Aragonesisms and Provençalisms: *dreita, feita, muito, peyor, leyer, pleno, pleguem, cortesa, dona, bela*, etc.

[33] The best account of this is found in R. Menéndez Pidal, *Poesía juglaresca y juglares*, pp. 150-259.

The Provençal poems in other cases served as entertainment and spectacle for the kings and their courtiers, not so much because of the texts of the poems (generally obscure and oversubtle) as because of the music of the jongleurs who sang them. This spectacle remained external to those who found pleasure and escape in it. The music and words of the songs can be compared with opera which, though sung in Italian, has delighted upper-class audiences in Spain from the eighteenth to the twentieth century without bringing about the birth of Spanish opera. Even the efforts to have foreign operas sung in Spanish have failed. Something similar must have been true of the Provençal songs in twelfth- and thirteenth-century Castile, even if we disregard their obscurity, sometimes abstruse, and this would explain why they did not become acclimated in the Peninsula. The essential reason was their lack of congruence with the Castilian form of life.

The Castilians replaced the songs of Provence with Galician adaptations of that poetry. The remote Galician language (although less remote than that of the troubadours) was like a disguise, behind which the Castilian could forget his inhibitions and his peculiar taboos. Alphonse X went so far as to write actual obscenities in Galician,[34] at the same time that he was singing praises to the Virgin. But neither of those two things could he do in his own Castilian. Galician served as an escape valve for his emotions, and as a gutter for his more unseemly notions.

Alphonse the Learned's Collaborators

We do not know anything about the manner and extent of effective assistance that Alphonse the Learned received from his collaborators save in the case of those who translated and edited the treatises on astronomy. But even if Christian scholars abounded—and such must have been the case—among the editors of the historical and legal works, it is difficult to attribute to them the decisive motivation behind the employment of the vulgar tongue for works of learning, which at that time was not within the perspective of European Christendom. It is evident, nevertheless, that the explanation of a phenomenon of this kind will never come from documents. But in spite of this we must try to understand the most decisive event in the history of the Spanish language. It is not enough to say that the king wanted it so, and so it was; for Al-

---

[34] Like the song that begins: "Joham Rodriguiz foy designar a Balteira/ Ssa midida, per que colha sa madeyra . . ." (*Cancioneiro da Biblioteca Nacional*, Lisbon, 1950, II, 343). La Balteira was a famous courtesan; see Menéndez Pidal, *op.cit.*, pp. 224, 230.

phonse X would not have thrown himself into composing in Castilian
the history of the world, astronomical science, and the legal encyclopedia
of his time, if he had not had beside him a group of scholars who revealed to him the science contained in Arabic and Latin works, and who
at the same time showed more interest in cultivating Romance than Latin, the language of Christian Europe. This interest must have been felt
above all by the Jews.[35] The innovation of writing historical and scientific
works in a Romance language occurs under the patronage of a monarch
whom the Jews compare with Alexander and Caesar, and who rewarded
their services and praises with magnificent favors. The king wrote nothing personal that would indicate that he knew enough about science in
his own right to be the master of his courtly scholars. The latter must
have carried weight with him and influenced his tastes and his plans, just
as the Galician jongleurs moved him to compose or to have composed
the *Cantigas* to the Virgin. Alphonse, more of a diplomat than a conqueror, and attracted by the sedentary pleasures of the cultivated life,
found himself, by virtue of circumstances he had not created, on a pinnacle from which he could discern imperial perspectives. All historians
agree that Alphonse had an indecisive and unenergetic character, and
that he was a very refined lover, with none of his father's chaste saintliness.[36] His palace counselors, among whom the Jews were prominent,

[35] The *Chronicon Mundi*, which was finished in 1236 under a commission from
Doña Berenguela, the mother of Ferdinand III, was written by Lucas, Bishop of Tuy,
who naturally had no thought of using the spoken language. Don Rodrigo Jiménez
de Rada (1180?-1247) composed his *Rerum in Hispania gestarum Chronicon* in
Latin. Still later, the Franciscan Juan Gil de Zamora, Sancho IV's tutor, wrote a
variety of historical works in Latin (*Liber de preconiis Hispanie*); Jofré de Loaysa,
archdeacon of Toledo (died between 1307 and 1310), wrote a chronicle of the
kings of Castile between 1248 and 1305; he composed his work in Castilian, but he
asked Armando de Cremona, Canon of Cordova, to translate it into Latin, and this
is the text that is preserved (B. Sánchez Alonso, *Historia de la historiografía española*,
I, 270-272; 218). We have, then, four Christian writers of the thirteenth century
who did not conceive of history written in any language except Latin. Those clerics
felt themselves well integrated in the Christian community of their time. When a
Spanish Jew like Abraham ibn 'Ezra lived outside of Spain, he had to use Latin as
the scientific language. His *Basis of Astronomical Tables* was dictated in Latin to an
amanuensis, while the author was living in Italy and France at the middle of the
twelfth century, and the same thing would have happened if he had lived there a
century later. (See J. M. Millás Vallicrosa, *El libro de los fundamentos de las tablas
astronómicas*, Madrid, 1947, pp. 17, 66.)

[36] "And by one lady he had a son whom they called Alphonse the Child. And by
another lady, who was called Doña Mayor Guillén, he had a daughter whom they
called Beatrice." ("Crónica de Alfonso X," in the *Biblioteca de Autores Españoles*,
LVI, 5.)

exerted a much greater influence over him.[37] It was no doubt easy to persuade him of the advantage of enriching Castilian science, poor "in its lack of the good philosophers' books," the enrichment to be effected through the bodies of knowledge familiar to the Jews, whose brokerage services thus had a unique market, as they had had all along in commerce and the administration of finance. This is how it happened that in Spain and nowhere else in Europe books of astronomy appeared in the vulgar tongue. These books, unpublished until 1867, were to remain like an island in Spanish civilization.

If there had been Christians like Vincent de Beauvais, Roger Bacon, or Thomas Aquinas around Alphonse X, he would not have asked them to bring their thought down to street level, where "the people talk to their neighbors," as Berceo said. But in the case which concerns us, the scholars were foreign people who imported their impersonal science with a view to offering attractive services. The ones who helped the language of Castile to develop into an organ of science were the King and his various Jewish, Moslem, and European collaborators.[38] One has only to look at the names of the men we positively know as participants in the preparation of the Alfonsine works: Yehuda el Coheneso (Yehuda ben Moshe); [39] Shemuel el Leví (Shemuel ha-Leví Abū-l-'Āfiya); [40] Rabbi Çag el de Toledo (Isḥaq ben Cid); [41] Don Xosse; [42] Don Abraham, the king's

[37] The king, however, watched their Castilian style very closely. The book entitled *De los juicios de las estrellas* (Prognostication by the Stars) by Abén Ragel (Ibn Abī al-Riyāl) was translated by Yehuda el Coheneso (Yehudá ben Moshe) under a commission from Alphonse X, but it was not included in the royal codex of the *Libros del saber de astronomía* (Books of Astronomical Learning). A glance at this work will show how that Hispano-Hebrew wrote Castilian when the king, or people he employed for the purpose, did not correct the style. A fragment of this book has been transcribed by the editor of the *Libros del saber de Astronomía*, III, x.

[38] In 1254, two years after ascending the throne, Alphonse X founded in Seville "a school of Latin and Arabic," about which we know nothing further (see J. Amador de los Ríos, *Historia de la literatura española*, III, 480).

[39] See M. Steinschneider, *Die hebräischen Übersetzungen des Mittelalters*, p. 979. For other Jewish collaborators of the king, cf. *Nueva Revista de Filología Hispánica*, 1951, V, 371-372.

[40] See M. Steinschneider, p. 986.

[41] Also called Rabí Abén Cayut. M. Rico y Sinobas (*Saber de Astronomía*, I, xcii), believed that they were two different persons, just as he divided Yehudá ben Mosé into Yhudá el Coheneso and Yhudá fi de Mosé fi de Mosca (i.e., Yehudá son of Moses son of Mosca; *ibid.*), an error caused easily enough by the vacillation between the Hebrew, Arabic, and Castilianized forms of their names. Names, like the other phenomena, are an aspect of the contexture of Hispanic life.

[42] Don Xosse Alfaquim, which is to say, "Don Yuçaf, physician," to whom, in 1253, the king gave "six *aranzadas* [one *aranzada* equaled anywhere from .9 to 1.1 acres] of vineyards and some tillable land, and some houses" in Seville (Baer, I, 50).

alfaquí (physician).[43] The astronomical works that came out of the royal household were written by Jews, by Moslems, or, if not, by other non-Castilians, as can be seen from the names of the other collaborators: Guillen Arremon d'Aspa (from Gascony, perhaps), Juan de Mesina, and Juan de Cremona (Italians). We cannot apply this remark to the authors responsible for the historical and legal works because their names are unknown. As for the king's participation in the composition of the *Crónica general*, the scholar who knows this work best says: "The much vexed question of the part played by the Learned King in the redaction of the *Primera Crónica general* is conclusively resolved by the important fact that the entire work was not written during his reign. This at once deprives the work of personality."[44] Nor is anything known about what minds inspired and organized the *Siete Partidas* and the *Grande e General Estoria*, which court flattery and the custom of centuries put under the name of Alphonse X, who made those great works possible, but who was not their author in the sense of a person who writes or dictates that which he has in his head. Alphonse X himself felt the necessity for clarifying the question, for he wrote or caused to be written in the preface to the *Libros de la ochava esfera* a passage which has been frequently quoted during the past century: "It was translated at his command by Yhudá el Coheneso, his *alfaquí*, and Guillén Arremón d'Aspa, a court cleric. . . . And then the aforesaid king corrected it and commanded it to be revised accordingly, and he removed the words that he thought were superfluous, and which were not in good Castilian, and he put in others which he thought proper; and everything in the language he revised himself."[45] The text translated by a Jew and by a Gascon must have been read over at the instance of the king, and he must have introduced

---

In the same document other fine gifts are made to Don Sisa, Don Çulemán, Don Todrós, and "Master Çag." Since this happens one year after the beginning of Alphonse's reign, it is reasonable to suppose that the Jews thus rewarded had captured the king's favor when he was still the heir apparent or that they had served well during the reign of Ferdinand III.

[43] He translated from the Arabic the so-called *Tablas alfonsíes*, in reality the work of Azarquiel (ibn al-Zarqālī), who lived in Toledo between 1061 and 1080 (M. Steinschneider, *op.cit.*, p. 590; Rico y Sinobas, III, 135). Azarquiel's work was first translated by Fernando de Toledo, who I would say was a converted Jew, principally because he knew Arabic, and in addition because the patronymic Toledo sounds Jewish. Bernardo de Toledo, a convert, translated Maimonides in the fifteenth century; Alfonso, Diego and Juan de Toledo figure in the list of converts given by Baer (I, 579-581). Fernando de Toledo's translation did not please the king or his advisers, and Don Bernardo *el Arábigo* and Don Abraham *el Alfaquí* made a new one.

[44] R. Menéndez Pidal, *Estudios literarios*, 1938, p. 144.

[45] Edition of Rico y Sinobas, I, 7.

appropriate corrections in the language to make it conform to the usage of his educated courtiers. But it cannot be believed that he had the time and patience to do such work on all the pages that came out of his *scriptorium*, especially if we include with them translations of the Old and New Testaments.[46] Yet in spite of the restrictions on the monarch's active participation in this labor, without him none of these valuable writings would exist, and the history of the language would not be what it is.

His desire for enlightenment does not remind one so much of an eighteenth-century sovereign as of Al-Ḥakam II, the Cordovan caliph (961-976) who sponsored all kinds of learning. In the works brought to birth by his enthusiasm, Alphonse X emphasized moral and juridical aspects, and this is what survived his own reign. His desire for purity and clarity of expression gave Castilian a definite character in contrast to ways of speech in the adjacent regions. The prose of the future was to be that of the juridical *Partidas* rather than that of the historical *Crónica general*. And in any case, we ought to stress more than we do the anonymous character of the juridical and historical works that are presented under the name of the king. Generally speaking, these are a conglomeration of translations, bound together by a communal type of learning. In the case of the books on astronomy, their authors and especially their translators should appear on their title pages, and not Alphonse X: "We, King Don Alfonso, deemed it a good thing and commanded the said Rabbi Zag to make this book quite thorough" (*Saber de astronomía*, IV, 3). The author, then, is the Jewish scholar and not Alphonse, however noble and indispensable he may have been in his role as promotor, Maecenas, and corrector of style.[47]

In conclusion, the extremely peculiar fact that a mountain of learned vernacular prose should have risen up around Alphonse X is explained in part, no doubt, by the monarch's energetic will to bring it into being. But this would not have happened, if there had been in Castile scholarly

---

[46] The Chronicle of his reign, far from exact at times, says that "King Ferdinand, his father, had begun to write the books of the *Partidas*, and this king, Alphonse, had them finished. . . . And likewise, he then commanded the scriptures of the Bible, and all of Ecclesiasticus, and the writings about the art of astrology to be turned into Romance" (Chap. IX). However it may have been in reality, it is curious that what seems most personal among the works of Alphonse X, the *Partidas*, could be regarded, in the middle of the next century, as the undertaking of two kings. The chronicler, through his crude and careless narration, reveals how the king appeared to a courtier of his great-grandson Alphonse XI.

[47] The same thing happens in other cases: "We commanded Samuel el Leví, of Toledo, *our Jew*, to write this book about the candle clock" (IV, 77).

personalities in harmony with twelfth- and thirteenth-century European Christendom; or, equally, if there had not been present, in the court, the learned Jews, who well knew the amount and type of culture possible and desirable for the blossoming Castile of Alphonse X, and who did not share the feeling of Christian catholicity of which the Latin language was an outward sign.[48] Being a Castilian, the king was interested in his personal situation, in his own language, rather than in the abstract idea of an international culture.

Now to fill in the preceding outline, I would say that it became possible for Jewish science to attain prestige in Castile in the thirteenth century not only because the Hispano-Hebrews shifted their attention from the Islamic to the Castilian world, but also because great multitudes of Jews had emigrated to Castile in the second half of the twelfth century when they found it impossible to endure the brutality of the African Almohades.[49] Castile received an increment of population which was Islamicized in its culture and which in its second generation, at the beginning of the thirteenth century, used Castilian as its own language. The translation of *Calila e Dimna* is a good example of that language in its literary form, full of Arabic words and turns of phrase and very much lacking in learned Latin words, which Christians strove for much more than Jews. In 1420 Mosé Arragel says that the language of Christian people had become much more learned than "in the olden times"; so much so, that it seemed as if Latin had changed into Castilian. In one first draft of his text of the Bible, Arragel used many Latinisms that he later tried to replace with words of a more popular character, thinking of the readers of his own people, *"because he did not want the Jews to*

[48] "Latin never replaced Arabic as a medium of Jewish culture. It was not only linguistically alien; it was spiritually hostile and historically inimical" (A. A. Neuman, *The Jews in Spain*, II, 99). This did not keep the rabbis and cultivated Jews from knowing Latin for reasons of practical utility. Neuman recognizes that the Romanic languages were regarded by the Hebrews as "our language" (*ibid.*, pp. 100-101). According to M. Steinschneider, *Die hebräischen Übersetzungen*, p. 461, "Latin, which the Jews called 'Roman' or 'Christian' and later 'clerical,' was little studied by them, except for the scientific texts, international, as it were, and not the special province of any religion or nationality. They were suspicious and afraid of Latin; it was the language of the destroyers of the Temple, of those who had brought God's chosen people to that situation of slavery and degradation and had called them deicides. Latin was the language of the Vulgate, the Bible brought into conformity with Christian dogma and contrary to the Biblical conception and tradition of the Jews; in that language had been composed the most horrible decrees against the Jews."

[49] This is recounted by the chronicler Abraham ha-Levi ben David (1110-1180); see B. Sánchez Alonso, *Historia de la historiografía*, I, 202.

take fright at the Latin."[50] This confirms my idea that the Jews lived at some remove from the Latin tradition, which was passed on to the Christians through the church. In spite of the widespread development of Latin humanism at the beginning of the fifteenth century, Arragel was afraid that his coreligionists would not know about such novelties and would not be interested in having any part of them; so they must have been much less interested in writing Latin during the reign of Alphonse the Learned. D. S. Blondheim observes that Jewish translations of the Bible in the Middle Ages show few traces of Church Latin.[51]

Other passages from Arragel reveal his sense of the superiority of Castilian Jews. The Grand Master of Calatrava, Don Luis de Guzmán, wrote his vassal the rabbi in 1420: "We are told that you are very learned in the laws of the Jews. Rabbi Mose: Know that we have desire of a Bible in Romance, with glosses and illustrations. We are told that you are quite able to make it" (Arragel's *Biblia*, p. 1). The rabbi opposed the suggestion at first, considering it a sacrilege to illustrate the sacred book with pictures. Later he gave in to his lord's demand. He wrote to him, nevertheless, in a tone that makes it quite clear what relations were between the learned Jews and the great lords, the latter far removed from the anti-Semitism of the lower class which for the preceding twenty-five years had been murdering Jews and robbing their communities:

"The kings and lords of Castile have had this advantage, that their Jewish subjects, reflecting the magnificence of their lords, have been the most learned, the most distinguished Jews that there have been in all the realms of the dispersion; they are distinguished in four ways: in lineage, in wealth, in virtues, in science. The kings and the lords of Castile have always been aware that almost everything the Jews know about law and science has been produced by Castilian Jews. Jews all over the world are governed by these very doctrines."

The rabbi refused to translate the Bible if it was to be accompanied with graven images. The Grand Master censured him for his "excessive haughtiness and pride and even in some cases fantasy" (p. 14), and gave him as a collaborator the Franciscan Arias de Enzinas, who persuaded the rabbi that the Grand Master wanted to read his glosses "not because of a lack of scholars amongst the Christians, as you see, but to the end of knowing, understanding, and informing himself from the Bible through the glosses of your modern doctors, which Nicholas of Lyra

[50] *La Biblia de Mosé Arragel de Guadalfajara,* of the Duke of Alba, 1, 20.
[51] *Les parlers judéo-romans,* p. xcv.

neither knew nor used" (p. 15). But in spite of their effort to save appearances, the Grand Master and the Franciscan had to ask a Jew for that which they did not have in their Christian world, at least among the Christians of Spain, and they permitted the rabbi to include his arrogant epistle in the very volume composed to be read by the Grand Master of Calatrava. This is an admirable example of tolerance in a country which was soon to forget that virtue altogether. But it is also a clear indication of how the learned Jews felt about their relations with the great lords and of the by then venerable custom of exchanging lordly splendors for Jewish wisdom expressed in an accessible language after the example of Alphonse X, whose reign was already remote in time.

During these same years—the early fifteenth century—Gómez Suárez de Figueroa, son of the Grand Master of Santiago Don Lorenzo Suárez de Figueroa, commissioned the convert Pedro de Toledo to translate Maimonides' major work, the *More Nebuchim* or *Enseñador de los turbados* (Guide of the Perplexed). Pedro de Toledo's work has not been published yet,[52] and it ought to be, regardless of the translator's mistakes, to show how a book on philosophical problems was understood and interpreted in an epoch in which nothing of such philosophical density had yet been expressed in Castilian.

At the end of the century, the Grand Master of Alcántara, Don Juan de Zúñiga, called the astronomer Abraham Zacuto to his palace in Zalamea, as I said earlier. I mention the matter again at this point to make it clear that Castilian came into use as an instrument of high culture thanks to the Jews who surrounded Alphonse X and excited his extremely refined curiosity. Two centuries later the situation had not changed, for it was the Jews and not the Christians who used the vulgar tongue for scriptural commentaries, philosophical prose, and astronomical studies. It is impressive that these three important events in Castilian culture took place, respectively, around the grand masters of each of the military orders, in marked contrast to the course taken by popular hatred during the same period. The great lords of the fifteenth century continued to live in the intellectual milieu of the Jews and the converts (Juan de Mena close to the King John II, Juan de Lucena closely connected with the Marquis de Santillana, Don Alonso de Cartagena conspicuous at the Council of Basel as the emissary of the king, etc.), because no class with intellectual curiosity had appeared outside the field in which the Jews had been well-established for centuries. Jewish interest in intellectual tasks confirmed the Christian in his conviction that such tasks were to be

[52] See Mario Schiff, *La bibliothèque du Marquis de Santillane*, 1905, p. 428.

performed by subject people. Disinterested curiosity scarcely existed, even among the Jews. No one realized the implications of those ideas which the Jews of the thirteenth century had attributed to the pen of Alphonse X: "We, King Alphonse, desiring that the great and marvelous virtues that God has put into the things which He made, should be discovered and known by learned men *so that they might be helped by them.*"[53] Those "great and marvelous virtues" of things were one day to be the laws of physics through the knowledge of which man would dominate nature. But the great Castilian lord and his Jewish servant scarcely looked beyond the naïve concepts of astrology. The Grand Master Don Juan de Zúñiga used the services of Abraham Zacuto to find out what was going to happen to his own person, not to find out what the stars were.

The Spanish Jew worked in the service of the aristocratic class, just as today men sometimes study the sciences in order to obtain positions in education or industry. He concerned himself only with matters interesting to his protectors, and did not write freely in Castilian on philosophy or theology, which the Church left uncultivated, for he was persecuted enough without this. The Jews confined themselves to performing tasks in the Christian milieu (different from the Arabic) which would bring them economic advantage or social prestige. Christians and Jews reacted on each other, and in this contact their opposite peculiarities were strengthened.

Jews in Medicine

It is very well known that medicine was one of the professions most widely practiced by educated Jews, and most neglected by Spanish Christians. We rarely find physicians in the royal household who are not Jews, and when we do, they are Frenchmen.[54] In the indexes of the documents collected by Fritz Baer, there are 55 mentions of Jewish physicians in Castile and 58 in Aragon. Apart from this, it was the habit of kings, lords, and prelates to have Jews for their private physicians. Thus, Haymn ha-Levi was physician to Don Pedro, Archbishop of Toledo in 1389 (Baer, II, 230). At the time of the expulsion, the Duke of Albuquerque was served by Rabbi Simuel, called Master Fabricio after he was converted. Rabbi Salomon Byton was physician to Queen Isabel in 1476. Henry IV had Master Samaya Lubel between 1456 and

[53] *Libros del saber de astronomía*, I, 8.
[54] In 1145 Alphonse VII mentions "Hugo monachus, magister et medicus meus et canonicus vester," i.e., of Archbishop Raymond (Baer, II, 14).

1465, and Rabbi Jaco Aben Núñez in 1472; the Marquis of Santillana had Don Çag Abocar in 1465; Doña Juana Pimentel, a cousin of John II, had Rabbi Salomon in 1453; etc.[55]

The records of the archives of the Crown in Aragon mention 77 Jewish physicians during the fourteenth century.[56] John II of Aragon underwent a famous operation on his eyes in 1468, and recovered his sight thanks to the skill of a Jewish surgeon and astrologer (Baer, I, 862). From the numerous data available, I shall choose a few for their curious and significant aspects. The town Talavera de la Reina paid 3,000 *maravedís* a year to Juda, a surgeon, in 1453; 5,000 in 1458. The physician Mamon received 2,000 *maravedís* in 1455; "Rabbi Abraham, Jewish physician," received 8,000 *maravedís* in 1477, and Mosen Isoque is relieved of the duty of billeting (as if he were a nobleman), and it is ordered that "he not be deprived of his mule, forasmuch as he has great need of it for visiting."[57] If such documentation had been preserved and explored for Castilian towns of any importance, the result would be the same. In a little place like Hita (Guadalajara), in 1492, the very year of the exile, there is mention of "Don Yuçaf, surgeon; Rabbi Mose Anacaba, physician; Rabbi Yoce Baquex, physician; Don Davi Baquex, surgeon," in the inventory of the expelled Jews' property. One of these doctors owned "some houses, 20 vats, 15 vineyards"; another, "a house, a wine-cellar, 3 vineyards, casks, vats." Yocé Baquex was the richest of them (Baer, II, 419-420). As we have seen in the case of Talavera, these men were not the doctors of only the Jewish community. Besides, with four Jews, there must have been little work left for any Christian doctors in Hita.

The Jews who were converted to Christianity continued to practice medicine, as I have said earlier. In a documentary mention of Alvaro

---

[55] Baer, II, 520, 341, 321, 336, 329, 325. See besides, A. A. Neuman, *The Jews in Spain*, 1942, pp. 213ff. According to H. Graetz, *History of the Jews*, VI, 73, the Dominicans got permission from Innocent VIII, in 1489, to continue to use Jewish doctors; see Neuman, II, 217.

[56] J. Rubió y Balaguer in *Estudis Universitaris Catalans*, 1909, III, 489-497.

[57] Fidel Fita in the *Boletín de la R. Academia de la Historia*, 1883, II, 318-321. Fita adds that the *aljama* of Talavera was so rich and powerful that "it contributed almost half the general quota for the support of the municipal expenses" (p. 338). As a datum for economic history it is interesting to compare the recompense received by these municipal physicians with that of the physicians in the royal household some two centuries before: "To Don Mosse, physician to the king, 1080 *maravedís*. To Don Çag, physician to the king, for his salary, 1080 *maravedís*." (From certain accounts for the year 1294, in R. Menéndez Pidal, *Documentos lingüísticos*, p. 470.)

de Castro and his descendants—a famous family in medicine who lent their services to the Counts of Orgaz in the fifteenth and sixteenth centuries[58]—it is not noted that they were converted Jews, yet Alvaro de Castro handled Arabic and Hebrew with perfect ease in the lexicon of materia medica which appears at the end of his *Ianua Vitae*. The study of medicine, being employed by great lords in a technical or professional capacity, and the mastery of the Hebrew and Arabic languages were unmistakable features of the Jewish tradition, so that one may safely say that Alvar Gómez de Castro, the famous humanist known for his biography of Cardinal Cisneros, was descended from converts.[59]

The caliphs of Cordova had Jewish physicians, and Saladin was attended by Maimonides. Thus we can see the Moslem origin of the custom of employing Jews as physicians in the royal and aristocratic families. The authority and prestige enjoyed by these doctors is reflected in the language of Juan Manuel's last will and testament (see footnote 5), as well as in his statement that Don Todros should stay in attendance on Queen Violante when Alphonse X went to confer with the pope (see footnote 26). It is curious that time and again laws were made prohibiting Christians from utilizing the services of Jews as doctors[60]—one more example of the inevitable incongruence between law and life, state and society, endemic in Spain as a result of her very structure of life. The laws which the king dictated but was incapable of enforcing were in the long run brutally and blindly applied by the anonymous masses. This anomaly is not due to any fact of inherent goodness or badness, of social orderliness or anarchism—labels with which we usually conceal our flight from historical problems. The motive or meaning behind this centuries-old disorder lies in the very reality of Spanish life—pure drive and sense of seigniory, unaccompanied by any interest in "things." The image of the good ruler who encourages the "arts of peace," work, in-

[58] J. M. Millás Vallicrosa, *Las traducciones orientales en los manuscritos de la Biblioteca Catedral de Toledo*, pp. 109, 129.

[59] Another convert was the "Master Juan Serrano, surgeon, citizen of Toledo," who figures in an Inquisitorial trial in 1515 (Baer, II, 544). The document states that in the house of this Juan Serrano stayed a Jewish ambassador of the Moorish king of Tlemcen, who had come to treat the king, that is, Ferdinand the Catholic. Baer gives an abstract of the trial in German. If this is the case, Ferdinand the Catholic was attended, in 1512, by a Jewish physician, who was acting as ambassador of a Moorish king in accordance with the tradition common to Spanish Moors and Christians.

[60] In 1412, in the time of John II of Castile, it is still prohibited "for any Jew or Jewess, or Moor or Mooress, to be a spice merchant, or an apothecary, or a surgeon, or a physician" (Baer II, 265).

dustry, and commerce, evokes as its background a Dutch meadow smoothly cropped by peaceful cows, a field of tulips, and a chubby burgomaster such as we know from Flemish paintings. Castile forged its soul in the process of extending the frontier of its bleak plateau, swept by a wind as raw and cutting as the fury of the Moslem raids and surprise attacks that laid waste to the land. The management and development of "things," not luxuries but necessities, was left more and more in the hands of Jews and conquered Moors or greedy foreigners. The ruling caste had to keep up its impetus and nourish its sense of seigniory at any cost, and it neglected everything else. The laws prohibiting various Jewish activities were formulated to calm the protests of a people who, when they were not making conquests and actively exercising their power, felt themselves foreigners in their own land. But these activities were already too indispensable to be effectively suppressed. The conflict lay in the contradiction between wishing to be, or having by nature to be, a certain kind of person and feeling compelled externally to yield to the pressure that was at first Jewish and later foreign. The Spaniards' very being was by history of a certain kind and they were compelled to subsist in a way different to their way. This idea, which I continue to hammer on, comes up again and again in this book. Here it is useful in understanding the absurdity of the Spaniards' forbidding the Jews to serve as doctors to Christians at the same time that the legislators and the people who were themselves trying to exterminate the Jews, could not possibly do without the services of the Jewish physicians when they had so much as a stomach ache.[61]

[61] It is not a part of my task to inquire as to the substance of this medical science, nor what the schools were that the doctors attended. They must have gone to some kind or other, for in 1491 Rabbi "Yucé Alabán," physician to Don Pedro de Luna, says that it was "about 17 or 18 years ago, when this witness was a student, that he came to this village of Cuéllar in search of Rabbi Samuel, physician to the Lord Duke of Cuéllar, because they were both to go to the school together" (Baer, II, 521). He must have learned the traditional materials of Hippocrates and Galen, transmitted and broadened by Avicenna and others. The Cordovan Maimonides (1135-1204), Saladin's physician, must have been a great authority for the Spaniards. Superstition and astrology were not absent from their medicine, but at the same time we find a tendency to treat ailments by proper diets and hygiene rather than by recourse to drugs (see D. Yellin and I. Abraham, *Maimonides*, p. 110. There is a good account of Arabic medicine, which was the basis of Hispano-Hebrew medicine, in Max Mayerhoff, *The Medical Work of Maimonides*, in *Essays on Maimonides*, 1941, pp. 264-299). A book by Maimonides which the Jewish doctors undoubtedly possessed is one that a Sephardic Jew translated in the seventeenth century, which contains advice about body hygiene and the proper governance of the soul, a mixture characteristic of Arab teaching: "*Tratado de moralidad y regimiento de vida*, by the

There is no point in recording anecdotally more facts since the meaning of the known facts is what really matters. It makes no difference for my purposes whether Jewish therapy was good or bad, scientific or astrological. What is beyond doubt is that the Christians, from the king down, consulted the Jewish doctors about their most intimate troubles, and the doctors were connected with the Islamic way of feeling and thinking. These doctors were, beyond shadow of doubt, one of the channels through which still flowed the didacticism, the sententious style, the integral expression of the person, the preoccupation with purity of blood,

---

very famous and very learned Señor Rabenu Mosé of Egypt. Translated from the Hebrew language to our Romance by David, the son of Ischac Cohén de Lara (may his soul dwell in glory), and dedicated to the most illustrious Señor Ischac de Sylva Solís. In Hamburg, the 12th of Siván, the year 5422 of the creation of the world. In the house of Georg Rebenlein [1662]." In the elegant prose of that Sephardi we get something of the private life of the medieval Spaniard in an echo which we should search for in vain in Christian texts. Here is a brief sample: "Some things there are which are notably harmful, which man must keep away from and not allow to enter his mouth. The large, rancid, salted fish, the old salted cheese, mushrooms and truffles, rancid salt meat, musty wine, stale food, and any kind of food that smells bad or is very bitter; all this is poison for the body. There are others that are less harmful, and man can eat of them in small quantities over a long period of time . . . , large fishes, cheese, milk 24-hours old, the flesh of the excessively large ox or he-goat, beans, lentils, vetch, unleavened bread, barley bread, cabbages, leeks, onions, garlic, mustard, and radishes. And since all the aforementioned kinds are pernicious, let him not use them at all during the summer; in the winter, yes, but very little, except beans and lentils, which he ought not to eat in either the one season or the other. Pumpkin he may eat if it be a little, in the summertime" (pp. 20-21). "When he goes into the hothouse to bathe (which he will do every seven days), let him take care that he be not desirous of eating, or that he be at the beginning of digestion after having eaten; and let him not wash himself in water so hot as to scald his body; and he will wash only his head with hot water, his body with warm water, and then lukewarm, and finally with cold water" (p. 24). "The wise man does not permit himself to live in a city which lacks the ten things following: physician, surgeon, bath, toilet, spring or river water, synagogue, schoolmaster, notary, treasurer of the alms which are distributed to the poor, officers of the law to arrest, flog, and punish" (p. 28). "When the wise man speaks, let it not be by shouting and bellowing like the beasts, nor let him talk very loud, but with gentleness and calm to all kinds of people. . . . The learned man is not to go about stiff-necked and puffed up . . . ; let him walk neither so slowly, one foot in front of the other, as women and insolent men do . . . , nor let him walk fast and running through the streets after the manner of fools, nor let him walk downcast and bent over like hunch-backs. . . . Even by his walk is it known whether a man is wise and discreet, or stupid and foolish" (p. 33). More information about Jewish medical science in Spain may be found in Antonio Cardoner Planas, *El médico judío Shĕlomó Caravida y algunos aspectos de la medicina de su época* (14th century), in *Sefarad*, 1943, III, 376-392. See too José Llamas, *El "Tratado de las fiebres" de Ishaq Israeli*, Madrid, 1945.

and many other phenomena of life (including the fierce passion of the Inquisition), which the converts were eventually to rivet into the Spanish consciousness. We have already seen that the first preeminence that Arragel assigned to the Jews of Castile was that of "lineage"; and, later, other characteristics common to Jews and Christian were to become evident. Centuries and centuries of medical attendance cannot be ignored or dismissed by history.

Tax Collectors and Tax Payers

Just as the kings, nobles, and ecclesiastics entrusted the Jews with the treatment of their aches and pains, so they were also to entrust them with the collection of public income as well as the management and development of other important sources of wealth. We do not realize clearly enough today what it meant to turn over essential branches of the public administration to the Hispano-Hebrews. If the latter had been a normal component of Spanish life, happily articulated in it, their activities as the managerial and banking caste would have had another meaning. Such articulation is historically unthinkable, because the Jew had no honorable place in the Christian idea of the state. England and France expelled the not very numerous Jews from their lands in the thirteenth and fourteenth centuries on the initiative of the ruling class. The case of Spain was entirely different. The Jews had remained there in large numbers up to 1492, as serfs of the kings, as enemies of Christianity, and as irritating guests, allowed to share the life of the dominant caste for reasons of necessity and interest. But the politically inferior caste—the Jews—performed functions essential for the collective life in the same way that, as physicians and administrators, they had a place in the private life of those who ruled Spain. The history of every day— not that of the great moments in warfare—came to be something like the product of the Jew's "inferiority" multiplied by the technical incapacity of the Christian—a very uncomfortable situation which disturbed the experience of values and their hierarchy. It is a serious affair when the services that we lend or are lent to us do not mesh with a system of mutual loyalties and common values, as they did where the feudal organization was an authentic reality.[62] In important areas of Spanish life, loyalty and esteem were replaced by the tyranny of the lord and

[62] Such, without being feudal, was also the healthy atmosphere which the Cid and his Castilians breathed in the *Cantar de Mio Cid*, a fine harmony of happy and reciprocal loyalties, within which it was just as valid to command as to be commanded.

the flattering servility of the Jews, forced to pay this price to subsist. This false situation was fatal, and equally so was the situation in which the common people had to accept a group whom they hated and despised, as their superiors, legally entitled to prey regularly upon their meager resources. And the more evident the superiority of the Jews turned out to be, the worse it became. From such premises it was impossible that there should be derived any kind of modern state, the sequel, after all, of the Middle Ages, hierarchic harmony. The belief "non est potestas nisi a Deo" implied a scheme in which all power was founded on justified reason (king or state), related to the right of the individual to govern himself.[63] The genesis of the organization of the state, which reached its culmination in the European nineteenth century, lay in the web of spiritual relationships which, starting with the king, spread downward through graduated levels to the lowliest subject. The feudal system duplicated in the realm of the human the divine organization of the Church. In Spain, however, the inescapable presence of the Moors and Jews in the Christian kingdoms prevented the implantation of the Christian-European social system, fixed by the coordinates of the papacy and the Carolingian Empire. The main paths that were open to the Christian feudal state were obstructed in Spain by the Jew, as necessary as he was foreign. Spain was left outside the feudal system for the same reason that she could bring Castilian prose to flower in texts of high learning, thus in the thirteenth century turning her back on the Latin of Europe. It is almost symbolical that the pope declined to recognize Alphonse X's indubitable legal rights to the imperial throne.

We may now begin our reflections on the dominating presence of the Jews in the most vital centers of the state organism. It is not known when or how they began to serve as fiscal agents for the Christian kings. During the many centuries of oppression and persecution by the Christians, the Jews became usurers and publicans in violation of the letter and spirit of their own law, because this was the only way they could keep afloat in societies that excluded them from the normal occupations.[64]

[63] The "raison d'état" of the seventeenth century was primarily a theory to justify the abuse of power.

[64] "We take no pleasure in trade . . . , we live on good land and cultivate it diligently" (Josephus, *Against Apion*, XII, 60). The Bible and the Talmud describe the existence of an agrarian community, and are both hostile to the idea of commerce (Béla Szekely, *op.cit.*, pp. 162, 203). The Jew of Rome did not attract attention for his wealth but for his poverty (Juvenal, III, 14-16; VI, 542-547; Martial, XII, 57; Rutilius Namatianus, pp. 385-386). The Roman Empire, when it had already become Christian, barred him from several trades as well as ownership of territorial property (Baron, *op.cit.*, II, 10-11). Later the Christian community identified itself

Traffic in merchandise, when it was not carried on by Jews, was carried on by Italians (Genoese, Lombards, etc.) in medieval Spain, although the hatred against the latter was not translated into constant persecution, because they were not "deicides" and because they had not formed a caste closely articulated within the public administration of Spain.

The Jewish merchants, normally exempt from military service, must have had a part in the supplying of the army, and probably in the first centuries of the Reconquest they had already become extremely useful officials in that poor, backward, and heroic milieu. Their cleverness in trading and in mediating between one party and another recommended them as diplomatic and fiscal agents, for the collecting of the monies owed to the king or the grandees was in the last analysis very much like collecting their own money.[65]

What it is not easy to understand is why, as the Reconquest advanced, Christian functionaries did not gradually emerge capable of doing the work of the fiscal agents and with fortunes large enough to offer the necessary guarantees in hard cash. Also, why were the rulers not more zealous in creating a moneyed middle class among the Christians, and why did they accept the collaboration of the Jews as something traditional and inevitable? The Christian endowed with intelligence and the impulse to do something, interested himself in ruling over lands, just as, inversely, the more capable Americans very often go into business rather than devote themselves to disinterested studies. The small-scale bustling about of the Spanish Jews seemed an unworthy occupation to the Chris-

---

allegorically with the chosen people of the Old Testament (cf., for example, the poem *De contemptu mundi* of the Cluniac monk Bernard, and the use therein of the terms *Hebraeus, Israelita, Sion*). Now just as the Bible forbade usury, canon law also forbade Christians to practice it. But this does not alter the fact that in the twelfth century in non-Spanish Christian Europe the clergy constituted the most important group of money-lenders (Baron, *op.cit.*, II, 16). This is how the Jew came to perform tasks abandoned by the Hispano-Christian. (I am indebted to Sra. María Rosa Lida de Malkiel for this note.)

[65] Charles the Bald (823-877) learns through Jude, "fidelis noster," how devoted the Barcelonans are to him. The same monarch writes that "per fidelem meum Judacot dirigo ad Frodoynum episcopum libras X de argento ad suam eclesiam reparare" (Baer, I, 1). We have already seen (Chapter 13) how Alphonse VI sent a Jew to collect the tribute from the Moorish king of Seville. In 1200 Peter II of Aragon sent Abenbenist as ambassador to the king of Morocco (Baer, I, 49); Ferdinand IV of Castile sent his finance minister Don Samuel as ambassador to Granada in 1303 (A. Giménez Soler, *Don Juan Manuel*, p. 286); in 1304 James II of Aragon ordered Azmel de la Portiella "to go to Castile to find out about affairs" (Baer, I, 177). They were used as secret agents of the kings even in relations between Christian kings. The Catholic Sovereigns (Ferdinand and Isabella), as I shall point out, were in their day to use them for important missions.

tian, and this feeling decided the course of Peninsular history. The history of the Spanish Christians began with an enormous imbalance in favor of the Moors and Jews, very much interested in the management of material things. The Christians later made up for this imbalance with their supremacy and distinction as ruling lords, but anything like a national commerce and industry was unknown in Spain until the middle of the nineteenth century.

Craftsmanship, trade, and the equivalent of banking institutions were the almost exclusive birthright of the Hispano-Hebrews in the Middle Ages. Something like this happened wherever there were Jews, but the situation in Spain reached unique extremes.[66] With the increased intensity of the popular protest against the Jews in the course of the fourteenth century, Henry II of Trastámara gave this answer to a request of the deputies at the *Cortes* of Burgos in 1367:

"To what we have been told . . . , that we farmed out to Jews the collection of the debts and the arrears which the cities and villages of our realm owed, without declaring what the amounts were; and that if this happened, it would be a great disservice to us and would cause people to abandon our land; and we were requested to have the debts collected by our treasurer, and to farm out the collection to Christians.

"To this we reply, that it is true that we farmed out the collection of said income to Jews, *because we found no others* to bid for it; and we commanded it to be farmed out to them with the proviso that every subject should be fairly treated. . . . But if any Christians should wish to collect said income, we shall command that the task be given to them for a much lower sum than the Jews are given for it."[67]

In 1367, Henry II was in the midst of a civil war against his brother Peter I, and he was very anxious to please his partisans. Nevertheless,

---

[66] "Because it had been the custom for a long time in Castile to have Jewish financial officials in the households of the kings, the king [Alphonse XI], for this reason and because of the request of Prince Phillip, his uncle, took as finance minister a Jew who was called Don Yuçaf de Ecija who held an important position in the king's household and great power in the kingdom through the favor which the king did him" ("Crónica de Alfonso XI," in the *Biblioteca de Autores Españoles,* LXIV, 199*a*).

[67] *Cortes de León y Castilla,* II, 15. In 1327 Alphonse XI discovered that his finance minister, "Don Yuzaf," was keeping money out of the royal treasury for himself, "and from then on the king commanded that Christians and not Jews should collect his income, and that these persons should not have the name of tax-collectors [almojarifes] but treasurers [tesoreros]," (*Crónica de Alfonso XI,* Chap. 82). But in 1329 "Don Yuzaf" appears again as *almojarife,* for he is addressed on this date by Alphonse IV of Aragon: "To you, Don Yuceff de Ecija, chief *almojarife* of the very noble king of Castile" (Baer, I, 262).

it was impossible for him to dispense with the services of the Jews. In the same *Cortes* the deputies raise their protest thus, according to the king:

"For as much as in some cities and towns and villages of our realm, the castles are held by Jews and Moors, we are requested the favor of commanding that the castles be taken back by ourself, and given to Christians in whom we trust." (See p. 209).

To which Henry replies that he will do so wherever it will not damage him, for otherwise "there is no sense in doing it" (*Cortes*, II, 146).

In 1367, then, there were still Moorish and Jewish castellans, because Spanish history still consisted in a Christian-Islamic-Jewish contexture. A hundred and two years later, in 1469, we find a similar picture. At the *Cortes* of Ocaña, Henry IV is reminded that Jews and Moors are prohibited from being tax-farmers and collectors of taxes; as the ancient record puts it, they were not allowed

"to be tax-gatherers or majordomos of the Christians, nor to hold other offices in the houses of the lords . . . , *but we see that said laws are not kept*; rather we see that the principal offices in the administration and collection of your rents and taxes are held by Jews; and we believe that if your rents were farmed at more reasonable rates, there would be Christians who would bid for them, and the latter should be given the collection of taxes for a lower bid, as the laws of your realm recommend. And another even worse thing is done in your realm: *many prelates and other clergy entrust their rents and tithes . . . to Jews and Moors*, who enter the churches to distribute the tithes and the offerings, to the great offense and injury of the Church." (*Cortes*, III, 803)[68]

Any task that required financial and administrative competence was

---

[68] This was an old practice, and the church commissioned Jews (and Moors too, apparently) to collect her tithes, just as the king entrusted them with the collection of his taxes. In 1352 the chapter of the Cathedral of Toledo authorized Don Mayr Abenhamías to perform this service (Baer, II, 177; see also pp. 203, 305, 347, 348, 387). All the goods handed over by the faithful as tithes (wheat, wine, kids, lambs, calves, etc.) were stored until Easter Sunday; then they were sold at auction "at the hour of high mass, inside the church" of each town. The law required that the tithe-farmers should sell to the highest bidder, and that they should deliver the money to the proper persons: one-third to the king and the rest to the Church (*Ordenanzas reales de Castilla*, Book VI, Title VI, law 1). This is what the Jews and Moors did inside the churches as tithe-farmers. The word *almoneda* (auction), which is Arabic, exists in Spanish from the eleventh century, thus proving that public sales were an affair of Moors and Jews. Arabic also is the Portuguese *leilão* (auction) from Arabic *layla* (night) with the suffix of *serão* (night gathering) because the *leilões* were held, as they still are, at night.

in Jewish hands. Four years before the expulsion, Ferdinand and Isabella appointed Don Abraham Seneor, for "the good and loyal services that we have received from you," nothing less than treasurer of the *Santa Hermandad* (the king's police force). His functions were to collect the taxes for the support of the institution most characteristic of that reign, and to pay the salaries of the members (Baer, II, 388). Likewise in 1488 the king and queen granted safe conduct to Don Simuel Abolafia so that the authorities would respect and protect him, because "he has done many and good services for us in the war" of Granada, and they now command him "to go with some people to certain places, both within our realm and outside it, as well by land as by sea, to attend to matters very useful to our service" (Baer, II, 390).[69] The Jews still figured in the diplomatic service of the Catholic Sovereigns, and were treated as valuable and indispensable officials at the same time that their complete ruin was being prepared. Essentially the relation between the Jews and the crown was the same as in the time of Alphonse VI, four centuries before, so that it is quite evident that the initiative in expelling them from Spain did not come from the sovereigns.[70]

Much space would be required to describe in detail the financial activities of the Jews. For our purpose a few facts by way of example will be sufficient. The *aljamas* (ghettos) were a prime source of wealth because each one of their members contributed to the treasury of the king, to whom, consequently, it was a matter of considerable interest that the Jew should not grow poor; the Christian commoners, who, unlike the *hidalgos*, were not exempt from paying taxes, delivered their money to the crown by way of the Jews who collected the taxes. In one way or another, the income of the treasury proceeded from Jews or had of necessity to pass through their hands. The same thing happened in city treasuries, for we have already seen that the income from the local *aljama* covered almost half of the expenses of Talavera. During the reigns of Alphonse X and Sancho IV the *aljamas* of Castile contributed

[69] Graviel Israel was an "interpreter and notary for Arabic documents" another position of strict trust and confidence (Baer, II, 398).

[70] As late as May 1491, the royal officials heard the complaints of the *aljama* of Zamora against a Fray Juan, a Dominican, who was stirring up the people against the Jews with his sermons. The constable Don Pedro Fernández de Velasco, Count of Haro (we would call him minister of war today), on this occasion issued two royal orders to the authorities of Zamora: "Herewith we take and receive the said *aljama* . . . and its properties under our security and protection and royal defense" (Baer, II, 400). The firm tone of these orders betrays no anti-Semitism whatsoever, nor any special sympathy for the Dominican monk.

6,000 *maravedís* daily (2,190,000 a year) as a kind of personal tax.[71]

The protection dispensed by the sovereigns until almost the eve of the decree of exile had its roots in such circumstances. In 1215 the Fourth Lateran Council ordered that the Jews wear a distinctive badge so that they might not be confused with Christians. When the papal order was about to be applied to Spain, the ghettos rioted and some important members of the synagogues threatened to go to Moorish territories, which at that time were still extensive and wealthy. King Ferdinand III and the Archbishop of Toledo begged the pope to suspend the decision of the council in regard to Castile because the largest portion of the royal revenue came from Jewish taxes. Honorius III yielded to the plea in 1219 in order that serious conflict might be avoided for the king, "cuius proventus in iudeis ipsis pro magna parte consistunt."[72] So it happens that the history of Spain has risen on the basis of a Jewish economy, and one must admit the fact with all its consequences. The history of Spain requires much less searching of archives than people say, but it does require that we pay attention to what is already known so that it will not be left lying about like so many *disjecta membra*, lifeless, meaningless. History is not a simple product of economic circumstances, as a naïve and mentally lazy positivism repeats; the economic system is a result of human circumstances, and in our case the productive ability of the Jew is as essential to history as is the Christian inability to utilize the resources of land and people, which were there and are still there, waiting for those who know how to make use of them. The Hispanic Christian imprisoned himself in his ineffectualness with regard to the production of material wealth—a situation which was both helpful and harmful to his life—and contemplated and suffered impassively the productive work of the Jew (and of the Moor), just as he later trusted in the golden manna which the Indies rained upon him. The human motivation of that economy, and not the physical milieu or the wealth itself, is the decisive factor.

What Ferdinand III, the Saint, said to the Pope is the same thing that the kings of Spain kept on saying afterward until the very moment of expulsion. Alphonse III of Aragon ordered his local governors in 1328 to proceed moderately with the Jews, for "as you well know, our predecessors and those of the said king of Majorca have tolerated and

---

[71] See Baer, II, 587, under "Abgaben." They paid 30 *dineros* from the age of 15, besides the tithes and first-fruits (in which they were always a little in arrears).

[72] F. Fita, in the *Boletín de la R. Academia de la Historia*, 1893, XVI, 574; Baer, II, 24.

suffered the Jews in their kingdoms and territories, and the Church of Rome tolerates them still, because *these Jews are the strong-box and treasury of the kings*. And if the Jews were to go away and be deprived of their property in the land of the said king of Majorca, that would harm him very much."[73]

In 1391 John I of Aragon condemned the massacres of Huesca gravely, because the Jews "are part of our treasure and are under our royal authority" (Baer, 1, 686).[74] In 1417, Alphonse V considered it necessary to rebuild the *aljama* of Saragossa after the persecutions by the people because it was about to disappear "with great harm and loss to ourselves and to our privileges" (Baer, 1, 839). In 1481 Ferdinand the Catholic severely rebuked the prior of the Cathedral of Saragossa for his violent action on Jews "who are the treasure chests of ourselves and of our patrimony"; he insists that "they are our treasure chests, and the defense of them belongs to us and to our officials" (Baer, 1, 898, 899). The king threatened to take away the bishops' temporalities, and bluntly ordered them to read in public a "cry" annulling one issued by themselves demanding that within thirty days the doors and windows of the ghetto that opened on the Christian section of the city should be closed, and forbidding the Jews to practice certain trades and to wear certain kinds of clothing, all this "by authority of the said bull," that is, the bishops' "cry." To the Royal Council, through which his letter was to be transmitted to one of the bishops, he wrote: "We are shocked that you have proceeded so inadvisedly and suddenly, without consulting our majesty, our most serene queen, our very dear and beloved wife having commanded you not to proceed with any action or proceedings by authority of the said bull." Ferdinand wrote the Royal Council that he wanted "our said *aljama* and the individuals in it to be able to live without danger, disturbances, or riots"; and if the prior of the cathedral and the other bishop, Pilares, failed to obey the royal order, the temporalities of both of them were to be taken over as a warning to those

[73] A. Rubió y Lluch, *Documents per l'historia de la cultura catalana mig-eval*, 1, 92.
[74] The protection given the Jews by the kings of Aragon sometimes overrode ecclesiastical scruples. In 1391, Queen Violante ordered Prince Martín, in Barcelona at the time, to stop the legal proceedings already begun by the Archbishop of Tarragona against certain books of Rabbi Mosé ben Maimón, which were said to contain errors against the Christian faith. Since the trial would cause a great disturbance "in our *aljama* in Barcelona," she kindly begged her brother, in the interests of avoiding trouble, not to allow the trial to be prosecuted in Barcelona or any place where there was an *aljama* of Jews (Baer, 1, 650-651). This and other cases yet to be brought up show how far from the Inquisitorial spirit the kings were. They were more interested in their political economy than in persecuting heresies.

who might dare to carry out "similar acts in our disservice" (Baer, 1, 900).

It was far from the mind of the Catholic King to expel the Jews from Spain in 1481. But what happened? The king's counsellors told him that the letters ought not to be given to the prelates of Saragossa, much less should their "cry" be revoked, because the people were on the point of breaking out in "riots, disturbances and sudden violence" (Baer, 1, 902). The king yielded to pressure from below, and announced his departure for Saragossa to resolve the thorny problem.

For some two centuries the king and the noblemen had been trying to contain the anti-Jewish onslaught of the Christian populace, the mendicant orders, and many ecclesiastics.[75] Like all the other problems in Hispanic history, this one also turned out to be insoluble, because the kingdom could not get along with the Jews and it could not get along without them, in view of the fact that national welfare cannot be founded on nothing but beliefs, passions, and desires. The sovereigns had to give up, and alter the policy that Castile and Aragon had followed for centuries. Ferdinand the Catholic was not a man to fight for lost causes; and just as he held back the letters to the Saragossan bishops in 1481, so he also decided to sign the decree of exile—because it was not possible to manage a kingdom in the face of opposition from the people and the minor church officials, especially if it was necessary to use the people to wage war in distant lands. Obviously, once he had taken the resolution, it was inevitable that he carry it out in league with the most powerful party. Conventional historians have seen in Ferdinand the Catholic either a monster of intolerance and fanaticism or the hand and sword of the divine will. The Jewish historians center their accounts around the dramatic story of Don Isaac Abravanel, who implored the king until he lost his voice; "but the king like a deaf serpent, sealed his ears. . . . Likewise the queen, who was at his right side *to corrupt him*, swayed him with powerful persuasion to carry out the work he had begun and to finish it." According to Abravanel, it was the conquest of

[75] My study (in *Aspectos del vivir hispánico*, 1949) of the Order of Saint Jerome in the fifteenth century made me realize that the expulsion of the Jews was a case of unbridled demagoguery in opposition to the policy of the kings. When the Hieronymites were on the point of not admitting baptized Jews into their order, the Catholic monarchs sent their chaplain, Juan Daza, to make the monks reverse their stand, inspired more by mundane pride than by Christian charity. The monarchs thought in this matter like Cardenal Don Pedro González de Mendoza and like the Duke of the Infantado.

Granada that decided Ferdinand: "In his tenacity and pride he felt emboldened, and he attributed his power to God."[76]

But the human forces at play in that slow process must be situated in a proper and adequate perspective. During the first centuries of the Reconquest, the king's treasury was filled principally out of the wealth snatched from the Moors and by the pilgrimages to Santiago. From the second half of the twelfth century on, the mass emigration of the Jews from the Moorish zone meant an immense help to the crown of Castile. As early as 1158 Sancho III was giving lands to his finance minister Boniuda in recompense "pro bono et fideli servicio, quod patri meo Imperatori et michi semper fecistis,"[77] which reveals that Alphonse VII, the Emperor, had already found the Jews useful. The *Poema del Cid* presents them as the only people able to lend money, in the well-known episode of Raquel and Vidas. Alphonse VIII gave lands in similar fashion to Avomar Avenxuxén, "dilecto et fideli almoxerifo meo," and in his will (in 1204) he acknowledged that he still owed the Jew 12,000 *maravedís*.[78] The documents that chance has preserved for us reflect only a part of what happened. The collection of taxes and the giving of money to the kings must have been a lucrative business, and the result was that at the beginning of the thirteenth century the Jewish communities felt so strong that they threatened Ferdinand III with leaving the kingdom if he forced them to wear the hateful badge.[79] The king asked the pope for permission to let his orders go unheeded, and in a perfectly tolerant way the interests of Church, king, and people were harmonized.

[76] Salomón ben Verga, *La vara de Judá*, tr. into Spanish by F. Cantera, p. 208. It can be deduced, even from this text, that before 1492 Ferdinand was not decided to expel the Jews from the kingdom, and that Isabel was more convinced than he of the necessity for such a measure. For reasons now obvious to the reader, Castile was more anti-Semitic than Aragon, and the Jews had been expelled from Seville and Cordova years before.

[77] F. Fita, *La España hebrea*, 1890, I, 20; Baer, II, 16-17.

[78] Baer, II, 20-21. The Jews of Zorita de los Canes were exempted from taxes and tributes by Henry I in 1215 because they had helped "multum in pecunia" Alphonse VIII, in whose reign there happened to be great needs. (*ibid.*, p. 23.)

[79] The laws respecting this matter were as unenforced as all the others. Time and again sumptuary laws were decreed to restrain the Jews in their luxury, and they were as disregarded as those prohibiting the Jews from serving as physicians to Christians. The Cortes of Valladolid, in 1258, forbade "any Jew to wear a white fur or sindon of any kind or to use a gilt-edged saddle or a silvered one, or crimson hose, or dyed cloth . . . except for those whom the king may command to do so" (*Cortes de León y Castilla*, I, 59). As a matter of fact, the Jews who were well-off or rich dressed like the Christians of the same class.

A century later the same relationship no longer prevailed among the king, the Church, and the Jews. It is especially surprising that the chapter of the Cathedral of Toledo, whose wealth had been enormous, had to have recourse to Jewish money-lenders. The canons' debts must have been considerable, for they went to the pope to get them out of their difficulties by means of a bull which exempted them from repaying their creditors the capital and the interest. Moreover, the bull provided that the Jews should return to the canons the interest already paid. The Jewish community turned to the king, their natural lord, and in 1307 Ferdinand IV twice addressed the chapter with an order to refrain from using papal bulls as instruments of law. The royal missives must have been quite violent, because Ferrant Ivánez Pantoja, one of the king's gentlemen, who read them, did not dare to read them in their entirety, for "there were still worse things in what was left of the letter to be read." The king says: "I am astonished that you dared to use such letters [from the pope], without my command, and thus to pass sentence on my Jews." The king prohibited the cancellation of the debts, "for you well know that all the Jews and what they have are mine." For any harm done the Jews the king demanded double indemnity from the canons.[80]

In this incident we have one of the first episodes in the struggle between the ecclesiastical and the Jewish camps, to be decided two centuries later in favor of the former. It was peculiarly characteristic of the Spain of that time for the Christian kings to oppose as strongly as they could the aspirations of the churchmen. The monarch wanted to take care of the goose that was laying the golden eggs, and the Church, backed by popular rancor, was trying to destroy it so as to have all the profits at once. The state regarded the Jews as a permanent source of wealth; the Church and the people saw in them valuable booty. Here we are at the very heart of the strangeness of Spanish history in the Middle Ages—lacking any kind of internal order that was connected with the general order of Christendom. Its internal problem in no way resembled the struggles between the papacy and the empire, or between the schismatic and the legitimate popes. The peculiarity of Spain was rooted precisely in the oriental wedge or splinter that was, and at the same time was not, the substance of Spain. The other European countries lived with a life, rich or poor, hard or easy, that they had created for themselves. Spain, when she was not conquering lands, lived by utilizing or coveting the wealth created by the Jews. Because a similar situation has not ex-

[80] The document was published by A. Benavides, *Memorias de Don Fernando IV*, II, 554; now in Baer, II, 111-113.

isted in any other occidental country, the history of Spain does not resemble any of them. It must be noted that the Jews disappeared from
England in the thirteenth century, and from France at the beginning
of the fourteenth, and that the Jews in those kingdoms never experienced
a situation remotely comparable to that of the Jews in the Iberian Peninsula. (We have already seen—see footnote 1—how they lived in Constantinople.)

A provincial council held in Zamora in 1313, taking as authority the
Council of Vienna and the constitutions of Clement V, warned the Jews
that they should not "dare to make counter statements or even defend
themselves *with the privileges granted by the kings.* . . . We ordain that
in all lawsuits the testimony of Christians shall be valid and prevail
against the Jews, and not that of Jews against Christians, nor are they
to be heard in testimony," under penalty of "the curse of God who is
powerful"—that is, who is more powerful than the law of the king.
The council decreed that Jews could not hold offices or dignities conferred by the kings or other secular princes, nor have Christian nurses
for their children; "that they may not practice with Christians, *no matter how learned and proven the Jewish doctors may be* [an inferiority
complex breaks out here]; they may not lend money to Christians, nor
may they claim payments of debts owed to them by Christians, for this
is forbidden by the constitution of Clement V, the Pope."[81]

All this remained a dead letter, because the combination of Church
and people was still not enough to override the interests of the kings in
the matter of the Jews. Beneath the violent tone of the decree is hidden
a hypocritical rancor, for the ecclesiastics themselves needed the Jews to
collect the tithes owed to the Church of Christ. But such ecclesiastical
statements followed and paralleled the continual demands of the deputies in the *Cortes,* of which we have already seen important examples.
The Jews were finally attacked physically in 1391 by the populace of
Seville, incited by Ferrant Martínez, archdeacon of Écija. In his person
converged the inveterate rage of the people against the Jews and the
animosity of the popular element in the Church against the state. The
savage archdeacon stirred up the masses, the "little people," against
the Jews in spite of the opposition of Archbishop Barroso, who excommunicated the archdeacon, declaring him "contumacious, rebellious, and
under suspicion of heresy."[82] Urged by the theologians and canonists to

[81] The Council of Zamora was incorrect in this. Baer has examined the constitution and finds no mention of the Jews in it (II, 120).
[82] J. Amador de los Ríos, *Historia de los judíos,* II, 346.

show the reasons for his unchristian conduct, he always retorted that he would not talk except "before the officials and people of the town." Archbishop Barroso died in 1390, and in blind fury the masses sacked the ghetto in Seville, murdered many people, razed the synagogues, and inflicted a mortal blow to Hispano-Hebrew civilization. The example of Seville was quickly imitated by other cities, and the kings had every time less power to control the excesses of the mob.

Taking a panoramic view of the problem now, we may observe that in 1215 Ferdinand III resolved the conflict between the pope's interests and his own without violence; in 1307 Ferdinand IV sent a knight to read threatening letters to the cathedral chapter in Toledo; in 1481 Ferdinand the Catholic wrote similar letters, but there was no longer anyone who would dare to deliver them to the bishops in Saragossa. Eleven years later the Jews left Spain.

The Jews were ejected from what they regarded as their fatherland because the people which had formed itself into "brotherhoods" against them at the beginning of the fourteenth century (see Chapter 11) was the same people which in 1492 figured in the Holy Brotherhood of Ferdinand and Isabella, now strengthened by the masses of converts that contributed so greatly to the cruelties of the Inquisition. The people would no longer tolerate the preeminent position of the Hispano-Hebrews now that Spain had conquered the last remaining Moors in the Peninsula and the people felt proud of belonging to a powerful and efficient nation, whose very strength and efficiency owed much to the Jews. The Christian populace (peasant, Franciscan, or Dominican, it was all the same in this respect) was irritated by the economic and technical superiority of its Semitic compatriots. The Christians wanted the Jews to get out, regardless of the consequences and knowing full well that no one would take care of many of the essential tasks that for centuries had been the occupations of the Jews. The more intelligent Spaniards of the past[83] as well as the present have understood this. In our

---

[83] Pero López de Ayala says of the massacres of 1391: "And all this was a thirst for robbery, it seemed, *more than devotion*" (*Crónicas*, ed. by Llaguna, II, 391). Fray José de Sigüenza says: "The fathers of the Order of Saint Francis, *as persons zealous in matters of the Faith*, greatly favored the side of the Old Christians; and we shall see how they later, both publicly and secretly, condemned *the poor Jews* without mercy, readily believing *the mob*, which, without judgment or restraint, followed its fancy in doing to them and saying about them whatever mass fury will dare to do and say" (*Historia de la orden de San Jerónimo*, I, 366). In defense of the descendants of the Jews, Father Juan de Mariana, an aristocratic mind, wrote: "The only cause for the persecution of the descendants of the Jews was the hatred felt toward their Jewish ancestors" (*Historia de España*, Book XXII, Chap. VIII).

own time Menéndez y Pelayo has written: "Nothing has been more repugnant than this conflict, the principal cause of decadence for the Peninsula. . . . The matter of race explains many phenomena and resolves many enigmas in our history."[84] The fact to ponder gravely is that the best and most enduring Spanish values were forged on the anvil of that long and inescapable agony.

Other Activities of the Hispano-Hebrews

We have no detailed, well-organized history of the life of the Spanish Jews, and even the richest collections of documents have great gaps that will never be filled. But since my purpose is to understand and not enumerate, the known materials are more than enough to give some confirmation to my ideas.

In 1342 Alphonse XI asked Pope Clement VI to permit the Jews of Seville to make use of the new synagogue built by his *almojarife* Don Juçaf de Écija—in spite, I might add, of the most severe legal restrictions. The reason was that the Jews were "supremely necessary, because they contribute to the needs of the city, and at times they even fight against the Saracens alongside the Christians, and they are not afraid to risk their lives" (Baer, ii, 163). Reconquered Seville was an ample city, and to fill it many Jews and Saracens had to be brought in, so that the existing synagogues were not enough (Baer, ii, 163). The king speaks of his Jews as he does of any other subjects, associating them with the national mission—the Reconquest—and extolling their heroism.[85] But the very fact that he mentions their services as soldiers reveals the necessity for saying so and the suspicion that the reader might not have expected it, although we know that the Jew felt Spain to be his home, especially during the reigns of Alphonse XI and Peter the Cruel.[86] In any case, these and other praises always betrayed special

---

[84] *Historia de los heterodoxos españoles*, iii, 398; v, 108. Menéndez y Pelayo, nevertheless, did not try to explain anything by developing this pregnant intuition, but went ahead rather as if this problem were disposed of in that lamentation, which was purely external and, at bottom, insincere.

[85] His good defense of Alfaro against the French was mentioned as late as in 1466 (Baer, ii, 333).

[86] In connection with all that I am saying it is worthwhile to have in mind how many Jews there were in Spain. In the fifteenth century the total population of the Peninsula was probably between 7 and 8 million inhabitants, and the Jews must not have exceeded 235,000, according to the figures of Isidore Loeb in the *Revue des Etudes Juives*, 1887, xiv, 161. Evidently, then, the importance of the Hispano-Hebrews consisted in the quality of their work and not in their numbers.

interests, and went hand in hand with allusions to the strange and ad-ventitious nature of the Jews.[87]

One would expect that the powerful military orders, with their im-mense properties and their complicated hierarchy, would have been able to administer their own affairs, as happened with the Templars, the bankers of France and Europe.[88] But the grand masters and knights com-mander did not know how to use their land advantageously, as a few examples will reveal. In 1272, 1273, and 1274 the Grand Master of Santiago, Don Pelay Pérez, farmed to Don Bono, Don Jacobo, and Don Samuel the collection of the order's rents in Murcia, Toledo, La Mancha, and the frontier of Granada, "with all our personal taxes that we have there and are supposed to have, from Moors as well as Chris-tians." The bid was for 52,000 *maravedís*, 1,200 *cahices* (1 *cahiz* equals about 12 bushels) of wheat, and 1,200 *cahices* of barley, rye, and oats; the grand master demanded an advance of 26,000 *maravedís*.[89] The Order of Santiago leased all its properties in Carmona (Seville) in 1281, in payment of a debt of 8,350 *maravedís* owed to a Jew, whom they or-dered to "repair the mills with good mortar, as they were in the time of the Moors, using all the old masonry they had in them, and let them be as wide as the old walls" (Baer, II, 78). Apparently the order lacked Christian administrators capable of making the property produce, and their mills had not been kept up since they had been taken over from the Moors thirty-three years before.[90]

The Christian lords shed their troubles by turning the care of their property over to the good Jewish bidders, skilled in the handling of tangible things. This transfer signified the breakdown of the moral unity between vassals and lords, and the making of the Jew into a

[87] "In 1340 King Phillip III [of Navarre] granted a commission to Fernando Eximino, Canon of Tudela, to Aparicio de Zaragoza . . . , and to Rabbi Azac, a Jew, to open an irrigation system from the river Aragon to Tudela" (J. Yanguas, *Diccionario de antigüedades del reino de Navarra*, III, 424). In 1380 that kingdom was left impoverished by the exodus of the Jews: "every day Jews would leave the kingdom, and the taxes were reduced and lost" (J. Amador de los Ríos, *Historia de los judíos*, III, 289).

[88] The French monarchy destroyed them with the object of nationalizing their financial services.

[89] Don Bono on another occasion had paid debts contracted by the grand master with merchants of Montpellier and Lucca (Baer, II, 64-65).

[90] Sancho IV farmed out to Don Abraham el Barchilón in 1284 the collection of all the crown's income: "taxes on cattle and sheep, fines, the income from salt-mines, iron, and mercury" (II, 77). In 1286 the king had leased the salt-mines he owned in Medinaceli.

specialist in the heinous task of milking the poor for the benefit of the rich. Thus a permanent abyss was carved between the people and the government, and also between the state and the Church, because in the Jew the kings had a convenient source of income and in the Church a rival that was taking it away from them. What the king got from the *aljamas* in the way of tribute, and the technical services and public loans from the Jews, were the *facts*, not the *reasons*, that kept them participating in a common life with the Christians. When the lawmaker of the *Partidas* in the thirteenth century faced this grave problem, he reflected the official doctrine of the Church, knowing that it was ineffectual in Spain even among the ecclesiastics. The Jews lived with the Christians "so that they could live as in captivity forever, and that they might be a reminder to men that they come from the lineage of those that crucified Our Lord Jesus Christ" (*Partidas*, VII, 24, 1); the ancient emperors held it as right "that no Jew should ever hold an honored place or public office from which he might exercise authority over any Christian in any way" (VII, 24, 3).[91]

Yet in spite of such laws and the protests of the church and the people, the Hispano-Hebrews had positions in the administration and government of the Christian kingdoms, at least from the eleventh century on. As early as 1081, Pope Gregory VII admonished Alphonse VI: "Do not in your kingdom permit Jews in any way to be lords of the Christians, or to have authority over them."[92] The king of Castile used Jews as emissaries because the Moslems did the same thing.[93] At the beginning of the thirteenth century Innocent III complains "of the favor which the king of Castile shows to Jews and Saracens."[94] Doubtless these are not the only documents emanating from the pope. Churchmen of lesser rank never ceased complaining of the favor shown the Jews by the Span-

[91] Alphonse X sent Don Mair, his tax-collector, on a diplomatic mission to Morocco (Baer, II, 53). In 1258 the Jews of Badajoz were seizing Christians for their debts, and Alphonse X prohibited "any Jew to make loans in usury or any other way in the person of a Christian" (Baer, II, 57). In 1264, Ciudad Real (at that time Villa Real) was depopulated because the Jews sold the houses of their debtors to collect the debts, an action prohibited by Alphonse X (II, 58). But occasional laws would not change a situation based on the Christian's necessity and the Jew's wealth.

[92] "Dilectionem tuam monemus, ut in terra tua judeos christianis dominari vel supra eos potestatem excercere ulterius nullatenus sinas" (Baer, II, 5).

[93] "A Jew who was the emissary of King Alphonse"; his contemporary Al-Qādir, the Moorish king of Valencia, had as his vizier another Jew (*Crónica general*, 552a, 551a). The texts are in Baer, II, 5.

[94] Bréquigny et La Porte du Theil, *Diplomata, Charta et Epistolae*, VIII, 5, quoted in Amable Jourdain, *Recherches critiques sur l'âge et l'origine des traductions latines d'Aristote*, 1843, p. 150.

ish monarchs; so that Spanish history turned into a sustained tug-of-war between royal and ecclesiastical power for more than 400 years. Hispanic problems have dragged out through the centuries, as they continue to do: both Alphonse VI and Ferdinand the Catholic made use of Jewish functionaries and ambassadors.

But in spite of all this, we would be falsifying the meaning of the Jewish participation in the vital centers of Christian society and of the ecclesiastical and popular protests, if we interpreted it according to our modern criterion, as a struggle between enlightened progressives (kings and noblemen) and dark reactionaries (conservative clergy and ignorant people ruled by passion). It has been possible for Disraeli to rule England in the nineteenth century and for the United States to have Jewish secretaries of the treasury in the twentieth because the nations of English speech rest on rational norms and earthly aspirations (power, prosperity) which serve as a common basis for believer and disbeliever alike. For their part, the Moslems of the ninth, tenth, and eleventh centuries included the Jewish collaborator in the system of the Koranic faith. But in the Christian kingdoms, the Jewish official was neither in keeping with rational principles (impossible at that time in Spain), nor with an authentic juridical order of religious tolerance (as practiced by the Moslems); he existed, consequently, as something chaotic and dislocated,[95] "illegally" tolerated outside the spiritual framework of the Middle Ages—like the Romance language of Castile when it, instead of Latin, was used for scientific writings. The papal admonitions quoted above were "calls to order," to the medieval order, to which Spain could lend no ear.

This situation came to an end when the wild, demagogic reactions of the lower classes prevailed over the political empiricism of the kings as a result of a slow advance that had lasted more than four centuries, a kind of internal "reconquest."[96] The major episode in this movement

[95] The *Usatges* of Barcelona (1053) still regarded the Jews as a separate people: "Judei jurent christianis; christiani vero illis unquam" (Baer, 1, 13). But by 1142 the *fuero* (statute laws) of Daroca (Aragon) were saying: "Christiani, judaei, sarraceni unum et idem forum habeant"; and the *fuero* of Salamanca (thirteenth century): "Let the Jews have a law like the Christians' " (edition of Onís and Castro, section 259). Thus, the more realistic municipal law gave the Jew a legal status denied him by the more general statutes of the *Siete Partidas*, a status such as he had enjoyed among the Moslems until the arrival of the *Almohades*.

[96] Here is one of the numerous skirmishes in the prolonged quarrel: "Don Yuzaf de Écija, finance minister to Alphonse XI, maintained a great household of many knights and squires," because he was the king's counselor. A powerful lady, Doña Sancha, "who was always wanting disturbances and uprisings," promoted a conspiracy, and "those in Valladolid who were a party to the plot, *stirred up the peas-*

was formed by the brutal massacres and pillagings of 1391, in precisely those cities whose life was most prosperous and luxurious: Seville, Valencia, and Barcelona.[97]

Jewish labor and commerce no doubt contributed to that prosperity.[98] Manual labor was an ancient tradition with a religious basis for the Jew, as it was later for the Protestants. One of the father's duties, according to the Talmud, was "to teach his son some kind of handicraft that is easy and yet requires skill." "Besides studying the Torah," it says, "try to master some form of labor as a means of livelihood and a source of income." The greatest authorities on the Talmud were workers and artisans of the most varied kinds,[99] and because practical jobs were so normal for them, they could fit very easily in the gap left by the Hispano-Christian's aspiration to an "absolute" life, which was removed from anything that was not awareness and expansion of the self, and which did not acknowledge the necessity for a humble concern with things.[100] This is not to say that there were no Christian doctors, or that Christians did not engage in manual labor outside of agriculture. The strange thing is the abundance of Jewish doctors and artisans, considering that the Jews were a small minority. In 1306 the ecclesiastics in Avila

---

ants and the little people . . . and they tried to kill Don Yuzaf and those who were with him" (*Crónica de Alfonso XI*, Chap. 68).

[97] The radical difference between the histories of Spain and France is to be noted in the fact that it was the French kings who confiscated the wealth of the Jews (Saint Louis, in 1251). On his deathbed Philip, Count of Boulogne, distributed the Jews that belonged to him to his subjects (1235). When the Jews were expelled by Philip the Fair at the beginning of the fourteenth century, many found refuge in Catalonia and Aragon. The grand master of Calatrava took in thirty families in Alcañiz (*Revue des Etudes Juives*, 1887, xv, 233; 1893, xxvii, 149).

[98] Also Italian trade. The Italians' form of life had more points of contact with the Jews than with the Spanish Christians. In the Middle Ages there were dynasties of great Genoese traders (the Grimaldi and the Centurioni); the Genoese continued to engage in banking negotiations between Spain and her American dominions when there were no Jews to do this (J. M. Ots-Capdequí, in the *Boletín del Instituto de Investigaciones Históricas*, 1935, xviii, 61).

[99] M. Kayserling, *Das Moralgesetz des Judenthums*, Vienna, 1882, p. 27.

[100] In 1465, Henry IV was encamped in Simancas with an insufficient army. To increase it he offered letters patent of nobility to those who would come to the royal tent with their arms and at their own expense; the records of the Cortes say that amongst the ones favored, "many of them were in your camp and in your army as the muleteers of others, and as foot soldiers and stewards and other mercenaries." By becoming noblemen they were relieved of paying the head tax to the king (*Cortes de León y Castilla*, iii, 782). The king told the deputies that he would annul the letters patent for those people (p. 784), but the significance of the fact stands just the same. The longing for noble status and personal rank—incompatible with work—existed long before the sixteenth century.

took a census of all the houses owned by the church,[101] and of the people who lived in them. In the part of the city owned by the ecclesiastics, one would expect an all but total predominance of Christian residents and artisans. Yet a good number of houses are mentioned as being occupied by Moors and Jews, and the number of these non-Christian artisans is as great as the number of Christian ones. We find there a painter, two cobblers, two pack-saddlers, a locksmith, three blacksmiths, a harness-maker, and a goldsmith. From other documents that Baer cites pertaining to Avila we learn that there were two Jewish dyers there in 1297; a scrivener and a surgeon in 1301; a silversmith and a brazier in 1371. In the above-mentioned census there is no mention of Christian artisans in iron, gold, silver, or brass.

The situation in Catalonia was similar. Baer (I, 409-415) has published a number of documents from the fourteenth century giving the names of shop-keepers and persons of many trades: silk-mercers, brokers, tailors, an anchor-maker, a "doctor scolarium," a cutler, a curtain-maker, a sin-don-weaver, a painter of woolen cloth, an instrument-maker (magister strumentorum), a turner, a maker of scales, silversmiths, cobblers, work-ers in coral, "curritor auri" (gold-broker), a dice-maker, apothecaries, button-makers, book-binders, dyers, lantern-makers, a caretaker of lions, a jubbah-maker, embroiderers, soap-makers (I, 495). In 1326, the Jews were prohibited from selling missals and prayer books with pictures of saints in Barcelona.[102]

In 1066 Ramón Berenguer I, Count of Barcelona, assigned two Chris-tians and the Jew David the concession of minting money. The *alfaquim* Abram built a bath in the garden of Ramón Berenguer IV in 1160. Jews appear as royal judges in Aragon in 1170, 1192, 1217, 1236, and 1248,[103] just as we have seen that they occupied castles belonging to the king of Castile in the fourteenth century.

Evidently, then, the Jew did everything there was to be done, in-cluding the intoning of funeral chants at Christian burials: "to the Jew-

[101] This document, along with others from Avila, was published in part by Baer, II, 104-106. It can now be read in its entirety in *Cuadernos de Historia de España*, Buenos Aires, 1949, XII, pp. 151-180.

[102] M. Kayserling, in the *Revue des Etudes juives*, 1894, XXVIII, 110. The Jewish shoemakers formed a brotherhood in Saragossa, and it was to Jewish labor that that city owed its prosperity in the thirteenth and fourteenth centuries. In 1285 Al-phonse III of Aragon authorized the Christians of Saragossa not to pay their debts to the Jews, even when they had sworn to do so (*ibid.*, p. 116).

[103] Baer, I, 4, 22, 27, 46, 53, 90, 97.

ish women dirge-singers, 15 *maravedís*."[104] We know nothing of the songs of these professional funeral poetesses, but it must have been of Islamic tradition, since it was sung by Jews, and it was later to be reflected in the Andalusian *saetas*, a kind of dirge.

The Jew of the eleventh, twelfth, thirteenth, and fourteenth centuries was no longer the Jew of the Visigothic period, effectively persecuted by the laws. No, he was a human element deeply involved with Christians and Moors, since the trajectory of Islamic existence in Spain carried automatically a Jewish component. In spite of the laws in the *Partidas*, the truth is that even Jewish orthodoxy was protected by law. The *Libro de los fueros de Castilla*, a codification of much earlier laws made in the middle of the thirteenth century, sets a punishment for Jews who do not observe the Sabbath: "If on the Sabbath day he carry a weapon that has iron in it, he must pay a fine of two solidi."[105] The *Fuero Real*, of around 1255, forbids "any Jew to dare to read books dealing with the Jewish religion and attacking it, nor may they keep such books concealed; and if anyone has them or finds them, let him burn them at the door of the synagogue, publicly" (IV, 2, 1).

The *Partidas* say that "many wrongs take place between Christians and Jews because they live and dwell with one another in the towns, and the ones go about dressed just like the others" (VII, 24, 11). "The Jews who lie with Christian women are guilty of great daring and presumption" (VII, 24, 9), although, in 1300, Jews and Moors were still indulging in intercourse with the Christian women of Niebla and Seville (Baer, II, 100). The legal prohibitions were not effective. When the *Partidas* (VII, 24, 8) prohibit the obtaining of medicines made by Jewish hands, this means that Jews did make medicines: and they went on making them, as is evident from the already mentioned prohibition of 1412, a century and a half later. The latter law (Baer, II, 265) made it an offense for Jews to make use of Christian servants "to light their fires on Saturdays, and to go after wine for them . . . ; nor may they have Christian wet nurses, nor ploughmen, nor gardeners, nor shepherds, nor may they attend Christian funerals, weddings, or burials: *nor may they be godmothers or godfathers of Christians, nor Christian men and women of*

[104] From the bill for the funeral of Doña Mayor Ponce, Toledo, 1344; the document comes from the Toledan convent of the Carmelites (Baer, I, 162).

[105] Edition of Galo Sánchez, p. 116, where other punishments for similar errors are recorded. In 1391 John I of Aragon ordered proceedings against Mosse Faquim because he showed disrespect for the Christian religion and Mosaic law: drinking Christian wine, eating pork, working on Saturday (Baer, I, 646).

them." Apparently the difference in religion did not keep the Jews from being sponsors at baptisms nor the Christians at circumcisions. They are not permitted to be "tax-farmers, deputies, finance officers, majordomos, collectors of the royal rents or those of the lords, brokers"; nor are they permitted to have their own judges in civil and criminal cases;[106] to visit the Christian sick, nor to lend them remedies; to bathe in the same public baths, nor to send the Christians "presents of pastries, or spices, or cooked bread, or dead birds"; nor could Jews call themselves "*don* in writing or speech"; nor could they be veterinaries, "nor farriers, nor cobblers, nor jubbah-makers, nor tailors, nor shearers of cloth, nor knitters of stockings, nor butchers, nor furriers, nor clothiers of Christians"; nor "muleteers, nor carriers of any kind of merchandise such as olive oil and honey and rice" (Baer, ii, 265-269).

Through this text—as strongly worded as it was impotent—we can see the typical city life of the fifteenth century, and sense the short distance between people and court, as well as the great social volume displaced by the Jewish minority. The solemn legislator had to descend casuistically to the petty level of the young girls who then, as now, in the small towns of Andalusia, must have gone about carrying gifts of pastry, or any of the other fine dishes at which a good Jewish cook was expert. The decree was issued; and the doctor, the veterinary, and the muleteer went on working at their traditional jobs. The law was still unable to do away with the Jews by a single stroke of the pen. All it could do was break them verbally into little bits.[107]

[106] An extremely peculiar feature of the Spanish ghetto was its system of autonomous courts. When the famous Rabbi Asher arrived from Germany, he could not conceal his astonishment: "When I first arrived here, I asked in amazement by what legal right Jews could today legally convict anyone to death without a Sanhedrin. . . . In none of the countries that I know of, except here in Spain, do the Jewish courts try cases of capital punishment" (A. A. Neuman, *The Jews in Spain*, i, 138-139). Here we see the strength and peculiarity of the Spanish Jews, whose community constituted a state within the state, just like a church; so that the nation never reached the point where it coincided fully with the state. A prohibition issued in the name of John II of Castile refers to the fact that "the *aljamas* of the Jews and Moors cannot have and henceforth shall not have Jewish or Moorish judges of their own to try their civil as well as their criminal suits," which henceforth were to be tried "by the judges of the cities. . . . But by my grace the said judges . . . will preserve the customs that until now the Jews and Moors have kept among themselves" (Baer, ii, 266-267). In the fifteenth century Spain still had a motley population from the legal standpoint, subject to Christian, Jewish, and Moorish laws and to the canon laws of the church. And to these laws are to be added the statutory peculiarities of the ancient kingdoms and regions.

[107] As I shall make clear later, the decree of 1412 must have been inspired and even written by a converted Jew. The detail of this decree and the acquaintance it

The law of 1412 followed the massacres and sackings of 1391,[108] which did not destroy, as one might have thought, all intercourse between the two peoples, who continued to be mutually indispensable. But this law and others like it do not reveal to us the great detail of everyday life in Christian-Judaic Spain, which we will perceive better if we observe certain phenomena of a religious character. The truth is that our ideas about Spanish Christianity in the Middle Ages are nebulous. To begin with, it is surprising that the *Fuero Real*, cited above, should have concerned itself with the Mosaic faith by forbidding the Jew to read heterodox books,[109] but there are other facts that are still more surprising. Alongside the religiosity of certain Dominicans like Saint Vincent Ferrer appear manifestations of indifference—tolerance would not be an adequate word for them. The intimacy in which the three religions lived together developed something of deism or indifferentism in the habits of the people. Otherwise, how could a Jew have been the godfather of a Christian, or have been charged with the collection of the Church's tithes? There are other facts no less significant. The plague attacked Seville in 1449, and the Christians organized solemn supplications. The images were brought out and accompanied in procession by *penitentes*.[110] For their part the Jews organized another procession which went through the city along streets covered with sedge and lined with hangings. In all its apparatus the Jewish procession with the Torah imitated the procession of Corpus Christi. There was a great scandal, for it turned out

---

shows with private life in the ghettos betray an author who has experienced this life from the inside.

[108] The community in Barcelona ceased to exist in 1393 (M. Kayserling, *Revue des Estudes Juives*, 1894, xxviii, 114). King John II of Aragon wanted to found a new *aljama* in 1392, but the Jews did not return. In 1424 Alphonse V of Aragon prohibited the creation of a new community; the Jews were authorized to stay in Barcelona as transients and only for fifteen days. This means that commercial and industrial life in Barcelona could get along without the Jews before that time; but it also means that the axis of political life did not pass through Catalonia. The royal power defended the Jews of Old Castile and Saragossa until almost the moment of expulsion.

[109] It is not enough to say that the kings watched over the religious conduct of the Jews with the object of benefiting from the fines imposed upon those who broke the law: "one who swears falsely must pay one hundred solidi to the king" (A. A. Neuman, *The Jews in Spain*, i, 128).

[110] The document was published by Stern, *Urkundliche Beiträge über die Stellung der Päpste zu den Juden*, Kiel, 1895, i, 48. Baer gives an extract (ii, 315). Chance reveals this fact to us which could not have been unique. In 1465 it was prohibited for the Jews to hold processions on the occasion of plagues (*Memorias de Enrique IV de Castilla*, ii, No. 109).

that the Jewish supplications had been authorized by the archbishopric of Seville, a vacant see at the time. The canon Antonio Ferrari protested violently, but the local Curia jailed him and denied his appeal to the pope. Even so the case got to Rome, and, quite logically, the finding was in favor of Ferrari, who, once he was set free, went straight to Rome to complain before Nicholas V. The pope ordered the bishop of Seville to punish the organizers of the Jewish procession if there was any reason to do so, and to indemnify Ferrari.

A part of fifteenth-century Spain—the kings, the nobility, many converts, the rich businessman, the humanist or epicurean clergy—must have regarded the wealthy Jews as a distinguished class in their society, incorporated in Spanish life since time immemorial, indispensable for the well-being of the privileged folk, and inoffensive to their beliefs. But however gratifying and humane the conduct of the kings and aristocrats may seem to our modern eyes, anyone who reflects a little on the matter cannot fail to be astonished at the temerity of those who ruled Spain for more than four centuries, for they were leaving behind, as an unassimilated and unassimilable mass, nothing less than the immense majority of the Spanish people. It will be said that they could do nothing else, given the condition of Spain, a country forged between the blows of ambitious Europe and obdurate Islam. Be it as it may, that living from day to day for centuries, without working out a homogeneous and congenial system of law from above and without the development of the general mores into harmonious forms of communal life, caused Iberia to enter upon what for other peoples has been the "modern era," with no other equipment than her grandiose and desperate personalism. For centuries the Christian masses, with no ideals save warfare, *hidalguía*, and faith, regarded the state and its organs as an enemy that preyed upon them through its agents, specialists in the ungrateful task of fleecing the poor —a situation without the compensations, one must emphasize, of the feudalism of Christian Europe. The Jew, for his part—what could he do but what he did? Rivers run through the channels they have in front of them.[111]

[111] Since there are no organic descriptions of medieval life it is not uncommon for people to imagine for themselves a romantically naïve picture of the relationship between the church and the faithful who paid her their tithes. The reality is that the people hated with equal passion all who exacted any kind of economic tribute from them, whether these persons were agents of the church or the state; and their only thought was how to defraud the church and their other overlords. An ordinance of the late fourteenth century says that even the prelates and other clergy did not regularly pay the tithes on the wealth that they owned privately (not, like the prop-

Lords, people, Jews, and Moors had to live, in the last analysis, on terms of mutual exclusion and mutual disturbance, and this becomes not living at all—quite literally—when compensations are not forthcoming to ease the situation. The lack of moral and religious unity produced the first eruption in the violent segregation of the Jews in 1492 and then of the Moriscos in 1609. Subsequent history has shown that among the Christians who remained in the Peninsula after the expulsion of both Jews and Moors, the ties that tended to bring about a satisfactory social unity were very feeble.

The fact that the kings and great lords attached more importance to the Jews' money than to their offenses against Christianity spurred the Dominican order on in the development of its inquisitorial spirit, gestated in almost three centuries of rancor against the royal power, a rancor parallel to that felt by the masses as victims of the fiscal rigors of the Jews. We have already seen that as late as 1491 Ferdinand and Isabella were willing to listen to the complaints of the Jews of Zamora against the attacks of the Dominicans, and this was a very old story. In general terms it can be said that in the Middle Ages the kings had no religious policy, or at least, they had nothing that would serve as a precedent for the Spain that Ferdinand and Isabella bequeathed to the future.[112]

---

erty of the church, exempt from tithing). This matter interested the king very much, because a third of the tithes belonged to the crown. "We deem it proper," says John I, "for the prelates and the clergy to give a full tithe of all the fruits of their properties . . . which do not belong to their churches; and because we find that much deception goes on in the giving of tithes, from henceforth we forbid that anyone dare to gather or measure his pile of wheat, and [we require] that he keep it, winnowed, on the threshing floor until first the bell be struck for the collectors of the royal thirds to come, or those who are supposed to collect the tithes; who, we command, are not to be threatened, driven away, or beaten for demanding their rights" (Ordenanzas reales de Castilla, Book I, title v, law II). If the clergy themselves defrauded the king and their church, what must the people not have done? Each one tried to measure his stack of wheat without the intervention of the tithe-collectors or the third-collectors; the latter generally were Jews and Moors who were in the habit of measuring the wheat "stealthily, by night." This law does not appear for the first time in the Ordenanzas reales. It had also formed a part of the Fuero real of the thirteenth century (Book I, title vi, law iv).

[112] The peculiarity of the Jews' situation in Spain stands out even more if we recall what happened in Sicily and the South of Italy at the end of the thirteenth century. There the Dominicans and their Inquisition managed to prevail over the tolerantly interested policy of the Angevin kings, Charles I and Charles II, and as a result the Jewish communities were either converted en masse or they were dispersed. At that time some of the converts showed great zeal in persecution, among them a certain Manuforte, who got an order from Charles I in 1269 preventing the converts from becoming Jews again (see Joshua Starr, "The Mass Conversion of Jews in Southern Italy" [1290-1293], in Speculum, 1946, xxi, 203-211). It is

In 1305 a Dominican named Sancho de las Caynas denounced Açac de Çalema to the authorities of James II of Aragon. Açac was "the richest and most learned Jew in that region," and he had mocked Christ saying: "You adore and take for the Son of God a man conceived and made in adultery." The Jew was imprisoned and all his property was seized, but the trial was reviewed by the royal court, and the accused was absolved in September of the same year.[113]

In 1318 the *infante* Don Alfonso of Aragon absolved a certain Lope Abnexeyl, accused of the most atrocious crimes: insulting God, the Virgin, and the saints, counterfeiting money, seducing women, robbery, murder, etc. (Baer, 1, 209-210). The reputation of David de Besalú, who had been condemned by the king and the Inquisition for uttering certain words "against our faith," was rehabilitated by Peter IV in 1356, and he was authorized to hold certain offices in the Jewish community (*ibid.*, 1, 360). In 1367 Peter IV forced the Bishop of Majorca to hand over to him Issach Analdi, detained in the ecclesiastical prison for having blasphemed against the Virgin and her virginity; the king threatened actions against the bishop's person and his property (contra vos et bona vestra) if the bishop did not comply (*ibid.*, 1, 391).

These examples—there is no point in multiplying them—when taken together with the attitude of Ferdinand the Catholic against the bishops of Saragossa in 1481 and the repeated declaration that the Jews were the major source of income for the Aragonese and Castilian crowns, make it possible to understand the royal policy with respect to the Jews and to the church. The interests and prerogatives of the crown were more important than any other consideration, though this did not imply an indifference to religious belief, for nothing really heterodox and threatening to Catholicism appears among the Hispano-Christians of the fourteenth and fifteenth centuries. The interests and prerogatives of the crown were also part of another "belief," opposed to the one represented by the ecclesiastics. A glance through the records of the Cortes of the fifteenth century is enough to make clear how stubborn the passive resistance of the churchmen was to any order emanating from the civil authority. The power of the lay authorities came up against an unbreach-

---

thus demonstrated one more time that outside of Spain the Jews were confronted with quite different social conditions. The Dominicans, a Spanish order, took almost three centuries to accomplish in their own land what had been so easy for them in foreign parts.

[113] "Ipsum insontem invenerimus . . . Idcirco . . . visis presentibus absolvatis nec deinceps ipsum propterea molestetis vel molestari ab aliis permittatis" (Baer, 1, 188).

able wall precisely because they could not argue their case; nor was there any way for them to do so if the essential activities of the public administration were in non-Christian hands. Therein lies one of the chief reasons for the failure of the civil power in Spain, a failure that is historically incomprehensible if we fail to examine the problem in its own terms.

Isabella's joke has more to it than is apparent: "She said that if you want to put a fence around Castile, then give it to the Hieronymites."[114] The Christian knew little of the art of producing and conveying wealth, and he looked with surprised and hostile eyes[115] upon the industry of the Jews and Moors, their diligence in manual labor, and, especially, the commercial internationalism of the Jews. The land and the life on it went on being limited by the religious orders and excluded from the operations of earthly interests, because religious belief was more and more in the foreground. In it the person without present or future acquired a perspective of eternity and with this, social dignity. Belief was becoming a "liberal" and luxurious art for the spirit by sheer contrast to the binding shackles of laborious and deliberate reasoning. Through belief one arrived at the truth with one stroke, just as with a sudden discovery of gold in the Indies one became rich overnight.

The kings' own land was slipping away from them; the religious orders were invading it and fencing it off, and the state was changing from an earthly to a heavenly entity. The Catholic queen, located *ex officio* between heaven and earth, gave a tinge of irony to her remark about the very prosperous children of Saint Jerome.

Purity of Blood and Inquisition

The new and very difficult situation of the Jews with respect to the Christians during the fifteenth century was much more decisive for the direction of Spanish life than the resurgence of classical letters, the con-

[114] Melchor de Santa Cruz, *Floresta*, No. 68.

[115] In 1473 the converted Jews of Cordova, pursued by a mob, tried to take refuge in Gibraltar. The Duke of Medina Sidonia was inclined to let them stay on Gibraltar, in opposition to the view of his friends, who alleged "the unsuitability of the New Christians for the defense of such an important town. . . . They added that those lazy men, *accustomed to an easy life*, and generally engaged in such humble trades as that of shoemaker or money-lender, were useless, or at least unworthy, to garrison the town. . . . Neither these reasons nor others like them made any dent in the Duke's mind, now moved only by the prospect of money," etc. (Alfonso de Palencia, *Crónica de Enrique IV*, Spanish translation from the original Latin by A. Paz y Melia, III, 132-133).

tact with Italy, or any other of the events by which the so-called Middle
Ages are customarily marked off from modern times. The savage persecution of the Jews modified the traditional relations among the nobility,
the church, the common people, and the Jews,[116] and it finally brought
about the emergence of that unique form of Spanish life in which religion
and nation confused their boundaries.

Distinguished Christian families had mixed with Jewish people during the Middle Ages, sometimes for economic motives, sometimes on
account of the frequent beauty of Jewish women. Before the fifteenth
century nobody was shocked by this, or at least the scandal was not great
enough (save the singular case, real or legendary, of the affair between
Alphonse VIII and the Jewess of Toledo) to leave any echo in literature. But in the period under discussion, people wrote freely on a theme
that inflamed the passions, that is, on the insoluble drama that rent the
two inimical Spanish peoples asunder. In abusive poems like the *Coplas
del provincial* and others, there is allusion to the Jewish provenience of
certain persons. To this certain converts make reply, as sure of their own
superiority as they are of the vulgarity of those impugning them. For
example, someone sent Don Lope Barrientos, Bishop of Cuenca and a
partisan of the converts, an allegation against a certain Pedro Sarmiento
and a bachelor of arts Marcos García Mazarambrós, who incited the mob
in the massacre and sacking of the Toledo ghetto in 1449.[117] In this
allegation, the author's foremost objection is the use of the term "converts" to designate the New Christians, "because they are sons and grandsons of Christians, and they were born in Christendom, and they know
nothing at all of Judaism nor of its rite."[118] The good converts ought

[116] The liberal professions were also affected. Regarding the riots in Toledo, to
which I shall presently refer, the convert Hernando del Pulgar wrote: "I recall
among the other things that I heard Fernán Pérez de Guzmán say, that the bishop
Don Pablo [de Santa María] wrote the old Constable who was ill in Toledo: 'I am
glad that you are in a city of notable physicians and fine medicines.' I do not know
whether he would say so now; for we see that the famous leather-bottle-makers [an
odrero had headed the movement against the converts] have driven the famous physicians away from there; and so I believe that you are now provided with much
better rabble-rousing bottle-makers than with good natural scientists" (see *Clásicos
castellanos*, Vol. 99, p. 24).

[117] See the "Crónica de don Juan II" in the *Biblioteca de Autores Españoles*,
LXVIII, 661-662.

[118] This text was published by Fermín Caballero, *Conquenses ilustres. Doctor
Montalvo*, 1873, pp. 243ff. The informant of the Bishop of Cuenca summons Marcos
García, the bachelor of arts Marquillos, and accuses him of having caused discord in
Toledo and of being a worthless person "even as a peasant from the village of Mazar-

not to pay for the bad ones, just as "we are not going to massacre the Andalusians merely because some of them turn Moors every day." There follows a long list of illustrious names, people who had Jewish relatives, and not excluding persons of royal blood: "*Going still higher,* it is not necessary to recount the sons and grandsons and great-grandsons of the noble and very powerful knight, the admiral Don Alonso Henríquez, who on one side is descended from the king Don Alonso [XI] and the king Don Enrique [II] the Elder, and on the other side is descended from this [i.e., Jewish] lineage." We may add that John II of Aragon married Doña Juana Henríquez, the daughter of the admiral mentioned above, as his second wife, so that their son Ferdinand the Catholic turns out to be Jewish on his mother's side.[119]

In two other well-known texts of the sixteenth century there are mentions of families with Jewish antecedents. One is the *Libro verde de Aragón,*[120] and the other *El tizón de la nobleza de España,* by Cardinal Francisco Mendoza y Bobadilla, Archbishop of Burgos,[121] in which the Cardinal demonstrates that not only his relatives, the Counts of Chinchón (accused of impure blood), had Jewish ancestors, but that almost all the aristocracy of that epoch also had them. If Spanish life had unfolded in a calm and harmonious rhythm, the mixture of Christians and Jews would not have started any kind of conflict, because Spain had been a contexture of three peoples and three beliefs since the eighth century.

---

ambrós. . . . It would be better for him to go back to ploughing as his father and his grandfather had done, and as his brothers and relatives do today" (p. 252).

[119] This is not a dubious inference but a known fact, as is proved by the following anecdote told by Luis de Pinedo, *Libro de chistes* (*Sales españoles,* collected by A Paz y Melia, Madrid, 1890, I, 279): "Sancho de Rojas [a first cousin of Ferdinand the Catholic], said to the Catholic King (as he was cutting out a hunting costume for him): 'I beg Your Highness that if any of this cloth is left over you will make me a present of it.' The King told him that he would do so gladly. The next day Sancho de Rojas said to the King: 'My Lord, was anything left over?' The King said: 'No, by your life, not even this much.' And he traced an O (such as the Jews customarily wore as a sign on their breasts) on his breast with his hand. Sancho de Rojas answered: 'The king was speaking his own language.'" Another anecdote (p. 268) suggests that Jewish origin was also attributed to the Duke of Alba: "Alonso de la Caballería asked Cardinal Pero Gonçález de Mendoça what he thought of Don Enrique Enríquez, who later became an admiral, and Don Fadrique de Toledo, who later became Duke of Alba. He said: 'I think that the further apart Jews get the more vicious they are.'"

[120] Used by J. Amador de los Ríos in Vol. III of his *Historia de los judíos,* and later published in the *Revista de España,* cv, cvi, 1885.

[121] The rarity of this work has forced me to rely on the summary in the *Enciclopedia Universal Ilustrada* (*Espasa*), the article "Nobleza." See the *Revue Hispanique,* 1900, VII, 246.

The Jew had acquired almost as much distinction as the Christian, in spite of all the prohibitions, and the kings themselves gave to some of their Jews the title of *don*, at that time a sign of high position in the hierarchy of the nobility. For instance, in 1416 Ferdinand of Aragón knighted Gil Ruiz Naiari.[122] The mixture of blood and the interplay of circumstances already described affected the inward forms of life, and the Jew of quality felt himself noble, fighting at times in the royal army against the Moor, and he built temples like the synagogue of the *Tránsito* in Toledo, on whose walls are emblazoned the arms of Castile and Leon. Let us remember that the greatest advantage which Rabbi Arragel assigned the Castilian Jews was that of "lineage," of having more noble blood than the non-Spanish Jews. The Bishop of Burgos, Don Pablo de Santa María (who before his conversion was Rabbi Salomon Halevi), composed a discourse on the *Origin and Nobility of His Lineage*.[123] The feeling of *hidalguía* and noble distinction was common to Christians and Jews in the fifteenth century, and accompanied the latter into their exile. Max Grünbaum says: "Anyone who attends the divine office in the splendid Portuguese synagogue of Amsterdam will notice the difference between the German and the Spanish Jews. The solemn and tranquil dignity of the worship distinguishes it from that of the German-Dutch synagogue. . . . The same Spanish *grandeza* is found in the Hispano-Jewish books printed in Amsterdam."[124] This feeling of superiority persists still in the Jews of the Spanish Diaspora, an inexplicable phenomenon if we do not refer to their horizon prior to 1492—the belief in the seigniory of the person, the soul of ancient Castile. Through that inner form of life, the Sephardim are vitally linked with their adversaries and persecutors of 450 years ago.

But now I want to consider the reverse influence, the effect the Jews had on the Christians. We have already seen that without taking the Jews into account it is difficult to understand the birth of learned prose in the thirteenth century. Likewise, the literature of the fourteenth and fifteenth centuries is indebted to the Jewish people for the works, to mention only the most important of many, of Don Santob, Don Alonso de Cartagena, Juan de Mena, Rodrigo de Cota, Hernando del Pulgar, and

[122] Francisca Vendrell, *Concesión de nobleza a un converso*, in *Sefarad*, 1948, VIII, 397-401.

[123] J. Amador de los Ríos mentions this work as unpublished in his *Estudios sobre los judíos de España*, 1848 (Buenos Aires edition, 1942, p. 333). I know of no other references to this manuscript of the Biblioteca Nacional in Madrid.

[124] *Jüdisch-Spanische Chrestomathie*, 1896, p. 4.

Fernando de Rojas. Later, Luis Vives, Fray Luis de León, and Mateo Alemán were to show the scar of their Jewish descent. But rather than dwell on such well-known matters, I should like to call attention to certain aspects of the Hispanic character that emerged with extraordinary vividness at the end of the fifteenth century. Among the medieval Christians of Spain we do not find the preoccupation with what was later to be called "purity of blood." If it had existed, the strong mixture maliciously denounced in *El tizón de la nobleza* (The Blight of the Nobility)[125] would not have been possible, nor would the Jews have occupied the eminent positions in which we have found them even at the moment of their expulsion.

The people who really felt the scruple of purity of blood were the Spanish Jews. Thanks to the translations of A. A. Neuman, we know the legal opinion (responsa) of the rabbinical courts, and these reveal unsuspected things. In these writings there is a punctilious concern for family purity and what one's neighbors will say about one, for the "cares of honor" so characteristic of seventeenth-century Spanish drama.[126] The minority Jew had always lived on the defensive in the face of the dominant Christian; but as a consequence of the persecutions in the fifteenth century, he became still more acutely aware of his exclusive particularism. When he was converted to Christianity, this feeling carried over and was sometimes exacerbated. In order to protect himself against the suspicion and persecution of the Old Christians, the New Christian built up his caste-consciousness as a protection against his own Jewish descent and as a protest of the total sincerity of his Christianity, an act of justification in his own eyes and the eyes of society. For his part, the Old Christian found that the expulsion and conversions of the Jews brought him little comfort, for he frequently observed that the New Christians still enjoyed one kind of importance or another, that they "were conspicuous for the acuteness of their minds," as one Inquisitorial trial puts it. So the Old Christians and the New, by inciting each other, reached a furious state of mutual exclusivism and persecution, to which the more enlightened Hispano-Christians had never been inclined before the expulsion,

[125] Among the prohibitions of the Decree of 1412, promulgated during John II's minority, is this: No Christian woman "may venture within the district where the said Jews and Moors live, neither at night nor in the daytime" (Baer, II, 268).

[126] Since literary themes are not ghosts that wander about through the abstract space of the centuries, I find that my studies of the sense of honor published in 1916 in the *Revista de Filología Española* are badly in need of revision. I thought them out as if Moors and Jews had not existed in Spain—an error made altogether too frequently.

and which did not become general for some time. We have seen how tolerant royal justice was with the Jews who blasphemed against the Christian religion, a leniency which it would be hopelessly naïve to attribute to the "corruption of the times"—the times are never incorrupt. For the medieval Spanish Christian the problem of first magnitude was not to preserve his faith and race incontaminate, but to conquer the Moor and utilize the Jew. In any case, at the end of the thirteenth or beginning of the fourteenth century it would be impossible to find a *Christian* document conceived in the terms of the following Jewish "responsum":

"I certify over my signature to all whom this document may reach that witnesses appeared before my teacher, Rabbi Isaac, son of R. Eliakim, who was presiding at the court session, and that he received proper and legal testimony from aged and venerable men of the country concerning the family of the brothers David and Azriel, to the effect that they were of pure descent, without any family taint, and that they could intermarry with the most honored families in Israel; for there had been no admixture of impure blood in the paternal or maternal antecedents and their collateral relatives. Jacob Issachar, son of R. Shalom."[127]

This certificate of purity was evoked because someone had said that one of the forbears of the young aristocrats in question had been a slave. Not content with the finding of the local court, the plaintiffs went to other eminent rabbis, and all the decrees were finally carried to the highest authority, the celebrated Shelomo ben Adret, of Barcelona, who wrote the following statement:

"When your letter reached me and I opened it, I stood terrified. The author of this wicked rumor, whatever his motive, has sinned grievously and deserved severer punishment than one who slaughtered his victim in cold blood. For a murderer slays but two or three souls, but this man has defamed thirty, forty souls and the voice of the blood of the whole family cries from the earth, groaning aloud. The defamer should be excommunicated. While the sages of the Talmud stated long ago, 'He who calls his neighbor slave shall be considered excommunicate,' it is not sufficient to leave the culprit under the general reproach of the ancient ban, but he should now be excommunicated by a living court, and I shall confirm their act and affix my signature to such a document."[128]

[127] A. A. Neuman, *The Jews in Spain*, ii, 5. The document is one of the *responsa* of Shelomo ben Abraham ben Adret, who lived in the late thirteenth and early fourteenth centuries.

[128] For other calumnies substantiated in the rabbinical courts, see Neuman, *op.cit.*, ii, 8.

We have before us, then, the earliest text of a proof of purity of blood in Spain, with witnesses examined in different places, a text without parallel among the Christians of that time. In the sixteenth and seventeenth centuries, the purity of blood had become a thought pattern of the noble and ecclesiastical society as a result of the preoccupations with which the converts had, as it were, injected it. For just as the "summum jus" gives rise to a "summa injuria," likewise the frantic opposition to the Jews was impregnated, through dramatic mimicry, with the habits of its adversary.

A Jewess in Coca (Segovia) carried on amorous relations with a Christian somewhere around 1319. Concerning this unnatural sin we have a decision from Rabbi Asher of Toledo, very important for the social background it reveals.[129] Yehuda ben Wakar, physician to the *infante* Don Juan Manuel, went to Coca with his lord in 1319, and there found out how a Jewish widow happened to be pregnant as a result of a love affair with a Christian, to whom, moreover, she had ceded a large part of her wealth. The Christians of Coca submitted the case to Don Juan Manuel, who adjudged the Jewish court competent. The Jewish woman gave birth to twins. One died, and the other was taken by the Christians to be baptized. Yehuda then asked Rabbi Asher "what should be done so that the law of our Torah should not appear to be trampled upon in the eyes of the people? . . . All the towns in the neighborhood of Coca are talking about it, and conversations about this lost woman are going on everywhere, so that our religion has become something to be scorned. . . . I suggest that, the case being so notorious, her nose be cut off so as to disfigure the face with which she pleased her lover."[130]

Let us notice how Yehuda is more disturbed by the divulgence of the scandal than by the wrong done by the pretty Jewess whose face he wanted to make hideous. The law in the *Partidas*, mentioned above, simply put a penalty upon illicit relations between Christian women and non-Christian men, reserving severe punishment only for those who offended repeatedly. The law of the *aljama*, on the other hand, emphasized the effect of transgressions of the law on public opinion, and identified the reputation-honor of the individual with that of the com-

[129] The *Partidas* (VII, 24, 9; 25, 10) condemn Christian women who sleep with Moors or Jews. For the first offense they must give up half their property to their parents; for the second they lose everything in the same way; and if there is a subsequent recurrence, they are condemned to death. If it was a case of a married woman, the husband could do as he wished in the matter—kill her or forgive her.
[130] Baer, II, 138, gives a German version of the original Hebrew.

munity. We do not find anything like this in the Castile of the Middle Ages, but we do among the Spaniards of the sixteenth century, who lumped together national honor-reputation with that of the individual, and considered it a collective disgrace for a single Spaniard to fall into heresy.[181] Just as peculiar is the fact that the Holy Office should concern itself with punishing lapses from morality such as concubinage even as it punished attacks against religion. In this the similarity to the Jewish tribunals is even closer.[182] Law, religion, morality, and social interdependence came then to be one and the same thing.

Thus we begin to realize that the peculiar identification established in Spain between Catholicism and the state in the sixteenth century is inseparable from the Christian-Islamic-Judaic contexture, within which it was no longer possible to recognize anything that is pure and abstract Christianity, Islamism, or Judaism. The new vital situation brought no change in the inner disposition of Hispanic history—a history made of belief and the self's awareness of how it—and not the world around it—is existing. The Inquisition and the concern over the purity of blood appear as an interplay of the possibilities and authentic inclinations of the Spaniards. Their psychology, as they entered the sixteenth century, rested upon foundations 800 years deep. During that time the Peninsula had been invaded by African *Almorávides* and *Almohades* (eleventh and twelfth centuries), anxious to reestablish in its former vigor the Islamic faith that had become lax under the kings of the *taifas*. The Christians of the north stubbornly resisted the penetration of foreign heresies (the Albigensians, for example), at the same time that they stifled in their own minds any thought dangerous to stability of their own belief. And it is no accident that the decisive book in bringing back those who had strayed from the faith of Moses was a work of Maimonides, a Jew of Cordova. Thus, those who have absorbed my idea of the concrete reality *of each* history will understand that the Inquisition and a zealous concern for the purity of blood do not imply any change in the structural functioning of Hispanic history, even though new contents are introduced into it.

No kind of Machiavellian reasoning presided over the course undertaken by the Spanish kings and peoples from the fifteenth century on;

[181] See Marcel Bataillon, "Honneur et Inquisition," in the *Bulletin Hispanique*, 1925, XXVII, 5-17. By spreading his heresies in foreign lands, Miguel Servet was dishonoring Spain. His own family tried to lure him back to his country so they might hand him over to the Inquisition.

[182] Neuman, II, 278.

no sort of genuine effort was made to avoid internal disturbances and preserve unity in order to wage foreign war with undivided attention. These arguments were adduced *a posteriori*. To see their inadequacy, one has only to recall that the Moriscos, politically more dangerous and less involved than the Jews in the public administration, were not exiled until 1609. Philip II did not carry out this move even after the bloody struggles in the Alpujarra. The state-church, a dual concept that actually stands for an organic unity, was a creation that came out of the spirit of those people who came to find themselves in an advantageous position for releasing impulses that they had been carrying within themselves for a long time. It was an almost revolutionary conquest achieved by resentful masses and by converts and the descendants of converts anxious to forget what they were. The molds of what had once been Jewish life were filled with anti-Jewish contents and purposes, with a fury directly proportional to their desire to get away from their origins. Centuries of tradition, Islamic as well as Judaic, burst out in the orgy of a belief which was now going to control the national mass without restraint or misgiving. This belief encompassed the whole of life. The establishment of the Inquisition is all of a piece with the messianism[133] that flourished in a wild state in the fifteenth and sixteenth centuries, together with mystico-sensual transport of the Illuminati, whose Islamic relationships Asín has established beyond any doubt.[134]

It is therefore not a paradox but an elemental truth that Spanish society grew more and more fanatic in its Christianity as more and more Jews disappeared or were Christianized. Sixteenth-century Spanish Catholicism, which was a totalitarian and state religion, does not resemble the Catholicism of the Middle Ages in any of its European forms, least of all, that of papal Rome, which did not scruple to grant asylum to many of the Jews expelled from Spain. Let us also keep clearly in mind the fact that Ferdinand the Catholic, in opposition to the preachments of the Dominicans, was still protecting the Jews of Zamora in 1491, still

[133] See *Aspectos del vivir hispánico*, pp. 217ff., for the messianism of that epoch. There was a general belief in the superhuman mission of the Catholic Sovereigns and Cardinal Cisneros; the latter in turn protected the nun Juana de la Cruz, a prophetess who expected to bring forth a new savior (M. Bataillon, *Erasme et l'Espagne*, p. 74). A Franciscan friar believed that he was called to beget a new prophet who would save the world, and he wrote Mother Juana de la Cruz, a pure virgin, to this effect. A Franciscan, Fray Melchor, a descendant of converted Jews, started conventicles of Illuminati and found disciples among the converts (*ibid.*, pp. 65-73). In 1520, a certain Jew named Juan de Bilbao passed himself off as Prince John and the redeemer of mankind (*Aspectos del vivir hispánico*, p. 51).

[134] See *Al-Andalus*, 1945 to 1948.

entrusting them with the administration of the Holy Brotherhood, still using them as ambassadors, etc. The end of the fifteenth century was marked by an intense upheaval which made impossible what had formally been quite usual. The infiltration of the converts into the Christian society gave rise to phenomena that have found a parallel in the history of our own day, when many extremists of the "right" or the "left" have changed their political allegiance overnight and the victims have suddenly turned into the hangmen.

Up to the fifteenth century, Christians had mixed with Jews without considering the crossing of blood an abomination. Thus it was possible even for Christians of royal descent to have love affairs with Jewish women, and for the mother of Ferdinand the Catholic to have Jewish blood in her veins. The normality of this situation is indicated by the silence over such mixtures before the fifteenth century, and the outcry they provoked after that time. Naturally a number of the converts—not all of them, of course—behaved in a perverse fashion, and some of these turned out to be the worst enemies of the Jews and of the converts themselves, who were to be found everywhere, sometimes in positions of high station.[135] Concerning the celebrated theologian and Dominican Don Juan de Torquemada, Cardinal of Saint Sixtus, we have the word of Hernando del Pulgar that "his grandparents were of the lineage of Jews converted to our holy Catholic faith,"[136] so that the first inquisitor, Fray Tomas de Torquemada (a relative of the Cardinal) also turns out to be *ex illis*. Hernando del Pulgar—a strange and subtle spirit—was another Jewish convert, although the histories of literature do not put him down for such. He wrote an ironic epistle to Don Pedro Gonzáles de Mendoza, the Great Cardinal of Spain, after the families of Guipuzcoa had been forbidden to marry converts and the converts had been forbidden to go and live in Guipuzcoa:

"Your Lordship no doubt knows the new statute made in Guipuzcoa, in which it was ordained that we should not go there to marry or to dwell. . . . Isn't it ridiculous that all, or many of them send their sons

---

[135] Strictly speaking, from the second generation on down the converts were not Jews; one would have to make a special human category for them determined by their not wanting to be Jews and exceeding the Old Christians in their orthodoxy.

[136] "Claros varones," in the series *Clásicos castellanos*, p. 119. A historian of the Dominican Order, Fray Hernando del Castillo, denied Pulgar's veracity in 1612 (*Historia de Santo Domingo y de su orden*, p. 572); but Pulgar knew his illustrious contemporaries for what they were, while Fray Hernando was only trying to add luster to his order and remove the stain of "infamy" that had fallen upon the famous cardinal.

here to serve us, and many of them as running footmen, and at the same time, they do not wish to be relatives by marriage of those who wish to be servants. . . . *These people [the Jews] are now paying for the prohibition that Moses made to his people, that they should not marry gentiles.*"[187]

Pulgar, secretary to the Catholic queen, historian of the acts of the king and queen, and at the same time fond of solitude, lived the drama of the social change in Spain in all its amplitude. With an accurate eye he was able to perceive the meaning of the events taking place around him, and we must now try, insofar as possible, to see things as he saw them. With a free spirit he told the Cardinal, a great aristocrat far removed from any sort of plebeian suspicion, that the exclusivism of his contemporaries, their concern over purity of blood, was a reply to that other hermeticism of Pulgar's own ancestors. The historical reality becomes intelligible to us only when seen to be possessed of both extremes: the exclusivism of Catholic Spain was a reply to the hermeticism of the *aljamas*.[138]

If the purity of blood was the answer of a society animated by anti-Jewish fury to the racial hermeticism of the Jew, the inclusion of all life within the religious framework and the violent rejection of any kind of study or doctrine that would endanger the supremacy of theology was in turn an exacerbated synthesis of the religious exclusivism of the three beliefs in which Spanish life had consisted for centuries. There are explicit antecedents of all this among the Jews. In 1305 the Jewish community of Barcelona manifested its opposition to having men younger than twenty-five study the works of the Greeks in natural science or metaphysics, to prevent the alienation of their hearts from the law of Israel.[139] The Jews of Provence, devoted to the tradition of Maimonides, berated the Barcelonans for narrow-mindedness—those of Provence "had always been distinguished from their brothers in Spain and France because of their interest in philosophy and scientific enterprises." In the disputes over what was permissible and what was pernicious material for study the narrow and suspicious spirit of the future Spanish Inquisition was already evident, a narrowness which the Jew had broken out of during the period of the great Moslem splendor, but which was very

[187] "Letras," in *Clásicos castellanos*, pp. 149-150.

[138] We have already seen how the belief in Santiago was magnified to oppose the faith in Mohammed. This does not mean that the belief in Santiago was Islamic or that the Inquisitorial reaction was Jewish, even though we cannot explain these phenomena without keeping in mind the situation of the Moors and the Jews.

[139] A. A. Neuman, *The Jews in Spain*, II, 131-140.

consistent with his belief that he belonged to God's chosen people. The Spain of the Catholic sovereigns and Charles V must have inherited this theomania in addition to the similar and no less intense feeling of the Moslem. In the famous action against Luis de Leon, who was summoned before the Inquisition for his effort to translate the Bible by combining faith with common sense, one might say that the enraged polemics between the Spanish and Provençal Jews, or the polemics carried on among Moslems over the interpretation of the Koran, were being revived.

We begin to understand how the strange and peculiar institution of the Spanish Inquisition was possible, a development that is incomprehensible if we limit ourselves to saying that it was instituted with the object of protecting the purity of the Catholic faith in Spain. Nothing new had happened in the field of Spanish theology, nor was anyone trying to found a new religion in the fifteenth century, nor to bring down the pillars of the existing one. Those who were burned in Europe (John Hus, Etienne Dolet, Miguel Servet, Giordano Bruno, etc.) expressed ideas ostensibly adverse to the doctrine of Rome. Those who were hanged and then burned as Jews by the Spanish Inquisition died because they practiced their forbears' religion, no longer tolerated by those sentinels of religious behavior, people given to gossip and talebearing, and oozing with hatred and covetousness. The peculiar innovation of the Inquisition lay in the subtle perversity of its ways, in its mysterious technique of inquiry, in basing its judgments on the word of informers and gossips, and in the way it combined the plundering of its victims with a pretended zeal for the purity of religious belief. There were no religious conflicts in Spain. She was the home of theological wisdom, not of new doctrines, whether organized in orthodox or heretical fashion. Spanish beliefs were what the wash of centuries had been accumulating in souls dyed with Christianity, Islamism, and Judaism— the thaumaturgic luxury of the saints, and the messianism and fatalism of the masses. Behind the Inquisition lay no doctrinal plan of any kind; only the shriek of popular hatred, which had as its explosive agent the poisoned souls of a number of converts, despised by the Jews and the Old Christians alike.

We must follow the trail of the Inquisitorial ways back into the obscurity of the Castilian and Aragonese ghettos, if we wish to learn anything of their origin. According to one Jewish scholar, the people who informed on the Jews in Catalonia at the end of the fourteenth century "were not ordinarily Christians, but those newly converted to Christianity, desirous of displaying their neophytes' zeal or satisfying ancient grudges."[140] The most dangerous inhabitant of the ghetto was the *malsín*, or slanderer, the twin of that sinister character, the *wāshī* or tale-bearer, who burrowed around in both Moslem and Christian courts. So dangerous and widespread was the type of the *malsín* that that Hebrew word came into everyday Spanish,[141] along with its derivative, the verb *malsinar*, as a testimony that in this matter there were no barriers between the ghetto and the Christian population. The *malsín* denounced his coreligionists to the Christian authorities. The latter treated the victim without mercy, with a view to extorting the largest possible amount of money from him, and this in turn explains the concern of the Christian laws for the purity of the Mosaic religion (as stated before) and the observance of its precepts. Informing brought the *malsín* a reward in money or the pleasure of revenge. The Jewish authorities pursued him with all possible vigor, while the officials of the king sought to benefit from the *malsín* and his victim as well, since the one man's property was booty just as desirable as the other's. "The poisoned tongue or pen was recognized as a national problem at the conference of *aljama* representatives in 1354."[142]

The trials in the Jewish courts that originated as a consequence of the slanderous reporting of informers were carried out without the normal

---

[140] Jean Régné, in the *Revue des Etudes Juives*, 1906, LII, 227.

[141] In the sense of "one who secretly informs the authorities about criminals, maliciously and out of self-interest" (Covarrubias, *Tesoro de la lengua castellana*, 1611). The word was frequent in the seventeenth century.

[142] A. A. Neuman, *The Jews in Spain*, I, 128-132. Here is an extraordinary example of how the royal officials and those of the *aljamas* were involved with one another: Don Juzaf Pichón, "a man honored among the Jews, had been King Henry [II]'s chief accountant, and some of the more important Jews of the *aljamas* who were about the court disliked him, and in the time of King Henry they accused him, and caused him to be seized . . . ; and afterwards he was released, and he accused the other Jews." During the festivities celebrating the coronation of John I (1379), certain Jews (Don Zulema and Don Zag) of the king's *aljamas* asked King John for letters patent authorizing the city governor to give the death penalty to a Jewish *malsín* whom they would designate, "for, they said, they were bound by custom to kill any Jew who acted as a *malsín*." They then went to the house of Don Juzaf Pichón and beheaded him. When the king perceived the Jews' trick "he was astonished and annoyed," because Don Juzaf Pichón had been "an official in the household of his father the king and had served him." The result of this was that John executed the Jews who figured in this play of mutual slander, a drama characteristic of life in the *aljama* with their dense, indeed choking, atmosphere of passion. "From that day forward the king commanded that the Jews should not have the power of blood justice over any Jew, as they had had up to that time, executing this power according to their laws and ordinances; and thus it was done" ("Crónica del rey don Juan I," in the *Biblioteca de Autores Españoles*, LXVIII, 66).

guarantees of due process of law, in secret, and without giving the accused an opportunity to confront those who had informed on him. "There are even to be found occasional traces of inquisitorial proceedings and the use of torture to secure confessions."[143]

In view of this, it is permissible and reasonable to suspect that the new and strange procedures of the Spanish Inquisition were a survival of procedures customary in the *aljamas*, and that the vehicle for such an adaptation is to be found in the numerous Jews who in the fifteenth century became bishops, monks, and even members of the Supreme Council of the Inquisition. Some of them wrote positively inhumane books against the people of their own race, as we shall see.

There is no better person than the Jesuit historian Juan de Mariana to confirm the impression that the Holy Office as it began operations in 1480, with its secrets and its *malsines*, was an unheard-of novelty—and at the same time "a heaven-sent remedy," according to Mariana. "*What was especially surprising to the people* was that the children paid for the crimes of their fathers; that the accuser was not known or indicated, nor confronted with the criminal, nor were the lists of witnesses made public, *entirely contrary to the ancient custom in the other courts*. Besides, it was thought to be a new thing that such sins should be punished with the death penalty. And the gravest thing of all was that through those secret inquiries people were deprived of the liberty of listening and talking to one another, for there were in the cities, towns, and villages *special persons* [here the *malsines* come in] to give warning of what was happening, a practice which some regarded as like *a servitude most onerous and on a par with death*." Although Mariana recalled that the Inquisition had existed before in other countries, he recognized that the Inquisitorial procedure in Spain was an innovation in the Church because "at times the ancient customs of the Church *are changed* in accordance with what the times require."[144] The establishment of the Holy Office meant for Spain the loss of her ancient customs, and the entrance upon a new regimen, "a servitude most onerous and on a par with death."

[143] A. A. Neuman, *The Jews in Spain*, I, 135, 145. Toward the end of the fourteenth century the *aljama* of Tudela named a commission of twenty members to punish the transgressors of their religious law (Baer, I, 983; J. Yanguas, *Adiciones al Diccionario de Navarra*, 1843, p. 166). No doubt there were other such cases.

[144] *Historia de España*, XXIV, 17. The peculiarity of the Spanish, as distinguished from the medieval, Inquisition is a well-known matter. "The Spanish Inquisition . . . is even more noted in history for its ingenious devices and severity in disciplining heretics than the papal tribunal established in 1215" (J. Hastings, *Encyclopedia of Religion and Ethics*, the article "Discipline," Vol. IV, 718b).

The methods of the new tribunal were as new and unheard-of in civil as in ecclesiastical courts; wherefore the astonishment that is so well reflected in the terse language of the Jesuit. The spirit of the ghetto, new and strange, spoke through the priests of Jewish extraction who managed the Inquisition.[145]

United in that enterprise were the age-old, amorphous hatred of the "little people" and the venomous and articulate passion of certain Jewish theologians, converted to Christianity to the detriment of Jews, of Christian spirituality, and of the Spanish people. Out of the nameless, formless mass burst the blind violence which at the end of the fourteenth century began to scourge the ghettos. Certain religious orders with a popular coloring and a broad base in the peasantry—and at the same time well populated with resentful converts—supplied the program for the attack through arguments which they shouted from their position of prestige in the pulpits, and which by and by must have had incalculable consequences. It was not enough for the kings to try to control the misguided wrath of those who were deprived of profitable jobs.[146] Their most compelling urge was to get their hands on the wealth created by the people they hated. Moreover, it would have been difficult indeed for the great lords to impose prudence upon their commoners, when they themselves had no other mission in life save to "live themselves up," exercising their valor and enjoying themselves in the spectacle of their own distinction. Before the Catholic king discovered a way to utilize the impatience of his knights for unrestrained combat, the restlessness of these men was leading them to destroy their own land.[147] In the mean-

---

[145] Juan de Mariana lived under the suspicion, groundless, perhaps, of belonging to a family of converts. Gracián alludes to it maliciously in El criticón (ii, iv).

[146] In Burgos "the lower classes of the people in the city went to such extremes in 1391 that in a few weeks the district of the ghetto was almost deserted. This was not prevented by the royal letter of 16 July 1391 demanding maximum respect for the persons and property of the Jews" (Luciano Serrano, Los conversos don Pablo de Santa María y don Alfonso de Cartagena, 1942, p. 27).

[147] Hernando del Pulgar describes Castile with bitter and surgical precision as he saw it in 1473: "The Duke of Medina together with the Marquis of Cadiz, and the Count of Cabra together with Don Alonso de Aguilar, have charge of destroying all the land of Andalusia, and call upon the Moors when any of them is hard-pressed. . . . The one who calls himself a grand master of Alcántara has charge of destroying the province of Leon. . . . This our kingdom of Toledo is in charge of Pedrarias, Marshal Fernando. . . . The constable and the Count of Triviño with the knights from the northern mountains are doing their best to lay waste the whole land [of Galicia] as far as Fuenterrabía. . . . There is no more Castile. If there were, there would be more wars" ("Letras," in Clásicos castellanos, Vol. 99, p. 127).

time tumultuous crowds, a rabble of low people, spurred on in fury by the sermons of certain monks,[148] fed on the spoils of the rich ghettos.

At such an anxious juncture, the life of many Jews was bound to assume strange and desperate attitudes. Since the end of the fourteenth century, kings and lords had not been able to protect them the way they wanted to, and the crown took a far less than firm line during the fifteenth century. Catherine of Lancaster, the queen of English origin who ruled Castile during the minority of John II, tried with one blow to destroy the free association of Christians and Jews with her decree of 1412, which I suppose to have been edited by a convert filled with heinous rancor. The constable Don Álvaro de Luna inspired the one of 1443, more humane and reasonable, in which Christians were permitted to work for Jews at the same time that such work was characterized as unworthy, with the object of winning popular tolerance.[149] Don Alvaro's protection of Jews and converts contributed greatly to his disastrous end.[150]

If the kings and the nobility at times were able to contain the violence of the mob against the Jews, no one, on the other hand, could restrain the theological fury of certain illustrious converts against their erstwhile

[148] Father José de Sigüenza describes the religious situation in Castile in 1461 through highly intentional irony and insinuation (the aristocratic Hieronymites, to which he belonged, did not hold the Franciscans in great esteem): "The fathers of the Order of Saint Francis, *being zealous in matters of faith,* took the side of the Old Christians; and as we shall presently see, *condemned the poor Jews without mercy,* putting easy credence in the *common people, who, without judgment or restraint,* attacked the Jews by word and deed in every way that an angry mob can dream of and with all the daring that such mass passion can beget. Preaching before the king [Henry IV], a certain Franciscan said that he had in his possession a hundred foreskins of circumcised Christians." This denunciation, made in the spirit of the *malsín,* was proved false, but, continues Sigüenza, "this father and the other in his order, acting as public prosecutors and showing much zeal for the faith, *provoked the wrath of the people against the poor Jews*" ("Historia de la orden de San Jerónimo," in the *Nueva Biblioteca de Autores Españoles,* i, 366-367. The first edition is of 1600.).

[149] "In such servile jobs and trades there is no dignity, nor thereby does one have or acquire positions of honor" (see J. Amador de los Ríos, *Historia de los judíos,* iii, 586).

[150] Don Alvaro was so suspicious of the converts that he even distrusted Alvaro de Cartagena, who risked his life to save Don Alvaro. This is how Don Alvaro spoke to his close friends: "You know how this Alvaro de Cartagena is from a family of converts, and you also know how much this family dislikes me, although I have done more for them than any other man in this kingdom has ever done in my time. And besides, this Alvaro de Cartagena is a nephew of the Bishop of Burgos [a convert], who in this matter is the greatest opponent I have, and I think that this nephew of his has come here more as a spy than anything else" (*Crónica de don Álvaro de Luna,* edition of Carriazo, p. 381).

brothers in faith. It seems incredible, but most severe blows against the Jews came from their own baptized rabbis. Terror and desperation played a part in such changes of front, but so did that terrible passion for preeminence that we have found reflected in the words of Rabbi Arragel. In the thirteenth and fourteenth century the Jew had dreamed of the possibility of dominating Castile, the new promised land. He had in his hands the promotion and administration of the wealth of the kingdom as well as the technical and scientific knowledge possible at that time. Like almost all the phenomena of Spanish life, his Judaism also knew no bounds or discretion, and thus it was finally dashed down from the greatest splendor to miserable disaster. After 1391 the Jewish flock dispersed like an army in defeat. There were those who continued to resist with heroism or resignation till the moment of expulsion. Others accepted baptism, and their children were no doubt like any other Christian children. A number of them lived with one foot in the synagogue and the other in the church, as circumstances might require. Finally, a small group made up of intelligent and learned men sacrificed everything to the passion for preeminence and for feeling securely established on the highest levels of society.

The first figure in the group was Salomon Halevi, born in Burgos and the chief rabbi of that city. He, his sons, and his brothers embraced Christianity in 1390, and from then on Salomon was Don Pablo de Santa María. From him stem all the theologians, jurists, and historians named Santa María, whose works fill fifteenth-century letters with distinction. Don Pablo received the degree of doctor of theology in Paris; in 1396 he was already a canon of the Cathedral of Burgos, and from then on, honors and distinctions rained upon him: chief chaplain to Henry III, papal nuncio of Benedict XIII in the court of Castile, tutor and chancellor to John II (whose decree of 1412 against the Jews he, perhaps, inspired and edited), and finally Bishop of Burgos. His evident intelligence and great learning made it possible for him to pass in a few years from the position of chief rabbi to that of bishop in the same city, an inconceivable phenomenon outside of Spain.[151] Up to this point Don

---

[151] This is by no means the first case of a converted Jew who occupied a high ecclesiastical position. "Maestro Andrés," a canon of Palencia in 1225, was a convert, as is evident from the bull of Honorius III addressed to him at the instance of the Bishop of Palencia. The pope was cognizant that the new canon had not only mastered the seven Liberal Arts, but also knew Hebrew, Chaldean, Arabic, and Latin, and declared him worthy of ecclesiastical benefices and dignities "preterquam ad episcopatum"—up to, but excluding, the episcopate. (C. H. Haskins, "Michael Scot in Spain," in *Estudios in memoriam de Adolfo Bonilla*, 1930, II, 133.) The

Pablo's life is above reproach—Paul, a second Saul of Tarsus—for as the converts of the fifteenth century so frequently said, Christianity began with Jesus Christ, a divine convert, and Jewish converts were his apostles. But if the conversion of Salomon Halevi is respectable in principle, the attitude that he assumed toward the Jews of Spain was of the purest villainy, no matter how easily it is to be explained within the complex movement of Spanish history. In his *Scrutinium Scripturarum*, written in his old age, this bishop of Burgos said that the Spanish Jews "by diabolical persuasion, . . . had risen to high stations in the royal palaces and the palaces of the grandees," and that through terror they had brought the Christians to submission, shamelessly endangering the latter's souls; that they were ruling Castile as they pleased, and that they regarded the kingdom as their own. Don Pablo praises the massacres of 1391, and thinks that the mobs were stirred up by God to avenge the blood of Christ (Deo ultionem sanguinis Christi excitante). The Ferrán Martínez who incited the populace of Seville was for the "Christian" bishop of Burgos "an unlettered man of praiseworthy life." See besides Mantua edition, 1474, ff. 243-244 (New York Public Library).[152]

The rabbi-bishop was conjuring up, as he wrote, the ghosts of his own life—shouting down the voice of his conscience. Don Pablo, as a convert, could easily rise to high station in the palace of the king and rule the kingdom of Castile as he pleased. His ancestors had done so as rabbis and *alfaquís*; he could no longer do the same thing save by abjuring his faith. In Don Pablo is sketched the sinister figure of the inquisitor of his own people.[153]

---

inference is that in 1225 a converted Jew encountered obstacles in the way of ecclesiastical preferment, which the pope had to remove, although he denied the convert access to the episcopate.

[152] See J. Amador de los Ríos, *Historia de los judíos*, III, 38-43.

[153] Fernán Pérez de Guzmán sketched a moral portrait of Don Pablo de Santa María in his *Generaciones y semblanzas*, with his usual elegance and precision: "Don Pablo, Bishop of Burgos, was a very wise man and an accomplished man in science; he was a native of Burgos, and he was a Jew, from a great family of that people. . . . He had an important position with King Henry III . . . , and no doubt it was with very good reason that he was loved by every prudent king or prince, for he was a man of good counsel, great discretion, and great confidence, which are virtues to make the man worthy of any prudent king's confidence." These were the traditional virtues of the Jews in their intercourse with the grandees, and it is thanks to these virtues that the Jews enjoyed royal and noble favor for centuries. Pérez de Guzmán censures those who say that all the converts are bad, arguing *ad hominem* from the example of Don Pablo and his family. He says that he has known good converts "like the bishop and his honorable son Don Alfonso, Bishop of Burgos, who composed writings of great usefulness to our faith. And if some say that they write these works

If the illustrious converts had kept their new beliefs for themselves, or had lived like some whom Pérez de Guzmán knew—"good monks who, of their own free will, are spending a hard, austere life in the orders"—then they would have done no harm at all. The harm comes from their sense of the urge to justify themselves by blotting out every trace and recollection of their Judaism. Among such abject characters the rabbi and, later, Franciscan, Master Alonso de Espina, stands out. One time when King Henry IV was in Madrid, resting from his labors, "Master de Espina came there with Fray Fernando de la Plaza and other monks of the observance of Saint Francis, to notify the king that there was a great heresy in his kingdom on the part of certain people who were practicing Judaism, keeping the Judaic rites, and, under the name of Christians, circumcising their sons; begging him *to have an inquisition made* about the matter so that they would be punished. On this theme some sermons were preached, and especially by Fray Fernando de la Plaza, who said that he had the foreskins of some sons of Christian converts. . . . The king had them called, and told them that the matter of the circumcised sons was a grave insult to the Catholic faith, and that it was his duty to punish it, and that they should therefore bring the foreskins and the names of those who had done the thing. . . . Fray Fernando answered that persons in authority had taken charge of the matter. The king demanded that he say who the persons were. He refused to say, so that it was found to be a lie. Then came Fray Alonso de Oropesa,[154] prior general of the Order of Saint Jerome, with some priors of his order, and he opposed the others, preaching before the king, so that the Franciscans were left somewhat confounded."[155]

Fray Alonso de Espina is the author of the *Fortalitium fidei*, which he completed in 1458 and which went through numerous editions in the fifteenth century and later (1485, 1494, 1511, 1525). It contains passages such as the following: "I think that if *a true inquisition* were made in this our time, innumerable persons found to be actually practicing Judaism would be sent to the flames. These people, if they are not punished in this world, will be burned in the eternal fires of hell more

___

out of fear of the kings and prelates, or because they want to appear more gracious in the eyes of the princes and prelates and *stand better with them,* I answer that unfortunately the law and the faith are not kept today with the rigor and zeal that would justify this fear and this hope" (edition of the *Clásicos castellanos,* pp. 94-95).

[154] Also from a family of converted Jews, but a better Christian than the others.

[155] "Crónica del rey Enrique IV," by his chaplain and chronicler Diego Enríquez del Castillo, *Biblioteca de Autores Españoles,* LXX, 130.

cruelly than those who publicly admit that they are Jews."[156] Fray
Alonso eventually became rector of the University of Salamanca, and
he spent most of his time writing and preaching against the Hebrew
people. By adding more and more fuel to the flames of popular wrath
and by hammering on the ears of the kings,[157] as the Jewish slanderers
had done in the *aljamas*, Fray Alonso and other ex-Jews succeeded in
establishing the Supreme Council of the Inquisition, and Fray Alonso,
his zeal triumphant, was thus able to enjoy his old age as a member of
the Supreme Council he had helped to create.

We have very imperfect knowledge of the activities of the deserters
from Israel prior to the Inquisition, although it is easy to imagine the
atmosphere of the Franciscan and Dominican monasteries in the fifteenth
century. In another work I have already analyzed the arguments for
and against converts in the Order of Saint Jerome. From what we know,
the conclusion emerges that the Inquisition had been in the making
since the beginning of the fifteenth century. The ferment of hatred had
been well prepared by a number of people, among them Don Pablo de
Santa María and his contemporary Josue Lurqui (that is, of Lorca, in
Murcia), another learned rabbi, who, upon conversion, took the name
of Jerónimo de Santa Fe. Like Don Pablo, he was a great friend of
Benedict XIII—the Anti-Pope Luna—who organized the Conference
of Tortosa in 1413, a conference in which Christianity and Judaism came
face to face. It was attended by fourteen rabbis, and ironically enough,
it is nonetheless true that the church spoke through the voice of Jerónimo
de Santa Fe, who, Talmud in hand, proceeded to destroy all the doctrines of the Hebrews. Of the fourteen rabbis, only two, Rabbi Ferrer
and Rabbi Joseph Albo, gave dignified resistance to the demolishing
argumentation of their ex-colleague. Twelve became Christians, thus
augmenting the great host of future inquisitors. The victims of the terror
found relief in terrorizing others, as now happens in certain totalitarian

---

[156] *Fortalitium fidei*, Lyons, 1511, ccxxxvir. In the *Noticia de los escritores
rabinos españoles* (*Biblioteca Española*, Madrid, 1781, p. 354), J. Rodríguez de
Castro says: "Fray Alonso de Espina, a friar of the Franciscan Order, a most learned
fellow, rector of the University of Salamanca, and officer of the supreme tribunal of
the Inquisition, was, before his conversion, the wisest or one of the most learned
Jews of his time."

[157] Espina lamented the fact that the Jews in Castile were not treated as a captive
people, as they were in France and England: "in hoc ergo regno judeorum non
gravatur captivitas, cum ipsi terrae pinguedinem edant et bona: non laborant terram,
nec eam defendunt. . . . In regno isto aliqui ipsorum nimis valent cum regibus, et ea
quae ad reges pertinent, pertractant; et talibus se immiscent quod habent sub jugo et
dominio christianos," etc. (*ibid.*, ccxxxiir).

countries. Jerónimo de Santa Fe ended his mission by writing the notorious work *Hebraeomastix* (The Scourge of the Hebrews), of which Amador de los Ríos says: "The things gathered together in this book could only have been imagined and written down in obedience to an intention of extermination."[158]

The absurd form of Spanish life during the Middle Ages was beginning to yield fruits of absurdity. To the common people, brave in battle and inept for technical work, the Jew was an octopus who lived by what his tentacles could suck out of them, and at the same time that he was freeing the great lords from the cares their position imposed upon them. Very few of the grandees were aware of their responsibility. This is brought into sharp relief by an act which, if it had been imitated with sufficient frequency, would have altered the course of Spanish history:

The family of the Counts of Haro was covered with well-deserved prestige in the fifteenth century. One, Don Pedro Fernández de Velasco, "since there were many Jews in some of his villages, and since it seemed to him that usury was causing poverty, ordered that no one should dare to lend money, under grave penalty. And after this had lasted for some time, his vassals complained to him, saying that they were being harmed much more by not being able to borrow money either at usurious rates or any other way, since, not finding any, they found it necessary to sell their cattle and wool and wheat and other things too soon. And therefore they begged him to allow usury. The count, wishing to remedy this situation, ordered three chests to be set out, one in Medina de Pomar, and one in Herrera, and one in Villadiego, putting in each one of them two hundred thousand *maravedís* and in the barns of each of these villages, two thousand fanegas of wheat; and he ordered the keys given to four aldermen . . . , instructing them that any vassal of his, needing money or wheat up to a certain amount, should, if he would leave a pawn or pledge, receive it on loan for a year. By this means he so protected the citizens of those villages that all lived free from need. This was surely done by a very Catholic and prudent man, very worthy of memory."[159]

In 1471, then, the Count de Haro simply founded the first farm-credit bank in Spain, thus making Jewish money-lending as unnecessary for the peasants in the towns of his domain as it was for the lords. In

---

[158] *Historia de los judíos*, Buenos Aires edition, II, 74. See also the same author's *Estudios sobre los judíos*, Buenos Aires, 1942, pp. 334ff.

[159] Mosén Diego de Valera, *Memorial de diversas hazañas*, Chap. LXII (Carriazo edition, p. 190).

institutions like this lay the possibility of normalizing the public economy, and of making of the Jews useful and not indispensable elements of society. But the Count of Haro's bank remained an isolated instance of an intelligent solution to the problem,[160] a testimonial to the virtues of the nobility in the fifteenth century, perhaps the only epoch, as I have said, in which the nobility of Castile showed any sense of the obligation inherent in their position.

Other stimuli unfortunately dominated in the long run. The simple folk of the fields and villages, lacking initiative or direction, fell upon the Jew, who was much their superior in social effectiveness. Terrified, the Jews changed religions to save their lives and their fortunes, but they went on doing the same things as before. They were favorites, physicians, and ambassadors of the kings; administrators of rents and finances; bishops and cardinals—just as they had once been rabbis. Two of the bishops of Burgos, the bishop of Coria, the cardinal of Saint Sixtus, and many others were converts. They were in the cathedral chapters as well as in the monasteries and nunneries. In the meantime, the Old Christians and the "New Christians" were coming to blows in Andalusia and elsewhere. The great aristocrat Don Alonso de Aguilar tried to control the violence against the converts in Cordova, just as, in 1391, the son of the King of Aragon had tried in vain to make the mobs that attacked the ghetto of Valencia respect him. But in Cordova, "shameless and without regard for Don Alonso, the plundering began, and a great riot took place there, and many of the townspeople threw stones at Don Alonso, so that he had to withdraw to the castle."[161] A little later, in 1473, the constable Miguel Lucas de Iranzo was assassinated in Jaén because he favored the converts. Among the converts, some, under the protection of their new faith, attacked the Jews, whether they were converts or not, impelled, as we have seen, by their fear and their ambition. The Jews, for their part, denounced the converts by way of reprisal, and Spain was choking in an atmosphere of espionage and counterespionage. Yet along with the poisons, chiefly the sinister Inquisition with its sinister innovations, that seeped into Spanish life, Spanish Christendom, in

---

[160] The Count of Haro's example was later followed by the Count of Ureña, who established a granary in Jaén in 1494. Cardinal Ximénez de Cisneros helped in the establishment of another in Alcalá de Henares in 1513 (E. Ibarra, *El problema cerealista en España*, 1944, pp. 57-58). But when this happened the Jews had already been expelled, and, besides, such impulses were isolated instances that could have no effect on the Spanish economy in general.

[161] Mosén Diego de Valera, *Memorial de diversas hazañas*, Chap. LXXXIII, ed.cit., p. 242. Valera was a convert.

the increment of forced converts, acquired the precious forbears of a Fernando de Rojas, a Luis Vives, a Saint Teresa, a Fray Luis de León, and many others, whose works would be inconceivable outside that zone of agony in which they did appear. As in so many other cases, the historians have spent all their time justifying or denouncing the Inquisition when they should have started out by wondering how such a monstrous and unusual enormity came to be possible. Three and a half centuries of Inquisition have made people believe that the Holy Office was a natural secretion of the Spaniard because he was a fanatic, just as, in Molière's comedy, opium put people to sleep "quia habet virtutem dormitivam." But in Mariana's own words, the unprepared Spaniard was struck by it as "a most onerous servitude and on a par with death." Hernando del Pulgar, who was in the confidence of the Catholic sovereigns, says, in one of his letters printed in 1486 and apropos of the outrages committed by the people of Fuensalida: "Since those citizens [of the province of Toledo] are great Inquisitors of the faith, behold what heresies they have found in the properties of the peasants of Fuensalida, which they robbed completely *usque ad ultimum*" (letter xxv).

Spain took many years to get used to breathing the rarefied air that was the legacy of the Judaic tradition; at the end of the sixteenth century she was still protesting against Inquisitorial barbarism. A traditional religious weapon of the Jewish authorities was the *ḥerem* or excommunication, which had been used in the ghettos for centuries with a breadth and intensity unknown in the rather lax society of the Castilian Christians. "Under biblical law, an Israelite having knowledge that might benefit his fellow is morally and religiously obligated to appear as witness," and when such witnesses were either unknown or unwilling, the publicly proclaimed ban of the *ḥerem* proved useful, as Neuman says,[162] "in leading them to appear in court. This method of securing testimony was especially effective in tracing slanderous rumors to their source and thus exonerating the wronged party." Infractions of moral or religious law were rigorously persecuted by the *Bet Din* (literally "house of the law," court) in accordance with the precept, "And ye shall remove the wicked from your midst." "Frivolous violations of private oaths were punished by flagellation," for there was no boundary between sin and crime. Excommunication, which included those guilty by association, fell, for example, upon embezzlers of public funds, a part of the penalty being in such cases that no one could speak to the excommunicated person

---

[162] A. A. Neuman, *The Jews in Spain*, I, 122-125.

or help him in any way, so that he was isolated as if he had the plague. The intermingling of religious and civil life, characteristic of the *aljamas*, was to pass over into the Christian society of the sixteenth and seventeenth centuries, and Spanish Catholicism of this later period, narrow and stifling, was to be as different from its European counterpart as from Medieval Spanish Catholicism itself. We can now perceive the remote origin of Quevedo's bitter jokes in the *Buscón*, as when Pablos threatens to denounce a woman to the Inquisition because she has called her chickens by saying "pío, pío," when Pío (Pius) is the name of popes: "I cannot fail to inform the Inquisition, for if I don't, I shall be excommunicated." The ex-rabbis who in the fifteenth century laid out the plan of organization for the Holy Office, conceived it as a *Bet Din*, full of cruel and subtle tricks, of denunciations by informers, of secrecy. The habit of mutual plundering that prevailed in the relations between Christians and Jews for several centuries, found a natural outlet in the Inquisition—*Bet Din*. Plundering "usque ad ultimum," as Hernando del Pulgar had described it, and as always has been the practice of unrestrained, totalitarian powers everywhere.[163]

Some Additional Facts about Aragon and Portugal

Although my history is based on evidence from life rather than on masses of data, it is perhaps advisable to supplement what I have said with evidence collected from certain documents. The Judeo-Christian contexture presents in Aragon the same appearance as in Castile. Instances of intransigence in Saragossa "were limited to a single episode, according to M. Serrano y Sanz, so that there is nothing strange about the fact that the respect and tolerance that generally prevailed between Christians and Jews should, in a certain way, result in a spiritual interpenetration. This is clear from the many words used by the Hebrews themselves: the members of a *cahal*, or synagogue, were called *parroquianos* (parishioners); the rabbi's assistants, *sacristanes* (sacristans); in the com-

---

[163] There are numerous documents referring to the *malsines* in Baer, 1 (see the references on p. 1,165). Here are a few examples: Peter IV of Aragon authorized the *aljama* of Mallorca to take action against the *malsines*: "cut off one or more of his members, or kill him . . . with or without trial, with or without witnesses, merely on the basis of suspicion (*sino solament ab indicis*) . . . according to any precedent sentence or gloss of one or more Jewish sages or scholars who have written or rendered decisions in such cases." If he is killed, the king must be given "seventy gold *reales* from the funds of the aljama" (Baer, 1, 538).

position of public documents the Jews did not oppose the use of the
date of the *Nativity of our Lord Jesus Christ*, and we rarely find dates
according to their own reckoning from the creation of the world; there
are scarcely any barriers between Jewish and Christian society; in many
instances, Jews are attorneys or administrators and even arbitrators in
friendly disagreements among Christians." In 1471 the Jews named a
Christian priest as arbitrator of one of their own disputes—Juan de
Viana, a cleric from the church of San Andrés. In 1414, to solemnize
an important contract, there was a meeting of the representatives of the
aljama of Saragossa "in the San Francisco monastery of that city, where
it has been the custom on various occasions to meet."[164]

The Christian's incapacity for carrying out tasks at which the Jews
excelled shows up once more in a license granted to the Jews to establish cloth shops freely in Saragossa (1390), considering that "the Jewish drapers, as is well known, are much better at selling cloth according
to its quality than the Christian drapers are" (Serrano y Sanz, *op.cit.*,
p. xxix).

The situation is the same if we move to Portugal, where in 1490 the
scene of 1367 in Castile was reenacted. The deputies wanted the Portuguese king (John II) to relieve the people "from subjection to the
Jews, who have great power over the Christians because they are tax-
farmers and collectors of our rents." The monarch gave the answer that
other Peninsular kings had been giving for centuries: there were no
Christians capable of performing such services.[165]

Pórtugal was more Judaized, if possible, than Castile and Aragon.
Saint Vincent Ferrer was not allowed to go there to preach against the
Jews, for the Portuguese tried to keep as far as they could from the
path followed by Castilian policies. No doubt there were other restrictive
laws like those of Dom Duarte (d. 1438) prohibiting the Jews from
auctioning off the tithes and offerings in the churches, as well as from
filling the role of administrators and major-domos in the households of

[164] M. Serrano y Sanz, "Orígenes de la dominación española en América," in the
Nueva Biblioteca de Autores Españoles, xxv, p. xxxii. Desiring to make known
Columbus's Aragonese friends and protectors, the author of this work has gathered
together valuable documents patiently dug up in the Crown Archives of Aragon, in
the Archives of Protocol in Saragossa, in the Archives of the Indies in Seville, etc.
As is generally known, the people who gave financial and moral support to Columbus
when everyone else refused him the means for carrying out his first voyage were
converted Jews. The rich mass of facts collected by Serrano y Sanz fits into my construction perfectly.

[165] J. Lucio d'Azevedo, *Historia dos christãos novos portugueses*, 1922, p. 18.

princes, bishops, abbots, and knights. But the Jews went on doing this in spite of the law, and, besides, they read the horoscopes of the kings at the moment of their coronation. The mass of the common people was not as overwhelming in Portugal as in Spain (the political structure was different, there were not so many important cities, etc.), although the Lisbon ghetto was sacked in 1449 as a consequence of the irritation caused by the influx of Jews from Castile. Alphonse V ordered many Christians executed. The punishment of "people of coarse and low condition" was stopped by the public outcry. A friar asked the king to give up his overseas conquests, and to suspend the economic aid he was receiving from the Jews, "for in the desire for greater profit, the Christian population finds itself subject to Jewish jurisdiction."[166]

But Jewish wealth and science were indispensable for the release of Christian Portugal's brilliant impulses to conquest and seigniory. Prince Henry, the precursor of maritime empire, called a Majorcan Jew to the School of Sagres, one Jaime Ferrer, "a man very learned in the art of navigation, a maker of maps and instruments . . . ," and he taught "his science to the Portuguese artisans engaged in that trade."[167] It was Master José and Master Rodrigo, Jewish physicians to John II, who composed the tables for the declination of the sun, so that one could navigate by the position of the sun, and therefore on the high seas and not just along the coast.[168] The same King John II sent the Jews Abraham of Beja and José Zapatero, of Lamego, to Asia. In Baghdad the latter heard of the wonderful port of Hormuz on the Persian gulf, which received the fabulous wealth of India. The Jews transmitted the geographic science of the Arabs to the Portuguese. The maps of the Majorcan Abraham Cresques, drawn between 1375 and 1385, show an extraordinary knowledge of southern Asia, and Nordenskiöld (*Periplos*) supposes them to be based on contemporary Arabic maps.[169] When the Portuguese reached the coast of Malabar, it was already an old story for Moorish and Jewish merchants from North Africa and Spain and Portugal to pay regular visits to the trade centers of the Orient: Aden, Hormuz, Calicut, and Malacca, the last being a destination for Spanish mercury.[170] Vasco de Gama was guided to Calicut from Melinde, as G.

[166] See J. Mendes dos Remedios, *Os judeus em Portugal*, 1895, pp. 210-239.

[167] Juan de Barros, *Decadas*, I, 1, 16 (quoted in Mendes dos Remedios, *op.cit.*, p. 250).

[168] R. Ribeiro dos Santos, *Memorias da Academia*, VIII, 166.

[169] See Gabriel Ferrand, *Introduction à l'astronomie nautique des Arabes*, Paris, 1928.

[170] See Gabriel Ferrand, *Mélanges René Basset*, I, 1923, pp. 202-208. Concerning

Ferrand has proved (*op.cit.*, 247), by the Arab pilot, Ibn Mājid.

Even when King Manuel, under the double pressure of his own populace and Ferdinand and Isabella of Spain, had taken the decision to expel the Portuguese Jews, he did all he could to invalidate his own decree, for he ordered that the conduct of the Jews should not be investigated for 21 years, which was the same as allowing them to practice their religion freely.[171] But in the long run, the situation in Portugal was no different from that in Castile, and the Inquisition fostered *malsinismo* and subjected the converts and their descendants to cruel and arbitrary pressures as the only means of keeping up the supply of money which it had to have for its operations. To obtain the funds to repay guiltless persons for property wrongly confiscated from them, it was necessary to prey upon other people of Jewish descent through the use of informants and with a total disregard of "friendship, gratitude, and honor. A vile instinct was transformed into the most eminent kind of virtue" (Lucio d'Azevedo, *op.cit.*, p. 90).[172]

The Inquisition has been too loosely and too frequently cited as the explanation of Spain's meager accomplishment as compared with the rest of Europe in science, political freedom based on reason, etc. It has not been seen that these inequalities proceed from circumstances prior to the Inquisition. The critical injury inflicted by that Holy Office is to be perceived rather in the blunting of morality and sensibility, in the insane perversion that drove many converts to pounce like silent hyenas upon their blood-brothers, first out of terror and in self-defense, and then as a matter of malignant custom—a perversion no longer aware of its origins and equally normal for ex-Jews and for Christians of venerable lineage. That furtive, sacred, and despotic policy brought security, honors, and economic well-being. All that was needed to carry it out was stupid persistence and a sadistic, stone-cold soul. Three centuries of the Holy Office greatly demoralized civil life in Spain and Portugal, but this has nothing to do with the Hispanians' capacity or incapacity for discovering, say, modern physics.

Indeed, this seems the proper point at which to make it clear that the Inquisition's dark lines stand out in history not so much because it prac-

_____

Castilian-speaking Jews in Malacca at the time of the arrival of the Portuguese, see Elaine Sanceau, *O sonho da India. Afonso de Albuquerque*, Porto, 1939, p. 223. Also, Jaime Cortesão, *Portugal na historia da humanidade*, pp. 56, 141-142.

[171] J. Lucio d'Azevedo, *op.cit.*, p. 57.

[172] See also Da Silva Bastos, *Historia da censura intelectual em Portugal*, pp. 368-369.

ticed religious persecution as because there were absent in the environment any new and productive ideas, any positively interesting activities. Perhaps the only interesting Spanish idea popular in Europa and which at the same time represented a positive value in the Spain of the declining seventeenth century was the quietism of Miguel de Molinos (in the *Guía espiritual*), admirable and important, but not pointing toward an Enlightenment. It was not Inquisitorial cruelty alone that put Spain in a difficult position with respect to Europe. Louis XIV in France was as barbarous and intolerant as the worst inquisitor.[173] It was by his order that the Huguenots were crushed and forced to flee to foreign lands to save their lives and the honor of their women. Hundreds of thousands of Frenchmen, no less industrious and intelligent than the Jews expelled by the Catholic Sovereigns, found refuge far from their homeland. Those taken in by Prussia gave a strong impetus to the cultural activities of that country, which at that time was not in the van of European civilization. But to impose Catholicism, Louis XIV's government forced the Protestant households to billet the most barbarous soldiers of the French Army (the so-called "Dragonnades"), who were left free to behave as they pleased in so far as violence, depredations, and the raping of women were concerned, until the families thus mistreated should accept the religion of a king as enlightened as he was inhuman. It is evident, nevertheless, that the revocation of the Edict of Nantes and the destruction of Port Royal (a center of rare intellectual and spiritual activity) have not sullied the glory of the "Grand Siècle." The explanation for this is that the same country that supported such outrages also produced the ideas and cultivated the sentiments that have made it possible to consider it monstrous barbarism for people to live in subjection to religious tyranny and arbitrary violence. Were this not the case, the French Revolution itself would today appear to us as a bloody and stupid chaos, and nothing more. History exists in a vital dialectic of things present and things absent, of positive and negative values.

But let us return to Spain. In Aragon the converts behaved as they did in the rest of the Peninsula. In 1417 the king reproached the Dominicans of Valencia for their excessive zeal in prodding the Jews to abandon the religion of their forefathers:

[173] Montesquieu confirms my idea when he puts the expulsion of the Jews by the Catholic Sovereigns and the expulsion of the Protestants by Louis XIV on the same level of barbarism: "On s'est mal trouvé en Espagne de les [i.e., the Jews] avoir chassés, et en France, d'avoir fatigué des chrétiens dont la croyance différait un peu de celle du Prince. On s'est aperçu que le zèle pour les progrès de la religion est différent de l'attachement qu'on doit avoir pour elle" (*Lettres persanes*, IX).

"We have learned that certain monks of your convent, following, it is said, *the suggestion of certain neophyte Christians of that city*, are saying things against the Jews of the *aljama* in the sermons they preach there. These things stir the people of that city to noisy rioting against the Jews. We are astonished that anyone dares to do such things, since it is known that the welfare and protection of the said *aljama* lies very near our heart." (Serrano y Sanz, *op.cit.*, p. xxxi)

The neophytes with the souls of inquisitors were two converts, Florente Vidal and Jaime Trigo, who had turned the Church of San Andrés into a center of anti-semitic propaganda.

The Caballería family, descended from Bonaffós de la Cavallería, figured in the Aragonese court during the entire fifteenth century, and also, of course, in the court of Ferdinand the Catholic. One of the family's most powerful members, *micer* Pedro de la Caballería, carried his audacity to the point of *forging an affidavit of purity of blood*, as was customary among Jews. Thus, all his progeny turned out to be "veri christiani veterani ac ex sanguine mundissimo, nullatenus judeorum aut maurorum labe infecto." Since this Don Pedro was one of Alphonse V's advisers and "maestre racional" (secretary of the treasury) of Aragon, the greatest lords of the nobility perjured themselves to please him. Not content with this, Pedro de la Caballería composed, in 1450, a *Tractatus Zeluz Christi contra Judaeos, Sarracenos et infideles*, which was printed in Venice in 1592. In the preface the author declares himself to be an expert in the Latin, Chaldaic, Arabic, and Hebrew languages, a fact which by itself places him among his true people, whom he insults and attacks viciously in the pages of this perverse tract.[174] And this work, like the others already mentioned, helps us to understand how it was possible for the Holy Office to be established. The part of Ferdinand the Catholic's court that had to do with finance and administration was composed largely of converts. Serrano y Sanz has made a documentary study of the more important ones among them: the families of Santángel, Sánchez, and Caballería. Some of the members of these families were persecuted by the Inquisition, among other reasons, for having tried to oppose the introduction of the sinister tribunal into Aragon, contrary to the privileges and freedoms of that kingdom. But is it not likely that someday, if a more complete documentation of the period can be found, a better knowledge of this same circle of high officials will help us to understand really how Ferdinand the Catholic passed almost without

[174] M. Serrano y Sanz, *op.cit.*, pp. cxc-cxci.

transition from a policy of tolerance to a policy of absolute aggressiveness? Were such abrupt changes not highly peculiar to the psychology of the converts? Wasn't Ferdinand the Catholic, after all, descended from converts through his mother?

The Presence of the Jew in Literature and Thought

Don Santob's New Poetic Style

THE MORAL PROVERBS, or *Counsels to King Peter*, by Don Santob, a Jew of Carrión de los Condes (Palencia),[1] are the first instance of authentic lyric expression in Castilian. Don Santob invaded the literary language of Castile with his Hebrew lyricism just as, a little earlier, the Archpriest of Hita had done with his poetry of Christian-Islamic inspiration. Whereas the Archpriest still needed the supporting matter of narrations, descriptions, or happenings through which to project his creative impulse, Don Santob presents us with a poetic reality as a primary thing expressing an objectified feeling independent of any kind of human event:

> When the rose dries up, its season over,
> The sweet-smelling, rose-infused water remains, the
>   best of it.[2]

Castilians had never before turned a rose into poetry for its own sake. Flowers are obliquely referred to in the *Razón de Amor*, not a Castilian work:

> Many other plants there were,
> But I didn't know their names.

[1] The Spanish title of the work is *Proverbios morales*, or *Consejos al rey Don Pedro*. Fritz Baer says the author's name was Shem Ṭob ben Isḥaq ibn Ardutiel. He was highly praised by the poet Shemuel ben Yosef Sason. In 1345 he wrote a *Disputa entre el cálamo y las tijeras* (Dispute Between the Pen and the Scissors) and two sacred poems in Hebrew, which, unfortunately, are not translated into any occidental language. For bibliography, see J. M. Millás Vallicrosa, *La poesía sagrada hebraico-española*, 1940, p. 150; and S. M. Stern, in *Romance Philology*, 1951, v, 242-247.

[2] In Spanish:
> Cuando es seca la rosa, que ya su sazón sale,
> queda el agua olorosa, rosada, que más vale.

See Santob de Carrión, *Proverbios morales*, edited by Ignacio Gonzáles Llubera, Cambridge University Press, 1947, ll. 9-10. Since the autograph is not preserved and since the existing fifteenth-century copies differ a great deal, I choose the readings with the greatest poetic value.

Or they appear in Berceo as an elemental physical phenomenon devoid of human accent:

> The sweet-scented flowers gave off a splendid odor.[3]

Santob's rose lives even while it dies, thanks to the migratory, gliding essence with which it has been endowed by an oriental imagination. Our melancholy sympathy follows it in its extinction, although, happily, its not-being is a greater value than its being, and it is immediately reborn as an invisible fragrance. Its visible aspect has vanished into odor—a miniature drama of death and resurrection. Thus, it was a Jew who first translated into lovely Castilian words a poetic experience that involved no external happening. The existence of his rose is confined in a tiny, beautiful *hortus conclusus* where feeling, which gives it reality, and the expression of the poet's experience mingle together. There is no other interacting element. We are at the gateway to Spanish lyric poetry, just as we earlier apprehended the Hispano-Hebrews in the very act of forcing the premature growth of scientific prose in the middle of the thirteenth century. The Hispano-Hebrew poets were to be to the literary court of King John II, in the fifteenth century, what the astronomers and moralists were to the court of Alphonse X.

Hispano-Hebrew poetry was inseparable from the Moslem tradition so far as themes and style are concerned, even though it is graver and more restrained and often brings the profound and solemn echo of the despair of Israel. Certain themes, however, are undoubtedly Arabic. With an assured daring of which even Juan Ruiz was not capable, the Palencian Jew could say:

> In my dream I once kissed a beautiful girl,
> She being very much afraid of those in her house;
> I found her mouth sweet-tasting, her saliva gently warm:
> I never saw a thing so sweet, yet bitter to leave. (63-66)[4]

This is the epoch of Alphonse XI, and a Jew was already daring to express in the language of Castile what had hitherto been impossible: bitterness over the unreality of oneiric pleasures. For the Archpriest it

---

[3] J. M. Blecua, *Las flores en la poesía española*, 1944, has collected all the references to flowers in Spanish medieval poetry.

[4] In Spanish:

> En sueño una fermosa besava una vegada,
> estando muy medrosa de los de su posada;
> fallé boca sabrosa, saliva muy temprada:
> non vi tan dulce cosa, mas agra a la dexada.

was still necessary to filter out the salacious elements of his Moslem models through a screen of Christian virtue. Santob for the first time broke the dikes that had been holding in check the tides of Arabic lyricism. Falling in love in one's dreams is one of the forms of falling in love recorded by Ibn Ḥazm. He tells, for instance, how it was with a slave girl in his dreams: "and when I awoke I found my heart was lost to her."[5] Then as now the allusion to saliva must have given a lascivious tinge to the occidental poem, although in Arabic literature this is a normal commonplace. Thus Ferazdaq in the seventh century: "She lets him drink of a saliva cool and pure as spring water."[6] And Ibn Ḥazm again, in the eleventh century: "I see in her saliva the water of life with positive certainty" (op.cit., p. 139). Similarly, ibn-Quzmān: "This that you have in your mouth, is it liquid sugar or saliva? . . . Between your lips there is something I like. God's name! Is it your saliva or is it sugared water?"[7] Yehudah Halevi (born in Toledo in 1086) had already said what I quote here in Nina Salaman's translation:

> Yea, between the bitter and the sweet standeth my heart:
> *The gall of parting*, and the honey of the kisses. (p. 48)

There are many other examples.[8] And equally Arabic is the theme of the watched and guarded woman, which we have already encountered in the *Libro de Buen Amor* and which is widespread in Islam ("She being very much afraid of those in her house").

The virtues prized by Santob are of an intellectual type and purely mundane: "Prudence and liberality, wisdom and a plain manner, and decorum" (1,007-1,008). Natural sequels to his high regard for intelligence are the value he attaches to relations between men and the tone of broad and easy humanism he imparts to his *Proverbios*, without parallel in fourteenth-century Christian Castile: ". . . the company of wise men never fails to be a pleasure: this pleasure increases more and more. You enjoy yourself with such men, and they with you; you understand them and they understand you. Thus the company of the learned friend —such a great joy there cannot be in the world" (1,015-1,020).

I find here the first appearance in Spanish of the theme of the tiresome

[5] *The Dove's Neck-Ring*, Nykl translation, p. 26.

[6] Farazdaq, *Divan*, Boucher translation, p. 143.

[7] *Cancionero*, Nykl translation, pp. 359, 362.

[8] Like other themes from Arabic literature, this one reappears in the poetry of Góngora:
"The sweet mouth inviting one to taste a humor distilled amidst pearls and not to covet that sacred liquor that Mount Ida's youth ministers to Jupiter. . . ."

or boring man: "A man who is boring . : . , to such a one, even though I were implored to, I should not like to talk; still less should I like to listen to him speak, sitting at my fireside" (1,071-1,074). "I had rather lie alone on the mountain top . . . in danger of serpents than to be in the company of dull, boring men. . . . Solitude to be sure is like death, but such intolerable company—it is better to be alone" (1,116-1,132).[9]

This refined rationalist, this rebel against boredom, rejects the commonplaces of those who denounce the world: "There is no evil in it save ourselves, *neither monsters*, nor anything else. . . . It becomes neither appeased nor enraged, it neither loves nor hates, it is not crafty, nor does it answer questions or cry out. . . . For the world is always one, and constant [i.e., the world has a constant being], just as is man's mortal body" (1,312-1,348). What the world and man are has been determined by the heavenly sphere. "Man is not . . . better or worse than where the sphere puts him" (1,283-1,284). Yet, in accordance with the religious significance that work had for the Jew (see Chapter 13, footnote 99), Santob does not counsel abandonment to any kind of quietism: "Let him labor and never cease, *as if* it were in man's own power to win and to lose" (389-390). This mixture of fatalism and assiduous striving brings to mind the combination of predestination and unrelenting toil in the later Calvinist communities, and indeed both attitudes derive from common Judaic-Christian sources. Don Santob's ethical views sounded like a very strange doctrine in Castilian, even though his works circulated in several manuscripts and attracted the attention of the Marquis of Santillana (fifteenth century), who found the *Proverbios* to contain "exceedingly commendable precepts." That way of life—marginal and inauthentic for Spain—never succeeded in putting down deep roots or flourishing widely.

Santob's verses are the only writings prior to the fifteenth century that contain occasional references to purely philosophical themes. However, his intellectual's horizon is still the East and not Christian Europe: "The arrow speeds to its proper target, and the science of letters stretches from Burgos to Egypt. . . . The arrow can only reach what can be seen; the written word reaches even the man in the East" (943-950). This

[9] L. Stein, *Untersuchungen über die Proverbios morales von Santob de Carrión*, 1900, p. 99, compares the foregoing passages with *Bocados de oro*, p. 406: "I never saw anything more depressing or painful than to suffer the annoyance of a bad neighbor," where the note of boredom is lacking. More relevant is the quotation from the *Pantchatantra*: "Playing with serpents or living with wicked enemies is preferable to associating with bad friends, lacking in wit, frivolous and uncultured, unendurable" (Otto von Böhtlingk translation, II, 202).

confirms the idea that the Hispano-Hebrew was little interested in the international community whose language was Latin, a negative attitude that lent support to the isolation and particularism of Christian Spain.[10]

Santob's praise of "the Book"[11] in the *Proverbios* emphasizes more its intellectual than its religious aspects:

> Knowledge is the glory and gift of God:
> Such a jewel or treasure is not to be found in histories,
> Nor better company than the Book, nor anything
> to compare with it;
> To grapple with it is better than peace. . . .
> The wise men one would wish to see, one will find them
> There, and one will always be able to speak with them:
> The sages, much praised, that one has longed for,
> Honorable philosophers one has coveted to behold . . .
> So there is no friend like the Book:
> For the wise, I say, for with the foolish
> I do not argue. (665-690).[12]

The praise of books, a commonplace of oriental literature, seems like a novelty in fourteenth-century Spain. But the aforementioned Mas'ūdī was writing as early as the tenth century: "The wise have rightly said

[10] The Jews must have given the impression that they had attained the highest possible reaches in learning. At least, all that we know about intellectual activities of a social character is connected with Jews. About 1478 there lived "in the town of Cuéllar a Jew named Rabbi Samuel, physician to the old duke (and he now lives in Medina del Campo, and is a Christian and is called Master Fabricio). And it was announced that, being a great philosopher, he would lecture or preach on philosophy in the synagogue. And this witness says that he does not know whether he lectured or preached on philosophy or not, or whether he preached Jewish sermons or not; but the suspicion was that he wanted to inject something of the Jewish faith. . . . Many Christians of the town went to the synagogue to hear him. . . . Great excitement broke out in the town of Cuéllar, especially in the monastery of San Francisco. . . . Many Christians, both converts and Old Christians, went to hear the sermons that Rabbi Samuel preached in the synagogue. Among them were various teachers and Doña Leonor, the duke's aunt, and many people of the palace and the town" (Baer, II, 520, 523). In view of the scanty documentation we have about private life in Castile in the Middle Ages, a document like this one gives us a valuable glimpse into the intellectual activities of the Jews. Rabbi Samuel probably did not speak only of Judaism, for if he had, the most cultured Christians of Cuéllar would not have attended his lectures.

[11] Books (for Santob "the Book"), besides expressing someone's wisdom, are an aspect, through their very words, of either divine or traditional revelation.

[12] The well-known passage from the *Discours de la méthode* comes to mind: "La lecture de tous les bons livres est comme une conversation avec les plus honnêtes gens des siècles passés."

that a book is the best and surest friend . . . ; it brings the remote together with the nearby, the past with the present . . . ; it is a dead man who speaks to you in the name of the dead and transmits to you the language of the living. . . . It saves you laborious searches and the humiliation of having to turn to those who are less than you. . . . You have only to glance at it and it brings you prolonged delights. . . ."[13] Alongside Mas'ūdī's pages, which should be read in their entirety, Santob's remarks seem thin and feeble. The Arab was tasting the pleasures of the intellect at a time when the existence of such pleasures was scarcely suspected in Christian Europe, and he made books a part of the awareness of the personal life. Santob's verses are a belated flicker of this enlightened and limited humanism.

Also Arabic is the play in Santob's poetry between the inward and the outward, that is, the alternation between contrary aspects, whose expression in the *Libro de Buen Amor* has already been analyzed. Says Santob:

> Si mi razón es buena, non sea despreciada,
> porque de hombre suena rahez; que mucha espada
> de fino azero sano sale de rota vaína,
> y del *fino* gusano se faze seda fina. (129-132)[14]

In spite of his debased condition, his utterances are good, just as a sword of fine steel may come out of a broken sheath. In the phrase "fino gusano" the term *fino* means *finado* (finished, dead), shedding its form onto the *fina* of *seda fina* by means of the now familiar process. All that is human is unstable, like the word-play and alternation of forms and values:

"Scarcely anything ugly or beautiful can one find in the world, save through its opposite." (259-260)[15]

Everything is deceptive:

"I wish to say very positive words about the world and its ways, and how I am doubtful about it." (151-152)

The image of the wheel of fortune around which a little later the

---

[13] *Les Prairies d'Or*, ed.cit., III, 136-138.

[14] In English: "If what I say is good, let it not be scorned, because it comes from a man of despicable condition; for many a sword of fine steel comes out of a broken sheath, and from the finished worm fine silk is made."

[15] This idea is repeated over and over: "The good thing is known through its opposite; through the bitter, the good-tasting; the front through the back" (275-276). "The sun makes salt hard, the pitch it makes soft (enblandesce); it makes the cheek black, linen it makes white" (enblanquesce) (64) where the Spanish verbs are analogical in form but not in meaning. Etc.

convert Juan de Mena was to situate his world, harmonizes smoothly with the uncertainty about everything man finds in his life. Santob says:

> For in a short time, if it so please the wheel,
> It turns a crown into a worn-out shoe. (1,275-1,276)

Like the good Islamicized Hispano-Hebrew that he is, Santob cannot refrain from mingling something of his own person with the abstract morality of his proverbs. The poet includes in his moralizing the anguish and uncertainty of a person who knows that he is writing for hostile readers, who will question the nagger's right to lecture them. A Christian would not have felt the need for justifying himself:

"I do not feel that the rose loses anything by being born on the thorn, nor good wine because it comes from the vine. The goshawk is worth no less for being born in a lonely nest, nor are good exempla, for being said by a Jew." (137-140)

This is the defensive attitude of a troubled spirit. It is odd that this personal stanza about the goshawk and his nest is the only one remembered by the Marquis of Santillana in his famous historico-literary letter. The Jew felt his own life as an example of the conflict between the total personality and its environment, between the consciousness of its own worth and society's resistance against recognizing it. This disquietude gave rise to the punctilious sense of honor and caste. Santob, it should be noted, is the first Spaniard to speak of the uneasiness that comes from realizing the irregularity of one's social position:

"Those whom the whole world should pity most of all are three who, I should say, live *in profound distress*: The *hidalgo* loses his dignity by submitting to the basely born for the help which he cannot get along without. To think that the born *hidalgo* who, accustomed to giving freely, is brought by fate into lowly hands! And what of the *just man* who is forced to obey a lawless master? And the third case, the *wise man* who is pressed into the service of a fool. Any other wretchedness is nothing beside this." (797-806)

It was the Hispano-Hebrew spirit that first gave expression to the sense of *la negra honra* (black, that is, cursed, honor) and the violent social criticism[16] that are fused in the eternal figure of the Squire in

---

[16] The satirical works of the fifteenth century are usually attributed to converts: the *Coplas de ¡Ay, panadera!* to Juan de Mena; the *Coplas de Mingo Revulgo* to Hernando del Pulgar; the *Coplas del Provincial* to Rodrigo de Cota, to Antón de Montoro, and to Alonso de Palencia (also, I suspect, a convert). Certainly Hernando del Pulgar wrote the commentary that accompanies the *Coplas de Mingo Revulgo*, a commentary that perhaps only the author could have written. The supreme pica-

Lazarillo de Tormes. In the fourteenth and fifteenth centuries no Christian experienced the psychological necessity for poking around in such dark corners or for writing like Santob in the quoted passages, which are in accord with everything we know about the importance the *aljamas* attached to purity of blood and to honor as a matter of public reputation. The defense of the sense of dignity is something different from the Castilian Christian's awareness of seignorial grandeur and the urge to attain it. The convert Juan de Lucena, in his *Libro de vida beata* (On the Happy Life), puts the defense of Hebrew lineage into the mouth of Don Alonso de Cartagena, a Jew by birth and eventually bishop of Burgos: "Do not think you can insult me by calling my forefathers Jews. They are, to be sure, and I am glad that it is so; for if great age is nobility, who can go back so far?" Many boast, the bishop goes on to say, of being descended from the Greeks or the Goths or the Twelve Peers. But to one who comes from the Levites or the Maccabees or the Twelve Tribes of Israel, "be he ever so virtuous, be ever so remote from vice," to such a one they say, " 'Go on, go on, he is a pig': a little less than the dust. . . . Suppressing the truth of the gospel, they say, contrary to it, that the *vera lux* does not lighten those that come to it."[17]

The Jew, "noble by birth" (as Santob says) and wise through effort, felt that his existence was dependent upon the "man of low birth," and this causes his "profound distress." This "distress" kept on worrying the converts. Thus, I am of the opinion that Mosén Diego de Valera's noble genealogy is but a mask that conceals his Jewish origin. To the question "whether the converts to our faith, who according to their law or sect were noblemen, retain their nobility of lineage after becoming Christians, I answer that not only do such persons retain their nobility or *fidalguía* after being converted, but rather I say that they increase it . . . , that among the Jews and Moors there are nobles just as amongst the Christians is evident enough to the *learned*, although the *ignorant* think the contrary. . . . Speaking of the Jews, *Deuteronomy* says, 'What other nation is so noble?' as if to say, none." And there follow from Mosén Diego de Valera several pages of argument so intense as to be inconceivable if the author did not have a lively personal interest in it, for, by contrast, he disposes of the question of Moslem nobility in a few lines.[18]

---

resque autobiography, *Guzmán de Alfarache*, is as intensely Jewish as its author, Mateo Alemán, who was Jewish on both his father's and his mother's side. *Lazarillo de Tormes* is a Jewish work also (see Chapter 15, footnote 18). The antisocial rancor in the *Celestina* comes from the same source.

[17] Edition of *Bibliófilos Españoles*, XXIX, 146-148.

[18] "Epístolas" of Mosén Diego de Valera, in *Bibliófilos Españoles*, XVI, 206-212.

The Literary Expression of Despair

The bitterness of the Jew, whether noble or learned, leads to a wealth of compensatory themes in Santob's *Proverbios*: flight from the world, contempt for human honors, esteem for socially inferior man marginally situated in society—a frame that includes both Lazarillo and his Squire:

"The *fidalgo* suffers anxiety in his cares. . . . The man so base and wretched that he has no shame, enjoys the full life that comes from neither thinking nor dreaming" (855; 815-816).

In Santob we perceive the first gloomy foreshadowings of the six-teenth-century asceticism, Guzmán de Alfarache, and Quevedo:

"Do you not remember that you were created from something vile, from a dirty drop, rotten and filthy? And you regard yourself as a precious shining star!" (610-612)

This was a familiar theme in the Jewish tradition. The Cordovan Baḥya ibn Paquda had written in the eleventh century: "Do you not live in a despised body, in a trampled carcass? It has come from a muddy source, from a contaminated spring, from a fetid drop. . . . It was hidden in an impure matrix, enclosed in a putrid belly from which it came forth

---

The great historian of Ferdinand and Isabella and of Henry IV had already been out of Spain on a diplomatic mission in the time of John II (see the study of J. de M. Carriazo in the preface to his edition of the *Memorial de diversas hazañas*, 1941). His father was physician to King John II, a very normal occupation for a Jew, convert or not. Certain characteristics of Diego de Valera's style betray his inner concerns. He says such things in his letters as: "Disregarding the lowliness of my estate. . . . Do not think that I do not recognize the lowliness of my estate and person. . . . Do not let what I say be scorned because of the pettiness of my estate [compare with Santob's similar statement, footnote 14]. . . . To write what is repugnant to my habit and lowliness of estate" (*Epístolas*, pp. 4, 14, 15, 17, 27). Notice his prophetic tone: "Beware, my lord. It is written by certain holy men that Spain will be destroyed again. . . . My lord, every man is to be listened to, for the spirit of God breathes everywhere" (pp. 7, 19, and also pp. 10, 31, 35). Very characteristic are the insistent references to the Trinity, a touchstone for Jews and converts: "Triune God . . . supplicating the Most Holy Trinity. . . . Begging the Holy Spirit" (pp. 34, 77, 13, 3, 9, 88, 61). In ridiculing the convert Alfonso Ferrandes Semuel, Alfonso Álvarez de Villasandino represents him as saying in his will: "He bequeaths to the Trinity, one new farthing; and to the crusade, two eggs; as a token of Christianity" (*Nueva Biblioteca de Autores Españoles*, XXII, 385). Diego de Valera knew much about matters of nobility and at the same time insisted that it was wrong to relate honor to social position (pp. 45, 211). His knowledge of small and very practical details in connection with the war in Granada, his life in the court, and other things that could be added, outline the personality of a cultured and intelligent convert of the fifteenth century for anyone familiar with the ways of life in that epoch. My supposition, based on Diego de Valera's style of life, has been confirmed with documents. See the *Revista de Filología Española*, 1946, p. 243.

in anguish and pain, to contemplate only emptiness and disorder."[19] Quevedo expresses himself in similar terms in the *Dreams*. One of the souls in hell describes his future rebirth: "I shall be lodged in somebody's kidneys, and then, with less pleasure than shame, bidding the urine to get out of my way, I must go and be the latrine's next-door neighbor; nine months must I feed on revolting menses,"[20] etc.

What is important here are the function and the social and artistic status of such commonplaces in the literature of the seventeenth, fourteenth, and eleventh centuries, and not that they are from the Bible, the Talmud, or the *Contemptus mundi*. When ideas are charged with emotion and energy, their authentic reality lies in the lives of those who have taken their stand by such ideas. The Christian tradition of Castile was not gloomy and desperate in the twelfth, thirteenth, fourteenth, and fifteenth centuries. The *Poema del Cid*, Berceo's poetry, Juan Ruiz, the Marquis of Santillana, and Jorge Manrique evoke impressions of pleasant and peaceful calm. And in the sixteenth century one does not find in Catholic literature outside of Spain anything comparable to the Spanish ascetic and picaresque developments, which connect with the somber tradition of Santob, Juan de Mena, Rodrigo de Cota, and Fernando de Rojas, a tradition that was later continued and expanded by legions of desperate converts for whom there was no comfortable place in this world. Things were bound to be that way among a people who for centuries had been living in insecurity and without a system of thought to confine and limit their beliefs. It was an ingrained habit for them to make little or no effort to change the world about them. Thus the converts' industriousness remained apart and unassimilated by the Old Christians into their way of life, just as the Jewish caste had remained apart from the Christians, and unassimilated, prior to 1492. Some Jewish beliefs, however (for instance, that the human world is basically evil) were accepted by those for whom the only real horizon consisted of hope or despair.

If we avoid history in the abstract and move closer to the vital situation—the drama of the New Christians in the sixteenth century—the historical perspective changes considerably.[21] The concept of Counter-

[19] *Choboth Halebaboth* (Duties of the Heart), translated into French by Edouard Fleg, in *Anthologie juive*, 1923, p. 117.

[20] *Biblioteca de Autores Españoles*, XLVIII, 363a.

[21] In the *Revista de Filología Hispánica* (1942, IV, 63) I called attention to the will of a certain Diego de Peralta, drawn up in Segovia in 1555. The testator had six marriageable daughters, and he forbade them to marry any of the New Christians he enumerated. Among these there figured a Pedro Izquierdo, a lineal descendant of

Reformation, the defense against Protestantism, does not adequately explain the pessimism, the attack on life, the desperation and disillusion by which broad fields of literature in the sixteenth century are at the same time inundated and fertilized. The desperate style is the form, the token, of a desperate existence. Long before Protestantism existed, in the middle of the fifteenth century, the convert Diego de Valera found pleasure in recalling and translating Saint Gregory thus:

The life of man is like the mist that rises from the earth and lasts but a little time; and all flesh is as grass; and all earthly glory is like the flower which is soon dried up by the air; and like the straw which the wind lightly bears up and lightly drops; and like smoke, and like fog, which lightly go up and lightly come down; and like the morning dew, which does not last till the evening.[22]

Or, speaking for himself, he will describe the consequence of the human passions: "Oh passion, that drives out reason, that cuts off memory, that destroys temporal wealth, that wastes the strength of the body, that is the enemy of youth, that brings death to old age . . . , that dwells in the empty breast," etc.[23] These commonplaces occur in the work of a writer who says time and again that he is aware of the lowliness of his state and person (footnote 14).

One must recall the perverse delight with which Rodrigo de Cota goads the Old Man in his famous *Diálogo* into yielding to the call of love, only to confront him with the wretchedness of his old age, with the unreality of his dream:

"What mistake could have made you think that your grey hair would

---

the Jew who at Christ's crucifixion "carried a trumpet about in front of the cross, and played it." Marcel Bataillon has already pointed out the influence of the converts in the messianism of the sixteenth century (*Erasme et l'Espagne*, p. 65). But this rich vein of thought must be followed back to the very root of Hispanic anguish. The convert aspired to achieve honor—*honra*—by taking refuge in the Church and the university. But the following report was made at the famous trial of Grajal and Luis de León, professors at Salamanca: "Because Grajal and Fray Luis de León are manifest converts, I think that they should not further seek to obscure our Catholic faith and should return to their own law, and therefore it is my vote that the said Fray Luis be seized and brought to the prison of the Holy Office" (M. de la Pinta Llorente, *Procesos inquisitoriales*, p. 91). Grajal, who came from a family of merchants, had studied at Louvain and Paris (p. 96), just like Luis Vives, also of Jewish descent.

[22] Quoted by J. de M. Carriazo in his edition of Diego de Valera, *Memorial de diversas hazañas*, p. xxxiv.

[23] "Tratado en defensa de virtuosas mujeres," in *Bibliófilos Españoles*, XVI, 141.

turn golden? . . . And those sunken lips and rotten teeth, did you think that they were sweet to kiss?"

He goes on to mention the Old Man's "mouth oozing phlegm, a gummy rag for his tearful eye." "You spit just straight enough to foul your beard," he says. "Your feet are full of corns, you are a living soul in a dry stalk, a living death and a dead life." This is a style possible only in Spain, for everything is said not ironically but seriously and on a literary plane that seeks to maintain itself at a certain high level.

At about the same time, Hernando del Pulgar, another convert, writes about the woes of old age in an equally desperate style: "If an old man acts old, people flee from him; if he acts young, people ridicule him. . . . He eats with effort, he empties his bowels with labor. . . . His eyes, his mouth, and his other features and other members grow deformed . . . he speaks much and does little. What greater deterioration can there be in life? . . . I do not know what Cicero could find to praise in old age" (*Letras*, ed.cit., p. 8). Pulgar's negativism embraces everything that exists, "because God is angry with humanity, which is rotten" (p. 91). Pulgar looks to Saint Augustine to confirm him in his state of mind, just as Valera had done with Saint Gregory. There is nothing to be found in the world but "griefs, fears, foolish pleasures . . . , oppression of innocent people, calumnies, circumventions, prevarications, false witnessings, wicked judgments, deeds of violence, robberies," etc. (104). "I see that all people go wandering about without any goal and without knowing what is happening to them and what can happen to them, *filled with the fear of their own falling* and filled with pleasure as they *regard the falling of others*" (107)—no longer an observation from the *City of God* (book 22) but from Pulgar himself, and reflecting better than anything the anguish and demoralization of many intelligent persons at the end of the fifteenth century. In it we can perceive the situation of post-Inquisitional Spain: ecclesiastical inflation (Pulgar's daughter entered a convent at the age of 12), the colonization of America considered as an absurd, exclusively Spanish, duel between the secular interest and the Church's longing for control (Las Casas). In this oppressive atmosphere the ascetic and picaresque genres were to flourish, the twin offsprings of a Judaism become church and of a Christianity with no faith in man and without the merciful and sweet smile of its Founder.

The convert Fernando de Rojas also set the final strains of his superb *Celestina* in the tonality of despair: "Where will I find refuge in my disconsolate old age? . . . Oh life filled with turmoil and beset with misery! Oh world, Oh world! fearlessly now, like one who can lose nothing, ... like a penniless traveler, who, without fear of highwaymen, goes singing in a loud voice [I shall cry out that] you seem to me a labyrinth of errors, a frightful desert, a place where wild beasts dwell, a game of men going around in a circle, a lake filled with slime, a region filled with thorns, a high mountain, a stony field, a meadow filled with serpents, an orchard that has bloomed and given no fruit . . . , your deceits, your nooses, your chains and snares. . . . Oh my shattered, broken daughter! . . . Why have you left me sad and alone *in hac lachrimarum valle?*"[24]

Although the first act of *La Celestina* cannot have been written by Juan de Mena, it has nonetheless and with a certain vital logic been attributed to him. The desperate, aggressive spirit of that convert shows itself in his *Dezir que fizo sobre la justicia* just as it does in the rest of his verses. Alexander's journey to heaven (an oriental-Lucianesque theme) allows him to observe the whole earth, where "Everything seemed vain to him." According to Juan de Mena, "from snare to snare, from pit to pit, we dash along to the precipice: instead of reaching the true jewel, we play at fencing with God. The devil shows us glories and delights, and keeps us abounding in dominions, beautiful women and clothing, mantles, divers well-prepared foods, treasures, riches, table-service, daïses, and precious jewels and other marvels; and since he keeps us sitting in such exalted places, he has us under his command as if we were his own. And thus, *all estates* bring forth in corruption, without fear of reckoning, popes, cardinals, bishops, prelates," etc.

It was the converts who secularized the gloomiest asceticism of the Bible and of the Middle Ages, and injected the later Spain with the feeling that the world was a chaotic phantasmagoria (the picaresque autobiography, asceticism, flight from the world, etc.). Again, Juan de Mena says:

"One blind man after another, one mad man after another, thus we go in search of good fortune; the more we have, the less we have, *a dream, as it were, and a moon shadow.* . . . You then, little worm . . . , *dream and wind, corrupted thing,* do you not see what a small thing your existence is?" (*Nueva Biblioteca de Autores Españoles*, XIX, 201-202)

It would not be correct to say that these are "commonplaces," and that one reads similar things in other languages. The truth is that a

---

[24] Although Pleberio's words derive from Petrarch, the difference is that what in Petrarch is an abstract *judgment* of life is spoken by the literary character as a lived experience. Pleberio is looking at his daughter "broken and shattered."

frame of mind is beginning to show itself as taking shape and becoming consubstantial with the Spanish life of the sixteenth and seventeenth centuries. Juan de Mena and Mateo Alemán are like twin brothers, members of the same desperate caste.

The birth of the modern novel and drama in the pages of the *Celestina* was not simply a matter of amusement. The authentic novel came out of a "tragic sense of life" because the life in which it was incubated and brought to birth was tragic. Where there was no tragic and epic sense of life there was neither novel nor drama. But this problem must be left aside. If I have made this incidental observation, it has been to remind the reader that my intention is constructive—as one might try to explain the fertility of a piece of ground by the volcanic lava that lies under it.

One wonders how it could have ever come to pass that what Father Mariana calls "grievous servitude on a par with death" should turn into nothing more than a subject for debate today between clericals and anti-clericals. Let us consider rather what was happening to *the lives* of those who were living *on a par* with death. Their voice is heard in the foregoing quotations, which could be multiplied many times. We can also hear it in a more prosaic tone by penetrating the inner feelings that are revealed in the Inquisitorial trials. The convert Pedro Cazalla, paymaster of the army and a man of influence, was summoned to appear before the Holy Office on the 22nd of September, 1530. But before he went, "he called his wife into a room where Francisca Hernández was, a room apart so that the members of his household would not hear him, and there he told his wife that we had no king, but a fool [that is, Charles V], and that the devil had brought the Empress Isabel of Portugal to Castile, and that she was a viper like her grandmother Isabel the Catholic, who had brought this misfortune, the Inquisition, to Castile."[25]

The converts were anxious to flee to any refuge where they would not be known as converts—to a religious order or into the unreality of any lovely, melancholy fantasy. It is no accident that the convert Jorge de Montemayor wrote the *Diana* and thus set Spanish letters on the narrative lyrical course of the pastoral novel. And those whose spirit had

---

[25] Quoted in M. Bataillon, *Erasme et l'Espagne*, p. 195. To protect themselves against Inquisitorial plundering, "they hid all their silver and the best of their personal property, and they ate from earthenware plates." Cazalla said that "if I had not built the house in Valladolid, I would go and live in Portugal."

absorbed too much bitterness chose the blind battle against the world that harassed them, as in the case of Mateo Alemán.

When Mateo Alemán, in 1607, had to cite the names of his parents in a public document, he called himself the "son of Hernando Alemán and of Doña Juana." Even then, 115 years after the expulsion of the Jews, the converts felt themselves in the grip of public hatred. Mateo Alemán omits his mother's surname because in Seville the surname *Enero* "smelled Jewish a hundred leagues away." On another occasion he disguised his name and called himself Mateo Alemán de Ayala. Rodríguez Marín has uncovered the interesting fact that Alemán was also descended from Jews on his father's side, although Alemán himself tried to explain his name as a patronymic indicating that his forebears were from Germany (Alemania), whence they had come to serve the Emperor. Rodríguez Marín observes that this is "manifestly a falsehood, as much a fraud as the coat of arms with the two-headed eagle that Mateo Alemán invented for his portrait, for he and all the Sevillans of that name were of the same lineage and descended from that Alemán who was major-domo of the city of Seville in the time of the Catholic Monarch and who was called 'he of the many Alemán sons' and who died in the Inquisition's fiery furnace."[26]

In self-defense many converts passed themselves off as *hidalgos*. Only in recent years have we learned the true story of the descendants of Fernando de Rojas, the author of the *Celestina*. Forty-three years after his death, his grandchildren forged an affidavit of nobility (see the *Revista de Filología Española*, 1925, XII, 385-396). And I shall presently point out that Luis Vives' noble genealogy, as Gregorio Mayans has it, is false. But most interesting of all, perhaps, is the very recent discovery that the family of Teresa of Jesus was also Jewish. The facts are to be found in an article by N. Alonso Cortés, "Pleitos de los Cepedas," in the *Boletín de la Real Academia Española*, 1951, pp. 86-110. At the beginning of the sixteenth century, the man who was to be Teresa's father was living with his brothers in the village of Majálbalago (province of Avila). The town council demanded that the Sánchez de Cepeda family pay the municipal taxes, since they were commoners and not *hidalgos*. But the family refused. A legal dispute ensued between the council and the self-styled *hidalgos*. Investigations proved that the father of the Cepeda family, Juan Sánchez, was not an *hidalgo*, nor could his sons have been such, because the Inquisition of Toledo in 1485 had

[26] "Documentos referentes a Mateo Alemán," in the *Boletín de la Academia Española*, 1933, XX, 216.

found him guilty of lapsing, as he confessed, into his former Judaism and of having "committed many and grave crimes and derelictions of heresy and apostasy against our holy Catholic faith" (p. 90). Juan Sánchez was condemned to wear "a little sanbenito with its crosses, and he wore it publicly on Fridays in the procession of the reconciled who made a penitential pilgrimage from church to church for seven Fridays" (p. 95). Saint Teresa's grandfather, and his sons after him, were rich merchants, royal tax- and tithe-farmers, etc. (pp. 94-98). In sum, they did the same things that Jews had long been doing before they became or came to call themselves Christians. But in spite of this, and disregarding the facts reported to them by the Inquisition of Toledo, the judges of the court of appeal in Valladolid found "the said Alonso Sánchez de Cepeda and his brothers should be allowed to keep possession of their *hidalguía*" (p. 100). From this, one may conclude either that the civil court was venal and allowed itself to be corrupted by the wealthy Cepeda's money, or that occasionally there were people in authority who reacted against the atrocious Inquisitorial principle, as contrary to the Spanish tradition as to the Christian spirit. Much thoughtful and detailed investigation would be necessary before this question could be decided. But in any case, it is evident that Saint Teresa is to be considered another great figure in the Christian-Oriental line. Her strong propensity for autobiography, the nature of her mystical experience, had previously led me to suspect Islamic or Judaic connections. Elsewhere I have suggested that Montaigne's similar propensity, uncommon in sixteenth-century France, is easier to understand if we bear in mind that his mother, Antonia López, was the daughter of Saragossan Jews expelled from Spain (see my *Aspectos del vivir hispánico*, p. 156). Let me add that in the case of Saint Teresa's family, her seven brothers all went to Peru. Very likely, in spite of their official nobility, the descendants of converts preferred to take themselves far away from Spain in order to escape painful gossip.

The contradiction that was the very core of such people's lives—the feeling that they were at the same time both citizens and outlaws who had to keep in the shadows—is latent and patent in the somber blossoms of the ascetic and picaresque style: "*The son of nobody*, who rose out of the dust of the earth, a frail vessel full of holes, broken. . . . I turn the breath of violets into poison, I stain the snow, with my thoughts I abuse and crush the new rose" (*Guzmán de Alfarache*, I, 2, 4; II, I, I). According to Fray Hernando de Zárate, those who "waste their lives in striving and in bettering their condition . . . are like those who in the middle of the night find themselves in a great lake of water and mud, mired up to the waist, trying to move from the place where they are or to improve their situation in order to escape, usually fall into a deeper place, because the bottom is miry all over."[27]

As early as the eleventh century, the Jew Isḥāq ibn-Gayyat, of Lucena (Cordova) could write: "Let every intelligent and discreet man realize that the worm will have everything in the end. . . . The honey that is distilled in this world bears within it deadly poison." According to Yosef Ibn Ṣaddiq, of Cordova (twelfth century), "the feces that are within me are the contamination of my soul."[28] The works of other authors are enveloped in the same heavy and gloomy atmosphere. The Hebrew people must have felt a continual increase in their agony as they lived between the walls of two religions that had already received the human-divine message through Christ and Mohammed while Israel waited in despair, with no consoling way-stations between human insignificance and divinity. For the medieval Christian the visions of hell and the terrors of the millennium were tempered by his belief in the Virgin Mary and the presence of his church. But the Jew was imprisoned between the strict terms of the disproportion, God: man, and his anguish cried out in desolate measures.[29]

The Spanish convert of the fifteenth and sixteenth centuries expressed himself in somber modes because circumstances drove him back to the deepest roots of his own existence. It is no surprise that the Jew should have expressed himself thus but it is surprising that Spanish Christianity should have taken on a darker and darker color until it reached the point of a negation of the world very close to total nihilism such as we would seek in vain in France[30] or Italy. And what is most striking in Spain is that writers from the laity like Mateo Alemán, Quevedo, Gracián, and many

[27] "Discursos de la paciencia cristiana," 1593, in the *Biblioteca de Autores Españoles*, XXVII, 446. A part of the same complex of vital flight is the imitation of the novel of Heliodorus, *Theagenes and Chariclea*, quite evident in *Guzmán*.

[28] The texts are in J. M. Millás Vallicrosa, *La poesía sagrada hebraico-española*, pp. 238, 245.

[29] I wonder whether it would be possible to compile a medieval Christian anthology exclusively on the theme of the quest for God like the one made by J. M. Millás Vallicrosa for medieval Hispano-Judaic literature. Medieval Christianity has nothing to equal Ibn Gabirol's *Keter Malkut* (Royal Crown) as an expression of the authentic thirst for God.

[30] Saint Francis of Sales, Bossuet, and Massillon in their times discounted earthly values, but they did not destroy them. Massillon says: "Mais si la gloire humaine est *presque* toujours dégradée" (*Sermon pour le dimanche de la Passion*). These French preachers were courtiers and intellectuals at the same time that they were Christians.

others, should display such a downcast manner without giving rise to the supposition that they were all necessarily Jews. Just as literary prose and lyric poetry, once they were created, were available to everyone, likewise the desperate style of the Judaic tradition became a possible form of expression for many Old Christians.[31]

Man's feeling and belief that he was living in the midst of uncertainties and phantasmagorias spread like creeping grass through the spiritual soil of Iberia. Although that vital situation can be abstractly related to the ideas present in the church fathers or in certain moralists of the Middle Ages, the phenomenon is actually a matter of ideas rooted in life, and not merely of ideas. Between the eleventh and the fifteenth centuries we have seen the course of Hispano-Jewish power take shape, rise, and tragically go to pieces. Under Alphonse X the Jews dreamed of initiating their era of glory, to which they gave the name "Alphonsine." Alphonse XI was still building synagogues for them and was writing to the pope about how they had heroically risked their lives for the cause of Christian Spain. Three grand masters of the kingdom's major orders were still making use of their skill in writing, philosophy, and astronomy in the fifteenth century. The collapse of what one might call their illegal empire founded on skilled labor, finance, public administration, and learning, began at the end of the fourteenth century. From that time on, the Jewish population is split into two groups. One firmly resisted the persecutions and faced all the trials of the diaspora of 1492.

[31] Jorge Manrique had said that "our lives are the rivers that go into the sea, which is our dying," feeling the flow of the rivers as a movement through a channel. But this notion of a peaceful flowing through a channel was disturbing to such people at the end of the sixteenth century as could not find any kind of existence that moved along a normal and well-regulated course. A certain Doctor Francisco de Ávila published some *Dialogues intended to take away the presumption and dash of the man made vainglorious and proud by the world's favor and prosperity* (*Diálogos en que se trata de quitar la presunción y brío al hombre a quien el favor y prosperidad del mundo tiene vanaglorioso y soberbio*, Alcalá, 1576). We read there of "those who with riches, treasure, and fame spent their lives in the world, charging with impetuous fury, as the rivers 'go to the sea, which is our dying'; and there perishes and ends the *noise and tumult* with which they have run through that short, brief moment that their lives have lasted them" (fol. 2r). This good doctor, who feels and speaks like the descendant of Jews in that epoch, converted Jorge Manrique's peaceful river into a furious and tumultuous torrent to the end of "taking away man's presumption," and making clear the discord between the purpose and values that are pleasing to man on the one hand, and the true course of his life on the other. The world is not only beyond the control of human will and thought but also outside the divine order. Mateo Alemán thinks that God would not be able to improve the world even by destroying it and creating it anew; for the new men "must necessarily be just like the old ones" (*Guzmán de Alfarache*, I, I, 7).

The other, weaker, began, at the end of the fourteenth century to disappear into Spanish Christendom, a process that went on at an ever-increasing rate, and to combine with the Christian forms of life their own, which were as profound and as rich in values as they were bitter and desperate. This is the way Castilian society was penetrated by a poetic lyricism with Arabic overtones,[32] by Judeo-Islamic mysticism, by the potentialities of the novel (*La Celestina*), by philosophic thought that found refuge in foreign lands (Luis Vives, Francisco Sánchez, Baruch Spinoza).[33] But other currents also flowed into the mainstream of Spanish life through these same channels; Inquisitorial fanaticism and recourse to slandering informants—what one might call in Spanish "malsinismo"—frantic greed and plundering, the concern over purity of blood (bound up with the defensive impulse that created the Inquisition), the concern with public reputation (which becomes the measure of personal dignity), the desire of everyone to be a nobleman (for example, Mateo Alemán, who, like many other New Christians, felt compelled to obliterate the scars of inferiority by assuming superiority); somber asceticism (in disharmony with medieval Spanish Catholicism and the general tone of Catholicism outside of Spain), the negative view of the world (Lazarillo, Mateo Alemán, Quevedo), disillusionment, and the flight from human values. The Jew and his adversary, the convert, were something more than the usual run of people: they carried in their souls the agony of their feeling that they were being dashed from the summits of fortune into the terror of massacres, burnings at the stake, torture, *sanbenitos*, and harassment by a crazed society, which continually pried into the Jews' actions and conscience, always subject to exposure through

---

[32] The *Cancionero de Baena* with its converts amongst the laity as well as the religious (Fray Diego de Valencia) should be situated within this framework. The themes and problems therein expressed and debated could be analyzed in the same terms as Santob's. The same is true for the poetry of Juan de Mena, Antón de Montoro, and others.

[33] Among other illustrious figures of Judaic provenience, besides Saint Teresa and Luis de León, already mentioned, the Blessed Juan de Ávila and Diego Laínez, the second general of the Society of Jesus, are to be remembered. Concerning the latter, see the work of Feliciano Cereceda, S. J., *Diego Laínez en la Europa religiosa de su tiempo*, Madrid, 1945, I, 18-22. In 1545 many people were begging for the return of Laínez to Spain, but Ignatius de Loyola did not authorize it. This case was like that of many other New Christians (Luis Vives, for example), who stayed away from Spain for fear of the anti-Jewish reaction, which had as one of its principal targets the recently founded Society of Jesus, full of "gente berría"—new people—as the Jesuits who knew Basque used to write confidentially (*berría*, Basque for "the new ones, the new Christians"). Concerning the Hebraism of Juan de Ávila, see Cereceda, *op.cit.*, p. 22.

torture. Don Isaac Abarbanel, shouting himself speechless before Ferdinand the Catholic, is a vivid picture of the Hispano-Hebrew who clings with already torn hands to the edge of the last precipice. He is the symbol of the great tragedy that has been lived by the Jews, locked with their persecutors in a symbiosis that went on for more than five centuries. The history of Spain cannot be understood if we think of all this as a troublesome incident, serious in its economic consequences and for the shadow of intolerance that it cast over the Catholic Sovereigns. History cannot be based only on public economy, reproaches, regrets, and fallacies.

Some Aspects of Hispano-Judaic Thought

On several occasions the presence of the Hispano-Oriental tradition has been clearly evidenced in the tendency to adopt certain spiritual modalities (illuminism, mysticism, or Erasmianism) or certain profane styles (the pastoral and picaresque narratives). It is impossible to separate the fact that Jorge de Montemayor and Mateo Alemán were descendants of converts from the meaning of the pastoral and picaresque fiction and other works, for in them we see the intent to show human life as a dreamlike ideal or as a materialism devoid of meaning—negative idealism. In the convert Luis de León the ability to interpret the Bible with rigorous scholarship is linked with his eagerness to escape lyrically to "the fertile earth (suelo), eternal provider of consolation." The oppressive circumstances in which New Christians found themselves revived their traditional tendency to take refuge in distant ideals. Furthermore, being Spaniards, they sensed the importance of the self, an importance which, at that moment in the sixteenth century, the most cultured people could base on the exaltation of the worth of man which Italy had been asserting for some time. The Italy of the treatises "de dignitate hominis" was seen from the heights of power of the Spaniards who dominated her politically. And as for the incredible maritime enterprises of the Portuguese and Spaniards, Jews and converts had contributed a great deal toward making these possible with their technical knowledge and economic aid. Precisely at this moment, then, when the Iberian empire was beginning to take on unmeasurable proportions,[34]

[34] On August 30, 1529, Luis Vives wrote to Erasmus: "Spain is the empress and director of everything. . . . You must have heard that the Emperor sailed from Barcelona with an extremely powerful armada. . . . Besides the court retinue and the flower of noble Spanish youth, as many as 10,000 sailors selected from all over Spain" (Obras completas, Spanish trans. by L. Riber, II, 1715-1716).

the Hispano-Hebrew felt himself ejected from his country, or persecuted and pushed aside within it.

A sharp consciousness of the individual and social value of the self[35] was necessary to inform the theme of escape from the world with literary possibilities; the persecution of the Hispanic Jew would not alone have shaped the evasive and yearning literature of the converts, so different from the medieval "de contemptu mundi." The literature and philosophy of the converts accentuated the value of the individual inwardness —a value which was unknown to abstract ascetic literature. Luis Vives, sure of his own fame, said he scorned it, because "the noise of it draws me out of myself, and I cannot fix on myself my eyes and my thoughts, which are forced to pay attention to those who applaud me."[36] The escape that characterizes literary asceticism fails to take into account the specific individual who flees. It is apparent, therefore, that the special character of the literature and thought of the Hispano-Hebrews is more closely connected with an inclination to express those things experienced in the depths of their anguished consciousness than with the circumstance of being socially persecuted. Without the Hispanic Jew's ability to express the phenomena of the consciousness effectively, Inquisitorial persecution would not have sufficed to motivate the splendid literary flowering that I have been analyzing. The *despuntar de agudos*, as the *vox populi* recognized—the Jews' conspicuous cleverness—was a decisive factor in this case.

Possibilities of new lines of thought were present in the act of knowing how to seek the inner self and of revealing in consummate form the result of that search; and it is desirable to examine these new ways of thought briefly, now that we have attained the necessary perspective. The Hispanic Jew, linked with the Hispano-Moslem tradition, envisioned man as a vital, shifting, and changeable reality, rather than as a being ontologically one and abstractly conceivable. We have already seen (see Chapter 12) how Ibn Ḥazm found the whole and unifying aim of man's life in the casting off of "anxiety"; the essence of the life of man, for him, was not to be sought in a transcendent but in an immanent motivation:

[35] How the expatriate Jew continued to feel this value is seen in Francisco Delicado's *La Lozana andaluza*, written in Rome a little after 1527: "This is a synagogue of Catalonians, and this one down here of women; and there are the Germans; and that other one is French; and this one is composed of Romans and Italians . . . ; but *our* Spaniards know more than all the others, for among them there are learned men and rich men, and they are very cultured. Look there where they are. How do you like them? This synagogue has the best" (Chap. xvi).

[36] Ed.cit., ii, 1715.

he saw man's whole activity to consist in the compulsion to free himself from anxiety.[37]

Some three centuries later, with acute penetration, Don Santob de Carrión separated the reality of man from whatever is not man. It is useful now to quote at greater length the texts to which I have previously referred:

> We speak ill of the world, and there is no other
> evil in it than ourselves . . .
> Each man thinks of it according to his own *doings*:
> It has neither friendship nor quarrel with anyone. . . .
> *It is one* [i.e., not changeable] even when it is reviled. . . .
> The happy man thinks it good and considers it a friend;
> The careworn man abuses it and considers it an enemy.
> Wise men find in it no change:
> The changes are in the minds of the receivers. . . .
> We lie always enclosed under one sky;
> We go from night to day, and naught else.
> To this distant earth we have given the name world.
> Whether it is true or false no man knows.

[37] One recalls the 19th book of *The City of God* (chapters 12 and 13), in which St. Augustine says that man and everything else that exists aspire to peace: "Those who observe nature and human things with me realize that just as there is no one who rejects pleasure, likewise there is no one who does not desire peace." Which is the same as thinking that everything tends toward order: "All things are in order when they are at peace" (Chap. 13). Even those who hope for war would like to achieve a glorious peace through it. This idea, as is well known, was developed by Luis de León: "All that is done in this life by all of us who live in it, and all that is desired and toiled for, is directed toward securing this good of peace" (*Nombres de Cristo*, ed. by F. de Onís, II, 137). In spite of the similarity between this idea and that of Ibn Ḥazm, it is necessary to emphasize the difference. Ibn Ḥazm says: "No one *is moved* to act, nor does one decide to say so much as a word, if he does not expect to get rid of anxiety" (see Chapter 12). Ibn Ḥazm did not develop his idea; or, at least, he did not do so in the works of his which are accessible to me. Let us note, nevertheless, that the quest for peace means for Saint Augustine reaching that unity of the being in which all contradictions are resolved. Human activity so envisioned is a path which leads to a transcendental goal; by following this path man approaches the supreme unity of God, the highest good. The ultimate goal of life interests St. Augustine; Ibn Ḥazm concentrates his attention on its functioning, on the immanent motivation of the vital movement. The distinction which I am establishing is not hair-splitting but a strict necessity, based on the different perspectives within which the two thinkers contemplate life. It has already been seen that the Archpriest of Hita concentrated his interest on vital movement, open and multiple, and not on securing a single good. If he had followed St. Augustine, the structure of his Book would have been different.

It is always one; but all those who are born
Are divided like the right side and the wrong.
What profits one man, harms the other. . . .
The day which is of pleasure to him who
Collects his debt, gives sorrow to him who must pay:
The day itself is the same; it has not changed. . . .
And the world is one and unchanged always,
And man too is *one in his body*;
His humor changes from merry to sad
And one man is injured by what pleases another. . . .
Man seeks to do himself ill with his own evil,
Never getting his fill of ardor or greed.
No other thing in the world is so dangerous as man,
Or so harmful or such an ill-doer.
Beasts, when they are sated, are content,
They do not try to do wrong and they are at peace. . . .
With a thousand quintals of gold man can never be sated.

The *expressive current* of Santob's own life prompted these theoretical judgments about human life and set him to writing the first philosophical page in the Spanish language.[38] The reality of man is interwoven with, and opposed to, what is not man—all that which is nature in its constancy; man is variable, changeable, unpredictable, and dangerous. The constitutive human element is man's "doing," and from the standpoint of his doing man conceives the world; he makes the mistake of attributing his own mutability to the essential character of the world. World thus is everything that comes within man's psychological and moral reach. Confined under the vault of the firmament, man experiences nightfall and dawn ("we go from night to day"). In a splendid line the philosopher-poet says that men call that distant thing (lueñe tierra) "world," and actually know nothing about it with certainty, "whether

[38] I refer also to those who wrote in Latin without originality, following the scholastic philosophy of other countries (see T. y J. Carreras y Artau, *Historia de la filosofía española. Filosofía cristiana de los siglos XIII al XV*, Madrid, 1939-1943). There are those who think that the *Ars Magna* of Raymond Lully (1235-1315) has value as a germ of the symbolic logic of our day. But Lully was a theologian and mystic who hoped to fuse the truth of faith and the truth of reason: and certainly it would be necessary to suppress the content of Lully's writings, and force into other fields the possibilities latent underneath his thought to make his philosophy of any interest today. Santob's conception, on the contrary, stands forth clearly: man's reality is presented to us as a changing and unpredictable doing opposed to the constant essence of that which is not human reality.

it is true or false." The only sure thing is that it is constant: "it is always one." Man "relativizes" the reality of what lies outside him when he interprets it in accordance with the changing and unsure movement of his life. In the realm of the "not his" that confronts man are the animals with their predictable conduct: when their appetites are satisfied, they are no longer dangerous. Man's physical body is also constant; without changing bodies man passes from joy to sorrow, changes his "humor," his frame of mind. So it is that the course of human life is unforeseeable, since there can even be people who are not satisfied with "a thousand quintals of gold." Hence, also, man's perilous state, for "one man is injured by what pleases another" (1,350).

Santob says nothing about the theoretical questions which occupied the philosophers of his time: the universals, the harmony between religious faith and rational faith, the agent intellect, etc. His point of departure is the naïve experiencing of the natural or human phenomena which are accessible to him. For Santob there is always something one and constant which causes diverse and inexplicable effects or reactions. Before the passage cited above he says that:

> The sun hardens salt and makes the pitch soft,
> It darkens the cheek and whitens linen;
> It is *one and the same thing*, there in the sky
> When the weather is cold as when it is hot.

God knows the reason for all this: let no one imagine "that he can do anything *by taking thought*" (210). Nevertheless, Santob does not calm his spirit, and continues to be surprised that "the doctor who reads medicine dies and the stupid shepherd gets well." Beneath the design of God, on high, the supreme explanation, there is here manifest a duality consisting in something one and fixed, and something multiple and relative. Man belongs to this latter inferior region in so far as he is conscious of himself; Santob does not grant him a rational essence over and above his manifold emotional reactions. From this lack proceeds the restless uncertainty of this incipient vitalistic psychologist:

> Therefore I can never cling to one pole,
> Nor do I know which is better—whether the white one or
> the black. (191-192)

Talking in a language that anticipates Sancho Panza's wisdom and taking as the point of departure one's own awareness of vital experience —this sounds very Spanish. Whether or not the coincidence is accidental, it is not unwarranted to recall the following statement written by the son of a Spanish Jewess: "Truly man is a marvellously vain, varying, and wavering creature, on whom it is difficult to found a consistent and uniform judgment" (Montaigne, *Essays*, I, I). Santob had said all this two centuries before, and so inaugurated the only philosophy which has ever truly interested Spaniards. In the twentieth century they have gone in search of it to Kierkegaard, Dilthey, and Heidegger.

Ibn Ḥazm and Santob were attracted more by the immediate problem of man's reality than by the problem of his chief end. Both were believers within the framework of their respective religions. But they concerned themselves by preference with life, with the soul as a multiple, contradictory activity, incalculable by the philosophic means their times afforded. They felt it more urgent to analyze life as a phenomenon than to define it conceptually, and therefore they plunge into the dangerous sea of their feelings and passions. Their thought moved on the path of autognosis, the conscious awareness of the process of one's own existence.[39] Since for the Spaniard, whether or not of Hebrew descent, there actually was almost no authentic world beyond that of his own self, it is understandable that the trend of oriental life should find fertile soil in Spain and achieve a strong growth—in the *Celestina*, in mystical writings, in the picaresque autobiography, in the drama, and in the Cervantine novel. The greater taste—or the greater capacity—of the Hispanic Jew for intellectual meditation made the works of a Santob, an Alfonso de la Torre, or a Luis Vives possible. And I think that this series ought to include the *Examen de ingenios* by Huarte de San Juan, who, it seems very likely to me, was of Jewish descent. Since man is an entity who achieves his reality according to "his doing" (Santob), the possibility is opened for a new anthropology (Vives) as well as for the study of differentiated types of character (Huarte). This way of thinking about human existence was obstructed—outside Spain—by the triumphs of logical thought in its application to nature. The mystery of man was

---

[39] The value granted to the consciousness of one's life increases among Semitic peoples in direct proportion to the scorn for what man may think about the material and ideal world which surrounds him. One example, among others, would be Ibn Khaldūn, who rejects the validity of universal judgments about corporeal and spiritual beings; the first, he says, appear only as particular beings; and reasoning cannot be employed about the second because we have no way of assuring ourselves of their existence. And he adds: "I except only what we find within ourselves, 'between our two flanks,' relative to the human soul and the nature of its perceptions, especially in dreams, which happen to all men. What is beyond and above that—the nature of the soul and its attributes—is so profound a subject that there is no way of coming to know it" (*Prolégomènes*, French trans. by De Slane, III, 233-234).

violently subjected to the immediately exact procedures that had yielded such satisfying results in physics and mathematics, whose means were not fitted to the human object, unknown because the reality of its life is not being but continual self-creation. This is how the "être humain" was conceived, despoiled of its body, of the agitation of its passions, and of its insecurity. Seneca's abstract rationalism won the day—the idea of a man "who was neither raised up nor broken down by the fortunes of life . . . , and whose greatest joy shall consist in disdaining all joys" (quem nec extollant fortuita nec frangant . . . , cui vera voluptas erit voluptatum contemptio) (De vita beata, IV, 2). The peculiar and changing quality in man, the channel of his authentic reality, was screened off: "When I set to thinking about man, I distrust my eyes; I prefer a steadier light that allows me to distinguish the false from the true" (Oculis de homine non credo; habeo melius et certius lumen, quo a falsis vera diiudicem) (ibid., II, 2). It is impossible to think of anything more contrary to the authentic Hispanic mode of facing man's reality and expressing it. The philosophy of Seneca did not give rise to any sort of original thought in Spain. It is a superficial element in Quevedo, where the authentic, living ideas connect with the anguished tradition of the Hispano-Semites: "I am a was, and a shall be, and a weary is."

The exceptional character of man's being within all that exists is brought out clearly in the Bible, a Semitic work par excellence: "And it repented the Lord that he had made man on the earth, and it grieved him at his heart. And the Lord said, I will destroy man whom I have created from the face of the earth" (Genesis, 6: 5, 6). The pessimistic approach to the question what is man—the "most dangerous thing in the world," says Santob—made it possible to ask the question seriously, what is man's reality. In the twelfth century, Alain de Lille had Nature, the vicar of God, express the lament over man's exceptional character in the face of the universal rule traced out by God: "Sed ab hujus universitatis regula solus homo anomala exceptione excluditur."[40]

But if the effort to understand man as an exception within the world of natural laws was made possible by the pessimistic view of man, the great leap, nevertheless, consisted in realizing that, good or evil, man is as he is, for Ibn Ḥazm a "worried" being, for Santob, a changeable

---

[40] "De Planctu Naturae," in Migne, Patrologia, ccx, col. 448. As is well known, Jean de Meun used this work in the Roman de la Rose; see the edition of Ernest Langlois, IV, 304. It is unnecessary to say that in Jean de Meun's work there is nothing of the problematical anguish of Santob and Luis Vives—for reasons that should now be obvious to the reader.

and perilous "doing," irreconcilable with the rigidity of the laws of natural reason. Alfonso de la Torre, a fifteenth-century convert, also stands in this line, though less original and profound than the other two thinkers. In the *Visión deleitable*[41] he writes: "All things in the world have been made and ordained by God, and they do not depart from the order which Nature has given them, and they are *uniform* and not changeable *in their operations*, and I see that only man exceeds the strict laws of nature and breaks them; and there is nothing in men that is well ordered or well governed, nor anything in them that is stable or firm . . . ; all is variable, a thing which we do not see in any created thing," etc.

It is of little interest whether these and other passages derive from Alain de Lille or from other writers. As a matter of fact, what we have here is a reappearance of Augustine's notion that man does what he does in order to achieve peace with himself: "To attain that good, real or apparent, men work in different ways, some at sea, as pirates or as fishermen; others on land, either at tilling or in arts and trades" (*Visión deleitable*, p. 379). Even suicide is an act motivated by the desire to avoid an obstacle: "He [the despairing man] sees that he cannot escape from grief, and therefore it seems better to him pass through the grief in one day than in many" (p. 380). There existed, then, a Hispano-Oriental tradition of thought about man as a reality that creates itself moment by moment, driven by longing and anguish. This reality was revealed through autognosis. Luis Vives, another Hispano-Hebrew,[42] wrote in 1538: "He who has not explored himself will ill be able to govern his inner self and likewise apply himself to working well. And indeed, the first thing to be known is the artisan, so that we may know what kind

[41] *Biblioteca de Autores Españoles*, XXXVI, 377. J. P. Wickersham Crawford demonstrated that Alfonso de la Torre had translated a large part of the *Guide of the Perplexed* of Maimonides (*PMLA*, 1913, pp. 188-212). See also E. R. Curtius, *Europäische Literatur und lateinisches Mittelalter*, pp. 526-528.

[42] My suggestion in the first, Spanish, edition of this book (pp. 682-685) that Luis Vives was a Jew has been confirmed by documents. Vives' father was burned at the stake in 1526. The Inquisitorial trial of Luis Vives' family will be published by Mr. Abdón M. Salazar, who has kindly allowed me to see the most essential part of his important findings. Luis Vives attended a clandestine synagogue with his family until the synagogue was discovered by the Inquisition in 1502, when Luis Vives was ten years old. "Master Tristany," whose school Vives attended as a boy, was prosecuted for practicing Judaism. The circle of Vives' acquaintances in both Paris and Bruges consisted chiefly of converts (Santángel, Coronel, Maluenda, the Ortegas of Burgos, the Pardos, Astudillos, Mirandas, Valldauras, etc.).

of works we have a right to expect from him" (*De anima et vita*).[43] Man's life becomes possible in matter, but life itself is not matter: "It is absolutely impossible that this vivifying principle should be the dough that we call matter, always stationary, and *only like unto itself*, incapable of drawing strength from its own character and nature. . . . Out of that strength and faculty of life we see marvelous productions originating" (II, 1,173-1,174). Occasionally Luis Vives is introspective in an auto-biographical way: "I myself, with the first or second bite that I take after a prolonged fast, cannot contain laughter; the explanation of this is that the contracted diaphragm is expanded by eating" (II, 1,280).

Dilthey, understandably enough, saw in Vives something more than ideas about the education of youth: "The first great systematic writer in the field of anthropology is the Spaniard Vives. He wants to get rid of the involved scholastic study of ideas and direct his thought along the lines of the experimental; and this point of view requires a new science of man."[44]

But my concern is not to explicate the philosophy of Vives, but to make the reality of Spain perceptible. I wish only to show the connection between what Vives did, thought, and expressed on the one hand and the possibilities available to a Hispano-Jewish genius at the beginning of the sixteenth century. In 1529 he writes that some people "*forget their homeland* and all their family relations," and go to live "in a place where life passes quietly and peacefully, either because of its customs and government, or because of the amiable sweetness of the character of its inhabitants. Such a place they regard as their homeland, there they think to find their parents, their dearly beloved, and their sweet names—there where justice, peace, and concord are revered. And they regard as the place of their exile the place where one citizen harasses another or a newcomer; where one curious or trouble-making neighbor annoys another; where one's spirit is disturbed by a relative, a friend, a slight acquaintance, or an utter stranger, and one is torn from his repose. It is not only impossible to endure this; to see it is so revolting that *many prefer to abandon their houses and their homeland*, which have also been those of their forefathers, and to go away to distant lands, where they will not perceive such disagreeable things with their senses: neither see them, nor hear, nor understand, nor, in short be aware of them in any

---

[43] Since the Latin edition is not easily accessible, I refer the reader to the accurate translation by Lorenzo Riber, *Obras completas*, 1948, II, 1,147.

[44] *Weltanschauung und Analyse des Menschen seit Renaissance und Reformation*, 1921, p. 423.

way whatsoever. Who can regard the dissensions of citizens or neighbors with pleasure, knowing that *the tempest will either suddenly or little by little engulf him?*"

The foregoing passage is charged with too much passion to be interpreted as an abstract and merely doctrinal statement. It occurs in what we would today call an essay with the title *De pacificatione*, addressed to Don Alonso Manrique, Archbishop of Seville and Inquisitor-General, because archbishop means—as Vives sharply reminds the Erasmian Don Alonso—"vicar and imitator of Christ, who was brought from heaven to earth by a mission of peace. . . . With this reason, which is so weighty, as you see, it pledges and guarantees the peace, is conjoined the position of Inquisitor of the heretics; and the Inquisitor's mission being so powerful and dangerous, if the one carrying it out should not know what its object is, he will sin the more grievously the more he endangers the welfare, property, reputation, and life of many people. *It is an astonishing thing* that such broad authority should be given to the judge, who does not lack human passions, or to the accuser, who too often is impelled to calumny by concealed hatred, unconfessable hopes, or some other perverse inclination."[45]

Vives felt the same way about the Inquisition as Hernando del Pulgar, Mariana, and many others. Lest that tempest should engulf him, he sought out a homeland that was not Spain. The idea of peace here is not simply an echo of Erasmus or the Renaissance. Vives expresses it and uses it in impassioned modes because the absence of peace has rent his own life, and has directed it along strange paths not frequented by his contemporaries: on the one hand, social action (the reform of education, propaganda in favor of political and religious peace, original projects of public assistance); on the other, anguished meditation on the inner reality of the human soul, whose passional activities created the horrors that afflict Luis Vives' life. Why are Christians not Christian? What does it mean to be a Christian if one does not act in a Christian fashion? Why are the Jews burned in Spain? If only Christ's ministers set themselves about it, religious peace would reign. The emperor Theodosius "a grave and glorious prince," was expelled from the temple by Ambrose, Bishop of Milan, because Theodosius "gave his consent for his soldiers really to butcher his *pagan* subjects in Thesalonica" (*op.cit.*, p. 285). Therefore difference in religion does not justify the extermination of the dissidents.

Experience, the awareness of his own private life, led Vives (as it had

[45] *Obras completas*, ed.cit., II, 256, 274, 275.

earlier led Santob) to formulate the new and lasting element in his thought, and to put aside the abstract, scholastic reasoning of his time. His Hispanic tradition—as we already know—inclined him this way. Man, Santob had said, is not *one*, is not a quiet essence but a mobile, multiple, and changing "doing." Vives says: "It is not too important for us to know *what* the soul *is*, but it is very important to know what the soul is like and what *its actions* are" (*De anima*, ii, 1,175).[46] Thus it was that he began to discover in human life the richness of its individual varieties: "It would be an endless task to describe each person's peculiar kinds of displeasure. There are those who cannot stand the grating of a saw, the grunt of a pig, the tearing of a piece of cloth, the breaking up of a live coal with tongs. There are those who are offended by certain gestures, the way people walk, the way they sit down, the way they move their hands, the way they talk. And there are even those who are beside themselves when they see a wrinkle in someone else's clothing. Who could explain all the follies of this *difficult animal*, who at times can be suffered by no one any more than he can suffer others—and this being the case with all men?" (*ibid.*, p. 1,284). Montaigne and Pascal must have read Vives more than they are thought to have.

The anguished Vives preached peace with all the persuasive resources of his Romano-Christian latinity. The meditative Vives found the motives of human disorder, both cruel and incorrigible, in the inexplicable roots of life. Beside this refined and desperate personality Erasmus seems rather pale. The great Dutchman could not, or would not, ask himself the radical questions.

Vives' "difficult animal" recalls Santob's "dangerous" man. But the earlier writer's incipient expression unfolded, in the later one, into a brilliant display of human phenomena. His description of the passions that "issue from the aspect of evil," that "exasperate and derange the human spirit" (Book iii, Chapters xi-xxi) is exceedingly penetrating. Of sadness, for instance, he says: "It would be easy to enumerate, after the doctrines of

---

[46] What I am emphasizing is the importance which Vives gives to the phenomena by which the soul manifests itself and the effectiveness with which he observes them. The idea that the soul cannot be known except through its works was a commonplace of the schools. "Perfect[a]e cognitionis integritas quamvis a causis originem contrahat, tamen anim[a]e notitia, qu[a]e a sensibili perceptione distat, ex eius operibus indagatur quippe cum eius essentia latente opera ab ea emanantia ipsam in propatulo manifestent" (Petrus Hispanus, *De anima*, edit. by M. Alonso, p. 51). But when he goes on to discuss the passions, Petrus Hispanus limits himself to giving worthless enumerations: "dilectatio, dolor, gaudium, ira, mansuetudo," etc. (pp. 342-343). Furthermore, Vives does not try to ascertain what the essence of the soul is.

the Stoics, the parts that make up this affliction; and I would have done so if I had thought that they had been transmitted with proper fidelity, and that Cicero understood them and explained them rightly; but I am not convinced of the one thing or the other" (Chapter xix). Assisted by the Greek and Latin classics, Vives observes for himself. Good or bad, the passions reveal the functioning of the soul, they are constitutive of man's existence. The intellective curiosity of the Hispano-Jewish tradition is magnified in Vives along with his bitter and disillusioned view of the world. In this "man of the Renaissance" there is nothing of the gaiety of the Renaissance.

Like a true convert, Vives made several pronouncements against his ancestors: "The Lord gave the Jewish nation a peculiar, hard and harsh [praefractam] law, which suited a people of such character."[47] Though to be sure, there is nothing here of the perverse spirit of certain converted Jews. Quite the contrary, Vives was a stalwart defender of tolerance, and in his treatise *On the Truth of the Christian Faith* he argues that the charity of the Gospels should be practiced even between Christians and non-Christians. Diabolical motives, Vives thought, had given rise to "the sad reality that both the public and private morals of Christians are too often evil and corrupt, and those of the impious are sound and laudable." Thus it happens that the non-Christians reject a religion which is "unable to improve those who profess it. . . . We profess the law of Christ, but we do not practice it." In ancient times the Asiatic hated the European, the Greek hated the barbarian, and the Jew hated the Gentile. Mutual hatred was permissible among them, "and mingling and conversing were abominable. Christ, with his law, abolished all these distinctions, and razed to the ground the walls dividing one people from another. He united man with man, whatever their condition . . . , for all were sons of the same Father who was God" (ed.cit., ii, 1,662). In this work the Christian, the Jew, and the Moslem carry on a debate. But the latter two do not yield to the arguments of the Christian, who aspires to convince them and not to do them violence.

Vives' position with regard to man as a physical being and as a social and religious person is more desperate than that of his contemporary, Calvin, whose anguish was eased by the religion and the church he founded. Vives remained within the bonds of a Catholicism whose social efficacy was one of his problematical concerns and whose ministers he did not hold in excessive esteem. Turned in upon himself, he opened new

[47] *Socorro de los pobres*, ed.cit., i, 1391; *Opera omnia*, Valencia, 1783, iv, 468.

perspectives to psychology and devised more humane forms of social life. In contrast to the Spanish Inquisition, which rent people's souls and forced them to flee to more peaceful lands, the Valencian philosopher preached the life of the blessed company in an ideal Christ, and the creation of social organizations to resolve the conflict created by poverty. In *De subventione pauperum* a way is proposed for correcting mendicancy by utilizing the civil and not the ecclesiastical power. Once more appears the juridico-administrative tradition of the Spanish Jew, habituated for centuries to occupying himself with matters of public administration. Religious charity had failed, and it was urgent to cleanse the churches of beggars. They begged "with no regard for where nor when, during the very celebration of the sacrifice of the mass. . . . They open a way for themselves through the thickest crowds with their repulsive sores, with the nauseating stench that their entire bodies give off. So great is their selfishness and so acute the scorn which they feel for the community that they do not worry about communicating the virulence of their disease to others." Many beggars live in abundance. They eat and drink in the midst of raucous shouting. "You would say, if you heard them, that it is a quarrel between harlots and ruffians." If they are reproached, they say: "We are Jesus Christ's poor." But Christ, Vives observes in a heavily pregnant phrase, "did not say that the poor in money were blessed, but the poor in spirit."[48] The beggars that infest and infect the temples are never seen at confession and communion. "Let us not admit that ecclesiastical discipline has fallen so low, as to do nothing without being paid for it. The diocesan bishop thinks that sheep so bare of wool do not belong to his fold and pasture."[49]

All beggars who can must be forced to work, for Saint Paul says: "if any would not work neither would he eat." And likewise, "it is not to be tolerated that anyone live idly in the community, where, as in a well-ordered household, everyone must be in his place, attentive to his task" (p. 1,393). The civil authority must see to it that work goes on in the shops, that trades are taught, and that the physically able beggars are occupied in the various tasks that the community has to have done. "Easy jobs should be indicated to the sick and the aged. . . . No one is such an invalid that he lacks the strength to do something" (p. 1,395). Vives' plan required a reorganization of the hospitals, whose income benefited the administrators more than the patients. "If all the invalid beggars cannot be accommodated by the hospitals, one or more houses, as many as necessary, must be established, and the beggars must be isolated in

---

[48] *Obras completas*, I, 1,366-1,367.   [49] *Ibid.*, p. 1,391.

them. Let a physician, manservants, and maidservants be engaged. This is the way it is done by the human body and by those who manufacture ships: in both cases all filthy matter is collected in a sewer so that it will not harm the rest of the body. . . . Let those who are infected with a repugnant or contagious ailment sleep apart and eat separately, so that they do not transmit either their repulsiveness or their infection to others, lest sicknesses never come to an end" (p. 1,396). Vives inverts the usual perspective of charity, and first of all thinks of the good of society. There is something here like an anticipation of Baltasar Gracián's harsh coldness: "Pity for the unfortunate should never cause one to fall into the bad graces of the fortunate" (*Oráculo manual*).

The organization and control of the agencies of public aid Vives put in the hands of the community, which would name every year "as overseers two gentlemen from the Senate, very serious and spotless in their probity." The Church was excluded. In early times "when the blood of Christ still boiled, all the faithful cast their riches at the feet of the Apostles to be distributed by them according to each person's needs." Later "that blessed boiling of Christ's blood got colder and colder. . . . The Church began to emulate the world and to compete with it in pomp, show, and luxury. . . . For these expenses a huge heap of money was needed. And so, by this deplorable process, the bishops and presbyters converted the patrimony of the poor into their own wealth and income." Vives thinks that "these bishops and abbots and the others of the ecclesiastical hierarchy, if they had but the desire, could, with their enormous incomes, relieve most of the needy." The money spent on funerals would be better used in hospitals. "Those who are leaving this world should have no care for glory and praise that is not God's alone. . . . As for what goes on here in Flanders, I don't know . . . ; but conversing with old men in Spain I have heard them say that there were many who had increased their own income fabulously with the income of the hospitals, thus supporting themselves and their own instead of the poor, increasing the population of their own houses and depopulating the hospitals; all these abuses were started by the access to such abundant and easy money. . . ." No doubt the author of this original project for public assistance was prevented by caution from saying that the same thing was happening in Flanders. And he continued his pungent criticism of the way the Church administered the interests of society with the warning that "priests should never invest the money of the poor for their own profit, under the pretext of piety and the celebrating of masses; they have enough to get along; they need no more" (pp. 1,398-1,401).

The allusion to his conversations with old men in Spain betrays the presence of tradition, the Hispano-Jewish tradition, in the writer's frame of mind, the tradition of a people concerned for centuries with the economic and administrative management of public affairs and having a secular and not an ecclesiastical view of life. The teachings of Erasmus concurrently reduced the ceremonies and practices of the Church to a minimum and presented, moreover, an image of primitive Christianity enveloped in the utopian dream of a golden age of the spirit. Both things fitted perfectly into the vital situation and the frame of mind of certain converts of fine sensibilities. Others, of coarser temperament, resolved their anguish by using the Inquisition to persecute those suspected of "heretica pravitas." Our great philosopher preferred the more humane and intelligent way.

Vives' work should be regarded and presented as a coherent realization of the diverse tense impulses that agitated his life, a life that was always prey to anxiety and problematical instability. Someone should make such a study. My interest has been only to establish a plausible relationship between the thinker's originality and the historical context of Hispanic life.

The Hispano-Hebrew's traditional inclination to play an effective part in public administration with practical ideas and activities was a historic reality, as another example will confirm. As one might expect, the Spaniards persisted in living in dependence on the numerous "beyonds" by which their life was ruled. But this did not keep them from sensing and lamenting the advances of poverty as early as the time of Philip II, as well as the growing hollowness of the immediate situations which they had to face every day. Vives tried to educate his contemporaries; he wanted to teach them to think and act more effectively by taking reason and the Gospel as guides. A century later I find the last case of a Hispano-Hebrew interested in bringing some kind of order into the social and economic chaos of Spain, this time the Spain of Philip III and Philip IV. The person and his task are very humble when compared to Luis Vives and his work, but the form and direction of the two lives are similar. In 1622 Duarte Gómez published a privately printed book in Madrid which today is extremely rare, and whose title page reads: *"Discourses on Trade with the Two Indies, Wherein Are Treated Important Matters of State and War, Addressed to His Sacred and Catholic Majesty, Our Lord King Philip IV*. Author, Duarte Gómez, native of the city of Lisbon. Year MDCXXII."[50] The author had spent many years in Portuguese India and returned from there with a fortune. Philip III's ministers had some dealings with him; in the work cited appear two letters to the Duke of Lerma written in 1612, in which Gómez speaks of the ships constructed by him on the king's orders and of money lent to the viceroy of India. He was not, then, one of the numerous wild schemers who swarmed thickly in the Spanish court; Gómez laments the fact "that so much credit is given to those who treat important things frivolously" (p. 7). Gómez knew how ships should be constructed and why those of Holland and England were superior to Spanish vessels. He tried to prod the leaders of Spain out of the lethargy into which they had fallen: "we are a people who, among other nations, glory most in being Catholic; it is well that our government be such that it seem to everyone the most successful, and I know that just as we surpass others *in worshiping God*, we know better how to govern in *human affairs*, since we are aided by the God whom we serve" (p. 238). The Hispano-Hebrew was trying to harmonize faith with reason, as other Christian peoples outside of Spain had been doing. But it was then late to attempt such an accord in the Peninsula.

The two great worries of Duarte Gómez were, first, to halt the growth of economic impoverishment and technical incompetence[51] and, second, to improve the social condition of the New Christians, with the purpose of converting them into elements useful for Spain, and of having them cease from their collaboration abroad with the king's enemies. I know no other document of the seventeenth century in which we may see more

---

[50] The Spanish title is: *Discursos sobre los comercios de las dos Indias, donde se tratan materias importantes de Estado y Guerra, dirigido a la Sacra y Católica Magestad del rey don Felipe Quarto nuestro señor.* The work has been made available to me by Professor Moses Bensabat Amzalak in an edition published by him in Lisbon in 1943.

[51] In 1604 Garcilaso the Inca described the financial chaos of the Spanish monarchy. Wishing to find out "what the value of the royal revenue was," he asked an expert, a certain Juan de Morales—"clerk of His Majesty"—who "after three months spent in making the necessary inquiries, responded as follows . . . : 'It is a matter that has never been settled, not even approximately; and the King, who wants to know the situation very much, has ordered that a special book be kept for it, and it has still not been begun, nor do we know that it will be begun, not to mention finished, because everything has such great ups and downs that one doesn't know how to go about it. And since money comes and goes through so many different channels, it seems impossible to gather everything together, or to make a rough guess without making very large mistakes.' " (*Historia general del Perú*, I, vii, edition of A. Rosenblat, I, 33). Yet Garcilaso had information about the royal revenues of the rest of Europe, even including Turkey.

clearly the conflict between the two groups of Spaniards. Basically, the situation was the same as before the expulsion: "Although many could prove by then that they came of four generations of Christians, people saw them more clearly as descended from many generations of Jews, even though they had professed to be Christians with the baptismal water. And as others of this kind were merchants and, with this trade, prosperous in worldly goods, if people could hate some because they were Jews, they could hate others because they were powerful and rich merchants. . . . Since the nobility could not bear the highly improved position of those who they thought had entered Portugal after the expulsion from Spain poor and with humble trades . . . , they spoke ill of them, considering them all as only feigned Christians. . . . They manage the money that the kingdom has, whether it be much or little" (p. 20). The more the Jews were persecuted, the more trade and public wealth decreased; "for which reason it was necessary to seek solutions through which all Spaniards *might become brothers*." Here is the same agonizing problem which made Vives think about means of pacification. Gómez proposed a compromise to the king: no honors should be granted to New Christians, in order not to provide the people with more reasons for hatred; true *hidalgos* should not marry them; on the other hand, those nobles with some Jewish blood should be allowed to do so; children of these marriages should be "qualified to take all posts and occupations" (p. 21). Portugal had no other important source of income besides custom-house receipts; commerce with India was interrupted by enemy ships which were superior to Spanish vessels. This whole situation created a vicious circle in which, from lack of money, there was neither navy, nor army, nor power; and vice versa. It is impossible, says Gómez, to do without the Jewish people, of whom Holland takes advantage. "It is of pressing importance that Your Majesty should order the institution of military study and maneuvers, this being another piece of advice which the Catholic Englishman [a friend of mine] gave me. . . . Nothing is of greater importance than for Your Majesty to command that much favor be given to those who distinguish themselves most as public servants. . . . Then we will understand the reason why the Dutch, from so small an island [in the East Indies], have so much oppressed the affairs of a monarch as great as Your Majesty; for, your vassals being, man for man, braver than they, our ships armed and being stronger in artillery, the outcome is always more advantageous for them, because they fight with the art and skill for which they have gained such great fame; for this advantage alone is sufficient to encourage them more and to discourage us, as was seen in the South, in the year 606 [i.e., 1606], when they fought with the viceroy Don Martín Alfonso de Castro" (p. 241). In a Spanish which occasionally stumbles, Duarte Gómez thinks and says what is usually considered characteristic of the Age of Enlightenment in a Feijóo or in a Jovellanos: "The beginning of knowledge is experience, and the end of it is truth; and the object of this paper is to explain what credit is, and what are the fruits of the truth and of the true art of trading; and experience engenders art, and stupidity disaster and misfortune; the experience of particular things is art," etc. (p. 131). Gómez proposed the construction of smaller ships, with non-rotting wood; because "these vessels which cross from Lisbon to India, have brought the kingdom and the merchants and sailors to ruin"; their poor quality is proved by the fact that the English and Dutch make no use of them when they capture them (p. 132).

Duarte Gómez was able to store up much experience because he had an open mind; conscious of the religious, technical, and economic difficulties around him, he put his acute intelligence at the service of the public interests, which was at the same time very much his own. With his work the line of theoretical-practical thought of the Hispano-Hebrews in Spain is broken off. What there is of objectifiable culture in their activities may have displayed variety; but these men are all alike in having made visible to us the internal form of their lives along with their ideas and feelings. The fluid, the problematic character of Santob's ideas (man's reality is not reducible to unity) or of Vives' (man is a difficult being, individualized in his emotional reactions, rebellious against Christianity, etc.) or of Duarte Gomez's (discord between the divine and the human)—these ideas or views of the inner and the outer world were conceived by people incapable of isolating themselves from the distress which agitated them, and disinclined to think fixed, serene ideas, bound up tightly in a closed system. The originality of these Hispano-Hebrews stands out in sharp contrast against the rest of European culture, and it is not surprising that their thought has remained either unknown or barren. They were neither advanced nor backward with respect to occidental culture. Rather, they were something that might have been and yet never attained plenary existence, an attempt, perhaps, to harmonize the divine and the human, to make of them a "squared" circle, wherein their conflicting perspectives—the infinite and the finite, the one and the multiple—might be integrated. I wonder whether the philosophy of Baruch Spinoza, an Iberian by descent, might not appear less strange and foreign to Europe if it were considered as the magnification of the possibilities latent in the Hispano-Hebrew tradition. However that may be, it is still true that Santob, Alfonso de la Torre, Vives, and Duarte Gómez lived, and created their works, as very much a part of Spain, and that they must be understood in terms of her tradition.

Toward an Understanding of Spain

THE IBERIAN CHRISTIAN arrived at the year 1500 with the awareness that he was facing immense and unsuspected possibilities. The sense of triumph over Moor and Jew after the events of 1492 made him feel secure in the plenitude of his power. The discovery of new worlds and the conquest of the kingdom of Naples indicated that the "beyonds" of his dreams were turning into close-by reality. The only requisite to fulfillment was to persevere in the traditional faith, to tense the will, and courageously defy death. "Men of high mettle, to whom was entrusted the honor of Spain"[1] were vanquishing the troops of the king of France in Calabria and Naples by emulating the characters in the tales of Amadis and Palmerin. The path to international prestige and greatness was valor; and the humane virtues stood at the forefront: "The Great Captain commanded that the prisoners should be treated with magnificent generosity, and this was intended to bring honor and fame to the Spanish nation" (p. 123). "The Spaniards fought with such virility and spirit that it was a wonderful thing to see; and the French put into that battle [Seminara, 1503] all their hopes for a lustrous page in the chronicles of their king" (p. 168). But on this and many other occasions, victory went to the Spaniards.

The plowman, "from childhood destined by his fateful star for the struggle and stubborn resistance of the hard earth," passed without transition from his clods to dominion over distant lands whose existence had only recently been suspected. "The ship departs on its journey from the sheltered ports of western Spain, . . . following as best she can the will of her master, eager to lay his eyes on new things and strange peoples, and to ennoble his spirit, expecting to increase his worth by increasing his knowledge" (Torres Naharro, *Propalladia*, 1517). Lands and seas surrender meekly. In a brief span of years, Hispanic valor had girdled the planet's surface. There was a general awareness of all this, and the more

[1] "Crónica del Gran Capitán," in the *Nueva Biblioteca de Autores Españoles*, X, 121.

gifted sensibilities expressed it in exquisite fashion, for arms and letters went together in intimate reciprocity. In Gil Vicente's *Auto da Fama*, Castile and Portugal both aspire to possess Fame:

"Well you know, high lady, the victories of Castile. . . . You have heard that in our time she has conquered everything she sought to subjugate. . . . The Italian fields recount their Roman deeds. And Granada, won with such hard effort, is a wondrous thing."

But Castile, in Gil Vicente's words, recognized the preeminence of Portugal, "because her victories are in far-distant places and for the faith."

The Hispanic conquests were not shaped after any historic pattern. Rome had adjusted the peoples she conquered to institutions in which empire, law, and religion were unified. Spain's overseas enterprises from the outset established the never-before-heard-of dispute as to whether the conquest was legitimate or not. The king, the church, and private individuals carried on debates, bloody at times, over their respective rights. One might have expected the common effort in imperial expansion to reduce the Iberian Peninsula to a compact unity, yet Castile, Portugal, and Aragon-Catalonia did not fuse into a single will. Thus, in the middle of the seventeenth century, when the invisible bonds that held the Iberian peoples together were loosened, Portugal, Catalonia, and even Aragon thought of breaking away from the peninsular union. Immediate interests were lacking to incite the units to common and coordinate efforts.

It is no less surprising that from the outset of the conquest of America it was the Spaniards themselves who incited the indigenous populations to rebel against Spain. This is the ultimate implication of the anarchic tendency, as we would say today, in the work of Father Las Casas. The Spaniard who lived in active opposition to the state within Spain also lived in conscious agony (vivía desviviéndose) as he confronted the fact of the domination of the Indians by the Spanish people. If ambition and avarice had been the only motives of the conquest, no one would have questioned the right of the conqueror. But Ercilla, in *La Araucana* (1569), shows his sympathy for the Araucanian Indian rebels. Before this, Antonio de Guevara had criticized Spanish imperialism in *El Villano del Danubio*. And Quevedo says: "Those who are gluttonous for provinces have always died of surfeit. . . . America is a rich and beautiful strumpet who was unfaithful to her spouses the Indians. . . . The Christians say that heaven has punished the Indies (las Indias) because they adore idols; and we Indians say that heaven is bound to punish the Christians because they adore Indian women (las indias)" (*La hora de todos*, 1638). The idea that it was vicious and wicked for the Spaniards to maintain themselves in their American dominions reappears in Cadalso: "The great treasures quickly acquired in the Indies distract many from cultivating the mechanical arts in the Peninsula and from increasing its population" (*Cartas marruecas*, III). In his *Noches lúgubres* the same author alludes to the gold that someone "brought to *tyrant Europe* from *unfortunate America*." And other texts could be added. There is no need, therefore, to look around among ideas gestated outside Spain for motives and incitements for the independence of the Hispano-American colonies. The principal reason lay in the very process of Spanish history, within which Las Casas' strange form of Christianity turned eventually into rational criticism.

It was not in the pursuance of shrewdly calculated plans that the Spaniards spread over the world. If they had had any such plans, their undertakings would have had much more modest proportions. Some went out in search of riches, spices, and gold, as had the Venetians; for many converted Spanish Jews and Moors the primary impulse was to find a peace that they did not have at home; the religious missionaries reproduced in sixteenth-century America the pattern of the spiritual conquest of the Moslems; at their side were men eager to exercise personal seigniory in a peculiarly Hispanic form, to the end of "winning honor," of creating for themselves halos of grandeur worthy of their nobility and their manly virtue. "Good men of noble aspiration must seek life and must go from the good thing to the better . . . and try to win honor," wrote Bernal Díaz del Castillo as he began his *History of the Conquest of New Spain*, reflecting the feeling of those who, after all, were the authentic conquistadors. The idea that avarice and cruelty were the only motives for Hispano-Portuguese expansion presupposes a total ignorance of the reality of history. All kinds of stars guided those men, whose spiritual energy came from a very special form of humanity in which strange fantasies and the most concrete realizations were harmonized. The territorial expansion of the Spaniards was something like a novel or a drama in which the characters actually lived and died, with no end save that of consuming themselves and expressing themselves in the tension of their own existence. It is symbolic, to begin with, that the two extremities of the Spanish dominions in America should bear names taken from the romances of chivalry: California, from the *Sergas de Esplandián*; Patagonia, from *Primaleón*.[2] In the center rises the incredible figure of

[2] The origin of the name of California was discovered in 1862 by E. E. Hale (see Ruth Putnam, *University of California Publications in History*, 1917, IV, 293).

Bishop Vasco de Quiroga, rigorously applying to the Mexican Indians everything that Thomas More imagined in his *Utopia*. To try to fit Spanish life only to economic and down to earth criteria is truly to waste time and not to understand history. Among the thousands who sailed from the "sheltered ports of western Spain," there were many, many indeed, who went looking for fantastic islands in the gloomy ocean, for giants and pygmies, the fountain of eternal youth, the seven enchanted cities, the virgin Amazons, the lake where the sun retired to sleep, the Golden King, or the footprints left by the Apostles.[3] Eight hundred years of a life comparable to nothing else in Europe had made this and much more possible.

This faith in a future and a "beyond" marvelous to contemplate was not the heritage of the common people alone. Men of learning were sustained by that confidence no more and no less than the naïve and ignorant peasants. In 1492 Antonio de Nebrija felt that the Castilian speech had already climbed to its highest peak, so high in fact that "one can more rightly fear its descent than hope for its elevation."[4] Nebrija compared the lofty position of Castilian to the supreme level reached by Hebrew in the Bible; by Greek in "the multitude of poets, orators, and philosophers who put the finishing touches not only on the Greek language, but on all other [Greek] arts and sciences"; and by Latin thanks to "the abundant and delightful authors: Cicero, Caesar, Lucretius, Virgil, Horace, Ovid, Livy. . . ." With self-assured boldness Nebrija wrote: "what we have said of the Hebrew, Greek, and Latin languages, we can demonstrate much more clearly for Castilian." As the basis for this comment he took the works of Alphonse the Learned, in which "the language began to show its strength." According to him, the only enduring values of Castilian in 1492 were contained in the *Partidas*, the *General Estoria*, and the "many books translated from Latin and Arabic." However, Nebrija compared his language with those of Antiquity not so much because of its cultural prestige but because it had spread through Aragon, Navarre, and Italy, "following the company of the princes we send to rule over those kingdoms." The greatness of

---

For the name of Patagonia, see María Rosa Lida de Malkiel, *Hispanic Review*, 1952, xx, 321. The text of *Las sergas de Esplandián* (1521) says: "Know that at the right of the Indies there was an island, called California, very close to the location of the Earthly Paradise, which island was populated by black women, with not one man among them, whose manner of living was quite like that of the Amazons" (Chap. CLVII).

[3] See Enrique de Gandía, *Los mitos de la conquista americana*, Buenos Aires, 1929.

[4] Preface to the *Gramática castellana*, 1492.

the language, then, was rooted not in the language itself but in the imperial urge that sustained it: the unity of Spain and the spread of her victorious arms. Awareness of political power was thus put on the same level with the universal values that had been expressed in Hebrew, Latin, and Greek. The Castilians felt their language as a summit attained because they felt themselves to be lords and because they had imposed their seigniory on the other men, that is, because they were aware of the importance of their personal achievements. The greatness of the language consisted in the fact of its geographical extension and in the belief that it was destined to spread still farther: "as soon as Your Highness brings under his yoke many barbarous peoples and nations of strange languages . . . , then, through this my grammar they will be able to become acquainted" with Castilian. The author did not compose his *Gramática* out of disinterested scientific motives; he was drawn to his task by his *vision* of an imperial future in historical time and earthly space, and he was carried along by his messianic belief and his confidence in a queen "in whose hand and power lies the present importance of our language as well as the decisions about all our things."

Nebrija, a student in Bologna for ten years, was not a humanist in the Italian style but in the Spanish. His form of life, like the Hebraico-Islamic, depended on belief in a future, not on a present rich in lasting works. The Semite lived in the *will be* of his hope, in prophecy, in messianism, in a temporal and spatial beyond, and without any goals separable from the activity of which they are the end. A person who thus puts at the center of his life the future of his belief and his hope does not make a problem out of the current process of his existence, he does not live in a state of inquisitive and *docta ignorantia* in which nothing is accepted on the warrant of received faith or knowledge. The world around appears to him as a solid and opaque whole, given once and for all as something to be won, as the sum of possible booty for the will and hope, not for reflective analysis. Before this future, which I call "messianic," the spirit either sinks into total inactivity, or launches itself upon daring enterprises of incalculable dimensions. In either case, the life of the person with a messianic hope does not objectify itself completely in its products, because these products are simply the projection of his existence and faith: outside this frame of reference, they have no reality. The product of reflective thought, on the contrary, is objectified in something which is not identified with any person's psychological and emotional situation. A theorem or an internal combustion engine defy the most deep-seated skepticism and are indifferent to the strength or weakness of the human will. That is to say, if maximum belief can lead to ignorance, the total objectification of thought in unquestionable realities can convert man into an abstract mechanism. The authentic believer in the expectation that his life is bound to keep on "befalling him" has confidence that the world will go on being continuously created by a provident deity, following the same rhythm as the hopes in which he creates himself and recreates his own existence. Opposite him rises the rationalized man, proud of his omnipotence, the supplanter of divinity. His creations do not need the direction of any kind of providence. Witness Hegel: "Logic must be taken as the system of pure reason, as the realm of pure thought. This realm is the naked truth, in and for itself. It can therefore be said that this content is the exposition of God as He is in his eternal essence, *before the creation* of nature and of a finite spirit."[5]

The God of the Old Testament and the God of Islam are rather like artists who could never set their work free as finished and perfect. The man created in *Genesis* faltered time and again, and had to be made over and saved by the Christian God. Islamic man and everything that exists for him are a continual endeavor in which the fingers of his creator are never still. His being and his truth cannot be fulfilled save at the moment of becoming one again in his point of origin, when man returns from the temporal to the eternal. Only the Greek, among the ancients, and his heir, the European rationalist, have believed it possible to make of man an absolute reality.

Novelty (novedad) and New (lo nuevo)

At this point in our reflections it is perhaps appropriate to make more precise the way in which Spaniards have understood the words *novedad* (novelty) and *nuevo* (new)[6] and the value they have attached to the concepts thereby signified; for through these words it will be possible to sense the pulse of Spanish life at the heart.

Innovation as an external thing was regarded as a disturbance of what the Spaniard deemed to be his authentic life. Whereas he felt it

[5] *Wissenschaft der Logik*, Stuttgart, 1928, pp. 45-46.

[6] As in the previous philological discussions that have figured in this book, the translator is trying to be both helpful to the reader unfamiliar with Spanish and faithful to the Spanish which is being translated. The discussion here is about the peculiar meanings of two Spanish words, *novedad* and *nuevo* (in its various inflections). In English the words will sometimes be translated one way and sometimes another, depending on the context.

legitimate to magnify or diminish the value of the individual as long as this value was something absolute within the system of standards authorized by tradition, he regarded as undesirable anything that incited the person to be different from himself, or that disturbed his sense of being the way he was supposed to be. Nothing seemed more dangerous than confronting new external realities, for these had no connection with the belief that one was where one belonged. Thus, in 1617 Dr. Carlos García could write (not in Spain but in Paris) that "the Spanish mind is afraid and cowardly in matters concerning the faith and governance of the Church; for the moment the Spaniard is invited to analyze an article of faith, he stops up all his knowledge, wisdom, and judgment."[7] For the same reason, the humanist Sebastián de Covarrubias had said that *novedad* (innovation) "is usually dangerous because it brings with it change from ancient usage" (*Tesoro de la lengua castellana*, 1611). Before that, in the fifteenth century, the Marquis of Santillana had exhorted Spain to recover the awareness of what she was: "If you would go back to yourself, and recover the ancient custom . . . , then I could believe that the most exalted, sovereign mercy of the magnificent, powerful, and sovereign God would deal mercifully with you."[8] Moving ahead again in time, we find that Ramón de la Cruz writes these lines for a dialogue between a rustic and a courtier in 1763:

FELIPE. In Lent the priest said: "Lovers who have anything to do with each other without the Church's blessing on their heads are excommunicate."

GARCÍA. What a joke! The way the priest talks about such bunk. . . .

FELIPE. If you let loose another remark like that, I swear to God that I will inform the Holy Office. We'll let them put packsaddles and cruppers on us, but we'll never let anyone change the Church.[9]

To keep his existence within the frame of his own character has been the Spaniard's highest aspiration. Quevedo gave the most powerful expression to this idea latent in the depths of Hispanic consciousness. Rome was ruined, according to him, through "the *new* introduction of Julius Caesar's empire. The world was ruined by wanting to be different, and the desire to be *different from themselves* ruins men. Innovation is so little pleased with itself that it is no sooner unhappy with

[7] *La oposición y conjunción de las dos grandes luminarias de la tierra*, Paris, 1617, Chap. XI.
[8] In *Le Chansonnier espagnol d'Herberay des Essarts*, ed. by Ch. V. Aubrun, 1951, p. 22.
[9] "La civilización," in the *Nueva Biblioteca de Autores Españoles*, XXIII, 100.

what it has been than it tires of what it is. And to maintain itself as innovation, it must stop being new; for the innovator, life consists of perpetual deaths and perishings. He must either stop being a seeker after
novelties or perpetually concern himself with ceasing to be."[10] Which
is to say that what is changing never *is*, because being implies permanence,
so that innovation must either stabilize itself or renounce being. Swept
along by his antipathy for external newness, Quevedo pretends to include the life of man in the region of abstract and immutable being. He
does not do this when he observes how his own vital experience goes:

> It is no longer yesterday; tomorrow has not yet come;
> Today passes, and is, and was, with a movement
> Which carries me headlong toward death.

Life, then, is the great innovator, an unavoidable succession of *is* and
no longer is: it is lacking in substantiality. It troubles Quevedo that the
world external to man is not immutable and essential, yet in his own case
he is resigned to the realization that his life is a flux that is working its
own destruction. This contrast brings out important aspects of Spanish
thought underlying the Spanish language and the course of Spanish life.[11]

This scorn for innovation was felt by other Spaniards. "As if the
novelty of things, more than their greatness, could move us to investigate
their causes," says Luis de Granada in the *Símbolo de la fe* (1, 1, 4).
Gracián accepts the continual renovation of the axiological attitude; he
values, as it were, innovation in the power to perceive values: "Men of
wisdom have always had recourse to reflection, using their imagination
to come into the world anew, by noticing its wonders—for everything
is wonderful" (*Criticón*, 1, 11). But he attacks with no less violence than
Quevedo those who delight in outward innovation: "We go around
begging for new and childish trifles to quiet our curious yearnings with
oddities. . . . We delight in new playthings, provided by both nature

---

[10] "Marco Bruto," in the *Obras completas*, ed. by Astrana Marín, p. 589.

[11] There is a difference between Quevedo and Montaigne, whom he was fond of
reading. In the *Essais* (1, 22) political and religious innovation is rejected because
Montaigne does not wish to see any further disturbance of public peace (he is
writing after the Saint Bartholomew's Day massacre). Montaigne points out the
stupidity of many customs, and he says that "les miracles sont selon l'ignorance en
quoy nous sommes de la nature, non selon l'estre de la nature; l'assuefaction endort
la vue de nostre jugement. . . . L'usage nous desrobe le vray visage des choses." But
for practical reasons it is better not to change the established order. In the last
analysis, the relativist Montaigne would follow the example of that Greek who
knew how "non seulement commander selon la loix, mais aux loix mesmes, quand
la necessité publique le requeroit."

and art, and do gross injustice to ancient wonders because they are well known to us" (*ibid.*, I, III).

Thus it was to be expected that the Spanish caste would be little attracted by innovation within the world of things and ideas and that it would prefer to turn backward in time rather than make plans for the future of its land and people. Its language moved slowly, so that after more than four centuries certain pages from Juan del Encina and Torres Naharro seem modern in vocabulary and syntax. And for the same reason, Lope de Vega's contemporaries did not find his frequent medieval themes "medieval." They did not feel what we call the Middle Ages as medieval.

If we establish the distinction between desirable subjective innovation and detestable outward innovation, we can understand certain meanings of the word *novedad* and its relatives in Old Spanish. Here are a few examples: "Las *nuevas* que *faze* el Campeador" (*Cantar de Mío Cid*, 1,343); "de grandes nuevas *son* los Yfantes" (*ibid.*, 2,084); "aquis' metió en *nuevas* mío Çid Campeador" (*ibid.*, 2,113); "ome *sin* grandes nuevas" (Berceo, *Milagros*, 312); "gigante *de grandes* nuevas, que fizo grant conquista" (Berceo, *Loores*, 10).[12]

In these examples *nuevas* refers to an aspect or a moment of the person's vital functioning, inseparable from him, just as in the Gracián text quoted above, the *new* was the *wise men's* act of coming, and nothing external to them. Consequently, when the *Cantar de Mío Cid* says: "Estas son las nuevas de myo Cid" (2,113), *nuevas*, besides meaning "news," or "account," means above all, "great deeds performed by someone." On the contrary, *noveles* in Old French and *niuwen maeren* in Middle High German do not include an inescapable reference to the creative act of the person as something incorporated in the telling of the story. When the *Chanson de Roland* says: "Des ore cumencet le plait et les noveles / De Guenelun, ki traisun ad faite" (3,747), *noveles* means the same thing it does in line 665: "De Guenelun atent li reis *nuveles*," (the king is waiting for news, for an account of something), for an account of an objectified something which is no longer a part of the person Ganelon. The semantic perspective that is absent in French and German

---

[12] As the next paragraph indicates, there is no way to translate the word *nuevas* in these phrases and keep the double meaning of the Spanish. The following are the literal renderings, but the reader must remember that *nuevas* (*news*) in these cases is felt as a genuine plural in Spanish and not as a collective singular: "the news that the Cid makes (*or* does)"; "the Princes are men of great news"; "the Cid plunged himself into news"; "a man lacking great news"; "a giant of great news, who made a great conquest."

was possible in Spanish because in this as in other cases there was a cross with the oriental view of life and the world.

In the glosses to his translation of the Bible (c. 1430), Rabbi Arragel has something that at first seems incompatible with the idea of the creation of world *ex nihilo*. He is explaining how it is that *Genesis* begins with the account of the creation: "It was necessary to tell of the *beginning* and *innovation* of the world" (Duke of Alba edition, 1, 97). The rabbi adds that the world "has received innovation from the Creator. . . . We believe the world to have been made *anew*."[13]

This is intelligible only if it be admitted that *innovation* is not something different, changed, with respect to what has existed before. When Arragel speaks of the *new* he is pointing out an aspect or moment of the immanent process of creation; he is referring to the fact that creation has realized itself as existence.[14] This was the way certain Arabic philosophers conceived this problem, and it was possible for them to express themselves in forms of language that are puzzling to us but which corresponded to the forms of their thought. The Arabic verb *ḥadatha* means "to be new, to happen, to relate something," and in derived forms "to create, to give rise to something." Hence, *ḥādith*, "news, notice, narration"; *ḥudūth*, "creation," with reference to the possibility of creation. Avicenna says: "Everything that begins to be, *kull ḥādith*, has been possible before it exists. . . . The *ḥādith* is preceded by a potentiality for being and by an agent," which is not to be understood as the subject or agent of an

---

[13] The respective quotations read in Spanish: "El *començamiento* e *ynovación* del mundo, nescesario dezir era" and "ynovación de Criador rescebido aver. . . . Nos creer el mundo *de nuevo* fecho seer."

[14] The glosses to Rabbi Arragel's translation of the Bible were written not only by the Rabbi himself but in some instances by Christian collaborators imposed upon him by Don Luis de Guzmán, Grand Master of Calatrava (for whom the translation was made). One of these collaborators realized that the "innovation" of the world and its creation *ex nihilo* were incompatible. That is, his Christian mind found the two notions incompatible. And he added these remarks: "Master Girona says: 'In the beginning God created all things without any previous element, except that he created a kind of very thin, impalpable matter; and this is what God created in the beginning'" (1, 97-98). Apparently, then, it was matter, which was a mass capable of receiving the form of anything; which thing is called the *hyle* by some and by others the primal matter; the matter was created *ex nihilo*, and the form did not have to be so created, but could be "innovated." Aristotle, by this interpretation, thus resolved the conflict between Arragel and the Franciscans who wrote some of his glosses. Master Girona referred to here must have been a certain Antonio Girona who wrote commentaries on Aristotle and Peter Lombard (see Carreras y Artau, *Historia de la filosofía española*, II, 498).

action but in the weaker sense of "that in which resides the thing's power to be."[15]

Without going into the philosophical problem itself, and leaving aside the question of the relationship between Arabic and Greek thought, for present purposes it suffices to bear in mind that Averroes also describes as "innovated" those beings which, unlike God, do have an origin.[16] Ghazzālī says the same thing: "The possible does not exist because of itself but because of something else. In this sense it is said to be *muḥdath* [innovated, that is, it has begun to be]. And since the world is possible, it is therefore *muḥdath*, which means that its existence comes from something else, and that it does not have existence of itself" (Goichon, *op.cit.*, p. 255).

Now we understand what was behind Rabbi Arragel's speaking of the "innovation of the world," of its "beginning," of its having been made "anew." And we can also understand the meaning of a certain passage in *Lazarillo de Tormes* which has up to now escaped our attention: "Everyone said to me . . . , 'Look for a master to serve.' And I said to myself, 'Where is such to be found, unless God, *as he created* the world, create him now *anew*?'" (Third Treatise).[17]

Thus it is that by examining literary expression and language, it is possible to arrive at an outline of the very form of Hispanic life; that is, we can perceive something of the preferential direction taken by the course of Spain's living disposition. The Spaniard has innovated himself, created himself from within, not from without. When he has needed or

[15] See A.-M. Goichon, *La distinction de l'essence et de l'existence d'après Ibn Sīnā (Avicenne)*, Paris, 1937, p. 249 and *passim*.

[16] Ibn Rochd (Averroès), *Traité décisif*, texte arabe, traduction française par León Gauthier, Algiers, 1948, pp. 13-15. Manuel Alonso, *Teología de Averroes*, Madrid, 1947, pp. 174-176.

[17] The expression "create the world *anew*" (criar el mundo *de nuevo*) is characteristic of Hispanic Jewish writers: "The world is created *anew*, because it is a body, and a body must be either in motion or at rest, and both are accidents that are *innovated* in it, the one coming after the other; and the one that comes after is new without a doubt, because it comes upon the other anew; and *the one that is past is new*, because if it were eternal it would not suffer cessation. So that both are created anew; inasmuch as it did not exist before the accidents, and since the accidents are innovated, it follows that it also is created anew" (*Cuzary*, diálogo filosófico, by Yehuda Ha-Leví [twelfth century], translated from the Arabic into Hebrew by Yehudá Ibn Tibbon, and from the Hebrew into Castilian by Rabbi Jacob Abendana. Edition of A. Bonilla y San Martín, Madrid, 1909, p. 326). Other passages referring to the innovation of the world are to be found on pp. 15, 31, 32, 277, etc. Abendana published his translation in Amsterdam in 1663. Therefore the author of *Lazarillo* was a convert (or a Jew) well-acquainted with the literary Hispano-Jewish tradition.

wanted external innovations, he has had to import them from other peoples, for he has preferred to raise (it is significant that the Spanish verb here is *criar*, a popular variant of *crear*, "to create") persons, plants, or animals as in an extensible process of vivification. The *newness* in such phrases as those applied to a person "de grandes nuevas" is an aspect of the person's capacity for creative action and not a reference to something separated from the person (news, event, etc.). Novelty imposed from outside the person was rejected by Quevedo as unreal—reality has to be something that belongs to someone, not a "res nullius." If personal judgment by chance finds an objective truth to which it corresponds, very well. If not, however, it must, as Count Lozano says in *Las mocedades del Cid*, be defended as if it were right—"defended, not emended." For it is the person that counts and not his objectifiable discoveries.

The Future as an Advent

Man creates, he "innovates," his own self in his own sealed-off consciousness. At the same time he makes hardly any innovations at all in nature of the arrangement of the world around him. Things and ideas persist unchanged in the external realm while within the soul there is a frenzied succession of situations and perspectives one on top of the other. Lope de Vega wrote in 1602:

> To faint, to dare, to be in state of fury,
> To be cross, tender, generous, aloof,
> Heartened, dying, dead, alive,
> Faithful, treacherous, cowardly, spirited;
> To find outside of your beloved no center of repose;
> To show yourself gay, sad, humble, haughty,
> Vexed, valiant, fugitive,
> Contented, offended, suspicious;
> To turn your face from disillusionment,
> To drink venom as sweet liquor,
> To forget advantage, to love abuse;
> To think that a heaven dwells in a hell,
> To give your life and soul for a delusion—
> This is love: he who's tried it knows.[18]

There was a strong contrast between the changing variety of the psychological panorama and the paralytic immobility in which the Spaniard

[18] Sonnet CXXVI of the *Rimas humanas*, 1602.

kept the world around him. External novelty, whenever it is to be found in Hispanic history, has come about in various ways: it has resulted indirectly from the high tension of the individual will (the discovery of new lands,[19] for example); or it has been an "advent"—something rained from heaven; or it has been the imported product of other people's skill (constitutions, railroads, etc.). Left to himself, Hispanic man has always lived in himself and in his hopes, trusting in his self and in every kind of providential benevolence. Immediate circumstances have always had for him the appearance of a veil, whether thin or thick, which conceals a future and a beyond that are not subject to the control of the mind.

The form in which the Spaniard has articulated his awareness of his own inner life and the awareness of his external action is unique. This uniqueness is compatible with the fact that there is an evident connection between the Hispanic position with respect to the future and the same thing among the Semitic peoples. The Semitic attitude in this matter has been elegantly clarified by Hans von Soden and Xavier Zubiri:[20]

"For the Greek, his clan, his *polis*, is a moment of nature. For the Hebrew, on the other hand, nature is the theatre in which the existence of his people goes on. . . . Thus, the Hebrew sees the world through the modes of his personal existence. 'Others' are not simply 'others,' they are 'neighbors,' that is, either near to him or far away. For the Hebrew it has always been a question, as is seen even in the Gospel parable, who is the neighbor, not in an abstract sense but in the sense of *my* neighbor. I can depend on this neighbor, or I cannot, in life; he is true or untrue to his word; I can use his word for support, or I cannot. The Hebrew called this support *aman*. From this comes the word *emunah*, meaning firmness, certainty. The firmness of the friend in his pledged word, in the signs of affection that he shows me, entitles me to call him a *true* friend. Truth is thus for the Hebrew fidelity, fulfillment of a promise, veracity; so that the Hebrew, as he lives in the midst of other things, has seen them

---

[19] In *Os Lusiadas*, by Luis de Camoens, Vasco da Gama, upon his arrival in India, is greeted thus by a Moor: "What great *destiny*, or what *good fortune*, has led you to venture on such a journey. There must indeed be some hidden and obscure cause to make one come from the distant Tagus and the unknown Minho, through seas never ploughed by any other keel, to kingdoms so remote and out of the way" (VII, 30). The voyages and conquests of the other European peoples were thoughtfully planned out in advance. It did not occur to the Dutch, the English, or the French to write a poem like *The Lusiads* to celebrate their discoveries of any New World.

[20] See Hans von Soden, *Was ist Wahrheit*, 1927, with which I am acquainted through Zubiri's remarks in the *Revista de Occidente*, 1933, CXVIII, 94ff.

as promises. For the Hebrew, the stone does not 'have' hardness, it 'is' not hard in the sense that the Greek would give to these words. The stone, because of what we call its hardness, is present in the Hebrew awareness as something remaining firm in the future, behaving solidly in the future. The stone 'is' hard means: the stone will remain. The truth is thus not an attribute of the present, but a promise of the future, whether it is a question of men or of things. . . . The organ of truth is not the *logos* as a declaration of what things are, but trust, faith that they will be what they promise to be. The truth is perceived in trust, in hope. . . . What things are, what their destiny is, will be clear when the consummation of the centuries is reached. . . . The Greek looks at the world and says 'it is'; the Hebrew looks at the world and says 'so be it'—amen. Instead of the vision of the whole which the Greek called *theoría*, we have here another vision of the whole, essentially different: *eschatology*."

It is fitting to complement the foregoing statement with what Unamuno wrote in 1906 in his essay bearing the same title as Hans von Soden's, *What is Truth?* (¿Qué es verdad?): "The reality that is believed in is worth more than the reality which is not believed in. For it is the lie, not error, that kills the soul. . . . If the lie should vanish, errors would disappear and the truth would be revealed to us little by little. . . . That which we call reality, objective or logical truth, is nothing but the reward bestowed upon sincerity, upon truthfulness. Nature would have no secrets at all for the man always and absolutely truthful and sincere. Blessed are the pure in heart, for they shall see God! And purity of heart is truthfulness, and truth is God." This, according to von Soden, is neither the Greek nor the Western way of thinking.

It would be a gross error to approach the similarity between the Semitic and the Spanish conceptions of truth as if this similarity represented a transfer of ideas from one people to another like, for instance, the adoption of the French parliamentary system by Spaniards and Italians in the nineteenth century. The belief that truth is equal to truthfulness is important in the present case as a value-habit of the inner processes of Hispanic life. The Hispano-Christians who came up against the Moors and Jews in the eighth century and who intermingled with them had, to be sure, their own beliefs. But the tremendous usefulness of these beliefs in the furtherance of the Christians' purposes in both war and peace was revealed to them by the enemy, as we have seen in the case of Santiago, by an enemy whose life rested totally and authentically upon his religious belief. The Germanic peoples had not subjugated the Roman

Empire through the stimulus of any religious belief. Their wars were not waged under divine inspiration, they were not "divinales," the word that Alonso de Cartagena (a converted Jew) used in the fifteenth century to distinguish at one stroke the Spaniards from the other Europeans (see Chapter 1). The "divinely-inspired war" was a Mohammedan invention, or at least it appeared for the first time in Europe under the aegis of Islam. Nothing like it had gone on in Iberia before the invasion of 711. Nine hundred years later Spaniards and Portuguese were conquering remote peoples "divinely," that is, in the full awareness that God's word and man's were the foundation of truth, and granting no importance to the truth of things, a truth that has its foundation in impersonal logic.[21]

Regarded under this light, Spanish and Portuguese history becomes clear and unified in its meaning and, at the same time, quite independent of Semitic history. Under the pressure of prolonged crises, a people can modify or energize its own vital tendencies through the continual example of another people with whom its life is intimately interwoven, yet without abandoning its own peculiar, unique course. Truth, for the Spaniards, has been a gift from heaven, or a reality guaranteed by the word of a neighbor. The future is not the result of forethought. What does not exist within or around us will befall us as a good or an evil. For Spaniards the promised truth was as true as scientific truth is today. The dominance of this Hispanic form of truth—from the victories won by Santiago to Unamuno's words quoted above—can be properly attributed to the connection between the Semitic and Hispanic method of judging values, a connection motivated by circumstances already well known. Let us not confuse this with the "transfer of ideas," as if human life consisted of transferable and adjustable units.

The writings of those who have expressed their conscious experience of being Spaniards confirm my interpretation of the reality of Spain. The Marquis of Santillana, a leading spokesman for Hispanicity in the fif-

---

[21] In his *Historia da India*, finished in 1635, Antonio Bocarro wrote: "We may well call this conquest . . . an extension and exaltation of the Catholic faith . . . ; only, it has not been as pure as it is now, because of the great interest that commerce has had in it. . . ." The great obstacle encountered by the Portuguese was that the East-Indian rulers, "out of covetousness or out of pride . . . kept neither faith nor friendship . . . , the contrary being such a firm principle among the Portuguese," that they very often missed splendid opportunities only because they would not break "the inviolable observance of their faith and word" (Lisbon edition, 1876, pp. 3, 41). It may be added that Antonio Bocarro was a convert (see J. Lucio d'Azevedo, *Historia dos Christãos Novos Portugueses*, 1922, p. 231).

teenth century, says in his *Lamentación de España*: "Well you know, afflicted Spain, that your *yes* was once *yes* and your *no* was once *no*; wherefore, you alone held within yourself the faith, truth, and fortitude of the world, and your God was honored and worshipped. And today you are despoiled of all this, and are converted into another *substance without order.*"[22] The ideal of the perfect human reality was founded on the presupposition that a promise formulated in words was an authentic promise, a guarantee of the future. Otherwise, the *substance*, the being of men and things, would lose its order. The essence of the person was in his veracity, in his being, rather than a present, a responsible future. This is why the Count of Haro, that paradigm of virtues for fifteenth-century Castilians, was called a "man in essence" (ome esencial): "He feared God and he was a *man of truth*, . . . he was a man *in essence*, caring nothing for appearances, and making no show of what he had or what he did" (*Claros varones*, III). To have or to do is not of the human essence. It is of the human essence that *yes* should be *yes* and *no, no*; that each present moment should be part of a future, of a divine or human "beyond." The meaning of the word *essence* cannot be captured in this case through rationalist logic; *essence* and *substance* mean that the man who possesses them fulfills the high hope put in him, not that he *is* this or that.

Let us now look still further back. It has already been seen in Chapter 3 that those who initiated the Reconquest—Galicians, Asturians, Cantabrians, Pyreneans from Navarre and Aragon—had no unity save that of the common purpose of their attacks against the Moslemry of the south, a unity counteracted by the lateral quarrels between one group of Christians and another. The centers of traditional culture within the Peninsula as well as those in foreign lands lay far away (Hispalis, Toletum, Caesar Augusta; Ireland, England, Byzantium, etc.). The Hispano-Christian of the eighth, ninth, and tenth centuries fashioned his life along the lines offered to him by occasional political weakness and the constant cultural superiority of the Islamic South. Sustained by his faith in the heavenly beyond and the incentive of Moorish riches, the Christian conquered lands and at the same time was molding his life within him. Three hundred years of continuous risk are a great many years. Living in the hope of having the nearby land and in the faith in Santiago and San Millán made the Christian feel as strong and as much a lord as his

---

[22] In *Le Chansonnier espagnol d'Herberay des Essarts*, edited by Ch. V. Aubrun, 1951, p. 22.

powerful enemy, whose spirit was also supported by a faith—in the Moslems' "if God wills" (ojalá) and in the Jews' "so be it" (amen).

The outward sign of this lack of adhesion to a stable present was the absence of a capital to serve as a center for all the Christians, whose lives opened toward the future promise of the conquest: "there," not "here," the magnificent, ideal capital was to be found. The rationalist French centered their history in the fixed point of their capital city, Paris, whereas the Hispanic capitals varied and shifted till 1560, a fact which reveals the migratory, frontier spirit of a people who existed in and for the land / camp-ground of their history. The *reconquistador's* life was a waiting for the call to war, the *apellido* that sent him forth to a distant horizon.[23] The only sure, unshakeable thing in him was his conscious experience of feeling himself as all readiness for a mission, for something that would befall him. He was born to life with the certainty of already being what he ought to be; the rest was a matter of time and confidence, just as the nobleman's son had every expectation of becoming a full-fledged nobleman when he reached the age for putting on armor. The foundation stone of all that was Hispanic was the feeling that one was the son of God or the "son of *algo*" (fijodalgo). It was enough to embark upon the ship of destiny, with its sails set for a beyond open to everyone: "God grant you good fortune, for you have no need of knowledge." Hence the Hispanic people's deep-seated feeling for the individual person and their sense of "caste," founded on a constitution which, since it is eternal, has never been written, and therefore escapes the critical action of temporal changes. Spanish democratism is at the opposite pole from the democracy based on "the rights of man," a rational construction that has never entered the Spaniard's head nor his life.

It is hardly necessary to say that the contents of Hispanic history have not been the same as those of the history of Israel, although it is at the same time undeniable that for Semites as well as Hispanians the quest for truth has had meaning only when it has affected their conscious experience of their existence and the conduct of their life. The celebrated medical science of the Spanish Jews was concerned more with the avoidance of ills to come than with present complaints. Their knowledge of the stars did not grow out of a desire for scientific knowledge of the

---

[23] Here one sees the vital meaning of the word *apellido* (from *appellare*, "to call"). This word for "surname" peculiar to Spanish developed out of circumstances external to the individual, out of the call to accomplish the mission of the group and of each individual. The Spaniard's name also pointed toward the "beyond" of his future.

structure of the universe but rather was aimed at how the stars influenced the lives of men. The Spaniards realized titanic and beautiful achievements in the lands that they discovered and colonized with the intention of honoring their faith and of honoring themselves as sons of God and as noblemen by nature. They left to others the preoccupation with discovering the physico-chemical properties of American cocaine and quinine, or with the cultivation of the potato. Such tasks did not interest those seekers after eternity. It had to be this way, given the possibilities of the "dwelling-place" of Hispanic life—the *vividura*, possibilities that were clearly perceived by the more intelligent. Witness Feijóo in the eighteenth century: "It must be confessed that physics and mathematics are almost foreigners in Spain" (*Teatro crítico*, IV, 14). And following in Feijóo's footsteps, Father Isla recognized that "in Portugal and even in all of Spain, there is scarcely any awareness of what real Physics is. . . . There has not appeared, nor is there likely to appear, for a long time, anyone who will study it and advance it, for before this can be done, many obstacles must be overcome, and in the national genius these are little less than invincible" (*Fray Gerundio*, Book II, Chap. 6).

In the fifteenth century things could not be said so plainly, but indirectly the poverty of Hispano-Christian thought was recognized in the fact that when anyone set about making an inventory of Hispanic learning, only Moslem and Jewish thinkers could be cited. Fernán Pérez de Guzmán can recall only Averroes and Maimonides:

"And the Commentary [on Aristotle] of the pagan Avén Ruiz, pleases us. . . . If the Hispanic realm recalls the Egyptian sage Rabbi Moysén [Maimonides], it will plainly see that not for nothing was Cordova called another Athens. . . ."[24]

It is significant that the name of Averroes was Hispanized as *Avén Ruiz*,[25] revealing that the Spaniards felt him to be one of their own, and it is on him that Pérez de Guzmán bases his pride as a Cordovan. (The Duke of Rivas was to do the same thing in the nineteenth century in *El moro expósito*). Spain, "always rich in martial spirits" (says Feijóo) and in energetic propagandists for her belief (Domingo de Guzmán, Vicente Ferrer, Ignacio de Loyola), reached the sixteenth century with the conscious conviction that she deserved all the promises that a propitious future might offer her, but with no exploitable wealth save that

[24] "Loores de los claros varones de España," in the *Nueva Biblioteca de Autores Españoles*, XIX, 738.

[25] Juan de Mena, *Ilíada en romance* (Gallardo, *Ensayo* . . . , n. 3014); Francisco Delicado, *La Lozana andaluza*, Chap. 18.

of her agriculture and the immense potential energy in the strong-willed spirit of her men. It seems evident to me, nevertheless, that without the *deus ex machina* of American riches, Spain would have been unable to maintain her European empire, or even to affirm herself as a self-ruled nation.

Castes, rather than Classes

The Jews' help had been inestimable. Living as an intermediary between Moors and Christians, they presented an "occidental" aspect impossible in the Moslem. Gifted in languages, hard-working, peripatetic, and always alert, they articulated with the Christian much more than with the Moor. The special character of their occupations, either inaccessible or contemptible for the Christian, converted them into a caste, since their different belief prevented them from gradually uniting with the Christians, who really formed likewise not another class, but a different caste. The tolerance of the Middle Ages and the intermingling of three incompatible creeds hindered the establishment of the graduated regimen that prevailed in European feudalism—peasants, artisans, nobles, clergy. Spanish society broke up into three different hierarchies, each independent of the others, and therein lies the explanation for the absence of a feudal society.[26] If, as we have seen, there were still in the fourteenth century Moors and Jews who held castles in fief from the king, what kind of well-ordered hierarchy could be organized on such a base?

But it is not only the fact (which might be an accident) that there

[26] The Moslem order is expressed in texts like the following: "The world is a garden, and its fence is the kingdom, and the kingdom is maintained by laws, which are established by the king, and the king is the shepherd and is maintained by the knights, and the knights are maintained by their wealth, which is gathered together by the people, and the people are the servants of justice, and the world is governed by justice" (*Buenos proverbios*, Chap. XIII, ed. of H. Knust, p. 276). Similar texts appear in *Poridad de poridades* and in the *Partidas*: "The kingdom is like a garden, and the king is like the lord of the garden; and the king's officers who shall judge and assist in carrying out justice are like tillers; and the noblemen and knights are hired to protect the garden, and the laws and statutes and privileges are like fences that surround it, and the judges and courts of justice are like walls and hedges because they protect it from those who would enter there and do harm" (II, x, 3). For Arabic texts with the same idea, see Knust, p. 227. This order is horizontal, not vertical; the person who wrote the passage from the *Partidas* sensed this arrangement very clearly when he insisted upon the symbols "fence, walls, hedges," and not something like pyramid or building, which would have been proper Christian or feudal symbols. Notice how this order follows along a plane surface in the interwoven pattern of an arabesque.

were Hebrew bailiffs in Aragon or Moorish and Jewish wardens in the castles of Castile that stood in the way of feudal organization in Spain. It is the meaning of the facts that explains history, not the facts, which are in themselves mere inert appearance. Life, individual as well as collective, goes on in obedience to one hierarchy or another of values. Otherwise human life is inconceivable. And so, the Hispano-Christian, with no other horizon than his beliefs, could not organize within the Christian community the whole of his system of values. He had to accept as inescapable realities various kinds of Moslem and Jewish superiority. Thus, the daughter of James II of Aragon, married to the highest lord of Castile, brought up her children under the tutelage of Jews (see Chapter 13, footnote 5). The Christian found himself in a situation of cultural colonialism and no more so nor less than did the Spanish Moors and Jews, whose place in one hierarchy was below and in another above that of the Christians. In contrast to Spain, the feudalism of Western Christianity had a tightly homogeneous hierarchic scale of respect, submission, privilege and duty. The lord constituted a total and absolute horizon for the vassal. The Spaniard, quite the contrary, had to divide his loyalties among three different authorities (Christian, Moslem, Jewish), with no clear sense of what was owed to Caesar and what to God. In this situation, feudalism of the European type became impossible.

We have seen how useless it was to pass laws preventing the Christians from utilizing the good services of Jews and Moors. The tolerant laws of the *Partidas* (which in any case was a purely theoretical code in the thirteenth century) accepted the existence of Moors and Jews, but they did not suggest that the Christians should bow before their occasional superiority. The Jews were tolerated so that "they would live as in captivity forever, and would be a reminder to men that they came of the lineage of those who crucified Our Lord Jesus Christ" (*Partidas*, VII, 24, 2). Christian life was therefore the product of an inevitable custom and a disregarded legal will. Logically, this was a senseless contradiction; but since the Christian kingdoms of Spain lived this way for more than five centuries, such an easy description as "senseless contradiction" would seem inadequate, and it would be more worthwhile to think that the form of life consisted in an inescapable compromise between two beliefs, between believing that the Jew was a deicide and believing that it was legitimate to accept him. The synagogue was also a house of God, according to the *Partidas*.

By accepting the occasional superiority of his unfaithful fellow-citizens, the Christian was deprived of his consciousness of being lord of his land.

The Christian did not believe in his own superiority for the same reasons as the nobility of feudal Europe—not, that is, because he was doing what the commoner could not do (noblesse oblige)—but because he was possessed of a better belief. This explains why the Christian had more a sense of caste than of class. The social class bases its rank on what it does; the rank of the caste depends on the mere existence of the person: in the last analysis, all the Hispano-Christians ended up by feeling themselves a superior caste by virtue of the fact that they were Christians and not Moors or Jews. The form of their daily existence, then, was analogous to that of their literary creation: a personal "integralism" Islamico-Judaic in root and serving as a vital common denominator to Moors, Jews, and Christians.

The two subject castes were joined to the political superior caste by means of what one might call a broken scale of values. That is, deeds and accomplishments were seen as valuable while those who performed them were held in low esteem. Artisans, businessmen, technologists, scholars, etc., produced all manner of good things, but these products were tainted from birth by the fact that their producers came from castes deemed inferior; and no matter how good the products were, the producers *were not converted into a legitimate social class.* The production of wealth did not become an index of value for the Christian caste, which both needed and scorned those who built up fortunes. In the absence of such an attitude, the hermetic caste of the Christians would have been broken and the infidel castes would have infiltrated it, thus endangering its existence as the ruling caste. Social functions had to be differentiated not according to their objective value but according to the castes that carried them out. The tailor (alfayate), the barber (alfajeme), the muleteer (harriero), the mason (albañil), the architect (alarife), the inspector of weights and measures (almotacén), the shoemaker (zapatero), etc., were Moors. The tax-gatherer (almojarife), the physician, the pharmacist, the veterinary (albéitar), the tradesman, the astrologer, the interpreter (trujamán) and other such were Jews. The Christian played a more circumscribed part in such activities. His goal was to be a nobleman or a priest, callings which, once attained or taken up, were regarded as inherent to the person, beyond the power of renunciation or cancellation. Victimized by nobles, ecclesiastics, and Jews, the shapeless mass of the Christian commonalty was left outside this framework in a state of perpetual fermentation produced by the longing of its constituents to move up to the nobility through military enterprise and thus to become members of the ruling caste of lords. As the Cordovan Juan Ginés de Sepúlveda said: "In our

Cordova no notice is taken of commerce, and it is considered the greatest distinction to excel at arms. And so, after the care of one's family, the greatest concern is with agriculture, an occupation that is honorable and close to nature, and which usually strengthens the body and the spirit and prepares them for travail and for war: to such an extent that the ancients preferred labor in the fields to commerce, and the Romans took many consuls and dictators from the plough. . . . Let us not worry, then, if for the moment Cordova has citizens whose strength exceeds their opulence" (*De appetenda gloria*, Madrid edition, 1780, IV, 206). We can now understand the broad scope of the saying "Either prince or peasant" (O corte o cortijo), or of this one: "Church or sea or royal house" (Iglesia, o mar, o casa real). People aspired to be direct administrators of the faith, or to undertake adventures that would lead to lordship, or to serve the king in some way, comfortable in the realization that they were nobles and not plebeians.

The awareness of being a nobleman by birth was especially a Castilian trait. As concerns this, Castile embraced the ancient kingdoms of Castile, Leon, and Andalusia, not excluding the Basques, the most honest and honorable people of the Peninsula and always preferred by the Crown for positions of strict responsibility. The Count-Duke of Olivares, the *de facto* king of Spain more than was his lord King Philip IV between 1621 and 1643, bears this idea out. In his instructions concerning government, written in 1625 to quicken the mind of the frivolous and drowsy monarch, he says: "It seems to me much to the advantage of Your Majesty that those vassals [i.e., the Portuguese] should live in the hope that your Majesty . . . should hold your court in Lisbon for a certain continuous period of time. . . . I also deem it Your Majesty's obligation to employ persons of that kingdom in the service of this one, and particularly in embassies and viceroyalties, presidencies of the royal councils, and in some of the posts in the royal household. And I also think it a good thing to do this with the Aragonese, the Flemish, and the Italians . . . who regard themselves as foreigners."[27] The Portuguese, he adds, resemble the latter-named peoples more than they do the Castilians. The Castilians comprise the best of the Spanish infantry, in which "one sees, along with their loyalty to their kings (greater than that of any other vassals), *the brio and liberty with which the sorriest commoner of*

[27] As late as 1564 Don Martín Pérez de Ayala was reluctant to accept the archbishopric of Valencia, because he disliked the idea of "living with new people *not entirely of our own nation*" ("Vida de don Martín de Ayala," in the *Nueva Biblioteca de Autores Españoles*, v, 236).

Castile treats any lord or noble, even though he be greatly unequal in power, showing in the wisdom of his impulse how much human hearts exceed human forces."[28]

Olivares was thinking about how he could use the royal prestige to bring the *disjecta membra* of the Spanish dominions in Europe into a unified relationship. The Aragonese, including the Catalonians and Valencians, seemed to be foreigners as late as 1625. The nucleus of Spain was still Castile, as it had been since the tenth century, precisely because its men had been what Olivares said they were. The humblest peasant sensed that he was a member of the seignorial caste, a potential *hidalgo*. This notion seems to me to fit the reality better than the notion of Castilian democracy, in which democracy can have no strict meaning. The way of life in Castile was never democratic; perhaps it was, to some extent, in Aragon. The Castilians were governed seignorially by the best or more fortunate members of the lordly caste, all of whose members aspired to the same privilege. This was the basis of its grandeur and of its final wretchedness. There was never any democracy in Castile in the Greek or the Franco-English sense of the word. The inverse case, although similar in its vital scheme, was presented by the Jews, who were prisoner-defenders of their own religious belief. The reason for their existence was also their religion, just as it was for the Hispano-Moslems. Nobility, industry, and labor: these three kinds of life existed in Spain, in the highest form, and "theoretically" there was no reason why a "normal" nation should not have been the result. But unfortunately this was not the case. It happened rather that the Jews became obsessed with the idea of becoming noblemen, and the Christians fell prisoners to the defensive, Inquisitorial tendency and the notion of purity of blood, going so far as to invent a new historical category, the "Old Christian."

The Christian had grown accustomed to having no need for a knowledge of nature and the handling of things, because this was not required in the huge task of conquering his land and organizing his state. The rest was left in the hands of Santiago, the French monks and immigrants,[29] the Genoese shipbuilders, the Moorish builders of houses and fortresses, and the Jews, who knew trades, who could heal ailments, who knew how to collect the money to buy the things needed by the kings,

[28] P. 426 of the text as published by G. Marañón, *El conde-duque de Olivares*, 1936.

[29] It is curious that the Hispano-Christian had no traditional word of his own for "tailor." *Sastre*, the word he uses, is a Gallicism from the south of France. (See A. Steiger, *Aufmarschstrassen des morgenländischen Sprachgutes*, Berne, 1950, p. 17.) The other word, *alfayate*, is Arabic.

the lords, the clerics, and the "good men" of the cities. The urgency of getting money explains why the Jew has always appeared in front of the footlights of history. The later importance of the precious metals of America was not the result of any economic doctrine: it was simply the sixteenth-century aspect of the need to acquire by indirect means the things that could not be created.

This way history is reclothed with meaning and explains itself. For the Hispano-Christian, peace had never been productive. Juan de Lucena made a very shrewd observation in 1463. "There is no trouble around the house when the pigs are gone to the woods. . . . What a glorious king we would have, what a wonderful lot of vassals, what a crown for Spain, if the clergy, regular and secular, should go against Granada, and the king's knights should erupt into Africa! . . . *Increasing the number of kingdoms would produce greater wealth than the heaping up of treasures.*"[30] The Christian in his own home felt himself with nothing to do, and he stirred up trouble in the kingdom. But once Granada was conquered, the great humanist Juan Ginés de Sepúlveda sensed a danger in the lack of an adequate enterprise in which the Spaniards might occupy themselves:

"According to the philosophers, nature, to enliven men's power, has endowed them with a certain inner fire which, if it is not poked and set to working, not only gives no light, but at times languishes and goes out. Therefore I sometimes wonder whether it would not have been better for us if the Moorish kingdom had not been preserved in Granada instead of disappearing completely. For if it is indeed certain that we have extended the kingdom, we have also thrown the enemy back beyond the sea, deprived the Spaniards of the opportunity to practice their valor, and destroyed the magnificent motive for their triumphs. Wherefore I fear a little lest, with so much idleness and security, the valor of many men grow weak."[31]

Apparently the wars of Charles V were not enough for Sepúlveda. This idea, strange at first glance, has not been an isolated occurrence, for I find it again in Fray Alonso de Cabrera, preacher to Philip II:

"Our grandfathers, my lords, lamented the winning of Granada from the Moors, because on that day the horses fell lame and the cuirasses

---

[30] "De vita beata," in *Bibliófilos Españoles,* pp. 126 and 166.

[31] From the dialogue called *Gonsalus seu de appetenda gloria,* XXVI. In the preface to the *Razonamiento sobre la navegación del Guadalquivir* by Hernán Pérez de Oliva, Ambrosio de Morales writes: "At that time [about 1520] Cordova was half-deserted, since the end of the conquest of Granada left her without the steady pursuit of warfare, in which her natives engaged with great honor."

and lances began to rust, and the shields to rot. And the most distinguished cavalry of Andalusia was finished, and it was the end of youth and all its well-known gallantries."[32]

The Spaniards had the liveliest kind of awareness that their existence was a process of self-creation and self-destruction. Ferdinand the Catholic, who knew his people well, offered them the bellicose, seignorial mission they longed for, the only thing they were really capable of. Then came the great enterprises in America and Europe, and the nation did not feel satisfied even with them, as we are told by Sepúlveda, Las Casas, Antonio de Guevara, Father Cabrera, Quevedo, and . . . Cervantes, well-qualified witness among many too numerous to mention. Gracián was to have the impression that he was living in an empty world, the same impression we get from the ascetics, the authors of the picaresque autobiographies, and Calderon's theatre.

The idea of castes whose only world is that of their own self-consciousness may explain this singular history. The guiding caste thought it could live alone, welded to its belief and its sense of superiority, and it noticed the irremediable vacuum in which it was submerged when it tried to come out of its incarceration in the self.

Prior to the sixteenth century no European country had produced such a profusion of heroes and chieftains who challenged the greatest obstacles nature could present, and always won—Vasco da Gama, Albuquerque, Cortes, Pizarro, Balboa, Magellan, Cabeza de Vaca, and a hundred others. Along with many friars fed by an equally titanic energy and illuminated by their religious belief, they ceaselessly consumed their selves as in a sacrificial holocaust to that strange deity, personal integralism, the whole living person. In opposition to the principle inherited from Greece that reality "is what it is," the Spaniard sustained the principle that reality was what he felt, believed, and imagined. "Having postponed fear"—a *leitmotiv* already in the fifteenth century—he installed himself in Italy, he rode victoriously over the heart of Europe and over the summits of the Andes.[33] As he felt no fear, so he felt no surprise, for

---

[32] "De las consideraciones sobre todos los Evangelios de la Cuaresma," 1601, in the *Nueva Biblioteca de Autores Españoles*, III, 60. This text provides an excellent perspective in which to situate the genesis of the *Quixote*.

[33] That army was still decisive in the affairs of Europe in 1634. The Spaniards fighting in the bloodiest battle of the Thirty-Years War, the battle of Nördlingen, are described thus by a contemporary foreigner: "Then, marching calmly and solidly massed, several Spanish regiments advanced. They were almost exclusively well-tested veterans—without a doubt, the most reliable and the strongest infantry that I have fought against in all my life." The German-Swedish army was routed (see

everything could be matched with fantasies already lived. Hernán Cortes' triumphal entry into Mexico seemed to his men like an episode from *Amadis*, or like an adventure with enchantment. Reality was a simple game with friendly or hostile wizards.

Will, courage, and imagination took the place of reflection, and created a form of life which it would be inept to characterize as primitive, backward, prescientific, etc. For this form of life developed according to an ascending scale of values. So-called "primitive" man is not aware of the risk he runs by being primitive. The Spaniard has always realized the high price he has had to pay for being Spanish.

It has been customary to base judgments of Spanish life on the principle that the most perfected forms of the so-called Western Civilization were the supreme goals toward which all the peoples of the earth should have directed their course. Those human groups which do not fall entirely within the area of the civilization that was begun in Greece, given political shape by Rome, and brought to its apogee by the dazzling discoveries of physical science, are regarded as primitive, backward, childish, or misguided. Those who believe in the efficacy of this form of life think that the people who are "backward" with respect to this form are living in a limbo where they await the light of a new revelation, just as the pagans, in medieval thought, had spent their lives marking time as they waited for the truth of Christ to reach them. In the eighteenth century the Christian idea was replaced by faith in progress. Those not versed in mathematics, in the French language, in the rational interpretation of the world, and in the graces of the Parisian salons were also regarded as people still waiting to be saved. The Spain of Charles V also had an absolute aspiration. This was, to bring the whole planet into the fold of her theocratic-aristocratic faith; and thus motivated, she displayed an arrogance not exceeded by the British in the nineteenth century, or by Americans in the twentieth.

Now such "democentric" (not egocentric) attitudes are evidence that the people who feel them and formulate them have a strong sense of their own value. But at the same time such views put a serious obstacle in the way of our efforts to make perceptible the values of a history that is strange in its course, values which reveal themselves only as we penetrate deeper and deeper into the strange character of this history. The Spaniards' way of living "with their whole being" (see Chapter 8) made splendid results possible, for the total life of the self proved to be

Pedro de Marrades, *Notas para el estudio de la cuestión de la Valtelina*, 1943, p. 174).

expressible in actions of singular grandeur or in artistic works of a new stamp.

Nevertheless, it cannot be denied that the Spaniards have suffered the consequences of their peculiar inner life more than the other peoples of Western Europe. Having neither things nor objectified ideas, the "caste" did not become a social class, it did not break out of its silent cocoon, and there were no social mutations motivated from within Spanish life. Western Europe, from Charlemagne to the twentieth century, has experienced changes in religion, philosophy, science, politics, and economy because there have been men who disengaged themselves from the beliefs in which they were submerged and forged the bases for new modes in religion, politics, and so on. The believers in the reality of the world according to the canons of realist philosophy had the possibility from the eleventh century on of conceiving reality according to the objectified ideas of nominalist philosophy. In the fourteenth century William of Ockham presented the possibility of separating the truths of theology from those of reason, and thus opened the way to purely scientific reasoning. The result of this was that the whole non-Hispanic world of the fifteenth century was alive with assorted and attractive forms of thought and religion. To cite a single example, in the sixteenth century the English came upon the objectified idea that, for the Lutherans, the true church was not the church of the priests but that of the believers, and they promptly moved into that new ideal edifice. Later the market place was occupied by the idea that peoples had greater rights than kings in the determination of popular matters, and the English chopped their king's head off. A century after that, the French suggested the strange idea that noble and ecclesiastical privileges were not legitimate, the privileges were annulled, and public power was handed over to a new social class, the so-called bourgeoisie. In connection with all this, certain Germans in the nineteenth century said that the power should pass from the hands of the rich to those of the poor. The perspective offered by this idea proved attractive to millions of Russian peasants, and so brought about a change in the condition of certain European and Asiatic peoples.

Immobility and Intranquillity

When we compare the Western-European mode of life with the existence of the Hispanic peoples, the latter has the appearance of an escarpment against which the seas of the histories of the world have been dashing for centuries with little effect. The curious thing about this situation is that the Hispanic peoples have neither adapted themselves to alien usages nor resigned themselves to a tranquil acceptance of their own peculiarity. They have overlaid their perennial tradition with certain foreign ideas and products, and at the same time they have defended themselves against any kind of radical foreignization. Spain has been attacked in every possible way since the sixteenth century, and she has always maintained her right to live on the margin of scientific and industrialized Europe with the same tenacity as Don Quixote displayed in protecting his Quixotism against all the priests, barbers, bachelors, and canons of rationality.

The adopted position was to become immutable, or rather, it was immutable by "history," because its very history involved the disinclination —one might as well say the inability—of Hispanic man to invent new personal circumstances. There was no bond between men, ideas, and things. For this reason, the inhabitants of the Spanish Empire did not unite with one another by means of horizontal interest (as I have repeatedly pointed out). They were rather like bundles of ascending lines that converged in a belief—in the *caudillo*, in the king, in Santiago, in God. Neither in Spain nor in Hispano-America did the various regions weave themselves together in a network of mutually complementary tasks. It is therefore quite normal, "historically" speaking, that there should be all kinds of separatism in both Spain and Hispano-America. The regions were united either by their faith in the crown or by some kind of external force imposed upon them.

It will be said, however, that the Hispania of today is not like the Hispania of the sixteenth or even the eighteenth century, because now there are trains, telegraph lines, automobiles, deputies, senators, and hypodermic injections. But just as now, so in the seventeenth century hundreds of things were imported that seemed like innovations: "Spain exports wool, wine, olive oil, gold, and silver, as well as other products *of intrinsic value*, and she takes in coarse Angevin linen, thread, eyeglasses, pins, inkstands, glass beads, jew's harps, flutes, whistles, and dolls, as well as thousands of other foolish things that would be scorned by the most barbarous tribes of Ethiopia."[34] The situation in the preceding century had been essentially the same, with the difference that the producers of things were then inside the country—the Moors and Jews, who were already *being used* by the Cid in the eleventh century. The Christians both then and later lived behind the barricade of their sense

[34] Pedro Fernández de Navarrete, "Conservación de monarquías," in the *Biblioteca de Autores Españoles*, xxv, 533.

of the "intrinsic value" of their land and their persons, and thus the rhythm of Hispanic life turns out to be essentially the same in the tenth century and in the twentieth: in the earlier period, Moslem importations; in the later, European ones. When in 1909 Unamuno uttered his much disputed exclamation "Let the others do the inventing!" he was speaking from the depths of history, a history interested in promoting, from a fixed position and a longing for eternity, a series of changes in decoration that would leave untouched the living dwelling-place of that history. The simultaneous existence side by side of the authentically permanent and the temporary has quite naturally given rise to the illusion that there have been two Spains. However, we have only to remember that this phenomenon has been going on for a thousand years and we will realize how unfounded such a notion is.

Every important innovation in Spain that has not been based on the intention to magnify and express the character and feelings of the self has always had its origin outside Christian Spain, even though the will to carry out such changes has always come from within. The following "things" have been found by the Spaniards to be appealing and desirable: the Cluniacs in the eleventh century, the Cistercians in the twelfth century, the Jews down to the end of the fifteenth century, the Moors till 1609, Erasmianism in the sixteenth century, literary Italianism in the same period, French ideas and institutions from the end of the seventeenth century on, the sciences and techniques of all Europe in the nineteenth century, German philosophy in the nineteenth century (Krausism) and the twentieth (historical vitalism, phenomenology). I consider it an inadmissible abstraction to say that Spain has been a crossroads for the "cultures" of the world, where the natives of the land have met and fused with Phoenicians, Romans, Goths, Moors, etc. This approach makes for confusion in the concept of culture and, ultimately, for chaotic thinking, because it deprives us of a *subject*, an agent, and an intelligible center to which we may refer this alluvion of events and "influences."

The medieval Castilians decided to practice tolerance and establish a code for it, to have military orders, to found schools like the one in Palencia; and at the same time they had little use for many things that they could have had and did not (such as lyric poetry). The fact that such decisions were imposed by unavoidable circumstances is no reason for denying the existence of a constant will, any more than we would deny the presence of a skillful captain on a ship being tossed by a storm, or in the doldrums.

The decisive moves did not always originate in the same part of the social organism, and a detailed history of Spain would have to make it clear just which individuals and groups started what. The lower classes, not the upper, were behind the expulsion of the Jews, who were protected by the upper classes for centuries against all manner of attack and abuse. In the fifteenth and sixteenth centuries, the New Christians of Jewish provenience took either of two opposite directions—aristocratic or plebeian: they are just as likely to be found among the enlightened as among the Inquisitorial. This sort of thing is often called a cultural crossing, but it would be better to understand the creation of Hispanic values as the result of the conflict between two opposing tendencies, two contrary motions, one away from, the other into, the self. This constant polarization of Spain's vital activity, this tension whose opposing forces draw their energy from the same source, continues to be evident in the eighteenth and nineteenth centuries and among the cultivated citizens as well as among the common people. Thus, in the eighteenth century we have Moratín, the *Caballeritos* of Azcoita,[35] and Ramón de la Cruz's "Majos"; and in the nineteenth, both the so-called *afrancesados*, that is, the Gallicized, who were the modern spokesmen for the spirit of Sancho the Elder of Navarre and Alphonse VI, and the guerrilla-fighters in the War for Independence, as hostile to France as was the champion Bernardo del Carpio. It took two bloody civil wars to establish something like a constitutional regime. After that, Spain went on importing and imposing on herself alien things and institutions deemed necessary by certain persons who were not satisfied with the life of a nation that did not seem to change with the changing ages but always to live in her own changeless age. Thus there came socialism, communism, and fascism, or the substitution of traditional belief for the free-thinking borrowed from France at the end of the eighteenth century. What is there about the Spain of today that could be called authentically Hispanic? Probably these things among others: monarchism, absolutism in religious belief, and the mixture of anarchism and syndicalism which has as its structural plan for the country a conglomeration of human units displaying a centauric combination of physical violence and visionary idealism.[36]

[35] The name popularly given to a small group of aristocrats ("little gentlemen") in the Basque country who sought to promote the Enlightenment in Spain.

[36] The ideal of a Spain without laws, with a cooperative and nonauthoritarian state, with an autonomy which reaches the smallest village, serves to inspire the works of such eminent jurists as Joaquín Costa (*La ignorancia del derecho*) and Pedro Dorado Montero (*Valor social de leyes y autoridades*). The example of traditional customs, still in force in many little towns of Spain, is for them as important as the doctrines of certain theologians and jurists of the sixteenth century. The tendency towards separatism in the Hispanic world is an aspect of the Spaniard's anti-statism.

When closely examined, Hispanic man is seen to give only lip-service to the foreign things he imports or imitates, and he ends up either by destroying them or by using them only for the purposes of his own authentic life. The objectified world of ideas (scientific, political, or social) has not established pervasive or genuine authority in any Spanish-speaking or Portuguese-speaking country. But this is not for reasons of backwardness or barbarism—a barbarous people would not have reaffirmed, century after century, its awareness of its own way of being, nor would it have developed a state of perpetual anguish by turning this very way of being into a problem, nor would it have produced personalities and human works of such high quality.

Individualism?

"Experience has shown that obedience to decrees and corrective laws is of short duration in Spain; for every private citizen (hombre *particular*) makes it a point of honor to go against them, deeming it an act of positive nobility to refuse to submit to laws."[37] These are the words of Pedro Fernández de Navarrete, writing at the beginning of the seventeenth century. Writing at the end of the nineteenth century, Galdós has one of his characters say: "What the government says belongs to it doesn't really belong to the government but to the nation, that is, to John Private-Citizen (Juan *Particular*). And to defraud the government is to give back to John Private-Citizen the stuff that belongs to him."[38]

In these two quotations the word "particular" implies the lack of social virtues or aptitudes. In modern times the Spaniard's way of conducting his life has been called "individualism," but this term is so vague as to be almost meaningless. Everyone is an individual, a human being who in one way or another individualizes his life without losing his identity as a member of some social group. What separates and characterizes peoples is not their singular or collective individuality, which is always present. Rather, it is the way each individuality is given content. Cases of extreme individualism abound outside of Spain. Take, for example, the case of Oscar Wilde: "I am far more of an individualist than I ever was. Nothing seems to me of the smallest value except what one gets out of oneself. My nature is seeking a fresh mode of self-realization. . . ." (*De profundis*). Oscar Wilde aspires to fashion his life and express it in symbols, just as an artist conceives the realization of his

---

[37] "Conservación de monarquías," in the *Biblioteca de Autores Españoles*, xxv, 529.
[38] "Fortunata y Jacinta," in *Obras completas*, 1942, p. 36.

work in a particular style of his own. The validity of what he believes will depend on whether the value of his creation will be meaningful for others. His individualism is thus the cause and condition for obtaining a result that is not individual at all—the social objectivity of his work.

Those who have branded Spain with the mark of individualism have not usually had in mind artistic or creative individualism. And the term is used just as readily to describe the British attitude in favor of free competition, free trade, and the differentiation of industrial tasks. When it is applied to Spaniards, it is usually with reference to their rebelliousness against any standard—a rebelliousness devoid of any view to establishing a different set of standards. They rebel against standards as such. There is a kind of personal separatism. This is evidently what is meant by describing Spaniards as individualists. And if it is, let us say so, and dispel the uncertainty that has resulted from such vague language. I would rather speak in the Spanish case of a certain withdrawal and small interest in the world outside, qualities to be discerned in the Hispanians' failure to explore the lands and histories of other peoples, even when the peoples are those formerly ruled by Spain and Portugal. If I had to locate, as it were, that which is most characteristic of Hispanic life, I would put it between the acceptance of inertia and the willful outburst through which the person reveals what there is—be it something insignificant or something of value—in the depths of his soul, as if he were his own theatre. Visible examples of this enormous contrast are the peasant and the conquistador—insensibility to the political and social situations and the insurrections and convulsions of the blind mass of the people, destroying everything; apathy toward the transformation of natural resources into wealth and the use of public wealth as if it were private; archaic and static ways of living and the hasty adoption of modern devices produced outside of Spain. The electric light, the typewriter, and the fountain-pen were popularized in Spain more quickly than in France. On the plane of the highest human values we find a manifestation of this sharp contrast in the poetic inwardness of Saint John of the Cross or of the quietist Miguel de Molinos, and the series of daring assaults to be found in Quevedo and Góngora, or in Goya's artistic transformation of the outer world.

Unamuno illustrates the problem of so-called Spanish individualism more than with his thought, with this bare analysis of himself: "Of all tyrannies, the one most hateful to me is the tyranny of ideas. . . . On the other hand, I never protest when someone declares himself superior to me. I calmly wait for him to prove it with deeds. I wait eagerly for him to try to impose his will on me and trample me. If he succeeds, I thank him, for he has proved himself my superior, and he has actually come to help me in my inferiority" (*La ideocracia, Más sobre la crisis del patriotismo*). Spaniards feel themselves, then, to be like so many radii whose very existence depends on a center in the form of another person. When these radii are numerous, the circle of political dictatorship emerges— sometimes as a kind of patriarchy—a political form highly expressive of the Hispano-Portuguese life structure, and within which little margin is left for the individuality of citizens, just as in the case of the religious community. No individualistic religious doctrine has ever prospered in Spain, nor has it ever occurred to anybody to invent one. Mysticism, needless to say, is not an objective system of beliefs.

It would seem, then, that the following conclusion could be drawn from these observations: The Spaniard gives up his individuality and disciplines himself as he enters the community created by faith in God or in the personal power of another man; or he assumes strong individuality when he accomplishes something of value—acts and creations that endow him with an individual personality as rich as that of any other European (the examples would run from Fernán González and the Cid in the tenth and eleventh centuries to Ramón y Cajal and Manuel de Falla in the twentieth). Set over against this way, the so-called Spanish individualism—the blunt rejection of general ideas and standards— would consist in a vital emptiness, in an attitude devoid of all *individualizable* content, that is, in the Spaniard's "no me da la gana" (I just don't want to), utterly irremediable. Unamuno, who did not approach this problem the way I do, nevertheless made certain observations that I find useful: "It is hard to understand how a person, without speaking, without writing, without painting anything, without chiseling a piece of sculpture, without playing any music, without transacting any kind of business, *without doing anything at all*, can expect that by the single act of being present he will be regarded as a man of extraordinary merit and outstanding talent. Nevertheless, here in Spain—I do not know whether such is the case elsewhere—more than a few examples of this extremely odd phenomenon are known" (*El individualismo español*).

The phenomenon observed by Unamuno and many others is indeed hard to understand if we look for a logical motivation behind a person's assumption of merits that he does not have. It will not do simply to admit that Spaniards are this way because an abstract psychological pattern is realized in them. The truth is that in many Spaniards the aspect of a historic past survives without the motivating forces than originally underlay it.[39] The Spaniard has preserved certain inner and outer ways that were proper to the time when he felt himself the member of an imperial caste, aware of his innate merit and of the operative virtue of his mere presence. How can this be understood any longer in a technocratic world with which the Spaniard has always lived at odds? And yet we should try to make clear the blurred perspective which once granted legitimate efficacy to a sword upheld by personal power, by faith, and backed up by the skill of men who knew how to command. It must not be forgotten that the Spaniard began to be aware of the imperial power of his nation long before the discovery of America. The conquest of Naples by Alphonse of Aragon, followed at the end of the fifteenth century by the capture of Granada, the victories of the Great Captain, the discoveries across the sea, and the accession of Charles V—all these confirmed the Spaniard in his belief that Spain was predestined to be the guiding center of world politics. The will to seigniory became a reality in the empire just as the wing of the bird and the air around join efficiently in the action of flying. Likewise, being Spanish and acting with imperious authority became in the end reciprocal functions of the same person. It is not, then, that Spain, an abstract national entity, had an empire; rather, it is that Spain, when she was acting imperially, achieved the maximum expression of her possibilities, of her *vividura*, at the same time that the empire was becoming a Hispanic reality. As the conquistadors brought the lands of America under the Spanish domain, they effectively converted the mass of the Indians into people of partially Hispanic blood, Hispanic language and manner, and Hispanic religion. There is no way to understand Spain and write her history without reliving the state of mind of a people who knew that the royal standard was flying from Antwerp to Sicily, and from Saint Augustine and Santa Fe to Buenos Aires and Concepción (Chile). This titanic effort, without precedent in its time, is still evident in the commanding beauty of many fortresses, churches, and palaces, and in millions of people vitally molded to the Spanish pattern, regardless of whether they are today aware of the fact.[40]

[39] In *La Prisonnière* of Marcel Proust, Albertine responds to every statement with "Is that so? Is it really so?" even when someone says to her, "It is raining." The lovely girl gave "the strange impression of being a person who is not able to notice things for herself." The truth is that Albertine had acquired that irrepressible habit in the days of her precocious beauty when, sure of fascinating men, she answered phrases like, "You know that I have never found anyone as pretty as you," with a doubting "Is that true?" which concealed a satisfaction that was not at all doubtful.

[40] The Arch of Triumph built for Alphonse of Aragon in the Castel Nuovo in Naples was the work of Italian artists. Triumphal arches had not been raised in Italy since the time of the emperors, and this one would not have existed except for the

A meaningful history of the Hispanic expansion would, by its own rhythm, make clearly perceptible how the form of life forged during the Reconquest gradually accented its features. Without realizing any of this, the Spaniard—be he a great lord or a ragamuffin, dull or intelligent —goes on nourishing in his soul the void of the vanished empire, the dream that the self, the person, by virtue of his mere existence, is at once everything. Thus it is possible to understand how a few naïve Spaniards have lately been able to believe that they have an empire just because they have shouted a pair of magic words: "Imperial Spain." The person is everything, and he needs only himself. "Let *the others* do the inventing," said Unamuno; and one of Baroja's characters exclaims: "Ten men with talent and initiative, and the revolution is made!" Don Quixote was also persuaded that he could stop the Turks' advance by hurling a handful of knights errant against them. But still, in 1686, when their monarchy was bleeding to death from the wounds inflicted by Louis XIV, the Spaniards made an effective contribution to the liberation of Budapest from the Turks.[41]

Let us not go on calling this rebellious and proud aloofness "individualism." It would be better to approach this strange and sometimes splendid kind of existence as a "personal absolutism." "I am the master of my hunger" was the answer of one very poor Spaniard to men who wanted to buy his vote for a deputy he didn't like. This is not stoicism or Senecanism, for this same Spaniard, master of his hunger, can abandon himself to instinctive rage when the imperialism of his person so demands. The abstract reason of the Stoics or of legal codes is not very appealing to the Spaniard, whose ideas about justice would support what I have been saying. Laws and judges do not take into account man's complex and wavering situation: "They have forgotten the soul, they take little pity on it," said Pero López de Ayala in the fourteenth century. A judge, if he were to be acceptable to the Spaniard, would have

---

will of the king to have a "Roman triumph" after his entry into Naples on June 2, 1447—ALFONSUS REX HISPANUS SICULUS ITALICUS PIUS CLEMENS INVICTUS. In order to be authentic, the triumphal arch must include both the material structure and the triumph that passes beneath it—art and life. It was built between 1452 and 1468 (*Dedalo*, Milan, 1932, XII, 439).

[41] *A Detailed Journal of what happened during the Famous Siege of Buda; and a Full Account of Its Capture by Attack on September 2 of this year, 1686* (Diario puntual de quanto ha passado en el famoso sitio de Buda; y relación cumplida de su presa por asalto el día 2 de setiembre del año presente 1686), Madrid, Melchor Alvarez, 1686. Spaniards served in the army of the Duke of Lorraine, and the exhausted treasury of Charles II gave a huge sum toward that honorable undertaking for reasons of imperial prestige.

to be like the superhuman daimons in Plato's *Laws* (IV, 713). The Spaniard wants a system of justice based on value judgments, not on firm and rationally deduced principles. It is not accident that casuistry was fostered by the Spanish Jesuits, nor that the Frenchman Pascal should find this casuistry perversely immoral. It is written laws that the Spaniard fears and despises: "I find twenty chapters against you and only one that is with you," says a lawyer to the unfortunate litigant in the *Rimado de palacio* by Pero López de Ayala. According to Juan de Mena (1411-1456), justice consists in "a hundred thousand deceptions, schemes, and tricks"; legal works, "full of opinions like grapes in a basket," foster a cheating spirit in judges and lawyers. And so it was that the "land of the Moors" was longingly thought of as the place where justice was truly just; for with the Moors the same judge disposed of both civil and criminal cases, basing his opinions not on laws but on "discretion and good doctrine." Even Cervantes expresses more than once a longing for Moorish justice, in spite of his long captivity in Algiers: "Among these barbarians, *if they are barbarians in this regard*, the cadi is a competent judge in all cases, and he sums them up on his fingernail and gives sentence with a single breath, and there is no appeal of his sentence to any other tribunal" (*El amante liberal*). This praise of Moslem justice was a protest against having to submit to the law, which was not respected either by judges or by litigants. Cervantes, Quevedo, and Gracián all express their emphatic contempt for courts of law. Gracián says that the judge exiles the thieves "because he wants to be the only one" (*Criticón*, II, 7). And in 1903 Miguel de Unamuno writes: "In Spain, whenever there is talk of governmental programs it is time to start trembling, and the moment we hear that such and such idea is going to be applied, we had better run for shelter. I prefer the application of what is called the 'loyal wisdom and understanding' of any old judge, *whatever the quality of his culture*, because this wisdom and understanding, when it is really loyal, is usually the expression of a whole, real man, and not of an abstract entity" (*Sobre el fulanismo*). Unamuno says the same thing that Juan de Mena said four centuries ago.[42]

Turning from these characteristic ideas about justice, we find the same

---

[42] I am familiar with what has been written by Rabelais, Montaigne, and others about the justice of judges and the excellencies of free and spontaneous justice. Nothing in their ideas authentically enters into a system of "personal absolutism" like that of the Spaniards, who, when they speak of justice, do so from the fullness of their lives, and not merely from rational thought.

kind of personal projection when we observe the names given to the cities founded or conquered by Spaniards. As the Castilians advanced southward in the eleventh and twelfth centuries they frequently gave their own names to the places that they were repopulating: Gomecello, that is, *Gómez Tello* (Salamanca); *Gómez Sarracín* (Segovia). In the province of Cuenca there are *Martín Miguel, Sanchonuño, Urraca Miguel, Diego Álvaro*, and numerous other examples that have been pointed out to me by Rafael Lapesa. "They are extraordinarily frequent in the southern basin of the Duero, populated about 1088," is the confirmation of our master, Menéndez Pidal. Nothing like this took place in the other Romanic countries. The reconquering Castilians were thinking more about their own names than about the nature of the terrain or any other objective circumstance. The meaning that I attach to these facts is confirmed by what happened during the Spaniards' imperial expansion. The English and the Dutch, when they called many places in America New-this-or-that, were reflecting the Puritan belief that they had come to a *new* world, free of the old spiritual oppression. *Newark* meant "New Ark of the Covenant." In this case, the religious belief and the word *new* that expresses it, have a generic character and are not personalized or concretized. In contrast to this, Bartolomé Colón called the city he founded Santo Domingo "because he got there on a Sunday [domingo], the Feast of Saint Dominic, and his father's name was Domingo; thus three causes coincided to make him call it thus." So says Garcilaso the Inca. "The city of Cartagena [in Colombia] was so called because of its good harbor, which, since it was much like that of Cartagena [in Spain], caused those who first saw it to say: 'This harbor is as good as that of Cartagena'" (*Comentarios reales*, Rosenblat edition, I, 24-25). The city of *Osorno*, in Chile, owes its name to the fact that the mother of its founder, Don García de Mendoza, was Countess of Osorno. The Granadine Jiménez de Quesada remembered his own *Santa Fe*, near Granada, when he founded *Santa Fe de Bogotá*; the Spaniards from the Cordova in Andalusia gave the name *Córdoba* to various cities situated at the foot of a mountain as was their own. Garcilaso explains that the effort to give the name *Nueva Toledo* to *Cuzco* failed "on account of the inappropriateness of the name, because *El Cozco* has no river to gird it like Toledo, nor does it resemble Toledo in its situation" (*op.cit.*, II, 101). In this and other cases the place names are a reflection of a particular person's emotional experience as he faced the place to which he was giving a name. So it happened that names came into being that were expressive of the personal religious devotion of the sponsor: Sierra de la *Sangre de Cristo* (*Christ's-Blood* Mountains), River of the *Mother of God*, etc.; or they were expressive of what the discoverers fancied about the places and peoples they discovered: *Amazonas, Argentina*, etc. In all these cases the names are in accordance with the subjective situation of the individual person, not with the objective circumstances of the places.

It is no less curious that also in Arabic Spain there was an abundance of place names formed from the names of persons. The Arabist Miguel Asín wonders what the explanation is of "this plethora of personal names in the Arabic toponymy of Spain. Attachment to the land, the deeply-rooted right of property, attributes common to all races and peoples, would not give us a full explanation of a phenomenon which, like this one, is so peculiar to our own soil."[43] Asín tries to explain the phenomenon as the result of the distribution of part of the Spanish territory among the Moslems that conquered it in the eighth century. But since the same thing is found in Moslem Asia, it is necessary to look for deeper motives, that is, in the projection of the person's awareness over his immediate environment—in "personal absolutism."

From what has been said, then, it would follow that the Spaniard feels himself united to other people only when in his view they amount to a magnification of his own person, and not because they may represent ideas with a universal validity. It has not been the Spaniard's habit to accept plans of collective life based on continuous effort and good sense. Rather, he has given himself to those who have proposed utopian projects, because, without wondering about the possibility of their achievement, he has *believed* in them: magical changes in society, a new world empire, etc. On the other hand, nonsubmission to laws has been regarded as a "positive act of nobility" (Fernández de Navarrete).

The person never forgets himself. The only social life he really believes in and participates in is based on coincidences of feeling, without any background of ideas or depersonalized enterprises.[44] This explains

[43] M. Asín Palacios, *Contribución a la toponimia árabe de España*, p. 35. There are of course cities in the United States, for instance, that bear the names of their founders, but this manner of naming has taken place in a vital context entirely different from that of Castilian history in the eleventh and twelfth centuries.

[44] People have often noted this fact, although they have not fitted it into the whole structure of Spanish life. In 1896 Ganivet observed how secular societies failed and religious communities prospered: "We are rebellious toward association, and, in fact, all the organizations we found perish in a short time; and, nevertheless, we are the country of religious communities. . . . We understand and practice community of property when there is an ideal goal; but we do not know how to bring funds together to make them grow and prosper. We revolt against all authority and

the social groupings whose unifying center is a *caudillo*, the local political boss, or a common messianic hope. On the other hand, Spaniards do not join together to carry out the anonymous and, for them, cold task of making the life of their cities richer and more comfortable. Ganivet wrote in 1896 that he had seen some of the "ancient free cities" of Europe, and he was delighted by "their family-like attitude towards everything inside their walls, as if these were the walls of a single house," and by the citizen's faith and confidence in his city. But Granada, the beautiful city that Ganivet loved so much, "what can she do but beg the national government if she is lacking in means? If she turned to her own inhabitants, which of them would feel any confidence in her? There is little confidence in the nation; but in the city, not at all" (*Granada la bella*).

Now the historian, besides noting and evaluating facts as isolated or successive units, must arrange them in a vital structure. And when this is done, the important conclusion is reached that the history of a people cannot be constructed on universal and abstract patterns. The history of Spain becomes meaningful when it is conceived not as a continent of objectively organized culture but as an immense archipelago of great individual and collective figures—heroes, kings, saints, religious orders, great lords, poets in prose and in verse, artists, guerrilla-fighters, insurrectionists, and every other kind of thing along this line. Persons and entities emerge from a quiet collective background that is at the same time longing for a hope and a promise in this world or the other. Each person and each generation has the sense of arriving at the world "anew" when the decision is reached to break out of the timeless immobility. In the middle of the seventeenth century Baltasar Gracián said that "Spain is in the same condition today as when God created her; her inhabitants have not improved her in any respect."

Throughout the nineteenth and twentieth centuries it has been customary to say that in Spain "everything is still to be done." The generations have not bequeathed to one another a tradition of enterprises and purposes, save the tradition of belief that immobilizes and the art of expressing the awareness of the continuity of one's existence. Even so, we have seen that many people have considered the last three hundred years to be a gap in Spanish life. The empty spaces between one generation and another have usually been filled with other peoples' cultures, already

organization and then voluntarily despoil ourselves of our civil personality and accept the hardest slavery" (*Granada la bella*). Ganivet attributed this strange way of life to mysticism (which was, according to him, "sensuality restrained by virtue and poverty").

objectified, with what Unamuno would call other peoples' inventions. But the authentic texture of this history continues to be human naked-ness, with no adventitious ornaments in the way of ideas or "things," for a real tradition of objectified culture (philosophy, technology, economy, politics, science) does not exist in Spain, although there are distinguished figures in each of these cultural fields. There is, to be sure, a literary tradition, that is, an expression of the absolute consciousness of the per-son, of his self-awareness in his world of feelings, cares, and hopes. Start-ing with Lope de Vega, we can contemplate the whole expressive past of the Spaniards, continued later in the writings of the Romantics and even in the contemporary poetry of García Lorca. With Ganivet, Unamuno, or Antonio Machado we can go back through the centuries and hear time and again the troubled, noble voices of which they are a magnificent echo. But it is useless to look for Spanish antecedents of Menéndez Pidal's philology or Ramón y Cajal's histology. And if history is this way, why shouldn't history be written this way?

My history based on great writers and artists, on heroes, anti-heroes, saints, apostles, martyrs, or exalted nincompoops has its own traditional antecedents in Fernán Pérez de Guzmán's *Generaciones y semblanzas*, in certain autobiographies, and in certain pages of Quevedo. Many Spaniards have done with their lives, and with the lives of others that have come within their embrace, what the artist does by means of verbal or pictorial expression. But how is it possible to bring these stars of greater and lesser magnitude together in one historical system? In spite of the difficulty of such a task, it is perhaps worthwhile to undertake it, leaving aside for the moment such artificial notions as the Middle Ages, the Renaissance, Baroque, etc. It is especially necessary to separate clearly the permanent values of this history from the discontinuous scientific, po-litical, and economic culture that has come out of this self-consuming life, out of the conflict between personal longing for "the absolute," and the idea that such an absolute is not sufficient unto itself.

Hidalguismo, the Sense of Nobility

The immediately foregoing remarks will gain strength from a sum-mary examination of the Spaniard's sense of nobility. The Hispano-Chris-tian entered his history with the dangerous feeling that it was possible for him, in one burst of energy, to scale its greatest heights. As early as the year 1000, the Castilian was beginning to think that he could really "take" the Moor, and that fabulous Cordova was within reach of his sword. The conquests of Toledo and Valencia (although the latter conquest was temporary) provided an eleventh-century confirmation of his feeling of superiority, based on an awareness of his "intrinsic value." The Archpriest of Hita was later to say: "It is by serving well that Spanish knights win victories." To serve well as a knight was in fact a supreme aspiration. A person's value depended upon the vigor of his conduct in this regard. This attitude predisposed the Hispano-Christian to adopt whatever might reinforce it, even to the point of raiding the spiritual camp of the enemy. Thus he was ready to adopt Arabic ways of expressing personal value (fijodalgo), or what there was good in Arabic actions (*fazañas*). *Fazaña*, "feat, prowess," originally "model of goodness, generous act," comes from the Arabic *ḥasanah* (good act, generosity).[45]

Fijodalgo and *fazaña* are clear evidence of the impression of superiority which the Moslem left with the Hispano-Christian a thousand years ago. Then, the Christian's feeling of superiority grew stronger and stronger. This must be the point of departure for understanding the inordinate urge to nobility and the sense of caste that took possession of the Hispano-Christian. I shall begin by citing texts that will put us in contact with the living reality of history. In a proclamation made in Valencia in 1410 against blasphemers who "soiled their lips and tongues by speaking ill of God and the Virgin Mary," plebeians were condemned to be publicly flogged and pilloried; "but if it be a *person of honor who does not work with his hands*, let him pay as a penalty fifty gold *maravedís*."[46] An abstract conception of history would treat such an idea as a "theme" or "commonplace," and would relate it to Plato's contempt for physical labor and his low regard for crafts, which reappears in the Middle Ages: "Opus humanum, quod natura non est, sed imitatur naturam, mechanichum, i.e. adulterinum vocatur."[47] But what good would it do here to compose a study of the contempt for manual labor through the ages? We are actually faced with a kind of people who composed their existence out of the vital "impossibility" of working at tasks deemed not honorable. "You have always kept me busy with the base things of your mechanical job," says the soul to the body in the *Diálogos de la fantástica filosofía de los tres en uno*.[48] The author could and may have taken his idea from a repertory of medieval commonplaces, but in

[45] J. Corominas, *Vox Romanica*, 1949, x, 67-72.

[46] F. Danvila, in the *Boletín de la Academia de la Historia*, 1886, viii, 388.

[47] Hugo of Saint Victor, in *Patrologia*, Vol. 176, col. 747 (quoted by E. R. Curtius, in the *Zeitschrift für romanische Philologie*, lviii, 23).

[48] By Don Francisco Miranda Villafañe, Salamanca, 1583, fol. 21r.

its historical context the idea has a peculiarly Spanish meaning, for it implies that great value is attached to that which was not mechanical work,
that is, the *intrinsic value* of the person.[49]

That value was not only a matter of high spirit, courage, or *brio* predicated as attributes of the person. It was the very substance of the person,
that which made him whole, all of a piece.[50] The Spaniard has been the
only example in Western history of a man whose purpose in life is
founded on the idea that the only calling worthy of a man is to be a
man, and nothing more. When Pedro Crespo entrusts his son to the
general, Don Lope de Figueroa, he reasons thus: "What would he do
here with me but idle his time away in a life of profligacy? Let him go
and serve the king."[51] Pedro Crespo, a successful peasant, feels that the
value of his prosperity lies not in the fact that his life has been materially productive but in the fact that his wealth will assure his son a
career in the ennobling service of the king.

No other European country so stigmatized manual labor, which was
not accorded legal dignity until the reign of Charles III in the eighteenth
century, in the course of the invasion of rationalist ideas from foreign
lands, an invasion which affected only the epidermis of Spanish life. But
it is also certain that belief in intrinsic value was continually shaken by
the worry of those who found themselves locked up in their consciousness
of caste as well as by the similar worry of those who realized the grave
dangers of Spanish exclusivism. Pedro Fernández de Navarrete writes:
"This court has been filled with many other persons of low degree:
lackeys, coachmen, saddle boys, water-carriers, wafer peddlers, porters.
. . . The harm that comes from the fact that these people are leaving
the work in the fields undone need not be emphasized." The porter is
singled out for special censure: "With the introduction of this not very
ancient occupation, it has begun to be the custom that, if a servant buys a
real's worth of fruit, he must give half to the porter who carries it, an

---

[49] Don Artal de Alagón, Count of Sástago, wrote: "I am not trying to condemn
all combat between individuals or to discourage men from preserving their honor
and standing up for the honor of God and of themselves in the way that one
should . . . ; rather I would want to encourage them and give them enthusiasm for
these purposes, such enthusiasm, I understand, being more necessary than cooling
their blood, which is already so cold that it is pitiful to see how *intrinsic value* has
grown weak in those men in whom it should be strongest" (*Concordia de las leyes
divinas y humanas*, Madrid, 1593, fol. 126r).

[50] This is something different from the "moral integrity" which preserves intact
the moral principles on which conduct is based. The idea of "wholeness" refers to
something which implies active fortitude and courage and which leaves aside everything else.

[51] Calderón, *El alcalde de Zalamea*, II, ll. 765-768.

extravagance tolerated only at the court of Spain."[52] This criticism is closely connected with another: "No sooner has a merchant or a worker or a peasant enough to buy a government pension worth 500 ducats a year than he buys with this income a pension for his eldest son, whereupon not only this son but all his brothers become ashamed to occupy themselves at the humble tasks with which that money was originally earned," for "those who are not nobles aspire to make themselves nobles, and those who are aspire to rise to higher places still" (ed.cit., pp. 473, 475).

In 1541 there were already in Castile and Leon 781,582 tax-paying commoners and 108,358 hidalgos; that is, 13 per cent of the families in the kingdom paid no taxes and performed no work of any kind,[53] and they lived like a closed caste. It was observed, however, that it was not possible "to preserve in good condition a republic that consists entirely of nobles, for, to assure mutual assistance between citizens, it is necessary to have a head to rule, priests to pray, counselors to counsel, judges to judge, noblemen to give orders, soldiers to defend, farmers to till, tradesmen to do business, and artisans to take care of mechanical matters."[54] The last two classes of activity had been precisely the ones that had belonged to the Moors and Jews.

When the Spaniards got to the Indies, they implanted and perpetuated their way of life there. In 1590 the inhabitants of Buenos Aires wrote to Philip II in desperation, complaining of the poverty of the Argentine land (which for the English Puritans would have been a paradise), because it is not the land which makes the man but the reverse, even though the importance of natural conditions and the historical moment are not to be denied. In Argentina there was no gold or silver, nor were there native cities, as there were in Mexico and Peru, and the Spaniard, incapable of creating things, did not know what to do: "We are so poor and needy that we could not be more in want, in proof of which, *we do our plowing and digging with our hands.* . . . Such is the need from which the settlers suffer that *their own women and children bring their drinking water from the river.* . . . Spanish women, noble and of high quality, because of their great poverty *carry their drinking water*

[52] "Conservación de monarquías," 1626, discourse XXVI (in the *Biblioteca de Autores Epsañoles,* XXV, 504*b*).

[53] "Relación de los vecinos no pecheros que hay en las 18 provincias del reino para el repartimiento del servicio de 1541, y de los hidalgos que se presupone podrá haber en cada una de las dichas provincias," in *Colección de documentos inéditos para la historia de España,* 1848, XIII, 521-528.

[54] Fernández de Navarrete, *Conservación de monarquías,* ed.cit., p. 472.

on their own shoulders." The superior of the Franciscan convent who was the author of this letter, sorrowfully confirms that "the people do their own work and [take care] of their cattle *with their own hands*, for I have seen it happen thus, and it is a pitiable state of affairs; the people wait on themselves as if it were the tiniest village in Spain."[55]

I know no document more significant, especially for making understandable the history of Hispano-America and the contrasts it presents with the rest of America. The Spaniard moved into the region of the Plata in the sixteenth century just as in the tenth and eleventh he had spread down over the south of the Iberian Peninsula, with the object of gaining honor and maintaining seigniory for himself. Since there were neither Moors nor Jews to do the work in Buenos Aires, and since the Indians quickly fled out into the pampa, what was eventually to become the Argentina we know today remained in rather a wretched condition until about a century ago. Houses in Buenos Aires were straw-covered adobe huts, for this was the only kind of masonry the conquistador knew how to obtain without his wealth and his vassals to carry out his orders. As late as 1852, the future city was a pest-ridden village: "the skeletons of oxen and horses lay about in the mud in the middle of the street; even in front of the doors of some of the houses you could see the putrefied remains of animals."[56]

But at the same time people in America and Europe were already familiar with *Facundo*, a brilliant historico-critical picture of Argentine life by Sarmiento, for to produce such a work of personal integration and expression there was no need of debasing manual labor. But work with the hands was precisely what Sarmiento was later to propose as the remedy for his country's ills, a program similar to that proposed in Spain by the licentiate Fernández de Navarrete in 1626: bring people in from the outside, make others work, give foreigners special privileges, let them "make the rivers navigable and dig ditches for irrigation. . . . The children of these foreigners would, in the second generation, be Spaniards who would fill out the population of Spain, which is the object toward which this discourse is directed" (p. 478). He went so far as to advocate the importation of negroes "to improve some of the many mines that Spain possesses." These negroes would, "by the second or third generation be white; if they were not, it would make no difference, since they were apt at manual labor and the cultivation of the soil"

[55] Emilio A. Coni, *Agricultura, comercio e industria coloniales*, Buenos Aires, 1941, p. 15.
[56] Rafael Alberto Arrieta, *Centuria porteña*, Buenos Aires, 1944, p. 37.

(482). Fernández de Navarrete foresaw what was to happen in Brazil.

At first glance, Fernández de Navarrete's program looks like an attempt to correct the course of Hispanic history. More closely examined, it turns out to be the contrary. His negative criticism and lamentations over the poverty and depopulation of the land could have been the utterances of any representative of the "Enlightenment," with the sole difference that the author did not in the least suspect that the lack of things, the sense of emptiness, belonged to the very direction of Spanish life. The proposed solutions were of a mechanical nature, requiring the addition of an element rather than the fundamental changing of any existing element in Spanish life, that is, they called for the addition of people to do what the Moors and Jews had long been doing without any thought that the dominant caste would cease to be what it was. That it was the working castes that were missed is clearly seen in this statement of utopian and nostalgic longing: "I am persuaded that if, before the Moors and Jews had reached the state of desperation that brought them into such bad odor, a way had been found to admit them to certain honors, to avoid keeping them under the brand and stigma of infamy, it would have been possible for them to enter *through the door of honor* into the temple of virtue and into the bosom and obedience of the Catholic Church" (p. 466). This is in agreement with the ideas of Duarte Gómez referred to earlier (see Chapter 14). Fernández de Navarrete's ignorance of his own history and the rationalistic naïveté of the statement are obvious. He was also dreaming of a unique utopian caste, without realizing that if the Moors and Jews should have attained an awareness of their "intrinsic value," they would have ceased to do the work whose lack was now ruining Spain.

In fine, this excellent treatise is discreet throughout and is full of the anguish of a person who sees clearly what the situation is and would like it to be different.[57] But Fernández de Navarrete is like the madman in the asylum (*Don Quixote*, 11, 1) who, just after he was adjudged sane and was about to leave, said to one of his fellow-inmates: "If that man

---

[57] The work even proposes the creation of shipbuilding schools, "through which Spain would be freed from dependence on the help of foreigners, who, because they are foreign and without obligations or pledges of faith or love, are apt to undertake any kind of treason" (p. 542). It is incredible (although readily explicable) that the work of Fernández de Navarrete has not been published, with a sound historical commentary, to serve as basic instruction for all those who have to do with the government of the Hispano-Portuguese peoples, who are all alike in this respect. In the twentieth century (just as in the seventeenth or in the twelfth), no Hispano-Portuguese country is capable of building its own ships without foreign help.

is Jupiter and won't rain, I, who am Neptune, . . . shall rain whenever I feel like it." According to Fernández de Navarrete's advice to the king, the pursuit of letters "usually engenders a certain melancholy that weakens the spirit by opposing the cheerful impulsiveness with which dangerous adventures are undertaken when reflection does not cause them to lag. And that is why the goddess of knowledge was called 'Minerva, *quasi minuens nervos*' [!], for the peoples that indulge excessively in the pleasure of learning easily forget the practice of arms. Spain has examples enough of this, *for as long as the ejection from Spain of the Saracens' heavy yoke lasted, she was raw and lacking in letters,* and to remedy this the universities and schools were founded by the kings" (p. 542)—as a foreign importation, it might be added.

Similar observations might be made about the writings of Diego de Saavedra Fajardo, Spain's representative at the preparatory conference for the Peace of Westphalia (1648) and a man widely read, widely traveled, and well-versed in foreign languages. He too laments the harm and poverty suffered by his country, and we might expect to find in him an advocate of Europeanization ready to shatter the forms of traditional Spanish life. But nothing of the kind. When the time comes to face the decisive issues, Don Diego feels like a Spaniard of the tenth century. His world is the world of belief: "Don Juan de Austria commanded his banners to be embroidered with the cross and this motto: 'With these arms I have conquered the Turks; with them I expect to conquer the heretics! . . . I avail myself of them and of the standard of Constantine to signify to the princes the confidence with which they should raise the banner of religion against their enemies. . . . Heavenly spirits will attend this banner; *two riding on white horses* were seen fighting in the vanguard when King Ramiro II conquered the Moors near Simancas. . . . At the battle of Mérida in the time of King Alonso IX there appeared that divine lightning bolt, Santiago, the son of thunder, the patron of Spain leading the squadrons with his blood-stained sword."[58]

This belief, genuinely Spanish, was the sap and bark of the tree of Spanish life. Those who have been part of it include Quevedo, Gracián, and all those who have expressed something of what they have felt about themselves and Spain. Belief, not thought,[59] intrinsic value, the sense of

[58] *Idea de un príncipe político-cristiano, representada en cien empresas*, XXVI.

[59] It was natural that foreigners should think of Spain as a strange and incomprehensible country. Voltaire could not understand, of course, how a Spanish ambassador in London could have taken for fools two English scholars who asked his aid for a scientific expedition (probably to some of the mountains of America). The ambassa-

nobility, the spirit of caste, one and the same thing—the triple-stranded contexture of Christians, Moors, and Jews, 900 years old.

Thought as a Great Danger

Every attempt at thought was cut off, and at the same time the Spaniards were continually surprised by the consequences of this procedure. León de Castro, a theologian of Salamanca, did everything he could to destroy Luis de León, who was a victim of his own intelligence, and to all intents and purposes he was successful. Luis de León was immortalized in his poetry, but the ideas in his head, which were imprisoned with him in the jails of the Inquisition, and which he might have given to his century, he took with him into eternity. But we still have a record, a certain confidence made by León de Castro to Antonio Pérez, the less than respectable secretary to Philip II: It happened that the king wanted to bring Pérez's rich library to the Escorial, and Pérez gave the library for appraisal "to the secretary Antonio Gracián and Master León de Castro of Salamanca, that great theologian and Greek scholar. . . . Amongst those books there were and are the works of Saint John Chrysostom, in an early manuscript. . . . Master León, who was my close friend, said: 'Señor Antonio, for your part contribute this book, and I, for mine, will contribute myself and my work, *and I will go to Paris*, and I will have all these works printed, and I assure you the business will be worth more than 50,000 crowns to us, and we will divide the profit half and half. . . . For there in San Lorenzo [i.e., the Escorial], although it have the grandeur of a royal library, those books will be a hidden treasure buried in the earth.' "[60]

But the manuscripts of the Escorial remained like hidden treasure precisely because of all the León de Castros there have been in Spain, a country whose authentic history is to be read more in the public and private confessions of Spaniards than in the official chronicle. In addition to the fact that there were few humanists in Spain, the humanities were not promoted there for fear of the danger that "just as the humanist

---

dor "les prit pour des fous: lui seul était peu sage." (Epistle LV, *De l'usage de la science dans les princes*.)

[60] Antonio Pérez, "Cartas," in the *Biblioteca de Autores Españoles*, XIII, 502. See G. Marañón, *Antonio Pérez*, I, 10. The low ebb of Hellenic studies in 1611 in Spain may be clearly seen in the royal privilege which authorized D. Lorenzo Ramírez de Prado to print his book *Pentacontarchos* in Antwerp; it could not be printed in Spain because "The said book consisted in large part of Greek letters and other curious things which the presses of these kingdoms sorely lack, . . . and in the said city of Antwerp it would be printed with great care" (Gallardo, *Ensayo*, IV, 35).

emends a passage in Cicero, he will likewise emend one in the Scriptures; such foolishness as this has me bewildered, and often makes me feel like not going on." This is what the Valencian humanist Pedro Núñez wrote to the historian Jerónimo de Zurita.

This anguish reaches no greater pitch, so far as I know, than it does in a passage by Father Juan de Mariana, the one who wrote that the Inquisition had made the Spaniards feel themselves "on a par with death." In Latin, and in a work never printed in Spain, he describes the effect caused by the trial of Fray Luis de León:

"The case had many people anxious while they waited to find out the result. The fact was that men distinguished for their wisdom and their reputation had to defend themselves while in prison against something that was no small danger to their lives and their good name. A sad situation, that of the virtuous man: as a reward for his supreme achievements, he is obliged to endure the hatreds and accusations of the very ones who should be his defenders. With such an example, the ambitions of many gifted men *were fated to decline,* and *their energies to grow weak and die.* The affair in question depressed the spirits of those who were contemplating another man's danger, and who saw what torment threatened those who freely stated what they thought. In this way, many moved over to the other side, or bent before the wind.[61] And what was to be done? There is no greater madness than to exert oneself in vain, and to weary oneself to achieve only hatred. Those who shared the popular opinions went on doing so with greater pleasure, and they encouraged ideas that were pleasing, ideas in which there was less danger but no greater concern for truth."[62]

The disagreement of certain distinguished Spaniards with the Inquisitorial policy is quite evident, and what Mariana said at the end of the sixteenth century connects with what Hernando del Pulgar had said a cen-

[61] The Jews had been doing this since the end of the fifteenth century, and the New Christians continued the practice in the sixteenth century.

[62] "Pro editione Vulgata," in J.-P. Migne, *Scripturae Sacrae Cursus Completus,* Paris, 1839, p. 588. Mariana adds (p. 691) that if commentaries in Greek are needed to understand Homer, Hesiod, and Pindar, and Latin commentaries in order to understand Virgil, then Hebrew commentaries are required in order to interpret the Bible. "Young men should not be discouraged by these recent difficulties. . . . We Spaniards are little given to such studies, and I think that we are lacking more in encouragement than we are in obstacles" (Neque sumus Hispani tantopere id genus studiis addicti, ut fraeno et non potius calcaribus egeamus). Mariana boldly defended the right of certain famous Spaniards to be intelligent; his summation of the arguments in favor of a reasonable interpretation of the Bible has never been published in Spain or translated into Spanish.

tury before (see Chapter 13). The Spaniards, believers by tradition, never thought of modifying their religion precisely because they did not invent any new ideas on which an attempt at revision might be based. This, however, did not keep many from feeling and saying that the Holy Office was intolerable for them. Considering the Inquisition's Hispano-Judaic character, lacking all connection with the Christian past of the Peninsula, this is not surprising. That struggle between two castes promoted mental ineptitude and the paralysis of those skilled in the use of their intellectual curiosity. The trials began on the flimsy basis of denunciations and suspicions, and the victims were left in jail for years, sometimes dying there before they were brought to trial.[63] Granting that the Spaniard had to begin with only a slight inclination to deep scientific research, terror of the Holy Office estranged him still more from such a dangerous occupation. Mariana says that "the ambitions of many gifted men were fated to decline, and their energies to grow weak and die." The famous exegete Diego de Zúñiga says that any interpretation of the Bible different from the currently accepted one was regarded as Jewish subversion: "The stupid clamor of those people [the Inquisition and its chorus-masters] has produced such a panic in many learned exegetes that they have ended up by retiring from their noble and holy task, because they believe that it is impossible for a person of culture to devote himself safely to the study of sacred letters."[64] About the same time, Alonso de Cabrera, preacher to Philip II, said in one of his sermons: "We have gone from one extreme to the other: in order not to be hypocrites, men have yielded both to being dissolute and to appearing so; just as the man who did not want to be a heretic chose to be stupid and refused to learn how to read."[65] Refusing to learn to read out of fear of the Inquisition must have become a popular commonplace, a counter-

[63] This was the fate of the Salamancan professors Gaspar de Grajal, Martín Martínez de Cantalapiedra, and Francisco Sánchez de las Brozas; also of Fray Alonso Gudiel, professor in the University of Osuna, and others.

[64] "Quorum inepti clamores adeo formidabiles fuere multis sacrarum litterarum studiosis hominibus, ut eos ab hoc honestissimo et sanctissimo studio vehementer deterrerent; docti vero homines sacris litteris vix tuto se versari putabant" ("Didaci a Stunica . . . ," in *Job Commentaria*, Toledo, 1584, Chap. x, pp. 472-473). This text is cited by M. de la Pinta Llorente, *Causa criminal contra el biblista Alonso Gudiel*, Madrid, 1942, p. 27. Also to be recalled are other Inquisitorial trials. See the following studies by M. de la Pinta Llorente: "El biblista Gaspar de Grajal" (in *Cruz y Raya*, Madrid, 1936), *Procesos Inquisitoriales contra Francisco Sánchez de las Brozas* (Madrid, 1941), and *Proceso contra Martín Martínez de Cantalapiedra* (Madrid, 1946).

[65] Edition of the *Nueva Biblioteca de Autores Españoles*, p. 37.

part to the fear of the scholars expressed by Zúñiga and Mariana. Cervantes introduced the following amusing dialogue into one of his interludes:

ALGARROBO. Can you read, Humillos?

HUMILLOS. No, of course not. Nor can it be proved that in all my lineage there has been anyone of so little judgment as to learn those chimeras that lead men to the stake and women to the brothel.[66]

The danger of the Inquisition to thought and culture was also felt by Don Luis de Góngora, who told his bishop in 1588 that his theological knowledge was slight, because "I have deemed it better to be damned for frivolity than for heresy."[67]

The five texts quoted above are representative of the totality of Spanish life, from the most refined to the most vulgar, at the end of the sixteenth century. Not to think, not to know, not to read were protections against the sadism and the plundering instincts of the Holy Office. The only way the Spaniard could compensate for the intellectual silence imposed on him by the Inquisition was through vitally expressive activities. Thought requires, above all, freedom; it is freedom. The petty fury of the Inquisitors meant the same thing for intellectual culture as the social and economic organization prior to 1500 had meant for the material life of the commonalty. Unfortunately, the Hispanic people were not prepared in the sixteenth century to fight on the open field of the intelligence. Perhaps something could have been tried by certain descendants of the Jews, but it was against them above all that the expert ferrets of the Holy Office, heirs to the age-old rancor of the *aljamas*, had sharpened the claws of their passion. People of purely Christian descent turned away from the fight, and Mariana ended up by saying (who knows how sincerely?) that the Inquisition was a gift from heaven. As he says, "There is no greater madness than to exert oneself in vain, and to weary oneself to achieve only hatred." It is characteristic of Mariana for him to take a step backward whenever he thinks he has gone too far ahead in his defiance of the social pressure of the Inquisition. That is why he writes sometimes in Latin and sometimes in Spanish. For the same reason, Cervantes let his pen run more freely in the first versions (published only in recent times) of *Rinconete y Cortadillo* and *El celoso extremeño* than in the versions he sent to the printers. Those who are unacquainted with the inner quality of Spanish life and who do not feel it,

[66] *Los alcaldes de Daganzo*, edited by Schevill and Bonilla, p. 47.
[67] M. Artigas, *Góngora*, p. 64.

do not like our term "hypocrisy" for this attitude. But the term does not imply that either Mariana, or Cervantes, or Quevedo, or others like them were insincere in their religion. They simply took precautions against the overwhelming power of what they judged to be overweening and dangerous stupidity, veiling their disapproval at times in caution, at times in irony and humor, when they were the masters of such arts, as in the supreme case of Cervantes. The most intelligent and freest of spirits (Cervantes, Lope de Vega, Fernández de Navarrete, Quevedo, the Count-Duke of Olivares, and many others to be mentioned) sensed that the country was suffering from a monkish tumefaction, and that this was one of the causes of the national decadence.

The Inquisition was as popular as it was unpopular, as much the protector of belief as the executioner of believers. Once the Holy Office was in power, there was no way on the one hand of escaping its blows nor on the other of accepting them as a heavenly grace. But it is no less true that the decisive arguments against that institution, basically stupid and yet enduring till 1833, had to be imported from the foreign quarters of rationalism. To describe the effect of the activity of the Inquisition one should turn not to the written word but rather to the pictorial art of Hieronymus Bosch or of Goya in his Caprices. Yet after all, Quevedo's and Gracián's styles, both of them completely purified of any sense of reality, along with the intimate letters of Lope de Vega, would also bring us close to the gesticulating nihilism of that investigation-ridden society, in which the eternal and the temporal contorted themselves together as in an unrestrained saraband.

Given the form of Hispanic life, it all had to be this way, and it is idle to waste time pointing out the evils caused by the exclusive rule of belief, or that backwardness and feeble thinking are in the last analysis like a cloud of dust left behind by peoples sustained by belief and essentially nothing else.

Culture as an Expression of Life

There is more to this historical paradox than a series of calamities and negations. If Spanish life found its way cut off in certain directions, it nonetheless found others that it could take. One might say of the Spain beset by the Inquisition the same thing that Jacinta says of herself in Alarcón's comedy, *La verdad sospechosa*:

> And so, lest I die,
> I will speak and amuse myself,
> For I get nowhere by tormenting myself.

Many Spaniards indeed did speak—with their pens. The treasure-house of Western European literature was eventually enriched by the greatest of these efforts. The *Celestina*, the picaresque autobiographies, the pastoral narratives, the mystic works of Saint Teresa and Saint John of the Cross, the drama of Lope de Vega, Tirso de Molina, Alarcón, and Calderón, the poetry of Luis de León and Góngora, and, finally, Cervantes' novel—none of this could have come to be in an atmosphere of placid religious and intellectual tolerance where the tranquillity of economic well-being would have permitted the luxury of critical thought about man and nature. And certain other expressions of life would likewise never have existed—the anguished philosophies of Luis Vives and Spinoza, uprooted from the homeland; the painting of El Greco, carried away by the visionary ecstasy of his fellow Toledans; the painting of Velázquez, detached and aloof in the awareness of the aristocracy of his art, coldly skeptical on occasion, and in his supreme moments, caught up in the experience of life's inner process (see later in this chapter).

The Spaniards came of age, culturally speaking, toward the end of the fifteenth century, not because of their dazzling imperial activity, but because they had taken account of the insoluble problem that was their existence as individuals and as fellows one of another. A hegemony based on skillful political accomplishments and economic prosperity might have made the Spaniards happy; and when the time came for the dissolution of the empire—none lasts forever—their history would have resolved into a remembrance of happy days monotonously equal in their insignificance. It did not happen thus. The empire was all but limitless, yet the individual was a prisoner within himself. The despair of solitude made possible the creation of new forms apt for expressing the situation in which the best men of Spain felt themselves engulfed—a paradoxical situation which permitted no rational resolution. This is the sense concealed in the preface to *Lazarillo de Tormes*: the author is writing "so that full notice will be taken of my person, and, besides, so that those who have inherited noble estates may consider how little is due them (for fortune has been partial to them), and how much more have done those to whom fortune has been adverse and who, rowing with might and skill, have come into a good harbor."

Spain rowed against the tides of fortune, and came into a safe harbor where her values received the recognition they deserve—peculiar values, to be sure, as are all those created by histories endowed with important meaning. As late as the end of the fifteenth century (*La Celestina*, 1499), Spanish literary expression (except the Romancero) found its models in the forms and themes of the classic, European, or oriental traditions: the epic is of Franco-Germanic descent; learned poetry uses a French meter (the fourfold way) and classic or European themes (Alexander, Apollonius, the miracles of Our Lady); other works draw on the *matière de Bretagne* or on the courtly tradition of Provençal poetry; and alongside these, there was oriental didacticism and fiction (the *Disciplina Clericalis, Calila e Dimna*, Don Juan Manuel's *Conde Lucanor*, etc.) and lyricism (from the *kharyas* and *zajals* of the *Cantigas* to the Hispano-Orientalism of Juan Ruiz and Don Santob).

As in literature so in the rest of Spanish life, the pendulum had oscillated between the Christian north and the Moslem south. This mode of life is symbolized on the one side by the importation of public institutions from Europe, for example, the Prince of Asturias in imitation of the Prince of Wales, the office of constable, the Council of Castile; and on the other by the usages imported from the south, for example, the frontier commander, called in Spanish *adelantado de la frontera* (translated from Arabic *muqaddam* "put forward, chief," as has been discovered by H. L. A. van Wijk, *Neophilologus*, 1951, p. 91). The Spaniard habitually advanced beyond his own borders, and on all such advances he collected both material and cultural booty.

Architectural monuments also reveal Spanish culture's bilateral process of receptivity up to the end of the fifteenth century. The Romanesque style came into Spain in the eleventh century, contemporary with the monks of Cluny, and it flourished in places where Arabic and Mozarabic art had previously served the cause of beauty. As J. A. Gaya Nuño says, the Romanesque combined "French rules and Spanish genius." Then, in the thirteenth century, French gothic spread over the Peninsula, while the Moorish style of the "mudéjares" (of which the finest example is the Alcázar of Seville) embellished southern and central Spain.

About the year 1500 Spain became Spain, and she turned from the receptive to the expansive attitude. The *Celestina* was the first work to enjoy international value through multiple translations. Europeans were captivated by its forthright, personal expression of longing and anguish. And from then on, Spain continued to be present in the consciousness and imagination of other peoples. Many works were translated or imitated, or simply read in Spanish: those of Antonio de Guevara, *Amadís*, Montemayor's *Diana, Lazarillo de Tormes*, and *Guzmán de Alfarache*; Saint Teresa, Luis de Granada, and Saint John of the Cross; the *Quijote* and Cervantes' *Exemplary Novels*; books about lands and peoples discovered by the Spaniards; the drama of the seventeenth century, Quevedo, Gracián; and many *dii minores* for whom there is no space in such a summary account.

There were, then, no importers in the rest of the world attracted by Spanish wares in the realm of imperial grandeur or splendor (that is, there was little here in the way of objective system) nor in the realm of philosophy or science (although one might remember Luis Vives, Francisco Suárez, and, to a degree, Spinoza). What Spain could and did export were the forms in which she expressed her own problematical life. Through these forms she pointed out new directions to the literature of Europe, new directions for the awareness that the European came to have of his total life—sensibility, religion, imagination, the sense of human life as drama, novel, and comedy.

To fill and develop the outline sketched here, one would have to write a history that would interweave the literary histories of Spain and of the rest of Europe, not in terms of abstract relationships such as borrowings, influences, etc., but in terms of the vital relationships I have set forth here. At the same time, one would have to take into account the formation and expansion of the Spaniards' artistic originality—in architecture, from the plateresque to the churrigueresque; in painting, from El Greco to Goya and Picasso; and the Spanish innovations would be seen in their projection to lead to the impressionism of the nineteenth century.

Spain created a certain type of culture while she was destroying the possibility of the "other" type that was to prevail and triumph beyond her borders. This is the Hispanic paradox whose meaning and values I am trying to make perceptible.

Let one thing be clear above all: the admirable achievements of the sixteenth and seventeenth centuries gave a new content to Spanish culture, but they did not interrupt the vital dialectic of possibilities (preferences) and impossibilities (reluctances and rejections) that comprised the action in the peculiar dwelling-place of Spanish life. Personal expression attained summits of quality that had not been previously imagined. But the attachment to belief did not diminish, and there was but a slight awakening of intellectual and depersonalized activities, not very attractive to Spaniards then, theretofore, and thereafter.

The Problem Reviewed

Now the problem here considered, whether it be important or insignificant, touches upon the Hispanic people's self-awareness, and it also affects the work of certain historians and scholars. Precise and irrefutable proof is not involved in these matters, although it cannot fail to be useful to correct my thinking—as it was expressed in the first Spanish edition of this book—where it is deficient and my expression where it is inept.

I am not writing a history of Spain and her civilization, nor am I defining the psychology of the Spanish people. I have simply tried to show how the Spaniards are situated with respect to themselves and the world around them—their orientation, their perspective, the boundaries that limit their possibilities as Spaniards. It seems to me that the primary task of the historian's history should be to show the basic position of a people inside its own inescapable life. What a people does and what happens to it are conditioned by this station in its own life. Wars may be won or they may be lost, but they are won or lost in the French, the German, or the Spanish fashion. Here I am interested in what the Spaniard has done and what has happened to him when the deeds and happenings include his awareness of his Spanishness. I have tried to make clear (doubtless imperfectly) how the Spaniards have come to be themselves, how they have continued to live in the historical dwelling they have built, how they have felt in it while working at the unforeseeable accomplishments—extraordinary or paltry—that fill the great compass of their history.

The individual or collective creation of a culture is always the result of a compromise between what was desired and was possible and what was not desired and could not be accomplished. Every human work shows, through a certain arrangement and ordering of its elements, the will and the capabilities of its creator as qualified according to the way each individual lives within the "dwelling" of his own life.[68]

[68] Let us recall some examples in order to avoid misunderstanding. We have already seen how the Gothic king Ataulfo took the decision that he could not and should not destroy the remains of the Roman Empire, so setting the future course of the Visigoths. Lope de Vega conceived his theatre as a concession to majority taste at the same time that he wanted to—and could not—create another type of literature: "At times I have written according to the art that few know . . . but now I write according to the art invented by those who have sought popular applause" (*Arte nuevo de hazer comedias*). Corneille wanted to compose dramas in France when there actually were none, but he had to accommodate his will to write with the necessity to seek models outside of France: "I did not dare to trust my own resources . . . , I turned to the great Seneca for support. . . . When I resolved to pass from the heroic to the natural, I did not dare to descend from such heights without being assured of a guide, and I allowed myself to be led by the famous Lope de Vega" (introductory *Epître* to *Le Menteur*). Cervantes says that his book "is contained and enclosed within the narrow confines of the narration, although he has the ability, capacity, and understanding to deal with the whole universe," and "he asks that his work not be scorned" (*Quijote*, II, 44). Here quite clearly may be

To be understood, a culture must be seen and felt in the problematic process of its creation. It cannot be understood when viewed as an objectified and immobile mass, or when it is only recreated in terms of the observer's experience. This latter process, however valuable it may be, is not history.[69] The historian must see a culture as a continual self-creation going on within the life of a people, who, as they create, do so necessarily as Greeks, Spaniards, Englishmen, or whatever. Any truly significant "ingredient" that we single out in history will, no matter how universal it is, appear—and this is what makes it meaningful—in terms of how a particular people senses its own situation at a given moment in its own vital abode. To call certain traits of the historical Spaniard Moorish or Jewish, as I have done, it is to give a possible explanation of how they came into existence. The traits themselves are really Spanish. The word *hazaña* was originally a radiation of Moslem prestige, even though it may not have occurred to the Moors to give the name *hasanah* to a great feat.

I have not defined anything, because the human reality is not definable, it is only "presentable." I have sketched the panorama of the Peninsula at the time of the Moslems' arrival, and I have observed that the Visigoths were not then Spaniards. When, between the tenth and eleventh centuries, the new written language of Castile (eventually the language of Spain), begins to reveal to us a new form of human existence, we are face to face with a human reality which is no longer that of the Visigoths.

Peoples always appear to us in history as something given, complete, like birds who, when they begin their flight, leave their nest and their progenitors behind. It is likewise true that man, not being a bird, out of his desire to have an ancestry creates one for himself. Thus the Spaniard has variously seen his own ancestry as Visigothic, or Roman, or Iberian. But it is no less true that the life of the Spaniard and his authentic and valuable works have been different in structure and meaning from the life and works of the Iberian, the Visigoth, and the Roman, existing on the same Peninsular lands. If the life structures of peoples were eternal and hermetic, there would have been only one kind of man on the earth. But these *vividuras* are multiple, and they exist in particu-

---

seen the difference between the way in which the Spaniards and the French confront the problems posed by the will.

[69] The *Chinoiserie* of Théophile Gautier is valuable as an expression of the Romantic longing for distant and mysterious horizons, but it does not help in the understanding of Chinese culture.

lar times and places as the correlate of the univocal meaning present in the name of each people. It is not the external practices but the habitual character of inner decisions that makes the life of a people a homogeneous continuity. The practices of the Spaniards in the fifteenth century are not those of today; but if we listen to the opinions they had of themselves then and those they have now, the unity that binds them is evident at once. My history, if there is any in this book, is the history of Spain's self-awareness as a dramatic character through ten centuries of life and action. The various kinds of data I have collected serve to indicate how the Spaniard has dwelt in his own life, how he has on occasion rebelled against his destiny, how he has tried to escape from it. I have attached a good deal of importance to the confessions of certain very representative Spaniards who have found their historical life of the last three centuries to be a void, to be lacking in any positive value (p. 58).

What impresses the historian is that when he posts himself at the beginning of this much despised period of three centuries, he hears the voices of those who foresee the ruin of the nation whose other voices have already declared it to be dead. In fact, it is precisely this sense of agony that makes these prophets Spanish. These lamentations, rising as in antiphonal chorus from the opposite sides of a putative void of three centuries, give a clear picture of a strange life of a people zealous like no other to live in a constant agony of hopes and negations. In 1617 a deputy to the Cortes told the king: "All the vassals to the crown are being lost because they are becoming monks and priests, and the estates that originally were supposed to pay taxes to Your Majesty are gradually being taken over by the Church, and if the situation is not remedied, in a very few years Your Majesty is not going to have anyone to serve him." Gerónimo de Zevallos, a churchman, wrote in 1623 that because of the immoderate extension of the ecclesiastical estate, "this monarchy is going to be utterly ruined, for it is like a borer, which, no matter how small it is, can destroy a beam." Fray Luis de Miranda noted that for the same reason "the towns are almost all depopulated and deserted." And he added these oracular words of gloom: "Our Spanish monarchy is being consumed away hour by hour and moment by moment, and morally speaking it is impossible for it to last if the remedy is not applied with utmost haste and diligence."[70] The religious orders were carrying off "the bravest men, the healthiest, the most upstanding, those with the best faces, the most talented and skillful. There is not among them a

[70] These and many more texts are in A. G. de Amezúa, *Lope de Vega en sus cartas*, II, 217ff.

cripple, nor hardly a dwarf, nor one that is ugly, or dull, or ignorant. ... In the world [remain] only the dregs and dross of men" (according to a statement made in 1646). The plethora of monks was inevitable for people who felt that they were a privileged caste standing upon the pinnacles of a world empire. The monks were nobles of the divine order, who made a positive contribution to the organization of the empire in distant lands, and to the saving of the lives of the American Indians.[71] To wish that there had been fewer monks in Spain is merely to reveal ignorance of the structure and life-course of the Spaniards. A comparison with the situation in the United States might be helpful. Here we have an abundance, perhaps a superfluity, of government bureaucrats, some of whom are accused of corruption, while the farmers have a hard time finding hands to help with the crops. The Spanish Empire was a religious institution. The horizon of the Spanish mind was entirely religious, so that facing his horizon, the individual felt that he was living shut up within himself in hermetic isolation, yet at the same time had a full awareness that the religious life was stifling the secular life, a secular life that no one in Spain could conceive of as valuable in itself, as a rational and reasonable organization of human stimuli. The critics of the friars would themselves not have known what to do in a land without friars. Like authentic Spaniards, the friars who criticized their own brethren would have liked to be the only monks themselves, not out of any individualistic impulse, but because they could not get a grip on any objective hand-hold outside the area of their awareness of themselves. The European individualist reduced his individualism to a theory and objectified it, with the result that he depersonalized it, as is clear for example in Max Stirner's once celebrated book, *Der Einzige und sein Eigenthum* (The Individual and His Property), 1845.

Neither the lamentations of the seventeenth century, nor those of the fifteenth or the twentieth have served, as we might have expected, to eliminate or reduce the lamented evils. The Spaniards have spent the centuries rebuking their shadow, as we have seen in the case of Fernández de Navarrete and Saavedra Fajardo. They would not and could not change the world around them, yet they have shown surprise at their own immobility. My task then has consisted in trying to reduce to a unity of meaning the thing over which the lamentation is being made and the state of mind of the person making it; and in trying to see what

[71] Marcel Bataillon has written some accurate and enlightening pages about this; in the end "the spirit of peaceful conquest" triumphed in America ("La Vera Paz. Roman et histoire," in the *Bulletin Hispanique*, 1951, LIII, 235-300).

possibilities of valuable action are latent in other times or at present under what appears to the naïve observer as nothing but sterility and dreary inadequacy.

There is no foundation for the abstract complaint that there have been no elite minorities in Spain, if one is looking for minorities similar to those in certain other European countries. A directing minority is effective when it grows out of the possibilities already existing diffused in the people as a whole, that is, when it is an expression of the national disposition of life. Thus, the minority groups that have sprung up in Spain through the imitation or importation of foreign ideas have never clothed themselves effectively with Spanish life, just as Spanish culture in general has lived in a continual dramatic conflict between what it is and what it is not. But the Spanish minorities have been effective when they have reflected in a superior and valuable way what many Spaniards have desired and understood. Certain bishops of the sixteenth century, Las Casas, Zumárraga, and Vasco de Quiroga, changed the political direction of the American colonization. Whether we like what they did or not, there is no doubt that they represented a refined form of Spanish belief, and that they found ready followers both in the court and among the people. Lope de Vega, too, was the leader of a minority as he molded the collective sensibility of the people, through a complex artistic technique that became popular, by turning himself into the spokesman for their poetic yearnings. The dramatic genre invented by him still enjoyed a considerable prestige in the eighteenth century. When Spain lost her vitality, her possible minorities grew weaker and weaker in what one might call their value-potential. But this is not true only in Spain. There are not in France today minorities like those of the eighteenth and nineteenth centuries, and in the United States there are very few who can guide the opinions and tastes of the drifting masses. And in any case, it is not permissible for the historian of the Hispanic world to charge the term "minority" with a meaning not compatible with the system of Spanish life, and then appear to be surprised when he finds that such minorities in Spain have always been a failure.

If, on the other hand, we look for more positive realities instead of easy negations, we will find occasion for surprise in a fact already noted at the beginning of this book: almost the entirety of the Spanish Empire was retained by its Spanish inhabitants after they had separated politically from the mother country in 1824. When one remembers what a ghost of her former self Spain was at the beginning of the nineteenth century and how flimsy the political structures of her immense dominions were, it is surprising that all of them were not occupied by various powers, like another Poland, only richer and more appetizing than the European one. But the failure of the English at Buenos Aires in 1807 showed that it would have been an arduous task. This means that on a certain level the system of relationships between minority and majority was still working effectively. Those who were ready to fight and die for the glorification of their Hispanic personal absolutism were supported by thousands of people who were ready to be killed for the same reason. San Martín, Bolívar, Sucre, and others were new Pizarros and Corteses, driving in the opposite direction but with a similar motivation, power, and trajectory. This connection between great personalities and anonymous masses has nothing to do with the minorities of enlightened despotism, of course. But the history of Spain must be asked questions that it can answer, questions out of life, not out of books.

There have been good scientists in Spain from time to time, but their science has not originated there. If there has never been in Spain any authentic scientific thought, why is it expected that programs of a scientific or technological type will triumph there? The Inquisition was a long calamity, but it did not stifle any great Spanish thought that might otherwise have matured in the life of the Spanish people. The very existence of such a stupid tribunal, which did not have a breath of holiness in it, was possible because of the lack of any intellectual energy around it. There was really no heresy to combat, for Spain could not have so much as hoped for a Calvin or a Melanchthon, to say nothing of a Luther. Inquisitorial persecution was a conflict between two castes, which kept going in the same place as much from inertia as for any other reason, once the Jews were exterminated. No heresy developed.

Scientific studies in the Spain of the twentieth century have been the isolated labor of a few eminent men whose spirits were disturbed as they observed the contrast between the rapid rhythm of their European neighbors and the immobility of their own people. Since their activity as a minority did not find any natural connection with existing traditional inclinations, the results obtained have been only fragmentary and have made no place for themselves in the total picture of Spanish social life. The situation is comparable to a vehicle with many engines, some of which are such that, no matter how well they run, they are not made to fit the gears that will transmit their power to the wheels and propel the vehicle. One of the original forces in this twentieth-century renaissance of science in Spain was the Andalusian Francisco Giner de los Ríos (1839-1915), a dedicated man who in his power of persuasion and even in his appearance resembled Juan de Ávila, "the apostle of Andalusia" in the sixteenth century. The essential difference between the two is that Juan de Ávila prepared people to dwell in heaven, whereas Giner tried to make life in this world more pleasant and more intelligent. Giner was charmed by the socio-political manners of the English and the scientific rigor of the Germans, both of which were combined in him with a religious sense of life that was Hispanic after all, in spite of its evidently Romantic European roots. Distinguished figures in various fields contributed to the cultural renovation of the Spaniards; for instance, the biologist Santiago Ramón y Cajal, the humanist Marcelino Menéndez y Pelayo, and the Arabist Francisco Codera. In 1892 Menéndez y Pelayo was lamenting the fact that the only physics that existed in Spain was that used by engineers and pharmacists in their practical pursuits.

The science—I use the word in its broad, not its narrow, sense—that was founded on these powerful individual impulses produced results sporadically and in no relation to one another, though in some cases original and important. Spanish society made no organic response to these advances. And this demonstrates that the absence of science in Spain has not been due to an accidental delay, but to the way the Spaniards—an ex-imperial people—spontaneously organize their life. The reform movement did not succeed in affecting the national consciousness. A few "apostles" developed isolated disciples, but the public institutions went on basically as they had been. The administration of the state went on functioning with its habitual, lazy awkwardness.

The revival of culture manifested itself in certain branches of science insofar as its results had a direct or indirect effect on medicine and industry; there was great progress in the study of Spanish civilization and scant interest for other cultures. Today in Spain humanistic studies scarcely transcend the boundaries of the Hispanic, for when the hermetic Spaniard considers man, he thinks about himself, not about other men. Non-Spanish culture, ancient or modern, does not invite the Spaniard to think with originality. This is the confirmation I find for my idea that intellectual minorities have not meshed with the authentic possibilities of the majorities, and that the desire for culture (always present in one way or another) does not by itself bring forth among any of the Hispano-Portuguese people a culture that is effective, creative of new horizons.

A contrast with the situation of science thus described is offered by the resurgence of poetry that the Hispanic peoples have been experiencing now for half a century. Rubén Darío had only to poke around in the embers of authentic Hispanic possibilities, and in Spain and Spanish

America a thousand-year-old tradition of great poetry and the total expression of life burst into flame. The multitudes answered readily and organized the new artistic values in a correct scale.

The same thing has happened with certain social values—values which for me bear a negative sign. *Caudillismo* prevails in almost all the Hispano-Portuguese countries because the will of a few to dominate and the desires of many meet in a happy engagement. If this were not the case, the dictatorships would not prosper. They have come into existence to fill the void that is caused by the absence of a social culture based on a system of ideas and objective interests. We have already seen how Unamuno rejected the "tyranny" of ideas, but was ready to yield to any man personally superior to him. The relationship between minorities and masses must be understood, then, within the structural system of each people. The historian must adapt himself to the reality whose history he is writing. The question of who are the better members of a society and who are the less good is "absolutely" relative to the process of each particular history.

Some readers and critics have found determinism in my way of constructing and interpreting history. But the truth is, I am not tracing out what the future is to be of the peoples today called Hispanic. I have traced out on the map of history the directions that people have decided or preferred to follow. Could they have followed different ones? I do not know, nor does it seem worthwhile to speculate on the question. I have confined myself to suggesting plausible motives for this human course in its beginnings, and how, once the course was adopted, it was followed in the passing of a thousand years. This has been my way of sketching the portrait of a human collectivity, and I have called the face Spanish. Will the features of this face change? The One who presides over human destiny may know. I do not. One thing seems certain to me, and that is, that, if the "inward" features should change to the point of no longer being identifiable with those of the present portrait, then the new face would have to be called something other than Spanish. The people who occupy the Italian Peninsula today cannot be called Romans. The basic and undeniable fact underlying my description is that the present features, the main trends of Spanish life, are not to be found before the tenth century, while it is evident that the features emergent in the tenth century are still present in our own time. Thus it is that we sometimes recognize an unmistakable resemblance between the face of an old man and a photograph of the same person when he was a child.

To call this determinism shows how external to life certain ideas are concerning history. Every abstract concept ("minorities," "challenge and response," etc.) loses its "unity" the moment it is examined in a real situation, in the history of a people. We have just seen this in the case of the minorities. Concerning historical challenge, we have only to observe how the inhabitants of Iberia, France, and Italy met the Moslem attack. The challenge here is like a common denominator, while the response is in each case a peculiar and unique numerator. This is always the way it works. The character of the response depends upon the vital disposition of the people who respond.

At this point an inevitable question comes up: "What is the value of Hispanic history, the subject of this book?" It is a complicated problem. To ask the question seriously implies assumptions as problematical as the question itself. Certainly, the high value of Spanish civilization, whether or not it is demonstrable, is evident to me, else I would not have written the present work. The mere existence of the Spanish people has a value in itself, as a work of art, like an extraordinary novel about a unique historical character: born in anguish, now sure, now vacillating in their self-awareness, they have never known a serene moment of self-fulfillment; their life has consisted of a continual alternation between lethargy and startled awakening; it even has consisted in their judging as null and void some of the centuries of their history. Such an event is in its totality unique and, for one who perceives its meaning, admirable.

As a consequence of believing that history consists above all in an indefinite number of modalities, I think that the value of a history cannot be estimated according to a single pattern of values. There is no hierarchy of criteria that permits us to decide in a universally valid way how the lives of the nations should go on. Man is the "subjet divers et ondoyant" that Montaigne said he was, and it is still "malaysé d'y fonder jugement constant." There is no consensus concerning why man has come into this world, why he disappears after a short term, why he struggles to subsist and survive, and why some men destroy others. Man's reason is at a loss here as in many other instances. Nevertheless, there is no end to the arrogant attempts to predict history by means of a system of causes and effects, to reason it out as a physical reality, or as a process directed toward an ultimate and universal perfectibility, following the same course as the scientific and industrial progress of Western European life since the 18th Century.

When examined alongside the other European cultures, the history of

Spain naturally appears as an utterly aberrant form of life. It has endured not only the contempt of its foreign spectators but the lamentations of its own actors. Spain has been the butt of every kind of insult: she is primitive, backward, lazy, invertebrate, fanatical, etc., etc. But the reality of Spain is not made clear in this way, nor is it by means of the tragic conception of life that Unamuno was fond of, for this view, though it is an expression of Unamuno's own Spanishness, leaves in parenthesis the concrete reality of Spain.

A half century ago it would not have been possible to present Spanish history as anything but a deficiency, as a human enterprise that took the road away from, rather than to, the plenitude of culture that it might have reached. Argument was not possible. All that the dissenting weaker side could do was surrender. The European universities had spread their rigorous system of knowledge, the "Bildung" that was to make possible the ideal of humanity constructed by the German Romantics. But now knowledge of all kinds exceeds the scope of our embrace, the mortality rate has declined, there are more people on earth than ever before, and the welfare of the average person in some countries is greater than that of kings in the past. At the same time the value of man as a self-conscious being has declined, and even the spurts of certain religious activities tend more to the acquisition of power and material well-being than to developing in man that which is unique and incommensurable in him. We have never lived more absent from ourselves. In vast regions of the earth, different kinds of inhumanity dwarf the atrocities of Attila or those of the Spanish Inquisition or of the wars and conquests of earlier times. Ideas and beliefs do not reduce or ward off evil of any kind. The rivalry among nations is founded on self-interest, not on constructive ventures for the good of the world. Christianity goes on but it does not make Christians of people, as Luis Vives observed in the sixteenth century. Nor do the universities and schools (ever increasing in numbers) correct the tendency to vulgarity; rather, perhaps, they promote it. T. S. Eliot has said what needs to be said about this.[72]

[72] "Education becomes something to which everybody has a 'right,' even irrespective of his capacity; and when everyone gets it—by that time, of course, in a diluted and adulterated form—then we naturally discover that education is no longer an infallible means of getting on, and people turn to another fallacy: that of 'education for leisure'—without having revised their notions of 'leisure.' . . . The majority of people are incapable of enjoying leisure—that is, unemployment *plus* an income and a status of respectability—in any but pretty simple forms—such as balls propelled by hand, by foot, and by engines or tools of various types; in playing cards. . . . The uneducated man with an empty mind, if he be free from financial anxiety or narrow limitation . . . , is, for all I can see, as well equipped to fill his

A situation of such enormous dimensions cannot be left out of our current judgments concerning the value of peoples and of their histories, judgments that are much less obvious than is generally believed. It is not to be doubted that authentic living is difficult for man when he takes no interest in what the reality is that surrounds him, but it is no less atrocious for man to turn himself into a soulless observer of the reality whose being he wishes to ascertain and define. Culture in this case is voided of all meaning, since as a thing in itself, it is nothing. Culture is what man does with it as he lives with it. Because they are afraid to live with a culture, many scholars are in the habit of devoting their attention to the most external and insignificant aspects of human creations, and thus the situation arises that is described by Mr. Eliot (writing, teaching, and learning vanities), a situation that is contemporary with the coldly calculated torture and murder of millions of men.

The German Erich Kahler wrote in 1937: "Nowhere have purer, more exalted, more profound thoughts been expressed [than in Germany]; nowhere have ideas been more profoundly ineffective" (*Der deutsche Charakter in der Geschichte Europas*, p. 39). The situation in Germany, then, is the reverse of that in Spain: in Spain, much personalism and poverty in ideas; in Germany, great ideas and scant personality. But has there ever been a time when there was complete harmony between these two extremes? If Christianity has not Christianized man, how can it be expected that the plethora of schools should create an abundance of intelligent and benevolent persons, humanly speaking? The external magnitude of the volume does not in this case affect the density of the contents.

It is quite understandable that various clear-minded Germans should have perceived the seriousness of this problem. In 1911 Georg Simmel said:

"The work of art is an incommensurable cultural value because it does not permit of any division of labor, that is, because in its case, the creator is intimately preserved in the creation. What might seem in Ruskin to be a hatred for culture is really a passion for culture. This passion requires a retreat from divided labor, which leaves the cultural content without a subject and gives it a soulless objectivity, whereby it is torn out of the cultural process itself. After this we see the tragic development that binds culture to the objectivity of contents, that surrenders the contents finally, through their objectivity, to a logic of their own, and with-

leisure contentedly as is educated man" ("Modern Education," in *Selected Essays*, Harcourt, Brace and Co., New York, 1950, p. 453).

draws them from possible assimilation by subjects. . . . The formlessness of the objectified spirit as a totality affords it a tempo of development such that the tempo of development of the subjective spirit is bound to be left behind at a rapidly growing distance." (*Der Begriff und die Tragödie der Kultur*, in *Logos*, 1911, II, 24)

Thirty years later, another German of great distinction, Ernst Cassirer, faced the troublesome problem raised by Simmel: "The doubt and objections which can be raised against culture do not diminish. . . . Culture is 'dialectical' because it is truly dramatic. It is not a simple happening, not a tranquil onward movement. It is rather a doing that must be undertaken ever anew and whose end is never certain. So it cannot give way simply to a naïve optimism, or to a dogmatic faith in the 'perfectibility' of man. . . . Such is the drama that Simmel has tried to describe, although he recognizes but two characters in it as it were: on the one side stands life, on the other, the realm of ideal values, objective and valid in themselves. The two factors never merge and penetrate each other completely. As the cultural process advances, the creations that result from it become the enemies of their creator. . . . It would be futile to deny these tragedies, or to dismiss them with superficial consolations. Nevertheless, they take on a different appearance if one pursues to its end the path opened here. For at the end of this path is not the work in whose stubborn existence the creative process rigidifies, but the 'you,' the other subject, who receives this work in order to incorporate it into his own life, and to reconvert it once more into the medium which it originally came from. Only at this point can we see what resolution 'the tragedy of culture' is capable of. Until this 'opponent' (Gegenspieler) to the I appears, the circle cannot close. . . . The life process of culture consists in its inexhaustible capacity for giving rise to such intermediaries." (*Zur Logik der Kulturwissenschaften*, Göteborg, 1942, pp. 119-121)

All that Cassirer says is true. The inexhaustible richness of culture manifests itself in the richness of its "renaissances" in the individuals or human groups that reinterpret it. The visions of Antiquity, from Petrarch to Goethe, have value as splendid renewals, and I do not think that Simmel was ignorant of this. But the question seems to be something else. The fact that Aristotle renews Plato, Racine renews Corneille, or that Dante, Cervantes and Shakespeare have not yet found "opponents" worthy of those creators, has little to do with our problem—the irradiating power of culture. The difficulty arises when the cultural values become accessible to the many. Christianity, gentle and sweet at its source, has caused torrents of blood to be shed, as innocent as the blood of the martyrs. Then came the democratic idea, the secular version of Christianity, which was received like a new Gospel. Democracy has permitted the organization of the collective life in a few countries so that many people are materially happy; the life of the community, however, has prospered at the price of impoverishing the human content of the individuals—their originality and their expressivity. The rationalist democracy of the eighteenth century, crossed with Hegelian idealism, has now given birth to totalitarian systems and their unexampled horrors, precisely because it was based on cold, carefully calculated cultural principles.

The tremendous problem would not exist if culture had continued to be the isolated flowering of a few exceptional lives. But this is inconceivable. Culture can be assimilated and relived, as Cassirer says. When the culture produces a materially useful object, a telephone, for example, this creation is not incorporated into the life of the users; that is, the use of it does not require any interest in or assimilation of the science that is behind it. But when the culture consists in ideas, beliefs, and expressed feelings, the recipients of this spiritual and intellectual matter end up by debasing its original meaning, however exalted it may have been, and in the end they pervert it completely. As values pass from the solitary grandeur of their original form and moment into traditions of ever-widening currency, they are attenuated rather than intensified. We must accept this fact without tears, because this is the fact we have to deal with.

The lack of any correlation between the exalted values of the past and the way of life practiced by most of the people of the same past has been attributed to the "dark ages," to superstition, hardness of heart, etc. But such an explanation falls to the ground in our day with its abundance of schoolbooks, and culture, and with its tradition of four millennia of humanity within the reach of anyone. Not long ago Sir Richard Livingston exclaimed: "Who thirty years ago would have believed a prophet who said that civilized people would be capable of the persecution of the Jews, the horrors of the concentration camps, the barbarism knowing neither justice, nor mercy, nor truth. . . . How astonishing we say that such things could happen in the 20th century." (*Leadership in Education*, 1950)

We have to face the reality of man as it is, without falling into nihilism, a naïve and ineffectual solution. Man is as he is, and we must calmly try to understand and express what he is. The contrast between culture and life (consisting in hopes and achievements) lamented by Sir Richard and by the countless victims of inhumanity, has always existed; but it attracts our attention especially now because we believe that life has reached a pinnacle of glory with the triumphs of science, material welfare, the postponement of death, and the improvement of the economic condition of the masses in certain countries. It should be observed, however, that the fabulous progress of the sciences does not resolve the problems that man poses to himself when he faces his awareness of his own existence. Man mistreats and destroys his own kind, both in his own country and outside it, just as in the epochs called barbarous, because man's will makes its own laws. Every day culture grows more fertile with rational possibilities, while the capacity for creating new and imponderable values, or even of keeping alive the existing ones, does not open a continuous and progressive course. The thinking man and the man sensitive to values of the highest order (those valid in themselves) rarely march exactly together, and the contrast between them is greater today than ever. The commensurable and useful things made by man are esteemed, but man himself is treated more and more as anonymous and replaceable. People no longer invent noble and exacting styles of human life in which man is valued for what he is, styles that might be sequels to the idea of the saint, the knight, the *honnête homme*, or the gentleman. Nor are there new and "affirmative" artistic styles; for the most original styles of our time derive their originality precisely from their reflection of the chaos and lack of self-confidence which are the uncertain foundations of our contemporary existence.

Thus, while certain potentialities of culture continue to find effective cultivators, others lie in sterile soil. Mathematical truth is continually realized in the precision of industrial invention, while the "truth" of the work of art or of exemplary conduct remains stagnant: The automobile engine is a realization of several centuries of constant advance in physics. Yet it can happen that both the inventor of the machine and the person who uses it will lead the most ordinary kind of life, completely unrelated to the cultural values created by other men before them. Life thus presents a tragic-comic character, somewhat as if the physicist were mounting his new, high precision apparatus on an ox-cart. It can even happen that the teaching of the values of culture will be in the hands of those who, as persons, are very much at odds with what they are teaching. Such is the structure of life now, and such has it been in the past, and it hardly makes sense for man to get angry about this situation, since he has nothing better to compare it with.

Culture, present as "objective spirit," carries with it in disguise the possibilities of barbarism, possibilities that are not recognized as such by those who have allowed their self-consciousness to fall asleep. It is legitimate to ask, then, whether we ought to consider merely as cultural "backwardness" a form of life that has as its preoccupation not the promotion of objectified culture but man's meditation, so to speak, on his consciousness of existing as an "absolute" person, in continual vigilance over himself. This living-in-oneself makes the person feel himself a lost stranger when he enters into the otherness of the world, where he runs the risk of ceasing to be himself at the same time that he does not make a real place for himself in the otherness. This is what the Spaniards have felt as they opposed external innovation, and it is what disturbed Don Juan Manuel in the intimate declaration quoted earlier (see Chapter 8). The person lives in watchful guard over his own wholeness, and this leads to the drama of being left without any world, precisely as the forms of life we call progressive lead to the drama of being left without any personal awareness. Both roads lead to summits of great value and to abysses of wretchedness. Both are perfectly human. And who knows but that it might be more valid for the historian to understand correctly the functioning of these opposite ways of life, instead of emphasizing so much their tragic, backward, or primitive aspects.

"The Throne of the Soul"

In the *Guía espiritual* (1675), Miguel de Molinos says: "You must know that your soul is the center, the habitation, and the dominion of God; but for the great King to repose upon the throne of your soul, you must try to keep it clean, motionless, vacant, and peaceful."

It has not been my purpose with this book to answer the famous question "Que doit-on à l'Espagne?" formulated by the Encyclopedists of the eighteenth century. The reality and ultimate value of a people's history does not depend on whether the nation has or has not been a benefactor of humanity, nor how that people's or nation's values are esteemed today in the international market. To contemplate the effect of one people's values upon the life of another no doubt enriches our historical perspective. But there is no sense in getting into quarrels over merits and priorities. In the clamor of the dispute over whether A was or was not the cause of B, the value of A and B themselves is lost sight of. To take an example at random, in the argument about whether Arabic poetry "influenced" the poetry of Provence or not, the essential charm of both poetries is left to one side. The poetries are approached as collections of skeletal and abstract characteristics so that the disputants can bring out the desired formal connections.

The history of Spain would gain little from a listing of certain benefits conferred by it on the world, for history is validated by its inner meaning and not by its poorly acknowledged gifts. The Reconquest has value as the forge in which the Spanish life structure was wrought, not as the dike that protected Europe against the Moslems. Spanish domination saved southern Italy from being occupied by the Turks, although the presence of the Spaniards there was merely an expression of their will to imperial grandeur, which was met by the Italian eagerness for new forms of grandeur in literature and art to compensate in a way for Italian national debility (Italian *grandioso* is originally a Spanish word). The new way of discovering and conquering worlds, initiated by the Portuguese and the Spaniards, served as model to other Europeans, who, however, never remotely dreamed, before the Spaniards, of finding it profitable to assimilate distant lands nationally, linguistically, and religiously.

The empire beyond the seas "realized" the Spaniards and Portuguese just as the eagle's existence is realized in the loftiness and majesty of his flight. No other approach will do, for there is no science to determine the size and character of the volume and contents of empires. The fact that the Belgians owe their present boundaries, and indirectly their nationality, to the domination of their land by the Spanish crown until 1713 does not relegate to second-class status the fact that it was the Spanish spirit of crusade that preserved the personality of Flanders against the double threat of the French and the Dutch. The Spanish theatre is not valuable for having made possible a French theatre—a benefit esteemed but slightly, if not scorned, by the French. The theatre of Lope de Vega and his followers expresses how the Spaniards felt about the human virtues, and how they gave form to their desire for beauty—a soaring escape from the inert and the transitory in well-developed significant forms. Finally (to shorten the enumeration that could be very long indeed), the novel of Cervantes and his precursors would be what it is in itself, whether or not it had made possible the English novel of the eighteenth, and the Continental novel of the nineteenth century. The urge to assign maximum importance to one's own self is bootless, naïve, and a symptom of insecurity: let us put it aside.

The only culture that the Spaniards have really sought to radiate has been that implicit in their Catholic faith. Hence the Society of Jesus, Spanish in its origin, and much combatted in Spain at its beginning for the "novelty" of some of its features. Because of the Jesuits, and their

Velázquez, *Las Meninas* (The Maids of Honor). (See p. 662.)

Velázquez, *Las Meninas* (The Maids of Honor). The artist's self-portrait. (See p. 662.)

Velázquez, *Las Hilanderas* (The Spinners). (See p. 662.)

El Greco, *The Burial of the Count of Orgaz.* (See p. 662.)

Hispanic methods of attack, Catholicism was preserved in southern Germany and even in Poland and Lithuania. Besides its beliefs, Spain diffused over Europe certain literary modes of sensibility and expression, of elegance and courtliness. Inside and outside his country, the Spaniard has gone on existing within the absolutism of his personal life, girded by his halos like Saturn and its rings.

If he had been able to develop freely the possibilities of his isolation, the Spaniard would have arrived at the only forms of religious dissidence possible in his case—if it is at all possible for something objective and durable to come out of an absolute solipsism. The problem is exemplified in the diffusion and ultimate failure of the sect of the Illuminati, of Islamic origin in Spain,[73] and severely persecuted by the Inquisition precisely because of its undefined character and the attraction it had for both the learned and the ignorant. Even the archbishop Bartolomé Carranza was accused of Illuminism, and he ended his days in an Inquisitorial prison. In his *Comentarios al catecismo cristiano* (1558) he refuses to fix the time and place for the granting of God's grace. And Quevedo says in *La cuna y la sepultura* (1633) that God should be asked for nothing: "Let us not impose on God, with our prayers and supplications, our notions of limits on evil and good. . . . What is your wisdom that you dare to give advice to God's? . . . How much better you would do if you kept silent so that your insignificance should not destroy you!" Solitude, not the reading of the philosophers, says Quevedo, is the path to virtue and wisdom. "Be persuaded at last that *within yourself* you have so much to do that, no matter how long your life may be, you will not have enough time."

In this "within yourself" lay the danger of breaking the bond with the hierarchic order of the church, in view of the pleasure taken by the Spaniard in being alone with himself—so alone that even communication with God can become an insuperable difficulty. This is the conclusion of Bartolomé de Torres Naharro in a lovely poem written at the beginning of the sixteenth century, wherein he realizes that praises to the Virgin have no meaning commensurate with their intention. He has been commanded to praise the Virgin Mary ("Aquí me mandan loaros. . . "), and he does not know how, since between "human knowledge and who you are and can be, there is no proportion." And if this happens with the Virgin Mary, how can it be possible to praise God? Nothing said by man can serve as the predicate in a judgment whose subject is the infinitude

[73] This is clearly demonstrated in a series of articles published by Miguel Asín in *Al-Andalus* starting in 1944, as I already have pointed out.

of God, and thus only God can bridge the immeasurable chasm: "And since our coarseness cannot approach your worth, from that One, the great creator, from whom sprang such a work [i.e., the Virgin Mary] let the praise come from Him." There is, then, no congruence between the praises of the Virgin and the object of the praises; consequently "all that we say, since we are sinners [i.e., men], is a going in and no coming out, a beginning without ending, and the painting of colors upon gold" ("Coplas en loor de la Virgen," in the *Propalladia*, 1517).

These wonderful stanzas, terse and elegantly daring, have generally escaped notice. The modesty which inspires them creates problems that may have their solution in theology. But in any case, Torres Naharro breaks with a centuries-old tradition of praises to the Virgin Mary. I speak of this matter simply by way of presenting a problematical attitude characteristic of the so-called Renaissance, issuing from the writer's experience. Torres Naharro does not surmount the obstacle by embracing any kind of illuminism or mysticism, and so he does not seek to establish communication with God, whether in interior darkness or in light. He poses the problem and lives within it: "it is a going in and no coming out." To "come out" could have been achieved only through a rational philosophy, ultimately heterodox. The problem found no philosophical solution in Spain, but it did find a mystical one; that is, it was solved by moving in another dimension of the soul living with itself apart. In the long run, churchmen did not tolerate those who lived in this isolation, for her mission would have been useless if people could communicate independently with God. This was the way taken by Saint John of the Cross, dissatisfied with the knowledge of God through normal ecclesiastical channels: "It is impossible to know and sense divine things as they are by any natural way [so far he is in agreement with Torres Naharro], but only by means of the illumination of this mystical theology" (*Dark Night of the Soul*). By means of mystical illumination, God will make himself accessible to Saint John, whereas He remains shut off in the words of those who try to explain Him: "Give up and really surrender to me. Send me no more messengers, who cannot tell me what I want to know," for "they all wound me the more, and something or other they keep stammering [Un no sé *qué que que*dan balbuciendo] leaves me perishing" (*Cántico espiritual*). The three *que*'s in the Spanish well express the anguishing sensation produced by the stammering of those trying to say what cannot be said—the divine—with human means. It was inevitable that such a rigorous isolation should make the mystic forget the world of finite things, among them the visible and earthly things of the church. The ecclesiastical organization and external practices were not attacked by Saint John of the Cross, but all mention of them was omitted, because they had no function in a work of pure beauty very close to the region of the supreme and terrible silences. Neither in this work nor in the letters of the poet-saint is there any use of the words "pope," "cardinal," "bishop," "canon," "parish priest," "chaplain," "sacristan," and many others that are usually found in religious writings. He speaks five times of the "communion," and in three of the instances he criticizes the "frequent receiving of communion" and the "sensuality" and "pleasure" that communion occasions. It is surprising, by contrast, to find that the passages relative to direct "communication" with God fill ten pages of the *Concordancias* compiled by Fray Luis de San José.

God becomes present to Saint John of the Cross in the will the saint feels to possess Him in love, rather than in the statements, the inadequate "stammerings" with which people try to explain Him. The form in which this will was expressed has, as flawless beauty, acquired a universal validity, at least for those able to feel it. The divine emotion, working in the poet's soul—from the immanent throne of God, as it were—carves out a poetic experience of extreme lyric subtlety as the expression of its inner processes, which achieve a kind of "innovation" from within, completely oblivious of all that is happening beyond the confines of the soul.

Divine or human, the Spaniard's finest creations have always been like this, works which combine in an integral relationship the agent, the action, and the thing done. The external elements have served as incitements, as instruments, but the place where it actually happens, where it is infused with genius, is the "throne of God in the soul," the watchtower and workshop of one's own life and of the other lives relived by it. "I am laden with myself," exclaims Quevedo, with a "myself" that is a continual flux, "innovated" as it creates itself: an alternating succession of creations and destructions: "Oh how you slip through my fingers; oh, my age, how you glide away from me!" The state of mind here reflected is not Quevedo's alone, for we have already seen, among other examples, that the Archpriest of Hita's central theme is the slipping from one "care" to another (Chapter 12). The people who have felt their own lives to be like this have also felt external reality (persons, things) as a continual self-creation—a feeling they have expressed in certain works of consummate art—in the *Quijote* (as I have shown elsewhere) and in Velázquez' paintings, for example.

[661]

In Velázquez' painting *Las Hilanderas* (The Spinners) the central character is the tapestry, created by the mind of the artist and the strong, skillful hands of those who weave it; the tapestry in turn is recreated by those contemplating it in the picture, and we can now traverse, forward or backward, the route that goes from the inert matter to the work of art and the people within it that are looking at it. The absolute Hispanicity of this cycle is evident, and is to be understood in connection with all the foregoing. The vigorous movements of the spinning woman with her bare feet and arms are to the tapestry what Rodrigo de Vivar, the prosaic owner of the mills of Ubierna, is to "My Cid, who girded on his sword in an auspicious moment"; what Alonso Quijano, who eats lentils every Friday, is to the Knight of the Lions, Dulcinea's lover.[74]

This vital technique is even more explicit in *Las Meninas* (The Little Ladies-in-Waiting), in which there is a perfect simultaneous expression of the figure of the creator, the theme of his work, the process of realizing the work, and the people who are looking both at the process and at each other. De Tolnay lends authoritative support to this idea: "This is the painter as sovereign creator who is capable, thanks to a divine gift, of recreating within himself the visible world"—working from the "throne of his soul," I would add. In *Las Meninas*, De Tolnay sees Velázquez painting "from memory [i.e., without directly looking at his models] in a state of dreamy rapture. He is the only person who is not aware of his entourage." He is in himself, in a state of creative solitude.

Equally astonishing in this respect is El Greco's *El entierro del conde de Orgaz* (The Burial of Count Orgaz), in which heaven and earth recreate each other through mutual contemplation. The two realms are connected by the soul, which has left the corruptible body below and taken on the form of an imprecise little figure whose final perfection will

[74] Charles de Tolnay, studying this disquieting picture from another point of view, confirms my mode of understanding it. (See the *Gazette des Beaux-Arts*, 1949, xxxv, 21-38.) The mythological theme of Pallas Athene and Arachne is no more important, it seems to me, than the fact that the abstract mythological figures are incarnated in Spanish spinning women and exquisite ladies. The theatre of the Velázquez period likewise showed the intermingled existence of village rustics and gentlemen of the court at the same time that it juxtaposed in artistic harmony the song of the peasant and the cultivated verse forms of Italian origin. De Tolnay states the problem very well: "The craftsmanship presupposes the 'idea' of the Fine Arts, which it executes, and conversely, the embodied idea leads back to the Fine Arts." And he adds: "The transcendent becomes immanent, the goddesses and heroes become everyday men and women, and reality consequently loses the heaviness of earthly life, becoming a poetical and spiritual realm" (p. 32).

be realized in the triangle outlined by Christ, the Virgin Mary, and Saint John. The heavenly and the earthly flow into each other just as the corporeal, temporal figure of Saint Stephen (the beautiful youth who is helping Saint Augustine hold up the body) exists simultaneously with the scene depicting his martyrdom, embroidered on the dalmatic in which he is vested—and just as, in the second part of the *Quixote*, the visible "living" figure of the hero is injected, as it were, with the figure out of the story in Part I, so that the two figures draw poetic life from each other. All these are processes of going and returning, that merge in the consciousness of the contemplator.

The fact that an artist like El Greco, coming to Spain from so distant a world, could succeed in penetrating to such a degree the modes of Spanish life, reveals that these modes, however strange they may have been, were not the signs of primitivism or failure. El Greco acquired something more than a Hispanic tonality. The work of his Toledo period shows him to be a spiritual *mestizo*, produced by the seductive power of a milieu filled with values that were represented by the refined minority who rewarded El Greco with intelligent sympathy. Something like this happened to Charles V, who, speaking no Spanish when he came to Spain, eventually felt its seductive power on "the throne of his soul."

We inevitably reach the conclusion, then, that Hispanic life has consisted, up to now, at least, in being situated within oneself, just as a sovereign, by the grace of God, believes it legitimate, right, to maintain himself on his throne. The activities that the Spaniard has invented for himself authentically (not those he has copied and superimposed on his existence)—those activities have always tended to magnify his inner kingdom, to make it really present, to give it value, and to find for it every possible kind of expression. This way of life has been the basis for constructions by one person that other persons could incorporate into their own total self-consciousness: temples to pray in, palaces to marvel at, religious works through which to meditate upon the eternal future of the person, literature in which awareness of the self is magnified, without issuing beyond the confines of the self. The person's dwelling in himself and the idea he has of his own dimensions are matters of belief, not the result of any kind of discursive analysis.[75] The problemati-

[75] If we wish to see at a glance how the Spaniard has conceived his life, we have only to examine the indexes of the *Bibliotheca Hispana* compiled by Nicolás Antonio, an excellent bibliographical work for its time (1672). There are 48 pages of titles of religious works; 40 of historical works of largely religious character; 13 of jurisprudence and law; 8 of profane literature; 7 of humanistic learning; 6 of medicine and natural sciences; 5 of philosophy (in support of theology and religion);

cal questions asked by the world outside (conflict with the silent reality of nature, doubts created by the use of reason) have elicited no response, and so there have been few Spanish inventions worth considering, either material or rational.[*]

Spanish time has been the time of belief and of its sequel, hope, a time that is either immobile or frenetic, in a life of traditional inertia that is broken only by sudden efforts to reform everything at once. Confined within itself, this life gradually stagnates in its own history, which is made of inner "innovations" and not of changes imposed from without. The drama begins when we notice that the Spaniard has never been entirely satisfied with the absolute confinement to which he condemns himself. In countries close by he could observe the passage of time in the changes introduced by the objectified efforts of other men: printed books, firearms, artifacts of all kinds, produced in a dizzying rhythm down to our times. The Spaniards have always been fascinated by what other people have done, at the same time that they have feared the danger of ceasing to be themselves. In 1480 Ferdinand and Isabella authorized the free importation of foreign books: "Lately certain of our merchants, both native and foreign, have brought in, and every day they continue to bring in, many good books. This seems to redound to the profit of everyone, and to the ennobling of our kingdoms." But in 1502, the same monarchs prohibited the sale of "any printed books" imported from other countries, until such books should pass both ecclesiastical and secular censorship. So that it was not Philip II who began to make intellectual communication difficult between Spain and the rest of the world. But the Spaniard likewise has always practiced—at irregular intervals—the adoption, in fragmentary form, of things and ideas from the outside. Strange and irregular situations have thus been created in a process whose only constant feature has been its irregularity, the authentic expression of self-consuming life, the *vivir desviviéndose*. The importations have not been mere playthings, as happens with the peoples called primitive. The Spaniards have expanded and contracted the objective zone of their life in a dramatic rhythm: they are not inclined to industrial activity, nor will they agree to live without industry. At certain moments the outward sallies, the efforts to break out of themselves, have brought on bloody catastrophes, as a result of the dialectical alternation between what is authentically Spanish and the importations that give rise to problems that have no "normal" Spanish mode of solution. This

4 of mathematics, astronomy, music, geography, nautical science, engineering, and architecture all together; 3 of political science.

dialectical polemic is constitutive of the Spanish life structure, which I have tried to bring clearly into focus. There are not two Spains. No people is *two*. It must be *one*, a unity not definable by logic or by conventional psychology. The vital unity of all that is Hispanic rests upon the inner continuity that I have here exposed to light, whether or not everyone will see it the same way. Additional facts and documents will complete and enrich the picture, but they will not destroy its outline. Spain is a human entity that made its appearance a thousand years ago (but not before the Moslem invasion) with the vital disposition that it still presents today.

In such a way of living, even as among the peoples that have grown out of Greco-Romano-Germanic rationalism, there can emerge both supreme and insignificant values. I do not believe, therefore, that the Hispanic mode is to be spurned, or that it is legitimate to present it as an abortive effort to assimilate the European mode. There have been moments when Europe nursed at the Spanish breast, and I am thinking, of course, of something more than imitations or "influences." The history of Europe could not be understood without the presence of Spain, a nation which has not discovered mathematical theorems or physical principles, but which *has been* something which Europe has not been able to do without, and which will come into its proper relief the day when the history of every human variety is conceived as a life in conflict with itself. The fact that its price is not quoted on the market of physical knowledge does not mean that the human series Fernando de Rojas (*La Celestina*), Hernan Cortes, Saint John of the Cross, Cervantes, Velázquez, and Goya has any less significance in the axiological world, the world of man's highest values, than the series Leonardo, Copernicus, Descartes, Kepler, Galileo, and Newton. When the pragmatic criterion of "practical" utility and intelligible objectification is no longer the only one employed to understand the human reality, history will humanize itself and perhaps such limited points of view will be forgotten.

It will be seen, besides, that Spain is a human entity that has functioned as a subject-agent. Once formed, her structure permitted her to adopt and Hispanize, which is what to adopt means in this case, her past and the present of other people. It is senseless to speak of a Tartesian or Celtic or Iberian or Roman or Visigothic Spain, since these alleged "Spains" were devoid of any self-awareness that can be linked with the authentically Spanish, self-awareness which is demonstrably continuous from the tenth century down to today. The Iberian and the Roman past were a *condition* for what I call Spain, but neither of them has acted on Spain more effectively than did Islamic life or European Christendom; still we do not for this reason apply the name of Spain to Islam or France, nor do we confuse the Spaniards with the Moors or the French. Ever since Spain has existed as such, she has reacted inwardly in the Hispanic manner in spite of the waves of foreign culture that have washed over her. The epics of the tenth to the fifteenth century were neither Germanic nor French; Galician poetry was neither Mozarabic nor Provençal; Catalonian law was neither Roman nor French. The Cathedral of Toledo, although in an imported (Gothic) style, developed its architecture in a Hispanic fashion down to the eighteenth century, even though the successive developments were, like the original style, of foreign origin. The same thing can be said for the other manifestations of Spanish civilization, filled with non-Spanish elements and yet always intensely Spanish. Cervantes owes much to Erasmus and to the Italians; but what is all this compared with the *Quixote?*

If we approach history peripherically, or on the assumption that a given people has always existed, we are bound to fall into a confusion of undifferentiated anecdote. But if instead we take our post at the guiding center of Hispanic history, that is, on the "throne of the [Hispanic] soul," the unruly materials take shape, and history gives docile answers to our questions. Each history has a sustained form and meaning. Let us not destroy them.

APPENDIX I

The Independence of Portugal

IF MY VIEW regarding the relationship between Portugal and Spain is to be accepted as valid, it is necessary to put in abeyance, at least temporarily, the way the Portuguese themselves feel about their history. Vitally speaking, to be sure, the Portuguese are not in error when they believe that Portugal was already in existence before the twelfth century, but objectively speaking this may be less than precise. The belief that Portugal brought herself into being and was not the result of forces external to her is part of the very existence of that nation. If the Portuguese had felt that they were an appendage of the Kingdom of Leon or the Duchy of Burgundy, they would not, I daresay, have achieved their wonderful discoveries, nor would we have the works of Gil Vicente and Camoens.

The cold facts of Portugal's past are to the Portuguese nation as the historically documented personage of the Cid is to the Cid of literature. The legend of Portugal, which is of course as much a part of the Portuguese reality as the facts are, asks us to believe that the region situated between the Miño and Douro rivers had, before the twelfth century, certain peculiar characteristics betokening a national self-awareness; the inhabitants were already looking toward Lisbon and Santarém, still in Moslem hands, as a prolongation of Portugal. But the cold fact is that what was to become Portugal did not, before it came under the rule of Henry of Burgundy, display any important features different from those characterizing Galicia. But even if a region is distinctively featured this does not mean that it is capable of constituting itself a political state. Yet it is no less true that in failing to be objective, the historical awareness of the early Portuguese produced an interpretation of the past that became a fruitful part of the authentic history of the Portuguese people: to exist as a Portuguese consists, among other things, in not feeling oneself to be an appendage of Spain. This dissociation impelled the Portuguese to increase their historical dimension backward in the past, and to seek imperial expansion in the present. The heroic impulse that carried as far as Hormuz and Malacca was but a part of the effort to find non-Spanish national roots.

According to certain historians, the people who dwelt between the Miño and the Tagus in the eighth and ninth centuries already displayed an attitude of expectation; that is, they were waiting to become themselves, Portuguese. The *Annales Portugalenses veteres* (from the beginning of the twelfth century) mention the taking of Coria by Alphonse VI of Leon and Castile in 1077. Some would take this remark as evidence that the Portuguese of that time already believed that the town of Coria was "the key to the Tagus valley, and certainly within their sphere of interest" (Pierre David, *Etudes historiques sur la Galice et le Portugal du VIe. au XIIe. siècle*, 1947, p. 332).

Portugal, *finis terrae*, had always dreamed of escaping her narrow confines:

> The Lusitanian realm,
> Where the land ends and the sea begins.
>
> (*The Lusiads*, III, 20)

It is impossible to understand the formation of the immense Portuguese empire solely in terms of economic or statistical analysis. During the sixteenth, seventeenth, and eighteenth centuries, Portuguese was the linguistic vehicle that brought Western civilization to the East Indies (David Lopes, *A expansão da lingua portuguesa no Oriente*, 1936). As early as in 1427 the Portuguese were already established in the Azores. And all that was achieved by a country which had but a few more than one million inhabitants.[1]

Spain and Portugal are not inwardly happy nations, and they never have been. To this inner disquietude shared with Spain, Portugal adds the resentful and therefore repressed awareness that her past has not been entirely her own. Portugal wanted and believed a history of her own, and she did this with such intensity that she was successful little by little in incorporating both an imagined history and the practice of imagining it into the process of her authentic existence. The imperial enterprises; the enduring imprint of Portugal in Brazil, in the East Indies, and in Africa; the imposing figures of Vasco da Gama, Affonso de Albuquerque, Ferdinand Magellan, and others; the works of Gil Vi-

---

[1] The enterprises were begun in the fourteenth century and finally carried through to a successful conclusion by Prince Henry the Navigator (1394-1460). For bibliography concerning this matter, see Fortunato de Almeida, *Historia de Portugal*, 1924, II, 26ff. The importance of the Portuguese efforts in Africa is properly appreciated in such works as the monumental *Anais de Arzila* by Bernardo Rodrigues, which covers the years 1508 to 1550 (edition of David Lopes, Lisbon, 1915); or in the *Chronica do descobrimento e conquista de Guiné*, which was completed by Gomes Eannes de Azurara in 1448 (edition of the Viscount of Carreira, Paris, 1841). That the Portuguese still maintain their African colonies is a natural projection of the national and international greatness of her past.

cente and Camoens—all this and more have motivated the recreation of the origins of Portugal. Historical consciousness has transformed that which had no intrinsic value as objective reality into human poetic reality. A great novelist does not work differently.

But let us now examine the objective background of this great history. A Brazilian scholar describes it correctly:

"The rebellion and independence [in the twelfth century] had meant the dismembering of the Hispano-Christian empire that was on the way to being established; and the existence of Portugal depended on her not accepting the Spanish imperialist ideas. Portuguese nationalism was a historical and moral position opposed to Spanish political ideology: the policy of Spain was to direct its forces centripetally; Portuguese policy, to find centrifugal moral and material forces that would provide it with a historical destiny outside the Spanish orbit. . . . Portugal found herself an illustrious past on the plane of universal history, but not within the perspective of Spanish history."[2]

In the twelfth century, the Portuguese structure of life was no different from the Galaico-Leonese; so the differentiation of Portugal from Leon could not consist in wishing to be, or in going on being, herself, but rather, in finding some way of not being like her relatives and neighbors. It is obvious, then, that the militant impetus and support for that Peninsular vivisection could not arise spontaneously from the Galician-speaking people who dwelt to the south of the Miño and were spreading out in the wake of victories achieved in the Reconquest by Ferdinand I and Alphonse VI of Leon and Castile. The initial motivation of that rebellion does not lie in the proto-Portuguese character of that county which Alphonse VI granted Henry of Burgundy in fief, but in the fact that the count was a Burgundian. There is of course no trace of such reasons in the historical consciousness of the Portuguese, for if the kingdom of Lusitania was to exist at all, it had to forget its real origin. And this consciousness in turn created retroactively a belief in the primordial reality of Portugal. In the process of human history, children can give life to their fathers, as well as the other way around. That is why two apparently contradictory ways of understanding the origin of Portugal—my own and that of the Portuguese historians who opposed it—can both be true. I would say metaphorically that our conception of history becomes true in a space of more than three dimensions.

It is easy to understand why the origins of the kingdom of Portugal

[2] A. Soares Amóra, *O Nobiliario do Conde D. Pedro*, São Paulo, 1948, p. 62.

are veiled in legend and obscurity. It has not been possible to locate the battle of Ourique (1139), the most important event in the Portuguese reconquest. The names of the defeated Moorish kings are equally unknown. The story of the taking of Santarém (1143) is found in an account that is by any critical standards apocryphal. Foreign participation in the reconquest of the land that eventually came to be Portugal was both considerable and decisive.[3] Of the reign of Affonso Henriques, the first Portuguese king (1128-1185), little is known. The Portuguese chronicles did not record the activities of foreigners who came to that far corner of Europe, although these foreigners bore the brunt of the war against the Moors, as did not happen in Spain, regardless of the number of foreigners present there. The contemporary accounts[4] of the conquest of Lisbon (1147) were composed by an Englishman and two Germans, and these left no doubt concerning the secondary role that fell to the Christians of the Peninsula in that enterprise. When the city surrendered, "the name of the Franks was glorified in all Spain. . . . One of our own, Gilbert of Hastings, was chosen bishop of Lisbon with the consent of the king" (p. 122). In 1149 Affonso Henriques gave this bishop thirty-two houses: "xxxii domos cum omnibus suis hereditatibus ubicumque illas invenire potuerit."[5] The fleet engaged in the conquest of Lisbon had weighed anchor in England with 169 ships provided and manned by Englishmen, Germans, Flemings, Frenchmen, and Gascons. The towers raised for the conquest of the city were the work of Flemings, Englishmen, and an engineer from Pisa. All the booty was for the foreigners, who, through a pact with the Moors, took for themselves the gold, the silver, clothing, the horses, and the mules, and gave the city to the king: "regi civitatem redderent" (pp. 129, 139). The chronicler of these international forces proudly writes that "the soldiers of the king of Spain [regis Hispaniae—he does not say Portugal] gave battle from a wooden tower," even though they were frightened by the Moors' missiles, until the Teutons came to their aid (donec Theutonici eis auxilio venerant). "When the Saracens saw the Lorrainese going up into the tower, such panic came over them that they gave up their arms" (pp. 132).

[3] See Carolina Michaëlis de Vasconcellos, *Cancioneiro da Ajuda*, II, 692-698. The erroneous etymology of Portugal in the fifteenth century is significant: "Portus Galliae." Count Henry and his son Affonso Henriques gave many towns and lands to the Burgundians and the French.

[4] Alfredo Pimenta, *Fontes medievais da Historia de Portugal*, 1948, I, 107-140.

[5] A. E. Reuter, *Documentos da chancelaria de Afonso Henriques*, Coimbra, 1938, p. 219.

Our information concerning the taking of Silves (1189) comes from a German writing in 1191. According to it, it was the crusaders or foreign adventurers who took the lead in the action (pp. 162-163). And foreigners also participated in the taking of other cities—Alcor and Alcacer.

The history of Portugal in the twelfth century is a tissue of shadows and gaps. David Lopes, through his fortunate acquaintance with Arabic sources, has added to our meager knowledge of Gerald the Fearless (Geraldo Sem Pavor), a chieftain contemporary with Affonso Henriques.[6] It was Gerald, not the king, who conquered Trujillo, Evora, Cáceres, Montánchez, Juromenha, and Badajoz. Falling out with the king, Gerald went to Morocco, where the Moors, fearing he would betray them, cut off his head. It is perhaps not surprising that the Portuguese should compare this figure with the Castilian Cid, because both personages became subjects of Moorish kings. But a great deal is known of the Cid, and of Gerald, very little. The one served as subject for poetry in Latin and Romance, whereas the other is remembered only in fragmentary Christian and Arabic anecdotes. Besides, Gerald seems to be a foreigner, judging not only from his name but also from his epithet (Sem Pavor), which seems French rather than Portuguese. In the middle of the tenth century, the third duke of Normandy was called "Richard Sans Peur." From the little of his life that has come down to us, Gerald appears to have helped the king on some occasions, and on others, not. His loyalty to the monarch is not like that of Rodrigo Díaz, the Cid. In any case, one wonders why neither the chronicles nor any other documents have anything to say about such a prominent person, no matter what his relations with the king may have been. Gerald was very likely quite as foreign as the dynasty that founded the Portuguese kingdom and as the conquerors of Lisbon.

Transcending the bare reality of those facts, the Portuguese created the work of art that was their history-life. They owed their independence from Leon and Castile to the fact that the lands to the south of Galicia had been given to a Burgundian house at a time when the Burgundians were the most dynamic and energetic people of Europe. Against this foreign background there later developed a distinctive national feeling which separated Portugal from the rest of the Peninsula but did not destroy the structure of life that it had developed as a part of the Peninsular community—belief, personal absolutism, heroism, intellectual quietism.

[6] "O Cid português: Geraldo Sempavor," in the *Revista Portuguesa de Historia*, 1941, I, 93-104.

APPENDIX II

Deism in Fourteenth-Century Castile

IN TREATING of religious tolerance (Chap. 7), I alluded to certain manifestations of deism in Castile comparable to those that are to be found in the writings of the Sufi and in Raymond Lully. The text in question is a portion of a Chronicle of Alphonse XI, as yet unpublished, but made available to me through the kindness of Sr. Diego Catalán Menéndez Pidal. The figure of fourteenth-century Castile that I have been outlining these last few years, when regarded in the light of the ideas of tolerance brought out in Chapter 7, is seen to accommodate the new fact so easily that the addition to the picture occasions no surprise. The Castilians of the middle of the fourteenth century were receptive to all modes of literary expression: the lyricism of Juan Ruiz and Santob; the highly personal tone of Don Juan Manuel; in the ballad (another literary novelty), the suppression of epic and novelistic events in favor of bringing out the emotional quality of human situations;[1] the expression of religious faith out of the depths of personal experience among the anchorites who founded the Order of St. Jerome, and in the poetry of the chancellor Pero López de Ayala; or, in fine, the intimate, emotional twist, as we shall see, given to his account by one of Alphonse XI's chroniclers.

This chronicle says that Prince Peter and Prince John lost their lives while fighting the Moors in the lowland, or *vega*, of Granada, and that their army suffered total defeat. Peter had signed a truce with the Moorish king of Granada, by virtue of which the Moors were to pay him tribute. While the truce was still in effect, the prince requested and received from the pope authority for a crusade; and the pope also ordered him, under pain of excommunication, to break the truce with the infidels, and not to enter into pacts with them. The prince then very

---

[1] For the jongleur of the epics, the important thing was the narration of heroic deeds; whereas the ballad-singer is interested in love affairs, jealousy, the description of feminine beauty, sensual attractiveness, the anxious waiting of an abandoned wife, the prisoner's solitude, the sadness of the deceived Moorish maid, the mariner's magic song, etc., etc. The presence of these new stimuli towards beautiful expression is more interesting than the prehistory of the new poetic form, brief and terse for the simple reason that intense emotional effect cannot be sustained over the stretch of a thousand lines and more. What I have continually emphasized is that before the fourteenth century, the human climate was not such as to make the *Romancero*—the ballads—possible.

gladly returned the tribute that had been collected, whereupon the king is reported to have said: "I am a Moor, the prince is a Christian. I wish to serve the truth established by God, and I do not wish to take back the money I have given the prince. Rather I seek to keep the charter of loyalty which he has given me. . . . And the prince has wronged me, for he has wreaked havoc over my land, and has pursued my Moors and slain them; and after he had done these wicked things to me, I paid him tribute so that he would let me live on my lands in peace. And now he would break the faith and word he has given me. And I call upon God to be the judge between us and to show His justice through a miracle, so that all men will know what faith and truth are" (chap. 19).

The chronicler does not confine himself to the narration of visible events; he tells us how his character feels in the depths of his soul. Situations of this sort must have existed earlier, but the means and possibility of expressing them were lacking. But let us continue. Hostilities began, and the *infantes* Don Juan and Don Pedro invaded the *vega* of Granada with a strong army. However, there was discord between the two princes, and each desired his rival's death: "But God, who is our father and powerful lord, and is the maker and the undoer of all things, did not wish any of the intentions that they had in their hearts to be fulfilled" (chap. 20). (Notice that we are continually shown the "inwardness" of the hearts as well as the "outwardness" of the deeds.) The army of 9,000 knights and countless foot-soldiers was met by 5,000 Moorish knights, and disaster followed. Prince Peter was killed through the fault of his own men; the army was disorganized before the fight began, and the disorganization turned into a rout; Prince John also perished, and the disaster was complete. And the chronicler says: "God had now passed sentence against the Christians, and the wheel of fortune had taken such a bad turn that without contest or battle and without any blows between Christians and Moors, the Christians were defeated. And such was the will of God, either because of the sins of the Christians, or because of the wicked intentions of the two dead princes— nobody knows. And so it is understood to have been a miracle and justice done by God; for God, in whom all power is fulfilled, is never served except by the truth, and metes out justice only as it is deserved, and therefore He knew what he had done, and it was done with His consent" (chap. 21).

The chronicler speaks more plainly on this subject when he anticipates it in chapter 18: "And of all things done by Prince Peter, men find none to bring up against him save this one only: that he broke the peace that he had set up with the king of Granada, and his word; and he broke the faith and loyalty which God has established among the community of men. And so men suspect that this was the cause for which this prince was killed, as you shall later hear."

In this view, then, the God of the Christian and the God of the Moor were the same, for above the difference in religions was "the loyalty which God has established among men." Truth and justice are one. This unity appears as the ideal vertex of three real beliefs forming a single vital contexture. The case of the Christians and the Moors in the Granadine *vega* provides the instance of an ordeal in which God is the supreme arbitrer; and He punishes the disloyal contender without regard for his religion. On such a base it would have been possible to erect a system of supreme justice, binding on all men; and this is the ideal that inspired the juridical doctrine of Francisco de Vitoria in the sixteenth century, as well as the rationalistic deism (unthinkable in Spain) of certain non-Spanish Europeans between the sixteenth and eighteenth centuries—from Guillaume Postel to Lessing.

Tolerance, and its sequel, deism, did very well in Spain while the three distinct religious castes were living together; and there would be more evidence of this if the Castilians prior to the fourteenth century had had the means of expression by which to reveal their inner selves. It is of some significance, moreover, that a Spanish chronicle should have remained unpublished, and that this chronicle is one in which God, the father of all righteous men, should decide a trial against a group of Christians whose defense is not only their faith but also a mandate from the Vicar of Christ.

When the right light is brought to play upon Spain, her authentic reality is revealed in ever clearer lines.

Index

Cartagena, Teresa de, 346
Carvajal, Miguel de, 218
Caspari, C. P., 148
Cassirer, Ernst, 654
Castañeda, V., 84
Castel Nuovo (in Naples), 622
castes, 607
Castile, 13, 14, 16, 17, 18, 21, 25, 27, 78, 254, 268; in the 14th century, 369ff.; moral objectivity, 314ff.
Castilian dialect, 254; epic, 253; land, 87; scientific prose, 483-489
Castillo, Hernando del, 530
Castor and Pollux, 131, 136, 149
Castro, Don Fernando de, 186
Castro, León de, 635
Castro, Martín Alfonso de, 587
Castro de Zubiri, Carmen, ix
Catalan language, 325
Catalán Menéndez-Pidal, Diego, 672
Catalans (called "Franks"), 179
Catalina, J., 108
Catalonia, 8, 78, 102, 161, 189, 208, 302, 325
Catherin of Lancaster, 536
Catholic Sovereigns, 529 and passim
caudillismo, 650
Cazalla, Pedro, 564
Celestina, La, 7, 562-565, 641
Celtiberians, 47
"centauric" structure, 277; style, 331
Centurioni (Genoese traders), 513
Cercamon, 440
Cereceda, Feliciano, 569
Cervantes, 5, 9, 10, 43, 46, 91, 110, 183, 195, 213, 236, 251, 275, 624, 638, 643, 658
Chanson de Roland, 34, 219, 263, 264, 270, 349, 597
chantefable, 440
Chapu, Guillaume, 369
Charlemagne, 149, 262, 264, 268
Charles I of Anjou, 519
Charles II of Anjou, 519
Charles II of Spain, 623
Charles III of Spain, 7, 125, 244
Charles V, 13, 24, 66, 92, 298
Charles VII of France, 15, 20
Charles the Bold, 498
Chartres, school of, 475
Chrétien de Troyes, 280, 482
Christianity, 652
Chronicle of the Pseudo Turpin, 177
Church Fathers, 41
Church of Rome, 8
Cicero, 54, 136
Cid, The, 270, 316

Cisneros, Cardinal F. Ximenez de, 529, 542
Cîteaux, Abbey of, 177
City of God, 262, 572
Civil War (in Spain), 123, 127
Clavería, Carlos, 76
Clavijo, battle of, 135
Clemencín, Diego, 184, 300
Clement V, 507
Clement VI, 509
Clovis, 63
Cluny, Order of, 130, 158, 161, 164, 170, 181, 219
Coca (Segovia), 527
Codera, Francisco, 649
Codex Calixtinus, 135, 177
Cohén de Lara, Ischac, 495
Coimbra, 152, 154
Coincy, Gautier de, 353, 366, 367
Colón, Bartolomé, 625
Columella, 54
communism, 127
"Communities" (against Charles V), 381
Conde, J. Antonio, 203
Condé, Prince of, 231
Conde Lucanor, 241
Condillac, 52
Coni, Emilio A., 632
Conon de Béthune, 280
"conscious awareness," 17
Constantine, Emperor, 63
Constanza (Alphonse VI's wife), 170
Coplas de "¡Ay, panadera!", 557
Coplas del Provincial, 522, 557
Coplas de Mingo Revulgo, 557
Coplas de Yoçef, 115
Corbacho, 457
Córdoba, 82
Córdoba, Gonzalo de, 43, 188
Coria, 182
Corneille, Pierre, 643
Cornu, J., 320
Corominas, J., 97, 104, 629
Cortés, Hernán, 182, 665
Cortesão, Jaime, 547
Cortes of Cadiz, 197
Cossío, M. B., 6
Costa, Joaquín, 618
Costes, R., 109, 184
Cota, Rodrigo de, 524, 557, 561
Coucy's "Chatelain," 440
Council of Basel, 11, 65, 490
Council of Braga, 79
Council of Compostela, 155
Council of Reims, 133
Council of Toledo, Third, 64
Council of Trent, 155
Council of Troyes, 205